STUDY GUIDE
FOR OREGON
REAL ESTATE
FINANCE
JOHN JEDDELOH
FOURTH EDITION

Published in the United States of America by
Real Estate Publishers, Inc.
8316 N. Lombard #329
Portland, Oregon 97203-3727

WWW.REALESTATEPUBLISHERS.COM
E-mail: INFO@REALESTATEPUBLISHERS.COM

Library of Congress Catalog Card Number 99-66090
ISBN 1-878572-16-4

First printing, September 2002
Second printing, June, 2003

Cover Design: Architectural elevation of house © 2002 Bruinier & Associates, Inc., Portland, Oregon, 800-379-3828, reproduced with permission. Bruinier & Associates sells stock building plans and plan books for residential, commercial, duplexes, rowhouses and multifamily. Plans are available in traditional format or on CD-ROM. They also do custom architectural design. You can see their work at HTTP://WWW.BRUINIER.COM, or e-mail PLANS@BRUINIER.COM.

Contents

Introduction

The STUDY GUIDE FOR OREGON REAL ESTATE FINANCE offers a thorough introduction to the study of Oregon real estate finance and is especially structured to prepare students to take the Oregon real estate license examinations. The text is part of the Study Guide series – other texts in the series include STUDY GUIDE FOR OREGON REAL ESTATE LAW, STUDY GUIDE FOR OREGON REAL ESTATE PRACTICES, STUDY GUIDE FOR OREGON REAL ESTATE CONTRACTS, STUDY GUIDE FOR OREGON REAL ESTATE AGENCY and STUDY GUIDE FOR OREGON PROPERTY MANAGEMENT. Used in conjunction with the other texts in the series, this text will give the reader an excellent foundation in real estate. It is an invaluable tool for anyone interested in real estate investments, property management, mortgage lending, title work, escrow and real estate development.

This book is divided into ten sections covering all aspects of the practical side of real estate finance, with special consideration to those topics which are covered on Oregon real estate licensing examinations. Because many people using this book will be preparing for the examinations, we have taken great care to ensure that all examination subjects are covered thoroughly, and in proportion to their importance on the real estate examinations. In addition, we have included sample examination questions, many of which have been used on past state exams.

The author, John Jeddeloh, began his real estate career in 1971 and since then has worked in brokerage, property management, appraisal and investing. There is nothing in the field of real estate that he has not done.

The sample questions and text material are from the author's personal knowledge of the real estate licensing examinations in Oregon and from his many years of teaching prelicense courses in both public and private schools in Oregon. The author has 20 years of classroom experience teaching prelicense real estate full-time. There is no one as familiar with the Oregon real estate licensing examinations as he is. Before entering the real estate field, Mr. Jeddeloh worked for a large commercial bank in Oregon and also taught public secondary schools. Mr. Jeddeloh has an undergraduate degree in Education and did his graduate work in Business Administration, Law and Finance. Students who have taken his live instruction classes are always impressed by his ability to explain complex subjects clearly and understandably.

The author's combination of knowledge and experience have resulted in this book being the most comprehensive text available for the study of real estate finance in Oregon.

Getting a Real Estate License

Real estate brokerage is a relatively young profession compared to other professional fields such as medicine and law. Real estate agents were almost totally unregulated until 1908 when the National Association of Real Estate Boards was formed (currently the National Association of Realtors®. In fact, the chief purpose for which the National Association of Real Estate Boards was formed was to create a Code of Ethics and to encourage government licensing of real estate agents.

Even then, membership and adherence to the Code of Ethics was voluntary. Oregon led the nation by creating the first effective real estate licensing law in 1919. Today, this law is known as the Oregon Real Estate License Law, and is augmented by numerous Administrative rules promulgated by the Oregon Real Estate Agency. The Real Estate License Law requires that you hold one of several different kinds of real estate licenses in order to engage in what the law refers to as "professional real estate activity." Which kind of license you obtain depends on what kind of real estate activity you plan to do, and whether you plan to work for another agent or be independent. Most of these real estate licenses require completion of a separate license examination.

Most persons new to the real estate profession must get a *brokers license* as their first license. A brokers license entitles you to engage in all kinds of professional real estate activity except appraisal. (Appraisal is considered a separate field and appraisers are licensed by the Oregon Appraiser Certification and Licensure Board.) A real estate broker can work independently or cooperatively with other brokers. If you wish to run a real estate company and have other brokers working for the company, then you need a *principal brokers license*. With some exceptions, you cannot get a principal brokers license in Oregon without meeting additional educational requirements and having three years of experience as a broker. The most notable exceptions to these rules are for out of state licensees or for persons who have held a license in another state and now

reside in Oregon. Partial or full waiver of the time requirement is also possible if you can demonstrate substantial experience related to real estate, although a full waiver is granted only in exceptional circumstances. Since each individual's situation will be unique, if you feel you might qualify for a waiver, and wish to apply directly for a principal brokers license, you should contact the Oregon Real Estate Agency to determine the exact requirements. Their address is: Oregon Real Estate Agency, 1177 Center Street N.E., Salem, Oregon 97310, Telephone (503) 378-4170.

Assuming, however, that you are new to the profession and do not have significant previous real estate experience, you will need to start with the regular brokers license if you wish to engage in real estate sales. If you wish to conduct property management activity, and your professional real estate activity will be limited to property management, then you may wish to consider the special property managers license (see *Property managers license* below).

There are four requirements to obtain a brokers license. You must
- Be 18 years of age,
- Be of good character,
- Demonstrate competence in Oregon Real Estate Law, Real Estate Finance, Real Estate Practices, Property Management, Real Estate Agency, Real Estate Contracts, and Real Estate Brokerage, and you must
- Take and pass the national and state (Oregon) real estate brokers exams.

Since most persons have no problem with the first two requirements, let us confine our discussion to the last two.

You must demonstrate competence in the seven subject areas by taking and passing a course in each subject area in a school where the course(s) have been approved by the Oregon Real Estate Agency.

The real estate examinations consist of the Oregon exam (also called the state exam) and the national exam. These exams are always given at the same time, which is every month on the third or fourth Saturday (except La Grande test center, which is only three times a year). You must pass both exams with a score of 75% or better. If you pass one exam, but fail the other, you need to retake only the exam you failed, provided that you finally pass it within 12 months of passing the first exam.

Both exams are made up of totally objective multiple choice questions. The Oregon exam consists of 50 questions and the national exam has 150 questions. Most states now split their examinations into a state portion and a national portion (also sometimes called "multi-state" or "uniform" exam). As a result, if you ever move to another state you will usually only have to take the state portion in the new state, since most states now recognize Oregon's national exam as meeting the same requirements as their national, multi-state or uniform exam.

In order for a course to be approved by the Oregon Real Estate Agency it must meet certain requirements. In particular, a course in Oregon Real Estate Finance must cover the material presented in this text. Another requirement is that you must actually spend the time taking the course, either in a tape presentation with an instructor present, in a live classroom setting, or by approved distance education (e.g., by the internet or through correspondence).

Property managers license: In early 1988 it became possible to obtain a special license as a property manager. The requirements for the property managers license are the same as for the brokers license, except that the examinations and courses are different. To obtain a property managers license you need to demonstrate competence only in Oregon Property Management. In addition you must take a general examination on property management consisting of 150 questions. You should bear in mind that a property manager licensee is limited strictly to property management; you cannot be involved in any real estate activity that involves a sale. For example, you could lease a property to a tenant, but you could not do a lease-option because if the option is exercised it would result in a sale. Note also that brokers and principal brokers can also do property management, so if you want to be involved in both sales and property management, then the brokers license is the one to get.

Applying for the Examinations: The deadline for applying for any real estate exam is generally the fifth day of the month in which you wish to take the exam. In other words, if you want to take an exam scheduled for the third Saturday in December, you must apply no later than December 5. Note that your application must be postmarked by December 5, not received in Salem by December 5.

However, you should mail your application as soon as possible. Many test centers have limited space (especially the Portland center). If the test center you have chosen is filled when your application is received, then you will be assigned the next closest center where space is available.

The fee for the examination is $75 for the brokers national and state (or either exam separately), and the property managers exam is also $75. In addition, you must submit a fingerprint card the first time you apply to take an examination. The fingerprint card must be completed by an official qualified to take fingerprints. The Real Estate Agency charges $40 for processing the fingerprint card. The fingerprint card will be submitted to the FBI for criminal activity check. You can take the examination(s) at any time, but no license will be issued until the check is completed. This can take several months, so the fingerprint card should be submitted immediately once you have made the decision to obtain the license. You can submit the fingerprint card with the fee for processing it alone and send in the exam application later. The fingerprint card must be obtained from the Real Estate Agency; generic fingerprint cards from other agencies are not acceptable.

You may obtain an exam application, fingerprint card and *Examination Information* booklet from the Oregon Real Estate Agency (see address and phone above). These materials are also available free of charge at the most real estate schools.

Study Hints

Successful students know that if you master the terminology of a given subject area, you will have mastered that subject. This is particularly true of real estate because you will encounter an overwhelming number of new terms to learn. Don't let a new word get by you without learning its meaning and how it is used. About half the exam items are really just vocabulary questions – testing your knowledge of real estate terminology. So if you know the language of real estate thoroughly, you will have the subject well in hand at exam time. To assist you in mastering real estate vocabulary, you will find a *Key terms* section at the end of the reading in each section. Each of the key terms listed is italicized where it first appears in the preceding text, so you can easily check on its meaning and usage.

Always be sure you understand a topic thoroughly before going on to the next topic. Since you will forget material as you progress through the course, you should start a program of systematic review of the material previously studied. A wise man once said "if you want to increase your vocabulary, use a new word three times a day for three days and it will be yours forever." This works because people learn best by a sequence of learning, forgetting, relearning, forgetting, relearning, and so on. Each time you learn-forget-relearn you double the time before you will forget the material.

Another good study trick is to look for common elements and ways to tie information together. If you try to memorize facts in isolation, it is very difficult to remember them for long enough to pass an exam. But if you get an overall picture, the individual facts are easier to remember. After all, individual facts make more sense when you have a framework to place them in.

Do not be alarmed if you find your retention is poor at first. It is not uncommon for students to retain only 20-30% of the information after just one reading. But if you do not give up, you will find that successive readings (plus attendance at the lectures for which this text was designed) will increase your memory remarkably.

Exam Techniques

At the end of each section in this text you will find various sample exam questions which are similar to the type of questions you will find on the real estate exams given by the Real Estate Agency. You should be sure you practice with these questions, as they are the most important part of the text if you are planning on taking licensing exams.

There are three basic question types. Probably the most prevalent type is the *completion* or *fill-in* type of question (see examples below). Almost as common is the *double true-false* format, and occasionally you will encounter a *Roman numeral* type of question. But regardless of the type of question, all test questions are comprised of two parts. The first part is called the **stem**, and it is the part that actually "asks the question." The stem is followed by three **distracters** or **foils**, which are the three wrong answer choices, and, of course, the correct answer.

For example, in the following question, the stem is in regular print, and the distracters or foils are underlined. The correct answer is in italics:

In real estate, a preliminary sales contract is called
(A) a listing agreement.
(B) a lease-option.
(C) *an earnest money agreement.*
(D) an offering.

Many students make silly mistakes answering questions because they were never taught the simple ground rules for answering questions. The rules are really very easy:

1. Read the stem and the first answer (answer A) as an entire sentence. Then decide whether the statement is true or false. Using your pencil, make a notation of your decision next to the answer.

2. Read the stem again, this time followed by the second answer (answer B). Again, decide whether the statement is true or false and mark your decision next to the answer. Repeat the process for the last two answers (C and D). It is important to remember to read the stem over again each time.

3. When you have finished, the correct answer will be obvious – whichever answer is the "odd man out" is the correct answer. In other words, if you marked three answers false and one answer true, then the one marked true must be the correct answer. Similarly, with some types of negative questions, you may mark three answers true and one answer false. Then the one marked false is the correct answer.

When you finish the above question, it should look like this:

In real estate, a preliminary sales contract is called
f (A) a listing agreement.
f (B) a lease-option.
t (C) an earnest money agreement.
f (D) an offering.

Be sure to mark your decision for each answer. Do not attempt to trust your memory. By the time you finish reading the fourth answer, you could easily have forgotten what you decided about the first answer. This technique is not only useful for avoiding silly mistakes, but also when you are not sure of the answer and must make a partial guess.

These questions are really the same type of question. The only difference is that in the fill-in question an actual blank appears in the question, while the completion question contains an assumed blank at the end of the stem. For example –

The _____ is the interest held by the vendor during the term of a land sales contract.
(A) equitable title (C) naked title
(B) marketable title (D) insurable title

or

The interest held by the vendor during the term of a land sales contract is the
(A) equitable title. (C) naked title.
(B) marketable title. (D) insurable title.

After you answered the above questions, your answer section should have looked like this
f (A) equitable title. *t* (C) naked title.
f (B) marketable title. *f* (D) insurable title.

The fill-in or completion format is especially useful for testing knowledge of vocabulary items. Since testing your familiarity with real estate terminology is a fundamental part of the real estate exams, you will find many fill-in and completion questions.

Double true-false questions

The second most commonly encountered exam question type is the double true-false question. These questions come in one of two formats, e.g.

According to the Real Estate License Law, the

I. Real Estate Commissioner is the seventh member of the Real Estate Board.

II. decisions of the Real Estate Commissioner cannot be appealed.

(A) I only (C) Both I and II

(B) II only (D) Neither I nor II

or sometimes the format is like this –

According to the Real Estate License Law,

(A) the Real Estate Commissioner is the seventh member of the Real Estate Board.

(B) the decisions of the Real Estate Commissioner cannot be appealed.

(C) both A and B are true.

(D) neither A nor B is true.

In answering the double true-false question, follow exactly the same rules as for the fill-in or completion question. That is, first read the stem and the first answer (Roman numeral I in the first example, and (A) in the second format). Decide whether the statement is true or false, and mark your decision next to the answer. Then read the stem again, followed by the second answer, and decide whether this statement is true or false. Again mark your decision next to the answer. When you have marked both answers, the correct choice is obvious.

Double true-false questions are popular with test makers because they are easy to write. They are hard on students, however, because if you have to guess at one of the answers, you have only a 50-50 chance.

After you have answered the above question, it should look like this:

According to the Real Estate License Law, the

t I. Real Estate Commissioner is the seventh member of the Real Estate Board.

f II. decisions of the Real Estate Commissioner cannot be appealed.

(A) I only (C) Both I and II above

(B) II only (D) Neither I nor II above

or

According to the Real Estate License Law,

t (A) the Real Estate Commissioner is the seventh member of the Real Estate Board.

f (B) the decisions of the Real Estate Commissioner cannot be appealed.

(C) Both A and B above are true.

(D) Neither A nor B above is true.

Roman numeral questions

A third type of question which occasionally occurs on the real estate exams is the Roman numeral question. This question is similar to the double true-false question above, but instead of having two answers (I and II), it has three or more answers. As a result, the choices (A, B, C and D) may have a variety of choice combinations. For example –

Which of the following would be an encumbrance on a real estate title?

I. A land sales contract

II. An easement

III. A trust deed

IV. A mortgage

(A) I, III and IV only (C) IV only

(B) III and IV only (D) All of the above

Answer the Roman numeral question the same way as you answered the preceding question formats. That is, read the stem followed by each answer in turn and decide whether it is true or false, mark your decision, and continue until you have marked each answer. Always re-read the stem for each answer. When you have marked all the answers, you can easily select the correct answer. After you have completed the above question, the Roman numeral section should look like this –

t I. A land sales contract

t II. An easement

t III. A trust deed

t IV. A mortgage

Notice that regardless of the question format, you always mark your true-false decisions next to each answer and always re-read the stem with each answer. The importance of this technique cannot be overstressed. It is very common for students to let the first answer color their thinking about the second answer. *You cannot do this*. Each answer is distinct and separate from each other and must be considered in isolation. Making your true-false markings as you decide about each answer is the only way to ensure that you will do this properly.

On rare occasions, you may encounter on the real estate exams a set of two or more questions which are related to each other. In other words, data from a question is referred to and used in one or more following questions. However, you will never find a set of questions where you must get the answer correct to the first one before you can get the answer correct for the following question(s). In other words, the questions may use common data, but they must be kept separate to the extent that missing a previous question will not cause you to miss a subsequent question.

Frequently, when this technique is employed, there will be a chart or graph to which a number of questions will be directed. These questions are unpopular with test makers because it becomes hard to store the questions individually and they become inflexible when trying to make up a new exam.

One situation on the real estate exams, however, does consistently make use of the question set technique. When testing your knowledge of listing agreements and earnest money receipts, the Real Estate Agency usually includes a "narrative" – that is, a story about how a transaction is to take place. The narrative is followed by a sample listing agreement or earnest money receipt. The listing agreement or earnest money receipt will contain blanks, several of which are numbered. One or more questions then follow, and each question asks what should be placed in one of the numbered blanks. Note that all the questions use the same common data (the narrative), but each question is separate and distinct from the others. That is, you can miss any one question but still have an equal opportunity to get all the others correct.

Ranking the answers

Many times, when answering a test item, you might find that you are unsure of the right answer. Since there is no penalty on the real estate exams for guessing, by all means you should answer the question. But some students have problems deciding which answer to choose. If this happens to you, it may be helpful to use a *ranking technique*, a modification of the true-false marking system discussed above. For example, suppose we had the same completion question we used previously,

The interest held by the vendor during the term of a land sales contract is the

(A) equitable title.   (C) naked title.
(B) marketable title.   (D) insurable title.

Except that this time, suppose you are not sure of the answer. Suppose that you read the stem and answer (A) and decide that it is definitely false, so you mark it false. Then you read the stem again with answer (B), and you decide that the answer is probably true. So you mark (B) as true. When you read the stem again followed by answer (C), you decide that this is a true statement also, so you mark (C) as true. Finally, you read the stem the fourth time followed by answer (D), and this time you also decide the statement is true. When you mark answer (D) as true, you are faced with a dilemma – which is the correct answer among (B), (C) and (D)? Only one answer can be true, but you answered three with true –

The interest held by the vendor during the term of a land sales contract is the

f (A) equitable title.   *t* (C) naked title.
t (B) marketable title.   *t* (D) insurable title.

The answer is to rank the ones of which you are unsure. It is usually easiest to do this in pairs. For example, ask yourself the question, "Do I like (B) better than (C)?" If you answer yourself that you like (C) better than (B), then eliminate (B) by marking it false. Next, decide between the two remaining choices, (C) and (D). Ask yourself which of these two you think is more likely to be true. If you decide (C) is more likely to be true than (D), then eliminate (D) by marking it false. By this process of elimination you have arrived at the decision that (C) is the correct answer. This method works because it is human nature to get confused when we have too many choices to make, but it is always easy to decide between just two items at a time.

Elimination technique

Sometimes you might encounter a problem where you have no idea whether any of the answers is right or not. In this situation, you might still be able to save the day. Many times you can get at the correct answer to a question by eliminating the answers you know are not correct. If you can eliminate three answers as definitely wrong, then you know the fourth answer has to be the correct one.

Use your subconscious mind

Another trick used by successful test takers is to exert a reluctance to change their answers. Good students know that the subconscious mind is a powerful force. They know that they may not be able consciously to remember the answer, but if they ever read the information in the past it is still stored somewhere in their unconscious mind. Therefore, a good rule of thumb when guessing is to stick by your first answer. Of course, when checking over your test at the end you may discover that you completely misunderstood the question, in which case you are certainly justified in changing your answer.

Work the answers backwards

There is another clever technique which is very useful for certain difficult math questions. While the math questions on the real estate exams are a lot easier than many people fear, still there may occasionally be a math problem that is especially difficult. For example, look at the following problem –

A seller told an agent that she wanted to net $160,000 from the sale of her lot, which she felt had a market value of about $180,000. She told the agent that the agent could have everything over the $160,000 as commission. However, the agent did not wish to take a listing on this basis, and decided to list it at a set price which would include the amount the seller wished to net plus a commission of 6%. At what price should the agent list?

(A) $160,000   (C) $170,213
(B) $169,600   (D) $180,000

Now, the way to calculate this correctly is to divide the $160,000 the seller wishes to net by 94%. This is because $160,000 is 94% of what the agent needs to list the property for. However, if you cannot remember how to do the problem, you can still get the right answer another way.

Obviously, one of the four answers above is correct. So you can figure out which is the correct answer just by calculating which one works. Take your calculator, subtract 6% of each answer from that answer in turn, until you find the answer that will leave you with $160,000. As you can see, this technique can make stubborn math problems a breeze.

Learn to smell the answers

Good test takers are usually people who have taken a lot of standardized tests and therefore have come to understand these principles. They have also developed a second sense – they almost seem to be able to "smell" wrong answers put in deliberately to mislead them. The best way for you to develop this second sense is to practice, practice, practice. Go over each and every sample test question without fail.

One thing you can do which will help you develop this second sense is to watch out for key words in a ques-

tion. Pay particular attention to negative words such as not, least, except, and so forth. Also pay close attention to words such as never, and always. In the real world, things are seldom absolute, so answers containing the words "never" and "always" tend to be untrue.

Pay attention also to the grammatical flow of the question. If there seems to be an abrupt change when you leave the stem and start reading the answer, this can be a clue that the answer is not true. On the other hand, answers which are long, wordy or full of qualifications tend to be true statements. Of course, all of this advice can really only be useful in those cases where you are reduced to guessing anyway. If you know the material, you won't need to worry about second-guessing the test makers.

Choosing the best answer

Many students complain that the test questions seem to have more than one correct answer. They report that one answer may be better than another, but it confuses them when two or more answers are both technically correct. In reality, students who find more than one correct answer are students who really do not understand the material thoroughly. In fact, very few questions have two correct answers and force you to choose the better of the two. The fact is that students who have learned some of the material, but not all of it, find they are able to discriminate down to the last two choices, both of which sound correct to them. But if they knew the material better, they would realize that only one of these last two is really correct.

Incomplete answers

Don't let an incomplete statement fool you. For example, suppose you read the stem of a question and the first answer and it reads "For a valid escrow to exist, there must be: (A) an escrow agent and escrow instructions." You immediately conclude that this is a false statement, because there are several other requirements to create a valid escrow in addition to "an escrow agent and escrow instructions." Wrong! If you read the statement all by itself, it is a true statement, because an escrow agent and escrow instructions are required for a valid escrow. The fact that there are other requirements is irrelevant to the truth of this statement.

Don't "what if" the question

One of the most common mistakes students make is to add material or facts to a question that is not stated. People tend to jump to conclusions and make unwarranted assumptions. This can lead to errors. Consider the following question –

> An office manager has assigned all the leads during one afternoon to Hans Schmidt, a broker licensed with the company. Consuelo Moreno, another of the company's brokers is also in the office at the same time. In the middle of the afternoon, Mr. and Mrs. Gomez come in to inquire about buying a property. If the broker assigns the buyers to Moreno,
> (A) this is steering.
> (B) the broker has violated the Fair Housing Act.
> (C) both A and B above are correct.
> (D) neither A nor B above is correct.

The correct answer is (C), because assigning clients to brokers on the basis of race, religion, national origin, sex, mental or physical handicap or familial status (having children), is a called *steering* and is a violation of the Fair Housing Act. But many students read this question and add the assumption that the buyers do not speak English. Then they add the assumption that the buyers do speak Spanish, that Schmidt does not speak Spanish, and that Moreno does speak Spanish! Notice that the stem and the answers do not address the language issue at all, so you must assume that everyone speaks English.

Do the easy questions first

You can maximize your probability of success if you do not let the difficult questions slow you down. If you are taking the national and Oregon exams, you will have almost two whole minutes per question. Since most questions won't take more than about 30 seconds, this will be plenty of time. But if you spend 15 minutes on one tough question, and as a result lack time to finish all of the easy questions, you will be the loser.

To avoid this, the best technique is to answer all the easy questions first. Leave the more difficult questions for a second pass later. After you have finished the easy ones, you will find that you have lots of time left to go back and do the harder ones. Furthermore, you will be more relaxed, more mentally conditioned to the test, and you may have found some material which jogged your memory about one of the harder questions you skipped earlier. Some students still skip some of the especially difficult questions on their second pass and save them for a third pass later. If you follow this approach, you can be sure that, if you run out of time, the questions you didn't have time to finish were the questions you had the least chance of getting right anyway.

Double-check your work

When you finally finish the exam, make a final double-check of your work. Don't forget to check your answer sheet – remember that you get no credit for the right answer unless it is clearly marked with pencil in the proper place on the answer sheet. If you skip a question, be especially careful to place your answers in the right space on the answer sheet. Also be sure that your name and other information is correct. When students talk over the exam afterwards with other students, they usually realize that they made at least one, stupid, silly mistake. In fact, the average error rate is about one silly mistake per 50 exam questions, even when you are trying your best to be careful. If you have time remaining, check your work over carefully; this is no time to get sloppy.

Get ahead of the game

As the day for the exam draws near, you will quite naturally feel nervous and apprehensive. This is really a senseless time for you to feel this way! If you studied well, then you are as prepared to take the exams as any of the other people you will meet at the test center. If you haven't done your work by now, well, it's probably too late anyway. So whether you are prepared or not, it makes no sense to worry. The best course of action for the last couple of days before the exams is to continue to review and study, but *relax*! Of course, it also helps to get plenty of rest, watch your diet, and don't let the rest of the world get in your way, but the most important factor is to stay relaxed.

Make your final preparations for the exam several days in advance. Since you may have to drive some distance, be sure to set the alarm clock early enough. Also tend to other mundane matters such as getting together your pencils, admission ticket, identification, calculator (don't forget fresh batteries), and even fill up the car with gas. Get your family to help you for the last couple of days by taking the rest of your usual chores off your back to allow you time to review in peace and quiet. If you can do all this, you can sit down to take the exam feeling confident that you are as prepared as it is possible to be and that ***nothing is going to stand in the way of your success!***

DOCUMENTS OF REAL ESTATE FINANCE

B Y THE TIME A REAL ESTATE LOAN HAS BEEN FINALIZED, THE LENDER'S FILE WILL contain numerous reports, forms and other documents, each of which is crucial to the lender's security. By far the most important of these documents are those which constitute evidence of the debt and which make the real estate collateral. In this chapter we will explore in detail the complexities of the documents which lenders use to perfect their legal rights.

In law, a legal document is called an ***instrument***. Therefore, in real estate finance, we refer to mortgages and other loan documents as the ***instruments of finance***. When the average lay person thinks of financing documents, the usual instrument that comes to mind is the mortgage. But, although the mortgage is an important instrument of finance, other instruments are more commonly used in modern Oregon loan transactions. In fact, today, most lenders rely on standard forms created by the ***secondary mortgage market***. The secondary mortgage market consists of lenders who purchase loans originated by local ***primary lenders*** (discussed in detail in the next section, Sources of Funds for Mortgage Lending).

Even though a lender may use a standard form, the documents will undoubtedly be one of three possibilities. Lenders in Oregon can use either a ***note and mortgage***, a ***note and trust deed***, or a ***land sales contract***. When a lender uses a note and mortgage, the note is the evidence of the debt, and the mortgage makes the real estate collateral for the debt by creating a ***lien*** on the borrower's real estate. For this reason, we say the mortgage is the ***lien instrument***. The same thing happens in a note and trust deed transaction, except that the lien instrument is a trust deed instead of a mortgage.

In a land sales contract, however, the legalities are completely different. For one thing, in a land sales contract, the note and lien instrument are not separate documents. Instead, the buyer promises to pay for the property in installments and the seller agrees

NOTES

to give the buyer a deed when the buyer finishes paying for the property. Note that, since the deed is not delivered to the buyer until the end of the contract, the buyer does not become the owner of the property until the loan balance is paid in full. Each of the three loan possibilities will be discussed in detail later in this section.

Notes

A ***note*** is also sometimes called a ***promissory note*** or occasionally, a ***bond***. As we observed above, the note is the evidence of the debt and must accompany a mortgage or trust deed. The note is, therefore, central to the loan transaction. Without the note as the evidence of the debt, the mortgage or trust deed would be useless – after all, if there is no debt, the lien instrument would have little purpose.

It is important to understand that in Oregon a note can be considered separately from the mortgage or trust deed. That is, it is the borrower's personal pledge, a promise to repay a debt, and can stand alone. In Oregon, a lender can sue the borrower on the note and ignore the collateral. This would result in a general judgment against the borrower which the lender can enforce by having the sheriff seize any of the borrower's assets (within certain limits).

$ _____   _____ _____
                                                  CITY AND STATE WHERE EXECUTED   DATE

     I/we, jointly and severally, promise to pay to the order of

_____

at (insert place payments to be made)

_____

the sum of _____ DOLLARS,

with interest thereon at the rate of _____ percent per annum from _____ until paid, payable in _____

installments of not less than $ _____ in any one payment. Interest shall be paid _____ ☐ in addition to ☐ and is included in (in-

dicate which) the minimum payments set forth above. The first payment shall be made on _____ , and a like payment

shall be made on _____ thereafter until the whole sum, principal and interest has been paid. If any installments is

not so paid, all principal and interest shall become immediately due and collectable at the option of the holder of this note.

    If this note is placed in the hands of an attorney or other third party for collection, I/we promise and agree to pay the holder's reasonable attorney's fees and/or

collection costs, even though no suit or action is filed. If a suit or an action is filed, the amount of such reasonable attorney's fees shall be fixed by the court(s), in which the suit

or action, including any appeal, is tried, heard or decided.

                                                       _____

                                                       _____

                                                       _____

Form No. 17 – Installment Note. NO   COPYRIGHT 1998 Stevens Ness Law Publishing Company

A standard promissory note, reproduced courtesy Stevens-Ness Law Publishing Company

---

A note is similar to a check or a draft, all of which are examples of a category of contracts called ***negotiable instruments***, but there are some differences. Of course, we are all familiar with checks. One of the major differences between notes and checks is that checks are due upon presentment, where notes are due on some date in the future. Another difference is that a check is an order to a third party (the bank) to pay the money to the payee, where a note is a promise to pay the money directly to the payee.

In a note the borrower is called the ***maker*** and the lender is the ***payee***. Sometimes there is more than one maker, in which case the terms of the note will obligate the makers "jointly and severally" – that is each borrower is personally liable for the full amount of the debt, or the lender could recover different portions of the debt from each borrower. When there is a co-signer the co-signer becomes the same as an additional maker and is fully liable. A co-signature is sometimes referred to as the co-signer's **guaranty**.

Notes and checks are called negotiable instruments because the payee can usually transfer his or her interest easily (sell the note) merely by **endorsement**. When a note has been endorsed to another there arises a question of **recourse**. Normally the new payee has recourse against the person from whom it was received, but only if the new payee is a **holder in due course**. A holder in due course is a subsequent payee who accepted a note which was –

- Complete in its terms and appeared to be enforceable, and
- Accepted before it was in default, and
- Accepted in exchange for valuable consideration, and
- Accepted in good faith without knowing or suspecting that it might not be honored.

However, notes are frequently endorsed **without recourse**, that is, the party endorsing the note does not accept any responsibility for payment. When a primary lender sells a loan in the secondary mortgage market, the note is occasionally endorsed without recourse. This means that if a foreclosure becomes necessary, the secondary lender has no recourse to the primary lender and must foreclose on the borrower in order to recover. Naturally, secondary lenders prefer to buy loans endorsed in blank (with full recourse), so that they can simply make the primary lender take the loan back if the borrower defaults.*

As noted earlier, a loan file contains numerous documents and, although the note is certainly the most important, there are others that are also critical. When a loan is sold, the usual practice is to endorse the note to the buyer of the loan, but **assign** the interest in the mortgage or trust deed, fire insurance policy, title insurance policy, etc. Most contracts are transferred by **assignment**; only negotiable interests are transferred by endorsement.

When describing the terms of a note there are various expressions common in the world of finance. A note where the entire principal balance is due at the end of the loan is called a **straight note**. In contrast, real estate loans are more commonly arranged with periodic payments of principal. When the loan is paid off in installments, it is called an **amortized note**. Amortized notes sometimes call for a lump sum payment toward the principal, called a **balloon payment**. Balloon payments are usually used to pay the loan off early, but the term is also used to describe any extra principal payment. For example, a loan with a balloon payment might call for regular payments, but also contain a clause requiring the borrower to pay "the then remaining principal balance" in full at some point. The requirement to pay off the loan early can be structured as a balloon payment or as a **call feature**. A balloon payment requires the borrower to pay the loan off in full at the stated time. A call feature, on the other hand, allows the lender to demand repayment in full any time after some point. Unless the lender calls the loan due, the borrower need not pay it off. The balloon payment is not as flexible as the call feature.

Borrowers should be careful to read the terms of the note. For example, if the loan calls for regular payments, it should also contain the expression "not less than" or "or more," or other language allowing the borrower to pay more than the minimum. If the note does not contain language allowing the borrower to pay extra, then the borrower is said to be **locked in**.

---

* Investors use the term "recourse" and "non-recourse" in another way. To an investor these terms refer to whether or not the lender can satisfy the debt from any of the investor's assets (recourse financing), or whether the property is the lender's sole recourse (non-recourse financing).

For the lender, probably the most important clause in the note is the ***acceleration clause***. Lenders will require an acceleration clause in all installment notes. The acceleration clause allows the lender to call the entire principal balance immediately due in the event the borrower should default. If an installment note does not contain an acceleration clause, then all the lender can do is sue to force the borrower to bring the loan current.

A ***demand clause*** is similar to an acceleration clause, but allows the lender to call the entire principal balance due in full even if the borrower is not in default. Demand clauses are seldom encountered today in residential lending, but are still common in commercial notes.

Priority of liens

A complete understanding of lien instruments requires knowledge of the priority of liens. Whenever there is a foreclosure the rights of the respective lienholders are determined by their priority. We use the term ***junior*** or ***subordinate*** lienholder to describe the lender whose interests are in second or subsequent position. A ***senior*** lienholder is a lender who enjoys priority over a junior or subordinate lienholder.

In general, priority is determined by the date the instrument was recorded in the public records. There are certain exceptions, however. The most notable exceptions are judgments, which can be recorded, but which are usually just placed on the court records. Certain other liens, such as city liens and income tax levies are also found in places other than the public records. Regardless of where the record of the lien is found, the date of its creation usually constitutes its priority date, although property tax liens are prior liens regardless of their date. Because the priority date is critical, lenders always make sure their lien instruments are recorded and verified as to priority before they allow the loan funds to be disbursed to the borrower. If a lien is not recorded at all, it is always last in priority.

Normal priority can also be altered if a senior lender agrees to ***subordinate*** to a junior lienholder. For example, suppose you buy a building lot and the seller carries your note for a portion of the purchase price, secured by a mortgage or trust deed on the lot. Later you go to build on the lot and wish to finance the construction with a bank loan. The bank wants a first lien, but the seller already has a recorded lien. In this case, you could convince the seller to agree to subordinate to the bank. The bank will then have a first lien, even though the bank's mortgage or trust deed will be recorded at a date later than the seller's mortgage or trust deed.

In a foreclosure priority is crucial, as the property will usually be sold at a public auction sale and the proceeds of the sale will be distributed to lienholders according to priority date. Depending on the type of lien instrument, junior lienholders sometimes participate in these proceeds, and sometimes not. Any lienholder can always file a foreclosure when the loan is in default, but junior lienholders must take title subject to the senior liens.

In general, foreclosure by a senior lienholder will extinguish all junior liens, provided the junior lienholder is properly notified of the suit and, in most cases, given the right to protect his or her lien by paying off the senior lien. In some cases, the junior lienholder may save his or her lien merely by bringing the senior lien current to reinstate it, rather than having to pay it off in full. In order to be sure of getting notice of a foreclosure by a senior lienholder, a junior lienholder frequently records a ***request for notice of default***.

It is important to understand that this pecking order of priority is not limited just to financing instruments. Leases, options, earnest money agreements, easements – all other interests are subject to the same rules. If you mortgage your property and then lease it to a tenant, foreclosure by the lender will extinguish the tenant's leasehold. But if the property is already leased and mortgaged later, the lender must take the property subject to the lease. A wise lender would insist on a subordination from the lessee to the mortgage.

Exercise a

The three instruments used in real estate finance are the _____ , its modern replacement, the _____ _____ , and the _____ _____ _____ , which is car-ried by a seller. The first two of these are called _____ instruments because they create a _____ on the borrower's real estate. They must be accompanied by a _____ , which is the evidence of the debt. Notes are also called _____ notes. A note is an example of a _____ _____ . A note is a promise to pay a sum of money in the _____ . In a note the borrower is called the _____ and the lender is called the _____ .

A lender can transfer a note (sell it) by _____ . A _____ in _____ _____ has _____ to the last endorser, unless the note is endorsed _____ _____ . A note signed without restriction is endorsed _____ _____ .

When a note calls for interest only, it is said to be a _____ note. If there are regular reductions of principal, we call it an _____ note. When there is an exceptional extra amount to be paid on the principal, this is called a _____ payment.

For the lender, the most important clause in the note is the _____ clause, which allows the lender to call the entire balance due in full in the event of the borrower's _____ . A clause allowing the lender to call the loan due at any time is called a _____ clause, although this clause is seldom found in _____ lending today.

When a lien instrument is recorded it establishes the _____ of the lien as against subsequent lienhold-ers. All later interests are said to be _____ or subordinate interests. In a foreclosure, the property will be sold and the proceeds will be paid to the lienholders in the order of their _____ . Foreclosure by a senior lienholder also _____ all junior interests. Property taxes, among other liens, are excep-tions to the normal order of priority, as would be a senior lienholder agreeing to a _____ to a junior lienholder. To protect a junior lien, the lienholder may record a _____ for _____ of _____ .

Creation of the mortgage

As we have seen in the preceding discussion, a mortgage is a **lien** on the property, but a mortgage alone is worth little without the note as evidence of the debt. When there is a lien on the property, we say that the title is subject to an **en-cumbrance**; that is, a lien is a special type of encumbrance which makes the property collateral for a debt.

Encumbrances are said to "run with the land" – if the owner sells the property, the buyer takes title subject to the encumbrance. Therefore, when a lender has a lien on the borrower's property, the borrower cannot get rid of the lien by sale, lease, additional liens, or any other means, short of paying off the debt. This makes a recorded lien an ideal protection for the lender.

Historically, mortgages were the first instruments ever used to make real estate collateral for a debt. Their history goes back to the earliest recorded beginnings of English common law. Originally, the mortgage was literally a conveyance of the title to the lender. The mortgage operated in a manner similar to a deed. Since the borrower would give the mortgage to the lender, the borrower was called the **grantor** and the lender was called the **grantee**, although the terms **mortgagor** and **mortgagee** are more common today. (In law, the "-or person" always gives the document to the "-ee person.")

In the earliest mortgages, when the title was conveyed to the mortgagee, the mortgagee took physical possession of the real estate. Later, as mortgage lending became a specialized field and mortgage lenders acquired more than just a few mortgage loans, it became impractical for lenders to oversee their many properties and mortgage instruments were changed to allow the mortgagor to remain in possession.

It is interesting to note that early mortgage instruments were really the conveyance of a **defeasible fee**. The mortgagor held a **right of reverter**, that is, the right to recover the title by paying the loan in full. According to the terms of these early mortgages, repayment would cause the title to revert automatically to the mortgagor. The clause setting forth this right was called the **defeasance clause**. The right of the borrower to clear title after paying off the loan is still called the defeasance clause, even in modern mortgages.

Originally the mortgagee was not required to file a suit to foreclose. If the borrower failed to pay off the loan by the due date, the buyer simply lost the right of reverter and the lender's title to the property would become vested absolutely. As time went by mortgagors gained more and more rights. Eventually mortgagees were required to file a suit and obtain judicial approval to keep the property. This became known as a **foreclosure**, that is, a suit to foreclose the borrower's interest in the property.

Much later, borrowers gained the right to redeem their property, even after foreclosure. Originally this right lasted for one year. In early England, most people lived close to the land and gained their living from agricultural pursuits. Since most farmers get paid once a year when they sell their crops, if the law is going to give a farmer a second chance, it should be at least one year. Today the time limit for redemption after foreclosure is set by individual state statutes. In Oregon the right of redemption today is 180 days.

Although borrowers in all states today can count on the right to judicial review of a foreclosure and of a period of time after foreclosure in which to redeem, a few states still follow the old concept that a mortgage is a conveyance of a defeasible title to the mortgagee. These states are called **title theory** states. Most states (including Oregon and other western states) follow the more modern theory that the mortgage is merely a lien against the borrower's title. Such states are called **lien theory** states. A major significance of being in a title theory state is that second mortgages are more difficult. Once the lender is in title to the property, the borrower has little to pledge as collateral for a second mortgage. Title theory states have had to enact special legislation to make a second mortgage possible.

As noted previously, when a mortgage loan has been made the mortgage is recorded to protect the priority of the mortgagee's lien. It is not customary to record the accompanying note, although some lenders incorporate the note into the mortgage document. Since the mortgage has been recorded in the public records, when the borrower pays off the loan, we must record another instrument in order to extinguish the lien created by the mortgage. This document is called a **satisfaction of mortgage**, or just **satisfaction**, for short. The term "satisfaction" is also used to describe instruments terminating many other liens – satisfaction of construction lien, satisfaction of judgment, and so forth.

FORM No. 7 – MORTGAGE – Short Form (Individual). COPYRIGHT 1999 STEVENS-NESS LAW PUBLISHING CO., PORTLAND, OR 97204

NN

MORTGAGE

_____

_____
_____
_____

Mortgagor's Name and Address

_____
_____

Mortgagee's Name and Address

After recording, return to (Name, Address, Zip):

_____
_____
_____

SPACE RESERVED
FOR
RECORDER'S USE

STATE OF OREGON,
County of _____ } ss.
I certify that the within instrument was received for recording on _____,
at _____ o'clock _____ M., and recorded in book/reel/volume No. _____, on page _____ and/or as fee/file/instrument/microfilm/reception No. _____, Records of this County.
Witness my hand and seal of County affixed.

_____
NAME   TITLE

By _____, Deputy.

WITNESSETH, That _____
_____ , mortgagor, in consideration of
_____ Dollars ($ _____),
to mortgagor paid, does hereby grant, bargain, sell and convey unto _____ ,
_____ mortgagee, the following described premises situated
in _____ County, State of _____, to-wit:

Together with the tenements, hereditaments and appurtenances thereto belonging, or in any way appertaining, and to have and to hold the premises with the appurtenances, unto the mortgagee, and mortgagee's heirs and assigns forever.
This mortgage is intended to secure the payment of one (or more) promissory note(s), in substantially the following form(s):

Mortgage. Note the language that sounds as though it is conveying title. This form reproduced here for educational purposes with the kind permission of Stevens-Ness Law Publishing Company.

The date of maturity of the debt secured by this mortgage is the date on which the last scheduled principal payment becomes due, to wit: _____ ,

The mortgagor warrants that the proceeds of the loan represented by the note(s) and this mortgage are:

(a)*   primarily for mortgagor's personal, family or household purposes (see notice below), or

(b)   for an organization or (even if mortgagor is a natural person) for business or commercial purposes.

Now, if the sum of money due upon the note(s) and this mortgage shall be paid according to the agreement herein expressed, this conveyance shall be void. In case default shall be made in payment of the principal or interest or any part thereof as above provided, then the mortgagee or mortgagee's personal representatives, successors or assigns may foreclose the mortgage and sell the premises with each and every of the appurtenances or any part thereof, in the manner prescribed by law, and out of the money arising from such sale, retain the principal, interest, attorney fees, and costs as provided in the note(s), together with the costs and charges of making such sale and the surplus, if there be any, pay over to the person(s) entitled thereto, as such interest(s) may appear.

WARNING: Unless mortgagor provides mortgagee with evidence of insurance coverage as required by the contract or loan agreement between them, mortgagee may purchase insurance at mortgagor's expense to protect mortgagee's interest. This insurance may, but need not, also protect mortgagor's interest. If the collateral becomes damaged, the coverage purchased by mortgagee may not pay any claim made by or against mortgagor. Mortgagor may later cancel the coverage by providing evidence that mortgagor has obtained property coverage elsewhere. Mortgagor is responsible for the cost of any insurance coverage purchased by mortgagee, which cost may be added to mortgagor's contract or loan balance. If it is so added, the interest rate on the underlying contract or loan will apply to it. The effective date of coverage may be the date mortgagor's prior coverage lapsed or the date mortgagor failed to provide proof of coverage. The coverage mortgagee purchases may be considerably more expensive than insurance mortgagor might otherwise obtain alone and may not satisfy any need for property damage coverage or any mandatory liability insurance requirements imposed by applicable law.

In the event any suit or action to foreclose this mortgage is commenced, the losing party therein agrees to pay the attorney fees, costs and disbursements of the prevailing party, including statutory costs and disbursements and costs of title report(s) and/or title search. If any appeal is take from any judgment or decree entered pursuant to such suit or action, the losing party on appeal therein promises to pay the attorney fees, costs and disbursements, including all statutory costs and disbursements, of the prevailing party. To the extent permitted by law, all such sums shall be and are secured by the lien of this mortgage and shall be included in the judgment or decree of foreclosure.

DATED _____ ,

*IMPORTANT NOTICE: Delete, by lining out, whichever warranty (a) or (b) is inapplicable. If warranty (a) is applicable, and if the mortgagee is a creditor, as such word is defined in the Truth-in Lending Act and Regulation Z, the mortgagee MUST comply with the Act and Regulation by making required disclosures. For this purpose, use Stevens-Ness Form No. 1319 or equivalent.

STATE OF OREGON, County of _____) ss.

This instrument was acknowledged before me on _____ ,

by _____ .

_____
Notary public for Oregon

My commission expires _____

Mortgage remedies

A default is a breach of a contractual promise. When a borrower defaults on a loan agreement, be it a note and mortgage, note and trust deed, or land sales contract, the default is usually a failure to pay when due. However, failure to pay is only one of many possible defaults. There are numerous clauses in any financing instrument, and failure to perform any of these clauses is just as serious a default as failure to pay.

For example, the mortgage usually requires the borrower to maintain insurance on the premises and to pay the property taxes when due. Another clause will typically require the borrower to maintain the premises in good condition. Many loans today also contain a clause prohibiting the sale of the property without paying off the mortgage.

If a mortgagor is in default of the mortgage the mortgagee can accelerate and, if the mortgagor does not pay the full balance after acceleration, the mortgagee can proceed with foreclosure. If a foreclosure is contemplated legal advice will be necessary, because a mortgage foreclosure must be a ***judicial foreclosure***, that is to say, a lawsuit must be filed. Other financing instruments (notably trust deeds) allow for non-judicial foreclosure, where an appointed trustee sells the property at public auction, without judicial review or the necessity of filing suit.

Lenders almost invariably win suits to foreclose; in fact, it is rare for a borrower to win a suit to foreclose. Even if the mortgagor wins, the best that can usually be hoped for is reinstatement of the debt, that is, the acceleration is denied and the mortgagee is required to continue to accept payments. Of course, in order to win reinstatement, the mortgagor would certainly have to be prepared to make up all back payments and cure any other defaults.

When the mortgagee has won, the court will enter a ***decree of foreclosure and sale***. The decree of foreclosure and sale allows the lender to have the property sold to satisfy the amount owing, which will include not only the balance of the debt, but the costs of foreclosure, unpaid interest and other charges. The lender must attempt to satisfy this amount by filing with the court a ***writ of execution***. The writ of execution becomes the order of the court to the sheriff to sell the property at public auction.

The sheriff must publish a notice of the impending sale in a newspaper of general circulation in the county where the property is located. The notice must be published at least once a week for four consecutive weeks, and the last notice must appear at least one week before the date set for the sale. The sheriff (or a deputy) will hold the sale at the time and place as advertised in the published notice. A common location is the front steps of the county courthouse.

Anyone may bid at the auction, including the mortgagee, the mortgagor, or any other party claiming an interest in the property, or any member of the public, although the sheriff or deputy holding the sale is not permitted to bid. No one is required to bid. All bids must be for cash, except that the mortgagee may bid up to the total balance owed without paying cash, since the mortgagee already paid that amount when the loan was made. If the mortgagee wishes to bid over the amount owing, the difference must be paid in cash. The mortgagee may also refuse to bid at all.

The successful bidder will receive a ***sheriff's certificate of sale***, which will entitle the successful bidder to a ***sheriff's deed***, subject to the redemption rights of the mortgagor or junior lienholders (discussed later). The successful bidder is also entitled to immediate possession of the property, unless there is a valid lease which was recorded prior to the mortgage. The successful bidder is entitled to any income from the property, but if the mortgagor or a junior lienholder later exercises a right of redemption, the net income goes to the benefit of the mortgagor.

The sheriff will turn the proceeds of the sale over to the clerk of the court for final disbursement to the mortgagee. If there is a surplus it must be paid to the mortgagor. The mortgagor has ten days in which to file objections with the court claiming irregularities in the sale procedures. If there are no irregularities then the mortgagee applies to the court for an order confirming the sale.

The mortgagor can halt the proceedings at any time prior to the actual sale by paying to the court the full amount due as stated in the decree of foreclosure and sale, together with the lenders costs incurred up to that point. This is called the ***equitable right of redemption***. Even after the sale, the mortgagor can still redeem the property for 180 days. This right is called the ***statutory right of redemption***. In order to exercise this right, the mortgagor must pay to the successful bidder the amount the successful bidder paid for the property, plus 9% interest from the date of the sale, plus any sums the successful bidder paid to maintain the premises up to the time of redemption, but less the net income received by the successful bidder. The successful bidder is entitled to recover only expenses incurred to prevent waste or for property taxes paid. Sums expended for improvements or additions to the property cannot be recovered. If the property is not redeemed, then when all redemption rights have expired, the sheriff will deed the property to the successful bidder.

Junior lienholders also have a statutory right of redemption which lasts for 60 days from the date of the sale. Their rights of redemption are substantially the same as the rights of the mortgagor. A junior lienholder who redeems steps into the same position the successful bidder was in, that is, if the mortgagor still has time remaining on the 180-day statutory right of redemption, the mortgagor may still exercise it. The only difference is that now the mortgagor would be redeeming from a junior lienholder, rather than from the successful bidder. If there is more than one junior lienholder, then each has a 60-day right of redemption, and if one junior lienholder redeems, the right of redemption of the other junior lienholders is extended to 60 days from the date of the last redemption by a junior lienholder.

Deficiency judgments Most of the time when a mortgagor borrows money the purpose is to obtain the funds to acquire the property. If the money is borrowed from a third party, such as a bank, then the mortgage is said to be a ***hard money mortgage***, because the lender advanced hard cash. On the other hand, maybe the mortgage is carried by the seller rather than a bank. In such a transaction, the seller would deed the property to the buyer, who would then give a note and mortgage back to the seller for part of the purchase money. This is called a ***purchase money mortgage***.

What if the property did not sell for enough at a sheriff's sale to satisfy the mortgage debt? Normally, the mortgagee may then file a motion with the court requesting a ***deficiency judgment***. This is a judgment against the mortgagor personally and can be enforced by execution on the mortgagor's other assets, subject to certain limitations. However, the mortgagee is entitled to this remedy only if the loan was for hard cash (i.e., it was a hard money mortgage). If it was a purchase money mortgage, then the mortgagee lent the equity in the property, and must be satisfied with taking the property back. It has therefore become a fundamental principle of common law that a purchase money mortgagee is never entitled to a deficiency judgment.

In 1975 the Oregon Legislature enacted a statute which expanded the definition of a purchase money mortgage. Now, purchase money mortgages include not only mortgages carried by sellers, but also mortgages carried by third party lenders if the original balance is $50,000 or less, the mortgage is on the borrowers primary or secondary residence, and the property is a single-family structure. Note that the effect of this statute was to prohibit deficiency judgments on personal residences with loans under $50,000.

The terms "purchase money" and "hard money" are applied to other financing instruments as well. In other words, a note and trust deed carried by a seller is called a "purchase money trust deed," but if carried by a third party it is a "hard money trust deed." Land sales contracts are always carried by the seller, so they are always purchase money instruments. Generically, lenders refer to all financing carried by the seller as "purchase money financing" and bank loans as "hard money financing." Similarly, the notes secured by mortgages and trust deeds can be referred to as "purchase money notes" and "hard money notes" respectively. The special Oregon statute making personal residence loans under $50,000 hard money mortgages, even if carried by the seller, applies only to mortgages in Oregon, and not to trust deeds as well.

Exercise b

In a note and mortgage transaction, the borrower is called the _____ and the lender is the _____. Oregon is a _____ theory state; this means that the mortgage is not considered a _____ of the property to the lender.

When the mortgage loan is paid in full, we record a _____ of _____ to remove the lien from the borrower's record title.

A mortgage foreclosure must be a _____ foreclosure. If the borrower successfully defends the foreclosure, the court will order _____ of the debt. If the lender wins, the court will enter a _____ of _____ and _____ .

After the lender wins the suit, a _____ of _____ can be filed with the court. This becomes the order of the court to the _____ to sell the mortgaged property at public auction to satisfy the debt. All bidders must pay _____ except the lender, who can bid up to the amount of the balance due without paying _____ . If the lender bids more than the amount due, any surplus must be paid in _____ . The successful bidder gets a _____ _____ of _____ .

If the proceeds of the sale are more than the amount necessary to satisfy the amount due the lender, the surplus is turned over to the _____ .

After the sale, the mortgagor gets a _____ of _____ which lasts for _____ days. Junior lienholders also have the same right, which lasts for ____ days. If no one redeems, the successful bidder is entitled to a _____ deed to the property.

If the property did not sell for enough to satisfy the amount due, the lender is entitled to apply to the court for a _____ _____ , which can be used to execute on the borrower's other assets, within certain limitations. This is not permitted, however, if the loan was a _____ _____ mortgage, which is a loan carried by the _____ , or by a third party if the original loan balance was under $ _____ and on the borrower's _____ _____ .

Creation of trust deeds

Trust deeds were used occasionally in Oregon as early as the 1800s, but did not become common until after the **Oregon Trust Deed Act** was created in 1959. Today, the modern provisions of the trust deed make it by far the most popular instrument with lenders. In fact, there is hardly a major lender left in Oregon who does not use the trust deed to the exclusion of all other instruments.

To understand trust deeds we must first understand the idea of the **trust**. A trust is an arrangement where a person (called a **trustor**), gives something (usually money or property), to someone (called a **trustee**), with the understanding that the trustee is to hold it for the benefit of a third party (called a **beneficiary**). An easy example is what would happen if you placed some assets in trust for your child. You would select a trustee, perhaps the trust department of a bank or a trust company, and transfer the asset to the trustee with instructions for how it is to be managed. Your child is the beneficiary in this arrangement. We use trusts today for dozens of purposes, usually to avoid taxation or legal liability. For example, if you were to set up those assets in trust for your child, a portion the income earned by the assets can become the child's income – not yours – and taxed at the child's tax rates, whose tax bracket is probably not nearly as high as yours. Trusts usually have all three of the parties above, trustor, trustee and beneficiary, and the rights and duties of each is spelled out in the trust agreement.

We will see how we can make use of this concept of the trust in a clever way to create a lien on real property. But first, if you recall, in a note and mortgage transaction the borrower gave a note and a mortgage to the lender. The note was the evidence of the debt, and in fact, could stand alone as an unsecured instrument if desired. The mortgage created the lien on the property –

In a mortgage transaction the borrower (called the mortgagor) gives a note to the lender (called the mortgagee). In exchange for the note the lender gives the borrower the cash. The borrower also gives the lender a mortgage which makes the borrower's real estate collateral for the note.

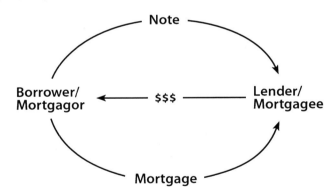

Now, when we substitute a trust deed for the mortgage, things are completely different, although the net result is similar, that is, the lender gets a note, and the lender also gets a lien on the property. However, the way the trust deed creates the lien is unique.

To create a trust deed lien the borrower (owner) deeds a right in the property to the trustee. This right is generally referred to as a limited **power of sale**. This power of sale gives the trustee the right to sell the property, but limited, in that the trustee can sell the property only if the borrower is in default. In the trust arrangement it says that the Oregon Trust Deed Act applies to this deed, and the Trust Deed Act stipulates exactly how the trustee can sell the property. This power of sale is a title right so it must be conveyed by a deed. Note that the borrower is the grantor of the deed and the trustee is the grantee of the deed. Since the deed creates a trust, we call it a trust deed or deed of trust. And since the lender receives the benefit of the trust, we call the lender the beneficiary.

You can see that the borrower could be called the owner, the borrower, the trustor, or the grantor. The trustee could also be called the grantee. In Oregon it is more common to refer to the borrower and the trustee as grantor and trustee, but in other states it is more usual to hear trustor and trustee. The lender is always referred to as the beneficiary.

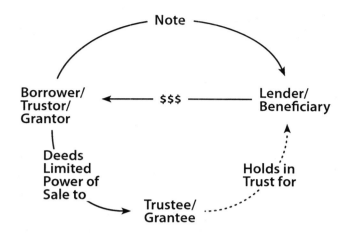

In a trust deed transaction the borrower gives a note to the lender in exchange for the loan funds, the same as in the mortgage transaction on the previous page. The difference is that the lien is created when the borrower deeds a limited power of sale to a third party, called a trustee. The trustee holds the limited power to sell the property in trust for the lender. Since the lender receives the benefit of the arrangement the lender is called the beneficiary.

The best part for the beneficiary is the simplicity of foreclosure. Essentially, a foreclosure can be effected just by telling the trustee that the note is in default and to sell the property at public auction according to the provisions of the Trust Deed Act. This saves having to file a suit and wait for the cumbersome judicial process to finish. Of course, for the protection of the borrower, the Trust Deed Act sets standards which the trustee must follow.

The trustee may not be the same entity as the beneficiary, nor may the trustee be an entity which is a subsidiary of or affiliated with the beneficiary. The Trust Deed Act specifically states that a trustee may only be an attorney, a bank or savings and loan, a trust company, a licensed escrow agent or title insurance company, or an agency of the U.S. government. However, it is important to note that the trustee is not neutral, but rather, owes allegiance to the beneficiary. A trustee may be an attorney who represents the beneficiary, even if the attorney is an employee of the beneficiary.

Now that you see the basic operation of the trust deed, what would happen when the grantor pays off the note? In a note and mortgage transaction, the mortgagee would give the mortgagor a satisfaction of mortgage to record. However, this time the lien was created by a conveyance of the limited power of sale to the trustee. Logically then, in order to undo the lien, the beneficiary simply orders the trustee to convey the limited power of sale back to the grantor. The instrument used is called a ***deed of reconveyance***.

Trust deed remedies

As we have seen, a beneficiary can foreclose the trust deed just by telling the trustee to sell the property. This is called a ***trustee's foreclosure*** or ***non-judicial foreclosure***. The beneficiary should be sure that the note is indeed in default. If the beneficiary wrongfully commences a trustee's foreclosure, the only way the grantor can have a day in court is to bring a suit to enjoin (bar) the trustee from holding the sale.

The first step in foreclosure is always to accelerate the debt. In a trust deed, the second step is for the trustee to record a ***notice of default and election to sell***. The notice of default and election to sell must also be served on the grantor or the grantor's successor in interest, any junior lienholders whose liens are recorded or known to the beneficiary, and on any other person who has recorded a special document called a ***request for notice of default***. The request for notice of default is usually recorded by junior lienholders whose liens are small judgments or other liens which are not of record.

FORM No. 881 – TRUST DEED (Assignment Restricted)   COPYRIGHT 1999 STEVENS-NESS LAW PUBLISHING CO., PORTLAND, OR 97204

NN

TRUST DEED

_____
_____
_____
Grantor's Name and Address
_____
_____
Beneficiary's Name and Address
After recording, return to (Name, Address, Zip):
_____
_____
_____

SPACE RESERVED
FOR
RECORDER'S USE

STATE OF OREGON,
County of _____ } ss.
I certify that the within instrument was
received for recording on _____,
at _____ o'clock _____ M., and recorded in
book/reel/volume No. _____, on page _____
and/or as fee/file/instrument/microfilm/reception
No. _____, Records of this County.
Witness my hand and seal of County affixed.

_____   _____
NAME   TITLE

By _____, Deputy.

THIS TRUST DEED, made on _____ , between
_____
_____ as Grantor,
_____, as Trustee, and,
_____
_____, as Beneficiary,

WITNESSETH:

Grantor irrevocably grants, bargains, sells and conveys to trustee, in trust, with power of sale, the property in
_____ County, Oregon, described as:

together with all and singular the tenements, hereditaments and appurtenances and all other rights thereunto belonging or in any way now or hereafter appertaining, and the rents, issues and profits thereof, and all fixtures now or hereafter attached to or used in connection with the property.

FOR THE PURPOSE OF SECURING PERFORMANCE of each agreement of grantor herein contained and payment of the sum of _____
_____
Dollars, with interest thereon according to the terms of a promissory note of even date herewith, payable to beneficiary or order and made by grantor, the final payment of principal and interest hereof, if not sooner paid to be due and payable on _____ .

The date of maturity of the debt secured by this instrument is the date, stated above, on which the final installment of the note becomes due and payable. Should thge grantor either agree to, attempt to, or actually sell, convey, or assigtn all (or any part) of the proeprty, or all (or any part) of grantor's interest in it without first obtaining the written consent or approval of the beneficiary, then, at the beneficiary's option*, all obligations secured by this instrument, irrespective of the maturity dates expressed therein, or herein, shall become immediately due and payable, The execution by grantor of an earnest money agreement** does not constitute a sale, conveyance or assignment.

To protect the security of this trust deed, grantor agrees:

1. To protect, preserve and maintain the property in good condition and repair; not to remove or demolish any building or improvement thereon; and not to commit or permit any waste of the property.

2. To complete or restore promptly and in good and habitable condition any building or improvement which may be constructed, damaged or destroyed thereon and pay when due all costs incurred therefor.

3. To comply with all laws, ordinances, regulations, covenants, conditions and restrictions affecting the property; if the beneficiary so requests, to join In executing such financing statements pursuant to the Uniform Commercial Code as the beneficiary may require and to pay for filing same in the proper public office or offices, as well as the cost of all lien searches made by filing officers or searching agencies as may be deemed desirable by the beneficiary.

4. To provide and continuously maintain insurance on the buildings now or hereafter erected on the property against loss or damage by fire and other hazards, as the beneficiary may from time to time require, in an amount not less than $ _____, written by one or more companies acceptable to the beneficiary, with loss payable to the latter. All policies of insurance shall be delivered to the beneficiary as soon as issued. If the grantor shall fail for any reason to procure any such insurance and to deliver the policies to the beneficiary at least fifteen days prior to the expiration of any policy of insurance now or hereafter placed on the buildings, the beneficiary may procure the same at grantor's expense. The amount collected under any fire or other insurance policy may be applied by beneficiary upon any indebtedness secured hereby and in such order as beneficiary may determine, or at option of beneficiary the entire amount so collected, or any part thereof, may be released to grantor. Such application or release shall not cure or waive any default or notice of default hereunder or invalidate any act done pursuant to such notice.

5. To keep the property free from construction liens and to pay all taxes, assessments and other charges that may be levied or assessed upon or against the property before any part of such taxes, assessments and other charges become past due or delinquent and promptly deliver receipts therefor to beneficiary. Should the grantor fail to make payment of any taxes, assessments, insurance premiums liens or other charges payable by grantor, either by direct payment or by providing beneficiary with funds with which to make such payment, beneficiary may, at its option make payment thereof, and the amount so paid, with interest at the rate set forth in the note secured hereby, together with the obligations described in paragraphs 6 and 7 of this trust deed, shall be added to and become a part of the debt secured by this trust deed, without waiver of any rights arising from breach of any of the covenants hereof and for such payments, with interest as aforesaid, the property hereinbefore described, as well as the grantor, shall be bound to the same extent that they are bound for the payment or the obligation herein described. All such payments shall be immediately due and payable without notice, and the nonpayment thereof shall, at the option of the beneficiary, render all sums secured by this trust deed immediately due and payable and constitute a breach of this trust deed.

6. To pay all costs, fees and expenses of this trust including the cost of title search as well as the other costs and expenses of the trustee incurred in connection with or in enforcing this obligation and trustee's and attorney's fees actually incurred.

7. To appear in and defend any action or proceeding purporting to affect the security rights or powers of beneficiary or trustee; and in any suit, action or proceeding in which the beneficiary or trustee may appear, including any suit for the foreclosure of this deed or any suit or action related to this instrument, including but not limited to its validity and or enforceability, to pay all costs and expenses, including evidence of title and the beneficiary's or trustee's attorney fees; the amount of attorney fees mentioned in this paragraph 7 in all cases shall be fixed by the trial court and in the event of an appeal from any judgment or decree of the trial court, grantor further agrees to pay such sum at the appellate court shall adjudge reasonable as the beneficiary's or trustee's attorney fees on such appeal.

It is mutually agreed that:

8. In the event that any portion or all of the property shall be taken under the right of eminent domain or condemnation, beneficiary shall have the if it so elects, to require that all or any portion of the monies payable as compensation for such taking, which are in excess of the amount required to pay all reasonable costs, expenses and attorneys fees necessarily paid or incurred by grantor in such proceedings, shall be paid to beneficiary and applied by it first upon any reasonable costs and expenses and attorney's fees, both in the trial and appellate courts, necessarily paid or incurred by beneficiary in such proceedings, and the balance applied upon the indebtedness secured hereby; and grantor agrees, at its own expense, to take such actions and execute such instruments as shall be necessary in obtaining such compensation, promptly upon beneficiary's request.

NOTE: The Trust Deed Act provides that the trustee hereunder must be either an attorney who is an active member of the Oregon State Bar, a bank, trust company or savings and loan association authorized to do business under the laws or Oregon or the United States, a title insurance company authorized to insure title to real property of this state, its subsidiaries, affiliates, agents or branches, the United States any agency thereof, or an escrow agent licensed under ORS 696.505 to 696.585.
*WARNING: 12 USC 1701j-3 regulates and may prohibit exercise of this option.
**The publisher suggests that such an agreement address the issue of obtaining beneficiary's consent in complete detail.

A common trust deed, reproduced courtesy Stevens-Ness Law Publishing Company

9. At any time, and from time to time upon written request of beneficiary, payment of its fees and presentation of this deed and the note for endorsement (in case of full reconveyance, for cancellation), without affecting the liability of any person for the payment of the indebtedness, trustee may (a) consent to the making of any map or plat of the property; (b) join in granting any easement or creating any restriction thereon; (c) join in any subordination or other agreement affecting this deed or the lien or charge thereof; (d) reconvey, without warranty, all or any part of the property. The grantee in any reconveyance may be described as the "person or persons legally entitled thereto," and the recitals therein of any matters or facts shall be conclusive proof of the truthfulness thereof. Trustee's fees for any of the services mentioned in this paragraph shall be not less than $5.

10. Upon any default by grantor hereunder, beneficiary may at any time without notice, either in person, by agent or by a receiver to be appointed by a court, and without regard to the adequacy of any security for the indebtedness hereby secured, enter upon and take possession of the property or any part thereof, in its own name sue or otherwise collect the rents, issues and profits, including those past due and unpaid, and apply the same, less costs and expenses of operation and collection, including reasonable attorney's fees upon any indebtedness secured hereby, and in such order as beneficiary may determine.

11. The entering upon and taking possession of the property, the collection of such rents, issues and profits, or the proceeds of fire and other insurance policies or compensation or awards for any taking or damage of the property, and the application or release thereof as aforesaid, shall not cure or waive any default or notice of default hereunder or invalidate any act done pursuant to such notice.

12. Upon default by grantor in payment of any indebtedness secured hereby or in grantor's performance of any agreement hereunder, time being of the essence with respect to such payment and/or performance, the beneficiary may declare all sums secured hereby immediately due and payable. In such an event the beneficiary may elect to proceed to foreclose this trust deed in equity as a mortgage or direct the trustee to foreclose this trust deed by advertisement and sale, or may direct the trustee to pursue any other right or remedy, either at law or in equity, which the beneficiary may have. In the event the beneficiary elects to foreclose by advertisement and sale, the beneficiary or the trustee shall execute and cause to be recorded a written notice of default and election to sell the property to satisfy the obligation secured hereby whereupon the trustee shall fix the time and place of sale, give notice thereof as then required by law and proceed to foreclose this trust deed in the manner provided in ORS 86.735 to 86.795.

13. After the trustee has commenced foreclosure by advertisement and sale, and at any time prior to 5 days before the date the trustee conducts the sale, the grantor or any other person so privileged by ORS 86.753, may cure the default or defaults. If the default consists of a failure to pay, when due, sums secured by the trust deed, the default may be cured by paying the entire amount due at the time of the cure other than such portion as would not then be due had no default occurred. Any other default that is capable of being cured may be cured by tendering the performance required under the obligation or trust deed. In any case, in addition to curing the default or defaults, the person effecting the cure shall pay to the beneficiary all costs and expenses actually incurred in enforcing the obligation of the trust deed together with trustee's and attorney's fees not exceeding the amounts provided by law.

14. Otherwise, the sale shall be held on the date and at the time and place designated in the notice of sale or the time to which the sale may be postponed as provided by law. The trustee may sell the property either in one parcel or in separate parcels and shall sell the parcel or parcels at auction to the highest bidder for cash, payable at the time of sale. Trustee shall deliver to the purchaser its deed in form as required by law conveying the property so sold, but without any covenant or warranty , express or implied. The recitals in the deed of any matters of fact shall be conclusive proof of the truthfulness thereof. Any person, excluding the trustee, but including the grantor and beneficiary, may purchase at the sale.

15. When trustee sells pursuant to the powers provided herein, trustee shall apply the proceeds of sale to payment of (1) the expenses of sale, including the compensation of the trustee and a reasonable charge by trustee's attorney, (2) to the obligation secured by the trust deed, (3) to all persons having recorded liens subsequent to the interest of the trustee in the trust deed as their interests may appear in the order of their priority and (4) the surplus, if any, to the grantor or to any successor in interest entitled to such surplus.

16. Beneficiary may from time to time appoint a successor or successors to any trustee named herein or to any successor trustee appointed hereunder. Upon such appointment, and without conveyance to the successor trustee, the latter shall be vested with all title, powers and duties conferred upon any trustee herein named or appointed hereunder. Each such appointment and substitution shall be made by written instrument executed by beneficiary, which, when recorded in the mortgage records of the county or counties in which the property is situated, shall be conclusive proof of proper appointment of the successor trustee.

17. Trustee accepts this trust when this deed, duly executed and acknowledged, is made a public record as provided by law. Trustee is not obligated to notify any party hereto of pending sale under any other deed of trust or of any action or proceeding in which grantor, beneficiary or trustee shall be a party unless such action or proceeding is brought by trustee.

The grantor covenants and agrees to and with the beneficiary and the beneficiary's successor in interest that the grantor is lawfully seized in fee simple of the real property and has a valid, unencumbered title thereto, except as may be set forth In an addendum or exhibit attached hereto, and that the grantor will warrant and forever defend the same against all persons whomsoever.

WARNING: Unless grantor provides beneficiary with evidence of insurance coverage as required by the contract or Joan agreement between them, beneficiary may purchase insurance at grantor's expense to protect beneficiary's interest. This insurance may, but need not, also protect grantor's interest. If the collateral becomes damaged, the coverage purchased by beneficiary may' not pay any claim made by or against grantor. Grantor may later cancel the coverage by providing evidence that grantor has obtained property coverage elsewhere. Grantor is responsible for the cost of any insurance coverage purchased by beneficiary, which cost may beadded to grantor's contract or loan balance. If it is so added, the interest rate on the underlying contract or loan will apply to it. The effective date of coverage may be the date grantor's prior coverage lapsed or the date grantor failed to provide proof of coverage. The coverage beneficiary purchases may be considerably more expensive than insurance grantor might otherwise obtain alone and may not satisfy any need for property damage coverage or any mandatory liability insurance requirements imposed by applicable law.

The grantor covenants that the proceeds of the loan represented by the above described note and this trust deed are (choose one):*

(a) primarily for grantor's personal, family or household purposes (see Important Notice below).

(b) for an organization, or (even if grantor is a natural person) are for business or commercial purposes.

This deed applies to, inures to the benefit of, and binds all parties hereto, their heirs, legatees, devisees, administrators, executors, personal representatives, successors and assigns. The term beneficiary shall mean the holder and owner, including pledgee, of the contract secured hereby, whether or not named as a beneficiary herein.

In construing this trust deed. It is understood that the grantor, trustee and/or beneficiary may each be more than one person; that if the context so requires, the singular shall be taken to mean and include the plural, and that generally all grammatical changes shall be made, assumed and implied to make the provisions hereof apply equally to corporations and to individuals.

IN WITNESS WHEREOF, the grantor has executed this instrument the day and year first written above.

*IMPORTANT NOTICE: Delete, by lining out, whichever warranty (a) or (b) is inapplicable. If warranty (a) is applicable and the beneficiary is a creditor as such word is defined in the Truth in Lending Act and Regulation Z, the beneficiary MUST comply with the Act and Regulation by making required disclosures. For this purpose, use Stevens-Ness Form No. 1319, or the equivalent. If compliance with the Act is not required, disregard this notice.

_____

_____

_____

State of Oregon, County of _____) ss.

This instrument was acknowledged before me on _____ ,

by _____ .

This instrument was acknowledged before me on _____ ,

by _____

as _____

of _____ .

_____

Notary Public for Oregon.
My commission expires _____ .

REQUEST FOR FULL RECONVEYANCE (To be used only when obligations have been paid.)

TO: _____ , Trustee

The undersigned is the legal owner and holder of all indebtedness secured by the foregoing trust deed. All sums secured by the trust deed have been fully paid and satisfied. You are hereby directed, on payment to you of any sums owing to you under the terms of this trust deed or pursuant to statute, to cancel all evidences of indebtedness secured by the trust deed (which are delivered to you herewith together with the trust deed) and to reconvey, without warranty, to the parties designated by the terms of the trust deed, the estate now held by you under the same. Mail the reconveyance and documents to _____

_____

DATED _____

Do not lose or destroy this Trust Deed OR THE NOTE which it secures.
Both should be delivered to the trustee for cancellation before reconveyance is made.

_____

_____
Beneficiary

The trustee must include in the notice of default and election to sell all information pertinent to the foreclosure, including the date, time and place set for the sale. The date for the sale must be a minimum of 120 days from the date the last person was served. During the time between the service and the sale date, the trustee must publish the notice of default and election to sell. The notice must be published once a week for four consecutive weeks, and the last publication must be at least 20 days before the date set for the sale.

A special provision of the Trust Deed Act allows the grantor, or any junior lienholder, to cure the default and reinstate the trust deed note, provided that the default is cured before the fifth day prior to the date set for the sale. In curing the default, the trustee and the attorney for the beneficiary are entitled to reasonable fees for their services in assisting the beneficiary to enforce the trust deed. Of course, all sums due to date, plus late charges, and other costs, must be tendered in order to reinstate the debt. The right of **reinstatement** essentially bars the lender from accelerating until the fifth day before the sale date. It is a major difference between the trust deed and the mortgage.

If the trust deed is not reinstated prior to the fifth day before the sale date, then the trustee proceeds to hold the sale. As in a mortgage foreclosure sale, anyone may bid, except that this time it is the trustee who is holding the sale, so the trustee may not bid. All bids must be for all cash, except that the beneficiary may bid up to the balance then due under the note and trust deed without paying cash. The beneficiary may decline to appear at the sale, yet may nevertheless deliver a bid to the trustee prior to the sale, to be announced by the trustee at the start of the sale. If the beneficiary bids more than the amount due, the surplus must be paid in cash. No one is required to place a bid, but it is customary for the beneficiary to bid the total amount due.

Following the sale, the trustee deeds the property to the successful bidder within ten days. The deed is called a **trustee's deed**. There is no right of redemption for the grantor or for junior lienholders. Possession is to be delivered to the successful bidder within ten days. Except for a lessee whose lease was entered into prior to the trust deed, anyone remaining in possession more than ten days after the sale date may be evicted forthwith. The trustee will disburse the proceeds of the sale, first to the costs of the sale, including the fees of the trustee, second to the beneficiary to the extent of what is due to the beneficiary, third to all junior lienholders in the order of their priority date, and finally, any remaining surplus to the grantor. If the proceeds of the sale are insufficient to pay the entire trust deed obligation the beneficiary will lose money on the loan because the beneficiary is never entitled to a deficiency judgment under a trustee's foreclosure.

As you can see, compared to a mortgage foreclosure, the trustee's foreclosure gives a reasonably balanced menu of benefits to both parties. The grantor gains the right to reinstate the loan and freedom from worrying about a deficiency judgment. The beneficiary gains inexpensive and fast foreclosure, and quick possession without having to deal with a possible right of redemption. Most institutional lenders prefer the trustee's foreclosure. After all, they only want to earn interest income on their loans, so if a grantor cures the default and reinstates the loan, so much the better. On the other hand, if the grantor cannot reinstate the loan, then better to have the foreclosure over with as quickly and inexpensively as possible. Of course, the lender must give up the right to a deficiency judgment but, as a practical matter, mortgage lenders rarely get anything out of a deficiency judgment anyway.

However, the Trust Deed Act states that a trust deed "at the option of the beneficiary, may be foreclosed by the beneficiary as provided by law for the foreclosure of mortgages on real property." (See ORS 86.710 in the Appendix, page 388.) In other words, the beneficiary can simply treat the trust deed as though it were a mortgage and proceed with a judicial foreclosure. This gives the beneficiary the option to accelerate and deny

FORM No. 887 – TRUSTEE'S DEED OF RECONVEYANCE   COPYRIGHT 1999 STEVENS-NESS LAW PUBLISHING CO., PORTLAND, OR 97204

NN

Trustee's Name and Address
To

After recording, return to (Name, Address, Zip):

Until requested otherwise, send all tax statements to (Name, Address, Zip):

SPACE RESERVED
FOR
RECORDER'S USE

STATE OF OREGON,
County of _____ } ss.

I certify that the within instrument was received for recording on _____, at _____ o'clock ____ M., and recorded in book/reel/volume No. _____, on page _____ and/or as fee/file/instrument/microfilm/reception No. _____, Records of this County.

Witness my hand and seal of County affixed.

_____
NAME   TITLE

By _____, Deputy.

DEED OF RECONVEYANCE

KNOW ALL MEN BY THESE PRESENTS that the undersigned trustee or successor trustee under that certain trust deed dated _____ , executed and delivered by _____ as Grantor, and recorded on _____, in the records of _____ County, Oregon in book/reel/volume No. _____ at page _____ , and/or as fee/file/instrument/microfilm/reception No. _____ (indicate which), conveying real property situated in that county described as follows

(IF SPACE INSUFFICIENT, CONTINUE DESCRIPTION ON REVERSE)

having received from the beneficiary under the trust deed a written request to reconvey, reciting that the obligation secured by the trust deed has been fully paid and performed, hereby does grant, bargain, sell and convey, but without any covenant or warranty, express or implied, to the persons legally entitled thereto, all of the estate held by the undersigned in and to the described premises by virtue of the trust deed.

In construing this instrument and whenever its context so requires, the singular includes the plural.

IN WITNESS WHEREOF, the undersigned trustee has executed this instrument. If the undersigned is a corporation, it has caused its name to be signed and its seal, if any, affixed by an officer or other person duly authorized to do so by its Board of Directors.

DATED _____ .

_____

_____

_____
TRUSTEE

State of Oregon, County of _____) ss.

This instrument was acknowledged before me on _____ ,

by _____ .

This instrument was acknowledged before me on _____ ,

by _____

as _____

of _____ .

_____
Notary Public for Oregon.
My commission expires _____

Deed of reconveyance, reproduced courtesy Stevens-Ness Law Publishing Company

reinstatement. But if the beneficiary takes this route, not only will it likely cost more, but more important, the grantor and junior lienholders have rights of redemption. The beneficiary's hands are tied until the rights of redemption expire. On the other hand, this explains why lenders today prefer the trust deed – a mortgage only has one remedy, where a trust deed could be foreclosed either through a trustee's sale or judicially as a mortgage.

The Trust Deed Act also provides that a beneficiary who sues judicially to foreclose a trust deed may gain a deficiency judgment, even if the trust deed is a purchase money instrument, provided that the trust deed was entered into after 1983 and was not a residential trust deed. A residential trust deed is –

"A trust deed on property upon which are situated four or fewer residential units and one of the residential units is occupied as the principal residence of the grantor, the grantor's spouse or the grantor's minor or dependent child at the time a trust deed foreclosure is commenced" [ORS 86.705 (3)]

It is of special interest to note that the Trust Deed Act not only makes it possible for lenders to gain a deficiency judgment on a trust deed but on a purchase money trust deed as well. The right to a deficiency judgment on a mortgage is determined by whether it is carried by the seller or not (purchase money mortgage). On a trust deed the limitation is that it cannot be on the borrower's personal residence.

Exercise c

A trust is created when a _____ entrusts something to a _____ who holds it in trust for a _____ . In a trust deed transaction, the owner/borrower is the trustor, more commonly called the _____ of the trust deed, who conveys to the _____ a title right called a _____ _____ of _____ . The _____ holds this title right in trust for the lender, who is the _____ . When a trust deed is paid off, the _____ releases the lien by delivering to the borrower a _____ of _____ .

To foreclose a trust deed, the lender orders the _____ to record and serve on the borrower a _____ of _____ and _____ to _____ , which must contain certain matters, including the sale _____ , which must be at least _____ days from the service. At any time up to the _____ day before the date set for the sale the borrower can _____ the trust deed loan by paying all sums due up to that point, including the costs the lender has incurred. If this is not done, the _____ will sell the property at public auction on the appointed date. Following the sale, the successful bidder will be entitled to a _____ _____ and the foreclosure will become final. There is no _____ of _____ following the sale.

As an alternative, the lender can foreclose _____ as though the trust deed were a mortgage. Unless it is a _____ trust deed, a _____ _____ against the borrower may be possible.

Creating land sales contracts

Even though their histories and the manner in which mortgages and trust deeds are created are very different, still mortgages and trust deeds are similar in major respects. Both create a lien on the borrower's title and both must be supported by a note as evidence of a debt. Not so the **land sales contract**. The land sales contract is also a very commonly used financing instrument, but it involves an entirely different concept.

When we talk of the land sales contract, we have to be sure all the parties know they are talking about the same thing. On occasion, you will hear buyers, sellers and real estate agents use endless synonyms for the land sales contract. Frequently heard are "real estate contract," "conditional sale agreement for real property," "real property contract," "contract for a deed," and the list goes on and on. Probably the most common expression in Oregon is "land sales contract," or simply "contract."

A contract is usually carried by a seller, so buyers commonly say they are "buying on contract." Unfortunately, buyers and sellers are not ordinarily very sophisticated, so when you investigate such a sale you frequently find that the actual instrument was a purchase money trust deed, or occasionally a purchase money mortgage, not an actual land sales contract. Usually the real estate agent must obtain a copy of the instrument, since it contains important information. For example, whether or not the loan can be assumed is a fact which can only be ascertained for sure by reading the exact language of the instrument.

The expression "contract for a deed" is an interesting synonym for "land sales contract," for that is exactly what it is. Reduced to its essential form, the land sales contract is a contract between an owner and a buyer for the future conveyance of the real estate. The owner agrees to give the buyer a deed to the property when the buyer has finished paying for it. The buyer agrees to make the payments called for in the contract. Make special note of the fact that the seller does not usually deed the property to the buyer until the buyer has made the final payment. The seller is said to retain legal title to the property until the buyer has fully performed his or her part of the bargain. Since the buyer's right to a deed is a substantial right, we use the word **equitable title** to describe the buyer's rights. The word "equitable" means "just" or "fair."

Under common law, the rights and responsibilities relating to any parcel of real property are vested in the owner (freeholder). It is always the owner who must pay the taxes, and who is responsible for the property. The owner is also the party who is entitled to possession, use and enjoyment of the property. When real estate is sold on a land sales contract, the seller retains the legal title, so, logically, the seller retains the right of possession, use and enjoyment. The seller also remains liable for the property taxes and any problems created by the property. But in the land sales contract, the owner wishes the buyer to assume the responsibilities and the buyer wants the rights of possession, use and enjoyment. Thus, a typical land sales contract specifically states that the buyer will pay the taxes and other liens and the buyer will save the seller harmless from any liability regarding the property during the time the buyer is paying for it. Similarly, contracts invariably have clauses giving the buyer the right of possession, use and enjoyment, as long as the buyer is not in default. When essentially all the rights and responsibilities of ownership are given to the buyer, we say that the seller's legal title is reduced to a **naked title**.

So far we have referred to the parties as the buyer and the seller. Most modern land sales contracts call them just exactly that, the buyer and the seller. Some more old-fashioned contracts refer to the parties as the **vendor** (seller) and the **vendee** (buyer), but modern attorneys prefer the simplest plain language wherever possible.

FORM No. 706 – CONTRACT – REAL ESTATE – Monthly Payments   COPYRIGHT 1999 STEVENS-NESS LAW PUBLISHING CO., PORTLAND, OR 97204

NN

_____

_____

_____

Seller's Name and Address

_____

_____

Buyer's Name and Address

After recording, return to (Name, Address, Zip):

_____

_____

_____

Until requested otherwise, send all tax statements to (Name, Address, Zip):

_____

_____

_____

SPACE RESERVED
FOR
RECORDER'S USE

STATE OF OREGON,

County of _____ } ss.

I certify that the within instrument was received for recording on _____, at _____ o'clock ____ M., and recorded in book/reel/volume No. _____, on page _____ and/or as fee/file/instrument/microfilm/reception No. _____, Records of this County.

Witness my hand and seal of County affixed.

_____

NAME   TITLE

By _____, Deputy.

CONTRACT – REAL ESTATE

THIS CONTRACT, Dated _____ , between

_____

_____, hereinafter called the seller,

and _____

_____, hereinafter called the buyer,

WITNESSETH: That in consideration of the mutual covenants and agreements herein contained, the seller agrees to sell unto the buyer and the buyer agrees to purchase from the seller all of the following described lands and premises situated in _____ County, State of _____, to wit:

for the sum of _____ Dollars ($ _____), hereinafter called the purchase price, on account of which _____ Dollars ($ _____) is paid on the execution hereof (the receipt of which is hereby acknowledged by the seller); the buyer agrees to pay the remainder of the purchase price (to wit: $ _____) to the order of the seller in monthly payments of not less than _____ Dollars ($ _____) each, _____

payable on the _____ day of each month hereafter beginning with the month of and year _____, and continuing until the purchase price is fully paid.

The true and actual consideration for this conveyance is $ _____. (Here comply with ORS 93.030.)

All of the purchase price may be paid at any time; all of the deferred payments shall bear interest at the rate of _____ percent per annum from _____ until paid; interest to be paid _____ and ☐ in addition to ☐ to be included in the minimum monthly payments above required. Taxes on the premises for the current tax year shall be prorated between the parties hereto as of _____ .

The buyer warrants and covenants with the seller that the real property described in this contract is
* (A) primarily for buyer's personal, family or household purposes,
* (B) for an organization or (even if buyer is a natural person) is for business or commercial purposes.

The buyer shall be entitled to possession of the above lands on _____ , and may retain such possession so long as buyer is not in default under the terms of this contract, The buyer agrees that at all times buyer will keep the premises and the buildings, now or hereafter erected thereon, in good condition and repaid and will not suffer or permit any waste or strip thereof; that buyer will keel the premises free from construction and all other liens and save the seller harmless therefrom and reimburse seller for all costs and attorney fees incurred by seller in defending against any such liens; that buyer will pay all taxes hereafter levied against the property, as well as all water rents, public charges and municipal liens which hereafter lawfully may be imposed upon the premises, all promptly before the same or any part thereof become past due; that at buyer's expense, buyer will insure and keep insured all buildings now or hereafter erected on the premises against loss or damage by fire (with extended coverage) in an amount not less than $ _____ in a company or companies satisfactory to the seller, specifically naming seller as an additional insured, with loss payable first to seller and then to the buyer as their respective interests may appear and all policies of insurance to be delivered to the seller as soon as insured. If the buyer shall fail to pay any such liens, costs, water rents, taxes or charges, the seller may do so and any payment so made shall be added to an become a part of the debt secured by this contract and shall bear interest at the rate aforesaid, without waiver, however, of any right arising to the seller for buyer's breach of contract.

(OVER)

*IMPORTANT NOTICE: Delete, by lining out, whichever warranty (A) or (B) is not applicable. If warranty (A) is applicable and the seller is a creditor, as such word is defined in the Truth in Lending Act and Regulation Z, the seller MUST comply with the Act and Regulation by making required disclosures; for this purpose, use Stevens-Ness Form No. 1319 or equivalent.

A common land sales contract, reproduced courtesy Stevens-Ness Law Publishing Company

WARNING: Unless buyer provides seller with evidence of insurance coverage as required by the contract or loan agreement between them, seller may purchase insurance at buyer's expense to protect seller's interest. This insurance may, but need not, also protect buyer's interest. If the collateral becomes damaged, the coverage purchased by seller may not pay any claim made by or against buyer. Buyer may later cancel the coverage by providing evidence that buyer has obtained property coverage elsewhere. Buyer is responsible for the cost of any insurance coverage purchased by seller, which cost may be added to buyer's contract or loan balance. If it is so added, the interest rate on the underlying contract or loan will apply to it. The effective date of coverage may be the date buyer's prior coverage lapsed or the date buyer failed to provide proof of coverage. The coverage seller purchases may be considerably more expensive than insurance buyer might otherwise obtain alone and may or may not satisfy any need for property damage coverage or any mandatory liability insurance requirements imposed by any applicable law.

The seller agrees that at seller's expense and within _____ days from the date hereof, seller will furnish unto buyer a title insurance policy insuring (in an amount equal to the purchase price) marketable title in and to the premises in the seller on or subsequent to the date of this agreement, save and except the usual printed exceptions and the building and other restrictions and easements now of record, if any. Seller also agrees that when the purchase price is fully paid and upon request and upon surrender of this agreement, seller will deliver a good and sufficient deed conveying the premises in fee simple unto the buyer, buyer's heirs and assigns, free and clear of encumbrances as of the date hereof and free and clear of all encumbrances since the date placed, permitted or arising by, through or under seller, excepting, however, the easements, restrictions and the taxes, municipal liens, water rents and public charges so assumed by the buyer and further excepting all liens and encumbrances created by the buyer or buyer's assigns.

And it is understood and agreed between the parties that time is of the essence of this contract, and in case the buyer shall fail to make the payments above required, or any of them, punctually, within 20 days of the time limited therefor, or fail to keep any agreement herein contained, then the seller shall have the following rights and options:

(1) To declare this contract canceled for default and null and void, and to declare the buyer's rights forfeited and the debt extinguished, and to retain sums previously paid hereunder by the buyer;*

(2) To declare the whole unpaid principal balance of the purchase price with the interest thereon at once due and payable; and/or

(3) To foreclose this contract by suit in equity.

In any of such cases, all rights and interest created or then existing in favor of the buyer as against the seller hereunder shall utterly cease and the right to possession of the premises above described and all other rights acquired by the buyer shall revert and revest in the seller without any act of re-entry or any other act of the seller to be performed and without any right of the buyer of return, reclamation or compensation for moneys paid on account of the purchase of the property as absolutely, fully and perfectly as if this contract and such payments had never been made; and in case of such default all payments theretofore made on this contract are to be retained by and belong to the seller as the agreed and reasonable rent of the premises up to the time of such default. And the seller, in case of such default, shall have the right immediately, or any time thereafter, to enter upon the land aforesaid, without any process of law, and take immediate possession thereof, together with all the improvements and appurtenances thereon or thereto belonging.

The buyer further agrees that failure by the seller at any time to require performance by the buyer of any provision hereof shall in no way affect seller's right hereunder to enforce the same, nor shall any waiver by the seller of any breach of any provision hereof be held to be a waiver of any succeeding breach of any such provision, or as a waiver of the provision itself.

Seller, seller's agents, and the holder of any existing encumbrance to which the lands and premises are subject may enter upon the lands and premises at reasonable times (upon reasonable prior notice to buyer) for the purpose of inspecting the property.

In case suit or action is instituted to foreclose this contract or to enforce any provision hereof, the losing party in the suit or action agrees to pay such sum as the trial court may adjudge reasonable as attorney fees to be allowed the prevailing party, in the suit or action and if an appeal is taken from any judgment or decree of the trial court, the losing party further promises to pay such sum as the appellate court shall adjudge reasonable as the prevailing party's attorney fees on such appeal.

In construing this contract, it is understood that the seller or the buyer may be more than one person or a corporation; that if the context so requires, the singular shall be taken to mean and include the plural and the neuter, and that generally all grammatical changes shall be made, assumed and implied to make the provisions hereof apply equally to corporations and to individuals.

This agreement shall bind and inure to the benefit of, as the circumstances may require, not only the immediate parties hereto but their respective heirs, executors, administrators, personal representatives, successors in interest and assigns as well.

IN WITNESS WHEREOF, the parties have executed this instrument in duplicate; if either the undersigned is a corporation, it has caused its name to be signed and its seal, if any, affixed by an officer or other person duly authorized to do so by order of its board of directors.

THIS INSTRUMENT WILL NOT ALLOW USE OF THE PROPERTY DESCRIBED IN THIS INSTRUMENT IN VIOLATION OF APPLICABLE LAND USE LAWS AND REGULATIONS. BEFORE SIGNING OR ACCEPTING THIS INSTRUMENT, THE PERSON ACQUIRING FEE TITLE TO THE PROPERTY SHOULD CHECK WITH THE APPROPRIATE CITY OR COUNTY PLANNING DEPARTMENT TO VERIFY APPROVED USES AND TO DETERMINE ANY LIMITS ON LAWSUITS AGAINST FARMING OR FOREST PRACTICES AS DEFINED IN ORS 30.930.

_____
*SELLER: Comply with ORS 93.030 et seq. prior to exercising this remedy.

State of Oregon, County of _____) ss.

This instrument was acknowledged before me on _____ ,

by _____ .

This instrument was acknowledged before me on _____ ,

by _____

as _____

of _____ .

_____

Notary Public for Oregon.

My commission expires _____ .

_____
ORS 93.635 (1) All instruments contracting to convey fee title to any real property, at a time more than 12 months from the date that the instrument is executed and the parties are bound, shall be acknowledged, in the manner provided for acknowledgment of deeds, by the conveyor of the title to be conveyed. **Such instruments, or a memorandum thereof, shall be recorded by the conveyor not later than 15 days after the instrument is executed and the parties are bound thereby.**
ORS 93.990 (3) Violation of ORS 93.635 is punishable, upon conviction, by a fine of not more than $100.

(DESCRIPTION CONTINUED)

As you can see, the seller's security interest during the term of the contract is really the title to the property. You may hear people refer to this as a ***vendor's lien*** although in reality it is not a lien in the same sense of the word as other liens such as judgments, mortgages, trust deeds, and the like. The land sales contract is really a claim, or possible right, which the buyer has in the seller's title. A ***cloud*** is what we call a possible interest or claim in another person's real property, so we must conclude that the land sales contract is a cloud. However, the cloud is not on the buyer's title – the buyer does not have a legal title. It is the buyer's equitable title which is a cloud on the seller's title.

In the past, it was popular for sellers not to record the land sales contract. This made it easy to get rid of a buyer who was in default – the seller could just eject the buyer, and the seller's record title was still clear so the property could easily be resold to another. The 1977 Legislature enacted a special statute requiring that all land sales contracts to be performed more than twelve months in the future be recorded within fifteen days of the date the parties are bound by the contract. Failure to do so does not render the contract unenforceable, but does subject the seller to a fine up to $100. The major purpose of this statute was to protect buyers on land sales contracts. As long as the contract is recorded, the seller cannot extinguish the buyer's rights without operation of law.

Real estate agents are happy when the seller is willing to assist in the financing of the property because this means the sale will not fall through due to the buyer not being able to get loan approval. But choosing a land sales contract as the security instrument means that an attorney must be called in. Real estate agents, escrows and other persons involved with the closing can usually fill in the blanks on most standard form documents without being guilty of unauthorized practice of law, but the land sales contract is clearly the domain of the legal profession. However, real estate agents need have no worries about having a lawyer write up the land sales contract, providing the earnest money or sale agreement is clear and precise about the terms of the contract.

Previously we saw that when a mortgage was paid in full we recorded a satisfaction of mortgage. And when a trust deed loan was paid off, we used a deed of reconveyance to release the lien from the borrower's title. When a land sales contract is paid off we simply record the deed called for in the contract. This deed is frequently referred to as the ***fulfillment deed*** since it is in fulfillment of the seller's final obligation to the buyer. The contract usually stipulates which form of deed is to be used. Commonly, the contract calls for the seller to give the buyer a bargain and sale deed or special warranty deed since these deed forms do not obligate the seller to make good on title problems caused by others. Because the buyer has been in possession of the property, the seller is usually unwilling to warrant the condition of the title beyond the seller's own actions.

Land sales contract remedies

Where mortgages and trust deeds have either common law or statutory remedies, the only remedies in a land sales contract are those remedies stated in the contract. As a rule, land sales contracts list three remedies – strict foreclosure, forfeiture, and specific performance.

Strict foreclosure A suit for strict foreclosure is substantially different from the procedures used in foreclosing mortgages and trust deeds. When a mortgage or trust deed is foreclosed, the result is an auction sale of the property, with the possibilities of deficiency judgment and right of redemption. When a land sales contract is foreclosed, it is called a ***strict foreclosure*** because the seller is asking for the property back, without a public auction sale. Strict foreclosure also asks the court to restore the seller's title, extinguish the buyer's rights under the contract, and for separate judgment against the buyer for the seller's costs and attorney's fees.

In a suit for strict foreclosure, the judge will determine how much the buyer owes the seller. Then the judge will order the buyer to pay this amount to the seller, even if everyone knows the buyer cannot do so. The judge will give the buyer a period of time in which to pay this amount. The time period is at the discretion of the court and varies from as little as 30 days to as much as a year, depending on what the judge feels is fair under the circumstances. For example, if the buyer has substantial equity in the property and there is good evidence that the buyer is capable of paying the contract off, the judge may give the buyer a long period of time. The judge's order that the buyer is entitled to this period of time is called an ***interlocutory decree***. Finally, if the buyer does not pay by the end of the period allowed in the interlocutory decree, then the judge will order the buyer's rights foreclosed. The buyer has no right of redemption following strict foreclosure.

Any junior lienholders must also be served and made a party to the foreclosure in order to extinguish their claims. Junior lienholders may also be granted a period of time in which to pay the balance due.

Forfeiture When a land sales contract allows the seller to declare a ***forfeiture***, if the buyer defaults, this means that the seller can declare the contract null and void. This remedy would appear to have a great advantage to the seller, because the buyer's rights can be terminated without court action. However, a substantial problem arises when the buyer is still in possession of the property. In order to remove an unwilling buyer, the seller would be required to file a suit for ejectment (similar to an eviction).

Nevertheless, many times the buyer voluntarily leaves and declaring a forfeiture may be the most expedient route. Oregon Revised Statutes Chapter 93 (see Appendix) allows the seller to declare a forfeiture without court action. The seller must mail to the buyer, by both certified and first class mail a notice of the nature and amount of the default and the date after which the buyer's rights will be extinguished if the buyer fails to cure the default. The buyer is entitled to at least 60 days but not more than 120 days notice, determined by the amount of the remaining balance as a percentage of the original purchase price. If the default is cured within the statutory time limit, the contract is reinstated; if not, the buyer's rights are extinguished. In order to cure the default, the buyer must pay the payments currently due plus the seller's actual expenses incurred, including late charges and attorney's fees not to exceed $350 and the cost of a title search. The seller must also mail, in the same manner, a similar notice to all junior lienholders and others claiming an interest in the property, who have the same right to cure and reinstate as the buyer.

In order to regain clear title, the seller merely records an affidavit stating that the default was not cured within the time limit and including a copy of the notice(s) and proof(s) of mailing. When the seller has recorded the affidavit it becomes conclusive evidence of good title to a purchaser in good faith. In other words, if the seller subsequently sells the property to a new buyer, the original buyer cannot challenge the new buyer's title.

Specific performance If the seller feels that the buyer has substantial assets and that the property is not worth the balance owing on the contract, the seller may find that a suit for ***specific performance*** of the contract is the best remedy. In a suit for specific performance the seller begins by acceleration of the entire balance. If the buyer does not pay the entire balance due, then the seller files a suit for this amount and asks the court for a decree of foreclosure and sale, similar to a mortgage foreclosure.

The judge will order the seller to tender the fulfillment deed to the court, and will order the buyer to pay the full amount of the purchase price. If the buyer does not pay the full purchase price, then the deed will be returned to the seller and the seller will be granted judgment against the buyer. The seller can then enforce the judgment by execution (sheriff's sale) on the property, again, similar to a mortgage foreclosure.

If the property does not sell for enough to cover the balance owing, then the seller is entitled to deficiency judgment against the buyer, even considering that the land sales contract is always a purchase money instrument. Furthermore, the buyer has no right of redemption, so the successful bidder at the sheriff's sale will receive a sheriff's deed, not a sheriff's certificate of sale. Also, as with any other foreclosure or forfeiture proceeding, junior lienholders and others with an interest in the property must be served and made a party to the suit so they will have the same right to redeem as the buyer.

Which instrument should the lender choose? Institutional lenders such as banks, savings and loan associations and mortgage bankers may have little choice, since the secondary mortgage market requires a uniform trust deed today. Institutional lenders typically use land sales contracts only if they are selling a property they own themselves, and even then they almost always use a trust deed. However, owners who sell their properties and carry back financing are generally free to choose any of the three instruments, although it is most common for them to use either a pre-printed trust deed or land sales contract. Precisely which instrument you should use depends on whether you are representing the borrower or the lender, as well as the exact language of the instrument in question.

Exercise d

In a land sales contract the seller promises to give the buyer a _____ when the buyer has finished paying for the property. This gives the buyer rights which are referred to as the buyer's _____ title. The seller retains a _____ title, although when all the rights and responsibilities of ownership have been given to the buyer, the seller's interest is commonly referred to as a _____ title. The older terms for the buyer and the seller are the _____ and the _____ . The recorded contract is a _____ on the _____ title.

Land sales contracts must be recorded within ____ days of the date the parties are bound, unless the contract is to be fully performed within ____ months, or the seller is subject to a _____ .

When the contract is fully paid off the seller gives the buyer a _____ deed, which is usually a _____ _____ deed or a bargain and sale deed.

When the buyer defaults the usual remedy is a suit for _____ _____ , in which the seller asks the court to give the property back without a public auction sale. Another remedy is for the seller to declare a _____ . The seller also has the option to file a suit for _____ _____ of the contract, which can result in having the sheriff sell the property and getting a _____ _____ against the buyer if the property fails to sell for enough.

Deed as a mortgage

Have you ever heard someone say "the bank lent me the money, but they made me give them my deed as collateral"? What would happen if a lender literally took a deed to the property instead of a mortgage or other financing instrument? Could the lender then just legally demand possession of the property as the true legal owner?

Normally, the courts will look at the transaction and try to determine the intent of the parties. If the court can find that the borrower truly intended to convey the property to the lender, i.e., the money was given in exchange for the deed and not as borrowed money, then the bank would own the property. However, if the intent was clearly to make the property collateral for a loan, then the court will grant the bank the rights of a normal mortgagee.

Guaranties and collateral agreements

Many times a lender will take a note and trust deed on real property, but will request the borrower give a **collateral agreement** listing certain personal property as additional collateral. Collateral agreements are not commonly used on residential loans where the requirements of the secondary mortgage market dictate that the property alone appraise for sufficient value to support the loan.

However, collateral agreements are found on commercial mortgage loans, typically where a business owner wishes to borrow against real estate owned by a corporation. In these circumstances, bankers frequently request that the borrower give them additional personal property, usually trade fixtures of the business, as collateral.

Do not confuse the collateral agreement with a **personal guaranty**. A personal guaranty is akin to a co-signature. Personal guaranties are used in commercial lending where the lender is lending money to a business, but asks the business owner (or principal stockholders) to guarantee the loan personally. Thus, if the business defaults, the lender can look to the individuals for repayment.

Security agreements

The term **security agreement** is a modern expression for **chattel mortgage**. As the expression "chattel mortgage" would imply, this instrument is used to make personal property (chattels) collateral for a debt. In other words, you would use a mortgage to make real estate collateral for a debt and you would use a chattel mortgage to make chattels collateral for a debt.

If you lend money and take a note and mortgage (or note and trust deed), then your first step would be to record the mortgage or trust deed. As we have seen, recording establishes your priority date. All this is fine for mortgages and trust deeds, but what would you do to give constructive notice and establish priority if you had a note and security agreement? Today you can file a formal **ucc financing statement** in the office of the Oregon Secretary of State. When the financing statement or security agreement has been filed it establishes the priority of the claim against the personal property.

Real estate agents commonly encounter ucc financing statements on crops, and on fixtures on real property (for example, furnaces, air conditioning units, attached appliances, and so on).

Soldiers and Sailors Civil Relief Act

In rare instances, a lender must consider the **Soldiers and Sailors Civil Relief Act**. This is a federal law which provides relief from foreclosure for those who have been drafted into any branch of the armed forces and, as a result of their military service, are unable to meet their loan obligations.

The law only applies to draftees and not to career military people or those who enlisted voluntarily. In cases where the law applies it provides that the court can delay foreclosure action until 90 days after separation from military service, or if the borrower has already been foreclosed on and has a right of redemption, then the right of redemption extends until separation from the service. All sums due accrue interest at 6% until separation from the service, regardless of the interest rate in the financing instruments.

Alternatives to foreclosure

In some cases a lender may find it expedient to recast a loan agreement or grant concessions to a borrower rather than foreclose if the concessions would make it possible for the borrower to repay the debt. In practice, this occurs most commonly among purchase money lenders who do not want their property back. It is far less common to find institutional lenders granting concessions to borrowers. Institutional lenders generally feel they cannot afford to establish a precedent – if they grant concessions to one borrower, soon all their borrowers will be demanding concessions.

A popular concession is to lower the monthly payments by lowering the interest rate, extending the repayment period, or negative amortization. Or, sometimes the lender will agree to a moratorium, a period of time during which the borrower need not make payments. Unpaid interest can be forgiven or added to the unpaid balance.

In the end, if a satisfactory solution to the default cannot be arranged, the lender must either foreclose or request a ***deed in lieu of foreclosure***, also known as an ***estoppel deed***. The deed in lieu of foreclosure is called an estoppel deed because it "estops" (bars) the lender from taking any further action against the borrower. The lender agrees to accept the property as full satisfaction of the obligation – if the lender is forced to take a loss on the resale of the collateral, the lender will have no recourse against the borrower, including any right to a deficiency judgment. The savings in legal expense can be significant, but lenders are usually under no requirement to accept a deed in lieu of foreclosure. If the property is not worth the amount owing, and the borrower has other assets that the lender knows about, then the lender commonly refuses to accept a deed in lieu of foreclosure. The borrower should be aware that an ordinary deed used to convey the title to the lender will not be a release from liability for a deficiency judgment. The borrower should be sure the deed contains the estoppel language.

Exercise e

When a lender asks a borrower to pledge additional assets, the lender is asking for the borrower to execute a _____ _____ , *but if the lender wants to make the borrower personally liable for a corporate debt, then the lender will ask the borrower to execute a* _____ _____ . *When personal property is the collateral, the lender takes a* _____ *which is filed of record in the office of the* _____ *of* _____ .

Typical clauses

The ***acceleration clause*** is invariably found in notes and lien instruments where there are periodic payments. The acceleration clause allows the lender to demand the entire unpaid principal balance in the event of a default. If the loan documents did not include the acceleration clause, then all the lender can do is sue to force the borrower to perform as agreed – the lender cannot foreclose and cannot sue for the entire balance owing.

A ***late charge*** is common in financing instruments. By statute in Oregon, the late charge cannot exceed 5% of the amount of the monthly payment and the borrower is enti-

LENDER REMEDIES

	MORTGAGE	TRUST DEED		LAND SALES CONTRACT		
	Judicial	Judicial	Trustee's Sale	Forfeiture	Strict Foreclosure	Specific Performance
Must go to court	YES	YES	NO	NO	YES	YES
Buyer can reinstate	NO	NO	YES	YES	NO	NO
Auction sale	YES	YES	YES	NO	NO	YES
Right of redemption	YES	YES	NO	NO	NO[1]	NO
Deficiency judgment	YES[2]	YES[3]	NO	NO	NO	YES
Typical time to foreclose	3 months to 2 years	3 months to 2 years	4 to 6 months	2 to 5 months	3 months to 2 years	3 months to 2 years

1. Buyer has right of redemption during interlocutory period
2. Only if it is a hard money mortgage
3. Only if it is a commercial trust deed

tled to a fifteen-day grace period on loans on single-family residences, except those guaranteed or insured by the FHA or VA or loans which have been sold in the secondary mortgage market. The grace period does not include the due date and, if the fifteen-day period ends on a Saturday, Sunday or holiday, then the grace period is extended through the next business day. A lender can only charge one late charge for each installment.

A *subordination clause* is sometimes encountered in second lien instruments. Suppose your property already has a first mortgage and you borrowed additional funds on a second mortgage from another lender. If you pay off the first, the second is the only mortgage remaining, so it now automatically becomes a first lien. But you might wish to retain the right to replace the first mortgage without changing the priority position of the second mortgage. You can get this right by having a subordination clause in the second mortgage.

Subordination clauses are also used on occasion in construction financing. A builder may ask the seller of land to carry a purchase money note and trust deed for part of the purchase price. The builder also commonly needs to borrow the construction funds from an institutional lender. The institutional lender will likely require a first position, yet the seller of the land will already have the first position. To solve the dilemma, the builder can ask the seller not only to carry a purchase money note and trust deed, but also to make the instrument junior and subordinate to a mortgage for the construction funds, to be recorded later. The difficulty with this arrangement is that the seller of the land could be in a very poor position in the event of the builder's default.

A junior lien instrument also frequently contains a *covenant to pay prior encumbrances*. Foreclosure by the first mortgagee would extinguish a second mortgage, so it becomes critical to the second mortgagee to be sure that the first mortgage is kept current. The covenant to pay prior encumbrances typically is worded so a default on the first mortgage is also considered a default on the second. This allows the holder of the second mortgage to cure the default on the first, and then foreclose the second. The second mortgagee can take the title subject to the first without paying it off. However, if the first mortgagee has already accelerated, it may be too late.

When a property is income property (and even on single-family homes today) it is common to find an *assignment of rents* clause in the lien instrument. If the property is rented and the borrower defaults, the assignment of rents clause allows the lender to collect the rent directly from the tenant and apply it to the outstanding debt. Without an assignment of rents clause, the lender may still be able to collect the rent from the tenant, but must first obtain a court order appointing a receiver.

An *exculpatory clause* (also called a *sole security* clause) is a clause which makes the property the sole source of repayment if the borrower defaults. The legal effect is to block any possibility of a deficiency judgment. Thus, a borrower who has signed a lien instrument with this clause can generally walk away from the property with no further obligations. To be totally effective the clause should block judgments arising from any foreclosure action, including judgments for attorney's fees, and should also block the lender from suing on the note in order to obtain a general judgment.

Many loan instruments today contain index clauses. The *index clause* ties the interest rate to a national index, such as the rate paid by the federal government on treasury bills, or the average interest rate on all mortgages purchased by the Federal Home Loan Mortgage Corporation for the previous two weeks. (There are several popular indexes in use by lenders today.) Lenders can change the interest rate on the outstanding loan balance as the index changes.

Usually the index is lower or higher than the rate the lender agrees to, so the loan will contain a *margin*. The margin is a constant amount, so the actual interest on the loan will be the amount of the index, plus or minus the margin. For example, suppose that you have a loan tied to the treasury bill rate, plus a margin of 2%. Then your interest rate will always be 2% higher than whatever the treasury bill rate is.

An **escalator clause** is similar to an index clause, in that it also causes the terms of the loan to change. However, when a loan contains an escalator clause the changes are predetermined and agreed upon by the parties at the time the loan is made. For example, if you and your lender agreed that the interest rate would be 8% the first year, but climb to 9% for the second and subsequent years, this would be an example of an escalator clause. Escalator clauses are also commonly used to change loan terms other than the interest rate. For example, perhaps you agree to make payments which are interest only the first year, the second year you are to pay the interest, plus $50 toward principal, and for the third and subsequent years you are to pay the interest, plus $100 toward the principal. Escalator clauses are typically used in private financing and infrequently in institutional loans.

Lenders on improved real estate need to be sure the insurance is current and that the insurance company has issued a **loss payable** clause as a part of the fire insurance policy. The loss payable clause means that the insurance company will pay the proceeds on any loss, first to the lender to the extent of the balance owing, and the surplus, if any, to the borrower. The standard loss payable clause required by most lenders also states that the insurance company will notify the lender of any cancellations and that the insurance will remain in force for ten days after the notice is mailed to the lender. This gives the lender time to contact the borrower and make sure the borrower has obtained a replacement policy, or place their own insurance on the premises.

Real estate lenders also have a special problem with real property taxes. Real property taxes do not follow the normal rules for priority of liens, i.e., in order by recording date. Regardless of when the taxes became a lien on the property or when the mortgage was recorded, real property taxes are a prior lien ahead of private liens. Thus, if the lender forecloses, the lender would have to take the title subject to any unpaid taxes. If the borrower has little equity in the property and the lender allows several year's taxes to accrue, the property may actually be overencumbered.

Lenders, therefore, need to be sure the taxes (as well as the fire insurance premiums) are paid by the borrower in timely fashion. Most lenders prefer to handle this by establishing a **reserve account**, also sometimes called an **impound** or **escrow account**. Simply stated, each month the borrower pays the monthly amount for principal and interest, plus one-twelfth the annual taxes and one-twelfth the annual fire insurance premium. The lender establishes a separate "reserve account" and places the amounts received each month for the taxes and insurance into it. Then when the taxes come due, the lender draws a check against the borrower's reserve account and sends it to the tax collector. Similarly, when the insurance premium comes due, the lender charges the reserve account for the funds to pay the insurance premium. The reserve account may include a reserve for taxes only, for insurance only, or for both. Real estate agents refer to loans where the monthly payment includes principal, interest, taxes and insurance as being paid "PITI." If the payment includes principal, interest and taxes, but not insurance, then the loan is said to be paid "PIT."

Oregon law (ORS 86.205 – 86.275 "Security Protection") allows the lender to require a reserve account, without paying interest on the funds, on insured and guaranteed loans, on loans where the loan balance exceeds 85% of the purchase price or appraised value, on loans made to be sold to secondary lenders, and in certain other cases. Otherwise, if the lender requires a reserve account the lender must pay interest on the reserve funds. The lender must also notify the borrower if the loan balance drops to the point where the borrower would be entitled to discontinue the reserve account. And the

NOTES

lender may not require the borrower to pay into the reserve account more than is reasonably necessary to pay the taxes and insurance when they come due.

In addition, the federal Real Estate Settlement Procedures Act prohibits lenders from setting the monthly amounts for the reserve account higher than would be necessary to cover two additional months worth of the anticipated expense. In other words, a lender knows that property taxes may increase, so establishing the monthly amount a bit higher than $\frac{1}{12}$ of last year's bill is reasonable, just so it is not more than 14 months worth.

Many conventional loans contain a clause requiring a ***prepayment privilege charge*** or ***prepayment penalty***. If the loan instrument contains such a clause, the lender may require the borrower to pay an additional amount in order to pay the loan off ahead of schedule. Prepayment privilege charges are not unusual on conventional loans, but never found on Federal Housing Administration (FHA) loans, Federal Veterans Administration (VA) loans, or loans made by the Oregon Department of Veterans Affairs (State GI). The amount of the prepayment privilege charge varies from lender to lender. Some lenders charge a flat dollar amount, others charge interest on the current balance for several months, yet others charge a flat percentage of the unpaid balance. Some lenders charge only during the first few years of the loan. Other lenders levy the charge any time the loan is paid off ahead of its maturity. Some lenders allow the borrower to pay a certain percentage of the loan balance in any one month without penalty. Other lenders levy the charge only if the loan is paid off in the process of refinancing the property, but forgive the charge if the loan is paid off because the property is sold. The modern practice, even on conventional loans, is not to charge a prepayment penalty at all, since lenders have discovered that it is very unpopular with borrowers.

Oregon statutes (ORS 82.160 and ORS 86.150) require the lender to state plainly in large bold or underlined type a notice that the loan contains a penalty for early repayment and the amount of the penalty. Failure to state the notice voids the penalty.

On rare occasions, a lender may wish to prohibit a borrower from paying off a loan at all before maturity. To do this, the ***not less than*** (or ***or more***) clause should be deleted where the monthly payment is stated, and a ***lock-in clause*** should be stated instead. To be enforceable under Oregon statutes (ORS 82.170), the lock-in clause must be clearly stated in large bold or underlined type.

Exercise f

The part of a loan document that allows a lender to declare the entire balance due in full is called the _____ *clause. If a lender agrees to become junior to another loan to be recorded later, the loan contained a* _____ *clause. A borrower would need a* _____ *to pay a* _____ _____ *clause if the seller is carrying the loan and owes money on an underlying loan. If the lender's sole remedy is to take the property without recourse to the borrower's other assets, then the loan contained an exculpatory clause, also called a* _____ _____ *clause. An* _____ *clause means the interest rate can go up or down. If the amount of the payments change according to a pre-agreed schedule, then the loan contained an* _____ *clause. A fire insurance policy on mortgaged property will contain a* _____ _____ *clause which requires the insurance company to pay the lender first in the event of a loss.*

Assumptions and novations

When a property is encumbered, the owner can always deed the property to a buyer subject to the encumbrance. This is true regardless of what kind of encumbrance it is – property taxes, leases, mortgages, trust deeds, judgments, clouds – any encumbrance. However, certain lenders in the past have attempted to bar the seller from selling the property subject to the lender's mortgage by placing a *due on sale clause* (also referred to as an *alienation clause*) in the lien instrument.

These clauses are typical in conventional loans, but do not occur in loans guaranteed by the Veterans Administration prior to March of 1988 and loans insured by the Federal Housing Administration (FHA) prior to December, 1986. The purpose of the due on sale clause is to force the borrower to pay off a low-interest loan or to force a new buyer to agree to a higher interest rate during a period when interest rates are rising

In any situation where the buyer takes the title subject to the loan, the lender will want the buyer to *assume and agree to pay* the debt. If the buyer assumes and agrees to pay, then the buyer has become personally liable for the debt the same as signing the note personally. If the buyer merely takes the title subject to the loan without assuming and agreeing to pay the debt, then the lender cannot hold the buyer personally liable for the debt. Of course, if the buyer fails to make the payments, the lender can still foreclose. Also, regardless of whether the buyer assumes and agrees to pay the debt or not, the original borrower (the seller) is not relieved of the obligation to pay the debt. So, if the buyer assumes and agrees to pay the debt, the lender has two individuals fully personally liable for the debt. Normally, the buyer assumes and agrees to pay by signing a separate assumption agreement.

Is there a way to relieve the seller of liability for the debt when the buyer takes over the loan? Yes, if the lender agrees to a *substitution of mortgagor*, which is a type of *novation*. Legally, a novation of a contract occurs where the original contract is cancelled and a new one replaces it. If the lender agrees to a substitution of mortgagor, this is deemed to be a novation of the debt agreement, so the original note and lien instrument are canceled. However, it is rare for a lender to agree to a substitution of mortgagor and, even if the lender does agree, the lender will require the buyer to qualify as thoroughly as if it were a new loan.

Loan types

A *blanket mortgage* (or blanket trust deed, blanket land sales contract, blanket encumbrance) encumbers more than one piece of real estate. Loans for development of vacant land and investment loans are kinds of real estate loans which sometimes involve a blanket encumbrance.

A blanket encumbrance typically contains a *lot release clause* (sometimes called a *parcel release clause* or *partial release clause*. The lot release clause allows the borrower to pay a stipulated portion of the debt in exchange for which the lender will give a satisfaction (or deed of reconveyance or fulfillment deed) for a particular parcel. Thus the borrower can get clear title to any given parcel by paying only a portion of the debt. How much the lender demands for each parcel is normally determined by the value of each parcel in relation to the total amount of the debt.

A *package mortgage* (also package trust deed, package land sales contract or package encumbrance) should not be confused with a blanket mortgage. A package encumbrance includes both real property and personal property as collateral. Package encumbrances are typically used by builders who include appliances with a new house, or in seller-financing of commercial structures such as apartments and office buildings.

Older real estate agents may still use the expression **budget mortgage** to refer to a loan which is being paid PITI (with a reserve account for taxes and insurance). When amortizing mortgages with equal monthly payments first gained favor with lenders during the 1920s, the payments on a budget mortgage were considered the equivalent in a homebuyer's budget as rent payments were to a renter.

The expression **participation mortgage** has two different meanings. Its more recent meaning is as a synonym for **equity participation loan**. In an equity participation loan, the lender charges a reduced rate of interest, but in exchange is entitled to a share of the profit when the property is sold in the future. In residential lending, these loans are sometimes referred to as **shared appreciation mortgages**. Equity participation loans of this nature have been used for decades in commercial loans such as office buildings and shopping centers, where the lender's future share in the profits is known as an **equity kicker**. However, equity participation loans on single-family residences have been used almost exclusively by private parties rather than institutional lenders.

An older meaning for the term "participation loan" is its use in commercial banking. Many times a commercial bank will be called upon to fund a business loan of many millions of dollars for a large corporate customer. If the bank wishes to make the loan, but does not wish to put so many eggs in one basket, the bank may solicit "participation" in the loan on the part of one or more of its competitors. Each bank advances a portion of the loan funds and takes a proportionate share of the interest and risk.

The expression **open mortgage** is a legal term which means that the loan has matured and is supposed to be paid off, yet there remains a balance owing. Perhaps this state of affairs was because the borrower missed a payment. More commonly today, the loan had a balloon payment clause requiring the loan to be paid in full at some point and the borrower did not do so. Regardless of the cause, open loans are subject to immediate foreclosure.

Do not confuse the open mortgage with an **open end mortgage**. An open end mortgage is like a credit line. The lender approves the property and the borrower as being eligible to borrow up to a certain amount. However, the borrower borrows only a portion of the maximum at any one time. From time to time the borrower borrows additional funds (up to the maximum) and from time to time the borrower repays funds previously borrowed. Sometimes this expression is used as a verb – as in "to open-end a mortgage," which occurs when the lender recasts an existing loan in order to advance additional funds to the existing borrower.

Wraparound encumbrances (also known as **all-inclusive encumbrances**) have gained a great deal of popularity in recent years. The basic idea is very simple. A seller whose property is encumbered with a loan (which does not contain a due on sale clause) agrees to sell the property to a buyer and carry back a wraparound land sales contract (or trust deed or mortgage). The balance the seller owes is included in the balance the buyer owes the seller. For example, suppose you owe $100,000 on an old FHA loan at 7%. You have a buyer willing to pay $160,000 for your property with $20,000 down, and is willing to give you 8% interest if you will carry a contract for $140,000. If you agree to this, the buyer will make the payments to you on the $140,000 and you, in turn, will continue to make the payments to your lender on the $100,000. Since the buyer will make higher payments to you on the $140,000 than you have to make to the bank on the $100,000, you can pocket the difference. Of course, you gain an additional advantage. The fact is that $100,000 of the $140,000 you lent to the buyer was never your money in the first place. You borrowed that $100,000 from the bank at 7% – and now you are re-lending it to the buyer at 8%. You are getting 1% interest on the bank's money. In fact, because of the interest differential, your yield on that land sales contract is significantly greater than the 8% the buyer is paying you. The exact yield is a complicated calculation and depends on the remaining maturities of the two loans. Financial aspects of wrap-around loans are covered in the section on Alternative Financing, pages 359-364.

A borrower on a wraparound loan needs protection in the event the seller fails to make the payments on the underlying loan. After all, foreclosure by the first lender will extinguish all the buyer's interest. To guard against this, sometimes the buyer and seller agree to use a collection service at a financial institution. The buyer makes the payment to the financial institution, which in turn subtracts the amount due on the underlying loan and remits it to the underlying lender, and then remits the difference to the seller. The buyer would also want to be sure the wraparound encumbrance contained a cove-nant to pay on prior encumbrances, and that a request for notice of default was recorded.

Exercise 9

A buyer taking over the seller's old loan must take the title _____ _____ the loan. The buyer does not take personal liability for the debt unless the buyer _____ and _____ to _____ the loan. To prevent a buyer from taking over a loan, the lender typically includes a _____ _____ _____ clause in the lien instrument, also known as an _____ clause. When the buyer takes over the seller's old loan, the seller is not relieved of personal liability unless the lender agrees to a _____ , also referred to as a _____ of _____ .

A _____ encumbrance is a loan which covers more than one parcel. Such loans typically have a _____ (or parcel) _____ clause. When the collateral includes personal property, we call it a _____ encumbrance. If the lender will share in future value increases, the loan is called an _____ _____ loan. If a borrower can borrow additional funds in the future, we call it an _____ _____ mortgage. A mortgage loan which has matured but which still has a re-maining balance due is called an _____ mortgage.

⚷ KEY TERMS

The key to understanding any new field is the vocabulary used in that field. To maximize your comprehension of the material presented in this chapter, be sure you know the meaning and significance of the following terms. Remember that the majority of test questions primarily test knowledge of vocabulary.

Acceleration clause	Assume and agree to pay
Alienation clause	Balloon payment
All-inclusive encumbrance	Beneficiary
Amortized note	Blanket mortgage
Assign	Bond
Assignment	Budget mortgage
Assignment of rents	Call feature

Certificate of sale

Chattel mortgage

Cloud

Collateral agreement

Covenant to pay prior encumbrances

Decree of foreclosure and sale

Deed in lieu of foreclosure

Deed of reconveyance

Defeasance clause

Defeasible fee

Deficiency judgment

Demand clause

Due on sale clause

Encumbrance

Endorsement

Equitable right of redemption

Equitable title

Equity kicker

Equity participation loan

Escalator clause

Estoppel deed

Exculpatory clause

Foreclosure

Forfeiture

Fulfillment deed

Grantee

Grantor

Guaranty

Hard money mortgage

Holder in due course

Index clause

Instrument

Instruments of finance

Interlocutory decree

Judicial foreclosure

Junior lien

Land sales contract

Late charge

Lien

Lien instrument

Lien theory

Lock-in clause

Loss payable clause

Lot release clause

Maker

Margin

Mortgage

Mortgagee

Mortgagor

Naked title

Negotiable instrument

Nonjudicial foreclosure

Not less than clause

Note

Notice of default and election to sell

Novation

Open end mortgage

Open mortgage

Or more clause

Oregon Trust Deed Act

Package mortgage

Parcel release clause

Partial release clause

Participation mortgage

Payee

Personal guaranty

Power of sale

Prepayment penalty

Prepayment privilege charge

Primary lenders

Promissory note

Purchase money mortgage

Recourse

Redemption

Reinstatement

Request for notice of default

Reserve account

Right of reverter

Satisfaction of mortgage

Secondary mortgage market

Security agreement

Senior lien

Shared appreciation mortgages

Sheriff's certificate of sale

Sheriff's deed

Soldiers and Sailors Civil Relief Act

Sole security clause

Specific performance

Statutory right of redemption

Straight note

Strict foreclosure

Subordinate

Subordination clause

Substitution of mortgagor

Title theory

Trust

Trust deed

Trustee

Trustee's deed

Trustee's foreclosure

Trustor

UCC financing statement

Vendee

Vendor

Vendor's lien

Without recourse

Wraparound encumbrance

Writ of execution

REFERENCES

The following is required reading to ensure your success on the exams. Many of the practice questions at the end of this chapter, as well as state exam questions, are drawn from the following reading.

Freddie Mac/Fannie Mae Uniform Note and Trust Deed (pages 38-47)

Appendix, Oregon Lending Statutes

    Repayment restrictions, ORS 82.150 – 82.170

    Mortgages, ORS 86.010 – 86.150

    Late charges, ORS 86.160 – 86.185

    Security protection, ORS 86.205 – 86.275

    Chattel mortgages, ORS 86.405 – 86.470

    Oregon Trust Deed Act, ORS 86.705 –86.795 (Very important)

    Uniform Vendor and Purchaser Risk Act, ORS 93.290 –93.300

    Forfeiture, ORS 93.905 – 93.945

ANSWERS

To chapter exercises. If you couldn't figure out what to put in the blanks, find the answer here!

Exercise a

The three instruments used in real estate finance are the ___MORTGAGE___ , its modern replacement, the ___TRUST___ ___DEED___ , and the ___LAND___ ___SALES___ ___CONTRACT___ , which is carried by a seller. The first two of these are called ___LIEN___ instruments because they create a ___LIEN___ on the borrower's real estate. They must be accompanied by a ___NOTE___ , which is the evidence of the debt. Notes are also called ___PROMISSORY___ notes. A note is an example of a ___NEGOTIABLE___ ___INSTRUMENT___ . A note is a promise to pay a sum of money in the ___FUTURE___ . In a note the borrower is called the ___MAKER___ and the lender is called the ___PAYEE___ .

A lender can transfer a note (sell it) by ___ENDORSEMENT___ . A ___HOLDER___ in ___DUE___ ___COURSE___ has ___RECOURSE___ to the last endorser, unless the note is endorsed ___WITHOUT___ ___RECOURSE___ . A note signed without restriction is endorsed ___IN___ ___BLANK___ .

When a note calls for interest only, it is said to be a ___STRAIGHT___ note. If there are regular reductions of principal, we call it an ___AMORTIZED___ note. When there is an exceptional extra amount to be paid on the principal, this is called a ___BALLOON___ payment.

For the lender, the most important clause in the note is the <u>ACCELERATION</u> *clause, which allows the lender to call the entire balance due in full in the event of the borrower's* <u>DEFAULT</u> *. A clause allowing the lender to call the loan due at any time is called a* <u>DEMAND</u> *clause, although this clause is seldom found in* <u>RESIDENTIAL</u> *lending today.*

When a lien instrument is recorded it establishes the <u>PRIORITY</u> *of the lien as against subsequent lienholders. All later interests are said to be* <u>JUNIOR</u> *or subordinate interests. In a foreclosure, the property will be sold and the proceeds will be paid to the lienholders in the order of their* <u>PRIORITY</u> *. Foreclosure by a senior lienholder also* <u>EXTINGUISHES</u> *all junior interests. Property taxes, among other liens, are exceptions to the normal order of priority, as would be a senior lienholder agreeing to a* <u>SUBORDINATION</u> *to a junior lienholder. To protect a junior lien, the lienholder may record a* <u>REQUEST</u> *for* <u>NOTICE</u> *of* <u>DEFAULT</u> *.*

Exercise b

In a note and mortgage transaction, the borrower is called the <u>MORTGAGOR</u> *and the lender is the* <u>MORTGAGEE</u> *. Oregon is a* <u>LIEN</u> *theory state; this means that the mortgage is not considered a* <u>CONVEYANCE</u> *of the property to the lender.*

When the mortgage loan is paid in full, we record a <u>SATISFACTION</u> *of* <u>MORTGAGE</u> *to remove the lien from the borrower's record title.*

A mortgage foreclosure must be a <u>JUDICIAL</u> *foreclosure. If the borrower successfully defends the foreclosure, the court will order* <u>REINSTATEMENT</u> *of the debt. If the lender wins, the court will enter a* <u>DECREE</u> *of* <u>FORECLOSURE</u> *and* <u>SALE</u> *.*

After the lender wins the suit, a <u>WRIT</u> *of* <u>EXECUTION</u> *can be filed with the court. This becomes the order of the court to the* <u>SHERIFF</u> *to sell the mortgaged property at public auction to satisfy the debt. All bidders must pay* <u>CASH</u> *except the lender, who can bid up to the amount of the balance due without paying* <u>CASH</u> *. If the lender bids more than the amount due, any surplus must be paid in* <u>CASH</u> *. The successful bidder gets a* <u>SHERIFF'S</u> <u>CERTIFICATE</u> *of* <u>SALE</u> *.*

If the proceeds of the sale are more than the amount necessary to satisfy the amount due the lender, the surplus is turned over to the <u>MORTGAGOR</u> *.*

After the sale, the mortgagor gets a <u>RIGHT</u> *of* <u>REDEMPTION</u> *which lasts for* <u>180</u> *days. Junior lienholders also have the same right, which lasts for* <u>60</u> *days. If no one redeems, the successful bidder is entitled to a* <u>SHERIFF'S</u> *deed to the property.*

If the property did not sell for enough to satisfy the amount due, the lender is entitled to apply to the court for a <u>DEFICIENCY</u> <u>JUDGMENT</u> *, which can be used to execute on the borrower's other assets, within certain limitations. This is not permitted, however, if the loan was a* <u>PURCHASE</u> <u>MONEY</u> *mortgage, which is a loan carried by the* <u>SELLER</u> *, or by a third party if the original loan balance was under $* <u>50,000</u> *and on the borrower's* <u>PERSONAL</u> <u>RESIDENCE</u> *.*

Exercise c

A trust is created when a <u>TRUSTOR</u> *entrusts something to a* <u>TRUSTEE</u> *who holds it in trust for a* <u>BENEFICIARY</u> *. In a trust deed transaction, the owner/borrower is the trustor, more commonly called the* <u>GRANTOR</u> *of the trust deed, who conveys to the* <u>TRUSTEE</u> *a title right called a* <u>LIMITED</u> <u>POWER</u> *of* <u>SALE</u> *. The* <u>TRUSTEE</u> *holds this title right in trust for the lender, who is the* <u>BENEFICIARY</u> *. When a trust deed is paid off, the* <u>TRUSTEE</u> *releases the lien by delivering to the borrower a* <u>DEED</u> *of* <u>RECONVEYANCE</u> *.*

To foreclose a trust deed, the lender orders the <u>TRUSTEE</u> *to record and serve on the borrower a* <u>NOTICE</u> *of* <u>DEFAULT</u> *and* <u>ELECTION</u> *to* <u>SELL</u> *, which must contain certain matters, including the sale* <u>DATE</u> *, which must be at least* <u>120</u> *days from the service. At any time up to the* <u>FIFTH</u> *day before the date set for the sale the borrower can* <u>REINSTATE</u> *the trust deed loan by paying all sums due up to that point, including the costs the lender has incurred. If this is not done, the* <u>TRUSTEE</u> *will sell the property at public auction on the appointed date. Following the sale, the successful bidder will be entitled to a* <u>TRUSTEE'S</u> <u>DEED</u> *and the foreclosure will become final. There is no* <u>RIGHT</u> *of* <u>REDEMPTION</u> *following the sale.*

As an alternative, the lender can foreclose _____JUDICIALLY_____ as though the trust deed were a mortgage. Unless it is a _____RESIDENTIAL_____ trust deed, a _____DEFICIENCY_____ _____JUDGMENT_____ against the borrower may be possible.

Exercise d

In a land sales contract the seller promises to give the buyer a _____DEED_____ when the buyer has finished paying for the property. This gives the buyer rights which are referred to as the buyer's _____EQUITABLE_____ title. The seller retains a _____LEGAL_____ title, although when all the rights and responsibilities of ownership have been given to the buyer, the seller's interest is commonly referred to as a _____NAKED_____ title. The older terms for the buyer and the seller are the _____VENDOR_____ and the _____VENDEE_____ . The recorded contract is a _____CLOUD_____ on the _____SELLER'S_____ title.

Land sales contracts must be recorded within _15_ days of the date the parties are bound, unless the contract is to be fully performed within _12_ months, or the seller is subject to a _____FINE_____ .

When the contract is fully paid off the seller gives the buyer a _____FULFILLMENT_____ deed, which is usually a _____SPECIAL_____ _____WARRANTY_____ deed or a bargain and sale deed.

When the buyer defaults the usual remedy is a suit for _____STRICT_____ _____FORECLOSURE_____ , in which the seller asks the court to give the property back without a public auction sale. Another remedy is for the seller to declare a _____FORFEITURE_____ . The seller also has the option to file a suit for _____SPECIFIC_____ _____PERFORMANCE_____ of the contract, which can result in having the sheriff sell the property and getting a _____DEFICIENCY_____ _____JUDGMENT_____ against the buyer if the property fails to sell for enough.

Exercise e

When a lender asks a borrower to pledge additional assets, the lender is asking for the borrower to execute a _____COLLATERAL_____ _____AGREEMENT_____ , but if the lender wants to make the borrower personally liable for a corporate debt, then the lender will ask the borrower to execute a _____PERSONAL_____ _____GUARANTY_____ . When personal property is the collateral, the lender takes a _____FINANCING_____ _____STATEMENT_____ which is filed of record in the office of the _____SECRETARY_____ of _____STATE_____ .

Exercise f

The part of a loan document that allows a lender to declare the entire balance due in full is called the _____ACCELERATION_____ clause. If a lender agrees to become junior to another loan to be recorded later, the loan contained a _____SUBORDINATION_____ clause. A borrower would need a _____COVENANT_____ to pay a _____PRIOR_____ _____ENCUMBRANCE_____ clause if the seller is carrying the loan and owes money on an underlying loan. If the lender's sole remedy is to take the property without recourse to the borrower's other assets, then the loan contained an exculpatory clause, also called a _____SOLE_____ _____COLLATERAL_____ clause. An _____INDEX_____ clause means the interest rate can go up or down. If the amount of the payments change according to a pre-agreed schedule, then the loan contained an _____ESCALATOR_____ clause. A fire insurance policy on mortgaged property will contain a _____LOSS_____ _____PAYABLE_____ clause which requires the insurance company to pay the lender first in the event of a loss.

Exercise g

A buyer taking over the seller's old loan must take the title _____SUBJECT_____ _TO_ the loan. The buyer does not take personal liability for the debt unless the buyer _____ASSUMED_____ and _____AGREED_____ to _PAY_ the loan. To prevent a buyer from taking over a loan, the lender typically includes a _DUE_ _ON_ _SALE_ clause in the lien instrument, also known as an _____ALIENATION_____ clause. When the buyer takes over the seller's old loan, the seller is not relieved of personal liability unless the lender agrees to a _____NOVATION_____ , also referred to as a _____SUBSTITUTION_____ of _____MORTGAGOR_____ .

A _____BLANKET_____ encumbrance is a loan which covers more than one parcel. Such loans typically have a _LOT_ (or parcel) _____RELEASE_____ clause. When the collateral includes personal property, we call it a _____PACKAGE_____ encumbrance. If the lender will share in future value increases, the loan is called an _____EQUITY_____ _____PARTICIPATION_____ loan. If a borrower can borrow additional funds in the future, we call it an _____OPEN_____ _____END_____ mortgage. A mortgage loan which has matured but which still has a remaining balance due is called an _____OPEN_____ mortgage.

NOTE

_____ , _____ , _____
[Date]   [City]   [State]

_____
[Property Address]

1. BORROWER'S PROMISE TO PAY

In return for a loan that I have received, I promise to pay U.S. $ _____ (this amount is called "Principal"), plus interest, to the order of the Lender. The Lender is _____. I will make all payments under this Note in the form of cash, check or money order.

I understand that the Lender may transfer this Note. The Lender or anyone who takes this Note by transfer and who is entitled to receive payments under this Note is called the "Note Holder."

2. INTEREST

Interest will be charged on unpaid principal until the full amount of Principal has been paid. I will pay interest at a yearly rate of _____ %.

The interest rate required by this Section 2 is the rate I will pay both before and after any default described in Section 6(B) of this Note.

3. PAYMENTS

(A) Time and Place of Payments

I will pay principal and interest by making a payment every month.

I will make my monthly payment on the _____ day of each month beginning on _____. I will make these payments every month until I have paid all of the principal and interest and any other charges described below that I may owe under this Note. Each monthly payment will be applied as of its scheduled due date and will be applied to interest before Principal. If, on _____, 20___, I still owe amounts under this Note, I will pay those amounts in full on that date, which is called the "Maturity Date."

I will make my monthly payments at _____ or at a different place if required by the Note Holder.

(B) Amount of Monthly Payments

My monthly payment will be in the amount of U.S. $ _____ .

4. BORROWER'S RIGHT TO PREPAY

I have the right to make payments of Principal at any time before they are due. A payment of Principal only is known as a "Prepayment." When I make a Prepayment, I will tell the Note Holder in writing that I am doing so. I may not designate a payment as a Prepayment if I have not made all the monthly payments due under the Note.

I may make a full Prepayment or partial Prepayments without paying a Prepayment charge. The Note Holder will use my Prepayments to reduce the amount of Principal that I owe under this Note. However, the Note Holder may apply my Prepayment to the accrued and unpaid interest on the Prepayment amount, before applying my Prepayment to reduce the Principal amount of the Note. If I make a partial Prepayment, there will be no changes in the due date or in the amount of my monthly payment unless the Note Holder agrees in writing to those changes.

5. LOAN CHARGES

If a law, which applies to this loan and which sets maximum loan charges, is finally interpreted so that the interest or other loan charges collected or to be collected in connection with this loan exceed the permitted limits, then: (a) any such loan charge shall be reduced by the amount necessary to reduce the charge to the permitted limit; and (b) any sums already collected from me which exceeded permitted limits will be refunded to me. The Note Holder may choose to make this refund by reducing the Principal I owe under this Note or by making a direct payment to me. If a refund reduces Principal, the reduction will be treated as a partial Prepayment.

6. BORROWER'S FAILURE TO PAY AS REQUIRED

(A) Late Charge for Overdue Payments

If the Note Holder has not received the full amount of any monthly payment by the end of _____ calendar days after the date it is due, I will pay a late charge to the Note Holder. The amount of the charge will be _____ % of my overdue payment of principal and interest. I will pay this late charge promptly but only once on each late payment.

(B) Default

If I do not pay the full amount of each monthly payment on the date it is due, I will be in default.

(C) Notice of Default

If I am in default, the Note Holder may send me a written notice telling me that if I do not pay the overdue amount by a certain date, the Note Holder may require me to pay immediately the full amount of Principal which has not been paid and all the interest that I owe on that amount. That date must be at least 30 days after the date on which the notice is mailed to me or delivered by other means.

(D) No Waiver By Note Holder

Even if, at a time when I am in default, the Note Holder does not require me to pay immediately in full as described above, the Note Holder will still have the right to do so if I am in default at a later time.

(E) Payment of Note Holder's Costs and Expenses

If the Note Holder has required me to pay immediately in full as described above, the Note Holder will have the right to be paid back by me for all of its costs and expenses in enforcing this Note to the extent not prohibited by applicable law. Those expenses include, for example, reasonable attorneys' fees.

7. GIVING OF NOTICES

Unless applicable law requires a different method, any notice that must be given to me under this Note will be given by delivering it or by mailing it by first class mail to me at the Property Address above or at a different address if I give the Note Holder a notice of my different address.

Any notice that must be given to the Note Holder under this Note will be given by delivering it or by mailing it by first class mail to the Note Holder at the address stated in Section 3(A) above or at a different address if I am given a notice of that different address.

8. OBLIGATIONS OF PERSONS UNDER THIS NOTE

If more than one person signs this Note, each person is fully and personally obligated to keep all of the promises made in this Note, including the promise to pay the full amount owed. Any person who is a guarantor, surety or endorser of this Note is also obligated to do these things. Any person who takes over these obligations, including the obligations of a guarantor, surety or endorser of this Note, is also obligated to keep all of the promises made in this Note. The Note Holder may enforce its rights under this Note against each person individually or against all of us together. This means that any one of us may be required to pay all of the amounts owed under this Note.

9. WAIVERS

I and any other person who has obligations under this Note waive the rights of Presentment and Notice of Dishonor. "Presentment" means the right to require the Note Holder to demand payment of amounts due. "Notice of Dishonor" means the right to require the Note Holder to give notice to other persons that amounts due have not been paid.

10. UNIFORM SECURED NOTE

This Note is a uniform instrument with limited variations in some jurisdictions. In addition to the protections given to the Note Holder under this Note, a Mortgage, Deed of Trust, or Security Deed (the "Security Instrument"), dated the same date as this Note, protects the Note Holder from possible losses which might result if I do not keep the promises which I make in this Note. That Security Instrument describes how and under what conditions I may be required to make immediate payment in full of all amounts I owe under this Note. Some of those conditions are described as follows:

> If all or any part of the Property or any Interest in the Property is sold or transferred (or if Borrower is not a natural person and a beneficial interest in Borrower is sold or transferred) without Lender's prior written consent, Lender may require immediate payment in full of all sums secured by this Security Instrument. However, this option shall not be exercised by Lender if such exercise is prohibited by Applicable Law.

The Fannie Mae/Freddie Mac Uniform Note

After Recording Return To:

_____

_____

_____

_____

—————————— [Space Above This Line For Recording Data] ——————————

DEED OF TRUST

DEFINITIONS

Words used in multiple sections of this document are defined below and other words are defined in Sections 3, 11, 13, 18, 20 and 21. Certain rules regarding the usage of words used in this document are also provided in Section 16.

(A) **"Security Instrument"** means this document, which is dated _____ , together with all Riders to this document.

(B) **"Borrower"** is _____ . Borrower is the trustor under this Security Instrument.

(C) **"Lender"** is _____ . Lender is a _____ organized and existing under the laws of _____ . Lender's address is _____ . Lender is the beneficiary under this Security Instrument.

(D) **"Trustee"** is _____ .

(E) **"Note"** means the promissory note signed by Borrower and dated _____ . The Note states that Borrower owes Lender _____ Dollars (U.S. $ _____) plus interest. Borrower has promised to pay this debt in regular Periodic Payments and to pay the debt in full not later than _____ .

(F) **"Property"** means the property that is described below under the heading "Transfer of Rights in the Property."

(G) **"Loan"** means the debt evidenced by the Note, plus interest, any prepayment charges and late charges due under the Note, and all sums due under this Security Instrument, plus interest.

(H) **"Riders"** means all Riders to this Security Instrument that are executed by Borrower. The following Riders are to be executed by Borrower [check box as applicable]:

☐ Adjustable Rate Rider   ☐ Condominium Rider   ☐ Second Home Rider
☐ Balloon Rider   ☐ Planned Unit Development Rider   ☐ Other(s) [specify] _____
☐ 1-4 Family Rider   ☐ Biweekly Payment Rider

OREGON--Single Family--Fannie Mae/Freddie Mac UNIFORM INSTRUMENT   Form 3038 1/01 *(page 1 of 17 pages)*

The Fannie Mae/Freddie Mac Uniform Trust Deed – Oregon form

If Lender exercises this option, Lender shall give Borrower notice of acceleration. The notice shall provide a period of not less than 30 days from the date the notice is given in accordance with Section 15 within which Borrower must pay all sums secured by this Security Instrument. If Borrower fails to pay these sums prior to the expiration of this period, Lender may invoke any remedies permitted by this Security Instrument without further notice or demand on Borrower.

WITNESS THE HAND(S) AND SEAL(S) OF THE UNDERSIGNED

_____ (Seal)
- Borrower

_____ (Seal)
- Borrower

_____ (Seal)
- Borrower

_____ (Seal)
- Borrower

[Sign Original Only]

MULTISTATE FIXED RATE NOTE—Single Family—Fannie Mae/Freddie Mac UNIFORM INSTRUMENT   Form 3200 1/01 *(page 3 of 3 pages)*

(I) "Applicable Law" means all controlling applicable federal, state and local statutes, regulations, ordinances and administrative rules and orders (that have the effect of law) as well as all applicable final, non-appealable judicial opinions.

(J) "Community Association Dues, Fees, and Assessments" means all dues, fees, assessments and other charges that are imposed on Borrower or the Property by a condominium association, homeowners association or similar organization.

(K) "Electronic Funds Transfer" means any transfer of funds, other than a transaction originated by check, draft, or similar paper instrument, which is initiated through an electronic terminal, telephonic instrument, computer, or magnetic tape so as to order, instruct, or authorize a financial institution to debit or credit an account. Such term includes, but is not limited to, point-of-sale transfers, automated teller machine transactions, transfers initiated by telephone, wire transfers, and automated clearinghouse transfers.

(L) "Escrow Items" means those items that are described in Section 3.

(M) "Miscellaneous Proceeds" means any compensation, settlement, award of damages, or proceeds paid by any third party (other than insurance proceeds paid under the coverages described in Section 5) for: (i) damage to, or destruction of, the Property; (ii) condemnation or other taking of all or any part of the Property; (iii) conveyance in lieu of condemnation; or (iv) misrepresentations of, or omissions as to, the value and/or condition of the Property.

(N) "Mortgage Insurance" means insurance protecting Lender against the nonpayment of, or default on, the Loan.

(O) "Periodic Payment" means the regularly scheduled amount due for (i) principal and interest under the Note, plus (ii) any amounts under Section 3 of this Security Instrument.

(P) "RESPA" means the Real Estate Settlement Procedures Act (12 U.S.C. §2601 et seq.) and its implementing regulation, Regulation X (24 C.F.R. Part 3500), as they might be amended from time to time, or any additional or successor legislation or regulation that governs the same subject matter. As used in this Security Instrument, "RESPA" refers to all requirements and restrictions that are imposed in regard to a "federally related mortgage loan" even if the Loan does not qualify as a "federally related mortgage loan" under RESPA.

(Q) "Successor in Interest of Borrower" means any party that has taken title to the Property, whether or not that party has assumed Borrower's obligations under the Note and/or this Security Instrument.

TRANSFER OF RIGHTS IN THE PROPERTY

This Security Instrument secures to Lender: (i) the repayment of the Loan, and all renewals, extensions and modifications of the Note; and (ii) the performance of Borrower's covenants and agreements under this Security Instrument and the Note. For this purpose, Borrower irrevocably

grants and conveys to Trustee, in trust, with power of sale, the following described property located in the _____ of _____ :
[Type of Recording Jurisdiction]   [Name of Recording Jurisdiction]

which currently has the address of _____
[Street]

_____, Oregon _____ ("Property Address"):
[City]   [Zip Code]

TOGETHER WITH all the improvements now or hereafter erected on the property, and all easements, appurtenances, and fixtures now or hereafter a part of the property. All replacements and additions shall also be covered by this Security Instrument. All of the foregoing is referred to in this Security Instrument as the "Property."

BORROWER COVENANTS that Borrower is lawfully seised of the estate hereby conveyed and has the right to grant and convey the Property and that the Property is unencumbered, except for encumbrances of record. Borrower warrants and will defend generally the title to the Property against all claims and demands, subject to any encumbrances of record.

THIS SECURITY INSTRUMENT combines uniform covenants for national use and nonuniform covenants with limited variations by jurisdiction to constitute a uniform security instrument covering real property.

UNIFORM COVENANTS. Borrower and Lender covenant and agree as follows:

1. Payment of Principal, Interest, Escrow Items, Prepayment Charges, and Late Charges. Borrower shall pay when due the principal of, and interest on, the debt evidenced by the Note and any prepayment charges and late charges due under the Note. Borrower shall also pay funds for Escrow Items pursuant to Section 3. Payments due under the Note and this Security Instrument shall be made in U.S. currency. However, if any check or other instrument received by Lender as payment under the Note or this Security Instrument is returned to Lender unpaid, Lender may require that any or all subsequent payments due under the Note and this Security Instrument be made in one or more of the following forms, as selected by Lender: (a) cash; (b) money order; (c) certified check, bank check, treasurer's check or cashier's check, provided any such check is drawn upon an institution whose deposits are insured by a federal agency, instrumentality, or entity; or (d) Electronic Funds Transfer.

Payments are deemed received by Lender when received at the location designated in the Note or at such other location as may be designated by Lender in accordance with the notice provisions in Section 15. Lender may return any payment or partial payment if the payment or partial payments are insufficient to bring the Loan current. Lender may accept any payment or partial payment insufficient to bring the Loan current, without waiver of any rights hereunder or prejudice to its rights to refuse such payment or partial payments in the future, but Lender is not obligated to apply such payments at the time such payments are accepted. If each Periodic Payment is applied as of its scheduled due date, then Lender need not pay interest on unapplied funds. Lender may hold such unapplied funds until Borrower makes payment to bring the Loan current. If Borrower does not do so within a reasonable period of time, Lender shall either apply such funds or return them to Borrower. If not applied earlier, such funds will be applied to the outstanding principal balance under the Note immediately prior to foreclosure. No offset or claim which Borrower might have now or in the future against Lender shall relieve Borrower from making payments due under the Note and this Security Instrument or performing the covenants and agreements secured by this Security Instrument.

2. **Application of Payments or Proceeds.** Except as otherwise described in this Section 2, all payments accepted and applied by Lender shall be applied in the following order of priority: (a) interest due under the Note; (b) principal due under the Note; (c) amounts due under Section 3. Such payments shall be applied to each Periodic Payment in the order in which it became due. Any remaining amounts shall be applied first to late charges, second to any other amounts due under this Security Instrument, and then to reduce the principal balance of the Note. If Lender receives a payment from Borrower for a delinquent Periodic Payment which includes a sufficient amount to pay any late charge due, the payment may be applied to the delinquent payment and the late charge. If more than one Periodic Payment is outstanding, Lender may apply any payment received from Borrower to the repayment of the Periodic Payments if, and to the extent that, each payment can be paid in full. To the extent that any excess exists after the payment is applied to the full payment of one or more Periodic Payments, such excess may be applied to any late charges due. Voluntary prepayments shall be applied first to any prepayment charges and then as described in the Note.

Any application of payments, insurance proceeds, or Miscellaneous Proceeds to principal due under the Note shall not extend or postpone the due date, or change the amount, of the Periodic Payments.

3. **Funds for Escrow Items.** Borrower shall pay to Lender on the day Periodic Payments are due under the Note, until the Note is paid in full, a sum (the "Funds") to provide for payment of amounts due for: (a) taxes and assessments and other items which can attain priority over this Security Instrument as a lien or encumbrance on the Property; (b) leasehold payments or ground rents on the Property, if any; (c) premiums for any and all insurance required by Lender under Section 5; and (d) Mortgage Insurance premiums, if any, or any sums payable by Borrower to Lender in lieu of the payment of Mortgage Insurance premiums in accordance with the provisions of Section 10. These items are called "Escrow Items." At origination or at any time during the term of the Loan, Lender may require that Community Association Dues, Fees, and Assessments, if any,

be escrowed by Borrower, and such dues, fees and assessments shall be an Escrow Item. Borrower shall promptly furnish to Lender all notices of amounts to be paid under this Section. Borrower shall pay Lender the Funds for Escrow Items unless Lender waives Borrower's obligation to pay the Funds for any or all Escrow Items. Lender may waive Borrower's obligation to pay to Lender Funds for any or all Escrow Items at any time. Any such waiver may only be in writing. In the event of such waiver, Borrower shall pay directly, when and where payable, the amounts due for any Escrow Items for which payment of Funds has been waived by Lender and, if Lender requires, shall furnish to Lender receipts evidencing such payment within such time period as Lender may require. Borrower's obligation to make such payments and to provide receipts shall for all purposes be deemed to be a covenant and agreement contained in this Security Instrument, as the phrase "covenant and agreement" is used in Section 9. If Borrower is obligated to pay Escrow Items directly, pursuant to a waiver, and Borrower fails to pay the amount due for an Escrow Item, Lender may exercise its rights under Section 9 and pay such amount and Borrower shall then be obligated under Section 9 to repay to Lender any such amount. Lender may revoke the waiver as to any or all Escrow Items at any time by a notice given in accordance with Section 15 and, upon such revocation, Borrower shall pay to Lender all Funds, and in such amounts, that are then required under this Section 3.

Lender may, at any time, collect and hold Funds in an amount (a) sufficient to permit Lender to apply the Funds at the time specified under RESPA, and (b) not to exceed the maximum amount a lender can require under RESPA. Lender shall estimate the amount of Funds due on the basis of current data and reasonable estimates of expenditures of future Escrow Items or otherwise in accordance with Applicable Law.

The Funds shall be held in an institution whose deposits are insured by a federal agency, instrumentality, or entity (including Lender, if Lender is an institution whose deposits are so insured) or in any Federal Home Loan Bank. Lender shall apply the Funds to pay the Escrow Items no later than the time specified under RESPA. Lender shall not charge Borrower for holding and applying the Funds, annually analyzing the escrow account, or verifying the Escrow Items, unless Lender pays Borrower interest on the Funds and Applicable Law permits Lender to make such a charge. Unless an agreement is made in writing or Applicable Law requires interest to be paid on the Funds, Lender shall not be required to pay Borrower any interest or earnings on the Funds. Borrower and Lender can agree in writing, however, that interest shall be paid on the Funds. Lender shall give to Borrower, without charge, an annual accounting of the Funds as required by RESPA.

If there is a surplus of Funds held in escrow, as defined under RESPA, Lender shall account to Borrower for the excess funds in accordance with RESPA. If there is a shortage of Funds held in escrow, as defined under RESPA, Lender shall notify Borrower as required by RESPA, and Borrower shall pay to Lender the amount necessary to make up the shortage in accordance with RESPA, but in no more than 12 monthly payments. If there is a deficiency of Funds held in escrow, as defined under RESPA, Lender shall notify Borrower as required by RESPA, and Borrower shall pay to Lender the amount necessary to make up the deficiency in accordance with RESPA, but in no more than 12 monthly payments.

Upon payment in full of all sums secured by this Security Instrument, Lender shall promptly refund to Borrower any Funds held by Lender.

4. Charges; Liens. Borrower shall pay all taxes, assessments, charges, fines, and impositions attributable to the Property which can attain priority over this Security Instrument, leasehold payments or ground rents on the Property, if any, and Community Association Dues, Fees, and Assessments, if any. To the extent that these items are Escrow Items, Borrower shall pay them in the manner provided in Section 3.

Borrower shall promptly discharge any lien which has priority over this Security Instrument unless Borrower: (a) agrees in writing to the payment of the obligation secured by the lien in a manner acceptable to Lender, but only so long as Borrower is performing such agreement; (b) contests the lien in good faith by, or defends against enforcement of the lien in, legal proceedings which in Lender's opinion operate to prevent the enforcement of the lien while those proceedings are pending, but only until such proceedings are concluded; or (c) secures from the holder of the lien an agreement satisfactory to Lender subordinating the lien to this Security Instrument. If Lender determines that any part of the Property is subject to a lien which can attain priority over this Security Instrument, Lender may give Borrower a notice identifying the lien. Within 10 days of the date on which that notice is given, Borrower shall satisfy the lien or take one or more of the actions set forth above in this Section 4.

Lender may require Borrower to pay a one-time charge for a real estate tax verification and/or reporting service used by Lender in connection with this Loan.

5. Property Insurance. Borrower shall keep the improvements now existing or hereafter erected on the Property insured against loss by fire, hazards included within the term "extended coverage," and any other hazards including, but not limited to, earthquakes and floods, for which Lender requires insurance. This insurance shall be maintained in the amounts (including deductible levels) and for the periods that Lender requires. What Lender requires pursuant to the preceding sentences can change during the term of the Loan. The insurance carrier providing the insurance shall be chosen by Borrower subject to Lender's right to disapprove Borrower's choice, which right shall not be exercised unreasonably. Lender may require Borrower to pay, in connection with this Loan, either: (a) a one-time charge for flood zone determination, certification and tracking services; or (b) a one-time charge for flood zone determination and certification services and subsequent charges each time remappings or similar changes occur which reasonably might affect such determination or certification. Borrower shall also be responsible for the payment of any fees imposed by the Federal Emergency Management Agency in connection with the review of any flood zone determination resulting from an objection by Borrower.

If Borrower fails to maintain any of the coverages described above, Lender may obtain insurance coverage, at Lender's option and Borrower's expense. Lender is under no obligation to purchase any particular type or amount of coverage. Therefore, such coverage shall cover Lender, but might or might not protect Borrower, Borrower's equity in the Property, or the contents of the Property, against any risk, hazard or liability and might provide greater or lesser coverage than was previously in effect. Borrower acknowledges that the cost of the insurance coverage so obtained might significantly exceed the cost of insurance that Borrower could have obtained. Any amounts disbursed by Lender under this Section 5 shall become additional debt of Borrower secured by this Security Instrument. These amounts shall bear interest at the Note rate from the date of disbursement and shall be payable, with such interest, upon notice from Lender to Borrower requesting payment.

All insurance policies required by Lender and renewals of such policies shall be subject to Lender's right to disapprove such policies, shall include a standard mortgage clause, and shall name Lender as mortgagee and/or as an additional loss payee. Lender shall have the right to hold the policies and renewal certificates. If Lender requires, Borrower shall promptly give to Lender all receipts of paid premiums and renewal notices. If Borrower obtains any form of insurance coverage, not otherwise required by Lender, for damage to, or destruction of, the Property, such policy shall include a standard mortgage clause and shall name Lender as mortgagee and/or as an additional loss payee.

In the event of loss, Borrower shall give prompt notice to the insurance carrier and Lender. Lender may make proof of loss if not made promptly by Borrower. Unless Lender and Borrower otherwise agree in writing, any insurance proceeds, whether or not the underlying insurance was required by Lender, shall be applied to restoration or repair of the Property, if the restoration or repair is economically feasible and Lender's security is not lessened. During such repair and restoration period, Lender shall have the right to hold such insurance proceeds until Lender has had an opportunity to inspect such Property to ensure the work has been completed to Lender's satisfaction, provided that such inspection shall be undertaken promptly. Lender may disburse proceeds for the repairs and restoration in a single payment or in a series of progress payments as the work is completed. Unless an agreement is made in writing or Applicable Law requires interest to be paid on such insurance proceeds, Lender shall not be required to pay Borrower any interest or earnings on such proceeds. Fees for public adjusters, or other third parties, retained by Borrower shall not be paid out of the insurance proceeds and shall be the sole obligation of Borrower. If the restoration or repair is not economically feasible or Lender's security would be lessened, the insurance proceeds shall be applied to the sums secured by this Security Instrument, whether or not then due, with the excess, if any, paid to Borrower. Such insurance proceeds shall be applied in the order provided for in Section 2.

If Borrower abandons the Property, Lender may file, negotiate and settle any available insurance claim and related matters. If Borrower does not respond within 30 days to a notice from Lender that the insurance carrier has offered to settle a claim, then Lender may negotiate and settle the claim. The 30-day period will begin when the notice is given. In either event, or if Lender acquires the Property under Section 22 or otherwise, Borrower hereby assigns to Lender (a) Borrower's rights to any insurance proceeds in an amount not to exceed the amounts unpaid under the Note or this Security Instrument, and (b) any other of Borrower's rights (other than the right to any refund of unearned premiums paid by Borrower) under all insurance policies covering the Property, insofar as such rights are applicable to the coverage of the Property. Lender may use the insurance proceeds either to repair or restore the Property or to pay amounts unpaid under the Note or this Security Instrument, whether or not then due.

6. Occupancy. Borrower shall occupy, establish, and use the Property as Borrower's principal residence within 60 days after the execution of this Security Instrument and shall continue to occupy the Property as Borrower's principal residence for at least one year after the date of occupancy, unless Lender otherwise agrees in writing, which consent shall not be unreasonably withheld, or unless extenuating circumstances exist which are beyond Borrower's control.

7. Preservation, Maintenance and Protection of the Property; Inspections. Borrower shall not destroy, damage or impair the Property, allow the Property to deteriorate or commit waste on the Property. Whether or not Borrower is residing in the Property, Borrower shall maintain the Property in order to prevent the Property from deteriorating or decreasing in value due to its condition. Unless it is determined pursuant to Section 5 that repair or restoration is not economically feasible, Borrower shall promptly repair the Property if damaged to avoid further deterioration or damage. If insurance or condemnation proceeds are paid in connection with damage to, or the taking of, the Property, Borrower shall be responsible for repairing or restoring the Property only if Lender has released proceeds for such purposes. Lender may disburse proceeds for the repairs and restoration in a single payment or in a series of progress payments as the work is completed. If the insurance or condemnation proceeds are not sufficient to repair or restore the Property, Borrower is not relieved of Borrower's obligation for the completion of such repair or restoration. Lender or its agent may make reasonable entries upon and inspections of the Property. If it has reasonable cause, Lender may inspect the interior of the improvements on the Property. Lender shall give Borrower notice at the time of or prior to such an interior inspection specifying such reasonable cause.

8. Borrower's Loan Application. Borrower shall be in default if, during the Loan application process, Borrower or any persons or entities acting at the direction of Borrower or with Borrower's knowledge or consent gave materially false, misleading, or inaccurate information or statements to Lender (or failed to provide Lender with material information) in connection with the Loan. Material representations include, but are not limited to, representations concerning Borrower's occupancy of the Property as Borrower's principal residence.

9. Protection of Lender's Interest in the Property and Rights Under this Security Instrument. If (a) Borrower fails to perform the covenants and agreements contained in this Security Instrument, (b) there is a legal proceeding that might significantly affect Lender's interest in the Property and/or rights under this Security Instrument (such as a proceeding in bankruptcy, probate, for condemnation or forfeiture, for enforcement of a lien which may attain priority over this Security Instrument or to enforce laws or regulations), or (c) Borrower has abandoned the Property, then Lender may do and pay for whatever is reasonable or appropriate to protect Lender's interest in the Property and rights under this Security Instrument, including protecting and/or assessing the value of the Property, and securing and/or repairing the Property. Lender's actions can include, but are not limited to: (a) paying any sums secured by a lien which has priority over this Security Instrument; (b) appearing in court; and (c) paying reasonable attorneys' fees to protect its interest in the Property and/or rights under this Security Instrument, including its secured position in a bankruptcy proceeding. Securing the Property includes, but is not limited to, entering the Property to make repairs, change locks, replace or board up doors and windows, drain water from pipes, eliminate building or other code violations or dangerous conditions, and have utilities turned on or off. Although Lender may take action under this Section 9, Lender does not have to do so and is not under any duty or obligation to do so. It is agreed that Lender incurs no liability for not taking any or all actions authorized under this Section 9.

Any amounts disbursed by Lender under this Section 9 shall become additional debt of Borrower secured by this Security Instrument. These amounts shall bear interest at the Note rate from the date of disbursement and shall be payable, with such interest, upon notice from Lender to Borrower requesting payment.

If this Security Instrument is on a leasehold, Borrower shall comply with all the provisions of the lease. If Borrower acquires fee title to the Property, the leasehold and the fee title shall not merge unless Lender agrees to the merger in writing.

10. Mortgage Insurance. If Lender required Mortgage Insurance as a condition of making the Loan, Borrower shall pay the premiums required to maintain the Mortgage Insurance in effect. If, for any reason, the Mortgage Insurance coverage required by Lender ceases to be available from the mortgage insurer that previously provided such insurance and Borrower was required to make separately designated payments toward the premiums for Mortgage Insurance, Borrower shall pay the premiums required to obtain coverage substantially equivalent to the Mortgage Insurance previously in effect, at a cost substantially equivalent to the cost to Borrower of the Mortgage Insurance previously in effect, from an alternate mortgage insurer selected by Lender. If substantially equivalent Mortgage Insurance coverage is not available, Borrower shall continue to pay to Lender the amount of the separately designated payments that were due when the insurance coverage ceased to be in effect. Lender will accept, use and retain these payments as a nonrefundable loss reserve in lieu of Mortgage Insurance. Such loss reserve shall be non-refundable, notwithstanding the fact that the Loan is ultimately paid in full, and Lender shall not be required to pay Borrower any interest or earnings on such loss reserve. Lender can no longer require loss reserve payments if Mortgage Insurance coverage (in the amount and for the period that Lender requires) provided by an insurer selected by Lender again becomes available, is obtained, and Lender requires separately designated payments toward the premiums for Mortgage Insurance. If Lender required Mortgage Insurance as a condition of making the Loan and Borrower was required to make separately designated payments toward the premiums for Mortgage Insurance, Borrower shall pay the premiums required to maintain Mortgage Insurance in effect, or to provide a non-refundable loss reserve, until Lender's requirement for Mortgage Insurance ends in accordance with any written agreement between Borrower and Lender providing for such termination or until termination is required by Applicable Law. Nothing in this Section 10 affects Borrower's obligation to pay interest at the rate provided in the Note.

Mortgage Insurance reimburses Lender (or any entity that purchases the Note) for certain losses it may incur if Borrower does not repay the Loan as agreed. Borrower is not a party to the Mortgage Insurance.

Mortgage insurers evaluate their total risk on all such insurance in force from time to time, and may enter into agreements with other parties that share or modify their risk, or reduce losses. These agreements are on terms and conditions that are satisfactory to the mortgage insurer and the other party (or parties) to these agreements. These agreements may require the mortgage insurer to make payments using any source of funds that the mortgage insurer may have available (which may include funds obtained from Mortgage Insurance premiums).

As a result of these agreements, Lender, any purchaser of the Note, another insurer, any reinsurer, any other entity, or any affiliate of any of the foregoing, may receive (directly or indirectly) amounts that derive from (or might be characterized as) a portion of Borrower's payments for Mortgage Insurance, in exchange for sharing or modifying the mortgage insurer's risk, or reducing losses. If such agreement provides that an affiliate of Lender takes a share of the insurer's risk in exchange for a share of the premiums paid to the insurer, the arrangement is often termed "captive reinsurance." Further:

(a) Any such agreements will not affect the amounts that Borrower has agreed to pay for Mortgage Insurance, or any other terms of the Loan. Such agreements will not increase the amount Borrower will owe for Mortgage Insurance, and they will not entitle Borrower to any refund.

(b) Any such agreements will not affect the rights Borrower has – if any – with respect to the Mortgage Insurance under the Homeowners Protection Act of 1998 or any other law. These rights may include the right to receive certain disclosures, to request and obtain cancellation of the Mortgage Insurance, to have the Mortgage Insurance terminated automatically, and/or to receive a refund of any Mortgage Insurance premiums that were unearned at the time of such cancellation or termination.

11. Assignment of Miscellaneous Proceeds; Forfeiture. All Miscellaneous Proceeds are hereby assigned to and shall be paid to Lender.

If the Property is damaged, such Miscellaneous Proceeds shall be applied to restoration or repair of the Property, if the restoration or repair is economically feasible and Lender's security is not lessened. During such repair and restoration period, Lender shall have the right to hold such Miscellaneous Proceeds until Lender has had an opportunity to inspect such Property to ensure the work has been completed to Lender's satisfaction, provided that such inspection shall be undertaken promptly. Lender may pay for the repairs and restoration in a single disbursement or in a series of progress payments as the work is completed. Unless an agreement is made in writing or Applicable Law requires interest to be paid on such Miscellaneous Proceeds, Lender shall not be required to pay Borrower any interest or earnings on such Miscellaneous Proceeds. If the restoration or repair is not economically feasible or Lender's security would be lessened, the Miscellaneous Proceeds shall be applied to the sums secured by this Security Instrument, whether or not then due, with the excess, if any, paid to Borrower. Such Miscellaneous Proceeds shall be applied in the order provided for in Section 2.

In the event of a total taking, destruction, or loss in value of the Property, the Miscellaneous Proceeds shall be applied to the sums secured by this Security Instrument, whether or not then due, with the excess, if any, paid to Borrower.

In the event of a partial taking, destruction, or loss in value of the Property in which the fair market value of the Property immediately before the partial taking, destruction, or loss in value is equal to or greater than the amount of the sums secured by this Security Instrument immediately before the partial taking, destruction, or loss in value, unless Borrower and Lender otherwise agree in writing, the sums secured by this Security Instrument shall be reduced by the amount of the Miscellaneous Proceeds multiplied by the following fraction: (a) the total amount of the sums secured immediately before the partial taking, destruction, or loss in value divided by (b) the fair market value of the Property immediately before the partial taking, destruction, or loss in value. Any balance shall be paid to Borrower.

In the event of a partial taking, destruction, or loss in value of the Property in which the fair market value of the Property immediately before the partial taking, destruction, or loss in value is less than the amount of the sums secured immediately before the partial taking, destruction, or loss in value, unless Borrower and Lender otherwise agree in writing, the Miscellaneous Proceeds shall be applied to the sums secured by this Security Instrument whether or not the sums are then due.

If the Property is abandoned by Borrower, or if, after notice by Lender to Borrower that the Opposing Party (as defined in the next sentence) offers to make an award to settle a claim for

damages, Borrower fails to respond to Lender within 30 days after the date the notice is given, Lender is authorized to collect and apply the Miscellaneous Proceeds either to restoration or repair of the Property or to the sums secured by this Security Instrument, whether or not then due. "Opposing Party" means the third party that owes Borrower Miscellaneous Proceeds or the party against whom Borrower has a right of action in regard to Miscellaneous Proceeds.

Borrower shall be in default if any action or proceeding, whether civil or criminal, is begun that, in Lender's judgment, could result in forfeiture of the Property or other material impairment of Lender's interest in the Property or rights under this Security Instrument. Borrower can cure such a default and, if acceleration has occurred, reinstate as provided in Section 19, by causing the action or proceeding to be dismissed with a ruling that, in Lender's judgment, precludes forfeiture of the Property or other material impairment of Lender's interest in the Property or rights under this Security Instrument. The proceeds of any award or claim for damages that are attributable to the impairment of Lender's interest in the Property are hereby assigned and shall be paid to Lender.

All Miscellaneous Proceeds that are not applied to restoration or repair of the Property shall be applied in the order provided for in Section 2.

12. Borrower Not Released; Forbearance By Lender Not a Waiver. Extension of the time for payment or modification of amortization of the sums secured by this Security Instrument granted by Lender to Borrower or any Successor in Interest of Borrower shall not operate to release the liability of Borrower or any Successors in Interest of Borrower. Lender shall not be required to commence proceedings against any Successor in Interest of Borrower or to refuse to extend time for payment or otherwise modify amortization of the sums secured by this Security Instrument by reason of any demand made by the original Borrower or any Successors in Interest of Borrower. Any forbearance by Lender in exercising any right or remedy including, without limitation, Lender's acceptance of payments from third persons, entities or Successors in Interest of Borrower or in amounts less than the amount then due, shall not be a waiver of or preclude the exercise of any right or remedy.

13. Joint and Several Liability; Co-signers; Successors and Assigns Bound. Borrower covenants and agrees that Borrower's obligations and liability shall be joint and several. However, any Borrower who co-signs this Security Instrument but does not execute the Note (a "co-signer"): (a) is co-signing this Security Instrument only to mortgage, grant and convey the co-signer's interest in the Property under the terms of this Security Instrument; (b) is not personally obligated to pay the sums secured by this Security Instrument; and (c) agrees that Lender and any other Borrower can agree to extend, modify, forbear or make any accommodations with regard to the terms of this Security Instrument or the Note without the co-signer's consent.

Subject to the provisions of Section 18, any Successor in Interest of Borrower who assumes Borrower's obligations under this Security Instrument in writing, and is approved by Lender, shall obtain all of Borrower's rights and benefits under this Security Instrument. Borrower shall not be released from Borrower's obligations and liability under this Security Instrument unless Lender agrees to such release in writing. The covenants and agreements of this Security Instrument shall bind (except as provided in Section 20) and benefit the successors and assigns of Lender.

14. Loan Charges. Lender may charge Borrower fees for services performed in connection with Borrower's default, for the purpose of protecting Lender's interest in the Property and rights under this Security Instrument, including, but not limited to, attorneys' fees, property inspection and valuation fees. In regard to any other fees, the absence of express authority in this Security

Instrument to charge a specific fee to Borrower shall not be construed as a prohibition on the charging of such fee. Lender may not charge fees that are expressly prohibited by this Security Instrument or by Applicable Law.

If the Loan is subject to a law which sets maximum loan charges, and that law is finally interpreted so that the interest or other loan charges collected or to be collected in connection with the Loan exceed the permitted limits, then: (a) any such loan charge shall be reduced by the amount necessary to reduce the charge to the permitted limit; and (b) any sums already collected from Borrower which exceeded permitted limits will be refunded to Borrower. Lender may choose to make this refund by reducing the principal owed under the Note or by making a direct payment to Borrower. If a refund reduces principal, the reduction will be treated as a partial prepayment without any prepayment charge (whether or not a prepayment charge is provided for under the Note). Borrower's acceptance of any such refund made by direct payment to Borrower will constitute a waiver of any right of action Borrower might have arising out of such overcharge.

15. Notices. All notices given by Borrower or Lender in connection with this Security Instrument must be in writing. Any notice to Borrower in connection with this Security Instrument shall be deemed to have been given to Borrower when mailed by first class mail or when actually delivered to Borrower's notice address if sent by other means. Notice to any one Borrower shall constitute notice to all Borrowers unless Applicable Law expressly requires otherwise. The notice address shall be the Property Address unless Borrower has designated a substitute notice address by notice to Lender. Borrower shall promptly notify Lender of Borrower's change of address. If Lender specifies a procedure for reporting Borrower's change of address, then Borrower shall only report a change of address through that specified procedure. There may be only one designated notice address under this Security Instrument at any one time. Any notice to Lender shall be given by delivering it or by mailing it by first class mail to Lender's address stated herein unless Lender has designated another address by notice to Borrower. Any notice in connection with this Security Instrument shall not be deemed to have been given to Lender until actually received by Lender. If any notice required by this Security Instrument is also required under Applicable Law, the Applicable Law requirement will satisfy the corresponding requirement under this Security Instrument.

16. Governing Law; Severability; Rules of Construction. This Security Instrument shall be governed by federal law and the law of the jurisdiction in which the Property is located. All rights and obligations contained in this Security Instrument are subject to any requirements and limitations of Applicable Law. Applicable Law might explicitly or implicitly allow the parties to agree by contract or it might be silent, but such silence shall not be construed as a prohibition against agreement by contract. In the event that any provision or clause of this Security Instrument or the Note conflicts with Applicable Law, such conflict shall not affect other provisions of this Security Instrument or the Note which can be given effect without the conflicting provision.

As used in this Security Instrument: (a) words of the masculine gender shall mean and include corresponding neuter words or words of the feminine gender; (b) words in the singular shall mean and include the plural and vice versa; and (c) the word "may" gives sole discretion without any obligation to take any action.

17. Borrower's Copy. Borrower shall be given one copy of the Note and of this Security Instrument.

18. Transfer of the Property or a Beneficial Interest in Borrower. As used in this Section 18, "Interest in the Property" means any legal or beneficial interest in the Property, including, but not limited to, those beneficial interests transferred in a bond for deed, contract for deed, installment sales contract or escrow agreement, the intent of which is the transfer of title by Borrower at a future date to a purchaser.

If all or any part of the Property or any Interest in the Property is sold or transferred (or if Borrower is not a natural person and a beneficial interest in Borrower is sold or transferred) without Lender's prior written consent, Lender may require immediate payment in full of all sums secured by this Security Instrument. However, this option shall not be exercised by Lender if such exercise is prohibited by Applicable Law.

If Lender exercises this option, Lender shall give Borrower notice of acceleration. The notice shall provide a period of not less than 30 days from the date the notice is given in accordance with Section 15 within which Borrower must pay all sums secured by this Security Instrument. If Borrower fails to pay these sums prior to the expiration of this period, Lender may invoke any remedies permitted by this Security Instrument without further notice or demand on Borrower.

19. Borrower's Right to Reinstate After Acceleration. If Borrower meets certain conditions, Borrower shall have the right to have enforcement of this Security Instrument discontinued at any time prior to the earliest of: (a) five days before sale of the Property pursuant to any power of sale contained in this Security Instrument; (b) such other period as Applicable Law might specify for the termination of Borrower's right to reinstate; or (c) entry of a judgment enforcing this Security Instrument. Those conditions are that Borrower: (a) pays Lender all sums which then would be due under this Security Instrument and the Note as if no acceleration had occurred; (b) cures any default of any other covenants or agreements; (c) pays all expenses incurred in enforcing this Security Instrument, including, but not limited to, reasonable attorneys' fees, property inspection and valuation fees, and other fees incurred for the purpose of protecting Lender's interest in the Property and rights under this Security Instrument; and (d) takes such action as Lender may reasonably require to assure that Lender's interest in the Property and rights under this Security Instrument, and Borrower's obligation to pay the sums secured by this Security Instrument, shall continue unchanged. Lender may require that Borrower pay such reinstatement sums and expenses in one or more of the following forms, as selected by Lender: (a) cash; (b) money order; (c) certified check, bank check, treasurer's check or cashier's check, provided any such check is drawn upon an institution whose deposits are insured by a federal agency, instrumentality or entity; or (d) Electronic Funds Transfer. Upon reinstatement by Borrower, this Security Instrument and obligations secured hereby shall remain fully effective as if no acceleration had occurred. However, this right to reinstate shall not apply in the case of acceleration under Section 18.

20. Sale of Note; Change of Loan Servicer; Notice of Grievance. The Note or a partial interest in the Note (together with this Security Instrument) can be sold one or more times without prior notice to Borrower. A sale might result in a change in the entity (known as the "Loan Servicer") that collects Periodic Payments due under the Note and this Security Instrument and performs other mortgage loan servicing obligations under the Note, this Security Instrument, and Applicable Law. There also might be one or more changes of the Loan Servicer unrelated to a sale of the Note. If there is a change of the Loan Servicer, Borrower will be given written notice of the change which will state the name and address of the new Loan Servicer, the address to which payments should be made and any other information RESPA requires in connection with a notice of transfer of servicing. If the Note is sold and thereafter the Loan is serviced by a Loan Servicer other than the purchaser of the Note, the mortgage loan servicing obligations to Borrower will remain with the Loan Servicer or be transferred to a successor Loan Servicer and are not assumed by the Note purchaser unless otherwise provided by the Note purchaser.

Neither Borrower nor Lender may commence, join, or be joined to any judicial action (as either an individual litigant or the member of a class) that arises from the other party's actions pursuant to this Security Instrument or that alleges that the other party has breached any provision of, or any duty owed by reason of, this Security Instrument, until such Borrower or Lender has notified the other party (with such notice given in compliance with the requirements of Section 15) of such alleged breach and afforded the other party hereto a reasonable period after the giving of such notice to take corrective action. If Applicable Law provides a time period which must elapse before certain action can be taken, that time period will be deemed to be reasonable for purposes of this paragraph. The notice of acceleration and opportunity to cure given to Borrower pursuant to Section 22 and the notice of acceleration given to Borrower pursuant to Section 18 shall be deemed to satisfy the notice and opportunity to take corrective action provisions of this Section 20.

21. Hazardous Substances. As used in this Section 21: (a) "Hazardous Substances" are those substances defined as toxic or hazardous substances, pollutants, or wastes by Environmental Law and the following substances: gasoline, kerosene, other flammable or toxic petroleum products, toxic pesticides and herbicides, volatile solvents, materials containing asbestos or formaldehyde, and radioactive materials; (b) "Environmental Law" means federal laws and laws of the jurisdiction where the Property is located that relate to health, safety or environmental protection; (c) "Environmental Cleanup" includes any response action, remedial action, or removal action, as defined in Environmental Law; and (d) an "Environmental Condition" means a condition that can cause, contribute to, or otherwise trigger an Environmental Cleanup.

Borrower shall not cause or permit the presence, use, disposal, storage, or release of any Hazardous Substances, or threaten to release any Hazardous Substances, on or in the Property. Borrower shall not do, nor allow anyone else to do, anything affecting the Property (a) that is in violation of any Environmental Law, (b) which creates an Environmental Condition, or (c) which, due to the presence, use, or release of a Hazardous Substance, creates a condition that adversely affects the value of the Property. The preceding two sentences shall not apply to the presence, use, or storage on the Property of small quantities of Hazardous Substances that are generally recognized to be appropriate to normal residential uses and to maintenance of the Property (including, but not limited to, hazardous substances in consumer products).

Borrower shall promptly give Lender written notice of (a) any investigation, claim, demand, lawsuit or other action by any governmental or regulatory agency or private party involving the Property and any Hazardous Substance or Environmental Law of which Borrower has actual knowledge, (b) any Environmental Condition, including but not limited to, any spilling, leaking, discharge, release or threat of release of any Hazardous Substance, and (c) any condition caused by the presence, use or release of a Hazardous Substance which adversely affects the value of the Property. If Borrower learns, or is notified by any governmental or regulatory authority, or any private party, that any removal or other remediation of any Hazardous Substance affecting the Property is necessary, Borrower shall promptly take all necessary remedial actions in accordance with Environmental Law. Nothing herein shall create any obligation on Lender for an Environmental Cleanup.

NON-UNIFORM COVENANTS. Borrower and Lender further covenant and agree as follows:

22. Acceleration; Remedies. Lender shall give notice to Borrower prior to acceleration following Borrower's breach of any covenant or agreement in this Security Instrument (but not prior to acceleration under Section 18 unless Applicable Law provides otherwise). The notice shall specify: (a) the default; (b) the action required to cure the default; (c) a date, not less than 30 days from the date the notice is given to Borrower, by which the default must be cured; and (d) that failure to cure the default on or before the date specified in the notice may result in acceleration of the sums secured by this Security Instrument and sale of the Property. The notice shall further inform Borrower of the right to reinstate after acceleration and the right to bring a court action to assert the non-existence of a default or any other defense of Borrower to acceleration and sale. If the default is not cured on or before the date specified in the notice, Lender at its option may require immediate payment in full of all sums secured by this Security Instrument without further demand and may invoke the power of sale and any other remedies permitted by Applicable Law. Lender shall be entitled to collect all expenses incurred in pursuing the remedies provided in this Section 22, including, but not limited to, reasonable attorneys' fees and costs of title evidence.

If Lender invokes the power of sale, Lender shall execute or cause Trustee to execute a written notice of the occurrence of an event of default and of Lender's election to cause the Property to be sold and shall cause such notice to be recorded in each county in which any part of the Property is located. Lender or Trustee shall give notice of sale in the manner prescribed by Applicable Law to Borrower and to other persons prescribed by Applicable Law. After the time required by Applicable Law, Trustee, without demand on Borrower, shall sell the Property at public auction to the highest bidder at the time and place and under the terms designated in the notice of sale in one or more parcels and in any order Trustee determines. Trustee may postpone sale of all or any parcel of the Property by public announcement at the time and place of any previously scheduled sale. Lender or its designee may purchase the Property at any sale.

Trustee shall deliver to the purchaser Trustee's deed conveying the Property without any covenant or warranty, expressed or implied. The recitals in the Trustee's deed shall be prima facie evidence of the truth of the statements made therein. Trustee shall apply the proceeds of the sale in the following order: (a) to all expenses of the sale, including, but not limited to, reasonable Trustee's and attorneys' fees; (b) to all sums secured by this Security Instrument; and (c) any excess to the person or persons legally entitled to it.

23. Reconveyance. Upon payment of all sums secured by this Security Instrument, Lender shall request Trustee to reconvey the Property and shall surrender this Security Instrument and all notes evidencing debt secured by this Security Instrument to Trustee. Trustee shall reconvey the Property without warranty to the person or persons legally entitled to it. Such person or persons shall pay any recordation costs. Lender may charge such person or persons a fee for reconveying the Property, but only if the fee is paid to a third party (such as the Trustee) for services rendered and the charging of the fee is permitted under Applicable Law.

24. Substitute Trustee. Lender may from time to time remove Trustee and appoint a successor trustee to any Trustee appointed hereunder. Without conveyance of the Property, the successor trustee shall succeed to all the title, power and duties conferred upon Trustee herein and by Applicable Law.

25. Attorneys' Fees. As used in this Security Instrument and in the Note, attorneys' fees shall include those awarded by an appellate court.

26. Protective Advances. This Security Instrument secures any advances Lender, at its discretion, may make under Section 9 of this Security Instrument to protect Lender's interest in the Property and rights under this Security Instrument.

27. Required Evidence of Property Insurance.

WARNING

Unless you provide us with evidence of the insurance coverage as required by our contract or loan agreement, we may purchase insurance at your expense to protect our interest. This insurance may, but need not, also protect your interest. If the collateral becomes damaged, the coverage we purchase may not pay any claim you make or any claim made against you. You may later cancel this coverage by providing evidence that you have obtained property coverage elsewhere.

You are responsible for the cost of any insurance purchased by us. The cost of this insurance may be added to your contract or loan balance. If the cost is added to your contract or loan balance, the interest rate on the underlying contract or loan will apply to this added amount. The effective date of coverage may be the date your prior coverage lapsed or the date you failed to provide proof of coverage.

The coverage we purchase may be considerably more expensive than insurance you can obtain on your own and may not satisfy any need for property damage coverage or any mandatory liability insurance requirements imposed by Applicable Law.

OREGON--Single Family--Fannie Mae/Freddie Mac UNIFORM INSTRUMENT   Form 3038 1/01 *(page 16 of 17 pages)*

BY SIGNING BELOW, Borrower accepts and agrees to the terms and covenants contained in this Security Instrument and in any Rider executed by Borrower and recorded with it.

Witnesses:

_____ (Seal)
                      - Borrower

Social Security Number _____

_____ (Seal)
                      - Borrower

Social Security Number _____

_____

[Space Below This Line For Acknowledgment]

OREGON--Single Family--Fannie Mae/Freddie Mac UNIFORM INSTRUMENT   Form 3038 1/01 *(page 17 of 17 pages)*

PRACTICE QUESTIONS

The following practice questions are representative of the questions you will find on the final examination and on the licensing examinations given by the Oregon Real Estate Agency.

1. To pledge property as security for a loan, such as in a mortgage, is to
    (A) hypothecate.
    (B) seek specific performance.
    (C) establish equity.
    (D) covenant.

2. When a property is given as security for a debt, but the owner does not give up possession, the owner has
    (A) converted a fee simple title to equitable title.
    (B) hypothecated the property.
    (C) devised the property.
    (D) conveyed the property.

3. To hypothecate is to
    (A) deliver a judicial opinion.
    (B) pledge a thing as security without the necessity of giving it up.
    (C) perform services in exchange for the satisfaction of a debt.
    (D) do none of the above.

4. Most purchasers of homes borrow the necessary funds and pledge the property as security for the debt while they retain possession of the property. This is known as
    (A) leverage.   (C) liquidation.
    (B) hypothecation.   (D) equity.

5. A purchaser pledges real or personal property as security for an obligation without surrendering rights of possession. This is usually accomplished by a mortgage or trust deed. This practice is called
    (A) hypothecation.   (C) amortization.
    (B) emblement.   (D) homesteading.

6. The conditions of most loan instruments require the borrower to pay all of the following when they are due except
    (A) principal and interest.
    (B) recording fees.
    (C) property taxes.
    (D) insurance premiums.

7. The Landslide Construction Company built a house and sold it for $290,000. They received $90,000 in cash and $200,000 on a note secured by a mortgage. The company wished to raise cash to build another house, so they decided to use the $200,000 note as security for a bank loan. The note would be
    (A) a chattel mortgage.
    (B) a purchase money mortgage.
    (C) a holding agreement.
    (D) a pledge.

8. A valid promissory note provides legally acceptable evidence of
    (A) debt.   (C) alienation.
    (B) hypothecation.   (D) liquidity.

9. A properly executed promissory note establishes
    (A) the amount of the debt.
    (B) who is borrower and who is lender.
    (C) the terms of repayment and the interest rate.
    (D) all of the above.

10. To be enforceable, a note must generally have
    (A) a promise to pay a certain amount.
    (B) a specific due date.
    (C) both A and B.
    (D) neither A nor B.

11. A note secured by real estate must generally have which of the following to be enforceable?
    (A) Be in writing   (C) A definite due date
    (B) Signed by the maker (D) All of the above

12. To be negotiable, a note does not need to contain
    (A) an acceleration clause.
    (B) a promise to pay a sum certain.
    (C) the signature of the maker.
    (D) a demand clause or provision making it due on a date certain.

13. A note is being signed by co-borrowers. To afford maximum protection to the lender, the note should state that the borrowers are obligated
    (A) jointly.
    (B) severally.
    (C) both jointly and severally.
    (D) neither jointly nor severally.

14. A "holder in due course" is one who has accepted a note
    (A) which appears to be regular.
    (B) before it was past due and without notice of previous dishonor.
    (C) in good faith and for valuable consideration.
    (D) under all of the above conditions.

15. You purchase a negotiable note from someone who endorses it to you. If you have no knowledge of any defects in the note, you are
    (A) a purchaser in good faith.
    (B) a holder in due course.
    (C) both A and B.
    (D) neither A nor B.

16. A lender is holding a note secured by a trust deed. In order to sell the note to another lender, the beneficiary must
    I. endorse the note to the secondary lender.
    II. assign the beneficial interest in the trust deed to the secondary lender.
    (A) I only   (C) Both I and II
    (B) II only   (D) Neither I nor II

17. A note
    I. endorsed without recourse becomes non-negotiable.
    II. must be endorsed by the maker to be negotiable.
    (A) I only   (C) Both I and II
    (B) II only   (D) Neither I nor II

18. A broker took a note from a buyer as earnest money on a transaction. The broker wanted to transfer the note to an escrow agent, but did not want to incur any liability in the event the buyer did not pay. The broker should endorse the note
    I. to the escrow agent without recourse.
    II. in blank.
    (A) I only   (C) Both I and II
    (B) II only   (D) Neither I nor II

19. A promissory note connected with a mortgage is signed by the
    I. lender.   II. borrower.
    (A) I only   (C) Both I and II
    (B) II only   (D) Neither I nor II

20. An endorser of a note who does not guarantee payment of the note to the person to whom the endorser immediately assigns it and to all future holders, endorses it
    (A) in blank.   (C) with recourse.
    (B) with protest.   (D) without recourse.

21. A potential homeowner wants to borrow money and is advised by the lender that the lender will only accept a negotiable instrument in exchange for the loan. Which of the following documents is not a negotiable instrument?
    (A) Promissory note   (C) Draft
    (B) Trust deed   (D) Check

22. Mortgages are negotiable if they are
    (A) recorded.
    (B) endorsed by the borrower.
    (C) endorsed by the lender.
    (D) Mortgages are never negotiable instruments.

23. The gradual repayment of a mortgage loan by regular payments to reduce principal and interest over a given period of time is called
    (A) amortization.   (C) accession.
    (B) accretion.   (D) prepayment.

24. A characteristic of a partially amortized loan is
    (A) no loan balance exists at the end of the loan term.
    (B) a balloon payment exists at the end of the loan term.
    (C) all have variable interest rates.
    (D) all have terms of 25 years.

25. A mortgage loan payable in monthly installments which are sufficient to pay the principal in full during the term of the loan is called
    I. a straight loan.   II. an amortized loan.
    (A) I only   (C) Both I and II
    (B) II only   (D) Neither I nor II

26. A promissory note that provides for payment of interest only during the term of the note would be
    (A) an installment note. (C) an amortized note.
    (B) a straight note.   (D) a non-negotiable note.

27. A promissory note used in connection with a mortgage or trust deed that permits the making of periodic payments to principal is called
    (A) a straight note.   (C) a hold check.
    (B) an installment note. (D) a non-recourse note.

28. Smith's loan is payable in monthly installments over five years. The last payment is a larger amount than the regular monthly payments. This is known as a
    (A) straight loan.   (C) balloon loan.
    (B) blanket loan.   (D) wraparound loan.

29. When the loan on real property requires periodic payments which will not fully amortize the loan by the final payment, the final payment is called the
    (A) release payment.   (C) balloon payment.
    (B) section payment.   (D) acceleration payment.

30. A loan is paid with interest-only installments during its term and with the further requirement that the entire unpaid balance be paid in full at the end of five years. This method of financing involved
    I. a balloon payment.   II. amortization.
    (A) I only   (C) Both I and II
    (B) II only   (D) Neither I nor II

31. A balloon payment is
    (A) the large down payment usually required at the outset of an amortized loan.
    (B) a large payment required on a specified date during the term of a mortgage or trust deed.
    (C) a large payment required at the end of the payment schedule of a mortgage or trust deed.
    (D) either B or C above.

32. Which of the following is true about a term mortgage?
    I. Interest is paid during the term of the loan.
    II. The entire principal is due at the end of the term.
    (A) I only   (C) Both I and II
    (B) II only   (D) Neither I nor II

33. A person bought a parcel of real property and obtained a 75% first loan. The seller took back a mortgage for a portion of the remainder. This additional encumbrance is called a
    (A) package money mortgage.
    (B) junior mortgage.
    (C) chattel mortgage.
    (D) wraparound mortgage.

34. In researching records at the county clerk's office, a first mortgage and a second mortgage on the same piece of property can usually be distinguished by
    (A) the date of the instrument.
    (B) the words "first" or "second" preceding the phrase "this indenture."
    (C) notations made by the recorder.
    (D) date of recording.

35. An agreement to waive some rights in favor of another is called
    (A) redemption.   (C) subordination.
    (B) an escrow.   (D) none of the above.

36. A clause in a mortgage making it secondary to a subsequent mortgage is called
    (A) a deed-escalation clause.
    (B) a sub-mortgage clause.
    (C) an alienation clause.
    (D) none of the above.

37. A subordination clause in a trust deed benefits the
    (A) beneficiary.
    (B) trustor.
    (C) trustee.
    (D) beneficiary of a subsequently recorded trust deed.

38. A subordination clause in a mortgage or trust deed
    (A) allows readjustment and alteration of the terms as stated in the trust deed.
    (B) puts the loan in an inferior position in regard to other liens and encumbrances against the property.
    (C) permits the obligation to be paid off prior to the end of the anticipated term.
    (D) prohibits the grantor from obtaining another loan before the original loan is paid in full.

39. A subordination clause is used in
    (A) a quitclaim deed.
    (B) a grant deed.
    (C) a listing agreement.
    (D) none of the above.

40. When a first lienholder has subordinated to a second lienholder, the first lienholder
    I.   is called an assignee.
    II. has no further collateral.
    (A) I only
    (B) II only
    (C) Both I and II
    (D) Neither I nor II

41. Mr. and Mrs. Adams purchased a piece of vacant property for $100,000. They put $30,000 down and the seller carried back a mortgage for $70,000 for a term of 10 years. The Adams plan to build on the property in five years prior to paying off the existing mortgage. The absence of which clause in their mortgage could cause them problems when they try to get financing to build their home?
    (A) Subordination clause
    (B) Subrogation clause
    (C) Alienation clause
    (D) Acceleration clause

42. A husband and wife wish to buy a lot for $100,000. They pay $20,000 cash, and the seller carries back a note and trust deed for the balance. They intend to build a home in five years. When they get ready to carry out their construction plans, the absence of which of the following clauses may cause them difficulties?
    (A) Alienation clause
    (B) Acceleration clause
    (C) Release clause
    (D) Subordination clause

43. A typical subordination clause contained in a mortgage
    (A) allows the obligation to be paid off ahead of schedule.
    (B) requires premature payoff under specified conditions.
    (C) allows an increase in the rate of interest.
    (D) allows another lien to take precedence.

44. An existing first mortgage loan can generally be changed to a second or junior lien by
    (A) a court order.
    (B) payment in full of the first mortgage.
    (C) a subordination agreement signed by the first mortgagee.
    (D) recording another mortgage.

45. The agreement in a junior lien permitting a first lien to be refinanced without suffering loss of priority is called
    (A) an acceleration clause.
    (B) a lien waiver.
    (C) a release provision in a mortgage.
    (D) a subordination clause.

46. Which of the following statements regarding financing is true?
    I.   First mortgages may be foreclosed without the consent of the second mortgagee.
    II. Second mortgages may be foreclosed without the consent of the first mortgagee.
    (A) I only
    (B) II only
    (C) Both I and II
    (D) Neither I nor II

47. A typical subordination clause in a deed of trust
    (A) places the trust deed in an inferior position to other liens on the property.
    (B) forbids placing another trust deed on the property unless the existing trust deed is paid off.
    (C) prohibits payoff of the loan amount prior to the due date.
    (D) allows periodic renegotiation and readjustments in the terms of the trust deed.

48. Builder Smith purchased 20 lots from Brown for immediate development. Smith paid 10% down and gave notes and trust deeds for the balance. Smith would want the trust deeds to contain
   (A) an exculpatory clause.
   (B) a subordination clause.
   (C) a safety clause.
   (D) a lock-in clause.

49. The clause in a second trust deed which allows a first note and trust deed to be refinanced without sacrificing the first trust deed's priority is the
   (A) acceleration clause.   (C) subordination clause.
   (B) release clause.   (D) lien waiver clause.

50. A mortgage in Oregon is
   (A) a chattel.   (C) an estate in land.
   (B) real estate.   (D) both B and C.

51. Mortgages may properly be regarded as
   I. contractual liens.   II. specific liens.
   (A) I only   (C) Both I and II
   (B) II only   (D) Neither I nor II

52. A mortgage is best defined as
   (A) a document conveying possessory interest.
   (B) a general lien.
   (C) a specific lien.
   (D) an involuntary lien.

53. When a mortgage is used in a real estate transaction, the evidence of the principal obligation is the
   (A) associated warranty.   (C) mortgage.
   (B) note.   (D) owelty.

54. A mortgage is usually accompanied by
   (A) a deed.
   (B) a conditional sales contract.
   (C) a title policy.
   (D) a promissory note.

55. When financing property with a mortgage,
   I. the promissory note serves as security for the loan.
   II. a promissory note must always accompany the mortgage.
   (A) I only   (C) Both I and II
   (B) II only   (D) Neither I nor II

56. A mortgage is
   (A) the amount of money the borrower owes the lender.
   (B) a pledge of property to secure a debt.
   (C) the amount of money owed at the time of foreclosure.
   (D) none of the above.

57. A mortgage is usually associated with a
   (A) deed.   (C) title policy.
   (B) land sale contract. (D) promissory note.

58. The lender in a mortgage is the
   (A) trustor.   (C) trustee.
   (B) mortgagee.   (D) mortgagor.

59. A mortgage on real estate must be
   I. recorded to be valid.
   II. in writing to be valid.
   III. signed by the lender.
   (A) I only   (C) II and III only
   (B) II only   (D) III only

60. Who holds the title to real property when a mortgage is given?
   (A) Mortgagee
   (B) Mortgagor
   (C) Specified lending institution
   (D) FHA

61. Since Oregon is a "lien theory" state, it follows that a
   I. mortgage of real property operates as a conveyance of title.
   II. mortgage lien is enforced by a statutory foreclosure suit.
   (A) I only   (C) Both I and II
   (B) II only   (D) Neither I nor II

62. The lien theory of mortgages
   I. is widely used in the United States.
   II. means the mortgagor gives a lien to the mortgagee during the indebtedness and retains legal ownership.
   (A) I only   (C) Both I and II
   (B) II only   (D) Neither I nor II

63. A borrower gave a lender a mortgage, pledging the property as security for a loan. The borrower
    I. conveyed the property to the lender.
    II. created a lien on the property.
    (A) I only
    (B) II only
    (C) Both I and II
    (D) Neither I nor II

64. A defeasance clause in a mortgage
    (A) requires that the balance be paid in full upon default of the loan.
    (B) indicates that the borrower has the authority to pledge the collateral.
    (C) stipulates that the borrower will be able to regain clear title after the mortgage is paid.
    (D) requires that the borrower maintain the collateral.

65. A borrower went to a lender to obtain a second mortgage. Which of the following is correct?
    I. To create a valid mortgage the borrower must sign a note as well as a mortgage.
    II. The borrower would be conveying a defeasible title to the lender.
    (A) I only
    (B) II only
    (C) Both I and II
    (D) Neither I nor II

66. A purchase money mortgage may be defined as one which normally
    I. is taken as all or part of the purchase price.
    II. is taken on several parcels of real property.
    III. provides for additional advances to the mortgagor without the necessity of writing a new mortgage.
    (A) I only
    (B) I and III only
    (C) II only
    (D) II and III only

67. A seller's financing of a part or all of the purchase of the seller's own property for the buyer is described as
    (A) a conventional mortgage.
    (B) a chattel mortgage.
    (C) a purchase money mortgage.
    (D) home financing.

68. If you sell a property for your client and the client takes back a purchase money mortgage in part payment, the client becomes a
    (A) mortgagor.
    (B) mortgagee.
    (C) trustee.
    (D) grantor.

69. A purchase money mortgage can sometimes be used as
    (A) a warranty of title.
    (B) a junior financing instrument.
    (C) a valid deed.
    (D) an equity of redemption.

70. A mortgage taken back by the seller as partial payment for the property is a
    (A) purchase money mortgage.
    (B) wraparound mortgage.
    (C) blanket mortgage.
    (D) takeout mortgage.

71. When does the purchaser normally acquire title when the property is financed under a purchase money mortgage?
    (A) On whatever date is stated in the earnest money agreement
    (B) On closing
    (C) When 50% of the mortgage has been paid
    (D) When the mortgage has been paid in full

72. The Kimbles purchased a house for $270,000. They made a down payment of $28,000 and agreed to assume the seller's existing mortgage, which had a balance of $175,000. The Kimbles financed the remaining $67,000 of the purchase price by executing a mortgage and note to the seller. This type of loan, by which the seller becomes the mortgagee, is known as a
    (A) wraparound mortgage.
    (B) package mortgage.
    (C) purchase money mortgage.
    (D) flexible payment mortgage.

73. If a deed is executed simultaneously with a purchase money mortgage
    I. the purchase money mortgage has priority over all liens which the buyer may place against the property.
    II. the seller still retains legal title.
    (A) I only
    (B) II only
    (C) Both I and II
    (D) Neither I nor II

74. When a mortgage is paid in full, it is said in legal terminology to be
    (A) retired.
    (B) satisfied.
    (C) fully amortized.
    (D) amortized.

75. A "satisfaction" is a writing that
    (A) records payment of a deed of trust indebtedness.
    (B) records and acknowledges a paid-off mortgage.
    (C) pays a landlord for damages to the property.
    (D) renders satisfaction to a lessor for personal damages.

76. The term "satisfaction" refers to which of the following?
    (A) The total payment of a mortgage.
    (B) A document filed upon final payment of a trust deed.
    (C) The extinction of the mortgage by a court of law.
    (D) The assumption of the mortgage by a third party.

77. The statement signed by the mortgagee acknowledging that a loan has been paid in full is called
    (A) an assertion of deraignment.
    (B) a satisfaction of mortgage.
    (C) an estoppel certificate.
    (D) a release of lien.

78. The instrument used of record to show that a mortgage is paid in full is a
    (A) satisfaction of mortgage.
    (B) deed release statement.
    (C) quitclaim statement.
    (D) estoppel certificate.

79. A mortgage lien can be released by
    I. foreclosure.
    II. sale of the property to the mortgagee.
    (A) I only   (C) Both I and II
    (B) II only   (D) Neither I nor II

80. Foreclosure is a procedure designed to
    I. enable a lender to acquire the value of the pledged collateral.
    II. terminate a borrower's interest in the mortgaged property.
    (A) I only   (C) Both I and II
    (B) II only   (D) Neither I nor II

81. When a mortgage is foreclosed, the action is
    (A) by breach of a covenant.
    (B) by confession of judgment.
    (C) judicial.
    (D) by estoppel.

82. The mortgagee sues the mortgagor to obtain a court order to sell the property. This is a
    (A) strict foreclosure.
    (B) voluntary foreclosure.
    (C) judicial foreclosure.
    (D) non-judicial foreclosure.

83. Generally, mortgage contracts are written so that a lender can foreclose on a real estate mortgage if the buyer does not pay the
    I. property taxes.
    II. hazard insurance premium.
    III. principal and interest.
    (A) I and II only   (C) I, II and III
    (B) I and III only   (D) II and III only

84. All of the following documents could be used in the foreclosure of a real estate mortgage except
    I. an indenture deed.   III. a lis pendens.
    II. a sheriff's deed.
    (A) I only   (C) II and III only
    (B) I and II only   (D) III only

85. In order to foreclose a mortgage, the mortgagee would first
    (A) notify the trustee of the default.
    (B) file an attachment.
    (C) accelerate the note.
    (D) notify the mortgagor of the default, giving at least 120 days in which to cure the default.

86. A court order directing the sheriff to sell property is called
    (A) a notice of lis pendens (notice of pendency).
    (B) a writ of execution.
    (C) an attachment.
    (D) a deficiency judgment.

87. At a mortgage foreclosure sale, the successful buyer will receive
    (A) a certificate of defeasance.
    (B) a certificate of title.
    (C) a certificate of sale.
    (D) a sheriff's deed.

88. A farmer is unable to meet the mortgage payments on the farm. After the foreclosure sale, the deed to the farm will be executed by the
(A) farmer.
(B) sheriff.
(C) judge.
(D) lender.

89. When a mortgagee buys a property at a foreclosure sale, a deed should be forthcoming from the
(A) owner.
(B) sheriff.
(C) trustee.
(D) clerk of the court.

90. If the amount realized at a sheriff's sale upon a delinquent mortgage exceeds the indebtedness, who gets the excess?
(A) The county
(B) The mortgagee
(C) The mortgagor
(D) The purchaser

91. If the foreclosure sale proceeds are less than the outstanding debt and foreclosure expenses, which of the following remedies is available to the mortgagee?
(A) The mortgagee may void the sale.
(B) The mortgagee must absorb the loss, since the mortgagor is liable only for foreclosure expenses.
(C) The owner has the statutory right of redemption.
(D) The mortgagee may be able to obtain a deficiency judgment against the mortgagor.

92. When property fails to sell at a court foreclosure sale for an amount sufficient to satisfy the unpaid mortgage debt, the mortgagee may sue for
(A) satisfaction of mortgage.
(B) damages.
(C) a judgment by default.
(D) deficiency judgment.

93. If the mortgagee has the property sold at a foreclosure sale and it brings an amount inadequate to pay off the loan, what can the mortgagee do?
I. Sue the mortgagor for the deficiency
II. Cancel the sale
(A) I only
(B) II only
(C) Both I and II
(D) Neither I nor II

94. If a commercial property sold at a court foreclosure does not sell for an amount sufficient to satisfy the mortgage loan debt, the mortgagee may be able to obtain
(A) a judgment by default.
(B) a deficiency judgment.
(C) a satisfaction of mortgage.
(D) damages.

95. A deficiency judgment is a
(A) judgment with no means for payment.
(B) judgment which reduces the debt through periodic payments.
(C) judgment due for the balance of a note remaining due after foreclosure sale.
(D) claim for interest allowed by law.

96. A deficiency judgment can take place when
I. a foreclosure sale does not produce sufficient funds to pay a mortgage debt in full.
II. not enough taxes have been paid on a piece of property.
(A) I only
(B) II only
(C) Both I and II
(D) Neither I nor II

97. A deficiency judgment is
(A) a general lien.
(B) a specific lien.
(C) both A and B.
(D) neither A nor B.

98. Just as the mortgagor's foreclosed property is about to be sold at public auction, the mortgagor appears with sufficient funds to prevent the sale by exercising the mortgagor's right of
(A) lis pendens (notice of pendency).
(B) umbrage.
(C) habendum.
(D) redemption.

99. A mortgagor's entitlement to reclaim the property after default is called the right
(A) of redemption.
(B) of reinstatement.
(C) to possession.
(D) to assign equity.

100. If there is a default on a mortgage, the mortgagor, after the foreclosure sale, has the right of
(A) reinstatement.
(B) redemption.
(C) estoppel.
(D) non-foreclosure.

101. Which of the following terms best describes the right to pay off a mortgage debt after default?
    (A) Foreclosure
    (B) Prepayment
    (C) Redemption
    (D) Escalation

102. John Brown's mortgaged property has been foreclosed and is about to be sold at a public auction. Before any bids are made, Brown appears with sufficient funds to prevent the sale by exercising his right of
    (A) lis pendens (notice of pendency).
    (B) deficiency judgment.
    (C) habendum.
    (D) redemption.

103. An equitable period of redemption refers to the time within which
    (A) a lender can foreclose on a borrower who is in default.
    (B) the debtor can reclaim the property by payment of the debt and costs.
    (C) a prospective purchaser can bid on the property.
    (D) the court may take possession of the secured property.

104. The mortgagor's right to reestablish ownership after default is known as
    (A) redemption.
    (B) reestablishment.
    (C) acceleration.
    (D) subordination.

105. The statutory right of redemption of an Oregon real estate mortgagor is terminated
    (A) upon entry of the judicial foreclosure decree of the court.
    (B) 60 days following the foreclosure sale.
    (C) 180 days following the foreclosure sale.
    (D) seven years following the foreclosure sale.

106. When a mortgage has been foreclosed and the borrower is in the redemption period, who is entitled to possession of the property?
    (A) The lender
    (B) The borrower
    (C) The sheriff
    (D) The county

107. Giving a deed in lieu of mortgage foreclosure is a voluntary act of the
    (A) trustee.
    (B) mortgagee.
    (C) mortgagor.
    (D) vendee.

108. The type of deed that conveys title from a mortgagor and prevents further legal action to recover the lender's funds is a deed
    (A) of surrender.
    (B) in lieu of foreclosure.
    (C) of release.
    (D) of reconveyance.

109. Which of the following statements concerning purchase money mortgages is true?
    I. A purchase money mortgage is an instrument given to the seller from the buyer to finance the purchase of a single family residence.
    II. The mortgagee may foreclose a delinquent mortgage and forego a deficiency judgment, or may waive the security and sue only on the note.
    (A) I only
    (B) II only
    (C) Both I and II
    (D) Neither I nor II

110. In a mortgage the lender can establish which of the following?
    I. The right of redemption
    II. The length of the redemption period
    (A) I only
    (B) II only
    (C) Both I and II
    (D) Neither I nor II

111. Trust deeds normally are used to
    (A) transfer title.
    (B) secure a contract.
    (C) secure a debt with real property.
    (D) secure a homestead.

112. To be a legally enforceable document, a trust deed must contain a clause requiring a grantor to
    (A) pay taxes and assessments before they become delinquent.
    (B) comply with all rules, regulations, health laws, and policy requirements.
    (C) keep the improvements on the property insured against fire.
    (D) do none of the above.

113. A trust deed in Oregon
    (A) is a voluntary lien.
    (B) is a conveyance of real property.
    (C) must be recorded to be valid between the parties.
    (D) is correctly described by all of the above.

114. Which of the following instruments would not be given to a purchaser of real estate?
(A) Special warranty deed
(B) Trust deed
(C) Warranty deed
(D) Bargain and sale deed

115. Oregon trust deeds are
(A) generally exempt from the Statute of Frauds.
(B) documents conveying real property.
(C) voluntary liens.
(D) correctly described by all of the above.

116. Property which is subject to a trust deed in Oregon may be
I. sold before the trust deed is paid off.
II. further encumbered with a second trust deed or mortgage.
(A) I only
(B) II only
(C) Both I and II
(D) Neither I nor II

117. Which of the following is not a party to a trust deed?
(A) Grantor
(B) Grantee
(C) Beneficiary
(D) Trustee

118. In conventional financing, the trustee of a trust deed
I. receives legal title. II. can be a beneficiary.
(A) I only
(B) II only
(C) Both I and II
(D) Neither I nor II

119. Payments on a note secured by a trust deed are made to the
(A) trustor.
(B) trustee.
(C) mortgagor.
(D) beneficiary.

120. The beneficiary of a trust deed in Oregon is the
(A) borrower.
(B) lender.
(C) neutral third party.
(D) surviving spouse.

121. The person who furnishes the funds for a loan secured by a trust deed is known as the
(A) trustee.
(B) beneficiary.
(C) grantor.
(D) trustor.

122. Which of the following statements regarding trust deeds is true?
I. There are only two parties involved in a trust deed.
II. The lender is the beneficiary and the borrower is the grantor.
III. The beneficiary always holds the power to sell in the event of default.
(A) I only
(B) II only
(C) III only
(D) I, II and III

123. A trustee in a trust deed can
I. be the borrower.
II. foreclose and sell the property in case of default.
(A) I only
(B) II only
(C) Both I and II
(D) Neither I nor II

124. The beneficiary of a trust deed in Oregon is the
(A) grantor.
(B) trustee.
(C) lender.
(D) surviving spouse.

125. In a trust deed entered into in Oregon, the borrower is called a
(A) grantor.
(B) beneficiary.
(C) trustee.
(D) mortgagee.

126. Which of the following statements about trust deeds is correct?
I. When a savings and loan is the beneficiary, it can also function as the trustee.
II. The beneficiary may receive legal title without a judicial foreclosure.
(A) I only
(B) II only
(C) Both I and II
(D) Neither I nor II

127. When money is borrowed on a trust deed, the payments are made to the
(A) trustee.
(B) grantor.
(C) beneficiary.
(D) contract purchaser.

128. The trustee in a trust deed executed in Oregon receives
I. full legal title to the real property described in the deed.
II. the power to sell in the event the grantor of the deed defaults.
(A) I only
(B) II only
(C) Both I and II
(D) Neither I nor II

129. In a trust deed transaction, the trustor is to the beneficiary in the same manner as
    (A) a mortgagor is to a mortgagee.
    (B) a vendor is to a vendee.
    (C) a grantor is to a grantee.
    (D) trustee is to the beneficiary.

130. A trust deed executed in Oregon
    (A) conveys title to the beneficiary.
    (B) provides a one-year redemption period in the event of foreclosure.
    (C) creates a voluntary lien on the grantor's property.
    (D) requires the trustee to seek a deficiency judgment in the event of default.

131. A trust deed is usually released by
    (A) reversion trust.
    (B) reconveyance deed.
    (C) quitclaim deed.
    (D) satisfaction agreement.

132. The instrument used to remove the lien of a trust deed from the county record is a
    (A) redemption of equity certificate.
    (B) satisfaction piece.
    (C) certificate of no defense, or estoppel certificate.
    (D) reconveyance deed.

133. What is a beneficiary obligated to do after the trust deed has been paid in full?
    (A) Make a request for reconveyance
    (B) Issue an acknowledgment
    (C) Issue a reconveyance of trust deed
    (D) Acknowledge satisfaction

134. A trust deed is satisfied on the public records
    (A) by posting a guarantor's bond.
    (B) by recordation of a deed.
    (C) when final payment has been made by the grantor.
    (D) when a reconveyance deed is recorded.

135. The instrument used to remove the lien of a trust deed from the record is called a
    (A) redemption of equity.
    (B) satisfaction.
    (C) certificate of no defense.
    (D) deed of reconveyance.

136. A reconveyance deed is signed by the
    (A) grantee.　　　　　(C) beneficiary.
    (B) grantor.　　　　　(D) trustee.

137. A trust deed creates
    I. a security interest in the property for the beneficiary.
    II. a fiduciary relationship between the trustee and the beneficiary.
    (A) I only　　　　　(C) Both I and II
    (B) II only　　　　　(D) Neither I nor II

138. The most common procedure for foreclosing a trust deed is called
    (A) strict foreclosure.
    (B) foreclosure by entry and possession.
    (C) foreclosure by sale.
    (D) foreclosure by writ of entry.

139. In a typical trustee's sale of property encumbered by a trust deed which is in default, which of the following would not be used?
    (A) Advertised notice of default
    (B) Deed of reconveyance
    (C) Trustee's deed
    (D) Affidavit of mailing the notice of sale

140. The owner of a house defaulted on the trust deed used to purchase it. The beneficiary's course of action would be to notify the
    (A) mortgagee so the mortgagee can notify the mortgagor and record a notice of default.
    (B) trustee so the trustee can notify the grantor and record the notice of default.
    (C) mortgagor so the mortgagor can notify the mortgagee and record the notice of default.
    (D) grantor so the grantor can notify the trustee and record the notice of default.

141. Felony Mortgage Company holds a second trust deed on a property on which there is still a first trust deed outstanding. In order to protect their interests in the event the holder of the first trust deed should foreclose, they should record
    (A) a notice of default.
    (B) an election to sell.
    (C) a request for notice of default.
    (D) a request for election to sell.

142. In exercising the power of sale clause in a trust deed at least 120 days must elapse after recordation of a Notice of Default and Election to Sell before the
    (A) grantor will be required to relinquish possession of the premises.
    (B) trustee can publish the Notice of Sale.
    (C) trustee can hold the sale.
    (D) statutory year of redemption begins.

143. Bill Anderson conveyed his house to a grantee for $250,000 and took back a trust deed and note for $100,000. Anderson immediately sold his note and trust deed at a discount to Mr. Baker for $70,000. Anderson signed the trust deed and endorsed the note with the words "without recourse" prior to his signature. If the grantor defaults before making any principal payments, which of the following methods would the buyer of the first trust deed utilize to receive the greatest amount of money in the shortest period of time?
    (A) Sue for specific performance
    (B) Foreclosure by trustee's sale to collect $70,000
    (C) Recover from Anderson, as the transaction was usurious
    (D) Foreclosure by trustee's sale to recover $100,000

144. In exercising the power of sale in a trust deed at least 120 days must elapse after recording the notice of default before
    (A) the trustee may publish the notice of sale.
    (B) the one-year right of redemption begins.
    (C) the trustee may hold the sale.
    (D) all of the above.

145. A distinguishing feature of the Oregon trust deed, when compared to a mortgage, is the
    I. power of sale clause in the trust deed.
    II. longer redemption period in the trust deed.
    (A) I only
    (B) II only
    (C) Both I and II
    (D) Neither I nor II

146. After the trustee's sale is held and the property has been sold to the highest bidder, the grantor has
    (A) 90 days equity of redemption.
    (B) 20 days to pay off the loan balance.
    (C) no recourse.
    (D) one year to redeem the property.

147. Curt and Betty Hamilton fell behind on the monthly payments due on their trust deed note. The beneficiary is Robert Marshall, from whom the Hamiltons purchased the property. Marshall was the successful bidder on the property at the trustee's sale for the unpaid balance, turned in his note and received a deed from the trustee. The Hamiltons' right to cure the default
    (A) will continue for a period of one year after the trustee's sale.
    (B) will continue for a period of 90 days after the trustee's sale.
    (C) ended when they became delinquent in their payments.
    (D) ended five days prior to the trustee's sale.

148. Wendell Smith is two months behind in payments on his note secured by a trust deed on his residence. A trustee's sale has been scheduled for the future. At this point Smith's interests in the property are protected by his right of
    (A) redemption.
    (B) reinstatement.
    (C) eminent domain.
    (D) reversion.

149. A borrower financed the purchase of a residence with an Oregon trust deed. One of the benefits of the trust deed to the borrower is that if the borrower defaults and the property is foreclosed by advertisement and sale, there is no possibility of
    I. redemption period.
    II. deficiency judgment.
    (A) I only
    (B) II only
    (C) Both I and II
    (D) Neither I nor II

150. A loan secured by a trust deed is in default and the trustee has scheduled the sale of the property. After the trustee's sale, the borrower will have
    I. one year in which to redeem the property.
    II. the right to possess the property for ten days more.
    (A) I only
    (B) II only
    (C) Both I and II
    (D) Neither I nor II

151. In the trustee's foreclosure of an Oregon trust deed the grantor
    I. may cure the default any time up to five days prior to the sale.
    II. has a one-year redemption period.
    (A) I only
    (B) II only
    (C) Both I and II
    (D) Neither I nor II

152. Which of the following is true concerning the foreclosure of a trust deed by advertisement and sale in Oregon?
    I. The trustee may personally place a bid on the property at the sale.
    II. The property is sold at auction.
    (A) I only
    (B) II only
    (C) Both I and II
    (D) Neither I nor II

153. Which of the following are allowed by Oregon law to make bids on property secured by a trust deed which is foreclosed by advertisement and sale?
    I. The beneficiary   III. The trustee
    II. The grantor
    (A) I only
    (B) I and II only
    (C) II and III only
    (D) I, II and III

154. When property secured by a trust deed is foreclosed by advertisement and sale, the
    I. trustee may personally make a bid on the property.
    II. lender may make a bid on the property.
    III. trustee executes a trustee's deed to the purchaser.
    (A) II only
    (B) I and II only
    (C) II and III only
    (D) I, II and III

155. A person who is the successful bidder on property which has been foreclosed under the provisions of the Oregon Trust Deed Act will receive
    (A) a sheriff's certificate of sale.
    (B) a trustee's deed of sale.
    (C) a trust receiver's deed.
    (D) either A or B.

156. Under Oregon law, a residential trust deed
    I. may be subject to a deficiency judgment.
    II. means, among other things, that the grantor occupies the property encumbered by the trust deed as a primary residence.
    (A) I only
    (B) II only
    (C) Both I and II
    (D) Neither I nor II

157. When a trust deed is foreclosed by judicial foreclosure, it
    (A) provides for a statutory redemption period.
    (B) is the same as foreclosing by a trustee's sale.
    (C) prevents a deficiency judgment.
    (D) accomplishes nothing because it would be illegal.

158. It is possible to obtain a deficiency judgment on a trust deed
    I. when the trust deed is foreclosed by a trustee's sale and the owner does not occupy the property.
    II. if the property is not occupied by the owner and the property is foreclosed by judicial procedure.
    III. if the property is occupied by the owner as his or her primary residence and the property is foreclosed by judicial foreclosure.
    (A) I only
    (B) II only
    (C) III only
    (D) II and III only

159. Benvenuto is the beneficiary of a $150,000 trust deed executed by Willkommen. Willkommen paid about $20,000 on the principal and then defaulted. Benvenuto subsequently had the property sold at auction for $100,000, leaving a deficiency of $30,000. Benvenuto can get a deficiency judgment unless
    (A) the trust deed was a purchase money trust deed.
    (B) Willkommen occupied the property as a principal residence.
    (C) the property is used for agricultural purposes.
    (D) either A or B is true.

160. Upon the completion of a trustee's sale, the borrower must vacate the premises
    (A) immediately.
    (B) within ten days.
    (C) when the judge orders it.
    (D) by the end of 180 days.

161. Bryan Schroeder owns real property encumbered by a trust deed. Since he wishes to convey title to the property to George Wand,
    (A) Schroeder must get permission from the beneficiary for this transfer.
    (B) Schroeder must pay off the beneficiary.
    (C) Wand must assume and agree to pay the trust deed.
    (D) Schroeder must use a deed to convey title to Wand.

162. Which of the following are differences between an Oregon trust deed and an Oregon mortgage?
    I. The trust deed in Oregon acts to convey real property to the beneficiary.
    II. Generally, when an Oregon trust deed is foreclosed on a personal residence the grantor will not be faced with a deficiency judgment.
    (A) I only
    (B) II only
    (C) Both I and II
    (D) Neither I nor II

163. Sue Jones, a real estate licensee, negotiated a first trust deed and a second trust deed on a parcel of real property which she is selling. At the closing of escrow, she instructed the title company to incorporate in the documents a Request for Notice of Default. This is included for the protection of the
    (A) trustee of the first trust deed.
    (B) grantor of the first trust deed.
    (C) lender who made the first trust deed loan.
    (D) lender of the second trust deed.

164. You, as the agent, have just sold a piece of property and have negotiated for a new first loan and also a second loan for the buyer. The first loan was made by the bank. The second loan was carried by the seller. You have been asked to record a "Request for Notice of Default." Usually this would be done for the protection of the
    (A) trustee for the bank loan.
    (B) lender of the bank loan.
    (C) grantor of the second loan.
    (D) lender of the second loan.

165. Land sales contracts are especially useful in real estate for selling
    (A) substandard property in declining neighborhoods.
    (B) remote property which has been rejected by ordinary lenders.
    (C) property where the buyer is unable to qualify for institutional loans.
    (D) all of the above.

166. Which of the following best describes an installment or land sales contract?
    (A) A contract to buy land only
    (B) A mortgage on land
    (C) A means of conveying title and possession immediately while the purchaser pays for the property in installments
    (D) A method of selling real estate whereby the purchaser takes possession and pays for the property in regular installments while the seller retains title until property is paid for in full

167. In Oregon, land sales contracts must be
    (A) in writing.
    (B) abstracted before recording.
    (C) amortized.
    (D) all of the above.

168. In order for a land sales contract to be enforceable between the parties, the documents must
    I. be recorded.
    II. include a title insurance policy.
    (A) I only
    (B) II only
    (C) Both I and II
    (D) Neither I nor II

169. Under Oregon law, sales of vacant land which will not be occupied by the buyer and which will be sold under a land sales contract, normally
    (A) must be recorded.
    (B) are valid.
    (C) are not valid, since lack of occupancy does not give notice to third parties.
    (D) Both A and B are correct.

170. In a land sales contract,
    I. an agreement prohibiting recording the agreement is enforceable.
    II. the lender is always the seller of the property.
    (A) I only
    (B) II only
    (C) Both I and II
    (D) Neither I nor II

171. By Oregon law, when property is sold on a land sales contract, the vendor must record
    (A) the contract in full within fifteen days of the date the parties are bound by the contract.
    (B) a memorandum of the contract within fifteen days of the date the parties are bound.
    (C) either the contract or a memorandum of it, within fifteen days of the date of the contract.
    (D) nothing.

172. Which of the following is true about the land sales contract method of financing the sale of real property?
    (A) It is used when the seller wants to convey title immediately without using a trustee.
    (B) It is similar to a lease; the buyer has the right of possession but no rights in the title.
    (C) The buyer has assurance of receiving title prior to specific performance.
    (D) The seller retains the title, and the buyer is the equitable owner.

173. A financing arrangement under which the buyer does not immediately become the legal owner of record is a
    (A) trust deed.
    (B) land sales contract.
    (C) purchase money mortgage.
    (D) quitclaim deed.

174. A buyer paid down a certain amount of earnest money and has been told that the seller will require monthly payments on the balance of the selling price. This will be done pursuant to
    (A) an installment contract.
    (B) a package money mortgage.
    (C) a blanket mortgage.
    (D) a listing agreement.

175. When the buyer and seller have signed a land sales contract the purchaser immediately receives
    (A) complete title.   (C) no title.
    (B) equitable title.   (D) naked legal title.

176. A real estate financing device which a seller can use to transfer equitable title to buyer is known as
    (A) a land sales contract.
    (B) an agreement of sale.
    (C) a real property sales contract.
    (D) all of the above.

177. When real estate is sold under an installment or land contract, possession is usually given to the buyer and title is
    (A) also given to the buyer.
    (B) kept by the seller until the full purchase price is paid.
    (C) generally required to be transferred to a land trust.
    (D) held by the broker.

178. A typical land sales contract financing arrangement includes which of the following?
    I. Possession of the property by the vendee
    II. Title of the property held by the vendor
    (A) I only   (C) Both I and II
    (B) II only   (D) Neither I nor II

179. Under a contract for the sale of real estate, the party who has the legal title during the term of the contract is the
    (A) vendor.   (C) mortgagee.
    (B) vendee.   (D) escrow agent.

180. The sale of real property on a conditional sales contract ordinarily transfers only
    (A) possession.   (C) an estate for years.
    (B) legal title.   (D) an estate for life.

181. Under a land sales contract, who retains legal title until certain specific conditions are fulfilled?
    (A) Buyer   (C) Beneficiary
    (B) Seller   (D) Trustee

182. Which of the following best describes a land sales contract?
    (A) A contract to buy land only
    (B) A means of conveying title immediately, while the purchaser pays for the property
    (C) A mortgage on real property
    (D) A method of selling real estate whereby the purchaser pays for the property in regular installments while the seller retains title to the property

183. Under a conditional land contract of sale, a buyer is considered to be
    (A) a severalty owner.
    (B) a tenant in common.
    (C) a prescriptive owner.
    (D) an equitable owner.

184. In a land sales contract, the buyer
    I. has equitable title to the property.
    II. is entitled to a conveyance of the legal title when all payments have been made.
    (A) I only   (C) Both I and II
    (B) II only   (D) Neither I nor II

185. At the outset, a land sales contract provides which of the following to the purchaser?
    (A) Fee simple title
    (B) Life estate
    (C) Equitable title
    (D) Estate for years

186. Which of the following statements concerning typical land sales contracts is correct?
    (A) The land sales contract is similar to a lease in that the buyer has a right of possession but no rights in the title.
    (B) Land sale contracts are the least secure method of financing for the buyer because the seller retains the title and the buyer is merely the equitable owner.
    (C) The buyer has absolute assurance of receiving title upon performance of the contract.
    (D) The buyer is usually not responsible to pay the property taxes until the seller has delivered a deed to the property.

187. When a purchaser signs a land sales contract he or she receives
    (A) legal title.
    (B) a remainder interest.
    (C) a reversionary interest.
    (D) equitable title.

188. Upon the signing of a land sales contract,
    (A) the legal title passes to the purchaser.
    (B) the equitable title passes to the purchaser.
    (C) no title to the real estate passes.
    (D) the seller keeps rights of possession.

189. At the time of signing a land sales contract the purchaser receives
    (A) fee simple title.
    (B) legal title.
    (C) an estate for years.
    (D) equitable title.

190. A land sale contract conveys
    (A) the full fee simple title to the purchaser.
    (B) an estate for years to the purchaser.
    (C) the legal title to the purchaser.
    (D) an equitable title to the purchaser.

191. Under a land sales contract, the buyer normally receives
    I. legal title.
    II. equitable title.
    III. possession.
    (A) I only
    (B) III only
    (C) I and III
    (D) II and III

192. The buyer under a land sales contract
    I. has equitable title to the property.
    II. is entitled to a conveyance of the legal title when all payments have been made.
    (A) I only
    (B) II only
    (C) Both I and II
    (D) Neither I nor II

193. A land sales contract transfers
    (A) ostensible title.
    (B) legal title.
    (C) a fee title.
    (D) equitable title.

194. In a land sales contract, the deed conveying legal title is delivered to the buyer when the contract is
    (A) fully paid and performed.
    (B) acknowledged and recorded.
    (C) agreed upon and signed.
    (D) recorded and adjudicated.

195. Upon the final payment of a land sales contract the buyer should receive a
    (A) novation.
    (B) deed.
    (C) obligation.
    (D) contract.

196. When an individual buys property using a land sales contract, delivery of the deed usually occurs
    (A) within two weeks after the preliminary title report is delivered.
    (B) when the buyer performs the contract requirements.
    (C) within ten days after the closing.
    (D) when the contract is signed.

197. In a land sales contract, the deed conveying legal title to the purchaser is delivered when the contract is
    (A) fully paid and performed.
    (B) acknowledged and recorded.
    (C) agreed upon and signed.
    (D) recorded and adjudicated.

198. When real estate is sold on a land sales contract, the seller must have marketable title at the time
    (A) when the contract is signed.
    (B) when the contract is recorded.
    (C) when the title insurance is ordered.
    (D) set for the delivery of the deed.

199. A buyer bought some land from a farmer on a land sales contract. The farmer was also buying the property from another person on an underlying land sales contract. For the protection of the buyer, what should be included in the new contract?
    (A) A lot or parcel release clause
    (B) A partial release clause
    (C) An estoppel agreement
    (D) A clause giving the vendee the right to pay on the underlying contract in the event of the vendor's default and deduct the amount paid from the amount due on the second contract.

200. When personal property is included in a land sales contract, the
    (A) agreement is void because a security agreement is required for personal property.
    (B) contract is valid if the personal property is specified as included in the sales price.
    (C) portion of the contract which refers to the personal property is unenforceable.
    (D) contract is voidable at the option of either party.

201. In a typical land sales contract, the buyer has which of the following duties?
    (A) Payment of taxes
    (B) Insuring the property
    (C) Maintaining the property
    (D) All of the above

202. Generally, the purchaser of real estate under a land sales contract
    I.   pays no interest charge.
    II. is not required to pay property taxes for the duration of the contract.
    (A) I only   (C) Both I and II
    (B) II only   (D) Neither I nor II

203. The purchaser under an Oregon land sales contract has the protection of
    I.   legal title to the property.
    II. a one-year grace period for redemption in the case of foreclosure.
    (A) I only   (C) Both I and II
    (B) II only   (D) Neither I nor II

204. The vendor in a land sales contract in Oregon
    I.   retains equitable title as security for payment of the purchase price.
    II. has only one legal remedy if the buyer defaults.
    (A) I only   (C) Both I and II
    (B) II only   (D) Neither I nor II

205. The vendor in a land sales contract in Oregon
    I.   retains legal title as security for payment of the purchase price.
    II. lacks recourse to foreclosure if the buyer defaults.
    (A) I only   (C) Both I and II
    (B) II only   (D) Neither I nor II

206. The seller's primary security under a land sales contract is the
    (A) purchaser's written promise to pay.
    (B) retention of legal title to the property.
    (C) grace period in the contract.
    (D) alienation clause in the contract.

207. In real estate, the term "strict foreclosure" is most closely associated with
    (A) the Statute of Frauds.
    (B) trust deeds.
    (C) mortgages.
    (D) land sales contracts.

208. The seller's remedy of strict foreclosure
    (A) takes court litigation.
    (B) requires the buyer's interest to be declared null and void.
    (C) results in a judicial sale of the property.
    (D) does both A and B above.

209. A parcel of real property was sold on a land sales contract which was recorded. The seller received no payments and took the property back. The seller decided to resell the property, conveying by warranty deed to a new buyer. In order to deliver a good marketable title to this buyer, what should the seller obtain from the original vendee?
    (A) A deed of reconveyance
    (B) A trustee's deed
    (C) A quitclaim deed
    (D) A release clause

210. A purchaser under a land sales contract in Oregon may redeem the property from strict foreclosure within
(A) ten days from the date of the sale.
(B) 30 days from the date of the sale.
(C) the time period set by the court.
(D) the one-year statutory period.

211. A vendor under a land sales contract discovered that the vendee has disappeared and left owing the vendor several payments. The contract has a clause allowing forfeiture and the vendor would like to use that remedy. If the vendor declares a forfeiture, the vendor will also have to file a suit
(A) for foreclosure and sale.
(B) to quiet title.
(C) for strict foreclosure.
(D) No suit would ordinarily be required.

212. A deficiency judgment against the buyer is possible in a land sales contract if the seller
(A) sues for strict foreclosure.
(B) sues for specific performance.
(C) declares a forfeiture.
(D) sues for foreclosure and sale.

213. Remedies that a buyer under a land sales contract might consider would be a suit for
(A) specific performance.
(B) rescission.
(C) either A or B.
(D) neither A nor B.

214. A land sales contract was recorded and the buyer defaulted shortly thereafter. Being in default, the buyer packed up and moved off into the night. This would create
(A) no problem, as the seller still has legal title.
(B) no problem, as the seller has the automatic right to possession of the premises at all times during the term of a land sales contract.
(C) no problem, as the seller has the right to declare a forfeiture in this case without going to court.
(D) an irreversible cloud on the title.

215. When a buyer under a land sales contract has fully performed the agreement, yet the seller refuses to convey title, the buyer would have the right to
I. sue for specific performance.
II. bring action to foreclose the seller's interest in the property.
(A) I only (C) Both I and II
(B) II only (D) Neither I nor II

216. Where legal, a chattel mortgage is an encumbrance on
I. real property. II. personal property.
(A) I only (C) Both I and II
(B) II only (D) Neither I nor II

217. Russell James built a house on speculation and sold it for $162,000. He received $52,000 cash and a $110,000 promissory note secured by a mortgage. In order to build a house on another lot, Mr. James wants to borrow $9,000. He decided to use the $110,000 note as security. The note would be
(A) a chattel mortgage.
(B) a purchase money mortgage.
(C) a holding agreement.
(D) a pledge.

218. An estoppel certificate is
(A) a satisfaction certificate.
(B) an assignment certificate.
(C) a certificate of no defense.
(D) a certificate of reasonable value.

219. An "estoppel certificate" or a "reduction certificate" is a document showing the
(A) method by which principal payments accelerate over interest payments in the later years of a mortgage.
(B) payment of an installment on an amortized loan.
(C) balance due on a mortgage at a specific time.
(D) mortgage is a lien.

220. A buyer taking title subject to an existing loan should request from the lender a
(A) reduction certificate.
(B) deficiency statement.
(C) satisfaction of mortgage.
(D) certificate of reasonable value.

221. If the lender with proper reason calls all sums due and payable eight months after the borrower entered into the loan contract, this is
    (A) illegal.
    (B) acceleration.
    (C) escalation.
    (D) subordination.

222. The clause in a mortgage, contract or trust deed which allows the lender to call the entire unpaid balance upon default is called the
    (A) balloon payment clause.
    (B) acceleration clause.
    (C) cancellation clause.
    (D) defeasance clause.

223. If the borrower defaults on the regular payments specified in a promissory note secured by a mortgage the lender has the option of calling the entire balance of the loan due and payable, provided the note included
    (A) a forfeiture clause.
    (B) a prepayment privilege.
    (C) a condemnation clause.
    (D) an acceleration clause.

224. A clause in a mortgage which causes the entire principal to become due upon default is called
    (A) a receiver clause.
    (B) a defeasance clause.
    (C) a brundage clause.
    (D) an acceleration clause.

225. An "acceleration clause" found in a promissory note or mortgage would mean that
    (A) upon the happening of a certain event, the entire amount of the unpaid balance becomes due.
    (B) payments must be made more frequently at a future specified date.
    (C) the interest rate can increase.
    (D) payments may not be made more frequently than specified.

226. A clause in a deed of trust or mortgage, or accompanying note or bond which permits the creditor to declare the entire unpaid sum due upon certain default of the debtor is called
    (A) an acceleration clause.
    (B) an elevator clause.
    (C) a forfeiture clause.
    (D) an excelerator clause.

227. Of the following, who most benefits by an acceleration clause in a mortgage or trust deed note?
    (A) The borrower
    (B) The lender
    (C) A party who acquires the property upon resale
    (D) The trustee

228. A provision which prohibits a borrower from paying the loan in full for a prescribed period of time without incurring additional charges is known as the
    (A) prepayment penalty clause.
    (B) acceleration clause.
    (C) lock-in clause.
    (D) non-alienation clause.

229. If a borrower pays the balance of the loan prior to its due date, the borrower may be liable for
    (A) an acceleration charge.
    (B) a prepayment penalty.
    (C) a discount.
    (D) a standby fee.

230. Some lenders charge extra if the borrower pays the loan off ahead of schedule. This is called the
    (A) overage fee.
    (B) prepayment penalty.
    (C) acceleration fee.
    (D) assumption fee.

231. The fee which the seller pays to the lender for the privilege of paying off the loan ahead of schedule is the
    (A) prepayment penalty.
    (B) assumption penalty.
    (C) liquidated damages penalty.
    (D) overage fee.

232. A prepayment privilege in a mortgage refers to the
    (A) right of lenders to demand full repayment of the outstanding principal if the payments fall into arrears.
    (B) lender's right to demand full payment of the outstanding balance at the end of the term of a partially amortized mortgage.
    (C) right of the borrower to pay off all or some of the outstanding balance during the term of the mortgage.
    (D) payment of a finder's fee to a mortgage broker as compensation for arranging a mortgage loan which is made prior to the advancing of mortgage funds.

233. A lender would find it advantageous to waive the prepayment penalty when
    I. funds are in short supply and there is strong loan demand.
    II. the Federal Reserve System lowers the reserve ratio and discount rate.
    (A) I only
    (B) II only
    (C) Both I and II
    (D) Neither I nor II

234. A clause in a loan document which makes the payments periodically increase is known as an
    (A) acceleration clause.
    (B) alienation clause.
    (C) escalator clause.
    (D) interest clause.

235. The inclusion of a variable interest rate in a real estate loan would imply which of the following?
    I. Interest rates could be increased in an inflationary economy.
    II. The lender could call in the balance of the loan if the loan is assumed without the lender's permission.
    (A) I only
    (B) II only
    (C) Both I and II
    (D) Neither I nor II

236. What is the name of the clause in a contract or note which allows the purchaser to make more than the stipulated payments?
    (A) Acceleration clause
    (B) Assignment clause
    (C) "Or more" clause
    (D) Contract of sale clause

237. David sold his home and agreed to take back a note and trust deed as part of the purchase price. He wanted to have the note become due and payable if the property was resold. To accomplish this, which of the following clauses should be in the note or trust deed?
    (A) Alienation clause
    (B) Subordination clause
    (C) Defeasance clause
    (D) Substitution clause

238. A provision in a mortgage requiring prior written notice to the mortgagee and the mortgagee's approval of the assumption of the mortgage
    (A) is voidable.
    (B) is contrary to public policy.
    (C) is valid.
    (D) violates the Statute of Frauds.

239. A provision in a real estate loan that prohibits its assumption without permission of the lender is known by one or more of the following terms. Identify the term or terms.
    I. A call provision
    II. A due on sale clause
    III. A lock-in clause
    (A) I only
    (B) I and II only
    (C) II only
    (D) II and III only

240. A late payment penalty is included as a provision in many real estate loans in order to
    (A) raise the lender's effective yield rate.
    (B) adjust the interest rate periodically.
    (C) penalize the borrower for any prepayment.
    (D) create the motivation for timely payments.

241. The assignment of rents provision in a standard trust deed
    (A) protects the trustor.
    (B) protects the beneficiary.
    (C) provides that the borrower will pay rent in case of default.
    (D) provides that the borrower will pay rent until title is transferred.

242. The existing mortgage which is taken by the purchaser as part of the selling price is called
    (A) a blanket mortgage.
    (B) an extension of mortgage.
    (C) a subordinated mortgage.
    (D) an assumed mortgage.

243. A buyer taking title subject to a mortgage should request a
    (A) satisfaction.
    (B) reduction certificate.
    (C) deficiency judgment.
    (D) new mortgage.

244. If property is conveyed "subject to" a loan, the
    I. buyer is personally liable for the debt in case of default sale and deficiency.
    II. seller's rights to foreclose against the original mortgagor remains the same.
    (A) I only
    (B) II only
    (C) Both I and II
    (D) Neither I nor II

245. When the deed in which you take title to a property contains the following clause, "subject to the existing loan,"
    (A) you are in danger of losing the property if the seller does not make the payments on the underlying loan.
    (B) the seller is permanently relieved of all liability.
    (C) the lender is guaranteed that you alone will pay off the loan.
    (D) you agree to assume the loan and make the payments directly to the lender.

246. A seller does not wish to be primarily responsible for an existing mortgage when the property is sold to a buyer. The seller should have the buyer
    (A) take the property subject to the mortgage.
    (B) assume and agree to pay the mortgage if the lending institution grants permission.
    (C) purchase the property on contract.
    (D) arrange to pay the mortgage under a subrogation agreement.

247. When a grantee takes title to real property "subject to" an existing mortgage, what is the grantee's maximum risk?
    (A) Loss of the equity
    (B) The possibility of a deficiency judgment
    (C) No risk because the grantee did not agree to "assume and pay" the mortgage
    (D) The threat of specific performance

248. Jones sold a house to Smith "subject to" an outstanding real estate mortgage. Two years later Smith fell behind in the loan payments and the house was sold under foreclosure proceedings. The foreclosure sale brought less than the amount owed on the loan. To collect the deficit amount, the lending institution can take action against
    (A) Jones only.
    (B) Smith only.
    (C) Jones and Smith together.
    (D) neither Jones nor Smith.

249. A mortgage using both real and personal property as security is
    (A) a blanket mortgage.
    (B) a package mortgage.
    (C) a wraparound mortgage.
    (D) none of the above.

250. A mortgage loan which is secured by a home and certain equipment in the home, is known as a
    (A) junior mortgage.
    (B) chattel mortgage.
    (C) blanket mortgage.
    (D) package mortgage.

251. Each of the following is an advantage to the purchaser of property who finances it by a package mortgage, except
    (A) the buyer deals with only one lender.
    (B) the interest rate is higher than through conventional installment financing.
    (C) the payments are distributed over a longer period.
    (D) total payments are uniform throughout the life of the loan.

252. A mortgage which allows the borrower to borrow additional sums up to a certain maximum amount is
    (A) a package mortgage.
    (B) an open end mortgage.
    (C) a purchase money mortgage.
    (D) a wraparound mortgage.

253. A loan secured by real property which provides that the outstanding balance can be increased in order to advance additional funds to the borrower up to the original sum of the note is called
    (A) a subordinated mortgage.
    (B) an alienation provision.
    (C) an open end mortgage.
    (D) a closed end provision.

254. What type of mortgage allows the home buyer to borrow additional funds up to a specified amount?
    (A) Open end
    (B) Blanket
    (C) Variable
    (D) Junior

255. A type of mortgage enabling one to borrow additional funds without negotiating a new mortgage is called
    (A) a conventional mortgage.
    (B) a second mortgage.
    (C) an open end mortgage.
    (D) a shared equity mortgage.

256. An open end mortgage is
    (A) a mortgage given to secure future loans made from time to time, usually back up to the original balance after partial repayment has been made.
    (B) partial satisfaction of a mortgage or trust deed.
    (C) a duly authorized endorsement of a note attached to a mortgage.
    (D) a mortgage which allows the lender to increase the security at its option.

257. An open end mortgage allows the
    I. mortgagor to borrow back up to the original amount, after some payments have been made.
    II. lender to increase the rate of interest at any given point in time.
    (A) I only
    (B) II only
    (C) Both I and II
    (D) Neither I nor II

258. The type of mortgage that covers more than one parcel of real property is called
    (A) a blanket mortgage.
    (B) an all-inclusive mortgage.
    (C) a package mortgage.
    (D) a wraparound mortgage.

259. The owner of six parcels of real property desires a mortgage loan and offers all parcels as security. The mortgage the owner will be required to execute will be
    (A) a package mortgage.
    (B) an amortization mortgage.
    (C) a blanket mortgage.
    (D) a building and loan mortgage.

260. A mortgage that covers several parcels of real property and which contains a provision for the sale of an individual property, thereby reducing the mortgage payments, is called
    (A) a declining balance mortgage.
    (B) a direct reduction mortgage.
    (C) an amortized mortgage.
    (D) a blanket mortgage.

261. When a mortgage covers two or more parcels of property simultaneously it is known as a
    I. wraparound mortgage.
    II. blanket mortgage.
    (A) I only
    (B) II only
    (C) Both I and II
    (D) Neither I nor II

262. A blanket mortgage is used for
    I. two or more properties under one mortgage.
    II. real and personal property under one mortgage.
    (A) I only
    (B) II only
    (C) Both I and II
    (D) Neither I nor II

263. A blanket mortgage
    I. covers several parcels of real property.
    II. finances the furniture and appliances in a dwelling.
    (A) I only
    (B) II only
    (C) Both I and II
    (D) Neither I nor II

264. A clause which relinquishes the lien on just one lot out of a mortgaged subdivision is
    (A) a satisfaction clause.
    (B) a prepayment clause.
    (C) an exoneration clause.
    (D) a partial release clause.

265. A "release" clause is most closely associated with which of the following liens?
    (A) Trust deeds against individual lots
    (B) Blanket mortgages
    (C) VA loans
    (D) Land contracts of sale

266. Cheryl Evans built a house and is selling it under a blanket encumbrance. Under normal procedure, she would request that the beneficiary give her a
    (A) partial reconveyance deed.
    (B) warranty deed.
    (C) grant deed.
    (D) quitclaim deed.

267. It is in the interest of the borrower that a blanket encumbrance on a large subdivision should contain
    (A) a subrogation clause.
    (B) a release clause.
    (C) a subordination clause.
    (D) none of the above.

268. Which of the following types of mortgage usually contains a partial release clause?
    (A) Blanket mortgage
    (B) Open end mortgage
    (C) Purchase money mortgage
    (D) Junior lien

269. A "release clause" in a mortgage is a provision which
    (A) provides for an option to renew a mortgage.
    (B) releases a co-guarantor from further liability under specified conditions.
    (C) creates a lien second only to the lien of taxes and assessments when part of the mortgage document.
    (D) allows portions of the property to be released from the mortgage lien.

270. In order to maintain a "release schedule," the lender of a blanket loan usually will charge a higher proportionate amount of money to release each lot than the loan proration indicated
    (A) because the better lots tend to sell first.
    (B) to have better security on the remaining lots.
    (C) to protect the investment as individual lots are sold.
    (D) for all the above reasons.

271. Mary Fairhaven obtained a business loan from a banker by agreeing that 1% of the equity ownership would be conveyed to the bank and by also paying a ½ of 1% discount. This kind of loan is called
    (A) a participation loan.
    (B) an equity loan.
    (C) ownership right.
    (D) a wraparound expansion loan.

272. A lender considering a loan on a large commercial property yielded to protestations of the borrower over interest charges and agreed to a ½ of 1% interest rate concession in return for a 2% interest in the equity. This is known as a
    (A) package loan.   (C) shut end loan.
    (B) participation loan.   (D) management loan.

273. In negotiating a mortgage on a large commercial complex, the lender agreed to reduce the interest rate on the loan by one-half of one percent in return for a two percent interest in the acquisition. This type of financing arrangement is known as
    (A) a participation mortgage.
    (B) a package mortgage.
    (C) a closed end mortgage.
    (D) an open end mortgage.

274. What kind of mortgage or loan allows the interest thereon to be increased or decreased for certain reasons?
    (A) Fluctuating   (C) Escalation
    (B) Variable   (D) Alienation

275. A mortgage that permits the interest charge to range up and down according to the money market is called
    (A) an escalation mortgage.
    (B) a net mortgage.
    (C) an open mortgage.
    (D) a variable rate mortgage.

276. A loan agreement in which the interest rate goes up or down according to some indicator is referred to as
    (A) a variable rate mortgage.
    (B) an adjustable mortgage loan.
    (C) a renegotiated rate mortgage.
    (D) any of the above.

277. A balloon payment is usually associated with a
    (A) blanket mortgage.
    (B) package mortgage.
    (C) variable mortgage that varies with the cost of living index.
    (D) large payment during the term or at the end of the payment schedule.

278. A mortgage wherein the lender takes over the responsibility of the first mortgage is called
    (A) a blanket mortgage.
    (B) a wraparound mortgage.
    (C) an open end mortgage.
    (D) a junior mortgage.

279. Financing that involves a loan that is junior to and subordinate to an existing lien, yet includes the existing lien is called
    (A) a land contract of sale.
    (B) a wraparound or all-inclusive loan.
    (C) an equity participation.
    (D) a collateral trust bond.

280. If title to real property remains in the seller's name after it is sold on a monthly payment plan, the buyer would have purchased it under
(A) an FHA insured mortgage.
(B) a land sales contract.
(C) a conventional mortgage.
(D) a VA guaranteed mortgage.

281. Which of the following documents will transfer title to real property?
(A) Trust deed
(B) Bargain and sale deed
(C) Purchase money mortgage
(D) Both A and B

282. A financing arrangement by which the buyer does not immediately become the owner of record would be a
(A) trust deed.
(B) land sales contract.
(C) purchase money mortgage.
(D) quitclaim deed.

283. The term "strict foreclosure" is most commonly associated with
(A) land sales contracts.
(B) mortgages.
(C) the Statute of Frauds.
(D) the Statute of Limitations.

284. A seller would most prefer to use a land sales contract rather than a purchase money mortgage because
I.   the seller does not want to convey title immediately.
II. the land sales contract or a memorandum does not have to be recorded.
(A) I only
(B) II only
(D) Neither I nor II
(C) Both I and II

285. A mortgage differs from a trust deed in which of the following particulars?
I.   Possession
II. Amortization
III. Number of parties
(A) I only
(B) I, II and III
(C) II and III only
(D) III only

286. The most significant difference between financing through the use of a mortgage and a trust deed is
(A) the type of property used as security.
(B) the length of time for repayment of the loan.
(C) the time period to complete foreclosure.
(D) a trust deed cannot be foreclosed.

287. Land sales contracts and trust deeds differ as to
(A) foreclosure remedies.
(B) who holds title during the term of the debt.
(C) both A and B.
(D) neither A nor B.

288. A conditional sale agreement for real estate and a purchase money mortgage are similar in that
(A) the title will be conveyed to the buyer immediately on closing.
(B) both give the buyer an equitable title.
(C) the seller lends equity in the property to the buyer.
(D) all of the above are correct.

289. A deed of reconveyance would be used in connection with
(A) a trust deed.
(B) a mortgage.
(C) a land sales contract.
(D) any of the above.

290. In a note and mortgage, the mortgagor would be the same party as which party in a trust deed?
(A) Grantor
(B) Beneficiary
(C) Grantee
(D) Trustee

291. Regarding instruments used in financing real property,
I.   a trust deed or mortgage is used to create a lien on the property.
II. the promissory note is generally essential to the enforceability if a trust deed or mortgage.
(A) I only
(B) II only
(C) Both I and II
(D) Neither I nor II

292. The seller can finance the sale of a property for the buyer through
(A) a trust deed.
(B) a purchase money mortgage.
(C) a land sale contract.
(D) any of the above.

293. Betty Goofsup borrowed $5,000 from a neighbor and gave the neighbor a note as evidence of the debt and a deed to her property. A court would likely construe the deed to be
    (A) an absolute conveyance.
    (B) a deed of trust.
    (C) a mortgage.
    (D) a contract for a deed.

294. All of the following concerning real estate financing are true except:
    (A) A mortgage is a lien on real property; an execution of a mortgage does not transfer title.
    (B) An owner who borrows and executes a trust deed is the grantor.
    (C) Selling a note for less than its face value is known as discounting.
    (D) A promissory note is the security for the trust deed.

295. The mortgagee sued the mortgagor and obtained a judgment and a court order to sell the property. This is an example of
    (A) strict foreclosure.
    (B) voluntary foreclosure.
    (C) judicial foreclosure.
    (D) non-judicial foreclosure.

296. A borrower went to a lender to obtain a $39,000 second mortgage on the borrower's home. Which of the following is (are) true?
    I.   In order to create a valid mortgage loan, the borrower must sign two separate instruments, a mortgage and a note.
    II. The lender could create a wraparound loan in this case.
    (A) I only   (C) Both I and II
    (B) II only   (D) Neither I nor II

297. Which of the following statements concerning real estate finance is true?
    (A) A trust deed or mortgage is given as security for a promissory note.
    (B) A promissory note secures a trust deed.
    (C) The trust deed is the evidence of debt.
    (D) A promissory note hypothecates the title to the property.

298. Which of the following statements regarding real estate finance is false?
    (A) A mortgage is a lien on real property.
    (B) A buyer who signs a trust deed is known as a grantor.
    (C) A trust deed is a lien on real property.
    (D) A promissory note is the security for the mortgage.

299. When a borrower obtains an FHA loan, title to the property is held by the
    (A) lender.
    (B) borrower.
    (C) FHA.
    (D) Office of Thrift Supervision.

300. Sam, a veteran, purchased and occupied a home by giving a mortgage as security for the loan. He lost his job and fell into default. He is protected against foreclosure by
    (A) the Veterans' Foreclosure Act.
    (B) the Homestead Exemption.
    (C) the Soldier's and Sailor's Relief Act.
    (D) none of the above.

301. A real estate agent representing the seller should inform his or her client about the potential for financial damages from taking a large
    I.   purchase money note.
    II. earnest money deposit.
    (A) I only   (C) Both I and II
    (B) II only   (D) Neither I nor II

302. A closely held corporation wishes to borrow money to construct a building. The bank will probably ask the majority shareholders for
    (A) their personal guaranties.
    (B) individual collateral agreements.
    (C) both A and B.
    (D) neither A nor B.

303. A chattel mortgage is a lien on
    I.   real property.   II. personal property.
    (A) I only   (C) Both I and II
    (B) II only   (D) Neither I nor II

ANSWERS

To practice questions. If you chose the wrong letter, here's the right one! The explanations are designed to clarify your understanding.

1. **A** Pledging an asset as collateral is called hypothecation. Specific performance is a legal action to compel a party to a contract to perform it as agreed.

2. **B** Pledging an asset as collateral for a loan is called "hypothecation." A devise is a gift of real property in a will. A conveyance is a transfer of title.

3. **B** Hypothecation is another term for pledging an asset as collateral for a loan.

4. **B** Hypothecation means pledging an asset as collateral for a debt. Leverage is controlling additional properties by financing their acquisition, as opposed to paying all cash. Liquidation is converting an asset to cash. Equity is the difference between the total of all liens and the value.

5. **A** Pledging assets as collateral for a loan is called "hypothecation." A right of emblement is a tenant's right to come back and harvest crops after a tenancy has been terminated. Amortization is the gradual payoff of a loan. A homestead is one's personal residence.

6. **B** Recording fees are incurred during the acquisition of the property and/or recording of the loan documents. Once paid, they never recur. Property taxes are a prior lien ahead of the lender's loan instrument and recur each year. Therefore, the loan document will undoubtedly require the borrower to keep the taxes current. Fire insurance premiums must also be kept current to protect the collateral.

7. **D** A chattel mortgage is the same as a security agreement, that is, it makes personal property collateral for a debt. A purchase money mortgage is a lien carried by the seller of real estate, as opposed to a hard money mortgage which is a lien carried by a third party lender. A holding agreement could be many things, but has nothing to do with real estate loans. A pledge is any agreement that makes an asset collateral for a debt.

8. **A** In a note and mortgage or note and trust deed transaction the note is the evidence of the debt and the mortgage or trust deed is the instrument that makes the property collateral for the debt. The note can exist without the mortgage or trust deed, in which case it will be an unsecured note.

9. **D** In a note and mortgage or note and trust deed transaction, the mortgage or trust deed is the lien instrument that makes the property collateral for the debt. The note is the evidence of the debt. Therefore, anything dealing with the debt itself would be contained in the note.

10. **C** The classic definition of a note is "a promise to pay a sum certain on a date certain." Without a due date the note would never become due, and would therefore be unenforceable. Without an amount there would also be no way to enforce payment.

11. **D** Oregon law generally requires a note to be in writing to be enforceable. The Oregon Statute of Frauds also requires documents to be "subscribed by the party to be charged," i.e., signed. If a note does not contain a due date, then it is never due, hence, unenforceable.

12. **A** The acceleration clause allows the lender to demand the entire remaining principal balance in the event of the borrower's default. A demand clause allows the lender to demand the entire balance even if the note is not in default. Although the acceleration clause and the demand clause are both common, neither is required in order for the note to be enforceable. It would be hard to enforce a note without an amount stated or the signature of the borrower, however.

13. **C** If the co-makers of a note are bound "severally," this means that each can be held responsible individually for the entire debt. If they are bound "jointly," then the lender has the option to collect a portion of the debt from each co-borrower.

14. **D** If the payee of a note endorses it to another, the new payee has recourse to the first payee and also to the maker. The legal term for the new payee is "holder in due course." To qualify as a holder in due course, the note must have been complete in its terms and appeared to be enforceable, the new payee must have accepted the note before it was in default, in exchange for valuable consideration, and without knowledge that it might be dishonored.

15. **C** A holder in due course is anyone to whom a negotiable instrument has been endorsed. A holder in due course is also a purchaser in good faith if the holder acquired the note with no notice of any defects.

16.   **C**   Negotiable instruments are transferred to another by endorsement. In a trust deed, the beneficiary is the lender. The beneficiary can transfer the interest in the trust deed by assignment. So a typical sale of a trust deed loan would involve endorsing the note and assigning the trust deed.

17.   **D**   Notes, by definition, are negotiable instruments. Endorsement does not make a note negotiable, since it already was negotiable the moment it was made. When a note is endorsed, the new holder has recourse against the person who endorsed it, unless it is endorsed "without recourse." Being endorsed "without recourse" has no effect on negotiability.

18.   **A**   If a note is endorsed without restriction or qualification, it is said to have been endorsed in blank. Endorsees always have a right of recourse against the endorser, unless the note was endorsed "without recourse."

19.   **B**   A mortgage makes real property collateral for a debt. The note is the evidence of the debt, so the two documents go together. The borrower would sign both of them.

20.   **D**   The principle regarding endorsements is that one always has recourse to the last endorser who, in turn, may have recourse to any previous endorsers. An exception is if the endorser places a restriction or limitation on the endorsement, such as "without recourse." If there is no restriction of limitation, the note is said to be endorsed "in blank."

21.   **B**   A negotiable instrument is a promise of payment, made by a "maker" and payable to a "payee." The most common negotiable instrument is a check. Notes and drafts are other examples. A trust deed is a lien instrument which makes real property collateral for a debt. The debt itself is evidenced by a note.

22.   **D**   Negotiable instruments are promises to pay money to another, such as checks, drafts and notes. Mortgages, like trust deeds, are lien instruments which make the property collateral for a debt. They are not negotiable instruments.

23.   **A**   There are two kinds of loan repayments – straight and amortized. A straight note is one with no payments toward principal at all until the end of the term, at which time the principal is paid in full. An amortized note calls for installments toward the principal over the term of the note.

24.   **B**   An amortized loan is one which is paid in installments, each of which include a partial payment of principal; as opposed to a loan in which the payments are interest only and the entire principal amount is paid at the end of the loan term. A partially amortized loan would be one which has some installments, but the remainder is to be paid in full in a balloon payment at some point.

25.   **B**   Loans which are paid in installments which include principal in each payment are called amortized loans. Loans where the entire principal balance is paid at the end of the loan are called straight loans.

26.   **B**   A straight note calls for payment of the principal in full at the end of the term of the loan, as opposed to an installment note which is paid off in regular periodic payments toward principal. Installment notes are said to be amortized.

27.   **B**   A straight note is a note with no periodic payments – the entire balance is due at the due date in one lump sum. The alternative is an installment note, where there are periodic payments to pay off the principal balance.

28.   **C**   Any special extra amount paid toward principal is called a balloon payment. A balloon payment is most commonly used as a final payment to pay off a mortgage earlier than it would be paid off by the scheduled installments.

29.   **C**   Any special payment toward principal is called a balloon payment. Balloon payments are usually used as a payoff at some point before the normal maturity of the loan.

30.   **A**   A loan is said to be amortized when there are regular payments toward principal. If all the payments are interest only, then the loan is not amortized. A balloon payment is any lump sum payment on the principal, usually a payment of the entire remaining principal balance.

31.   **D**   Any time there is a large, special payment toward the principal it is called a balloon payment. The usual (but not the only) use of a balloon payment is as an early payoff.

32.   **C**   A term loan is one which has no payments toward principal during the term of the loan, as opposed to an amortized loan. In a term loan the entire principal balance is due at the end. During the term of the loan the borrower usually pays interest as it accrues.

33.   **B**   The terms "senior" and "junior" refer to the priority of liens. For example, a second mortgage is junior to a first mortgage. A bank making a 75% loan will insist on being in first position, therefore any other encumbrances would have to be junior to the bank's lien.

34.   **D**   The priority of liens is ordinarily established by the recording date. Whether the instrument is labeled "first," "second," or whatever is irrelevant.

35. **C** The priority of liens is normally established by the recording date. On occasion one lender will agree to step down in favor of another. The document to do this is called a subordination agreement.

36. **D** When a senior lienholder agrees to become junior to another lien which will be recorded later, this is a subordination clause in the lien instrument.

37. **D** The priority of encumbrances is established by the recording date (except for property taxes, construction liens, and a few others). Subordination occurs when one lienholder voluntarily agrees to become junior to another lien, even though the other lien was recorded later. In a trust deed, the beneficiary of a is the lender, the trustor is the borrower, and the trustee is a third party who holds the power to sell the property for the beneficiary.

38. **B** The priority of liens is ordinarily established by the recording date. For various reasons, a lender in senior position may be willing to be junior to another lien to be recorded later. To accomplish this the lender must agree to a subordination clause in the original lien.

39. **D** Subordination occurs when a senior lienholder agrees to become junior to another lienholder. Therefore, the only documents which would contain a subordination clause would be a financing instrument.

40. **D** Recording a lien establishes its priority by the date of recording. An agreement of a senior lienholder (recorded first) to become junior to another lien, to be recorded later, is called a subordination agreement. The lienholder who becomes subordinate still has collateral. All that has happened is that the priority of claim has changed. An assignee is one who steps into another's position in a contract.

41. **A** When the seller's mortgage was recorded (at closing) it became a first lien on the property. If the buyers later wish to obtain a construction loan to build a home, the lender will insist on a first lien. In anticipation of this, the buyers should have negotiated a subordination clause in the mortgage with the seller. The subordination clause would state that the seller's mortgage would become junior to a construction loan to be recorded later.

42. **D** If they need a construction loan to pay for the home they wish to build in the future, they will have a problem. The seller's trust deed is a first lien. However, a bank lending construction funds will insist on a first lien also. The only way around the problem is for the seller to agree that the seller's trust deed will become subordinate (junior) to a construc-

tion loan, to be recorded later. The subordination agreement must be negotiated at the time of purchasing the lot. If it is not in the trust deed at closing, the seller will have no obligation to agree to it later.

43. **D** Subordination occurs when a senior lienholder (recorded first) agrees to become junior to another lien (recorded later).

44. **C** Priority of liens is normally established by the recording date. If the holder of a senior lien agrees, the lien can be made to be junior to another lien which was recorded later. This is done by a subordination agreement. It is commonly used when a seller finances land for a builder, and the builder later needs to obtain a construction loan.

45. **D** The priority if liens is normally established by recording date. Any time a lender agrees to be junior to another in spite of the fact that the recording date gives the lender the right to be senior it is called a subordination.

46. **C** The holder of any lien may always foreclose without anyone's permission, but if the lienholder is a junior lienholder, the buyer at the foreclosure sale will take title subject to any senior liens. If the lien being foreclosed is a senior lien, the foreclosure will extinguish all junior liens.

47. **A** The priority of liens is ordinarily established by recording date. A subordination clause in a lien instrument, regardless of what kind of lien instrument it is, makes the lien junior to another lien which will be recorded later.

48. **B** Subordination is an agreement by a senior lienholder to become junior to another lien. It is common in lot sales if the builder must finance the acquisition of the land. When the builder goes to get a construction loan, the bank will want a first lien, yet the holder of the financing on the lot already has a first lien. To get around this, the first lien will contain a clause stating that it will become junior to a construction loan which will be recorded later.

49. **C** Suppose you bought a property and assumed the seller's old loan, and the seller also carried a second. You want the ability to refinance the seller's old loan at some point in the future. Priority is normally established by recording date, so the instant the first mortgage is satisfied, the seller's second automatically becomes a first. A bank will insist on being in first position, so you would also have to pay off the second. A subordination clause in the second would allow you to refinance the first and still keep the second.

50.   **A**   A mortgage is a lien, and is considered personal property, not an estate in real property. The term "chattel" is a synonym for personal property.

51.   **C**   A contract is defined as an enforceable promise, which a mortgage certainly is. Specific liens are those which reach only specified property, as opposed to general liens, which reach all the property the debtor owns. Since a mortgage must state the description of the property it is a specific lien.

52.   **C**   A mortgage creates a lien on real property, making it collateral for a debt. General liens are liens which reach all property of a debtor. Specific liens reach only specified property. If you fail to make the payments on a mortgage, the lender can foreclose only on the property described in the mortgage, not on every property you own. Therefore the mortgage is specific.

53.   **B**   In a mortgage loan transaction the mortgage is the lien instrument which makes the real estate collateral for the debt. The debt is evidenced by the note.

54.   **D**   Mortgages and a trust deeds are lien instruments, i.e., they make the property collateral for a debt. Without a debt, they are worthless. Therefore, they must be accompanied by a note, which is the evidence of the debt.

55.   **B**   A mortgage creates a lien, making the property collateral for a debt. The debt itself is evidenced by a note. A mortgage without a debt is worthless.

56.   **B**   A mortgage creates a lien on real property to make it collateral for a debt. The debt is evidenced by a note. Therefore, when the borrower signs a mortgage, the borrower pledges the real estate described in the mortgage as collateral for the note.

57.   **D**   A mortgage creates a lien on real property to make it collateral for a debt. The debt is evidenced by a note. The mortgage is worthless without a note, so they always go together.

58.   **B**   A mortgage is a two-party document. The borrower gives a mortgage to the lender, creating a lien on the borrower's real estate to make it collateral for a note. Therefore, the borrower is the mortgagor (giver of the mortgage) and the lender is the mortgagee (receiver of the mortgage). A trustor and a trustee are parties in a note and trust deed transaction, not a mortgage loan.

59.   **B**   A mortgage is a lien on real estate. It is valid without being recorded, although unless it is recorded it will always be last in priority in the event there are other liens against the property. The borrower is the only person who must sign the mortgage for it

to be valid. The Statute of Frauds requires all contracts involving real estate to be in writing and to be signed by the party to be charged, lest the contract be void.

60.   **B**   In a title theory state the mortgage is deemed to be a conveyance of title to the lender. The majority of states are lien theory states (as is Oregon), where the mortgage merely creates a lien against the borrower's real estate. The borrower remains vested in title. In a mortgage, the borrower is the mortgagor and the lender is the mortgagee.

61.   **B**   In a title theory state the mortgage is held to be a conveyance of title to the lender, although the borrower retains possession. In a lien theory state the mortgage creates a lien against the property, and the borrower retains ownership.

62.   **C**   The original theory of a mortgage (title theory) was that it constituted a conveyance of title to the lender. A few states still follow this theory. The majority of states, however, hold that the mortgage creates a lien on real property (lien theory), and the borrower retains legal ownership.

63.   **B**   In some states, the mortgage is deemed to convey title to the lender. These are called title theory states. Oregon is a lien theory state, where the mortgage creates a lien on the mortgagor's property, but does not convey title.

64.   **C**   The original mortgage was a conveyance of a defeasible title to the lender, that is, the lender became the owner of the property, subject to the right of the borrower to regain title by paying the loan in full. Although Oregon is a lien theory state, in which the mortgage is no longer considered to be a conveyance of title, we still use the term "defeasance clause" to describe the right of the borrower to regain clear title upon payment in full.

65.   **A**   The mortgage makes the borrower's real property collateral for a debt. The debt is evidenced by a note. Therefore, the two documents must be used together. In title theory states, the mortgage is deemed to be a conveyance of title to the lender. Oregon is a lien theory state, not a title theory state, so the mortgage is deemed to create merely a lien.

66.   **A**   If a seller carries a note and mortgage then the buyer used them as part of the purchase money, so we call it a purchase money mortgage. If a third party lender (e.g., a bank) carries the financing, then the lender gave hard cash for the note and mortgage, so we call it a hard money mortgage.

67.   **C**   The term "conventional mortgage" is used to describe bank loans which are not government

insured or guaranteed. A chattel mortgage makes personal property (chattels) collateral for a loan. If the buyer gives the seller a note and mortgage, the buyer used them as part of the purchase price, so the mortgage is called a purchase money mortgage.

68. **B** In a mortgage transaction the borrower gives a mortgage to the lender, so the borrower is the mortgagor (giver) and the lender is the mortgagee (receiver). "Trustee" and "grantor" are parties in a trust deed transaction.

69. **B** A purchase money instrument is a loan carried by a seller. Seller-carried financing is frequently a second mortgage or trust deed, where the buyer assumed the seller's old loan but did not have enough cash to pay the seller's equity in full. A second lien would be junior financing.

70. **A** When the seller carries a note and mortgage it is because the buyer used it in lieu of cash for part of the purchase price. Therefore, a seller-carried mortgage is called a purchase money mortgage.

71. **B** There are three instruments a seller can use to finance the property for a buyer: A note and mortgage, a note and trust deed, or a land sales contract. The mortgage and the trust deed are used to create a lien on real property to make it collateral for a debt. A borrower must be in title, since you cannot lien property you do not own. Therefore, if the seller carries either a mortgage or a trust deed, the seller must deed the property to the buyer first. A land sales contract, on the other hand, is a "contract for a deed." That is, the seller agrees to deed the property to the buyer when the buyer has paid the contract in full.

72. **C** If the seller carries a note and mortgage, then the buyer used the note as part of the purchase price, so we call it a purchase money mortgage. The mortgage carried by the seller in this case is a second mortgage (junior financing). If the seller had carried a contract for $242,000 and had agreed to keep the underlying first mortgage current, then the $242,000 encumbrance would have been a wraparound loan. A package mortgage is a mortgage in which the collateral includes personal property as well as real property.

73. **A** Priority of liens is normally established by the recording date. If the purchase money mortgage is recorded immediately after recording the buyer's deed, then it will be the first lien. The deed from the seller to the buyer will convey title to the buyer, so the seller will no longer have title.

74. **B** A mortgage debt which is paid in full can be said to be fully amortized, but that is the account-

ing term. The legal expression is "satisfied," which means that the lien has been extinguished.

75. **B** The term "satisfaction" is used when many liens are paid off, including mortgages. The act of recording a satisfaction extinguishes the lien from the borrower's record title. To extinguish the lien of a trust deed we use a deed of reconveyance instead of a satisfaction.

76. **A** A satisfaction is a document signed by a lienholder that the lien is no longer valid, normally issued only when the debt is paid in full. When recorded, the lien is extinguished from the title. It is used for all liens, except trust deeds. The document to extinguish the lien of a trust deed is a deed of reconveyance.

77. **B** The usual document used as evidence that a mortgage lien is paid off is a satisfaction. A lender has no defense to a properly executed satisfaction – the lien is extinguished when the satisfaction is recorded. An estoppel certificate is a statement made by a lender as to the current balance due under the note. It could be argued that an estoppel certificate showing a zero balance owing would be the same as a satisfaction, but this would be technically incorrect, as the estoppel certificate does not extinguish the lien.

78. **A** A satisfaction is used when a lien is paid in full. This is true of judgments, construction liens, and most other liens as well as mortgages. Once recorded, the satisfaction extinguishes the lender's lien.

79. **C** There are three ways that a mortgage lien can be extinguished. The normal way is for the borrower to pay the loan off and have the lender execute and record a satisfaction. However, if the lender forecloses, this also extinguishes the lien – after all, the borrower no longer owns the collateral. And if the lender acquires title to the property the lien is also extinguished because it would be absurd to consider holding a lien your own favor on a property you also own.

80. **C** Regardless of the instrument or the method by which a lender forecloses, once the foreclosure is complete and any rights of redemption are past, the borrower has no further right or interest in the property. A foreclosure allows the lender to have the property sold at public auction and the funds paid to the lender, or in the event of a strict foreclosure, the lender gains title to the property directly without a public auction sale.

81. **C** Mortgages must be foreclosed judicially, that is, a suit must be filed and the foreclosure must be ordered by a judge. Other instruments, such as trust deeds and land sales contracts provide for pri-

vately held sales of the property or forfeiture of the property to the lender.

82.   **C**   Strict foreclosure is a remedy used in a land sales contract. Since the land sales contract is always carried by a seller of property, a seller using the remedy of strict foreclosure is asking the court to restore clear title in the seller and extinguish the buyer's interest, but without selling the property at public auction. In a mortgage, the lender's remedy is judicial foreclosure and sale.

83.   **C**   Property taxes are a lien which is ahead of a mortgage, trust deed or land sales contract. If the county forecloses for non-payment of taxes, the foreclosure will extinguish the lender's lien. Therefore, the loan instrument will always require the borrower to pay the property taxes in timely fashion. Similarly, if the property is not insured for fire and other hazards, the lender's collateral is at risk.

84.   **A**   Following the foreclosure of a mortgage, the lender will ask the court to order the sheriff to sell the property at public auction. The successful bidder will receive a sheriff's deed when the statutory right of redemption has expired. If the property does not sell for enough at the sheriff's sale to cover the balance due and the lender's costs of foreclosure, the lender may be entitled to a deficiency judgment. The lender can use the deficiency judgment to reach any other assets of the borrower. A lis pendens is a paper filed with the court asking the court to lien the borrower's other assets in anticipation of obtaining a deficiency judgment. An indenture deed was a deed used in ancient times which was written in two identical copies on one sheet of paper. The two copies were torn apart, the idea being that it would be easy to verify that they were the same because the tear would match.

85.   **C**   In a non-judicial foreclosure of a trust deed the beneficiary notifies the trustee of the default and orders the trustee to sell the property at public auction, after 120 days notice to the borrower. In a mortgage, however, the only option is to file a suit. The mortgagee cannot successfully sue to foreclose unless the entire balance is owing, so the first step would be to invoke the acceleration clause.

86.   **B**   Any time the court orders the sheriff to sell property to satisfy a debt the creditor must file a writ of execution with the court. The judge signs it and forwards it to the sheriff. Attachments and notices of lis pendens (pending litigation) are used to create a lien on property after filing a suit against the owner of the property in order to keep the owner

from liquidating the assets during the court proceedings. Since a mortgagee already has a lien on the property, an attachment or a notice of lis pendens would be pointless. Deficiency judgments are sometimes granted if the property does not sell for enough at the sheriff's sale to satisfy the debt. The deficiency judgment is a general lien which allows the lender to reach all the borrower's other assets.

87.   **C**   When a mortgagee has won a suit to foreclose the judge will enter a decree of foreclosure and sale. The mortgagee will then present the court with a writ of execution which the judge will sign and forward to the sheriff. The writ of execution orders the sheriff to sell the property at public auction and turn the proceeds over to the clerk of the court. The clerk will disburse the proceeds to lienholders according to the rules of priority. The successful bidder at the sheriff's sale will receive a "sheriff's certificate" or "(sheriff's) certificate of sale." The sheriff's certificate entitles the holder to a sheriff's deed to the property unless the debtor or a junior lienholder redeems the property. The statutory right of redemption is 180 days for the mortgagor and 60 days for junior lienholders after the date of the sheriff's sale.

88.   **B**   Following the foreclosure, the judge will order the sheriff to sell the property at public auction (sheriff's sale). The successful bidder will receive a sheriff's certificate of sale, which can be turned in for a sheriff's deed after the statutory 180-day right redemption.

89.   **B**   The successful bidder at a sheriff's sale is entitled to a sheriff's certificate of sale and, if no one redeems within the statutory time limit, a sheriff's deed. It does not matter if the successful bidder is the mortgagee, a junior lienholder, or anyone else.

90.   **C**   A mortgage foreclosure culminates in a public auction of the collateral by the sheriff (sheriff's sale). If the proceeds of the sale are in excess of the amount necessary to satisfy the debt, plus all the costs incurred by the creditor, the surplus is sent back to the borrower.

91.   **D**   Only the sheriff has the right to cancel the sale, which is rarely done. If it is a purchase money mortgage (seller carried), the mortgagee must be satisfied with the amount that the property brings at the sheriff's sale. If it is a hard money mortgage (third party loan), then the lender is entitled to a deficiency judgment against the borrower if the property fails to sell for enough to cover the debt and costs. The lender can use the deficiency judgment to reach all

other assets of the borrower. A right of redemption is a borrower right, not a right of the mortgagee.

92.   **D**   A mortgage foreclosure by a hard money mortgagee (third party lender) allows the lender to obtain a deficiency judgment, which can be used to reach all assets of the borrower. The deficiency judgment is an automatic right.

93.   **A**   It is possible for a sheriff's sale to be canceled, but at the discretion of the sheriff, not the mortgagee. The sheriff would do so only in the event there were irregularities or questions about the validity of the sale. A hard money mortgagee (third party lender) has the right to a deficiency judgment against the mortgagor in the event the property fails to sell for enough at the sheriff's sale to cover the debt and the lender's costs. The lender can use the deficiency judgment to reach all other assets of the borrower.

94.   **B**   A deficiency judgment is available to a hard money mortgagee (third party lender). The deficiency judgment allows the lender to go after the borrower's other assets as well as the mortgaged property.

95.   **C**   If a mortgagee forecloses and the property fails to sell for enough at the ensuing sheriff's sale to cover the amount due plus the mortgagee's costs of the foreclosure, the mortgagee may be entitled to a deficiency judgment. The deficiency judgment allows the mortgagee to reach any other assets of the borrower. A deficiency judgment is not available for a purchase money mortgagee (seller carried mortgage), nor is it possible on the judicial foreclosure of a residential trust deed.

96.   **A**   If the property fails to sell for enough at a sheriff's sale to cover the amount due plus a mortgagee's costs of the foreclosure, the mortgagee may be entitled to a deficiency judgment. The deficiency judgment allows the mortgagee to reach any other assets of the borrower. A deficiency judgment is not available for a purchase money mortgagee (seller carried mortgage), nor is it possible on the judicial foreclosure of a residential trust deed. Failing to pay the taxes may result in foreclosure, but not directly in a deficiency judgment.

97.   **A**   The original mortgage was a specific lien (reached only specified property), but a deficiency judgment is a general lien which allows the lender to reach any additional assets of the borrower.

98.   **D**   The final event in a mortgage foreclosure is the sheriff's sale. Before or after the sheriff's sale, the borrower (mortgagor) has a right of redemption. The

right of redemption can be exercised up to 180 days after the sheriff's sale. Since the lender has accelerated the debt by that time, in order to redeem prior to the sheriff's sale, the borrower must pay the entire balance in full, plus all the lender's costs associated with the foreclosure. After the sheriff's sale the amount required to redeem is whatever the property sold for at the sheriff's sale, plus 9% interest and any funds the successful bidder had to expend to prevent waste.

99.   **A**   A right of redemption is the borrower's right to recover the property after a sheriff's sale. To exercise it, the borrower must pay the amount paid by the successful bidder, plus 9% interest and anything the successful bidder had to pay to prevent waste. A right of reinstatement allows a borrower to bring the loan current and restore the loan, in other words, the lender cannot enforce the acceleration clause. The right of reinstatement exists only on trust deeds being foreclosed by trustee's sale.

100.   **B**   In a mortgage, the borrower is the mortgagor and the lender is the mortgagee. The borrower always has a statutory right of redemption for 180 days following the sheriff's sale. A right of reinstatement means the lender cannot accelerate and the borrower can save the property by merely bringing the loan current. The only loan where this can be done is a trust deed foreclosure where the lender has initiated a trustee's foreclosure.

101.   **C**   A mortgage does not allow the borrower a right of reinstatement, only a right of redemption. To redeem prior to the sheriff's sale, the borrower must pay the entire loan balance and all the lender's costs. After the sheriff's sale, the borrower must pay whatever the successful bidder paid, plus 9% interest and anything the successful bidder paid to prevent waste.

102.   **D**   Before or after a sheriff's sale, the borrower (mortgagor) has a right of redemption. Since the lender has accelerated the debt by the time the suit to foreclose was filed, in order to redeem prior to the sheriff's sale, the borrower must pay the entire balance in full, plus all the lender's costs associated with the foreclosure. After the sheriff's sale the amount required to redeem is whatever the property sold for at the sheriff's sale, plus 9% interest and any funds the successful bidder had to expend to prevent waste.

103.   **B**   A right of redemption allows a debtor to recover the property after default by paying the debt or the amount the property sold for. If the debt is a mortgage, or judicially foreclosed trust deed, or any other judgment or lien, the time period is 180 days

after the sale. For property taxes, it is two years after the foreclosure. The time periods are established by Oregon statutes.

104. **A** Oregon allows a mortgagor a 180-day statutory right of redemption following the sheriff's sale. To redeem the borrower must pay whatever the successful bidder paid for the property, plus 9% interest and anything the successful bidder paid to prevent waste. The borrower could also redeem prior to the sheriff's sale, but then the amount the borrower would have to pay would be the entire loan balance, plus the lenders costs incurred.

105. **C** When a mortgagee forecloses a mortgage the mortgagor has a statutory right of redemption of 180 days. To redeem, the mortgagor has to repay to the successful bidder at the sheriff's sale whatever the successful bidder paid for the property. Therefore, the right of redemption could not start until after the sheriff's sale. Junior lienholders have a 60-day right of redemption, except for the federal government, which has a 120-day right of redemption.

106. **A** The successful bidder is entitled to possession during the statutory right of redemption following a mortgage foreclosure sale, although the borrower is entitled to receive any income the property generates in the event the borrower elects to redeem. If the borrower does not redeem, the successful bidder may retain the income.

107. **C** In a mortgage transaction, the borrower gives a mortgage to the lender, so the borrower is the mortgagor (giver) and the lender is the mortgagee (receiver). The vendee is the buyer on a land sales contract, not a mortgage. The trustee is the third party between the borrower and lender in a trust deed transaction.

108. **B** A borrower and a lender may agree that the borrower will voluntarily relinquish the property to the lender. The deed to convey the title to the lender is called a deed in lieu of foreclosure. The borrower should be sure that the deed in lieu of foreclosure contains language which prohibits the lender from obtaining a deficiency judgment against the borrower in the event the property should later sell for less than the balance due on the loan. The language is said to "estop" (bar) the lender from asserting any further claims against the borrower. For this reason, deeds in lieu of foreclosure are sometimes referred to as "estoppel deeds."

109. **C** The definition of "purchase money mortgage" is a mortgage which the borrower gave to a seller as part of the purchase money, as opposed to a mortgage which a borrower might give to a third party lender to obtain the funds to buy the property. Because the third party lender lends hard cash, the law allows such a lender to obtain a deficiency judgment if necessary to recover the cash. A purchase money mortgagee is not allowed a deficiency judgment. Either a purchase money or hard money mortgagee may sue on the note independently of the mortgage, ignoring the collateral. This will result in a general judgment against the borrower, which the lender can use to reach all the borrower's assets, not just the mortgaged property. The disadvantage of doing so is that, if the borrower files a bankruptcy, the bankruptcy court will consider the mortgagee an unsecured lender, and the mortgaged property will be considered part of the general assets that all creditors can share in.

110. **D** Unlike a land sales contract, all rights of the parties in a mortgage or a trust deed are established by law. Individuals cannot contract to change the law.

111. **C** A trust deed is a deed only technically. Its function is to create a lien on real property to make the property collateral for a debt.

112. **D** A trust deed typically contains a lot of matters which the borrower must agree to, but the only provisions that are essential is that it convey a limited power of sale to a trustee, to hold for the benefit of the lender (beneficiary).

113. **A** Liens are classed as voluntary and involuntary. Mortgages, trust deeds and land sales contracts are all debt instruments entered into voluntarily by the borrower. A trust deed is a conveyance of a limited power to sell the property to a trustee, who holds it for the benefit of the lender. It is a conveyance of a small interest in property, not the entire title. Recording gives constructive notice and protects the parties from the claims of third parties. However, all contracts are valid between the parties without recording.

114. **B** A buyer receives a deed at closing, unless buying on a land sales contract. Deeds are either warranty, special warranty, bargain and sale, or occasionally, a quitclaim deed. A trust deed, while technically a deed, is really a financing instrument used to create a lien on real property.

115. **C** The Statute of Frauds requires all contracts involving real property to be in writing and signed by the party upon whom enforcement is sought, lest they be void. Liens are classed as vol-

untary and involuntary. Mortgages, trust deeds and land sales contracts are all debt instruments entered into voluntarily by the borrower. A trust deed is a conveyance of a limited power to sell the property to a trustee, who holds it for the benefit of the lender. It is a conveyance of a small interest in property, not the entire title.

116.   **C**   A trust deed is a lien against the borrower's title. An owner may always sell his or her property, although if there are any liens or other encumbrances, the buyer will take title subject to them. If the encumbrance is a lien with a due on sale clause, the lender may accelerate and foreclose, but the seller can still convey title. A trust deed is a conveyance of a limited power to sell the property to a trustee, who holds it for the benefit of the lender. This right can be given to the trustees for numerous lenders, whose priority will be according to the date their trust deeds were recorded. Both a mortgage and a trust deed are lien instruments, that is, either will make real property collateral for a note. Therefore, a mortgage could be used over a trust deed, or vice-versa.

117.   **B**   A trust deed is created when the borrower deeds a limited power of sale to a trustee, who holds the power of sale in trust for the lender (beneficiary). Therefore, the parties are the borrower (who can also be called the trustor, as well as the grantor of the trust deed), the trustee, and the lender, who receives the benefit of the trust (beneficiary). Technically, the trustee is also the grantee of the trust deed, but the Oregon Trust Deed Act refers to the parties as "grantor" (borrower), "trustee" and "beneficiary (lender)."

118.   **D**   To create a trust deed a borrower deeds a limited power of sale to a trustee. The trustee holds the power of sale during the term of the loan in trust for the lender. Since the lender receives the benefit of the trust arrangement, the lender is called the beneficiary. Although the trustee is the grantee of the trust deed, the only thing that was conveyed was the limited power of sale, not legal title. The Oregon Trust Deed Act requires that the trustee and the beneficiary be different parties.

119.   **D**   A trust deed is a conveyance of a limited power to sell the property to a trustee, who holds it for the benefit of the lender. The lender is, therefore, the beneficiary of the trust arrangement.

120.   **B**   In a trust deed, the owner (trustor) deeds one stick from the owner's bundle of rights to a trustee. The stick is a limited power to sell the property. The power is limited because the trustee can exercise it only if the debt is in default. The trustee holds the power to sell the property for the benefit of the lender. The lender is, therefore, called the beneficiary of the trust deed.

121.   **B**   A trust deed is a conveyance of a limited power to sell the property to a trustee, who holds it for the benefit of the lender. The lender is, therefore, the beneficiary of the trust arrangement.

122.   **B**   Both a mortgage and a trust deed are lien instruments, that is, either will make real property collateral for a note. A trust deed is a conveyance of a limited power to sell the property to a trustee, who holds it for the benefit of the lender. The lender is, therefore, the beneficiary of the trust arrangement. A trust deed is a special kind of deed. The parties to a deed are the grantor and the grantee. Since the borrower is the one who deeds the limited power of sale to the trustee, the borrower could be called the grantor, as well as the trustor, the borrower, or the owner. The essence of a foreclosure is for the trustee to sell the property at public auction to satisfy the debt (trustee's sale). The trust deed is, therefore, a three-party document. In a mortgage transaction the borrower gives the lender a note, the same as if it were a trust deed, and for the lien instrument, gives a mortgage directly to the lender. Therefore, the mortgage is a two-party transaction.

123.   **B**   A trust deed is a conveyance of a limited power to sell the property to a trustee who holds it for the benefit of the lender. The essence of a foreclosure is for the trustee to sell the property at public auction to satisfy the debt. The trustee may not be the same person or entity as the lender, nor can the trustee be the borrower. While not exactly neutral, the trustee is a third party in the transaction.

124.   **C**   In a trust there are always three parties, a trustor, who gives some asset to a trustee, who holds the asset in trust for a third party, called the beneficiary. In a trust deed, the owner deeds a limited power to sell the property to a trustee. The trustee holds the power to sell the property for the benefit of the lender. Therefore, the borrower (owner) could also be called the trustor, and the lender can be called the beneficiary.

125.   **A**   In a trust there are always three parties, a trustor, who gives some asset to a trustee, who holds the asset in trust for a third party, called the beneficiary. In a trust deed, the owner deeds a limited power to sell the property to a trustee. The trustee holds the power to sell the property for the benefit

of the lender. Therefore, the borrower (owner) could also be called the trustor, and the lender can be called the beneficiary. It must also be remembered that the trust deed is an ordinary deed to which the lender has added certain conditions. The parties to a deed are the grantor and the grantee. Since the owner deeds the limited power of sale to the trustee, the owner could be called the grantor and the trustee could be called the grantee.

126.   **B**   In trust deed an owner deeds a limited power of sale to a trustee (third party). The trustee holds the power of sale in trust for the lender. Since the lender receives the benefit of the trust agreement, the lender is called the beneficiary. The Oregon Trust Deed Act provides that the beneficiary and the trustee must be different entities. The main benefit of a trust deed is that, in the event of a default, the beneficiary can order the trustee to hold a private auction sale of the property without having to file a suit to foreclose (a non-judicial foreclosure).

127.   **C**   In a trust deed, the owner (trustor) deeds one stick from the owner's bundle of rights to a trustee. The stick is a limited power to sell the property. The power is limited because the trustee can exercise it only if the debt is in default. The trustee holds the power to sell the property for the benefit of the lender. The lender is, therefore, called the beneficiary of the trust deed.

128.   **B**   In a trust deed, the owner (trustor) deeds one stick from the owner's bundle of rights to a trustee. The stick is a limited power to sell the property. The power is limited because the trustee can exercise it only if the debt is in default. The trustee holds the power to sell the property for the benefit of the lender.

129.   **A**   In a mortgage transaction the borrower is the mortgagor and the lender is the mortgagee. To create a trust deed an owner deeds a limited power of sale to a trustee (third party). The trustee holds the power of sale in trust for the lender. Since the lender receives the benefit of the trust agreement, the lender is called the beneficiary. The borrower is called the trustor. Therefore, the borrower and lender in a trust deed are the trustor and beneficiary, analogous to mortgagor and mortgagee in a mortgage transaction.

130.   **C**   A trust deed is a conveyance of a limited power to sell the property to a trustee, who holds it for the benefit of the lender. It is a conveyance of a small interest in property, not the entire title. The essence of a normal foreclosure of a trust deed is for the trustee to exercise the power to sell the property. In this case,

the trustee is required to hold a public auction sale. The sale is absolute and the successful bidder receives a deed from the trustee right after the sale. The borrower has no further right of redemption or interest in the property. At the same time, a deficiency judgment would require court action. Since the foreclosure was by private sale, no suit was filed, therefore, the law does not allow a deficiency judgment. Mortgages, trust deeds and land sales contracts are all debt instruments entered into voluntarily by the borrower.

131.   **B**   The release instrument for most liens is a satisfaction. For a trust deed, however, we need to reverse the procedure that created it in the first place. A trust deed is created when the borrower deeds a limited power of sale to a trustee. To extinguish it, therefore, the trustee needs to deed the power of sale back to the borrower. Thus, the release instrument for a trust deed is a deed of reconveyance.

132.   **D**   To release a trust deed lien we need to reverse the process that created it. A trust deed is created when the borrower deeds a limited power of sale to a trustee. To extinguish it, therefore, the trustee needs to deed the power of sale back to the borrower. A satisfaction is the release instrument for most other liens. An estoppel certificate (certificate of no defense) is a statement from the lender as to the remaining balance owing on the debt.

133.   **A**   In a trust deed the trustee holds the power of sale for the benefit of the lender (beneficiary). When the loan is paid in full the lien is released by having the trustee deed the limited power of sale back to the borrower. The instrument to do so is called the deed of reconveyance. Since the beneficiary is the one receiving the payments, the beneficiary must order the trustee to give the borrower the deed of reconveyance when the loan is paid in full. The document to do this is called the request for reconveyance.

134.   **D**   In a trust deed the trustee holds the power of sale for the benefit of the lender (beneficiary). When the loan is paid in full, the lien is released by having the trustee deed the limited power of sale back to the borrower. The instrument to do so is called the deed of reconveyance.

135.   **D**   A trust deed is created when a borrower deeds a limited power of sale to a trustee to hold for the benefit of a lender (beneficiary). When the trust deed has been paid in full, the lien can be removed by reversing the process — that is, the trustee deeds the limited power of sale back to the borrower. Therefore, the release instrument is called a deed of reconveyance.

136. **D**   A trust deed creates a lien on the borrower's property when the borrower grants a limited power of sale to a trustee. The trustee holds the power of sale for the benefit of the lender (beneficiary). When the loan is paid in full, the lien is released by having the trustee deed the limited power of sale back to the borrower. The instrument to do so is called the deed of reconveyance. It could be argued that the trustee is the grantor of the deed of reconveyance, but the most direct answer is trustee.

137. **C**   A trust deed is deemed to be a lien instrument, not technically a conveyance. The trustee must be a different entity than the beneficiary, but is nevertheless the beneficiary's agent and has a duty of loyalty to the beneficiary. The trustee is a third party, but not a neutral party.

138. **C**   Trust deeds can be foreclosed in Oregon judicially, that is, in the same manner as a mortgage, with the exception that a deficiency judgment is possible only if the trust deed is on non-residential property. The more popular method of foreclosure is for the lender to order the trustee to sell the property at public auction (trustee's foreclosure).

139. **B**   The Oregon Trust Deed Act requires that the trustee must first serve the borrower with a Notice of Default and Election to Sell. The sale must be set at least 120 days from the service. The trustee must then publish the Notice of Default and Election to Sell at least once a week for a minimum of four weeks. Within ten days after the sale, the trustee gives the successful bidder a trustee's deed. A deed of reconveyance is used when the borrower pays off the debt in normal fashion. It is a deed from the trustee to the borrower, to deed the limited power of sale back to the borrower.

140. **B**   In a trust deed, the parties are the grantor (or trustor – the borrower), the trustee (the third party), and the beneficiary (lender). The terms "mortgagor" and "mortgagee" are used with mortgages, not trust deeds. The usual method of foreclosing a trust deed is for the beneficiary to notify the trustee that the loan is in default and order the trustee to proceed with a public auction sale of the property. The first step the trustee takes is to record the notice of default and serve it on the borrower.

141. **C**   In a trust deed the beneficiary (lender) has two possible remedies. The beneficiary can foreclose by filing a suit, in much the same manner as though the trust deed were a mortgage. Such a foreclosure is called a judicial foreclosure. Or the beneficiary can avoid the expense of a suit and direct the trustee to sell the property at public auction. Either way, junior lienholders must be notified of the foreclosure in order to extinguish their liens. If a junior lienholder (or any other interested party) wishes to protect his or her interest, it is possible to record a "request for notice of default," which requires the beneficiary to notify the person named in the request for notice of default.

142. **C**   The Oregon Trust Deed Act requires that the trustee must first serve the borrower with a Notice of Default and Election to Sell. The sale must be set at least 120 days from the service. The trustee must then publish the Notice of Default and Election to Sell at least once a week for a minimum of four weeks. Within ten days after the sale, the trustee gives the successful bidder a trustee's deed. In the foreclosure of mortgages, the borrower has a 180-day statutory right of redemption following the sale of the property. In the case of trust deeds, however, there is no right of redemption following the trustee's sale.

143. **D**   Normally, a holder of a note in due course has recourse to the last endorser. But when a note is endorsed "without recourse," the holder in due course can only go after the original maker. Therefore, the holder in due course has no alternative but to go after the original borrower, either by trustee's foreclosure, judicial foreclosure, or suing on the note to obtain a general judgment. Regardless of the remedy chosen, the amount of the debt is $100,000. The price paid for the note is irrelevant.

144. **C**   The Oregon Trust Deed Act requires that the trustee must first serve the borrower with a Notice of Default and Election to Sell. The sale must be set at least 120 days from the service. The trustee must then publish the Notice of Default and Election to Sell at least once a week for a minimum of four weeks. In a mortgage transaction, the borrower has 180 days after the sheriff's sale of the property in which to redeem. In the case of trust deeds, however, there is no right of redemption following the sale of the property. Instead, the Trust Deed Act requires the lender to allow the borrower to reinstate any time up to the fifth day before the date set for the trustee's sale.

145. **A**   Both a mortgage and a trust deed are lien instruments, that is, either will make real property collateral for a note. The mortgage must always be foreclosed by a suit. A trust deed may also be foreclosed judicially, the same as a mortgage, but the normal foreclosure of a trust deed is by trustee's sale. A trust deed is a conveyance of a limited power to sell

the property to a trustee, who holds it for the benefit of the lender. The essence of a foreclosure is for the trustee to sell the property at public auction to satisfy the debt. In a mortgage transaction, the borrower has 180 days after the sheriff's sale of the property in which to redeem. In the case of trust deeds, however, there is no right of redemption following the sale of the property.

146. **C**   The essence of a foreclosure is for the trustee to sell the property at public auction to satisfy the debt (trustee's sale). In a mortgage transaction, the borrower has 180 days after the sheriff's sale of the property in which to redeem. In the case of trust deeds, however, there is no right of redemption following the sale of the property. Instead, the Oregon Trust Deed Act requires the lender to allow the borrower to reinstate any time up to the fifth day before the date set for the trustee's sale.

147. **D**   In a mortgage transaction, the borrower has 180 days after the sheriff's sale of the property in which to redeem. Redemption means paying back whatever the successful bidder paid for the property. In the case of trust deeds, however, there is no right of redemption following the sale of the property. Instead, the law provides that the lender must accept reinstatement up to the fifth day before the date set for the sale. Reinstatement requires only that the borrower bring the loan current, including all late charges, interest, and whatever other expenses the lender had incurred up to the point of reinstatement.

148. **B**   In a mortgage transaction, the borrower has 180 days after the sheriff's sale of the property in which to redeem. Redemption means paying back whatever the successful bidder paid for the property. In the case of trust deeds, however, there is no right of redemption following the sale of the property. Instead, the law provides that the lender must accept reinstatement up to the fifth day before the date set for the sale.

149. **B**   The essence of a normal foreclosure of a trust deed is for the trustee to exercise the power to sell the property. In this case, the trustee is required to hold a public auction sale. The sale is absolute and the successful bidder receives a deed from the trustee right after the sale. The borrower has no further right of redemption or interest in the property. At the same time, a deficiency judgment would require court action. Since the foreclosure was by private sale, no suit was filed, therefore, the law does not allow a deficiency judgment.

150. **B**   In the foreclosure of mortgages, the borrower has a 180-day statutory right of redemption following the sale of the property. In the case of trust deeds, however, there is no right of redemption following the trustee's sale. The successful bidder is entitled to a trustee's deed within ten days following the auction.

151. **A**   The Oregon Trust Deed Act requires that the trustee must first serve the borrower with a Notice of Default and Election to Sell. The sale must be set at least 120 days from the service. Within ten days after the sale, the trustee gives the successful bidder a trustee's deed. In the foreclosure of mortgages, the borrower has a 180-day statutory right of redemption following the sale of the property. In the case of trust deeds, however, there is no right of redemption following the trustee's sale. Instead, the law provides that the lender must accept reinstatement at any time prior to the fifth day before the date set for the sale.

152. **B**   The Oregon Trust Deed Act provides that the sale must be held as a public auction by the trustee or the trustee's representative. Anyone may bid except the person holding the sale, including the borrower, the lender, junior lienholders, or anyone else.

153. **B**   The Oregon Trust Deed Act provides that the sale must be held by the trustee or the trustee's representative. Anyone may bid except the person holding the sale, including the borrower, the lender, junior lienholders, or anyone else.

154. **C**   The Oregon Trust Deed Act provides that the sale must be held as a public auction by the trustee or the trustee's representative. Anyone may bid except the person holding the sale, including the borrower, the lender, junior lienholders, or anyone else. Within ten days following the sale, the trustee delivers to the successful bidder a deed. This is called the trustee's deed, not to be confused with the trust deed, the original lien instrument.

155. **B**   Following a trustee's sale, the trustee is required to give a trustee's deed to the successful bidder within ten days. A sheriff's deed is used following a mortgage foreclosure.

156. **B**   The Oregon Trust Deed Act provides that, at the lender's option, a trust deed may be foreclosed as though it were a mortgage (called a judicial foreclosure), in which case, all the usual rules for a mortgage foreclosure apply. However, there is one substantial difference. In the foreclosure of a mortgage, if the property fails to bring enough at the sheriff's sale, the lender may go back to the court and ask for a deficiency judgment, which will be granted unless the

mortgage was being carried by the seller (a purchase money mortgage). In the case of a judicial foreclosure of a trust deed, the rules are different. A deficiency judgment is permitted only if the trust deed was not a "residential trust deed." The statute defines a residential trust deed as one where the collateral is not the borrower's primary residence.

157. **A** The Oregon Trust Deed Act allows the beneficiary of a trust deed to foreclose "in the manner provided by law for the foreclosure of mortgages." The only difference is that a deficiency judgment is available only if the collateral is a commercial (non-residential) property. If residential, the deficiency judgment is not allowed. The issue of purchase money vs. hard money financing is irrelevant. The statutory right of redemption is the same as for a mortgage foreclosure.

158. **B** The normal foreclosure of a trust deed is for the lender to instruct the trustee to hold a trustee's sale. However, the Oregon Trust Deed Act provides that, at the lender's option, a trust deed may be foreclosed as though it were a mortgage (called a judicial foreclosure), in which case, all the usual rules for a mortgage foreclosure apply. However, there is one substantial difference. In the foreclosure of a mortgage, if the property fails to bring enough at the sheriff's sale, the lender may go back to the court and ask for a deficiency judgment, which will be granted unless the mortgage was being carried by the seller (a purchase money mortgage). In the case of a judicial foreclosure of a trust deed, the rules are different. A deficiency judgment is permitted only if the property is not the borrower's personal residence.

159. **B** Deficiency judgments are possible on trust deeds only if the trust deed is not on the borrower's personal residence and the foreclosure is judicial, or if the lender sues on the note without foreclosing on the property. Whether or not the trust deed was a purchase money instrument is relevant only for a mortgage, not for a trust deed. The use or type of property is also irrelevant.

160. **B** The borrower is entitled to retain possession of the property for ten days following the trustee's sale. A borrower who remains in possession longer than ten days after the trustee's sale is a tenant at sufferance and can be evicted without further notice.

161. **D** A trust deed is a financing instrument that may or may not have a due on sale clause. If so, the grantor may need permission from the lender (beneficiary), or pay off the lender. The beneficiary may require the buyer to assume and agree to pay the trust deed. But regardless of the status of the trust deed lien, the seller must use a deed to convey title to the buyer.

162. **B** A trust deed is a conveyance, but not considered a conveyance of real estate. It conveys a limited power of sale to a trustee, who holds it for the benefit of the lender. At the lender's option, a trust deed may be foreclosed as though it were a mortgage (called a judicial foreclosure), in which case all the usual rules for a mortgage foreclosure apply. However, there is one substantial difference. In the foreclosure of a mortgage, if the property fails to bring enough at the sheriff's sale, the lender may go back to the court and ask for a deficiency judgment, which will be granted unless the mortgage was being carried by the seller (a purchase money mortgage). In the case of a judicial foreclosure of a trust deed the rules are different. A deficiency judgment is permitted only if the trust deed was not a "residential trust deed". The statute defines a residential trust deed as one where the collateral is not the borrower's primary residence.

163. **D** Before initiating a foreclosure, the Oregon Trust Deed Act requires the lender to check the public records relating to the property. The foreclosure notice must be served on all parties with a recorded interest in the property, plus anyone who has recorded a Request for Notice of Default. Foreclosure by a senior lienholder always extinguishes all junior liens, so holders of second and subsequent liens are the ones who usually record the Request for Notice of Default. By receiving notice prior to the foreclosure sale, they can pay to reinstate the first rather than having to pay it in full.

164. **D** A request for notice of default is a document which requires a lienholder to notify a junior lienholder before filing a foreclosure. The junior lienholder records it to make sure of the ability to pay off the underlying loan in order to protect the junior lien.

165. **D** Land sales contracts, by their very nature, must be carried by the seller, therefore any time seller financing is called for, the instrument is likely to be a land sales contract. Of course, a property can also be seller financed with a trust deed or mortgage, but the land sales contract is the most popular instrument.

166. **D** In a land sales contract the seller retains legal title until the buyer has finished paying for the property. The buyer's right to tender the balance and demand a deed is called the buyer's equitable title. Although the fact that the seller has retained legal title would ordinarily entitle the seller to retain pos-

session, it would be unusual to find a land sales contract which did not contain a clause granting possession to the buyer.

167.   **A**   The Statute of Frauds in Oregon requires all contracts involving real property to be in writing and signed by the person to be charged, lest they be void. Abstracts have been replaced with title insurance in Oregon. A land sales contract usually calls for installments (regular amortization), but lump sum payments are also common.

168.   **D**   A land sales contract must be recorded within fifteen days of the date the parties are bound, unless the term of the contract is less than one year. If the contract is not recorded, the seller is subject to a fine, however, the contract is still valid and enforceable between the parties. Although a buyer would be foolish to buy property on a land sales contract without title insurance, there is no legal requirement for it.

169.   **D**   The fact that the property is vacant land or that it will not be occupied by the buyer is completely irrelevant. However, land sales contracts must be recorded within fifteen days of the date the parties are bound by the contract, unless the contract is short term, to be fully performed within twelve months. Failure to record the contract does not render it unenforceable, but does subject the seller to a fine.

170.   **B**   Land sales contracts must be recorded within fifteen days of the date the parties are bound by the contract, unless the contract is short term (to be fully performed within twelve months). Failure to record the contract does not render it unenforceable, but does subject the seller to a fine. The contract is the buyer's promise to pay for the property later, and the seller's promise to deliver a deed to the buyer when the buyer has done so. Therefore, the land sales contract is always carried by a seller.

171.   **C**   Land sales contracts must be recorded within fifteen days of the date the parties are bound by the contract, unless the contract is to be fully performed within twelve months. Failure to record the contract does not render it unenforceable, but does subject the seller to a fine. Instead of recording the whole contract, a memorandum of the contract can be recorded.

172.   **D**   During the term of a land sales contract, the seller remains the owner (retains legal title), and the buyer obtains the right to pay the balance in full and demand the deed. The buyer's rights are called the equitable title. A trustee is used in a trust deed, not a land sales contract. Specific performance is performing a contract according to its terms.

173.   **B**   In a land sales contract the buyer agrees to pay for the property in installments, and the seller agrees to deed the property to the buyer when the buyer has finished paying for it. During the term of the contract the seller retains legal title. For a mortgage or trust deed to work the buyer must be in title. Both are lien instruments – and you cannot lien a property you do not own.

174.   **A**   There are many synonymous expressions for a land sales contract, including an installment contract for the sale of real property.

175.   **B**   A land sales contract is an agreement between a buyer and seller where the seller agrees to deed the property to the buyer when the buyer has finished paying for it. The seller retains legal title until that time. Nevertheless, the buyer has significant rights in the property, including usually the right of possession, use, enjoyment, and the right to pay the balance and demand the deed. We call these rights the buyer's equitable title. The seller is said to have retained merely naked title.

176.   **D**   There are three ways to finance real property – note and mortgage, note and trust deed, and land sales contract. The land sales contract goes by many synonyms.

177.   **B**   The essence of a land sales contract is that the seller retains legal title until the buyer has finished paying for the property. The buyer's right to tender the balance and demand a deed is called the buyer's equitable title.

178.   **C**   In a land sales contract the buyer (vendee) promises to pay the balance to the seller (vendor), usually in installments, and the seller promises to deliver a deed to the buyer when the purchase price has been paid in full. Therefore, the seller retains legal title until the buyer has finished paying for the property. Although the fact that the seller has retained legal title would ordinarily entitle the seller to retain possession, it would be unusual to find a land sales contract which did not contain a clause granting possession to the buyer.

179.   **A**   In a land sales contract the seller retains legal title until the buyer has finished paying for the property. The vendor is the seller and the vendee is the buyer. A mortgagee is a lender under a mortgage. An escrow agent is the party who closes a real estate transaction.

180.   **A**   The essence of a land sales contract is that the seller retains legal title until the buyer has finished paying for the property. The buyer's right

to tender the balance and demand a deed is called the buyer's equitable title. Although the fact that the seller has retained legal title would ordinarily entitle the seller to retain possession, it would be unusual to find a land sales contract which did not contain a clause granting possession to the buyer. An estate for years is a lease. An estate for life is an ownership for a person's lifetime.

181. **B** In a land sales contract the buyer promises to pay the balance to the seller, usually in installments, and the seller promises to deliver a deed to the buyer when the purchase price has been paid in full. Therefore, the seller retains legal title until the buyer has finished paying for the property. A beneficiary is a lender in a trust deed and a trustee is a third party who holds a power of sale in a trust deed.

182. **D** The essence of a land sales contract is that the buyer promises to pay the balance to the seller at a later date (usually in installments), and the seller promises to deliver a deed to the buyer when the purchase price has been paid in full. The land sales contract can be used for any real property. A mortgage, while a valid financing instrument, is completely different from a land sales contract.

183. **D** Under a land sales contract, the buyer's right to tender the balance and demand a deed is called the buyer's equitable title. When property is owned in severalty, it means there is one owner, as opposed to a co-tenancy. A tenancy in common is an example of a co-tenancy. A prescriptive owner is one who holds an easement obtained by long and continued use.

184. **C** In a land sales contract the seller retains legal title until the buyer has finished paying for the property. The buyer's right to tender the balance and demand a deed is called the buyer's equitable title.

185. **C** In a land sales contract the seller retains legal title until the buyer has finished paying for the property. The buyer's right to tender the balance and demand a deed is called the buyer's equitable title. Fee simple title is the highest ownership interest one can have in real property, and is probably what the seller has retained. A life estate is an ownership for one's lifetime. An estate for years is a lease.

186. **B** In a land sales contract the seller retains legal title until the buyer has finished paying for the property. The buyer's right to tender the balance and demand a deed is called the buyer's equitable title. Although the fact that the seller has retained legal title would ordinarily entitle the seller to retain possession, it would be unusual to find a land sales

contract which did not contain a clause granting possession to the buyer. Similarly, the seller would be responsible for the property taxes, except that a land sales contract almost always contains a clause requiring the buyer to pay them. The buyer may have the right under the contract to demand legal title upon payment of the final amount, but if the seller cannot or will not deliver, the buyer's sole remedy is to sue the seller for specific performance or damages.

187. **D** In a land sales contract the buyer promises to pay the balance to the seller, usually in installments, and the seller promises to deliver a deed to the buyer when the purchase price has been paid in full. Therefore, the seller retains legal title until the buyer has finished paying for the property. The buyer's right to tender the balance and demand a deed is called the buyer's equitable title. A reversionary interest and a remainder are future estates which follow a life estate.

188. **B** In a land sales contract the buyer promises to pay the balance to the seller, usually in installments, and the seller promises to deliver a deed to the buyer when the purchase price has been paid in full. Therefore, the seller retains legal title until the buyer has finished paying for the property. The buyer's right to tender the balance and demand a deed is called the buyer's equitable title. Since the seller remains legally in title the seller would be entitled to possession. Since this is not what the parties typically desire, land sales contracts normally contain a clause giving the buyer possession as long as the buyer is not in default.

189. **D** Fee simple title is the highest ownership interest one can have in real property. In a land sales contract the buyer promises to pay the balance to the seller, usually in installments, and the seller promises to deliver a deed to the buyer when the purchase price has been paid in full. Although the seller remains the owner of the property (retains fee title) until the deed is delivered to the buyer, the buyer has the right to tender the balance in full and demand the deed. We call this interest the buyer's equitable title. An estate for years is a lease.

190. **D** Fee simple title is the highest ownership interest one can have in real property. In a land sales contract the buyer promises to pay the balance to the seller, usually in installments, and the seller promises to deliver a deed to the buyer when the purchase price has been paid in full. Although the seller remains the owner of the property (retains fee title) until the deed is delivered to the buyer, the buyer has the right to tender the balance in full and demand

the deed. We call this interest the buyer's equitable title. An estate for years is a lease.

191.   **D**   In a land sales contract the buyer promises to pay the balance to the seller, usually in installments, and the seller promises to deliver a deed to the buyer when the buyer has paid the purchase price in full. Although the seller remains the owner of the property until the deed is delivered to the buyer (retains legal title), the buyer has the right to tender the balance in full and demand the deed. We call this interest the buyer's equitable title. Although having legal title would entitle the seller to retain possession, it would be highly unusual to find a land sales contract without a clause granting possession to the buyer.

192.   **C**   The essence of a land sales contract is that the buyer promises to pay the balance to the seller at a later date (usually in installments), and the seller promises to deliver a deed to the buyer when the buyer has paid the purchase price in full. Although the seller remains the owner of the property until the deed is delivered to the buyer, the buyer has the right to tender the balance in full and demand the deed. We call this interest the buyer's equitable title.

193.   **D**   The essence of a land sales contract is that the buyer promises to pay the balance to the seller at a later date (usually in installments), and the seller promises to deliver a deed to the buyer when the purchase price has been paid in full. During the term of the contract, the seller remains the owner (retains legal title), and the buyer obtains the right to pay the balance in full and demand the deed. The buyer's rights are called the equitable title.

194.   **A**   The essence of a land sales contract is that the buyer promises to pay the balance to the seller at a later date (usually in installments), and the seller promises to deliver a deed to the buyer when the purchase price has been paid in full.

195.   **B**   In a land sales contract the buyer promises to pay the balance to the seller at a later date (usually in installments), and the seller promises to deliver a deed to the buyer when the purchase price has been paid in full. A novation is recasting a contract and extinguishing the original contract.

196.   **B**   The essence of a land sales contract is that the seller retains legal title until the buyer has finished paying for the property. When the buyer has paid the contract in full the seller delivers the deed to the buyer.

197.   **A**   In a land sales contract, the seller agrees to deed the property to the buyer when the buyer has finished paying for it. Until then, the buyer has equitable title and the seller retains legal title.

198.   **D**   Marketable title means free and clear of financial encumbrances. It is very common for a seller to sell property on a land sales contract even though the property is encumbered with an underlying encumbrance. By the terms of a typical contract the seller only has to have clear title when delivering the deed to the buyer. Ordinarily, then, the buyer will make payments to the seller on the contract, and the seller will continue to pay on the underlying loan. Real estate agents usually structure the repayment of the land sales contract so that the underlying loan will be paid off at least as fast as the contract is being paid. Otherwise the seller could be faced with having to deliver a free and clear deed to the buyer, but still owe money on the underlying loan and not have the funds to pay it off.

199.   **D**   Foreclosure by a senior lienholder will extinguish all junior interests. So if the seller defaults on the underlying loan, the resulting foreclosure will extinguish the interest of the new buyer.

200.   **B**   Personal property can be part of the collateral covered by a land sales contract, mortgage or trust deed. The only requirement for enforceability is that the instrument describe the personal property with certainty and state clearly that it is considered part of the collateral.

201.   **D**   In a land sales contract the seller retains legal title until the buyer has finished paying for the property. The buyer's right to tender the balance and demand a deed is called the buyer's equitable title. As the legal owner, the seller would be responsible for the property taxes, except that a land sales contract almost always contains a clause requiring the buyer to pay them. Similarly, standard contracts also require the buyer to keep the property insured and maintain the property.

202.   **D**   A land sales contract is always carried by the seller, but otherwise imposes on the buyer much the same requirements as a mortgage or trust deed would on a borrower. For example, property taxes are a prior lien ahead of a private lien instrument, so a lender must always make sure the buyer pays the taxes, whether the lender is a bank or a seller carrying a land sales contract.

203.   **D**   In a land sales contract the seller retains legal title until the buyer has finished paying for the property. If a seller sues for strict foreclosure of a land sales contract, there is no right of redemption.

The court may allow the buyer a period of time in which to pay the balance in full before the court will give the property back to the seller, but the amount of time is discretionary with the judge.

204.   **D**   In a land sales contract the seller is the vendor, and retains legal title until the buyer (vendee) has finished paying for the property. The buyer's right to pay the balance in full and demand a deed is called the buyer's equitable title. If the buyer defaults, the seller can file a suit for strict foreclosure (ask for the property back), sue for specific performance of the covenant of indebtedness in the contract (seek a general judgment against the buyer), or declare a forfeiture.

205.   **A**   In a land sales contract the seller retains legal title until the buyer has finished paying for the property. If the buyer defaults, the seller can file a suit for strict foreclosure (ask for the property back), sue for specific performance of the covenant of indebtedness in the contract (seek a general judgment against the buyer), or declare a forfeiture.

206.   **B**   In a land sales contract the buyer promises to pay the balance to the seller at a later date (usually in installments), and the seller promises to deliver a deed to the buyer when the buyer has paid the purchase price in full. The seller retains the legal title until the buyer has paid the balance in full and the seller has delivered the deed. The buyer's promise to pay (the covenant of indebtedness) is also of benefit to the seller, because the seller could file a suit for the buyer's breach of the covenant and obtain a general judgment. However, when it comes to security, retaining legal title is what the seller usually looks to first.

207.   **D**   The seller in a land sales contract has several remedies. The most common is to file a suit for strict foreclosure. This is a suit which asks the court to extinguish all the buyer's rights in the property and restore the seller's title, but without an auction sale of the property. Another possible remedy is a suit for specific performance, which can result in a sheriff's sale of the property and possibly a deficiency judgment against the buyer. Or the seller can declare all the buyer's interest in the property forfeit. Declaring a forfeiture requires giving the buyer a right to reinstate, but is nevertheless popular because it is a non-judicial remedy. In most cases the seller can also sue the buyer on the promise to pay (called the covenant of indebtedness), and seek a general judgment against the buyer. This would be the equivalent of suing on the note in a note and mortgage or note and trust deed transaction.

208.   **D**   Strict foreclosure is a special remedy available only to sellers on land sales contracts. It is different from most foreclosures in that there is no public auction sale of the property. Instead, the court orders that the buyer's interest in the property is extinguished and the seller's title is restored as it was before the land sales contract.

209.   **C**   In a land sales contract the seller (vendor) retains legal title until the buyer (vendee) has finished paying for the property. The buyer's right to tender the balance and demand a deed is called the buyer's equitable title. Since there is no assurance that the buyer will make the payments and be able to demand the deed, the buyer's interest in the seller's title is a mere possibility, or claim. This is the definition of a cloud; in other words, the land sales contract is a cloud on the seller's title. When the holder of a cloud is willing to release his or her claim, the instrument that is most commonly used is a quitclaim deed. Therefore, the seller should get a quitclaim deed from the buyer to extinguish the buyer's equitable title.

210.   **C**   If a seller sues for strict foreclosure of a land sales contract, there is no right of redemption. The court may allow the buyer a period of time in which to pay the balance in full before the court will give the property back to the seller (interlocutory decree), but the amount of time is discretionary with the judge.

211.   **D**   Declaring a forfeiture is a non-judicial remedy. To declare a forfeiture, Oregon statutes require the seller to send the buyer by certified mail (or personally serve the buyer) a letter stating the nature of the default and giving the buyer between 60 and 120 days in which to cure it. The number of days is determined by the buyer's equity in the property. The letter must be sent to all other persons with an interest in the property. If no one cures the default, the seller can record an affidavit setting forth the facts of the case and thereupon all the buyer's interest in the property, and the interests of anyone else whose interest depends on the buyer's interest, are extinguished. Thus declaring a forfeiture can get the seller clear title without necessarily having to file a suit.

212.   **B**   In a land sales contract, the seller has various possible remedies. The most common is a suit for strict foreclosure, which asks the court to extinguish all the buyer's interest and return the property to the seller without a public auction sale. The seller could also declare a forfeiture, which also seeks to recover the property and extinguish the buyer's interest, but without a suit. If the seller sues for spe-

cific performance of the promise to pay, the seller can gain a judgment against the buyer for the entire balance owing, which can then be used to reach all the buyer's assets, in much the same manner as a lender in a mortgage can use a deficiency judgment.

213. **C** A suit for specific performance is a suit asking the court to order the defendant to perform a contract per the terms of the contract. If the seller has refused to deliver the deed as promised, even though the buyer has finished paying for the property, the buyer might consider a suit for specific performance of the contract to force the seller to deliver the deed. A rescission of a contract would require the parties to be placed in the same position they were in before they entered into the contract, as far as possible. In the case of a land sales contract that has been performed for a time, the courts generally let the seller keep the payments the buyer has made, as though they were rent, but require the seller to return the down payment. A party to a contract is only entitled to demand a rescission under certain specific conditions. In a land sales contract, the buyer might claim that the seller misrepresented the condition of the property. If successful in the claim, the court would allow rescission.

214. **C** Most land sales contracts have a clause allowing the seller to declare a forfeiture. This allows the seller to have the buyer's interest in the property extinguished and recover possession as well as clear title. Forfeiture is a non-judicial remedy.

215. **A** Foreclosure is a remedy exclusively for a seller or lender, not a buyer or a lender. A suit for specific performance is a suit asking the court to order the defendant to perform a contract per the terms of the contract.

216. **B** A mortgage is an encumbrance on real property which makes the real property collateral for a debt. When personal property (chattels) are used as the collateral, the instrument used is a chattel mortgage, although today the preferred term is "security agreement."

217. **D** When an asset is used as collateral for a loan we say the asset has been pledged. This is true whether the asset is real property or personal property, such as a note receivable. A chattel mortgage is an older term for "security agreement," which is a lien on personal property.

218. **C** An estoppel certificate is a statement from a lender as to the remaining balance on a loan. It estops (bars) the lender from asserting a higher remaining amount. A synonym is a certificate of no defense.

219. **C** An estoppel certificate is a statement by a lender as to the remaining balance owing on a loan. It is also called a reduction certificate or a certificate of no defense. Once the lender has issued it the lender is estopped (barred) from asserting any higher amount due. Estoppel certificates are typically issued annually as a report to the borrower, and also whenever the borrower requests it, e.g., in preparation for selling the property or having a buyer assume the loan.

220. **A** "Reduction certificate" is another synonym for "estoppel certificate." If a lender misstates the loan balance and an innocent party relies on the misstatement, the lender can generally be held to the statement. For this reason, when a loan is being paid off, assumed by a buyer, or when a junior lien is being created, it is common to demand from the lender an "estoppel certificate" setting forth the loan balance.

221. **B** Being able to call the loan balance due in full in the event of default is a right created by the acceleration clause. The lender cannot foreclose until the entire balance is due, so the acceleration clause is critical to the lender.

222. **B** A lender cannot foreclose until the entire balance is due. The acceleration clause allows the lender to declare the entire balance due in the event of a default.

223. **D** The lender must have a way to call the loan due in full in the event of a default, because the lender cannot initiate foreclosure until the entire balance is due. The acceleration clause gives the lender this right.

224. **D** A lender cannot foreclose unless the entire principal balance is due. Therefore, the lender needs a way to call the loan due in full at once in the event of a default. The clause that gives the lender this right is the acceleration clause.

225. **A** Any loan calling for installments will contain an acceleration clause. The acceleration clause allows the lender to call the entire balance due in full in the event of default. The lender cannot foreclose unless the entire balance is due, so the acceleration clause is critical.

226. **A** The clause allowing the lender to declare the entire remaining balance due in full in the event to a default is called the acceleration clause. The lender cannot foreclose until the entire balance is due, so the acceleration clause is essential. Without it, the lender would have to wait until the end of the loan term before foreclosing.

227. **B** The acceleration clause allows the lender to call the entire loan balance due in full at once in

the event of a default. The lender cannot foreclose unless the entire balance is due.

228. **A** A prepayment penalty requires that the borrower pay an additional fee in order to pay the loan off in full. A lock-in clause prohibits payoff completely. The acceleration clause allows the lender to demand the entire balance in full in the event of default. A non-alienation clause would prohibit selling the property while encumbered.

229. **B** Prepayment penalties occur on some conventional loans. The prepayment penalty allows the lender to demand an additional amount if the borrower wishes to pay the loan off faster than its scheduled amortization.

230. **B** Although not common on new loans today, a prepayment penalty requires the borrower to pay extra in order to pay the loan off early. Oregon law requires the lender to give the borrower a special notice when making a loan with a prepayment penalty.

231. **A** The seller is a borrower, paying off the seller's loan early because the property is being sold. A prepayment penalty is a fee which the loan document allows the lender to charge if the loan is paid off early.

232. **C** The term "prepayment privilege" is usually stated as "prepayment penalty" – i.e., an amount the borrower must pay in order to pay the loan off ahead of its normal period.

233. **A** If funds are in short supply and there is strong loan demand, interest rates will be rising and borrowers would want to pay off existing lower interest loans. If the Federal Reserve System lowers the reserve ratio and discount rate, this would cause interest rates to go down, which means lenders would not be able to re-lend mortgage funds at higher rates. Therefore, under such conditions, lenders would prefer to discourage borrowers from paying off loans early.

234. **C** An acceleration clause allows a lender to demand the entire remaining principal balance in full in the event of default. "Alienation clause" is a synonym for "due on sale clause." The interest clause states the interest rate. An escalator (or escalation) clause allows an increase in one or more of the terms of the agreement.

235. **A** Variable interest rate provisions are more popular in times of high interest rates. Because of the variable interest rate provision the lender generally agrees to a lower interest rate than for fixed rate loans. Being able to call the loan due if the loan is assumed without the lender's permission is a accomplished with a due on sale clause.

236. **C** The acceleration clause allows the lender to call the entire balance due at once in the event of default. Notes must state the payment terms, which are normally followed by the words "or more," or sometimes the payment amount is stated as "not less than" – e.g., "360 equal monthly payments of $1,000 or more." Either way, it is called the "or more" clause and allows the borrower to pay additional amounts toward the principal.

237. **A** The clause which requires the borrower to pay the loan in full in the event the property is sold is called the "due on sale clause," also sometimes called the "alienation clause."

238. **C** This provision is normally called a due on sale clause or an alienation clause. At one time such clauses were unenforceable in some states, but due to overriding federal legislation, the courts now hold such clauses to be legal.

239. **C** A call provision allows a lender to call the loan due in full any time after a certain period of time, even if the loan is not in default – somewhat similar to a balloon payment, although a balloon payment is automatic where the call feature requires the lender to make formal demand for payment in full. A lock-in clause prohibits the borrower from paying the loan off ahead of schedule. A due on sale clause allows the lender to accelerate in the event the borrower sells the property without the lender's permission. The due on sale clause is also sometimes called an alienation clause.

240. **D** Late payment penalties are important to lenders because the loan amortization schedule is calculated on a month-to-month basis, rather than actual days. In other words, the interest charged for the month is the same whether the payment is made on the first or last day of the month. Therefore, the sooner the lender receives the funds, the better for the lender.

241. **B** The assignment of rents clause is standard in mortgages, trust deeds, and land sales contracts. It provides that, in the event of default, if the property is rented, the lender can demand that the tenant pay rent directly to the lender. The lender in a trust deed is the beneficiary.

242. **D** When a buyer takes title subject to an existing mortgage the lender generally requires that the buyer assume and agree to pay the debt in order to make the buyer personally liable for the obligation.

243. **B** A reduction certificate (also known as an estoppel certificate) is a statement by a lender as to

the remaining balance owing on a loan. Once issued, the lender is estopped (barred) from asserting that a higher amount is owing, thus it protects a buyer who is assuming an existing loan.

244. **B** When a buyer takes title to a property and the seller does not pay off the existing loan, then the buyer takes title subject to the loan. If that is all that happens, then the seller remains personally obligated for the debt, but the buyer cannot lose any more than his or her equity in the property – the lender cannot come after the buyer for a deficiency judgment, for example. If the buyer takes title subject to the loan, and assumes and agrees to pay it as well (enters into an assumption agreement with the lender), then the buyer becomes personally liable for the debt. Even then, the seller remains liable as well.

245. **A** If you take title subject to a loan which the seller is supposed to keep current, you could lose your equity in the property to foreclosure if the seller fails to do so.

246. **B** When a buyer takes title to a property subject to the existing mortgage, the seller is still personally liable for the debt. If the buyer assumes and agrees to pay, this just makes the buyer equally personally liable – the original borrower is still not relieved of liability. The only way for the original borrower to get out of liability for the debt is for the lender to agree to a substitution of mortgagor (a kind of novation). However, the lender has no obligation or motivation to agree to this, so it is not usually an option. Having the buyer assume and agree to pay is the best that can usually be done. The seller and the buyer are then equally liable, but the buyer will have the primary motivation to keep the loan current, as the buyer is the one with the potential to lose the equity in the property.

247. **A** When you buy a property and the seller deeds it to you without paying off the underlying loan, you take title subject to the loan. If that is all that happens, the seller remains fully personally liable for the debt, but you incur no liability other than the potential loss of your equity if the lender forecloses. The lender cannot come after you for a possible deficiency judgment because you did not agree to the debt. If you "assume" the loan, then you have agreed to the debt and become personally liable for it. Note that technically in both cases you take title "subject to" the loan, but in the real estate business agents use the term "subject to" as a contrast to "assume," meaning "no personal liability."

248. **A** When a buyer takes title and there is a pre-existing loan which the seller does not pay off, then the buyer takes title subject to the loan. If the buyer assumed the loan as well (entered into an assumption agreement with the lender), then the loan becomes the buyer's personal obligation. If there is no assumption agreement, then the buyer can lose only the equity in the property; the lender cannot go after the buyer for a deficiency judgment. The seller, however, remains fully liable for the debt, including liability for a deficiency judgment, whether the buyer takes title merely "subject to" or subject to the loan and assumes it. In real estate terminology, agents use the term "subject to" and "assumption" or "assume" as opposite terms – disregarding that the buyer who assumes also, technically, takes the title subject to the encumbrance.

249. **B** When the collateral includes both real and incidental personal property it is called a package loan. A blanket encumbrance covers more than one parcel of real estate. A wraparound loan is carried by a seller and includes the balance owing on the seller's old loan.

250. **D** When personal property is included as part of the collateral the loan is called a package loan. A chattel mortgage covers just personal property (chattels). A blanket encumbrance covers more than one parcel of real estate.

251. **B** A package mortgage is one which includes personal property as part of the collateral in addition to the real property. In residential financing it might include appliances added by a builder in a new home. If the buyer had to finance the appliances separately, it would be less convenient and possibly more expensive, especially considering that financing contracts for consumer goods are typically at higher interest rates than residential mortgage loans.

252. **B** An open end mortgage is like a credit line. The lender agrees to lend to the borrower up to a certain amount, but the borrower might draw only a portion of the total at first. The term is also used as a verb – e.g., a homeowner has a mortgage but wishes to build an addition which will require additional financing. The homeowner could go to the lender who holds the existing loan and "open end" the loan, allowing the homeowner to obtain additional funds.

253. **C** Open end financing is like a credit line, secured by real estate. The borrower is given a limit, and can borrow up to the limit as the borrower chooses.

254. **A** An open end mortgage is like a credit line, which gives the borrower a limit and leaves it up to the borrower to decide when and how much to bor-

row. Blanket encumbrances cover more than one parcel. A variable (rate) mortgage allows the lender to adjust the interest rate according to an index. Junior liens are later in priority in the event of a foreclosure.

255.   **C**   An open end mortgage is like a credit line, allowing the borrower to decide when and how much to borrow, up to a prescribed limit.

256.   **A**   An open end mortgage is like a credit line, where the lender gives the borrower a limit and the borrower can take all or any portion up to the limit.

257.   **A**   An open end mortgage is like a credit line secured with real estate. The borrower is given a limit, and it is up to the borrower to decide how much and when to borrow, as long as the borrower does not exceed the limit. In a mortgage the borrower is called the mortgagor.

258.   **A**   Blanket encumbrances are liens which reach more than one parcel. "All-inclusive mortgage" is a synonym for "wraparound mortgage." A package mortgage is one which includes personal property as part of the collateral as well as real property.

259.   **C**   When the collateral is more than one parcel, the loan is called a blanket encumbrance. A package mortgage is one which includes personal property as well as the real property.

260.   **D**   Blanket encumbrances cover more than one parcel. Typically there will be a release clause allowing the borrower to pay a sum less than the entire remaining balance and thereby gain clear title to one of the parcels. It may also contain a provision where the payments are adjusted if such a partial payment is made, although not necessarily.

261.   **B**   Any encumbrance that covers more than one parcel is called a blanket encumbrance. A wraparound encumbrance occurs when a loan is made which includes the balance due on an underlying loan, as where a seller sells a property on a land sales contract without paying off the seller's underlying mortgage.

262.   **A**   Blanket encumbrances cover more than one parcel of real estate. An encumbrance which includes personal property as well as real property is called a package encumbrance.

263.   **A**   A package encumbrance is financing where the collateral includes personal property as well as real property. Blanket encumbrances cover more than one parcel.

264.   **D**   A mortgaged subdivision is normally encumbered with a blanket encumbrance (an encumbrance whose collateral is more than one parcel). Blanket encumbrances typically contain a lot release clause (also known as a parcel or partial release clause). The release clause allows the borrower to pay a certain amount on the principal and thereby get clear title to one of the parcels.

265.   **B**   Blanket encumbrances cover more than one parcel. The borrower may want clear title to one parcel in the future without having to pay off the entire obligation. A release clause allows the borrower to do so, specifying the amount for each parcel.

266.   **A**   A blanket encumbrance covers more than one property. A common provision in a blanket encumbrance is a clause requiring the lender to release the lien on any given parcel upon the payment of a portion of the debt (called the lot, or parcel release clause). If the blanket encumbrance is a trust deed, then the release instrument would be a partial reconveyance deed (deed of reconveyance).

267.   **B**   A blanket encumbrance creates a lien on more than one parcel. Blanket encumbrances are typical of loans made on an entire subdivision, where the encumbrance reaches each lot. It is also typical of such loans that they contain a lot release clause (also called a parcel or partial release clause). The lot release clause allows the borrower to pay a portion of the principal balance and receive clear title to an individual lot without having to pay off the entire obligation.

268.   **A**   A partial release clause (also called a lot or parcel release clause) allows a borrower to pay a portion of the principal balance and thereby receive clear title to one property covered by a blanket encumbrance.

269.   **D**   In a blanket encumbrances there will generally be a release clause. This allows the borrower to pay a portion of the remaining principal, and thereby gain clear title to one of the encumbered properties.

270.   **D**   A blanket encumbrance is typical of a loan on a subdivision taken out by a developer where the lien reaches all the lots. In order to get clear title to an individual lot, the developer will insist on a lot release clause, allowing the developer to pay a portion of the principal instead of the entire remaining balance. The lender, on the other hand, wants to be sure that the remaining lots still constitute adequate collateral for the remaining balance. Therefore, it is customary to "front-load" the payoffs, so the amount required to release the first lot is higher than the second lot, and so on. It is also customary to require a higher payment for those lots which are clearly worth more than others.

271.   **A**   Since the lender will participate in the profits, it is called a participation loan, or sometimes

equity participation loan. The slang term for the incentive offered to the lender is "equity kicker."

272.   **B**   Because the lender will participate in the equity, it is called a participation, or equity participation loan. The lender's share is also called an equity kicker.

273.   **A**   Since the lender will participate in the profits of the borrower when the property goes up in value, it is called a participation, or equity participation mortgage. The incentive (the 2% equity interest) is sometimes called an "equity kicker."

274.   **B**   When the interest rate floats according to an index the loan is said to be adjustable or variable. An escalation clause allows the lender to increase the amount of the payment or the interest rate according to a pre-agreed schedule, as opposed to being tied to an index. "Alienation clause" is a synonym for "due on sale clause."

275.   **D**   An escalator (escalation) clause in a mortgage allows the lender to increase the amount of the payment. If the lender has the option to increase the interest rate according to an index it is called a variable or adjustable rate mortgage.

276.   **D**   There are various expressions used in the lending industry to describe loans where the interest rate is tied to an index. The most common is "adjustable rate mortgage," but "variable rate mortgage" and "renegotiated rate mortgage" are also heard.

277.   **D**   Balloon payments are normally used as a device to force early payoff. The loan is typically amortized with normal monthly payments, with a clause requiring a lump sum to pay it in full at some point. However, "balloon payment" is also used to describe any extra payment on principal outside of the normally scheduled payments.

278.   **B**   The classic example of a wraparound loan is where a seller carries a contract when selling the property, but without paying off an underlying loan. The buyer makes payments to the seller on the contract, and the seller continues making payments on the underlying loan. The contract, therefore, "wraps around" the underlying loan. The same thing could happen with a third-party lender instead of the seller. Instead of having the seller carry a contract, the buyer could have a third-party lender purchase the property and assume the seller's old loan, then immediately sell to the buyer on a contract.

279.   **B**   When an owner sells a property that has an existing assumable loan on the property the buyer can assume the loan. If the buyer doesn't have enough cash, the seller could carry a second for the difference. The buyer would make two payments each month – one to the lender of the assumed loan and one to the seller. As an alternative, the seller could sell to the buyer on a contract or trust deed with a balance equal to the amount of the first the buyer would have assumed, plus the second which the seller would have carried. Now the buyer will make one payment each month to the seller. The seller, in turn, will continue making payments on the first. This is an example of a wraparound. Note that the wraparound could be a land sales contract, a trust deed, or a mortgage. What makes it a wraparound is not the instrument used, but the fact that the balance due on it includes the amount the seller owes underneath. The seller's wraparound document will be recorded subsequent to the seller's old loan, so the seller will be in second (junior) position to the original lender.

280.   **B**   In a land sales contract the seller retains legal title until the buyer has finished paying for the property, usually in installments. FHA, VA, and conventional loans are all made by institutional lenders, who use trust deeds only, not land sales contracts.

281.   **B**   A trust deed, while technically a deed, is considered a financing instrument. A mortgage is a conveyance in a few states, but not Oregon. A bargain and sale deed is an ordinary deed, commonly used to convey title.

282.   **B**   In a trust deed, the seller deeds the property to the buyer, and then the buyer gives a trust deed to a trustee for the lender. While the trust deed creates a lien on the buyer's title, the buyer is nevertheless the owner of the property. A purchase money mortgage is a mortgage carried by the seller. If the seller carries a mortgage, the seller still deeds the property to the buyer first, then the buyer gives a mortgage back to the seller. In a land sales contract the buyer promises to pay the balance to the seller, usually in installments, and the seller promises to deliver a deed to the buyer when the purchase price has been paid in full. Therefore, in a land sales contract the seller retains legal title until the buyer has finished paying for the property.

283.   **A**   In a land sales contract, if the buyer defaults, the seller can file a suit for strict foreclosure (ask for the property back), sue for specific performance of the covenant of indebtedness in the contract (seek a general judgment against the buyer), or declare a forfeiture. "Strict foreclosure" is contrasted with "foreclosure and sale" where the court orders the property sold to satisfy the debt. In strict fore-

closure the seller simply asks for the property back. Strict foreclosure is, therefore, a remedy only under a land sales contract.

284. **A** In a land sales contract the seller retains legal title until the buyer has finished paying for the property. Recording gives constructive notice and, as to financing instruments, establishes the priority date. Although a lender would be foolish not to record, it is optional under the law. An exception is the land sales contract, which must be recorded within fifteen days of the date the parties are bound, unless the contract terms provide for it to be paid in full within one year. It is permissible to record a memorandum of contract instead of the full document.

285. **D** Mortgages and trust deeds are both lien instruments which make the property collateral for a debt. The debt can be identical. However, a mortgage involves only a borrower and a lender (mortgagor and mortgagee, respectively). In the trust deed, the borrower deeds a limited power of sale to a third party (trustee). The trustee holds the power of sale in trust for the lender (beneficiary). Therefore, the trust deed is a three-party instrument.

286. **C** A mortgage and a trust deed have the same function – that is, each makes the property listed in the instrument collateral for a note. The terms on the note can be identical. Each can be foreclosed, but the procedures are different. A trust deed can be foreclosed as a mortgage, or it can be foreclosed by a trustee's sale. The time necessary to complete a trustee's sale is considerably shorter, and the borrower has no right of redemption afterward.

287. **C** In a land sales contract, the seller retains legal title during the term of the contract. The buyer promises to pay for the property in installments, and the seller agrees to deliver a deed to the buyer when the buyer has fully performed. The seller under a land sales contract can sue for strict foreclosure, declare a forfeiture, or sue the buyer for specific performance of the promise to pay. In a trust deed, the owner of a property (borrower) deeds a limited power of sale to a trustee (third party), who holds it in trust for the lender (beneficiary). The most common lender remedy in a trust deed is for the beneficiary to order the trustee to sell the property (non-judicial trustee's sale). As an alternative, the lender can sue the buyer for foreclosure and sale, the same as in a mortgage.

288. **C** A "conditional sale agreement for real estate" is a synonym for land sales contract. In a land sales contract, the buyer receives title only when the property is fully paid for. Until then, the buyer has equitable title. A purchase money mortgage is a mortgage carried by a seller of the property. To do so, the seller first deeds the property to the buyer, and then the buyer gives the seller the note and mortgage back. The only thing the two have in common is that both are carried by the seller.

289. **A** In a trust deed the borrower deeds a limited power of sale to a trustee. The trustee holds it in trust for the lender during the term of the loan. When the loan is paid off the trustee deeds the limited power of sale back to the borrower. This deed is called a deed of reconveyance. The release instrument for a mortgage is a satisfaction. When a land sales contract is paid off, the seller deeds the property to the buyer.

290. **A** In a mortgage transaction the borrower is the mortgagor. In a trust deed loan the borrower is the grantor of the trust deed.

291. **C** The original financing instrument is the mortgage. A mortgage creates a lien on the borrower's real estate to make it collateral for a note, which is the evidence of the debt. Without the note, the mortgage is useless. A trust deed is a modern replacement for a mortgage, creating a lien on the borrower's real estate to make it collateral for a debt. Like the mortgage, the trust deed is worthless without a debt, so it must be used with a note also.

292. **D** Sellers can carry the balance from the buyer on any of the three instruments used for real estate finance – mortgage, trust deed, or land sales contract. In Oregon today, the two most popular are the land sales contract and the trust deed.

293. **C** As long as the intent was clearly to create a lien on the property rather than a conveyance of it, a court would hold that the deed is a lien. Since the mortgage predates the trust deed and is considered the basic financing instrument, it would be construed as a mortgage on the real estate, rather than a trust deed or a land sales contract.

294. **D** Since Oregon is a lien theory state, a mortgage is deemed to create merely a lien. It is not a transfer of title. A trust deed is a three-party instrument, where a borrower (grantor) deeds a limited power of sale to a trustee, who holds it in trust for the lender (beneficiary). When a loan is sold for less than the face amount owing, the buyer receives a higher rate of return than the note rate. This is called loan discounting, or selling a loan at a discount. Mortgages and trust deeds make real property collat-

eral for a debt. In both cases, the debt is evidenced by a note.

295.   **C**   There are three kinds of foreclosure. If the instrument is a mortgage it must be foreclosed judicially (going to court) and the property must be sold at a sheriff's sale. A trust deed may be foreclosed by a trustee's sale, or in the same manner as provided for mortgages. In either case, the property will be sold at public auction and the lender will receive the sales proceeds. A land sales contract is always a purchase money instrument (seller carried). The collateral was originally the seller's property. Therefore, the law allows strict foreclosure of a land sales contract. Strict foreclosure means the seller gets the property back and the rights of the buyer under the contract are extinguished. There is no public auction sale in a strict foreclosure.

296.   **C**   When a mortgage is used, its function is merely to make the property collateral for a debt. The debt is evidenced by a note, so it is correct to call it a "note and mortgage" transaction. A wraparound loan is a loan whose balance owing includes the amount due on an underlying encumbrance, which the lender will keep current. The borrower makes payments to the lender on the larger balance, and the lender continues making the payments on the smaller underlying loan.

297.   **A**   Both mortgages and trust deeds create liens on real estate to make the property collateral for a debt. The debt is evidenced by a note in both cases. "Hypothecation" means pledging an asset as collateral for a debt, so the mortgage and trust deed are both hypothecation agreements.

298.   **D**   Both mortgages and trust deeds create liens on real property to make the property collateral for a debt. In both cases, a note is required as the evidence of the debt. A trust deed is a three-party instrument, where a borrower deeds a limited power of sale to a trustee and the trustee holds the power of sale in trust for a lender (beneficiary). The borrower is the grantor of the trust deed, which is the instrument which conveys the limited power of sale.

299.   **B**   The Federal Housing Administration (FHA) does not lend money; it simply insures a loan against default. The mortgagee, therefore, is a bank or other institutional lender. Regardless of who the lender is, FHA loans will be on a trust deed or mortgage. Neither conveys title to the lender. Both merely create a lien on the borrower's property to make it collateral for a note.

300.   **D**   There is no such thing as the "Veterans Foreclosure Act." The homestead exemption pro-

vides an exemption for a homestead of up to one city block, or 160 acres if outside an incorporated city, in an amount up to $25,000 for a single homesteader, or $33,000 for a married couple. The homestead exemption provides protection strictly against judgment creditors; it is of no force and effect against any other lienholder, including mortgage loans, property tax liens, construction liens, etc. The Soldiers and Sailors Civil Relief Act prohibits a lender from foreclosing on the homestead of a person while on active duty overseas. It has no effect unless the serviceperson is actually overseas on active duty during a declared hostility.

301.   **A**   In a traditional real estate transaction the seller is the principal and the broker is the agent. The agent owes a fiduciary duty to the principal. A purchase money note is a note used in lieu of cash to buy property. For example, if you buy a house for $200,000, give the seller $40,000 cash down payment and a note for $160,000, the note is a purchase money note. The seller takes a risk of having to foreclose if the borrower fails to pay. Earnest money is a good faith deposit which accompanies an offer to purchase (earnest money agreement). The earnest money agreement typically stipulates that the earnest money will be forfeit if the buyer fails to perform. Therefore, a large earnest money deposit benefits the seller.

302.   **C**   When a corporation borrows money the lender is usually in a precarious position. Because the corporation is a legal entity, it can disburse the funds to the stockholders as dividends, and then file bankruptcy. To protect the lender, it is common practice to demand that majority stockholders sign personal guaranties for the corporate debt. A personal guaranty is legally equivalent to a co-signature. A collateral agreement is also usually required. Collateral agreements make everything the signer owns collateral for a debt.

303.   **B**   "Chattel mortgage" is an older term for a security agreement, that is, an instrument which makes personal property collateral for a loan.

SOURCES OF FUNDS FOR MORTGAGE LENDING

THE REAL ESTATE AND CONSTRUCTION INDUSTRIES ARE WHAT ECONOMISTS CALL capital-intensive businesses. If you think about it, you will realize that a healthy real estate industry uses vast quantities of capital. In fact, no other industry is so dependent on capital as real estate. When credit dries up or becomes expensive, real estate sales drop dramatically, and when interest rates decline and capital is readily available, we prosper. Mortgage loans total over $6 trillion in the United States today. Where this capital comes from, and why the supply and cost of capital are forever changing, is a subject which real estate agents must understand thoroughly in order to survive. Knowing how financial conditions affect the cost and supply of capital is also crucial if a real estate agent is to be able to advise clients properly.

Let us start our discussion by taking a look at the various type of lenders — where you might go to obtain a mortgage loan on real property. Some of these lenders are referred to as *institutional lenders* because they are formal institutions created primarily to lend money. Institutional lenders include commercial banks, savings and loan associations, mutual savings banks, credit unions, mortgage bankers, finance companies and government lenders such as the Oregon Department of Veterans Affairs (ODVA).

Commercial banks constitute the single largest source of loan funds in the nation, but historically commercial banks used to shy away from heavy involvement in real estate loans, preferring instead to be providers of short term working capital to business and industry. Today, however, commercial banks are significant lenders in residential real estate.

Savings and loan associations, *mutual savings banks* (known collectively as *thrift institutions*, the *thrift industry*, or just *the thrifts*) for decades were the primary source of residential real estate loans. Unfortunately, most did not survive the bad economic times of the early 1980s. Many today have changed their name to *savings banks*, perhaps in an effort to disassociate themselves from their troubled past, and others have simply reorganized as full service commercial banks. Today there are few true thrifts left in residential lending.

Government loan programs, such as the Oregon Department of Veterans Affairs, sell tax-exempt bonds and use the funds to make low-interest loans for special purposes the government wishes to promote. Because the bonds are tax-exempt, they can be sold at low interest rates. The savings can be passed on to the borrower in the form of a low interest loan. In addition to the Oregon Department of Veterans Affairs, loans and other services funded by tax exempt bonds are available through the Oregon Department of Housing and Community Services (formerly the Oregon Housing Agency).

A *mortgage banker* is a firm which makes loans using its own funds, and then immediately sells the loans in the secondary market (see discussion of the secondary mortgage market later in this section). The sale of the loans restores the funds so the mortgage banker can make new loans. Mortgage bankers typically make their profit on the loan fees and on fees for *servicing* the loan (collecting the payments) for the secondary lender. Mortgage bankers frequently use the term "mortgage company" in their name.

Finance companies (sometimes called *small loan companies*), like mortgage bankers, do not use capital from depositors, because finance companies do not offer checking and savings accounts. Typically, finance companies borrow their funds from commercial banks or by selling corporate bonds and other corporate securities.

Insurance companies, private and public funds, real estate investment trusts (REITs), real estate mortgage trusts (REMTs) and mortgage brokers are organizations which sometimes become sources for real estate loans. Some people refer to these institutions as *quasi-institutional lenders* because they are institutions, but their primary purpose is not always to make loans, or at least not directly.

For example, insurance companies are organized primarily to provide insurance, not to make real estate loans. But insurance companies have billions of dollars in reserves to pay claims from, and these reserves must be invested. Sometimes insurance companies find real estate mortgage loans to be an excellent investment. Insurance companies invest in real estate mortgages both directly as primary lenders (when they make the loan themselves) and indirectly as secondary lenders (when they purchase pools of loans).

When we use the term *fund* we include pension funds, endowment funds, state government treasuries and private investment groups. One such fund in Oregon is the Oregon Public Employees Retirement Fund, which frequently makes loans on large commercial projects in Oregon.

Real estate investment trusts (REITs) are *business trusts* in which an investor buys shares of beneficial interest, in much the same way as stockholders buy stock in a corporation. Typically, a REIT is constituted so that the income it earns is not taxed, although the shareholders must pay tax on the earnings when they are distributed. A variant is the *Real estate mortgage trust* (REMT), which invests only in mortgages, where the REIT invests primarily by purchasing the real estate as an owner.

A *mortgage broker* is a party who locates a borrower and a lender, brings them together and arranges the loan, and collects a fee for the service. Unlike a mortgage banker, a mortgage broker does not service the loan.

Non-institutional lenders include private parties (paper buyers) and sellers who carry land sales contracts and other purchase money instruments. Most of these loans are small loans, frequently second position (junior) loans.

Some of these lenders are referred to as *financial intermediaries* because they act as intermediaries between people who have money (depositors) and people who need money (borrowers). Financial intermediaries include commercial banks, savings and loan associations, mutual savings banks, and credit unions. Mortgage bankers, mortgage brokers, finance companies, pension funds, insurance companies, and similar institutions are not financial intermediaries because they do not have customer deposits.

All financial intermediaries are also referred to as *fiduciary lenders* or *financial fiduciaries* because they have a fiduciary (trust) relationship with their depositors or investors and must follow safe and prudent lending practices to ensure the safety of their depositor's money.

Yet other lenders are referred to as *semi-fiduciary lenders* because they owe some obligations to the persons from whom they obtained their capital, but the obligation is not as strong as it is with a fiduciary institution. Examples of semi-fiduciary lenders are insurance companies, mortgage brokers, REITs and government bond programs.

Finance companies, private parties (paper buyers) and sellers who carry purchase money loans are referred to as *non-fiduciary lenders* because they are lending their own money directly and have no responsibility to anyone but themselves.

In the following section we will discuss in greater detail the real estate loan activity of each of these lenders.

Categories of Real Estate Lenders

Financial fiduciaries	*Financial intermediaries (Have customer deposits)* — **Commercial banks**, **Savings and loan associations**, **Mutual savings banks**, **Credit unions**
	Insurance companies, **Pension funds**
Quasi-fiduciaries	**Mortgage bankers**, **Mortgage brokers**, **Trusts (REIT/REMT)**, **Government bond programs**, **Private funds**
Non-fiduciaries	**Private lenders**, **Seller financing**

Institutional lenders

Non-nstitutional lenders

Exercise a

Commercial banks, savings and loans, mortgage bankers, mortgage brokers, finance companies and funds are referred to as _____ lenders. In contrast, private parties who lend money on real estate are called _____ - _____ lenders.

The majority of money in depository institutions is found in _____ _____ . A traditional source for real estate loans, however, is the _____ industry, which includes savings and loan associations and mutual savings banks. A mortgage _____ is a lender which is not a financial

_____ , *but makes real estate loans which it sells in the secondary market, yet for which it retains the servicing. In contrast, a mortgage* _____ *is a lender who arranges a loan between a borrower and a lender.*

Commercial banks

Of all the institutional lenders, the most prevalent is the commercial bank. The vast majority of lendable funds in the private sector is on deposit at commercial banks. Commercial banks have existed since ancient times, but the commercial bank as we know it today evolved largely from the banks of 17th century England.

In this country commercial banks were mostly unregulated until the National Bank Act of 1863, which required that federally chartered banks be supervised by the Comptroller of the Currency. In 1913, the Federal Reserve Act established the **Federal Reserve Bank System** (discussed in greater detail later in this section), and most banks today are regulated to some extent by the Federal Reserve Bank.

Commercial banks can be state chartered or federally chartered. While the Federal Reserve Bank System provides most of the regulation of federally chartered banks, state chartered banks are regulated by individual state regulatory agencies. In most states this gives them somewhat greater freedom, although even state chartered banks are subject to some regulation by the Federal Reserve Bank.

Customer deposits in commercial banks are insured up to $100,000 by the **Federal Deposit Insurance Corporation** (FDIC). The FDIC was organized under the provisions of the Banking Act of 1933 and originally insured deposits only in the commercial banks. The purpose of FDIC insurance was to strengthen the credibility of the private commercial banking system of the country.

The FDIC not only insures depositors against losses, but it also supervises member banks in order to prevent improper practices which could lead to failure of the bank. The FDIC conducts regular examinations of the institutions it insures and when it encounters problems, it can take corrective action. Powers of the FDIC include ordering management to change bank policy, lending funds to troubled banks and even requiring a change of bank personnel. When a member bank does fail, the FDIC acts as a receiver and proceeds to collect as much of the failed bank's assets as possible. In some cases the FDIC arranges a merger of the failed bank into a stronger local bank, or in other cases the failed bank is disbanded and the FDIC pays off the depositors directly.

Funds for operations and to pay losses are derived from premiums charged to member institutions. The reserves to pay losses (premiums paid in) comprise the **Bank Insurance Fund** (BIF). The FDIC also insures thrift institutions today, but their premiums are paid into a separate fund call the **Savings Association Insurance Fund** (SAIF). Although the FDIC has jurisdiction over both funds, bank losses can be paid only from the BIF and losses from thrifts can be paid only out of the SAIF. It is important to remember that when you put money on deposit in an insured bank or thrift the institution had to pay the premiums to keep your deposit insured. The premium is generally about ⅕ of 1% of all deposits. For each of the major banks and thrifts doing business in Oregon today that expense comes to millions of dollars a year.

Commercial banks are frequently a source of real estate loans for both residential and non-residential properties. Even today, however, commercial banks retain a strong sense that their primary role should be to provide working capital for business and industry, not long term real estate lending. Another hallmark of the commercial bank is their insistence on maintaining a high degree of liquidity. ***Liquidity*** refers to the ease with which an asset can be converted to cash.

Both of these attitudes are derived from sense of history. Before 1913 there was no Federal Reserve Bank to supply liquidity, and before 1933 there was no Federal Deposit Insurance Corporation to ensure the safety of customer deposits. As a result, runs on banks were common and national financial panics sometimes occurred. Bankers had to be able to convert their loan portfolio to cash (call the loans due) in such circumstances. Long term real estate loans simply could not be called due because, even if the loan instrument contained a demand clause, the borrower did not have the funds anyway. Businesses, on the other hand, could usually pay a loan off, by refinancing at another institution, if necessary. Loans to business and industry are also typically short term, which allows the lender to renegotiate the interest rates periodically in order to maintain the loan portfolio at market rates.

As a result, commercial banks generally only make residential real estate loans which can be sold in the secondary mortgage market. Originally these included only loans insured by the Federal Housing Administration (FHA), or guaranteed by the federal Department of Veterans Affairs (federal GI loans). Today conventional loans can also easily be sold in the secondary market, so commercial banks are now active in the conventional loan market as well. In lender terminology, a ***portfolio loan*** means either a loan which cannot be sold in the secondary market, or which the lender at least has not yet sold. Portfolio loans are rare today for any lender, but are least likely to be granted by a commercial bank than by other institutional lenders.

Commercial banks are also a source of temporary construction financing (also called ***interim financing***), particularly for commercial construction projects and subdivisions. Loans for home improvements are also commonly available from commercial banks. Note that these loans are not as easily sold in the secondary mortgage market, so a bank will likely insist that they be short term loans.

Commercial banks also participate indirectly in real estate lending by lending funds to other real estate lenders, such as REITs (discussed in more detail later), as well as finance companies and mortgage bankers. Also, commercial banks sometimes make real estate loans indirectly by owning a mortgage banking firm, finance company or other lending institution. Many commercial banks have trust departments which manage large sums of money which is part of an estate or employee pension fund. These bank trust departments sometimes make low-risk real estate loans as an avenue to invest these funds.

In recent years one of the most popular real estate loans for commercial banks is the home equity loan – generally short term, small dollar amount, and with above-market yields. Notice how such loans fit well with the historical attitude of the commercial bank.

Savings and loans

Among thrift institutions, mutual savings banks predominate only in New England. Everywhere else in the country, savings and loan associations outnumber mutual savings banks by a large margin. This is true in spite of the fact that mutual savings banks and savings and loan associations grew up practically side by side.

The first home purchase financed with a loan from a savings and loan association was in 1831 in Philadelphia. Savings and loan associations (originally called ***building and loan associations***) grew slowly but steadily. They were founded on the concept of being a community-based non-profit alternative to the commercial bank – much the same philosophy as is found at credit unions today.

Today, however, there are few mutual non-profit savings and loans; almost all are investor owned for-profit institutions. Today's savings and loan associations typically offer a full range of banking services, but savings accounts and residential mortgages remain their primary business activity.

Savings and loan associations went largely unregulated until 1932 when the Federal Home Loan Bank System was created. Where the Federal Reserve Bank regulates and provides liquidity for member commercial banks, the Federal Home Loan Bank (FHLB) was created to do the same for member thrift institutions. In recent years, however, a great many thrift institutions became insolvent. Although the reasons for this are complex, the result was that regulation of thrift institutions was removed from the FHLB and transferred to a new agency, the Office of Thrift Supervision (OTS), a subsidiary organization under the U.S. Treasury.

Mutual savings banks

Mutual savings banks originated on the east coast during the early and middle 1800s. The vast majority of mutual savings banks are still located in New England states, although occasional mutual savings banks are found in other states. Their original purpose was to provide a place where working people could deposit their savings and be paid attractive interest rates, while at the same time providing consumer loans to the same class of customers, largely for home acquisition.

Note that this is essentially the same philosophy upon which savings and loans are based, which is why real estate agents tend to place mutual savings banks in the same class as savings and loans. The important difference with mutual savings banks is that they are always mutual — that is, the profits are distributed to the depositors as dividends. Today there are practically no true mutual savings banks left. Almost all that survived the financial crisis of the 1980s converted to for-profit regular banks.

Credit unions

Credit unions are always mutual, non-profit organizations. They are insured by the National Credit Union Administration (NCUA) which performs the same role for credit unions as the FDIC does for commercial banks and thrift institutions. Since credit unions are non-profit organizations they are able to offer higher interest rates to depositors and lower interest rates on loans. Because this gives them an advantage over commercial banks and thrifts, their membership is restricted in some manner. They tend to refer to their customers as "members" in order to promote a sense of mutual interests.

Although credit unions make relatively few mortgage loans, they are legally empowered to make any kind of real estate loan. Credit unions are a common source for junior financing, but first mortgage financing is difficult for most credit unions because of their size. Credit unions are generally small organizations and cannot usually afford to hire staff with sufficient expertise to make a first mortgage loan and sell it in the secondary market. Nevertheless, some of the larger credit unions do become active in the first mortgage market, and real estate agents should not overlook even the smaller organizations as sources for junior financing.

Insurance companies

Most life insurance policies are really insurance coupled with an *annuity*. That is, when you buy a typical (whole life) insurance policy you are insured and the full amount of the policy will be paid if there is a claim, but every time you make a premium payment you also build up a *reserve*. Eventually, your policy will be paid up, and then the insurance company will start paying you the money back. In effect, most life insurance is really insurance coupled with a retirement savings account.

Insurance companies must invest these reserves. Most life insurance companies prefer to invest the bulk of their reserves in the bond market. Depending on market conditions, this will range from 30-40% of their total assets. However, real estate mortgages are their second most popular type of investment, accounting for 20-40% of their assets, again, depending on market conditions. As mortgage lenders, life insurance companies can be very competitive because their cost of funds is very low. They are able to pay rates on the reserves to their policyholders which are much less than the rates the policyholder could get from a savings institution because they are also giving them insurance at the same time. Also, net premiums after claims payments from term insurance (straight insurance without the annuity build-up) must be invested as well, and there is no cost for these funds.

Insurance companies are regulated by the insurance laws and regulations of the states where they do business. These laws and regulations set the loan to value ratios and other lending requirements. However, insurance companies are the least regulated of all institutional lenders.

Insurance companies, primarily life insurance companies, account for relatively few residential loans, but are a frequent source of funds for large commercial projects such as office buildings and shopping centers. Not only do they prefer large commercial projects. but they also prefer loans which are very safe. Typically, a loan from an insurance company would not exceed 80% loan to value ratio and frequently as low as 70-75% of the value.

Another common feature in insurance company financing is an **equity kicker** – a low interest rate in exchange for a participation in the equity build-up when the property is sold. If the property is not sold, then the mortgage usually requires an appraisal at some point in the future, at which time the lender's share of the equity build-up is added to the loan balance. Such loans are also referred to as **equity participation loans**, or **shared appreciation loans**.

Many insurance companies service their loans themselves, but most employ mortgage brokers to arrange the loans. Increasingly, however, insurance companies employ the services of a mortgage banker (discussed later) to service loans as well as originate them. Insurance companies also participate in the residential field by purchasing loans as a secondary lender.

Funds

There are various types of funds which operate as mortgage lenders. Some of these are private, such as investment corporations and pension funds for private companies. Other funds are public agencies such as state treasuries, public pension funds, and the like. Their assets range from a few million dollars to hundreds of millions of dollars.

Those funds which are retirement funds are the most heavily involved in real estate lending. The interesting thing about the billions of dollars held in pension funds is the similarity between this pool of money and the funds held in life insurance reserves. Both are paid into the fund in installments over many years and both are very stable with a large dollar amount available for long term investment.

Approximately one-half of all non-government workers are covered by some form of private pension plan (usually company sponsored), other than Social Security. In addition, about three-fourths of all government personnel are enrolled in private retirement plans. In the past, the pension funds have not contributed directly as real estate lenders, although some (mostly private investment funds) have mimicked the life insurance companies and invest in mortgage loans on large commercial projects. Many people in the real estate field hope to see the pension funds put more of their assets to work in residential real estate. However, the likelihood is that if they begin to invest in residential real estate they will most likely do so as purchasers of securities issued by the secondary mortgage market, not as direct primary lenders.

Mortgage bankers

The term ***mortgage banker*** sounds as though it means a person who works for a lender and makes mortgage loans. In fact, the term refers to a company, not an individual, which originates mortgage loans and sells the loans to investors. The mortgage banker continues to service the loan – collects the payments, sees that the taxes are paid, and even supervises a foreclosure – which is why they are also occasionally called ***loan correspondents***. In many cases, the borrower does not even realize the loan has been sold.

Mortgage banking existed as far back as the turn of the century, but did not become a serious force in mortgage lending until the Federal Housing Administration (FHA) was created in 1934, and the Federal National Mortgage Association (Fannie Mae) was added in 1938. The FHA created standardized loans which meet minimum requirements and which are insured against default by the FHA, an agency of the federal government. The fact that these loans all conform to minimum standards and are insured by the FHA makes them attractive to investors. As a result, Fannie Mae was created to purchase the loans as a secondary lender. Mortgage bankers came into existence to make the FHA loans and service them for Fannie Mae.

Following World War II loans guaranteed by the federal Department of Veterans Affairs (formerly the Veterans Administration) came into being, and mortgage bankers began making "VA" loans as well. Both FHA and VA loans could be sold to Fannie Mae. In more recent years, Fannie Mae and other newer secondary lenders have become the primary purchasers of conventional loans also. As a rule, mortgage bankers must sell the loans they originate because they have limited funds of their own. Since FHA, VA and conventional loans are all salable today, mortgage bankers now make virtually any kind of residential loan. Furthermore, today there are a multitude of secondary mortgage lenders (investors) in addition to Fannie Mae, and practically all of them buy mortgages from mortgage bankers.

It is important to understand that a mortgage banker is not a "banker" in the traditional sense. You cannot go to a mortgage banker and open up a checking or savings account. Mortgage bankers use their own funds (funds invested by stock- and bondholders) to make the loan. The profit in mortgage banking is derived from the loan origination fees and the servicing fees.

In fact, servicing the loan is sufficiently profitable that lenders frequently sell the servicing contracts on their loans. This practice has created a great deal of confusion for borrowers. A borrower may suddenly be told to make future payments to a different lender. This can happen repeatedly, with obvious potential for lost and misposted payments. As a result, Congress has enacted legislation to regulate the sale of servicing contracts.

Larger mortgage banking firms supply their own capital to make the loans, and then package them for sale to secondary lenders in large blocks. However, smaller mortgage bankers engage in a practice called ***warehousing***. A mortgage banker who does not have the funds to complete the package will go to a commercial bank to borrow the funds, frequently pledging existing loans already on the books as collateral. This suits the commercial bank because their major function is to provide short term working capital. When the mortgage banker completes the package, it is sold in the secondary market and the proceeds of the sale are used to pay back the commercial bank.

Mortgage brokers

The Depository Institution Deregulation and Monetary Control Act of 1980 (DIDMCA) made sweeping changes in the regulations of financial intermediaries. One of these changes is important to note here. Prior to 1980, financial intermediaries were permitted to make mortgage loans only within certain geographical limits, usually only within their state boundaries. DIDMCA removed most of these geographical restrictions.

This had a profound effect on mortgage lending, for it turned the mortgage market from a local market to a national market practically overnight. Suddenly, local banks, savings and loans, mutual savings banks and mortgage bankers found themselves receiving stiff competition from similar institutions in other states. In retaliation, each institution attempted to gain loans from other areas. Of course, the final result was beneficial for both consumers and lenders. Consumers benefit when there is greater competition, and the lenders benefit from greater diversification in their loan portfolios.

However, this creates a problem. How can you originate a loan in a community unless you have a branch office there? The answer is simple – employ the services of a local **mortgage broker**. The concept of mortgage brokerage has been in existence since practically the day the first loan was created. The basic idea is simple. A mortgage broker brings a borrower and a lender together, collects a fee (commission) for acting as go-between, and departs the scene. Unlike a mortgage banker, the mortgage broker does not service the loan. In fact, mortgage brokers today are as likely to represent mortgage bankers as they are to represent any other kind of lender.

Most lenders today charge **loan origination fees** (usually called simply **loan fees**) to increase their profitability. On some FHA insured loans and on all federal GI guaranteed loans, the government sets the maximum amount of the loan fee, usually about 1% of the loan balance. On conventional loans, there is no maximum, although competition tends to hold the rate at around 2% of the loan balance. Among commercial banks, thrift institutions and mortgage bankers there has always been an unwritten philosophy that the loan origination fees should pay for maintaining the office and the salaries of the loan officers and staff required to get the loan on the books. Other expenses of operation should be paid out of the profit on the loan – the spread between the cost of the funds (interest paid out) and the interest earned on the loan. Or, if the loan has been sold in the secondary market, the servicing fees should pay for the rest of the expenses and profit.

Now, if a mortgage lender doesn't have to maintain a branch office and pay loan officers' salaries, then all the loan fee is available to pay as a commission to a local mortgage broker. This is exactly what has happened since 1980. We now have mortgage brokers who take applications from borrowers and place the borrower's applications with lenders the broker represents. Since the mortgage broker knows each lender's particular requirements, the broker can match the borrower with the lender most likely to make the loan. The lender allows the broker to retain the loan fee as a commission.

Of course, mortgage brokers also broker loans other than residential loans. In fact, only since 1980 have mortgage brokers been active in residential loans. In the past, mortgage brokers tended to specialize in certain types of loans, usually loans for large commercial projects, vacant land, or other less common situations, and some mortgage brokers still provide these services.

Real estate trusts

Real estate trusts come in two main categories – **real estate investment trusts** (**REITs**), and **real estate mortgage trusts** (**REMTs**), although there are also real estate trusts which are called **combination**, or **hybrid trusts**, which take on aspects of both types of trust.

Real estate investment trusts invest in real estate equities, that is to say, they purchase properties for investment. A REMT lends money as a mortgage lender. Combination trusts sometimes invest as owners and sometimes as mortgage lenders. A REIT which invests solely as purchaser of real estate is called an ***equity REIT***.

Real estate trusts came into being as a result of the enactment of the Real Estate Investment Trust Act of 1960, which allowed the creation of trusts to invest in real estate equities and/or real estate mortgages as tax-exempt entities. In this respect, REMTs and REITs operate in much the same way as mutual funds do in the stock and bond markets. For example, a mutual fund invests shareholders' funds and distributes the profits to the shareholders by way of dividends. If the mutual fund meets the criteria required by the law, the mutual fund is tax-exempt – so all the profits are passed through directly to the shareholders. Of course, the shareholders must pay tax on their earnings, but double taxation is avoided. Real estate trusts operate the same way. As long as the trust qualifies, it pays no income taxes.

Real estate mortgage trusts have had a significant impact in financing of commercial projects. A typical REMT attracts capital not only by selling shares to investors, but also by borrowing from a commercial bank, or even sometimes from a REIT. It is not uncommon for a commercial bank or a REIT to sponsor or even own the REMT. Real estate mortgage trusts require higher interest rates than other mortgage lenders, partly because their investors demand a higher return and also because capital borrowed from commercial banks must be at market prime rate. Lending by real estate trusts is generally short term and usually as junior financing, primarily for large commercial projects.

In order to qualify as a REIT or REMT, the trust must meet various requirements, including the following –

- The trust may own real property, but not as a dealer for resale,
- There must be at least 100 investors,
- The top five investors must not own more than 50% of the total shares,
- The trust must be organized as a business trust which issues shares of beneficial interest, and not as a corporation which issues shares of stock,
- 95% of the trust's income must be derived from investments,
- 75% of the trust's income must be derived from real estate investments (equities or mortgage loans),
- A maximum of 30% of the annual income can come from securities held for less than twelve months, or real estate held for less than four years, and
- Each year the trust must pay out at least 95% of its profits to the shareholders.

Mortgage bonds

With some exceptions, state governments are allowed to borrow money by issuing bonds which are exempt from federal income tax. That is to say, investors who buy the tax-exempt bonds do not pay federal income tax on the interest income. If the state passes a statute exempting a bond issue from state income taxes as well, then the interest income will be what investors call ***double tax-exempt***. Because the interest income is double tax-exempt, the issuing agency can sell the bonds at very low rates.

If the funds from the bond sale are used to fund mortgage loans, the interest rate on the loans can be correspondingly low. States commonly use bond issues to make low-interest mortgage loans available to promote special government purposes such as urban renewal, low-income housing, and so forth. Of course, bondholders eventually have to be repaid, so the bond issue will structured in a manner to ensure that the revenue generated from loan repayments will be sufficient to repay the bonds.

In Oregon we have two examples of mortgage revenue bond programs. The Oregon Department of Veterans Affairs (ODVA) at one time was the largest residential mortgage lender in the state. Although its role is considerably diminished from its heyday in the 1970s, it is still the largest mortgage revenue bond program in Oregon. The ODVA makes loans directly and services them itself. Started in 1945 to make farm and home loans to eligible veterans, the program has been very popular. The ODVA currently holds several billion dollars in mortgage loans, and has a corresponding bonded indebtedness. Details about ODVA loans are covered in the section on Government Financing Programs.

Oregon's other mortgage revenue bond program is the **Single Family Mortgage Purchase Program**, which was begun in 1974 as an effort to provide low-interest financing for low- and moderate-income borrowers. You may hear people still refer to the program under the name of a discontinued similar program called "Loans to Lenders." The Single Family Mortgage Purchase Program is administered by the Oregon Department of Housing and Community Services (formerly the Oregon Housing Agency). The Department sells tax-exempt revenue bonds, and uses the funds to purchase mortgages which are originated by private primary lenders, such as local commercial banks, thrifts and mortgage bankers. The lender agrees to make the loan according to the standards and at a below-market interest rate set by the Department. Then the Department purchases the loan. Even though the interest rate is below market, the Department can buy the loan at face value because they have acquired the funds at double tax-exempt rates. Operations of the Oregon Housing Agency are covered in more detail in the section on Government Financing Programs.

Private lenders

Financing can sometimes be arranged from private lenders. Private lenders can generally be grouped into those who are private parties (who usually buy loans originated by sellers, rather than lend directly themselves) and those which are more institutional in nature, such as finance companies and other small loan companies.

These lines of distinction become somewhat gray, because some private paper buyers become large enough to have an office and start looking fairly institutional. And some finance companies not only make loans themselves, but also buy real estate paper generated by others. Finance companies in Oregon must be licensed, so there is some regulation. However, even though licensed, they are largely unregulated as to the type of loan which they can make. Most finance companies prefer junior liens in small dollar amounts, although some commercial banks have spawned fairly large finance companies as subsidiaries for the express purpose of lending on junior liens for large commercial projects, as well as residential loans. The private party lender is, of course, totally unregulated, but usually likes to limit exposure to 80% of the value of the property. Both private parties and finance companies insist on very high yields.

Seller financing

The seller of the property is a common source of funding for a real estate purchase. The percentage of transactions which involve seller financing varies dramatically with market conditions. Usually the seller would prefer to be cashed out, but some properties are just not amenable to outside financing. For example loans to finance vacant land, and loans to finance unique special purpose properties are difficult to place with outside lenders.

The seller will likely have to discount the sales price dramatically to attract an all-cash buyer. Also, in difficult times when interest rates are high, the seller may find it expedient to carry the loan, in fact, it may be the only way to sell the property. Seller

NOTES | financing involves every conceivable kind of instrument – land sales contracts, purchase money trust deeds, junior liens, wraparounds, balloon payments, sale leasebacks – and every other creative device that real estate agents have been able to conjure up. This area is so complex that all of the section on Alternative Financing has been devoted to it.

Exercise b

Funds on deposit in commercial banks are insured up to _____ by the Federal Deposit Insurance Corporation (FDIC). Historically, commercial banks avoided real estate loans because they insisted on _____ . Therefore, commercial banks generally do not make _____ loans.

Thrift institutions include _____ and _____ associations, as well as _____ _____ banks, which are not common outside of New England. Thrifts are regulated by the _____ of _____ _____ , a branch of the U.S. Treasury.

Credit unions are always _____ - _____ institutions, organized for the benefit of their customers, who are called _____ . Credit unions are a common source of financing, but _____ mortgage loans are difficult for all but the larger credit unions.

Insurance companies invest a large part of their _____ in real estate mortgages. When they lend directly, it is usually for a large _____ project, in which they frequently use an _____ _____ . In residential financing, they usually participate by purchasing pools of loans as _____ lenders. They tend to be very _____ lenders.

A _____ _____ has no customer funds on deposit, but rather uses its own funds to originate the loan, and then _____ the loan in the _____ market. It earns its profit on the loan _____ fees and on the fees for _____ the loan over its life.

A lender who brings a borrower and lender together but does not service the loan after it is made is called a _____ _____ .

Provided they meet certain criteria, income earned by a real estate _____ is exempt from taxation. These institutions are commonly called _____ s and _____ s, depending on whether they invest in real estate equities or in real estate mortgages. Those who do both are called _____ , or _____ _____ .

The Oregon Department of Veterans Affairs and the Oregon Department of Housing and Community Services both sell _____ - _____ revenue bonds at low interest rates and use the money for real estate loans.

Real estate cycles

The real estate market tends to run in cycles of boom and bust. For the most part, these cycles are caused by the availability and cost of mortgage funds. When mortgage funds are in short supply and interest rates are high, not as many buyers can qualify for the monthly payments necessary to amortize the debt. This causes fewer sales. Conversely, when interest rates are low, the real estate market picks up and sales volume is good.

General economic conditions can also contribute to the cycle. For example, the wood products industry is one of Oregon's major industries. When it is in a slump due to a national slowdown in the demand for its products or due to extreme competition, Oregon's entire economy slows down. Even if mortgage funds are readily available and interest rates are reasonable, it will be difficult to have a good real estate market under these conditions. Of course, in Oregon we have a double problem with interest rates, for when interest rates are high in Oregon, they are also high in the rest of the country. This causes the real estate market in the rest of the country to be slow also. This, in turn, causes there to be fewer construction starts nationwide, which further lowers the demand for wood products.

What causes these cycles of high and low interest rates? Why can't we just have a set interest rate that varies only a little over the years? This would be an ideal, but in a free-market economy, it is difficult to achieve. These are some of the questions to which we will turn our attention next.

The supply and cost of loan funds is determined by various complex institutions and their reactions to economic conditions. Not the least of these institutions is Congress and the Office of the President, both of whom want nothing but good economic times, particularly in an election year.

Every year Congress and the President create a budget for the coming fiscal year. In response to budgetary considerations, Congress and the President also change the tax rates from time to time. We all know that this process frequently creates a deficit. How big the deficit is, how it is funded, how high the tax rates are, are all controlled by Congress and the President. The Federal Treasury is charged with the responsibility of managing not just the deficits, but the entire national debt. This is referred to as **fiscal policy**, and is an important force in determining the course of the economy.

However, a more powerful force is the Federal Reserve System. In theory, the Federal Reserve System is supposed to manipulate and control the economy to smooth out the effects of fiscal policy. This is called **monetary policy**. Other institutions which have some effect on mortgage lending (but not on lending in general) are the Federal Home Loan Bank, the Office of Thrift Supervision, and the institutions of the secondary market (Fannie Mae, Freddie Mac, and Ginnie Mae, among others).

The Federal Reserve System

The Federal Reserve System was established by the Federal Reserve Act of 1913. As the nation's central bank, it attempts to ensure that the growth of money and credit over the long run is sufficient to provide a rising standard of living for Americans.

Over the short run, the Federal Reserve Bank System seeks to adapt its policies in an effort to combat deflationary or inflationary pressures. And as a lender of last resort, it is responsible for making and adjusting policy decisions as necessary to forestall national liquidity crises and financial panics.

The Federal Reserve System (sometimes called the Federal Reserve Bank, but usually referred to by bankers as "the Fed") is a central banking system composed of twelve federal reserve districts, each of which contains a federal reserve bank. The operations of the twelve federal reserve banks are coordinated and governed by a seven-member Board of Governors.

All federally chartered banks are required to be members of the Federal Reserve System. In addition, some state chartered commercial banks and some thrifts are members. In order to join, a member bank must agree to the regulations of the Federal Reserve System, and must purchase capital stock in the Federal Reserve Bank equal to 3% of the institution's net worth. Banks receive many benefits from membership, but one of the most important is that the Federal Reserve Bank will lend them money.

NOTES

The monetary policy of the Federal Reserve System includes three major functions (called ***instruments of credit policy***). These functions are the regulation of the reserve ratios of member banks (percentage of the bank's deposits that it must keep invested in federal securities), adjustment of the discount and federal funds rates (the rate charged when a member bank borrows from the Federal Reserve Bank or from another bank) and open market activity (purchase and sale of federal securities). These are discussed in detail below.

One of the requirements the Federal Reserve imposes on all banks (not just its members) is to maintain a ***reserve ratio***. Part of the purpose of the reserve ratio is to ensure that the bank remains solvent and has enough funds available to serve depositors' ordinary day-to-day banking needs. However, this is no longer the main purpose of the reserve requirement. Today, the Federal Reserve System changes the reserve requirement as a means of manipulating the economy. If the percentage is raised by, say, one percent, then one percent of the funds in all member banks would suddenly have to be invested in federal securities, and unavailable for loans to customers. If the supply of lendable funds shrinks, with no change in demand, interest rates will go up, which in turn will slow down the economy.

But, while it would slow down the economy, it would also have the side effect of increasing unemployment rates. So, perhaps it would be politically better to lower the reserve ratio. The effect of lowering the reserve ratio would be to increase the funds member institutions have available for lending. Assuming no change in demand, interest rates would go down. This would stimulate the economy. However, in an economy in which there is an excess of demand, merchants and suppliers are able to charge more, and this translates into inflation. So the Federal Reserve System changes the reserve ratio with care, and in conjunction with the other instruments of credit policy, to keep the economy on an even keel. The reserve ratio varies from about 3% for long term deposits to 22% for checking accounts.

The Federal Reserve System is comprised of 12 Federal Reserve Banks, some of which have branches. The twelfth district (shaded on this map) is served by the Federal Reserve Bank of San Francisco. The Federal Reserve Bank of San Francisco has branches in Los Angeles, Portland, Salt Lake City and Seattle. Note that the twelfth district is geographically the largest district. This is because the districts were apportioned roughly according to population as it existed in 1913 when the system was created. Federal Reserve Banks are also located in Atlanta, Boston, Chicago, Cleveland, Dallas, Kansas City, Minneapolis, Richmond, St. Louis, New York and Philadelphia.The Board of Governors meets in Washington, D.C.

When the Federal Reserve Bank lends funds to a member bank, it charges interest on those funds. The rate the Federal Reserve Bank Board of Governors sets on these funds is called the ***discount rate***. Changes in the discount rate affect the interest rates that the borrowing bank must charge its customers. Of course, this has a profound effect on the nation's economy. Lowering the discount rate lowers interest rates member banks charge their customers, and heats up the economy, and raising the discount rate will slow down the economy because member banks will have to charge their customers more.

If the Federal Reserve Bank raises the discount rate a member bank in need of additional funds will be stimulated to seek the funds elsewhere. A logical alternative is to borrow from another bank. Most commercial banks have borrowing relationships with other banks, usually banks in a different region – after all, you wouldn't want to owe money to a competitor across the street. When a bank borrows from another bank it is called borrowing ***federal funds***. Note that this process nullifies the effects the discount rate. If the Fed raises the discount rate, banks will just borrow from each other instead. So, in order to use the interest rate on borrowings by commercial banks as a tool to manipulate the economy, the Fed also manipulates the rates banks charge each other on federal funds. Today the Fed almost always maintains the rate on federal funds lower than the discount rate, so the real regulation is the federal funds rate. The purpose of setting the federal funds rate lower than the discount rate is to encourage banks to borrow from each other instead of borrowing from the Federal Reserve Bank.

Prime rate Every bank establishes its own ***prime rate***, which is the rate it charges its best corporate customers. While the discount rate and the federal funds rate have an influence on a bank's prime rate, there is no direct relationship. Banks are free to set their own prime rate as they wish. Of course, every bank feels intense competition from other banks, so when one bank changes its prime rate other banks in the community generally follow suit immediately. For this reason it may appear to the public that the prime rate is somehow set by a regulatory body, but that is not the case.

The third instrument of credit policy is ***open market activity***. This is controlled by the Federal Open Market Committee (FOMC). The FOMC is made up of the Board of Governors of the Federal Reserve System (all seven members), plus four of the presidents of the twelve district banks, and the President of the Federal Reserve Bank of New York. Open market activity consists of buying and selling federal securities, such as treasury bills, notes and bonds and bond issues of federal agencies.

The FOMC meets monthly to decide when, how many, and which kind of federal securities the Federal Reserve System should sell. When the Federal Reserve System sells securities it absorbs money from the private banking system – that is, banks will buy the securities rather than invest in loans. If the Federal Reserve System buys securities back, it pumps money into the banking system. Selling securities slows down the economy, and buying securities heats it up.

The U.S. Treasury

While the Federal Reserve System is responsible for monetary policy, the Treasury is responsible for fiscal policy – including management of the federal debt, as well as day-to-day operations. The Treasury's funds come from tax receipts. These funds are kept on deposit in the twelve Federal Reserve Banks and in private banks which are members of the Federal Reserve System. In fact, these institutions act as agents for the Treasury in the collection of employers' withholding taxes.

The Treasury issues three basic types of security – ***treasury certificates***, which have maturities from five to ten years, ***treasury notes***, with maturities of from one to five years, and ***treasury bills***, which have maturities of three months, six months, and sometimes one year. The total national debt is made up of a mix of these securities. How the Treasury funds the debt, which securities it issues and when, can have a major effect on the supply of lendable funds in the private sector. In theory, selling securities should remove money from the economy and slow things down, while repaying securities as they come due should pump money into the economy and heat things up.

In real life, the decisions of the Treasury are not always motivated by economic considerations. For example, if there is a huge deficit, the Treasury has no choice but to borrow additional funds (issue more securities). Thus it becomes the task of the Federal Reserve Bank to minimize the effect of this borrowing. The Federal Reserve System would probably do so by buying some or all of the securities itself. To do so, it might issue its own federal reserve notes (print currency) to raise some or all of the funds. Unfortunately, this would increase the money supply, which ultimately will result in inflation.

Another important function of the Treasury has been to supply the initial funds to start many of the institutions on which we depend today to create stability in real estate lending. The Federal Home Loan Bank (FHLB), the Federal National Mortgage Association (Fannie Mae) and a few other institutions, are capital stock organizations (owned by stockholders). The initial stock subscription was purchased by the Treasury in order to get these organizations going. Without the initial investment by the Treasury, these organizations would not exist today.

The Federal Home Loan Bank System

In 1932 Congress created the Federal Home Loan Bank System (FHLBS). The purpose of the FHLBS was, and remains, to provide financial stability for member institutions. Savings and loans, mutual savings banks and life insurance companies may be members of the FHLBS.

The FHLBS is patterned after the Federal Reserve Bank System. There are 12 Federal Home Loan Banks, each serving the needs of one of the twelve Federal Home Loan Bank districts (although the boundaries are not the same as the boundaries of the twelve federal reserve districts). The system is governed by a three-member board, plus the Federal Savings and Loan Advisory Council which is composed of 18 members, twelve of whom are elected (one from each district) and four of whom are appointed by the Board. The Council advises the Board on policy decisions.

All federally chartered savings and loans must be members of the FHLBS. State chartered institutions, mutual savings banks and life insurance companies may also join. Even state chartered institutions in Oregon are likely to be members of the FHLBS. Membership in the FHLBS requires that the institutions purchase FHLBS capital stock equal to 3% of their total assets.

The FHLBS provides regulation and liquidity to its member institutions, in much the same way as the Federal Reserve Bank System does for commercial banks. Regulations include a reserve ratio, which is adjusted from time to time as market conditions dictate. However, the percentage of reserves required is lower than the percentage the Federal Reserve System requires of commercial banks, because accounts in savings institutions are more stable and for longer terms.

In addition to the funds from the sale of capital stock to its members, the FHLBS raises money by selling securities to investors. These securities are sold for the FHLBS through the open market activity of the Federal Reserve System. Member institutions may borrow from their district Federal Home Loan Bank. Most Federal Home Loan Bank lending is to enable a member institution to forestall insolvency by restructuring the organization.

For real estate lenders, one of the most significant actions of the FHLBS was the creation of the Federal Home Loan Mortgage Corporation (Freddie Mac), a subsidiary of the FHLBS. Freddie Mac purchases loans as a secondary lender. It also publishes a journal in which it publishes various interest rates. Many lenders use these interest rates as indexes for variable and adjustable rate loans. Other operations of Freddie Mac are discussed in greater detail later in this section.

Exercise c

Real estate cycles are primarily caused by fluctuations in _____ rates on mortgage loans, although local economic conditions can also affect real estate cycles.

Operations and decisions of the Treasury are referred to as _____ policy. The Federal Reserve System creates _____ policy. This policy is implemented by three _____ of credit policy. The Federal Reserve Bank will _____ money to a member institution.

The Federal Reserve Bank can manipulate the supply of money by changing the reserve ratio, that is, the percentage of a member bank's _____ which it must keep invested in federal obligations. If the Federal Reserve System raises the reserve ratio, member banks have _____ money to lend. If the reserve ratio is lowered, member banks will have _____ money to lend. The Federal Reserve System can also manipulate the supply of money by changing the discount rate, which is the rate that is charged member banks who _____ from their Federal Reserve Bank. Raising the discount rate tends to ❑ heat up ❑ slow down the economy, while lowering it tends to ❑ heat up ❑ slow down the economy.

The Fed can also control the economy through its open market operations, which consists of buying and selling federal _____ . Buying tends to ❑ heat up ❑ slow down the economy, while selling tends to ❑ heat up ❑ slow down the economy.

The Federal Home Loan Bank System is made up of _____ district banks. The major purpose of the FHLBS is to provide stability and _____ for its member institutions. To accomplish this, the FHLBS sells securities through the _____ _____ _____ of the Federal Reserve Bank System, and then re-lends the funds to member institutions. The FHLB also establishes a _____ _____ for its member institutions through the operations of the Federal _____ _____ _____ Corporation.

The secondary mortgage market

When a lender sells a loan, the originating lender is called the primary lender and the lender who buys the loan is called the secondary lender. As a group, secondary lenders make up what is called the secondary mortgage market.

When a primary lender sells the loan to the secondary lender someone still has to collect the payments, see that the property taxes are paid, and generally look after the asset. This process is called loan servicing, and is usually done by the primary lender. In other words, a primary lender makes the loan, sells it to the secondary lender, but continues to collect the payments, which are remitted to the secondary lender as they are received from the borrower. Typically, the borrower is not even told that the loan has been sold. Of course, loan servicing is not free – the secondary lender must agree to a servicing fee. Today, servicing fees run about ⅜ of 1%. So, a secondary lender buying an 8½% loan, really only receives an 8⅛% yield, the remaining ⅜ of 1% is retained by the primary lender for servicing the loan.

Before the great depression of the 1930s, the idea of a secondary market was really only a dream. Occasionally, a primary lender would be able to sell a block of loans to a secondary lender – for example, a commercial bank might sell a block of loans to an insurance company. But this practice was infrequent. The idea of selling loans to investors was an attractive idea to lenders, but investors were not interested in loans without uniform standards. One bank might do an excellent job of making loans, but another bank might do a terrible job. How was an investor to know whom to buy loans from?

The problem was eventually solved when the Federal Housing Administration (FHA) was created in 1934. The FHA is a government-owned insurance company. With rare exceptions, the FHA does not lend money. Instead, the FHA insures loans against default. The loans are actually made and funded by private lenders such as commercial banks, mutual savings banks and mortgage bankers. In FHA terminology, these lenders are called ***participating lenders***, because they have been approved to participate in the FHA mortgage insurance program. The FHA will bear the loss if the loan must be foreclosed and the property does not sell for enough to cover the balance due, so the FHA insists that each loan meet certain minimum standards.

Since the FHA is huge, it insures millions of loans. And each loan meets minimum standards. Once the FHA got underway, many investors were attracted to FHA insured loans as an investment, and a true secondary mortgage market became possible.

Fannie Mae

Within a short time it became apparent that, in spite of FHA standardization and insurance, there were just not enough investors available to purchase all the loans that participating lenders wished to sell.

So, in 1938, a federal secondary lender was established. Its original name was the National Mortgage Association of Washington, which was later changed to the ***Federal National Mortgage Association*** (FNMA). It quickly gained the nickname "***Fannie Mae***" among investors. Today, FNMA has adopted the name "Fannie Mae" as its official corporate name, although it also goes by "Federal National Mortgage Association."

Fannie Mae grew quickly. Originally the idea was to sell federal securities to secure funds and then either lend these funds as direct loans under FHA Section 207 (construction loans for small apartment buildings), or to purchase other types of FHA loan originated by primary lenders. Originally only FHA loans would be purchased; conventional loans would not be added until the 1970s.

During this time, the FHA set (and changed from time to time) the maximum interest rates that a lender could charge on FHA loans. This rate was always a little below market, which meant that secondary lenders would discount the loans (pay less than face value for it) in order to raise their yield. However, Fannie Mae's cost of funds was below market, since its source was the sale of federal securities, which are not only direct federal obligations, but also exempt from state income taxes. Fannie Mae was able to buy the FHA loans at face value, and still make a profit for the government. Thus Fannie Mae became an indispensable partner for the success of the FHA program.

At the close of Word War II, Congress enacted the GI Bill, one of whose provisions was the authority of the Veterans Administration (at that time organized under the Department of Defense) to guarantee home loans for eligible veterans. In 1948, Fannie Mae was authorized to purchase these popular new VA guaranteed loans.

Fannie Mae continued to grow, fueled by the post-war housing and construction boom. Finally, in 1954, Fannie Mae was completely reorganized and Congress granted

Fannie Mae a new charter. The Charter of 1954 was designed to turn Fannie Mae eventually into a private organization. For its ownership interest (100% at that time), the Treasury was issued preferred stock. Common stock was authorized also, to be issued to private investors. Primary lenders doing business with Fannie Mae were required to purchase a portion of the common stock. Today, these primary lenders hold about 10% of Fannie Mae's outstanding stock. In addition to selling stock, Fannie Mae was authorized to sell bonds and other corporate debt instruments publicly in order to raise capital to buy mortgages. And the Charter of 1954 discontinued Fannie Mae's authority to make direct loans. From then on Fannie Mae would be strictly a secondary lender.

The Charter of 1954 specified three functions for Fannie Mae. First, Fannie Mae was charged with continuing its secondary market activities in order to stabilize and provide liquidity to the mortgage market. This included not only being a mortgage buyer, but now Fannie Mae would be able to sell loans from its portfolio as well. Second, Fannie Mae would continue to manage and collect for all FHA and VA loans acquired prior to 1954. And third, Fannie Mae would be the vehicle through which Congress could create special housing assistance programs. All three of these functions were kept in separate departments.

The Charter of 1954 also allowed Fannie Mae to buy mortgages at whatever yield was necessary to provide an adequate return to the investors in Fannie Mae. Since FHA and VA interest rates were still set slightly below market, this meant that Fannie Mae would start buying these loans at a discount. The private investors in Fannie Mae also began to insist on other changes. Not being satisfied with the standards of the FHA and of the VA, Fannie Mae announced that only loans which met Fannie Mae's somewhat more stringent credit requirements would be purchased. Eventually, the FHA and the VA raised their standards to Fannie Mae's standards.

One of the most significant functions of the "new" Fannie Mae would be the special housing assistance programs which Congress wished to begin. Programs were developed to encourage mortgage lending in geographic areas where mortgage loans were normally not available. There were also programs to fund projects such as urban renewal, disaster relief, low-income housing, and many other programs considered to be in the national interest.

Fannie Mae continued its functions under the Charter of 1954, growing stronger and helping to make the American dream of homeownership a reality. However, 1967 and 1968 were difficult years for real estate. In response, Congress enacted the Housing and Urban Development Act in 1968, which changed Fannie Mae's Charter once again. Under the Charter of 1968, Fannie Mae became a totally private organization. Fannie Mae was authorized to issue a large block of common stock, which was sold to the public. The proceeds of the stock sale were used to buy back the preferred stock held by the Treasury.

Fannie Mae still operates today under the Charter of 1968 (amended) as a private corporation. It is governed by a Board of Directors consisting of 18 members. Although Fannie Mae is now completely privately owned, it is still heavily government controlled. After all, it is only authorized to do what its charter allows, and its charter is issued by Congress. Congress has the authority to amend or even revoke its charter at will. Furthermore, of the 18 members of the Board of Directors, 13 are elected by the stockholders, but the other five are appointed by the President. These five members must be chosen from the mortgage banking, construction and real estate industries.

Another significant change resulting from the Housing and Urban Development Act of 1968 was the creation of the ***Government National Mortgage Association*** (GNMA), or as it is more commonly called, ***Ginnie Mae***. Ginnie Mae immediately took over two of Fannie Mae's departments – collection of pre-1954 FHA and VA loans, and buying mortgages for special assistance programs. After 1968, Fannie Mae would no longer be required to buy mortgages created for special assistance programs without receiving a market rate of return. Future secondary markets for these programs would be provided by Ginnie Mae.

Fannie Mae was also given some additional authorities. In order to fund Ginnie Mae's continuing mortgage purchases, the government wished for it to be able to sell securities. Fannie Mae's Charter of 1968 granted it authority to buy the securities issued by Ginnie Mae. The new Charter also gave Fannie Mae the authority to issue securities which were backed by specific blocks of mortgages in Fannie Mae's portfolio. These are called mortgage-backed securities. Investors buying these securities could be assured that, even if Fannie Mae went broke, they still had the value of the mortgages which had been pledged by Fannie Mae as collateral. And in 1970, Congress gave Fannie Mae the authority to purchase mortgages other than just FHA and VA mortgages. By 1972, Fannie Mae was using this new authority to buy conventional loans.

In order to sell loans to Fannie Mae, an approved Fannie Mae lender calls Fannie Mae to find the current commitment rates. Fannie Mae posts several rates, which change as often as daily. The best rate is for a 10-day commitment — that means that the lender is willing to commit to deliver the loans to Fannie Mae within 10 days. There are also 30-day, 60-day and 90-day commitment rates. Fannie Mae will buy as few as one loan at a time (minimum $25,000.00), or as large a block as Fannie Mae has capital available.

Today, Fannie Mae buys FHA (all types), VA, and conventional loans. Conventional loans can be fixed rate or adjustable and can be first mortgages or second mortgages. Fannie Mae buys loans for all kinds of residential property, including condominiums and multifamily housing. In addition, if a lender wishes to make loans which do not meet any of Fannie Mae's current programs, Fannie Mae may create a special program to buy loans from that lender. Fannie Mae also offers a unique program for public housing agencies who sell tax-exempt bonds and use the proceeds to make mortgage loans for special targeted areas and borrower groups. Fannie Mae will buy the loans these agencies have made by exchanging them for Fannie Mae mortgage-backed securities. The public housing agency can then pledge the mortgage-backed securities as collateral for the bonds.

Ginnie Mae

The Housing and Urban Development Act of 1968 divested Fannie Mae of two of its programs, collection of pre-1954 FHA and VA loans, and special housing assistance. These were picked up by the Government National Mortgage Association (Ginnie Mae), created at the same time, under the provisions of the Urban Development Act of 1968. Ginnie Mae operates under the supervision of the Department of Housing and Urban Development (HUD). (The FHA is also organized under HUD). Ginnie Mae is wholly government owned.

Ginnie Mae has helped fund loans for urban renewal, housing for the elderly, below-market loans for low-income borrowers (mostly FHA 235 and 236 loans), and experimental housing projects, among other special assistance programs. Most of these loans are either below market rate or involve higher than market risk, and so are unsalable in the normal secondary market. Ginnie Mae has the full authority of the federal government, so Ginnie Mae guarantees the payments on risky loans to make them salable to other secondary lenders, chiefly Fannie Mae.

Ginnie Mae has also received grants of money from Congress to subsidize below market rate loans. When possible, these loans would be sold directly to investors. However, when money became tight, Ginnie Mae would sell these below-market mortgages to Fannie Mae under the tandem plan. Under the tandem plan, the primary lender received a commitment from Ginnie Mae to buy the mortgage at par (face value without discount). This assured the primary lender a market for the mortgage. By previous arrangement, Fannie Mae agreed to buy the mortgage from Ginnie Mae, but at a discount, since Fannie Mae must have a market yield to satisfy its stockholders. When the primary lender had funded the loan, it would be sold directly to Fannie Mae, and Ginnie Mae would pay Fannie Mae the discount. Since Ginnie Mae only had to come up with enough money to pay the discount, this stretched Ginnie Mae's funds available for special assistance loans. New special assistance programs were discontinued in 1984, although mechanisms such as the tandem plan could be revived if desired in the future.

Ginnie Mae's most significant activity has been its ***mortgage-backed security*** program. A primary lender can issue and sell securities directly to investors to raise capital to make loans. In order to make the securities attractive, the primary lender pledges a pool of mortgages, which it already holds in portfolio, as collateral for the securities. The mortgages must be FHA insured or VA guaranteed. Rural Economic Community Development Corporation insured loans are also eligible, but are not commonly used.

The securities to be sold will equal the dollar value of the mortgages. When the primary lender has the details worked out, application is made to Ginnie Mae to guarantee the securities. Ginnie Mae reviews the application and, if the pool qualifies, issues its guaranty. The GNMA guaranty carries the full faith and credit of the U.S. Government. Principal and interest payments on the mortgages are funneled through to the investors, since it is these principal and interest payments which will pay back their investment. When the primary lender has sold the securities, the sales proceeds will replenish the lender's cash reserves, the same as if the mortgages had been sold directly to Ginnie Mae.

These securities are called ***pass-through securities*** because the principal and interest pass directly through to the investors. Ginnie Mae guarantees that the investor will receive both the principal and interest. In the original GNMA program the securities were sold in denominations of $15,000 — in other words, if you bought one of these securities, you bought a $15,000 participation in the pool. Since the early Ginnie Mae pools were usually $1 million pools, your share would be 1½% of the pool ($15,000 ÷ $1,000,000 = 0.015). Each month you would receive 1½% of the total principal and interest payments due from the borrowers. Your $15,000 investment would be evidenced by a ***participation certificate***.

Ginnie Mae securities are considered among the safest investments possible, and are therefore favored by pension funds, insurance companies and other conservative lenders. There are various kinds of Ginnie Mae pass-through securities — some are backed by fixed rate mortgages only, others are backed by adjustable rate mortgages. The dollar amounts of the pools also vary. Because of the variety, it is difficult for private individuals to participate directly, so mutual funds and other investment vehicles have been developed to allow investment in Ginnie Mae securities with professional fund management.

Freddie Mac

The Emergency Home Finance Act of 1970 created the ***Federal Home Loan Mortgage Corporation*** more commonly referred to as ***Freddie Mac***. Its original purpose was to provide a secondary market for savings and loan associations which are members of the Federal Home Loan Bank System. Freddie Mac is supervised by three members of the Federal Home Loan Bank Board of Governors, but is nevertheless a private capital stock organization whose stock is largely owned by member thrift institutions.

The years 1967-1968 saw financial intermediaries in a state of crisis. Loan demand was strong, and at the same time the Treasury found it necessary to sell a large dollar volume of federal securities to fund a larger than usual federal deficit. Meanwhile, inflationary trends made the Federal Reserve Bank decide to curtail the creation of new money. The resulting crunch caused interest rates on federal securities to rise to (at that time) unheard of levels. When these rates climbed, people withdrew money from their savings accounts to buy federal securities. This process is called ***disintermediation*** (money flowing out of financial intermediaries). Hardest hit were the thrifts, who found themselves with practically no funds to make new mortgage loans.

Freddie Mac was formed to solve this problem. As a secondary lender, it could buy existing portfolio loans from the thrifts that were members of the Federal Home Loan Bank System in order to pump cash back into these institutions. To get the funds to buy the mortgages, the twelve district Federal Home Loan Banks bought the initial stock subscription. Freddie Mac was authorized to sell securities in order to raise additional cash. Freddie Mac would buy mortgages and pledge them as collateral for the securities issues. In addition, the securities would be guaranteed by Ginnie Mae.

Since thrift institutions deal mainly in conventional loans, the most important function of Freddie Mac became the purchase of conventional loans. Fannie Mae, as you will recall, was also granted authority in 1970 to purchase conventional loans, and began doing so in 1972. Today, the majority of the secondary market for conventional loans is shared by Freddie Mac and Fannie Mae, who compete with each other for the mortgage production of primary lenders. Freddie Mac and Fannie Mae are also authorized to buy FHA and VA loans, but most of the loans they buy are conventional loans.

At the time Freddie Mac began purchasing conventional loans, standards had existed for FHA and VA loans for decades, but there were few standards among conventional lenders. The first major effect Freddie Mac had on mortgage lending was the creation of standardized instruments – uniform notes, trust deeds/mortgages, credit application and appraisal forms, and the like. In addition, uniformity in underwriting standards (loan approval requirements) was totally lacking. Although they compete with each other, Fannie Mae and Freddie Mac have agreed to use the same uniform instruments, and most of their underwriting standards are also the same. This enables a primary lender today to make a conventional loan, knowing that it will be salable to either Fannie Mae or Freddie Mac.

Fannie Mae and Freddie Mac have also taken a leaf out of Ginnie Mae's book. Ginnie Mae, technically speaking, does not buy loans, but rather issues a guaranty for a mortgage-backed securities issue. This is called ***securitizing*** the loans. Fannie Mae and Freddie Mac today engage heavily in the same practice, although both make direct purchases of loans as well.

From a historical standpoint we have changed the mechanisms and in the process freed up more capital for housing, but housing is still funded mostly from the same basic pool of capital. Before the advent of FHA and the secondary market in the 1930s, people provided for their retirement by putting their money into savings accounts in banks and thrift institutions. These financial intermediaries would use these funds to make mortgage loans. Today, people provide for their retirement by investing primarily in insurance annuities and public and private pension funds. These funds, in turn, invest heavily in secondary market mortgage-backed securities, which provides the funds for mortgage loans.

Federal Agricultural Mortgage Corporation

The ***Federal Agricultural Mortgage Corporation***, more commonly known as ***Farmer Mac***, was formed by the Agricultural Credit Act of 1987 to securitize pools of agricultural loans. In this respect it functions similarly to Ginnie Mae. Once a pool of loans has been underwritten by Farmer Mac investors in the pool enjoy a federal guaranty the same as investors in a pool of residential loans underwritten by Ginnie Mae.

While a securities issue by Fannie Mae or Freddie Mac may be securitized with hundreds of individual loans, pools underwritten by Farmer Mac may have only a handful of loans. The reason is that agricultural loans usually run into many millions of dollars. It doesn't take many such loans to make a pool of a substantial amount.

Real Estate Mortgage Investment Conduits

The Tax Reform Act of 1986 created **Real Estate Mortgage Investment Conduits** (REMICS), which have a feature in common with mutual funds and REITS — they are created to avoid double taxation. They can issue pass-through securities collateralized with real estate mortgages, where only the investor who owns the securities is liable for the tax on the income. These securities are issued in **tranches**, which are participations in **multiclass securities**.

Multiclass securities are securities which are collateralized with various types of loans, unlike the older Ginnie Mae, Fannie Mae and Freddie Mac securities, which generally had to be collateralized with loans of all the same type. For example, a loan pool could contain a mixture of adjustable rate loans, fixed rate loans, multi-family loans, and many other types. This allows much greater flexibility and has attracted a lot of investor capital to secondary market investments.

Exercise d

A lender who originates a loan is called a _____ lender. When the loan is sold, it is sold to a _____ lender. Organizations which buy loans make up the _____ _____ _____ . When a loan is sold, the lender who originates the loan usually retains the _____ of the loan.

The creation of _____ loans made it possible to originate and sell mortgages because _____ loans are all insured and meet minimum _____ . Eventually these loans were packaged and sold to the Federal _____ _____ _____ , now called Fannie Mae. Following World War II, Fannie Mae began buying loans _____ by the Veterans Administration. Today Fannie Mae is owned by _____ . Fannie Mae buys mortgages today, but most of their activity is in _____ mortgages for primary lenders.

Ginnie Mae, the common name for the _____ _____ _____ Association was created in 1968 primarily to provide a secondary market for _____ _____ program loans. Today, Ginnie Mae is the main conduit between primary lenders and investors for _____ and _____ loans. Ginnie Mae does this by issuing a _____ with the full faith and credit of the U.S. Government for mortgage-backed securities.

Freddie Mac, whose original name was the Federal _____ _____ _____ Corporation, was created by the Federal Home Loan Bank System and is owned by its member thrift institutions. It buys mostly _____ loans, for which it competes most heavily with Fannie Mae. Freddie Mac also _____ mortgage-backed securities issued by primary lenders as well as making direct purchases of loans.

One of the most significant contributions of Fannie Mae and Freddie Mac has been the creation of _____ loan documents and underwriting standards so that a primary lender can originate a conventional loan and sell it to either institution.

🔑 KEY TERMS

The key to understanding any new field is the vocabulary used in that field. To maximize your comprehension of the material presented in this chapter, be sure you know the meaning and significance of the following terms. Remember that the majority of test questions primarily test knowledge of vocabulary.

Annuity

Bank Insurance Fund

Building and loan association

Business trust

Combination REIT

Commercial bank

Credit union

Discount rate

Disintermediation

Double tax-exempt

Equity kicker

Equity participation loans

Equity REIT

Fannie Mae

Farmer Mac

Federal Deposit Insurance Corporation

Federal funds

Federal Home Loan Bank

Federal Home Loan Mortgage Corporation

Federal National Mortgage Association

Federal Reserve Bank System

Federal reserve note

Fiduciary lender

Finance company

Financial fiduciary

Financial intermediary

Fiscal policy

Freddie Mac

Fund

Ginnie Mae

Government National Mortgage Association

Hybrid REIT

Institutional lender

Instruments of credit policy

Interim financing

Liquidity

Loan correspondent

Loan origination fee

Loan servicing

Monetary policy

Mortgage banker

Mortgage broker

Mortgage-backed security

Multiclass security

Mutual savings bank

Non-fiduciary lender

Non-institutional lender

Open market activity

Participating lender

Participation certificate

Pass-through securities

Portfolio loan

Primary lender

Prime rate

Quasi-institutional lender

REIT

REMIC

REMT

Reserve ratio

Reserves

Savings and loan association

Savings Association Insurance Fund

Savings bank

Secondary lender

Secondary mortgage market

Securitizing

Semi-fiduciary lender

Servicing fee

Shared appreciation loans

Single Family Mortgage Purchase Program

Small loan company

Thrift industry

Thrift institution

Tranch

Treasury bill

Treasury certificate

Treasury note

Warehousing

 **ANSWERS**

To chapter exercises. If you couldn't figure out what to put in the blanks, find the answer here!

Exercise a

Commercial banks, savings and loans, mortgage bankers, mortgage brokers, finance companies and funds are referred to as _____INSTITUTIONAL_____ lenders. In contrast, private parties who lend money on real estate are called _____NON_____ - _____INSTITUTIONAL_____ lenders.

The majority of money in depository institutions is found in _____COMMERCIAL_____ _____BANKS_____ . A traditional source for real estate loans, however, is the _____THRIFT_____ industry, which includes savings and loan associations and mutual savings banks. A mortgage _____BANKER_____ is a lender which is not a financial _____ITERMEDIARY_____ , but makes real estate loans which it sells in the secondary market, yet for which it retains the servicing. In contrast, a mortgage _____BROKER_____ is a lender who arranges a loan between a borrower and a lender.

Exercise b

Funds on deposit in commercial banks are insured up to _____$100,000_____ by the Federal Deposit Insurance Corporation (FDIC). Historically, commercial banks avoided real estate loans because they insisted on _____LIQUIDITY_____ . Therefore, commercial banks generally do not make _____PORTFOLIO_____ loans.

Thrift institutions include _____SAVINGS_____ and _____LOAN_____ associations, as well as _____MUTUAL_____ _____SAVINGS_____ banks, which are not common outside of New England. Thrifts are regulated by the _____OFFICE_____ of _____THRIFT_____ _____SUPERVISION_____ , a branch of the U.S. Treasury.

Credit unions are always _____NON_____ - _____PROFIT_____ institutions, organized for the benefit of their customers, who are called _____MEMBERS_____ . Credit unions are a common source of financing, but _____FIRST_____ mortgage loans are difficult for all but the larger credit unions.

Insurance companies invest a large part of their _____PORTFOLIO_____ in real estate mortgages. When they lend directly, it is usually for a large _____COMMERCIAL_____ project, in which they frequently use an _____EQUITY_____ _____KICKER_____ . In residential financing, they usually participate by purchasing pools of loans as _____SECONDARY_____ lenders. They tend to be very _____CONSERVATIVE_____ lenders.

A _____MORTGAGE_____ _____BANKER_____ has no customer funds on deposit, but rather uses its own funds to originate the loan, and then _____SELLS_____ the loan in the _____SECONDARY_____ market. It earns its profit on the loan _____ORIGINATION_____ fees and on the fees for _____SERVICING_____ the loan over its life. A lender who brings a borrower and lender together but does not service the loan after it is made is called a _____MORTGAGE_____ _____BROKER_____ .

Provided they meet certain criteria, income earned by a real estate _____TRUST_____ is exempt from taxation. These institutions are commonly called _____REIT_____ s and _____REMT_____ s, depending on whether they invest in real estate equities or in real estate mortgages. Those who do both are called _____HYBRID_____ _____TRUSTS_____ , or _____COMBINATION_____ _____TRUSTS_____ .

The Oregon Department of Veterans Affairs and the Oregon Department of Housing and Community Services both sell _____TAX_____ - _____EXEMPT_____ revenue bonds at low interest rates and use the money for real estate loans.

Exercise c

Real estate cycles are primarily caused by fluctuations in _____INTEREST_____ rates on mortgage loans, although local economic conditions can also affect real estate cycles.

Operations and decisions of the Treasury are referred to as _____FISCAL_____ policy. The Federal Reserve System creates _____MONETARY_____ policy. This policy is implemented by three _____INSTRUMENTS_____ of credit policy. The Federal Reserve Bank will _____LEND_____ money to a member institution.

The Federal Reserve Bank can manipulate the supply of money by changing the reserve ratio, that is, the percentage of a member bank's _____DEPOSITS_____ which it must keep invested in federal obligations. If the Federal Reserve System raises the reserve ratio, member banks have _____LESS_____ money to lend. If the reserve ratio is lowered, member banks will have _____MORE_____ money to lend. The Federal Reserve System can also manipulate the supply of money by changing the discount rate, which is the rate that is charged member banks who _____BORROW_____ from their Federal Reserve Bank. Raising the discount rate tends to ❑ heat up ■ slow down the economy, while lowering it tends to ■ heat up ❑ slow down the economy.

The Fed can also control the economy through its open market operations, which consists of buying and selling federal _____SECURITIES_____ . Buying tends to ■ heat up ❑ slow down the economy, while selling tends to ❑ heat up ■ slow down the economy.

The Federal Home Loan Bank System is made up of __12__ district banks. The major purpose of the FHLBS is to provide stability and _____LIQUIDITY_____ for its member institutions. To accomplish this, the FHLBS sells securities through the _____OPEN_____ _____MARKET_____ _____OPERATIONS_____ of the Federal Reserve Bank System, and then re-lends the funds to member institutions. The FHLB also establishes a _____SECONDARY_____ _____MARKET_____ for its member institutions through the operations of the Federal _____HOME_____ _____LOAN_____ _____MORTGAGE_____ Corporation.

Exercise d

A lender who originates a loan is called a _____PRIMARY_____ lender. When the loan is sold, it is sold to a _____SECONDARY_____ lender. Organizations which buy loans make up the _____SECONDARY_____ _____MORTGAGE_____ _____MARKET_____ . When a loan is sold, the lender who originates the loan usually retains the _____SERVICING_____ of the loan.

The creation of __FHA__ loans made it possible to originate and sell mortgages because __FHA__ loans are all insured and meet minimum _____STANDARDS_____ . Eventually these loans were packaged and sold to the Federal _____HOME_____ _____LOAN_____ _____MORTGAGE_____ , now called Fannie Mae. Following World War II, Fannie Mae began buying loans _____GUARANTEED_____ by the Veterans Administration. Today Fannie Mae is owned by _____STOCKHOLDERS_____ . Fannie Mae buys mortgages today, but most of their activity is in _____SECURITIZING_____ mortgages for primary lenders.

Ginnie Mae, the common name for the _____GOVERNMENT_____ _____NATIONAL_____ _____MORTGAGE_____ Association was created in 1968 primarily to provide a secondary market for _____SPECIAL_____ _____ASSISTANCE_____ program loans. Today, Ginnie Mae is the main conduit between primary lenders and investors for __FHA__ and __VA__ loans. Ginnie Mae does this by issuing a _____GUARANTY_____ with the full faith and credit of the U.S. Government for mortgage-backed securities.

Freddie Mac, whose original name was the Federal _____HOME_____ _____LOAN_____ _____MORTGAGE_____ Corporation, was created by the Federal Home Loan Bank System and is owned by its member thrift institutions. It buys mostly _____CONVENTIONAL_____ loans, for which it competes most heavily with Fannie Mae. Freddie Mac also _____GUARANTEES_____ mortgage-backed securities issued by primary lenders as well as making direct purchases of loans.

One of the most significant contributions of Fannie Mae and Freddie Mac has been the creation of _____UNIFORM_____ loan documents and underwriting standards so that a primary lender can originate a conventional loan and sell it to either institution.

PRACTICE QUESTIONS

The following practice questions are representative of the questions you will find on the final examination and on the licensing examinations given by the Oregon Real Estate Agency.

1. The real estate industry is
   I. highly dependent on the flow of funds into the mortgage market.
   II. adversely affected by severe disintermediation.
   (A) I only
   (B) II only
   (C) Both I and II
   (D) Neither I nor II

2. If the demand for houses remains constant and the supply
   (A) increases, the value will increase.
   (B) remains the same, the value will increase.
   (C) remains the same, the value will decrease.
   (D) decreases, the value will increase.

3. Which of the following would you consider an institutional lender?
   (A) A mortgage banking firm
   (B) A mutual savings bank
   (C) A commercial bank
   (D) Any of the above

4. Commercial banks view their primary role in society as
   (A) providers of short term working capital for business and industry.
   (B) lenders on long term portfolio mortgage loans.
   (C) consumer financing lenders.
   (D) lenders of long term capital for local, state and federal government activities.

5. Commercial banks must be
   I. insured by the Federal Deposit Insurance Corporation (FDIC).
   II. members of the Federal Reserve Bank System.
   (A) I only
   (B) II only
   (C) Both I and II
   (D) Neither I nor II

6. Commercial banks
   (A) have always made more mortgage loans than any other kind of loan.
   (B) prefer mortgage loans which can be readily sold in the secondary mortgage market.
   (C) are the best place to get a loan for a small apartment building.
   (D) seldom make conventional loans.

7. Commercial banks make long term mortgage loans primarily because funds are available from
   I. savings of depositors.
   II. the secondary mortgage market.
   (A) I only
   (B) II only
   (C) Both I and II
   (D) Neither I nor II

8. Savings and loan associations are most interested in what type of loan?
   (A) FHA and federal GI loans
   (B) 80%, 90% and 95% conventional loans
   (C) Loans to finance the construction of large apartment buildings
   (D) Permanent financing for large commercial projects

9. A savings and loan association would not be likely to make a loan on
   (A) a vacant lot.
   (B) a single-family house.
   (C) an apartment building.
   (D) older residential property.

10. Mortgage bankers
    (A) are subject to the regulations of the Federal Reserve Bank System.
    (B) are regulated by federal, rather than state securities laws.
    (C) act as secondary lenders.
    (D) make their money on loan origination fees and servicing contracts.

11. A mortgage banker
    (A) arranges real estate loans, but does not collect the payments for the lender.
    (B) arranges real estate loans, and services the loans for the lender.
    (C) is a real estate loan officer in a commercial bank or thrift institution.
    (D) is a term used to describe any employee of a savings and loan association.

12. A mortgage banker would not
    (A) have savings deposits.
    (B) collect the payments on loans the mortgage banker is holding.
    (C) sell loans in the secondary mortgage market.
    (D) lend funds other than on single-family residential property.

13. A mortgage bank can do which of the following?
    I. Service loans for its clients
    II. Use its own money to make loans
    (A) I only   (C) Both I and II
    (B) II only   (D) Neither I nor II

14. Mortgage companies usually contract with the lending institutions for whom they originated the loan to service the loan. When servicing the loan, the mortgage company
    (A) does not provide for foreclosure in the event of a default.
    (B) does not require impounds on home loans.
    (C) usually charges the lender less than ¾ of 1% of the outstanding balance.
    (D) can only accept government insured or guaranteed mortgages.

15. Mortgage bankers typically
    (A) do not finance construction loans.
    (B) originate a large number of loan transactions and then sell these mortgages at a discount to large investors in the secondary market.
    (C) are the ultimate lenders in most non-government loan transactions.
    (D) will not act without the consent of their principals.

16. Mortgage companies
    (A) prefer negotiating loans that are salable in the secondary market.
    (B) are organized under federal laws and are subject to vigorous supervision.
    (C) do not service loans which they originate.
    (D) are not active in the field of government insured loans.

17. A mortgage broker
    I. takes applications and arranges loans with lenders.
    II. is a lender.
    (A) I only   (C) Both I and II
    (B) II only   (D) Neither I nor II

18. It is characteristic of mortgage brokers that they
    I. function to bring borrowers and lenders together for a real estate loan.
    II. seldom make and service loans on their own account.
    (A) I only   (C) Both I and II
    (B) II only   (D) Neither I nor II

19. Which of the following statements regarding mortgage brokers is true?
    I. After the loan is closed, a mortgage broker usually collects the regular monthly payments for the lender.
    II. Mortgage brokers generally make loans with their own funds, then seek to sell these receivables to the highest bidder.
    (A) I only   (C) Both I and II
    (B) II only   (D) Neither I nor II

20. A mortgage broker, also called a mortgage loan correspondent, arranges loans using
    (A) money belonging to the mortgage broker's clients.
    (B) money from financial institutions.
    (C) the mortgage broker's own money.
    (D) both A and B above.

21. A mortgage broker
    I. usually lends the mortgage broker's own money.
    II. will arrange loans using money belonging to other firms.
    (A) I only   (C) Both I and II
    (B) II only   (D) Neither I nor II

22. In today's real estate market, if you desired a second mortgage on your home, the most likely source, and the source which would likely offer the best interest rate, would be
    (A) a private party dealing through a mortgage broker.
    (B) a finance company.
    (C) an FHA loan through a participating commercial bank or savings and loan association.
    (D) a savings and loan association or mutual savings bank.

23. Life insurance companies generally operate as
    I. long term lenders.   II. short term lenders.
    (A) I only   (C) Both I and II
    (B) II only   (D) Neither I nor II

24. Life insurance company mortgage holdings are greatest in
    (A) farm loans.
    (B) conventional residential loans.
    (C) large commercial and apartment loans.
    (D) FHA and VA residential loans.

25. A lender that invests a major portion of its assets in long term real estate loans, prefers large loans on commercial properties, and does not like to service its own loans is a
    (A) savings and loan association.
    (B) life insurance company.
    (C) commercial bank.
    (D) credit union.

26. Insurance companies
    I. are generally very conservative lenders.
    II. prefer large projects when they lend as primary lenders.
    (A) I only   (C) Both I and II
    (B) II only   (D) Neither I nor II

27. As real estate lenders, insurance companies lend
    I. on new commercial structures such as office buildings and shopping centers.
    II. as secondary lenders by purchasing blocks of residential loans from primary lenders.
    (A) I only   (C) Both I and II
    (B) II only   (D) Neither I nor II

28. Insurance companies sometimes take equity positions as part of a loan agreement. They typically do this with loans on
    (A) single-family homes.
    (B) small shopping centers.
    (C) both A and B.
    (D) neither A nor B.

29. Life insurance companies are generally
    (A) short term lenders.   (C) both A and B.
    (B) long term lenders.   (D) neither A nor B.

30. Higher risk loans are usually made by
    (A) federally chartered savings and loan associations.
    (B) state chartered savings and loan associations.
    (C) private lenders.
    (D) pension funds or life insurance companies.

31. If you are seeking an FHA loan you should be aware that
    I. commercial banks are not allowed to make FHA loans, however, they may have wholly-owned subsidiaries who make FHA loans.
    II. FHA loans are made primarily by savings and loan associations.
    (A) I only   (C) Both I and II
    (B) II only   (D) Neither I nor II

32. A tight money market would indicate
    I. a buyer's market in real estate.
    II. a seller's market in real estate.
    III. high interest rates.
    IV. low interest rates.
    (A) I and III only   (C) II and III only
    (B) I and IV only   (D) II and IV only

33. In a tight money market," one would expect to find
    (A) potential borrowers delaying projects, expecting interest rates to fall.
    (B) lower interest rates than in an "easy money market."
    (C) marginal borrowers forced out of the credit market.
    (D) both A and C.

34. It would be to the advantage of the lending institution to waive the prepayment penalty in a mortgage loan when
    I. funds are in short supply and demand for loans is high.
    II. the Federal Reserve System drastically lowers the discount rate and reserve requirement.
    (A) I only
    (B) II only
    (C) Both I and II
    (D) Neither I nor II

35. Each year the conditions affecting the availability of loan funds change. When would it be to the advantage of lenders to waive a prepayment penalty provision in a note?
    (A) In a tight money market
    (B) When the Federal Reserve lowers its discount requirements
    (C) In a deflationary period
    (D) When money is readily available for real estate loans

36. The Federal Reserve System
    (A) supervises and operates the VA.
    (B) supervises and operates the FHA.
    (C) is the equivalent of a national bank for the U.S.
    (D) is under the control of the Treasury.

37. One of the functions of the Federal Reserve Bank System is to
    (A) issue cashier's checks.
    (B) insure FHA loans.
    (C) manage the economy.
    (D) guarantee GNMA securities.

38. When business is slow and we are in a recessionary period, if the Federal Reserve Bank System lowers the discount rate
    I. interest rates will decrease.
    II. there will be a danger of increasing inflation.
    (A) I only
    (B) II only
    (C) Both I and II
    (D) Neither I nor II

39. When we refer to the "open market activity" of the Federal Reserve Bank System, we are referring to the purchase and sale of
    (A) government savings bonds.
    (B) commercial paper.
    (C) stocks and bonds.
    (D) U.S. treasury securities.

40. One way the Federal Reserve System can regulate interest rates on lendable funds is through its open market operations. Through this process the Federal Reserve can
    (A) require lenders to raise or lower interest rates by regulation.
    (B) buy or sell government bonds at either higher or lower interest rates to banks, thereby either increasing or decreasing the bank's supply of funds.
    (C) require banks to hold more or less of their deposits as reserves.
    (D) persuade banks to voluntarily increase or decrease the amount of funds they are willing to lend.

41. To put the brakes on an inflationary trend, the Federal Reserve System may
    (A) buy government securities in the open market.
    (B) raise the discount rate charged member banks.
    (C) lower the reserve requirement of member banks.
    (D) lower the prime rate.

42. The Federal Reserve Board would do which of the following to tighten up money and make less credit available?
    I. Sell government bonds
    II. Raise the prime interest rate
    (A) I only
    (B) II only
    (C) Both I and II
    (D) Neither I nor II

43. The Federal Reserve System normally affects the supply of money in the economy by all of the following except
    (A) changing reserve requirements.
    (B) buying or selling bonds.
    (C) adjusting the discount rate.
    (D) buying or selling gold on the international market.

44. Which of the following actions of the Federal Reserve Board would relieve a tight money market?
    (A) Sell U.S. government securities on the open market
    (B) Issue new regulations for accreditation of banks
    (C) Lower the cash reserve requirement
    (D) Raise the discount rate

45. During a period of high inflation, the Federal Reserve Board can limit to some degree the expansion of the money supply by
    (A) increasing the income tax.
    (B) decreasing the income tax.
    (C) increasing reserve requirements of member banks.
    (D) decreasing reserve requirements of member banks.

46. If the Federal Reserve Bank feels that there is an inflationary trend developing in the U.S., it can do which of the following?
    I.   Increase the discount rate
    II. Adjust the amount of reserves required of member banks
    (A) I only   (C) Both I and II
    (B) II only   (D) Neither I nor II

47. The Federal Reserve Board can control the flow of money by
    (A) raising the discount rate to member borrowers.
    (B) increasing the reserve requirement of its member banks.
    (C) selling bonds.
    (D) all of the above.

48. If a member bank of the Federal Reserve Bank System falls below its reserve requirement, it may obtain additional funds by
    (A) selling mortgage loans from its portfolio.
    (B) borrowing from other banks.
    (C) borrowing from the Federal Reserve Bank.
    (D) any of the above.

49. When money flows out of depository institutions and there is a net deposit loss, this is called
    (A) hypothecation.   (C) equity.
    (B) disintermediation.   (D) leverage.

50. The FDIC insures
    (A) FHA loans.   (C) FMHA loans.
    (B) bank deposits.   (D) federal office buildings.

51. The U.S. Treasury functions as
    (A) manager of federal fiscal policy.
    (B) the nation's stockbroker.
    (C) manager of federal monetary policy.
    (D) all of the above.

52. Federal policies influence mortgage rates through
    (A) influencing corporate dividend policies.
    (B) raising and lowering interest rates on federal securities which compete with mortgage funds in the capital markets.
    (C) rationing goods and services.
    (D) fixing the prices on federal securities.

53. The interest rate a lender will charge a borrower depends most heavily on the
    (A) term of the loan.
    (B) amount of down payment the borrower is making.
    (C) lender's cost of capital.
    (D) borrower's income and credit rating.

54. Which of the following would be the primary consideration of a lender in setting interest rates?
    (A) The borrower's credit rating and ability to repay
    (B) The value of the property on which the loan is made
    (C) The location and condition of the property on which the loan is to be made
    (D) The overall interest rate the lender has to pay for lendable funds

55. The interest rate on real estate mortgages is
    (A) fixed by the state real estate commission.
    (B) fixed by federal law.
    (C) regulated by the Federal Reserve Board.
    (D) determined by competition between the money and capital markets.

56. Mortgage interest rates are determined by complex economic, social and legal factors. Under normal conditions, which of the following would be a significant economic factor?
    I.   Activities of the Federal Reserve Bank System
    II. Congressional action to change the tax rates
    (A) I only   (C) Both I and II
    (B) II only   (D) Neither I nor II

57. Samuel Johnson was beneficiary on a second trust deed that had an unpaid balance of $250,000.00. He sold this paper for $200,000.00. This act on his part is most commonly described as
    (A) liquidation.   (C) acceleration.
    (B) prepayment.   (D) discounting.

58. A promissory note with an unpaid balance of $100,000 was sold for $80,000 to a private investor. This is an example of
    (A) evaluating.   (C) depreciating.
    (B) subrogating.   (D) discounting.

59. Discounting a mortgage loan is a common practice in the secondary mortgage market. Discounting refers to the practice of
    (A) charging the borrower an additional fee for making a loan.
    (B) reducing the contract rate of interest on an outstanding mortgage loan.
    (C) buying or selling an existing mortgage loan for less than its current outstanding balance.
    (D) raising the contract rate of interest on an existing loan before offering the loan for sale.

60. Discount points
    (A) decrease yields to the lender.
    (B) increase yields to the lender.
    (C) increase yields to the seller.
    (D) decrease yields to the seller.

61. Discount points are used to
    (A) decrease yields to the lender when short term rates are higher than long term rates.
    (B) increase yields to the lender.
    (C) increase the yield to the seller of the property.
    (D) do both B and C.

62. Lending on real estate by pension funds, either as primary or as secondary lenders, is
    (A) increasing.   (C) staying the same.
    (B) decreasing.   (D) insignificant.

63. The secondary mortgage market is
    I. a source of second mortgage loans.
    II. made up of investors who provide mortgage funds by buying mortgage loans from originating institutions.
    (A) I only   (C) Both I and II
    (B) II only   (D) Neither I nor II

64. When we talk about the "secondary mortgage market" we are referring to
    (A) the sale of federal securities.
    (B) the origination of FHA and federal GI loans.
    (C) lenders who make second mortgage loans.
    (D) lenders who purchase loans as an investment.

65. The "secondary mortgage market" refers to the market wherein
    (A) secondary financing may be obtained.
    (B) FHA loans are originated.
    (C) existing loans are bought and sold.
    (D) conventional loans are originated.

66. The secondary mortgage market functions to
    I. enable primary lending institutions to free the funds they have invested in mortgage loans by selling those mortgages to lenders having capital available for real estate investments.
    II. minimize fluctuations in the supply of funds available to meet the demand for mortgage loans.
    (A) I only   (C) Both I and II
    (B) II only   (D) Neither I nor II

67. The national secondary mortgage market acts to redistribute funds from
    I. insured loan proceeds to non-insured loan proceeds.
    II. money-rich areas to money-poor areas.
    (A) I only   (C) Both I and II
    (B) II only   (D) Neither I nor II

68. Which of the following is true about the primary and secondary mortgage markets?
    I. The primary market holds or "warehouses" mortgage loans.
    II. The secondary market originates mortgage loans.
    (A) I only   (C) Both I and II
    (B) II only   (D) Neither I nor II

69. The primary mortgage market is the market in which
    (A) secondary financing may be obtained.
    (B) mortgages are originated.
    (C) existing mortgage loans are bought and sold.
    (D) mortgage insurance may be secured for existing mortgage loans.

70. The major source of funds to originate conventional loans is
    (A) savings deposits in thrift institutions.
    (B) Fannie Mae (FNMA) and Freddie Mac (FHLMC).
    (C) mutual funds.
    (D) real estate investment trusts (REITS).

71. Funds for conventional loans are received directly from
    I. Government National Mortgage Association.
    II. private parties and non-government institutions.
    III. the Federal National Mortgage Association.
    (A) I and II only (C) II only
    (B) I, II and III (D) II and III only

72. Which of the following statements concerning the secondary mortgage market is true?
    I. The Federal National Mortgage Association can purchase Federal Housing Administration, Federal Veterans Affairs, and conventional first mortgages.
    II. The Federal Home Loan Mortgage Corporation can purchase Federal Housing Administration, Federal Veterans Affairs and conventional first mortgages.
    (A) I only (C) Both I and II
    (B) II only (D) Neither I nor II

73. A mortgage banker arranges a credit line at a commercial bank. The mortgage banker is engaging in
    (A) mortgage investment.
    (B) warehousing.
    (C) mortgage brokerage.
    (D) loan discounting.

74. In real estate lending, the term "warehousing" has to do with
    (A) lending on commercial loans which are in default.
    (B) foreclosed properties held in a lender's inventory.
    (C) management of mortgage loan portfolios.
    (D) making portfolio loans.

75. Which of the following is not a secondary lender?
    (A) FDIC (C) Ginnie Mae
    (B) Fannie Mae (D) Freddie Mac

76. The majority of loans originated today by financial fiduciaries are
    (A) hypothecated to the Federal Reserve Bank.
    (B) sold in the secondary mortgage market.
    (C) sold to mortgage brokers and mortgage bankers.
    (D) maintained in portfolio.

77. The purpose of the Federal National Mortgage Association (Fannie Mae) is to
    I. provide an easy vehicle for channeling capital into housing.
    II. increase the liquidity of primary lenders' loan portfolios.
    (A) I only (C) Both I and II
    (B) II only (D) Neither I nor II

78. The Federal National Mortgage Association (Fannie Mae)
    I. supervises the activities of primary lenders.
    II. provides underwriting standards for the primary mortgage market.
    (A) I only (C) Both I and II
    (B) II only (D) Neither I nor II

79. The Federal National Mortgage Association (Fannie mae) was created for the primary purpose of
    (A) supervising lending institutions.
    (B) lending money to urban renewal projects.
    (C) increasing the amount of money available for credit financing of housing.
    (D) lending money on FHA loans when institutional lenders cannot.

80. The Federal National Mortgage Association ("Fannie Mae") functions in the secondary mortgage market to
    (A) purchase and service federally guaranteed loans exclusively.
    (B) decrease the liquidity of lending institutions in periods of tight money.
    (C) buy government-guaranteed debentures at market interest rates.
    (D) buy mortgages which are originated by other lending institutions.

81. The Federal National Mortgage Association was created for the primary purpose of
    (A) buying FHA loans from lending institutions to stabilize the mortgage market.
    (B) lending money on FHA Title II loans when banks will not.
    (C) buying Title I FHA loans.
    (D) advancing funds to mass production builders in or near large cities.

82. Fannie Mae's primary responsibility is to
    (A) provide special assistance for government lending programs.
    (B) maintain an active secondary market for mortgages.
    (C) manage and liquidate previously acquired mortgages.
    (D) place FHA and VA loans.

83. Fannie Mae
    I. provides mortgage funds directly to borrowers whose loans are either insured by the FHA or guaranteed by VA.
    II. is the common name for the Federal National Mortgage Association.
    (A) I only
    (B) II only
    (C) Both I and II
    (D) Neither I nor II

84. Fannie Mae purchases
    (A) government guaranteed mortgage loans.
    (B) government insured mortgage loans.
    (C) conventional mortgage loans, both insured and uninsured.
    (D) all of the above.

85. Fannie Mae does not purchase
    (A) chattel mortgages.
    (B) FHA mortgages.
    (C) conventional mortgages.
    (D) VA guaranteed mortgages.

86. Fannie Mae (FNMA) buys mortgage loans from
    I. thrift institutions. III. mortgage bankers.
    II. commercial banks.
    (A) I only
    (B) 1, II and III
    (C) II only
    (D) II and III only

87. Fannie Mae today secures funds by
    I. borrowing from the U.S. Treasury.
    II. selling mortgage-backed securities.
    III. selling capital stock.
    (A) I and II only
    (B) I, II and III
    (C) II only
    (D) II and III only

88. Debt instruments issued by Fannie Mae are sometimes guaranteed by the
    (A) Federal Housing Administration.
    (B) Ginnie Mae.
    (C) U.S. Treasury.
    (D) Federal Home Loan Bank.

89. The quasi-public institution which serves as a ready secondary mortgage market participant to purchase insured or non-insured existing loans is called the
    (A) Federal National Mortgage Association.
    (B) Government National Mortgage Association.
    (C) Federal Housing Mortgage Association.
    (D) National Mortgage Loan Association.

90. Fannie Mae
    (A) provides financing for the FHA.
    (B) guarantees loans sold through REMICs.
    (C) is listed on the New York Stock Exchange.
    (D) is active in buying commercial loans.

91. The Federal National Mortgage Association (Fannie Mae) is
    (A) owned and supervised by the Federal Reserve Bank.
    (B) a publicly owned corporation, supervised by Congress.
    (C) jointly owned by private investors and the U.S. Treasury, and supervised by Congress.
    (D) privately owned, and supervised by the Federal Home Loan Bank.

92. Government National Mortgage Association (GNMA) activities include all of the following except financing
    (A) urban renewal projects.
    (B) housing for the elderly.
    (C) new subdivisions.
    (D) experimental housing.

93. Ginnie Mae functions in the secondary market by
    (A) insuring FHA and VA loans.
    (B) making new first mortgage loans.
    (C) guaranteeing securities offerings backed by mortgages.
    (D) direct lending for special assistance programs.

94. When referring to liquidity and marketability, a mortgage banker is concerned with
    I. Fannie Mae.   II. Freddie Mac.
    (A) I only
    (B) II only
    (C) Both I and II
    (D) Neither I nor II

95. The purpose of the Federal Home Loan Bank Board is to
    I. provide a reserve credit system for thrift institutions.
    II. regulate the operations of member institutions.
    (A) I only
    (B) II only
    (C) Both I and II
    (D) Neither I nor II

96. One of the purposes of the Federal Home Loan Bank (FHLB) is to lend money to
    (A) member thrift institutions.
    (B) member commercial banks to provide funds for residential lending.
    (C) the Government National Mortgage Association (GNMA).
    (D) all of the above.

97. The primary purpose of the Federal Home Loan Mortgage Corporation is to
    (A) buy FHA and federal GI loans in order to further government housing goals.
    (B) sell mortgages for primary lenders.
    (C) buy conventional and government loans in order to stabilize the market.
    (D) guarantee payments on mortgage-backed securities offered by primary lenders.

98. The Federal Home Loan Mortgage Corporation (Freddie Mac) secures funds for its operations by
    I. borrowing from the U.S. Treasury.
    II. selling mortgage-backed securities.
    III. selling capital stock.
    (A) I, II and III
    (B) II only
    (C) II and III only
    (D) III only

99. The function of REMICs is to
    (A) insure loans being sold in the secondary market.
    (B) provide investments in tranches.
    (C) create tax-free investments in mortgage pools.
    (D) make tax-exempt mortgage loans.

100. Tax-free bonds are used in Oregon to finance housing through
    (A) the Oregon Department of Veterans Affairs.
    (B) the Oregon Department of Housing and Community Services.
    (C) both A and B.
    (D) neither A nor B.

101. An investor would use which of the following as a hedge against inflation?
    (A) Investment equity assets
    (B) Mortgages
    (C) Bonds
    (D) Savings accounts

ANSWERS

To practice questions. If you chose the wrong letter, here's the right one! The explanations are designed to clarify your understanding.

1.   **C**   No other industry is so capital-intensive as real estate. Real estate agents simply cannot make sales without enormous amounts of capital available at reasonable rates. Disintermediation refers to funds flowing out of financial intermediaries (banks, thrifts, credit unions) to seek higher rates elsewhere, usually U.S. Treasury obligations. When the money flows out of the financial intermediaries they have fewer funds to lend and interest rates tend to rise.

2.   **D**   Supply and demand is the most basic of all concepts in economics. If supply of a commodity remains the same, value will go up when demand increases, and down when demand decreases.

3.   **D**   The term "institutional lender" refers to any lender which is a recognized entity, such as a bank, savings and loan, or even insurance company or mortgage banker. The only lenders which are clearly not institutional lenders are private parties and sellers who carry purchase money financing for their buyers.

4.   **A**   Although commercial banks engage in all the listed activity, historically they have been providers of short term capital. Commercial banks have always been concerned with their liquidity position. Short term working capital loans for business and industry are the easiest to call due in a hurry, so this has always been their traditional role. In today's market that role is changing, but they still prefer business loans to consumer loans.

5.   **D**   Although it would be difficult to find a commercial bank that is not FDIC insured, it is not impossible. There are states where insurance is not required, and there are states which provide a state insurance pool as an alternative to FDIC insurance. Similarly, there is no requirement that a commercial bank be a member of the Federal Reserve System, although all banks are subject to certain Federal Reserve Regulations, whether members or not.

6.   **B**   Commercial banks, the same as other institutional lenders, do not readily make real estate loans that are not salable in the secondary market. The main stock in trade of commercial banks is lending to business and industry.

7.   **B**   All lenders today are reluctant to lend on residential real estate unless the loan is salable in the secondary market. In the past, the most significant source of mortgage funds was savings deposits. Today, secondary market activities have turned the primary capital markets into the largest source of lendable funds for mortgage loans.

8.   **B**   From a historical standpoint, the vast majority of loans originated by savings and loan associations have been conventional loans. For some, this is the only type of loan they have ever made. In today's market, thrifts have sought diversification and many have entered the FHA and VA market. Nevertheless the conventional loan remains their primary type of loan. Thrifts have also historically seen their role as providers of home loans, not mortgage loans for business and industry.

9.   **A**   Vacant land is the most difficult type of real estate to find financing for. Loans for development of land are available, typically from commercial banks, but loans for long term investment in land are considered highly risky. For one thing, land generally produces no income, so the only source of repayment is the borrower's income. Improved property, on the other hand, can be rented and the rent income is a potential source of repayment in the event of a default.

10.   **D**   Mortgage bankers are the least regulated of all lenders, since they do not have customer deposits. What they do with their own money is not considered a matter of public concern. Mortgage bankers are primary lenders, not secondary lenders. Mortgage bankers make their profit on the loan origination fees and on the fees they charge the secondary lender for servicing the loan.

11.   **B**   A mortgage broker is one who arranges a loan. A mortgage banker lends its own funds to make the loan, then sells the loan in the secondary market to recover the capital in order to make additional loans. Mortgage bankers make their profit on the loan origination and servicing fees.

12.   **A**   A mortgage banker is a firm which lends its own funds, not the funds of depositors. Mortgage bankers make their profit on the loan origination

fees and on the fees they charge the secondary lender for servicing the loan. Mortgage bankers have no customer deposits to make loans with, so they are completely dependent on selling their loans in the secondary market to recover the capital for making additional loans.

13. **C** Unlike a financial fiduciary like a savings and loan or a commercial bank, mortgage bankers do not have customer deposits. Their source of funds for mortgage loans is the investment of the stockholders. Since this is not enough to continue making loans indefinitely, a mortgage banker must sell its loan production in the secondary market. When it sells the loans it has originated, it continues to service them. A mortgage banker makes money on the loan origination fee and the fees it charges the secondary lender for loan servicing.

14. **C** Loan servicing contracts usually (but not always) provide for full service, including foreclosure, if necessary. Reserves for taxes and insurance (impounds) are required on FHA and federal GI loans, so the agency providing the servicing will have to maintain the impounds. Since the secondary market buys all kinds of loans, any loan can be serviced. The fee is negotiated in a competitive environment, and is usually about ⅜ of 1%.

15. **B** Mortgage bankers do not have customer deposits like banks. Therefore, they are completely dependent on being able to sell their loans in the secondary market. Loans sold in the secondary market are frequently discounted. There is no organized secondary market for construction loans.

16. **A** Mortgage companies (also known as mortgage bankers) do not have customer deposits. Their source of money is only the amount the stockholders have invested. This is not enough to continue making loans for long, so they sell their loans in the secondary market. They make their money on the loan servicing and loan origination fees. They are private organizations. Since they do not maintain customer deposits they are largely unregulated. They will make any kind of loan which can be sold in the secondary market.

17. **A** A mortgage broker is a go-between, in much the same way as a real estate broker. A mortgage broker brings a borrower and a lender together and charges a fee for the service. Once the loan is made, the mortgage broker's job is finished.

18. **C** Mortgage brokers are merely go-betweens. They bring a borrower and a lender together for a fee, in much the same way as a real estate broker brings a buyer and a seller together for a commission. They do not service the loan.

19. **D** Mortgage brokers bring a borrower and a lender together for a fee. They do not service the loan after it is closed, nor do they fund the loan.

20. **D** Mortgage brokers do not lend their own funds. They are go-betweens who arrange loans between borrowers and lenders. Mortgage brokers represent all kinds of lenders, including financial institutions.

21. **B** Mortgage brokers serve the same function in the lending world as a real estate broker performs in the real estate business – that is, to bring a borrower and a lender together. The mortgage broker charges a fee for doing so, usually paid by the borrower. The mortgage broker performs no further services once the loan is made.

22. **D** Private parties and finance companies are both characteristically the most aggressive when it comes to charging high interest rates. FHA loans might have reasonable rates, but second mortgages under FHA are not commonly available. In today's market, a thrift institution or commercial bank would be the most likely source, especially if they already hold the first mortgage.

23. **A** Life insurance companies have few loan personnel, so they tend to make large, long term loans on major projects.

24. **C** Life insurance companies have billions to invest, and few personnel to administer loans. Therefore, they tend to prefer very large loans. In the past they have concentrated mostly on large commercial projects and large multi-family structures. They also operate to purchase packages of smaller loans as a secondary lender.

25. **B** Savings and loan associations and commercial banks make primarily residential mortgage loans and only occasionally lend on larger projects. Credit unions do not make many real estate loans, but when they do, they are usually smaller loans such as second mortgages for their members. Life insurance companies have billions to invest and generally prefer large commercial or multi-family income properties.

26. **C** Insurance companies have billions of dollars in reserves they must hold on their insurance policies. These must be invested, but the investment must be conservative. Since the reserves are a stable pool of money, they are ideally suited to long term

investments such as bonds and mortgages. Insurance companies prefer to invest in mortgages either directly on large commercial projects, or in the residential market as secondary lenders.

27.   **C**   Insurance companies must invest the reserves they hold on insurance policies. A portion of these are invested in real estate mortgages. Since insurance companies do not have extensive loan servicing departments, they lend either on large commercial projects, or on pools of residential loans which they buy as a secondary lender.

28.   **B**   An equity participation loan is a loan where the lender will share in a certain percentage of the increase in equity as the property value increases. At some agreed-on point in the loan, the property will be appraised and the lender's share of the increased equity will be added to the loan balance. In exchange for this, the lender agrees to a lower than market interest rate. This is typical in commercial projects, and rarely found in residential lending.

29.   **B**   Insurance companies must invest the reserves they hold on insurance policies. These reserves are long term, stable sources of financing. A portion of these are invested in real estate mortgages. Because the source of funds is stable, insurance companies prefer long term loans.

30.   **C**   Although there is growing interest in high risk loans by institutional lenders, most lenders simply reject any loan that does not meet their standards. This leaves only one source for financing a high risk loan, and that is the seller or a private party.

31.   **D**   In the past, savings and loan associations were always primarily conventional lenders. Today some FHA loans are made by savings and loan associations, but most are made by mortgage bankers. Commercial banks are allowed to make any kind of residential loan.

32.   **A**   "Tight money" means lendable funds are in shorter supply than usual. When supply is decreased, but demand remains constant, the price goes up. The price of money is the interest that lenders charge. Therefore, in a tight money market interest rates will be higher than normal. Because real estate is almost always financed, this tends to curtail demand and make it harder for sellers to find willing buyers. A buyer's market favors buyers, and a seller's market favors sellers.

33.   **D**   When funds are in shorter supply, interest rates will go up. This will curtail demand, as real estate purchases are usually financed. The higher interest rates will create higher monthly payments, making it more difficult for buyers to qualify for financing.

34.   **A**   A prepayment penalty discourages early payoff of a loan, so a lender would want to waive it any time the lender wanted the loan paid off early. This would be typical of a market situation where the loan was at a fixed rate that was well below current market rates. By getting the funds back, the lender could re-lend them at the new, higher rate. Lowering the discount rate and reserve requirement would tend to lower interest rates in the marketplace.

35.   **A**   Waiving a prepayment penalty would be an incentive for borrowers to pay off their loans early. Therefore, a lender would waive the prepayment penalty for loans on the books at low fixed rates when market conditions are such that the funds could be re-lent at higher rates on new loans. This would be typical of a tight money market.

36.   **C**   There are twelve banks in the Federal Reserve Bank System. Their functions are similar to what a national bank does in other countries, i.e., lending money to private banks, functioning as the outlet for new currency, regulating private banks, etc.

37.   **C**   The Federal Reserve Bank System has several functions. Its most important function is to serve as a "banker's bank" for member institutions. In that capacity it lends money to member banks to help them maintain liquidity. It also regulates its members (and even non-members, to some extent). But for real estate agents its most important function is its manipulation of the economy by implementation of the three instruments of credit policy.

38.   **C**   The three instruments of credit policy are 1) changing the discount rate, 2) changing the reserve ratio and, 3) open market activity. The discount rate is the interest rate the Federal Reserve Banks charge their members on borrowed funds. Raising the discount rate causes banks to charge higher interest rates to borrowers, thus slowing down the economy, and vice-versa. The reserve ratio is the percentage of a member banks total reserves which must be invested in federal securities. Raising the ratio takes lendable funds out of circulation, causes interest rates to rise, and consequently slows down the economy. Lowering the reserve ratio has the opposite effect. Open market activity refers to buying and selling federal securities. Since most federal securities are bought by member banks to meet their reserve requirements, selling securities tends to absorb lendable funds in the private sector, raising interest rates and slowing down the

economy. Buying back federal securities pumps cash into the economy and heats it up.

39.   **D**   Open market activity refers to buying and selling federal securities. Since most federal securities are bought by member banks to meet their reserve requirements, selling securities tends to absorb lendable funds in the private sector, raising interest rates and slowing down the economy. Buying back federal securities pumps cash into the economy and heats it up.

40.   **B**   Open market operations means buying or selling government securities (e.g., treasury bills) to the public, primarily to banks. Selling them soaks up available capital in the private sector and decreases available lendable funds which, in turn, increases interest rates. Buying them has the opposite effect.

41.   **B**   There are three tools the Federal Reserve Bank can use to influence interest rates – changing the discount rate, changing the reserve ratio, and open market activity. The discount rate is the rate the Federal Reserve Bank charges on loans to banks. Raising the discount rate increases a bank's cost of funds, forcing them to raise interest on loans to their customers which, in turn, decreases loan demand and slows down demand for goods and services. Less demand for goods and services will be counter-inflationary. The reserve ratio is the percentage of customer deposits that a bank must keep invested in federal securities. Increasing the ratio means banks have fewer funds to lend, which will drive up interest rates, and again, lower demand in the marketplace. Open market activity means selling government securities (e.g., treasury bills) to the public. This soaks up available capital in the private sector and decreases available lendable funds which, in turn, increases interest rates and decreases demand in the marketplace. The prime rate is the rate a bank charges its best corporate customers. The Federal Reserve Bank can influence the prime rate, but does not have any direct control over it.

42.   **A**   Open market activity means selling government securities (e.g., treasury bills) to the public. This soaks up available capital in the private sector and decreases available lendable funds which, in turn, increases interest rates and decreases demand in the marketplace. The prime rate is the rate a bank charges its best corporate customers. The Federal Reserve Bank can influence the prime rate, but does not have any direct control over it.

43.   **D**   The reserve ratio is the percentage of customer deposits that a bank must keep invested in federal securities. Increasing the reserve requirement means

banks will have fewer funds to lend, which will drive up interest rates and lower demand in the marketplace. Open market activity means selling government securities (e.g., treasury bills) to the public. This soaks up available capital in the private sector and decreases available lendable funds which, in turn, increases interest rates and decreases demand in the marketplace. The discount rate is the rate the Federal Reserve Bank charges on loans to banks. Raising the discount rate increases a bank's cost of funds, forcing them to raise interest on loans to their customers which, in turn, decreases loan demand and slows down demand for goods and services. Gold is merely a commodity.

44.   **C**   Open market activity means buying or selling government securities (e.g., treasury bills). Selling them soaks up available capital in the private sector and decreases available lendable funds which, in turn, increases interest rates and decreases demand in the marketplace. The reserve ratio is the percentage of customer deposits that a bank must keep invested in federal securities (cash reserve requirement). Decreasing the ratio means banks have more funds to lend. The discount rate is the rate the Federal Reserve Bank charges on loans to banks. Raising the discount rate increases a bank's cost of funds, forcing them to raise interest on loans to their customers which, in turn, decreases loan demand and slows down demand for goods and services. Rules for accreditation of banks may affect the number of banks in existence, but will have no effect on the amount of funds available in the economy.

45.   **C**   The reserve requirement is the percentage of customer deposits that a bank must keep invested in federal securities. Increasing it means banks have fewer funds to lend, which will drive up interest rates, and lower demand in the marketplace. Income tax rates have an effect on the economy, but the Federal Reserve Board has no control over income tax rates.

46.   **C**   The discount rate is the interest rate the Federal Reserve Bank charges on loans to banks. Increasing the discount rate increases a bank's cost of capital, which increases interest rates in the marketplace, thus lowering demand. The reserve ratio is the percentage of customer deposits that a bank must keep invested in federal securities. Increasing the reserve requirement means banks will have fewer lendable funds, and interest rates will go up. Both of these actions would lower demand for goods and services, which will halt or slow down inflation.

47.   **D**   There are three tools the Federal Reserve Bank can use to influence interest rates – changing

the discount rate, changing the reserve ratio, and open market activity. The discount rate is the rate the Federal Reserve Bank charges on loans to banks. Raising it increases a bank's cost of funds, forcing them to raise interest on loans to their customers and lowering it allows banks to lower interest rates. The reserve requirement is the percentage of customer deposits that a bank must keep invested in federal securities. Increasing the ratio means banks have fewer funds to lend, which will drive up interest rates, and lowering it has the opposite effect. Open market activity means selling government securities (e.g., treasury bills) to the public. This soaks up available capital in the private sector and decreases available lendable funds.

48. **D** The reserve requirement is the percentage of customer deposits that a bank must maintain in reserve and cannot lend. If the bank has gone below its reserve requirement, it needs additional deposit funds, which can come from regular depositors, loans from other banks, or loans from the Federal Reserve Bank.

49. **B** Depository institutions are called "financial intermediaries" because they take money from depositors and lend it to borrowers. Depositors could lend the money directly, but using an intermediary is more efficient. When money flows out of financial intermediaries, usually because of higher yields in another market, it is called disintermediation.

50. **B** The Federal Deposit Insurance Corporation (FDIC) originally insured deposits only in commercial banks. Due to failures of thrift institutions, their insuring agency, the Federal Savings and Loan Insurance Corporation, was unable to meet the losses. As a result, deposits in all depository institutions today are insured by the FDIC.

51. **A** How to use the three instruments of credit policy to manipulate the economy is called monetary policy. This is handled by the Federal Reserve Bank and the Federal Open Market Committee. Fiscal policy, on the other hand, refers to the actions of the Treasury in borrowing to meet the deficits, managing the national debt, and paying current bills.

52. **B** Corporate dividend policies have nothing to do with mortgage interest rates. Investors buying pools of mortgages as secondary lenders are the real source of mortgage capital. These investors consider corporate bonds and federal securities as competitive alternatives.

53. **C** There is a common misconception among the public that the greater the risk, the higher the interest the lender will charge. While this notion is not entirely untrue, in real-world lending most lenders would be more likely to turn down a marginal loan altogether rather than make the loan at a higher interest rate. The cost of lendable funds is far more important in determining what rate a lender demands from a borrower.

54. **D** In real-world lending, most lenders would be more likely to turn down a marginal loan altogether rather than make the loan at a higher interest rate. While there are some lenders who specialize in marginal loans, for the majority of lenders the rate they demand from borrowers is determined by the lender's cost of funds.

55. **D** Interest rates are always set by competitive forces in the marketplace. It is true that the Federal Reserve Board can influence the market for money and capital, but the most direct force is still competition.

56. **C** The Federal Reserve Bank Board of Governors and the Federal Open Market Committee have various tools they use to influence the supply and cost of credit, and thereby influence the economy. Tax rates influence the economy by affecting people's ability to buy. All of these would have an effect on loan demand, and therefore interest rates.

57. **D** Selling a loan for less than the face amount due is called loan discounting. It is a means of increasing the yield to the investor who buys the loan above the rate of interest the borrower is paying.

58. **D** Selling a loan for less than the remaining unpaid balance is a way to increase the yield to the investor who buys the loan. The practice is called loan discounting.

59. **C** Loan discounting has occurred since the days when the first loan was sold. If an investor buys a loan for less than the face amount due, the investor's yield is effectively higher than the note rate. This is because the borrower will eventually pay the full amount, even though the investor's investment is less than the full amount.

60. **B** When a lender sells a loan to an investor the investor will get a higher yield than the note rate if the investor buys the loan for less than the face amount due on the loan. This is called loan discounting. The amount of the discount is measured in points. One point equals one percent of the loan balance.

61. **B** Loan discounts are measured in points. One point is one percent of the loan balance. By selling a loan at less than the full balance due, the yield

to the purchaser is increased. The seller of the loan suffers a corresponding loss. The seller of the loan is typically a primary lender who originated the loan. The primary lender probably knew the loan would have to be sold at a discount, and therefore charged the borrower the anticipated discount at closing.

62. **A** As pension funds have grown, so has their interest in real estate lending. Pension funds are long term and must be invested conservatively. Mortgages are therefore an ideal investment vehicle. Most pension fund investing in residential property has been as secondary lenders.

63. **B** A primary lender is a lender who originates a mortgage loan. A secondary lender is a lender who purchases loans as an investment from a primary lender. Do not confuse "secondary lender" with a lender who makes a second mortgage loan. Second mortgage loans are examples of junior financing, not secondary financing.

64. **D** The secondary market refers to investors and large institutions who purchase loans from primary lenders. Primary lenders are the loan originators.

65. **C** Do not confuse "secondary mortgage market" with "junior financing." The secondary mortgage market is made up of large organizations and investors who purchase blocks of loans originated by primary lenders. "Junior financing" refers to second mortgages.

66. **C** The secondary mortgage market is made up of numerous large organizations which purchase loans from primary lenders, or package bundles of loans originated by primary lenders and arrange for their sale to investors. This assures primary lenders a source of capital to continue making loans.

67. **B** Primary lenders originate and service real estate loans. The function of the secondary mortgage market is to ensure the availability of funds to primary lenders by providing them with a place to sell their loans. Whether or not a loan is insured is irrelevant.

68. **D** The primary mortgage market is made up of lenders who originate loans and continue to service the loans after they are made. The secondary market is composed of large organizations to whom and through whom primary lenders can sell their loans.

69. **B** Primary lenders are those who originate loans. Secondary lenders are those who purchase loans from primary lenders. "Secondary financing" means a junior lien (second mortgage).

70. **B** Today, the major source of funds for conventional loans is the same as for any other residential loan, that is, investors in the primary capital markets. Most residential loans today are sold in the secondary market, which in turn pledges them as collateral for securities issues which are sold to investors.

71. **C** The Government National Mortgage Association and the Federal National Mortgage Association are secondary lenders. They do not make loans. Their sole function is to buy loans originated by local lenders.

72. **C** Although originally founded for more restricted purposes, today both the Federal National Mortgage Association and the Federal Home Loan Mortgage Corporation are authorized to purchase any kind of residential loan from any primary lender.

73. **B** Since a mortgage banker may have limited funds, it is not uncommon to pledge existing loans as collateral for a short term working capital loan at a commercial bank. The working capital loan can allow the mortgage banker to complete a larger pool of loans before selling them in the secondary market. The larger the pool, the more favorable the terms when selling the loans. Pledging the loans as collateral for a short term working capital loan is called "warehousing."

74. **C** Lenders with limited capital, such as mortgage bankers, have no choice but to sell their loan production in the secondary market to recover the capital for making additional loans. The larger the pool of loans, the more favorable terms in the secondary market. Therefore, it is common for mortgage bankers to pledge existing loans as collateral for a short term working capital loan from a commercial bank. When the pool of loans is sold, the bank loan is paid off. This is called loan warehousing. A portfolio loan is one which is held in a lender's own portfolio, usually because it is not salable in the secondary market.

75. **A** "FDIC" stands for "Federal Deposit Insurance Corporation." Its sole function is to insure deposits in financial institutions. Fannie Mae and Freddie Mac purchase loans as secondary lenders. Ginnie Mae does not purchase loans, but is considered a secondary lender because its function is to guarantee securities issued by Fannie Mae and Freddie Mac.

76. **B** At one time, real estate loans were funded from customer deposits in local thrift institutions. Today, such deposits provide the funds to originate loans, but practically all lenders sell their entire production in the secondary market.

77. **C** The Federal National Mortgage Association (Fannie Mae) is the oldest of the secondary lenders. It was formed to create liquidity for primary

lenders by making available a market where they can sell their loan production. Investors buy stock and securities issued by Fannie Mae, thus channeling investment capital into housing loans.

78.   **B**   The Federal National Mortgage Association (Fannie Mae) has no supervisory or regulatory functions, although it does indirectly establish lending guidelines (underwriting standards) in conjunction with other secondary lenders, chiefly the Federal Home Loan Mortgage Corporation.

79.   **C**   The Federal National Mortgage Association (Fannie Mae) does not originate loans; its sole function is to purchase loans originated by primary lenders.

80.   **D**   The Federal National Mortgage Association (Fannie Mae) is a secondary lender, i.e., it purchases loans originated by primary lenders. The primary lender continues to service the loan after it is sold, remitting the payments of principal and interest to Fannie Mae. Fannie Mae is authorized to purchase any kind of residential loan. Its secondary market activities increase the liquidity of the primary lenders.

81.   **A**   The Federal National Mortgage Association (Fannie Mae) is a secondary lender, that is, it purchases loans which were originated by primary lenders. It can buy any kind of residential loan, although at its inception in 1938 it was restricted to just FHA loans. An FHA Title I loan is for home improvements. Title II loans are for home acquisition.

82.   **B**   Fannie Mae is strictly a secondary lender, that is, it purchases loans originated by primary lenders. Fannie Mae does not service the loans it acquires, relying instead on the primary lender to continue servicing the loan.

83.   **B**   Fannie Mae is authorized to purchase any kind of residential loan. It does not originate loans, however. Its sole function is to purchase loans from primary lenders. Its original name was the "Federal National Mortgage Association." Investors shortened the name to "Fannie Mae" as a slang term. Eventually the board of directors voted to adopt "Fannie Mae" as the official name of the organization, although they also maintain rights to the old name.

84.   **D**   Originally, Fannie Mae was allowed to purchase FHA loans only. Later, federal GI loans were added. Since 1970, Fannie Mae has been authorized to purchase any kind of residential mortgage loan.

85.   **A**   The Federal National Mortgage Association (Fannie Mae) was originally formed to purchase only FHA loans. In the 1970s this restriction was lifted and it can now purchase any kind of residential real estate loan. Chattel mortgages are security instruments which make personal property collateral for a debt.

86.   **B**   Fannie Mae will buy from any primary lender or even from other secondary lenders, regardless of the type of organization. Primary lenders must meet Fannie Mae standards and be approved as to their creditworthiness, but the type of organization is irrelevant.

87.   **D**   One of Fannie Mae's major activities is selling mortgage-backed securities in the primary capital markets to raise capital for additional loan acquisitions. In the early days Fannie Mae obtained funds by borrowing from the U.S. Treasury, but this has not been the case for several decades.

88.   **B**   The Government National Mortgage Association (Ginnie Mae) does not actually buy or sell loans; its sole function is to act as a guarantor. In that capacity it has the authority to extend the full faith and credit of the U.S. Government to securities issues in order to make them more attractive to investors. The more attractive the securities issue, the lower the interest rate, and therefore the lower the cost of mortgage funds. Although not a common occurrence, Ginnie Mae has also guaranteed Fannie Mae securities under certain special programs.

89.   **A**   The Federal National Mortgage Association (Fannie Mae) is privately owned by investors. Its stock is listed on the New York Stock Exchange. However, because it performs such a vital role in providing capital for the nation's housing market, it is regulated by the federal government. The Government National Mortgage Association is a wholly government-owned organization. The Federal Housing Mortgage Association and the National Mortgage Loan Association do not exist.

90.   **C**   The original purpose of Fannie Mae was to provide a secondary market for FHA loans. Later VA loans were added and, in 1970, conventional loans as well. Although it started as a government-owned organization, in 1954 it was reorganized and given the authority to issue capital stock to investors. In a second restructuring in 1968 it redeemed all stock held by the government and became totally privately owned.

91.   **B**   The Federal National Mortgage Association (Fannie Mae) was originally a purely federal agency. With the Charter of 1954, private investors were invited to purchase stock. In 1968 the government interest was completely bought out by

private investors. However, its corporate charter is issued by Congress, not a state government, as is the case with most corporations. It can only do what its charter allows it to do, so it would be correct to say that it is supervised by Congress.

92. **C** The Government National Mortgage Association is a wholly government-owned secondary lender. As such, it is the vehicle through which Congress authorizes special assistance loan programs such as housing for the elderly, urban renewal, and the like.

93. **C** Ginnie Mae was created as a spin-off from Fannie Mae in the restructuring of 1968. Although it is a secondary lender, it has never purchased a loan. Instead, primary lenders on FHA and VA loans sell investment certificates backed by the mortgages to investors. GNMA guarantees the securities with the full faith and credit of the U.S. government.

94. **C** Both Fannie Mae and Freddie Mac are secondary lenders which purchase loans from primary lenders such as mortgage bankers. This allows the primary lender greater liquidity and access to lendable capital.

95. **A** The Federal Home Loan Bank System was created to serve the needs of thrift institutions in a manner somewhat parallel to the way the Federal Reserve System serves the needs of commercial banks. Originally, it also regulated member institutions, but that function is now carried out by the Office of Thrift Supervision, an agency under the Treasury.

96. **A** The purpose of the Federal Home Loan Bank is to provide liquidity for member thrift institutions by acting as a "banker's bank" to them. It does not lend money to any other entities.

97. **C** The Federal Home Loan Mortgage Corporation (Freddie Mac) was formed as a subsidiary of the Federal Home Loan Bank System to provide a secondary market for institutions which are members of the System, largely thrift institutions. It is authorized to purchase any type of loan today from any kind of lender, whether a member of the FHLBS or not.

98. **D** The original capitalization of the Federal Home Loan Mortgage Corporation (Freddie Mac) was provided by the twelve Federal Home Loan Banks. Subsequently, additional capital stock was sold to member thrift institutions. Today, funds are also raised by pledging mortgage loans as collateral for securities issues which are sold in the primary capital markets. Although Fannie Mae at one time borrowed funds from the U.S. Treasury, Freddie Mac has never done so.

99. **B** Real Estate Mortgage Investment Conduits (REMICs) were created by the Tax Reform Act of 1986. They sell tranches to investors, which are participations in pools of mortgages where the participations are not direct pass-throughs of principal and interest.

100. **C** The Oregon Department of Veterans Affairs sells tax-exempt bonds at low interest rates, and makes direct loans to eligible veterans with the funds. Since the cost of the funds is low, the Department can make loans to veterans at below-market rates. The Oregon Department of Housing and Community Services also sells tax-exempt revenue bonds, but rather than make direct loans, they use the funds to purchase special assistance loans from Oregon institutional lenders.

101. **A** When inflation increases, money loses its value. To counter this effect investors look to investments in commodities which have an intrinsic value and can always be traded for money. By holding such commodities over the inflationary period, when the commodity is exchanged later for money, it will command more dollars. Favorite investments during inflationary times include gold and other precious metals, art, classic cars, coins and stamps, and the like. However, because real estate investments can be easily financed, real estate is by far the favorite investment as a hedge against inflation. In contrast, any investment whose return consists of interest will lose value during an inflationary period.

GOVERNMENT FINANCING PROGRAMS

A LTHOUGH NON-GOVERNMENT LOANS PROVIDE FINANCING FOR MOST RESIDEN-
tial borrowers today, real estate agents would make far fewer sales if the various
government financing options were not available. Even more important, government loan programs have made home ownership possible for millions of Americans who
could not have qualified without them. America has developed the highest level of home
ownership of any country in the world, and the success of government loan programs
over the last seven decades is a large part of the reason.

A government loan is any loan that is insured or guaranteed or made directly by
the federal, state or local government. In contrast, conventional loans are private contracts strictly between the lender and the borrower without any government involvement
of any sort.

Among government loan agencies, the largest is the Federal Housing Administration (FHA). On a national level, loans to veterans guaranteed by the federal Department of Veterans Affairs are the second largest source of government loans. For
rural properties loans through various federal agencies such as Farm Credit System
and the Farm Service Agency are also important sources of mortgage funding. And
no one in Oregon can ignore the Oregon Department of Veterans Affairs, which holds
mortgages on thousands of Oregon homes. The Oregon Department of Housing and
Community Services is another state agency which provides financing for special
housing needs including below-market rate loans for first-time home buyers and buyers of homes in specially targeted areas. The various programs offered by these agencies with specific purposes and qualifying requirements are what we will explore in
this section.

The Federal Housing Administration

The **Federal Housing Administration** (FHA) was created under the provisions of the National Housing Act of 1934. Its original purpose was to create jobs by stimulating housing construction and also to upgrade the nation's housing stock by promoting loans for home improvement. Under the original provisions of the National Housing Act, Title I was for home improvement loans and Title II spelled out the programs for home acquisition and refinance loans. Later many other titles were added to the original Act, creating programs for rent and interest rate subsidies, among a multitude of other purposes.

Real estate agents owe a great deal to the FHA. Although the FHA is not technically a lender, no other institution in the field of residential lending is as large. FHA loans are responsible for approximately 800,000 home purchases every year. Over the years the FHA is the only agency large enough to be able to experiment and try new approaches to residential lending. Practically all innovations in residential lending began with the FHA, later being copied and adapted by conventional lenders. The FHA pioneered minimum property standards and established standard qualifying procedures. And most importantly, FHA loans made the secondary market possible, without which real estate lending would be at the mercy of local economic conditions.

Today, the FHA loan program is operated by the Department of Housing and Urban Development in Washington, D.C. For purposes of administering FHA loans, HUD has divided the nation into ten regions, and each region has area offices in major cities. Oregon is in Region 10, whose headquarters are in Seattle with area offices in Portland, Spokane, Anchorage and Boise.

Although the FHA has been a direct lender on occasion in the past, it functions today almost exclusively as an insurer of loans. As a federal agency, it places the credit of the U.S. Government behind the borrower by insuring the borrower's loan against default. The loan itself is made by an institutional lender (called a **participating lender** in FHA terminology), such as a bank, thrift institution, mortgage banker, or any other organization that wishes to make totally secure loans. In the event of a default, the lender can recover losses from the FHA insurance pool.

The FHA insurance is called **mutual mortgage insurance** (MIP), to distinguish it from insurance provided by private insurance companies for conventional loans. Premiums for the mutual mortgage insurance are paid by the borrower and are calculated to be sufficient to cover anticipated losses and overhead. The FHA insurance program is designed to be self-liquidating and cost the taxpayers nothing.

The beauty of FHA insurance is that it entices lenders to make riskier loans with higher loan to value and more liberal income to debt ratios than they would otherwise be willing to make. Although anyone can get an FHA loan, FHA programs are structured primarily for first-time buyers.

Throughout most of the history of the FHA the mutual mortgage insurance premium was ½ of 1% (0.5%) per annum of the principal balance. The borrower would pay ¹⁄₁₂ of this annual premium with each payment. Lenders would collect the premium and place it in a reserve account for the borrower. Each year the lender would remit the premium to the FHA to continue the insurance for the coming year. Millions of loans were made this way, a few of which remain on the books even today.

In 1983 the method for collecting the mutual mortgage insurance was changed. Instead of paying ¹⁄₁₂ of ½ of 1% of the loan balance monthly, the borrower would pay 3.8%

of the principal balance at the beginning of the loan, which provides insurance for the entire first ten years. No additional amounts are collected on these loans. However, 3.8% of the principal balance is a lot of money for most borrowers, so FHA rules allow the lender to increase the loan amount by adding the premium to the balance due. Since the loan balance is higher, the monthly payments are higher, but then, the total monthly payment is probably not significantly different from what it would have been under the old system.

In 1991 calculation of the mutual mortgage insurance was modified again. The borrower paid the 3.8% premium in advance *plus* the monthly ¹⁄₁₂ of ½ of 1% of the loan amount. Although this made the program somewhat unattractive, we must bear in mind that the program is designed to be self-liquidating. The same economic conditions which caused the massive failures of savings and loan associations also caused the FHA mutual mortgage insurance fund to suffer fairly serious losses for several years. Raising the premiums was the only way to ensure the solvency of the FHA program.

Because the high premium charges made the program undesirable, the upfront premium was subsequently lowered to 2¼% of the loan balance for loans over 15 years, which is the vast majority of FHA loans. For borrowers in central cities who complete a 16-hour homebuyer education program the upfront fee is reduced to 1½% of the loan balance. The borrower still pays the ¹⁄₁₂ of ½ of 1% as well.

If a borrower pays the loan off early, there will be a partial refund of that portion of the premium which was prepaid (the 1½ or 2¼%). Similarly, if a borrower sells the property and the new buyer takes over the borrower's loan, it is customary for the new buyer to reimburse the original borrower for the portion of the premium which remains prepaid.

Real estate agents should be aware that a lender with an FHA insured loan will never lose money on the loan, but will also never profit from a foreclosure. If the lender forecloses on an FHA loan, the FHA usually requires the lender to open the bidding at the foreclosure sale with the total amount owed. All bidders other than the lender must pay all cash, so if the lender is outbid, this means the lender will be cashed out, and there is no further need for the FHA insurance. If the lender wins the bidding, the lender will then take title to the property. The lender then trades the property to the FHA for FHA bonds which mature at the same term as the remaining term on the loan, and bear the same interest rate as the original note. The lender does not receive cash, which could then conceivably be used to make a new loan at a higher rate to someone else. Because there is no way to profit from a foreclosure, the lender sees a foreclosure only as a last resort. As a result, lenders usually demonstrate greater forbearance with FHA loans than with conventional loans.

The FHA has many different programs, but for all FHA programs there is a maximum loan amount. The FHA changes the maximum amounts from time to time, and the maximums also vary from county to county. Of course, the FHA has different loan to value ratios for different programs, so the actual maximum loan amount can vary. To determine the current maximum loan amount requires consultation with a participating lender.

Traditionally, a borrower wanting an FHA loan would make application at a participating lender. Until recently, the lender would gather all the documents necessary to approve the loan – the verification of employment, credit report, copies of the earnest money agreement, and so forth – and send the documents to the area FHA office for ***underwriting approval***. The term "underwriting" is used here as a synonym for "insurance." In other words, since the ultimate risk is being carried by the FHA, it is the FHA which will want to be sure the borrower and the property qualify for the loan.

Today, most FHA loans are processed in a different manner. FHA now tells lenders what is required to approve an FHA loan. A lender can apply to be a ***direct endorsement*** lender, which allows the lender to approve the loan without sending the paperwork to the FHA for underwriting approval. To ensure compliance with FHA standards the FHA conducts spot audits of lenders' loan files. However, even direct endorsement lenders are not allowed to approve all loans. If a loan does not meet direct endorsement standards, it must be sent to the FHA for underwriting approval. Nevertheless, direct endorsement allows almost all FHA loans to be approved without waiting for FHA approval.

Another recent innovation to the FHA program is the possibility of co-insurance. Co-insurance, as the term would imply, means that the lender shares any losses with the FHA. The advantage to the lender is that the FHA gives the lender complete authority over loan approval. The disadvantage is the potential for greater losses in the event of a downturn in the economy that causes defaults.

The FHA sets maximums on the amount lenders can charge for borrower expenses such as loan origination fees, credit report fees, appraisals, and the like. Until 1983, the FHA also set a maximum interest rate that a lender could charge on an FHA loan. This interest rate was almost always set a little below market. After all, the goal of the FHA was to make housing affordable, and keeping the interest rate down would further that goal.

However, setting a maximum interest rate which was below market created a problem when the primary lender tried to sell the loan in the secondary market. Secondary market investors demand a market rate, so the loans had to be sold at a discount.

Suppose a loan were made at a below-market rate, and then sold to a secondary lender at a discount. If the secondary lender bought the loan for, say, 96¢ on the dollar, then the discount was 4%. The 4% discount was calculated on the loan balance, so if the loan balance in our example was $100,000, the discount would be $4,000 ($100,000 × 0.04 = $4,000). The secondary lender actually invested only $96,000, but is getting a return on the investment as though the investment were the full $100,000. After all, the sale of the loan does not change the borrower's obligation to repay the full $100,000. This effectively raises the secondary lender's yield on the $96,000 investment.

To keep from confusing the percentage of discount with the percentage of interest (interest rate) on the loan, we refer to the interest on the loan with the word "percent," as in "eight percent interest"; but we refer to percentage of discount with the term ***points***. In other words, the 4% discount in the above example would more commonly be stated as "four points" or "four points discount."

Real estate agents have a rule of thumb about discount points. Lenders have more sophisticated methods of calculating the discount, but real estate agents have discovered that there will usually be about eight points of discount (8% discount) charged for each whole percent of difference between the loan interest rate and market interest rate. In other words, if a lender makes a loan at 7% interest, but secondary lenders demand a rate of 8%, the secondary lender will discount the loan about eight points. Similarly, if the differential between the note rate and market rate is ½ of 1%, then you can anticipate about four points discount, and so on.

Of course, the primary lender will suffer a loss when the loan is sold in the secondary market. In our example above where a $100,000 loan was sold for 96¢ on the dollar, the loss would be $4,000. Obviously, the lender would decline to make FHA loans unless someone agreed to reimburse the lender for this loss. The logical candidate would be the borrower, since the borrower is getting the benefit of the below-market interest rate. But making the borrower pay an additional loan discount would not further the FHA's goal of making housing affordable, so the FHA made a rule that the borrower could not pay any part of the discount points. The only other person in the transaction with enough cash to pay the discount was the seller, so it became common practice to insist that the seller pay the discount points.

This made FHA loans unpopular with sellers. Sellers would, quite naturally, try to raise the price of the house to cover the anticipated discount. Sometimes this worked, although other times the appraisal would not come back high enough to allow the seller to recover the discount.

As a result, in 1983 FHA changed the rules. There is no longer a maximum interest rate on most FHA loans. Therefore, if the borrower agrees to pay a market rate, there will be no discount. On the other hand, the seller could agree to pay a certain number of points to buy the interest rate down for the borrower. A seller might agree to do this as a sales incentive. At the same time the FHA also rescinded the rule that borrowers were not allowed to pay the discount. So if a borrower wants a lower interest rate and the seller will not pay the discount, the borrower is now free to do so.

Not only do FHA loans provide more liberal qualifying terms for the borrower, they also have another great advantage. Unlike most conventional loans, all FHA loans are assumable. The rules on assumptions have changed, however, and the assumability today depends on when the loan was originated.

When a buyer "assumes" a loan the buyer enters into an *assumption agreement* with the lender. In this case the seller (original borrower) remains liable, and the buyer also takes personal responsibility to pay the loan. Think of an assumption as being the equivalent of the new buyer co-signing the note. A buyer could also take title subject to the loan without entering into an assumption agreement with the lender, in which case the buyer would incur no personal obligation to pay. The lender could still foreclose, but if the property failed to sell for enough at the foreclosure sale, only the original borrower could be held liable for any deficiency.

Of course, lenders want the buyer to enter into an assumption agreement and they want the buyer to submit to credit approval as well. As a result, it became common practice to offer the original borrower an incentive to get the new buyer to submit to credit approval and to assume the loan. The inducement is to offer to release the original borrower from liability if the new buyer will submit to credit approval and assume the loan.

When a buyer takes title without entering into an assumption agreement, real estate agents call this taking title *subject to* the loan. Technically speaking, the buyer takes title subject to the loan when the buyer enters into an assumption agreement as well, but real estate agents generally refer to this as an *assumption*. When the buyer assumes without going through credit approval, this is commonly called a *blind assumption* or sometimes a *simple assumption*. When a buyer assumes, goes through credit approval, and the original borrower is released from liability, this is called a *substitution of mortgagor*, or in terms of contract law, a *novation*.

In the past, all FHA loans could be assumed by a buyer and the FHA made no requirements of the buyer. Starting with loans originated after December 1, 1986, the loan documents require a new buyer to submit to credit approval and enter into an assumption agreement if the loan is taken over during the first two years of the loan. After the loan was two years old, the old rules applied and the lender could no longer require the new buyer to assume or submit to credit approval. And even if the loan was assumed during the first two years, the lender could not require a change in the interest rate.

In March of 1989 the rules were changed again. For loans made after that date, the new buyer only needed to submit to credit approval and assume the loan if it was taken over during the first year of the loan. And both the original borrower and the new buyer would be equally personally obligated for five years, after which the original borrower would be released from liability. And as before, even if the loan was assumed during the first year, the lender could not require a change in the interest rate.

Then the rules changed yet again. For all loans originated after December 15, 1989, the new buyer must always submit to credit approval and enter into an assumption agreement; blind assumptions are no longer possible. Both the original borrower and the new buyer remain fully liable until the entire loan is paid in full. Furthermore, the new buyer must agree to occupy the property; investor assumptions are prohibited. The only advantage is that the lender still cannot require a change in the interest rate.

When assuming an FHA loan it is important to know when the loan was made. Whatever the rules were when the loan was made are the rules which govern its assumption. This is because the rules were written into the note and trust deed, so neither the lender nor the FHA can change them after the fact.

Another advantage of FHA loans (and all government loans) is that there is never a prepayment penalty. The borrower can pay the loan off at any time without extra charges. This is not always true on conventional loans.

FHA programs

Over its history, the FHA has developed dozens of different loan programs. Many of these programs are no longer being used. Others are programs to finance large residential complexes, frequently to provide elderly, handicapped and low-income housing. A complete discussion of all FHA loan programs is beyond our scope here, but we should examine at least the more commonly encountered programs.

The most popular FHA program is the ***Section 203 (b) Loan Program***. This is the primary program and many other programs are based on it. Any resident of the United States can obtain an FHA 203 (b) loan, whether a citizen or not. An FHA 203 (b) loan is a fixed rate loan with a term of up to 30 years. Lenders sometimes limit the term to 20 or 25 years if the property has a short remaining economic life. Many lenders also offer a 15-year term at a slightly lower interest rate, even if the property has a long remaining life. But those are individual lender requirements; the program itself allows loans up to 30 years. Section 203 (b) loans can be used to buy or refinance one- to four-family properties. Manufactured housing also qualifies if the borrower will own the land. To acquire a home, the borrower must agree to occupy the property.

For most FHA loan programs, the maximum loan to value ratio is a complicated calculation, and 203 (b) loans are no exception. FHA allows the borrower to finance some of the ***allowable closing costs***. The allowable closing costs vary according to the amount of the purchase price. FHA has created a chart of maximum allowable closing costs which is based on their estimate of what the actual average closing costs ought to be. The chart is available from area FHA offices or from local lenders. Note that the borrower will ultimately pay the actual closing costs at close of escrow; the purpose of the chart is just to estimate the closing costs for purposes of calculating the maximum loan amount.

The calculation is to add the financeable portion of the allowable closing costs to the sales price. If this comes to more than $50,000, then the maximum loan amount is 97% of the first $25,000 and 95% of the rest.

The borrower can also ask the seller or third party to pay all or part of the allowable closing costs. In this case, the procedure to calculate the maximum loan amount will be slightly different because some or all of the allowable closing costs cannot be added, although the loan to value ratio will still be very high compared to conventional loans.

Since the goal of the FHA is to make housing affordable, it should come as no surprise that there are rules establishing maximum amounts that can be charged to the borrower. For example, the maximum loan fee the borrower is allowed to pay is one percent. In addition, the borrower may not be charged for document preparation, notary services, and a number of other charges that lenders like to pass on to borrowers.

An ***FHA Section 203 (b) (2)*** loan is a special type of 203 (b) loan for eligible veterans. Real estate agents sometimes call these "FHA/VA" loans, but note that they should not be confused with loans guaranteed by the federal Department of Veterans Affairs.

Section 203 (b) (2) loans are the same as regular 203 (b) loans except that only single-family properties (including manufactured housing on owned land) are acceptable, and the loan to value ratio is more liberal. For most properties the loan to value ratio will be 100% of the first $25,000, including allowable closing costs, and 95% of the balance. For new construction less than one year old, or manufactured housing which has been in place for less than one year, the maximum loan to value ratio is 90%. Of course, the borrower must be a qualified veteran who has served at least 90 days of continuous active duty and has obtained a Certificate of Veteran's Status from the federal Department of Veterans Affairs.

Section 203 (h) loans provide special terms for victims of disasters.

Section 203 (i) loans are similar to 203 (b) loans, but for properties in outlying areas.

Section 203 (k) loans are designed to allow the borrower to obtain a fixed or adjustable rate loan to acquire and rehabilitate a home. Most lenders are unwilling to make 203 (k) loans because of the extensive documentation required. Extra paperwork is required because the loan can be closed and funds disbursed to acquire the property, but the remainder of the loan must remain in escrow to be disbursed as work is completed. One important advantage of this program is that the upfront mortgage insurance premium is waived.

Section 221 (d) (2) loans are not commonly encountered today because the maximum loan amounts are too stringent. This program was originally created to assist people displaced by the freeway construction projects of the late 1950s and 1960s, but continues today and is available for all borrowers who qualify for its special provisions.

Section 222 provides special lower down payment loans for career military personnel.

Section 223 (e) loans are loans for properties in older, declining areas.

Section 234 (c) provides loans to acquire a unit in a condominium which is being converted from apartments, by a renter in the building.

Section 237 is a special program for borrowers who are poor credit risks.

Section 245 (a) loans are graduated payment loans (GPMs) with a fixed interest rate for the acquisition of a single-family home only. Graduated payment loans are not popular today, but during periods of high interest they can be a useful financing tool. A GPM loan has monthly payments at the beginning which are deliberately calculated to be too low even to cover the interest, let alone repay (amortize) the debt. This results in **negative amortization**, a situation where the balance owing increases over the first years of the loan. The amount of the monthly payment is increased each year, so that eventually the negative amortization is reversed and the borrower starts paying off the loan. Of course, GPM loans will be popular only when borrowers believe that increasing property values will cover the increasing debt. In any other kind of market, a GPM loan is potentially a disaster.

Section 234 (c) is a section of the National Housing Act that makes special provisions for condominium loans under the other programs. Section 234 (c) provides that condominium loans can be made only in complexes that have been approved by FHA, the federal Department of Veterans Affairs, or Fannie Mae. To gain approval, the bylaws and operations of the homeowners' association must be scrutinized and the ratio of owner occupied units to rental units must meet minimum standards.

Section 251 allows loans under Section 203 (b), 203 (k) and 234 (c) to be made with adjustable interest rates, using the one-year Treasury Constant Maturities Index to determine interest rate changes, with an annual cap of 1% and a lifetime cap of 5%.

The above programs are for single-family dwellings up to fourplexes. Although less popular, there are additional programs for properties in excess of four units. These include a wide variety of purposes, including rental housing for the elderly, people with

NOTES | disabilities, single room occupancy projects, projects in urban areas targeted for revital-ization, mobile home parks, as well as ordinary rental investments.

Exercise a

In real estate finance "FHA" stands for _____ _____ Administration, which was created under the National Housing Act in 1934. Title ____ loans are for home improvement and rehabilitation and Title ____ loans are for home acquisition and refinance. The FHA does not actually lend money, but rather _____ loans against default. The loan is made by a _____ lender. The premium paid by the borrower on an FHA loan is called the _____ mortgage _____ premium. On older FHA loans this premium was usually _____ of _____ of each month, included in the payment. Now, the borrower also pays _____ % of the original loan balance up front on most FHA loans. Today most FHA loans are approved by the lender because most lenders are _____ _____ lenders today.

Which of the following may pay discount points on an FHA loan?

❑ Borrower   ❑ Lender   ❑ Broker   ❑ Seller   ❑ Borrower's friends and relatives

When we speak of discount points, how many points would likely be charged on a loan if the note rate was 7% but the secondary market demanded 7¾%? _____

The basic FHA loan program is Section _____ . Special terms for veterans are available under Section _____ . Loans to acquire and rehabilitate a property are available under Section _____ . Mortgages for low and moderate income borrowers are available under Section _____ . Adjustable interest rate FHA loans are available under Section _____ . Section _____ applies to loans for condominiums. Loans under Section _____ are available for older, declining neighborhoods. Loans under Section _____ are for properties in outlying areas.

Federal Department of Veterans Affairs

Hard on the heels of World War II victory, Congress passed the Servicemen's Readjustment Act of 1945, more popularly called the "GI Bill," and now officially referred to as Title 38 U.S. Code. The GI Bill provided medical benefits, pensions, educational opportunities and many other advantages to promote the welfare of returning veterans. For real estate agents, the most significant of these other benefits is the right to borrow money for a home and have the federal government guarantee the loan.

Most real estate agents call these loans *federal GI* loans or *federal VA* loans, although the latter term is no longer technically correct. The loans originally were obtained through the Veterans Administration, an agency under the Department of Defense. In 1988 the Veterans Administration was elevated to its own cabinet post and renamed the **U.S. Department of Veterans Affairs** (DVA), so "federal VA" should probably be changed to "federal DVA," although it's not likely people will stop using the old term.

Federal GI loans are similar to FHA loans in one respect – like the FHA, the U.S. Department of Veterans Affairs does not ordinarily lend money. Instead it entices private banks, thrift institutions, mortgage bankers and others to make loans to eligible veterans by guaranteeing the loan against default. There is one major difference, however. Where the FHA *insures* the loan against default, the Department of Veterans Affairs *guarantees* the loan. The technical difference is significant. The word "insurance" implies that a premium is paid, which is definitely the case with FHA loans. A "guaranty" is like a co-signature, for which there is no charge.

Officially there is no charge for the guaranty. Today, however, the DVA charges a ***funding fee***. Currently the funding fee is 2% of the loan amount for a loan with no down payment. This is reduced to 1½% of the loan balance if the veteran borrower makes a 5% down payment, and to 1¼% for a 10% down payment. The funding fee is ¾ of 1% higher for reservists. The funding fee may be added to the loan amount, even if this would cause the loan amount to be greater than the appraised value of the property.

Unlike other loan programs, the DVA requires no down payment. Nor does the DVA set any maximum loan amount. There is, however, a maximum ***guaranty*** or ***entitlement***. In 1945 the original entitlement was $2,000, but today is $36,000 for homes valued up to $144,000, and $60,000 for homes valued over $144,000.

The interesting thing about the entitlement is that lenders will treat it the same as down payment, from a security standpoint. The most important reason for a down payment is to protect the lender in the event of a foreclosure. Since properties rarely sell for their highest market value when they are sold for cash in a forced auction sale, lenders want a cushion for protection. Traditionally, lenders have considered that a 75% loan to value ratio is safe and prudent.

Now, if the U.S. Department of Veterans Affairs will guarantee a maximum of the top $60,000 of the loan, a lender will generally consider that guaranty the same as down payment from a security standpoint. Therefore, the question is, how big a loan would a lender be willing to make if the top 25% of the loan was $60,000? The answer is simple – four times the $60,000, or $240,000. In other words, at a loan of $240,000, the top 25% of the loan is $60,000.

As a practical matter then, lenders will not make federal GI loans over $240,000. Note that this maximum is set by the *lender*, not by the DVA. The DVA sets no maximum loan amount. And, in fact, in high cost areas of the country, it is customary to find lenders willing to exceed the $240,000 maximum. However, they will exceed the $240,000 only if the veteran borrower makes a down payment of 25% of the amount of the purchase price which exceeds $240,000. Such a down payment keeps the lender from exceeding the 75% risk level. Note that it is not the original lender who makes the rule – the rule is from secondary mortgage market investors who buy securities backed by federal GI loans. To make a loan over $240,000 requires the primary lender to find an alternate market.

Of course, the loan also cannot exceed the amount of the sales price or appraised value, whichever is less, plus the funding fee. The DVA will have the property appraised and the appraisal report is called a ***certificate of reasonable value***, or just ***CRV*** for short. Note that the veteran is free to pay more for the property than the appraised value – it is only the loan amount that cannot exceed the appraised value plus funding fee.

The DVA does allow junior financing, but only as long as the total of the DVA guaranteed first lien and the junior lien does not exceed the amount of the CRV. Although loans can be as high as 100% loan to value ratio, there may be lenders unwilling to lend the full 100%, therefore junior financing can sometimes occur. The second lien document must be approved by the DVA, the interest rate cannot exceed the rate on the first, it must be amortized over at least five years, and there can be no balloon payments.

Occasionally the question comes up if a veteran who already used his or her entitlement can obtain another loan. There are several ways this can be done. If the veteran has sold the property and the loan is either paid in full or assumed by another veteran who uses his or her own entitlement, the original borrower can apply to the DVA for a complete restoration of entitlement. Or a veteran could get an additional DVA loan if the veteran has not used all of his or her entitlement. For example, suppose a veteran bought a home years ago when the entitlement was lower. Since Congress has raised the entitlement, now the veteran may have unused entitlement. Since lenders will generally lend four times the amount of the entitlement without requiring a down payment, it may be possible for many veterans to obtain a second federal GI loan. Veterans may also have their complete loan entitlement restored for purposes of refinancing an existing federal GI loan in order to obtain a lower interest rate.

To qualify for a federal GI loan the borrower's first step is to request a Certificate of Eligibility from the Department of Veterans Affairs. The eligibility requirements are complex and most real estate agents find it is more convenient to have a potential veteran buyer go or write directly to the Department of Veterans Affairs and let them determine the veteran's eligibility. After, all the veteran has to get the Certificate of Eligibility sooner or later, so why not get it before even beginning to look for a home? Oregon is served by a DVA regional office in Portland, so it is not difficult for veterans to do this.

However, there are certain persons who are entitled to a federal GI loan guaranty even though they are not technically "veterans." For example, service personnel currently on active duty who have been on continuous active duty for at least 90 days are entitled to a federal GI loan. Unmarried surviving spouses of veterans who died from service connected injuries also qualify, as well as spouses of service persons who have been missing in action or prisoners of war for at least 90 days. The Department of Veterans Affairs will even grant a Certificate of Eligibility to U.S. citizens who served in the armed forces of another country which was a U.S. ally during World War II.

Many lenders who make federal GI loans are qualified as ***automatic lenders***. This is the equivalent of an FHA direct endorsement lender, in fact, FHA direct endorsement lenders probably also qualify as federal GI automatic lenders. Automatic lenders are allowed to approve the loans themselves, and the Department of Veterans Affairs spot audits their loan files to ensure that they are following required underwriting standards.

Federal GI loans are always assumable but, like FHA loans, the rules have changed over the years. Loans made before March 1, 1988 had no due on sale clause, and any buyer, whether a veteran or not, could take title subject to the loan with or without assuming and with or without qualifying. As with FHA loans, lenders would sometimes offer to release the original veteran borrower from liability if the buyer would assume and submit to credit approval. Loans made after March 1, 1988 have a due on sale clause which requires the buyer to be qualified for the credit and assume the loan. However, the lender cannot use the due on sale clause to raise the interest rate, as is common on conventional loans.

As with FHA loans, there is never a prepayment penalty on a federal GI loan. The borrower can pay the loan off at any time without extra charge.

Federal GI loans can be used to acquire or refinance a one- to four-family property, but the veteran must occupy the property – investor loans are not available. A veteran can also use his or her federal GI entitlement to finance a manufactured dwelling, including a manufactured dwelling on rented land. Condominiums can also be financed with federal GI loans.

The federal Department of Veterans Affairs has three different loan programs. The original program is a traditional fixed rate loan amortized up to 30 years. This remains the most popular program today. Many lenders also offer shorter terms if the borrower desires to pay the loan off more quickly. It is also common for a lender to require a down payment, even if the DVA makes no such requirement.

Growing equity mortgages are also available under the federal GI guaranty. A *growing equity (GEM)* loan is a loan which may start out with payments lower than even the monthly interest charge (resulting in negative amortization similar to a graduated payment mortgage), but with regular increases to the payment over the entire life of the loan. The federal Department of Veterans Affairs does not allow their GEM loan to have negative amortization and the amount of the payment increases must be reasonable so the veteran borrower can handle them without difficulty.

The third federal GI loan program is a *graduated payment mortgage (GPM)*. The payments are initially set below the amount necessary to cover the interest, resulting in negative amortization. The payments increase by 7½% each year for the first five years and then remain the same for the remaining term of the loan, which can be up to 30 years. Federal DVA graduated payment loans require a down payment equal to the highest amount the negative amortization will climb to at the end of the fifth year.

Exercise b

Federal GI loans area available to qualified veterans and _____ *spouses. To qualify, a veteran must obtain a* _____ *of* _____ *.*

Federal GI loans are _____ *by the U.S. Department of Veterans Affairs. The property must be appraised. The appraisal is called a* _____ *of* _____ _____ *. The veteran must pay a* _____ _____ *which is used to offset partially the costs of the program. The maximum entitlement today is $* _____ *, which means the maximum practical loan amount is normally $* _____ *. The loan also cannot exceed the higher of the sales price or the amount on the* _____ *of* _____ _____ *. A veteran can have his or her loan entitlement* _____ *if the property has been sold and the loan paid in full or assumed by a veteran who uses his or her entitlement, or in order to* _____ *the property. Lenders who are permitted to make loan decisions are called* _____ *lenders. Federal DVA loans can be assumed, but if the loan was made after March 1, 1988, the new buyer must* _____ *for the loan and must* _____ *it. Standard fixed rate federal DVA loans are the most popular, but there are also* _____ *and* _____ *loan programs available.*

Agricultural Credit

The *Farm Service Agency* (FSA) is organized under the Department of Agriculture. It has a multitude of rural loan programs, including loans for –

• Purchase of land, farms and ranches,

• Construction and rehabilitation of farm homes and outbuildings, and

• Beginning farmers to acquire farms and for operating expenses.

Some programs have a maximum loan amount of $200,000 and others can be up to $782,000. Loans can be made by institutional lenders and guaranteed by the Farm Service Agency or, in some cases, direct loans. For some beginning farmer loans the Farm Service Agency makes direct loans for 40% of the purchase price and the remainder (up to 90% loan to value ratio) will be funded by an institutional lender, whose share of the loan will be guaranteed by the Farm Service Agency. Beginning farmer loans have a maximum maturity of 15 years, but other programs offer maturities up to 40 years. Interest rates are typically very attractive, usually one percent or more below market. The Agency uses federal funds for its direct lending, which are frequently exhausted and the applicant has to wait for additional appropriations. Part of the annual appropriation is reserved for loans to socially disadvantaged farmers and ranchers. Farm Service Agency loans can be sold in the secondary market, generally through Farmer Mac (see below).

Rural Housing Service is another agency of the Department of Agriculture that provides rural real estate lending. It offers programs for –

• Home ownership,

• Housing rehabilitation and preservation,

• Housing for farm labor, and

• Assistance to developers of multifamily projects, including assisted housing for the elderly and disabled.

Like Farm Service Agency, some of Rural Housing Service loans are direct loans and others are guaranteed. Loans generally must be in rural areas or towns with a population of 20,000 or less. For home ownership, loans can be direct loans at below-market interest rates, or by an institutional lender up to 100% loan to value ratio and guaranteed by Rural Housing Service. Loans are also available for people to provide their own labor to build a home, up to 65% of the work. There are also grants and loans for home repairs for low income families and persons with disabilities.

Farm Credit System

The *Farm Credit System* holds over $60 billion in loans to more than half a million farmers, ranchers and rural homeowners, among others. The Farm Credit System is made up of six regional Farm Credit Banks, one Bank for Cooperatives, and one Agricultural Credit Bank.

Banks within the Farm Credit System do not take customer deposits. Instead, they raise funds by selling bonds and notes in the primary capital markets. Selling the securities is a function of the Federal Farm Credit Banks Funding Corporation. Although government sponsored and regulated by the federal Farm Credit Administration, the banks within the system are customer-owned entities. The system provides loans for all kinds of agricultural needs, including long-term mortgages to farmers and ranchers.

The Agricultural Credit Act of 1987 created the *Federal Agricultural Mortgage Corporation* (Farmer Mac) to provide a secondary market for agricultural loans. It functions in this manner the same as Ginnie Mae – that is, it provides a government guaranty for mortgage-backed securities issued by the originating lender.

The Oregon Department of Veterans Affairs

In 1944 Oregon voters amended the Oregon Constitution to create the *Oregon Department of Veterans Affairs* (ODVA). Oregon is one of only five states which have state home loan programs for veterans. Beginning students should be careful not to confuse the ODVA with the federal Department of Veterans Affairs, a totally separate organization.

Not many of today's real estate agents were selling real estate at the time the ODVA was created, although many remember the frantic real estate market of the 1970s, when ODVA loans were the most favorable financing for home sales. Today, new loan originations are a fraction of what they once were. In any event, real estate agents must understand the immense impact the ODVA has had on residential lending in Oregon.

The program is patterned after a previous program adopted in 1921 to benefit World War I and Spanish-American war veterans. That is, tax-exempt bonds were to be sold and the proceeds used to make loans to veterans of World War II. Bonds could be sold up to 3% (8% today) of the total assessed valuation of all property in the state. Since the interest income on the bonds would be exempt from both state and federal income taxes, investors would be willing to buy the bonds at very low rates. The savings would be passed on to the veteran in the form of a loan at rates well below market.

The first bonds were issued on October 1, 1945 for a total of $1 million. At that time, loans to purchase farms and homes could be made up to 75% of the purchase price (not to exceed $3,000) to be repaid over 20 years. The interest on the bonds was only 0.75%, and the loans to the veterans were made at 4%, so a comfortable profit margin was assured.

The bonds were interest-only bonds, however, with the principal all due at maturity (10 years). Since the veterans were repaying their loans with monthly payments of principal as well as interest, the veterans' monthly payments were placed in a separate ***Oregon War Veterans Sinking Fund***, so they could be used to pay interest to the bondholders, fund administration of the program, and leave the principal and surplus available to retire the bonds when they came due. Of course, since the bonds were issued for a maximum of 10 years, but loans were made with 20-year maturities, it was possible that not enough money would be available to pay the bonds. In this case, the plan was to use funds from subsequent bond sales to re-fund the previous issue. Later issues included bonds with differing maturity dates, so the bonds would mature at about the same time as the loan repayments would come in.

The program proved to be popular from the start — so much so that additional bond sales were quickly made. Of course, as time went by, property values increased and loan limits were raised. Eligibility was also expanded. Both factors caused massive increases in the dollar amount of bond sales. During the late 1970s and early 1980s bond sales of $150 to $300 million were common, sometimes as frequently as every three months.

Voters approved numerous changes to the eligibility requirements, the latest of which was in 1996. Program participation is now limited to those who served for a minimum of 210 days, any part of which was between September 15, 1940 and December 31, 1976, although eligibility must be used within 30 years of leaving the service. Eligibility requirements are written into the Oregon Constitution, so expanding the scope to include veterans who served after 1976 requires a vote of the people. It is likely that the eligibility will be expanded in the future.

In 1951 the program was changed to allow veterans to have their loan rights restored. At that time, veterans could obtain a new loan only if the original home was lost due to fire, natural disaster or condemnation. Today the reasons have been expanded to include job transfers, divorces, change in family size, or the need to move in order to attend school. Because multiple loans threatened to create problems, the 1979 Legislature limited the number of loans to any veteran to two. (Most loans made prior to October 4, 1977 do not count toward the limitation, however.)

At the same time that the eligibility criteria were expanding, the types of loans that could be made were increasing. In 1975, mobile homes and floating homes were added, although at a lower loan to value ratio. And when condominiums became popular in the mid-1970s, they were accepted the same as any other home; even condominiums on leased land became eligible. Construction loans and refinances were also authorized, although both have been discontinued today.

In 1979, home improvement loans were added. Today, such loans are not granted if the improvements are luxury items, such as swimming pools, saunas, or elaborate landscaping, or if the veteran intends to sell the property within one year. But improvements for weatherization and/or alternative energy devices are considered desirable purposes for additional financing.

Periodic increases in the maximum loan amount were met favorably. Maximum loan amounts were increased 14 times between 1945 and 1991. In 1991 voters approved an amendment to grant the Director the authority to set the maximum loan amount at up to 75% of the maximum loan amount accepted by Fannie Mae.

While the maximum loan amounts were increased, the down payment was decreased. By 1971 the loan to value ratios were 95% for a home, 90% for a farm and 85% for manufactured and floating homes. Although the loan to value ratio was lowered in 1992, today the maximum loan to value ratio is back to 95%.

Additional bonded debt was incurred to fund property taxes for veterans. State GI loans are paid "PIT" – that is principal, interest and 1/12 the annual taxes. The borrower pays his or her own insurance. The taxes, however, are not placed in a reserve account as they are with other loan programs. Instead, the extra amount for taxes is taken off the principal each month. Then on November 15 (property tax due date), the ODVA pays the taxes for the veteran and adds the amount paid to the principal balance.

For the first 25 years of the program, loans were made at a fixed 4% interest rate, while the statutes authorized the sale of bonds at rates not to exceed 4%. But by 1967 interest rates in the bond market had escalated to the point where the legislature was forced to authorize the sale of bonds at rates up to 5% in order for the program to continue. Of course, borrowing at 5% and lending the funds at 4% meant red ink. Nevertheless, the program could afford to suffer a slight loss on these loans. There were millions in outstanding bonds at rates well below 4%, so the profitable loans could subsidize the new unprofitable ones for a short time until rates declined.

However, rates on new bond sales did not decline. By 1970, bonds were being sold at rates varying from 6% to 7%. In response to this problem, the program underwent a complete revision. From 1971 forward, loans would be made at a variable interest rate (initially at 5.9%), rather than the fixed 4% rate. According to the language in the mortgage used at that time, the Director of the Department of Veterans Affairs would have authority to raise the interest on all variable rate loans as necessary to insure the solvency of the program. By that time, interest rates on bonds being sold had dropped from the high rates of 1970 to an average of 5.1725% – a comfortable range below the new 5.9% rate.

During the 1970s, the real estate market became a seller's market. Inflation drove up property values and everyone tried to buy a home before prices got any worse. In response to the demand for home loans, the ODVA sold bonds worth billions of dollars. Although a few of these were issued at rates in excess of 5.9%, the great majority were sufficiently below the mortgage rate that the program was not in immediate financial difficulty. However, in late 1979 the Department discovered that it had acute financial problems.

Numerous studies were conducted which determined that the Department would suffer a serious shortfall sometime by the year 2000. Part of the problem was that interest rates went up on bond issues, but the Department did not move quickly enough to raise the interest rates on the post-1971 variable rate loans. Massive foreclosures during the recession of 1979-1983 worsened the problem.

In response to the crisis numerous measures were implemented which allowed the Department to save millions of dollars in costs. For several years the Department had discontinued making new loans, but once financial affairs were returned to a sound basis, new loan production resumed.

Today, new loans are financed by selling tax-exempt bonds as in the past. However, current new loans have a different twist. The ODVA makes loans insured by private mortgage insurance companies. All new loans must meet standard Fannie Mae guidelines for qualifying the borrower and the property. New loans require reserves for taxes and insurance, the same as ordinary secondary market requirements for conventional loans. The old way where the Department paid the taxes for the veteran and added the amount paid to the principal balance does not meet current secondary market guidelines.

Loans continue to be made at below-market rates, since the source of funding is still from the sale of double tax-exempt bonds. The ODVA uses institutional lenders throughout the state as agents to originate the loans. Veterans will be able to make loan application at these institutional lenders as well as through the ODVA in Salem. The loans are still made directly by the Department, even if made through an institutional lender. The function of the institutional lender is merely to act as agent of the ODVA to take the loan application and process the paperwork.

Much of the ODVA's activity is in processing assumptions of existing loans. ODVA loans are currently assumable by either veterans or non-veterans, although the interest rate is increased on assumption. Because of the changes to the program over the years, existing loans have a multitude of different interest rates, and real estate agents find they must call the ODVA for the assumption rate for each loan individually. The new buyer must qualify in all cases; blind assumptions are not permitted. And, as with other government loan programs, there is no prepayment penalty on state GI loans.

Real estate agents have a lot to thank the ODVA for. So do home builders, construction workers – everyone in Oregon has benefited from the stimulus to our economy that the ODVA has provided over the years. And, of course, the veterans who have bought homes, which many times they would otherwise not have been able to afford, have been among the biggest beneficiaries.

Housing and Community Services

In Oregon the **Department of Housing and Community Services** was formed in 1991 from the merger of the Oregon Housing Agency and the Oregon Department of Community Services. The Oregon Housing Agency provided loans and other assistance to low- and moderate-income borrowers and was becoming more active in rental assistance areas. One of the chief functions of the Department of Community Services was to assist the homeless in finding housing, so a merger of the two organizations seemed logical.

The Oregon Department of Housing and Community Services has federal authority to sell double tax-exempt bonds to promote housing for first-time borrowers whose income does not exceed the median income for the area. Borrowers must not have owned a home during the preceding three years and must agree to occupy the home they are financing under the program. Only single-family homes qualify and the purchase price cannot exceed the median purchase price for homes in the area. For specially targeted areas higher purchase prices are allowed and the requirement that the borrower not have owned a home in the preceding three years is waived.

The program was originally called **Loans to Lenders** when it was first begun in 1977. Since then the program underwent modifications and is now officially called the **Single Family Mortgage Program**, although many people still use the older term. Loans are made by institutional lenders throughout the state who have contracted with the Department to originate the loans.

NOTES

Loans must be insured by the FHA, guaranteed by Farm Service Agency, or insured by private insurers approved by the Department (insured conventional loans). When the institutional lender has made the loan it is sold to the Department. When the Department buys the loan they buy it at face value (par). Of course, they can do this because their source of funds is double tax-exempt bonds. Unfortunately, the authority to sell bonds is limited, so funds are not always available. And each time a new bond issue is sold, the loan interest rate changes to reflect the rate at which the bonds had to be sold. Since income limits change as well as property prices, the Department also usually adjusts the maximum income limits and purchase prices periodically.

The Department also provides a ***mortgage credit certificate*** which entitles the holder to a federal income tax credit equal to 20% of the annual interest paid on a home mortgage loan. The requirements are similar to those for the Single Family Mortgage Program. Borrowers can obtain a mortgage credit certificate, or a loan through the Single Family Mortgage Program, but not both.

Nehemiah grants The **Nehemiah Housing Opportunity Grant Program** makes available an interest-free second mortgage loan up to $15,000 to help reduce the cost of housing for qualified first-time home buyers. The loan is held by HUD and no payments are required until the home is sold. To qualify, an applicant must earn no more than the median income for the area. Borrowers may couple this program with the Single Family Mortgage Program from the Department of Housing and Community Services.

Exercise c

The letters "RECDC" stand for the _____ _____ _____ _____ _____ , *which provides loans in a rural setting. It is organized under the* _____ *of* _____ . *Its function is to* _____ *loans. The* _____ _____ _____ *holds over $60 billion in agricultural credit. It is made up of* _____ *regional Farm Credit Banks, plus one* _____ _____ _____ *and one* _____ _____ _____ . *The purpose of the* _____ _____ _____ _____ *is to provide a* _____ _____ *for agricultural loans by issuing a federal guaranty for mortgage-backed securities issued by private lenders.*

Exercise d

The Oregon _____ *of* _____ _____ *sells revenue bonds which are* _____ *tax-exempt and uses the funds to make loans to eligible veterans at interest rates below market. Eligible veterans must have served at least* _____ *days of continuous active duty between September 15, 1940 and December 31, 1976. The entitlement lasts for up to* _____ *years after separation from the service. Eligible veterans con obtain* _____ *additional loan(s) if they lose the property due to various circumstances beyond their control. An ODVA loan can be used for*

❑ *Adding a bedroom*   ❑ *Adding a windmill electric generating system*

❑ *Constructing a new personal residence*   ❑ *Buying a condominium built on leased land*

❑ *Buying a manufactured home*   ❑ *Adding extensive landscaping*

❑ *Buying a floating home*   ❑ *Buying a home for an ex-spouse*

KEY TERMS

The key to understanding any new field is the vocabulary used in that field. To maximize your comprehension of the material presented in this chapter, be sure you know the meaning and significance of the following terms. Remember that the majority of test questions primarily test knowledge of vocabulary.

Allowable closing costs

Assumption

Assumption agreement

Automatic lender

Blind assumption

Certificate of reasonable value

Department of Housing and Community Services

Direct endorsement

Entitlement

Farm Credit System

Farm Service Agency

Federal Agricultural Mortgage Corporation

Federal Housing Administration

Funding fee

Graduated payment mortgage

Growing equity mortgage

Guaranty

Mortgage credit certificate

Mutual mortgage insurance

Negative amortization

Nehemiah Housing Opportunity Grant Program

Novation

Oregon Department of Veterans Affairs

Oregon war veterans sinking fund

Participating lender

Point

Simple assumption

Single family mortgage program

Subject to

Substitution of mortgagor

U.S. Department of Veterans Affairs

Underwriting approval

ANSWERS

To chapter exercises. If you couldn't figure out what to put in the blanks, find the answer here!

Exercise a

In real estate finance "FHA" stands for ___FEDERAL___ ___HOUSING___ *Administration, which was created under the National Housing Act in 1934. Title* _I_ *loans are for home improvement and rehabilitation and Title* _II_ *loans are for home acquisition and refinance. The FHA does not actually lend money, but rather* ___INSURES___ *loans against default. The loan is made by a* ___PARTICIPATING___ *lender. The premium paid by the borrower on an FHA loan is called the* ___MUTUAL___ *mortgage* ___INSURANCE___ *premium. On older FHA loans this premium was usually* ___½₁₂___ *of* ___½___ *of each month, included in the payment. Now, the borrower also pays* ___2¼___ *% of the original loan balance up front on most FHA loans. Today most FHA loans are approved by the lender because most lenders are* ___DIRECT___ ___ENDORSEMENT___ *lenders today.*

Which of the following may pay discount points on an FHA loan?

■ *Borrower*   ■ *Lender*   ■ *Broker*   ■ *Seller*   ■ *Borrower's friends and relatives*

When we speak of discount points, how many points would likely be charged on a loan if the note rate was 7% but

the secondary market demanded 7¾%? ____SIX POINTS____
The basic FHA *loan program is Section* ___203 (B)___ . *Special terms for veterans are available under Section* __203 (B)(2)__ . *Loans to acquire and rehabilitate a property are available under Section* __203 (K)__ . *Mortgages for low and moderate income borrowers are available under Section* _221 (D)(2)_ . *Adjustable interest rate* FHA *loans are available under Section* ___251___ . *Section* __234 (C)__ *applies to loans for condominiums. Loans under Section* __223 (E)__ *are available for older, declining neighborhoods. Loans under Section* __203 (I)__ *are for properties in outlying areas.*

Exercise b

Federal GI *loans area available to qualified veterans and* _____SURVIVING_____ *spouses. To qualify, a veteran must obtain a* ____CERTIFICATE____ *of* ____ELIGIBILITY____ .
Federal GI *loans are* ____GUARANTEED____ *by the U.S. Department of Veterans Affairs. The property must be appraised. The appraisal is called a* ____CERTIFICATE____ *of* ____REASONABLE____ ___VALUE___ .
The veteran must pay a ___FUNDING___ ___FEE___ *which is used to offset partially the costs of the program. The maximum entitlement today is $* ___50,750___ , *which means the maximum practical loan amount is normally $* ___203,000___ . *The loan also cannot exceed the higher of the sales price or the amount on the* ____CERTIFICATE____ *of* ___REASONABLE___ ___VALUE___ . *A veteran can have his or her loan entitlement* ___REINSTATED___ *if the property has been sold and the loan paid in full or assumed by a veteran who uses his or her entitlement, or in order to* ___REFINANCE___ *the property. Lenders who are permitted to make loan decisions are called* ___AUTOMATIC___ *lenders. Federal* DVA *loans can be assumed, but if the loan was made after March 1, 1988, the new buyer must* ___QUALIFY___ *for the loan and must* ___ASSUME___ *it. Standard fixed rate federal* DVA *loans are the most popular, but there are also* _GEM_ *and* _GPM_ *loan programs available.*

Exercise c

*The letters "*RECDC*" stand for the* ___RURAL___ ___ECONOMIC___ ___COMMUNITY___ ___DEVELOPMENT___ ___CORPORATION___ , *which provides loans in a rural setting. It is organized under the* ___DEPARTMENT___ *of* ___AGRICULTURE___ . *Its function is to* ___INSURE___ *loans. The* ___FARM___ ___CREDIT___ ___SYSTEM___ *holds over $60 billion in agricultural credit. It is made up of* __SIX__ *regional Farm Credit Banks, plus one* ___BANK___ ___FOR___ ___COOPERATIVES___ *and one* ___AGRICULTURAL___ ___CREDIT___ ___BANK___ . *The purpose of the* ___FEDERAL___ ___AGRICULTURAL___ ___MORTGAGE___ ___CORPORATION___ *is to provide a* ___SECONDARY___ ___MARKET___ *for agricultural loans by issuing a federal guaranty for mortgage-backed securities issued by private lenders.*

Exercise d

The Oregon ___DEPARTMENT___ *of* ___VETERANS___ ___AFFAIRS___ *sells revenue bonds which are* ___DOUBLE___ *tax-exempt and uses the funds to make loans to eligible veterans at interest rates below market. Eligible veterans must have served at least* __210__ *days of continuous active duty between September 15, 1940 and December 31, 1976. The entitlement lasts for up to* _30_ *years after separation from the service. Eligible veterans con obtain* __ONE__ *additional loan(s) if they lose the property due to various circumstances beyond their control. An* ODVA *loan can be used for*

- ◼ *Adding a bedroom*
- ◼ *Constructing a new personal residence*
- ◼ *Buying a manufactured home*
- ◼ *Buying a floating home*
- ◼ *Adding a windmill electric generating system*
- ◼ *Buying a condominium built on leased land*
- ❑ *Adding extensive landscaping*
- ❑ *Buying a home for an ex-spouse*

The maximum loan amount for a single-family residence is _75_ % *of the maximum loan amount in Fannie Mae guidelines for conventional loans, and the maximum loan to value ratio is* _95_ %. *ODVA loans are assumable if the buyer* ___QUALIFIES___ , *assumes the loan and agrees to an increase in the interest rate.*
The Oregon Department of Housing and Community Services sells ___DOUBLE___ *tax-exempt revenue bonds and uses the funds to buy* ___CONVENTIONAL___ *and* FHA *loans made by institutional lenders at below-market rates. Borrowers must not earn more than the* ___MEDIAN___ *income for the area and the purchase price must not exceed the* ___MEDIAN___ *purchase price for the area, although higher limits are allowed in* ___TARGETED___ *areas. In most cases, the borrower must not have owned a home during the preceding* _3_ *years. The Department can also issue a* ___MORTGAGE___ *Credit* ___CERTIFICATE___ *to a borrower who meets the same qualifications. This will allow the borrower an income tax credit equal to* _20_ % *of the interest they will pay on their mortgage.*

PRACTICE QUESTIONS

The following practice questions are representative of the questions you will find on the final examination and on the licensing examinations given by the Oregon Real Estate Agency.

1. The amount of a loan expressed as a percentage of the value of the real estate offered as security is the
   (A) usury percentage.
   (B) amortization.
   (C) loan to value ratio.
   (D) mortgage to equity ratio.

2. The loan to value ratio is the ratio of the
   (A) value of the mortgage loan principal divided by the appraised value or the sales price of the property, whichever is lower.
   (B) actual amount of the mortgage divided by the assessed value of the property.
   (C) market value of the mortgage divided by the market value of the property.
   (D) annual payments on the loan divided by the market value of the mortgage.

3. In real estate finance, the initials "FHA" stand for
   (A) Federal Housing Authority.
   (B) Farm and Home Agency.
   (C) Federal Housing Administration.
   (D) Farmers Housing Authority of the Department of Housing and Urban Development.

4. Funds for an FHA loan come directly from
   (A) lending institutions.
   (B) the state.
   (C) the federal government.
   (D) Congressional appropriation.

5. Money for FHA loans comes directly from
   I. the Federal Housing Authority.
   II. Fannie Mae
   (A) I only
   (B) II only
   (C) Both I and II
   (D) Neither I nor II

6. The major source of funds for loans insured by the Federal Housing Administration is
   (A) the Federal Housing Administration.
   (B) private investors.
   (C) mutual funds and unit trusts.
   (D) the Department of Housing and Urban Development (HUD).

7. The Federal Housing Administration was originally organized to do all of the following except
   (A) stimulate jobs in the construction industry.
   (B) facilitate the sale of existing homes.
   (C) stabilize the real estate market.
   (D) assist in financing commercial properties.

8. FHA loan underwriting has been responsible for
   I. encouraging home ownership.
   II. increased quality of housing.
   (A) I only
   (B) II only
   (C) Both I and II
   (D) Neither I nor II

9. FHA has made major contributions to mortgage lending in the United States by
   (A) pioneering underwriting standards which are now used by other lenders.
   (B) helping to create a secondary mortgage market.
   (C) helping to make home ownership a reality for the average American.
   (D) all of the above.

10. The Federal Housing Administration
    (A) insures loans made by private lenders.
    (B) guarantees loans made by private lenders.
    (C) buys mortgages from private lenders in the secondary market.
    (D) makes loans directly to qualified home buyers.

11. Under Title I of the National Housing Act, the FHA will insure lenders against losses on loans made to
    (A) finance repairs, improvements, or alterations of existing residences.
    (B) construct rental housing projects located on or adjacent to military bases.
    (C) qualified veterans and war widows.
    (D) farmers and ranchers who have difficulty obtaining uninsured conventional loans.

12. Which of the following statements concerning the Federal Housing Administration (FHA) is true?
    I. The FHA issues long term residential loans.
    II. The FHA issues long term commercial loans.
    (A) I only   (C) Both I and II
    (B) II only   (D) Neither I nor II

13. The Federal Housing Administration does not
    (A) allow a new buyer to assume an existing mortgage.
    (B) expand the housing financing opportunities.
    (C) insure title.
    (D) insure loans for multi-family dwellings.

14. From the purchaser's standpoint, which of the following is an advantage of Federal Housing Administration financing?
    I. Low mortgage insurance payments to protect the borrower
    II. FHA financing has led to general improvement in housing standards
    (A) I only   (C) Both I and II
    (B) II only   (D) Neither I nor II

15. An FHA mortgage is one which
    (A) the principal stays the same each month.
    (B) the original financing is from FHA money.
    (C) one has to be a veteran to receive.
    (D) the lending agency is insured against default.

16. To a buyer today, the greatest advantage of an FHA loan is
    (A) a low down payment.
    (B) below-market interest rates.
    (C) assurance that the property conforms to minimum property requirements.
    (D) assurance of an FHA appraisal to be sure the price is fair.

17. Who lends money directly for loans insured by the Federal Housing Administration?
    (A) Fannie Mae
    (B) Federal Housing Administration
    (C) Federal Department of Veterans Affairs
    (D) Private lenders

18. To help a buyer get an FHA loan, a real estate broker should put the buyer in contact with
    (A) a lending institution approved by the FHA.
    (B) the FHA.
    (C) the Federal Home Loan Mortgage Corporation.
    (D) Housing and Urban Development.

19. An FHA mortgage loan is secured through which of the following?
    (A) Qualified lending institutions
    (B) Any government agency
    (C) The Federal National Mortgage Association
    (D) The Federal Deposit Insurance Corporation

20. The Federal Housing Administration (FHA) obtains its funds, which are used to insure private lending institutions against losses on certain loans, by
    (A) depending on the general revenues of the federal government.
    (B) imposing charges on the lending institutions.
    (C) imposing charges on the borrowers.
    (D) floating annual issues of stock.

21. If a borrower defaults on a Federal Housing Administration (FHA) mortgage, any losses sustained in foreclosure are reimbursed through
    (A) an attachment lien against the borrower.
    (B) an assessment against the lending institution.
    (C) a mutual mortgage insurance plan.
    (D) the Federal Treasury.

22. Federal Housing Administration insured loans have mutual mortgage insurance, which
    (A) protects the buyer if the buyer should become unemployed.
    (B) warrants against loss to the lender.
    (C) warrants against loss by fire.
    (D) warrants as to the death of the principal.

23. The mutual mortgage insurance which the Federal Housing Administration charges for
    (A) protects the lender in case the borrower dies.
    (B) protect the borrower from a loss suffered by a fire.
    (C) protects the lender in case the borrower defaults.
    (D) is paid for by the lender.

24. The mortgage insurance premium on an FHA loan is paid by the
    (A) mortgagor.
    (B) mortgagee.
    (C) seller.
    (D) Federal Housing Administration.

25. Federal Housing Administration loan insurance protects the
    (A) lending institution.   (C) borrower.
    (B) buyer.   (D) federal government.

26. Who is the recipient of the mortgage insurance premium charged on an FHA insured loan?
    (A) Mortgagor
    (B) State real estate organization
    (C) FHA
    (D) The lending institution

27. When a mortgage is insured by FHA, the fee for the appraisal of the property is normally paid by the
    (A) mortgagor.   (C) seller.
    (B) mortgagee.   (D) trustee.

28. The party who usually pays the loan origination fee on a Federal Housing Administration loan is the
    (A) lending institution.   (C) seller.
    (B) borrower.   (D) broker.

29. The FHA loan fee that is paid by the borrower is called
    (A) an origination fee.
    (B) a discount fee.
    (C) an acceptance fee.
    (D) an accommodation fee.

30. If a borrower on an FHA loan wishes to sell the property, the loan may be
    I. assumed without any change in the interest rate.
    II. paid off without any prepayment penalty.
    (A) I only   (C) Both I and II
    (B) II only   (D) Neither I nor II

31. The penalty for complete prepayment of an FHA insured loan during the first ten years is
    (A) 2% of the face value of the note at time of payment.
    (B) 90 days interest on the remaining balance.
    (C) 1% of the original amount of the loan.
    (D) none of the above; there is no penalty for prepayment.

32. Which of the following is true regarding FHA insured mortgages?
    (A) The building given as security for the debt must comply with construction standards set by the FHA.
    (B) The interest rate must be the market rate or going rate for real estate loans in the community.
    (C) There is no set ratio of loan to property value.
    (D) Government funds are used for FHA loans.

33. An eligible veteran may obtain from the federal Veterans Affairs a loan guaranty for the purchase of any of the following except a
    (A) single-family home.
    (B) condominium.
    (C) mobile home.
    (D) five-unit apartment building.

34. A federal Department of Veterans Affairs mortgage loan is
    I. made by a private lending institution.
    II. guaranteed by the federal Department of Veterans Affairs.
    (A) I only   (C) Both I and II
    (B) II only   (D) Neither I nor II

35. The laws, rules and regulations that govern mortgages guaranteed by the Federal Veterans Affairs provide that
    (A) the veteran is insured and his or her payments are made by the Federal Veterans Affairs if the veteran is unable to pay.
    (B) lending institutions are guaranteed against loss within certain limits on their loans to veterans.
    (C) families of veterans are insured against losing their homes in case of the veteran's death.
    (D) builders are guaranteed against losses on homes constructed for veterans.

36. The federal Department of Veterans Affairs
    (A) services its own loans.
    (B) guarantees loans.
    (C) discounts loans.
    (D) insures loans.

37. When the federal Veterans Affairs "guarantees" a loan, it does so to protect the
    (A) lending institution.
    (B) seller of the property.
    (C) veteran borrower.
    (D) assets of the Federal National Mortgage Association.

38. Which of the following statements regarding Federal Veterans Affairs (VA) loans is true?
    I. A qualified veteran's eligibility for a VA guaranteed home loan is available for only one loan.
    II. When securing a VA guaranteed loan on a duplex, the eligible veteran need not occupy one of the apartments.
    (A) I only   (C) Both I and II
    (B) II only   (D) Neither I nor II

39. The minimum down payment for a federal GI loan is
    (A) 0%.
    (B) 3%.
    (C) 5%.
    (D) determined by the federal government.

40. Who provides the direct funds for a loan guaranteed by the Federal Veterans Affairs?
    (A) Federal National Mortgage Association
    (B) Federal Housing Administration
    (C) Federal Home Loan Bank Board
    (D) Private lenders

41. Loans made under programs from the federal Department of Veterans Affairs are made
    (A) exclusively from VA funds.
    (B) from general government funds.
    (C) by private lending institutions.
    (D) in all of these ways.

42. The Federal Veterans Affairs
    I. will normally make direct loans to veterans.
    II. directly regulates lending institutions that make VA loans.
    (A) I only   (C) Both I and II
    (B) II only   (D) Neither I nor II

43. "CRV" is a common phrase in the real estate business. It stands for "Certificate of Reasonable Value." It is issued by the
    (A) Federal National Mortgage Association.
    (B) Federal Veterans Affairs.
    (C) Federal Housing Administration.
    (D) Farm Land Bank.

44. A certificate of reasonable value is issued by the
    (A) Federal National Mortgage Association.
    (B) federal Department of Veterans Affairs.
    (C) Federal Housing Administration.
    (D) Oregon Department of Veterans Affairs.

45. Before the federal Department of Veterans Affairs will guarantee a loan on real property,
    I. the property must be appraised.
    II. the borrower must provide signed verification that he or she will live on the property as owner-occupier.
    (A) I only   (C) Both I and II
    (B) II only   (D) Neither I nor II

46. In order to offset the cost of establishing a new loan, the lender typically charges a
    I. higher interest rate.   II. loan origination fee.
    (A) I only   (C) Both I and II
    (B) II only   (D) Neither I nor II

47. An appraisal for a loan through the federal Department of Veterans Affairs
    I. can be ordered before a veteran buyer is found.
    II. is called a certificate of reasonable value.
    (A) I only   (C) Both I and II
    (B) II only   (D) Neither I nor II

48. Regarding loans through the U.S. Department of Veterans Affairs (DVA), which of the following statements is correct?
    I. Before closing, the DVA will transfer the loan to another property if the veteran requests.
    II. Secondary financing is not permitted.
    III. The sales price cannot exceed the amount of the CRV.
    (A) I and II only
    (B) II only
    (C) II and III only
    (D) None of the above

49. When property is being financed by means of federal Department of Veterans Affairs guaranteed financing
    I. the sale price must not exceed the appraised value of the property.
    II. secondary financing is rarely used.
    (A) I only
    (B) II only
    (C) Both I and II
    (D) Neither I nor II

50. To secure a loan guaranteed by the federal Department of Veterans Affairs, the
    I. veteran must sign a document that he or she intends to live on the premises.
    II. VA will transfer the loan to other property if the veteran requests.
    (A) I only
    (B) II only
    (C) Both I and II
    (D) Neither I nor II

51. A discharged serviceman who wishes to obtain a federal Department of Veterans Affairs mortgage guaranty must first get a certificate of
    (A) reasonable value from the Federal Housing Administration.
    (B) eligibility from the Federal Veterans Affairs.
    (C) rehabilitation from the Defense Department.
    (D) need from a local lending institution.

52. Ted O. Lemon, a retired chief petty officer who has lived in The Dalles for six years, wants to get a mortgage guaranty from the federal Department of Veterans Affairs. He should apply for a certificate of
    (A) qualification from the Navy Department.
    (B) eligibility from the federal Department of Veterans Affairs.
    (C) reasonable value from the Federal Housing Administration.
    (D) disability from the Oregon Department of Veterans Affairs.

53. A discharged serviceman who wishes to obtain a GI Bill loan guaranty should apply for a certificate of
    (A) reasonable value from the Federal Housing Administration.
    (B) eligibility from the Federal Veterans Affairs.
    (C) rehabilitation from the Defense Department.
    (D) need from a local lending institution.

54. The amount of the prepayment penalty when a veteran pays off a $152,000 loan guaranteed by the Federal Veterans Affairs is
    (A) 1% of the original loan.
    (B) $520.
    (C) ½ of 1% of the original loan.
    (D) nothing.

55. The prepayment penalty on a Federal Veterans Affairs guaranteed loan is
    (A) ½ of 1%.
    (B) 1% of the original loan.
    (C) limited to $100 maximum.
    (D) zero.

56. Normally, if a non-veteran purchases a property subject to a federal GI loan, the
    (A) veteran is released from liability.
    (B) veteran is still liable for mortgage payments.
    (C) transaction is void.
    (D) loan must be paid off.

57. If a non-veteran purchases a property subject to a federal GI loan made after March, 1988,
    (A) the interest rate may be changed at the option of the lender.
    (B) the lender may call the loan due at any time unless the borrower qualifies.
    (C) both A and B are correct.
    (D) Non-veterans may not take over a federal GI loan, with or without the lender's approval.

58. When a veteran has a federal GI loan, he or she may be able to
    (A) sell the property subject to the loan.
    (B) repay the loan ahead of schedule without penalty.
    (C) gain a release of liability if the property is sold subject to the loan.
    (D) do all of the above.

59. Which would be an advantage of a loan through the federal Department of Veterans Affairs (DVA)?
    (A) New mortgage loans require no down payment.
    (B) There is no loan origination fee.
    (C) Loan costs such as appraisal and credit report fees are not subject to review by the federal DVA.
    (D) The federal DVA sets a maximum prepayment penalty of 1% of the original loan balance.

60. The Rural Economic Community Development Corporation is
    I. an agency of the Department of Agriculture.
    II. a source of funds for low-income borrowers.
    III. generally a source of funding for rural property only.
    (A) I only
    (B) I and II only
    (C) II and III only
    (D) all of the above

61. The Rural Economic Community Development Corporation was established primarily to
    (A) make and insure loans to farmers and ranchers unable to secure credit from other sources.
    (B) insure home mortgage loans for farmers shifting from rural to urban areas.
    (C) provide direct government loans for World War II veterans resuming agricultural careers.
    (D) enable tenant farmers to get purchase mortgages from local lending institutions.

62. The Rural Economic Community Development Corporation provides financing for
    I. homes for low-income farmers.
    II. rural housing for the elderly.
    (A) I only
    (B) II only
    (C) Both I and II
    (D) Neither I nor II

63. An eligible veteran may obtain a loan from the Oregon Department of Veterans Affairs to
    (A) refinance an existing loan.
    (B) purchase a personal residence.
    (C) install a swimming pool.
    (D) acquire a single-family rental property.

64. An Oregon veteran may borrow money from the Oregon Department of Veterans' Affairs to
    (A) acquire rental property.
    (B) refinance a conventional loan.
    (C) construct investment property.
    (D) acquire a residence.

65. The Oregon Department of Veterans Affairs makes direct loans to eligible veterans who intend to
    I. purchase investment property.
    II. occupy the property purchased as the veteran's principal home.
    (A) I only
    (B) II only
    (C) Both I and II
    (D) Neither I nor II

66. A loan from the Oregon Department of Veterans Affairs (ODVA) is available for
    (A) acquiring a newly constructed single-family detached residence.
    (B) acquiring a farm, even though it is not being worked as a farm.
    (C) any remodeling if the borrower already has an existing ODVA loan on the property.
    (D) acquiring a single-family rental property.

67. The Oregon Department of Veterans Affairs makes direct loans to eligible veterans who intend to
    I. purchase a home, manufactured dwelling or floating home in Oregon.
    II. occupy the property as the veteran's principal residence.
    (A) I only
    (B) II only
    (C) Both I and II
    (D) Neither I nor II

68. April Showers has not used her entire state GI loan entitlement. She can borrow additional funds for all of the following except
    (A) installation of solar panels.
    (B) additional insulation.
    (C) new rugs.
    (D) an electrical generation windmill.

69. When a veteran purchases a home under the Oregon Department of Veterans Affairs (ODVA) loan program, the ODVA
    I. will require that the seller provide a warranty as to structural problems.
    II. can compel a builder or seller to remedy defects or live up to a contract.
    (A) I only
    (B) II only
    (C) Both I and II
    (D) Neither I nor II

70. When a veteran applies for a state GI loan he or she must provide
    I. an honorable discharge.
    II. a notice of separation from the service.
    (A) I only
    (B) II only
    (C) Both I and II
    (D) Neither I nor II

71. To obtain a loan from the Oregon Department of Veterans Affairs (ODVA), a borrower must provide
    I. a mortgagee's title insurance policy.
    II. evidence of fire and extended coverage insurance.
    III. life insurance in at least the amount of the loan with the ODVA as beneficiary.
    (A) I and II only
    (B) I, II and III
    (C) II only
    (D) II and III only

72. An Oregon State Department of Veterans Affairs loan entitlement can be reinstated if
    (A) the borrower moves voluntarily to take advantage of new employment.
    (B) a divorce decree requires the veteran to relinquish the property to a spouse.
    (C) the property is destroyed.
    (D) any of the above occur.

73. The Oregon Department of Veterans' Affairs can restore a veteran's loan rights because of which of the following?
    I. Fire, flood, or condemnation
    II. Voluntary job change to another city to improve economic standing
    (A) I only
    (B) II only
    (C) Both I and II
    (D) Neither I nor II

74. Stuart Holmes, an Oregon veteran, may be granted an additional Oregon DVA loan for a new property where he has previously lost or disposed of his former real property, previously encumbered with an Oregon GI loan, through no fault of his own. The reason may be due to
    (A) loss by fire or flood.
    (B) moved by his employer to another city.
    (C) voluntary change of job to improve his economic standing.
    (D) any of the above.

75. A veteran whose home is financed by the Oregon Department of Veterans Affairs may sell the property
    I. and transfer the loan balance to a new owner occupied property.
    II. to a non-veteran, who can assume the existing loan.
    (A) I only
    (B) II only
    (C) Both I and II
    (D) Neither I nor II

76. The prepayment penalty on a state GI loan is always
    (A) 1% of the remaining loan balance.
    (B) 90 days' interest on the remaining loan balance.
    (C) 90 days' interest on 80% of the remaining loan balance.
    (D) There is no prepayment penalty on a state GI loan.

77. Regarding mortgage loans obtained with federal government support,
    I. a loan insured by FHA is similar to a loan guaranteed by the Federal Veterans Affairs in that both require a penalty for payment prior to maturity.
    II. a veteran may be released from his or her liability under a loan guaranteed by the Federal Veterans Affairs by obtaining a written release from both the lender and the DVA.
    (A) I only
    (B) II only
    (C) Both I and II
    (D) Neither I nor II

78. Which of the following statements about housing loans with federal government support is false?
    (A) The federal government supplies funds to the lending agency.
    (B) The federal government insures the lending agency against losses.
    (C) FHA may insure mortgages for either apartment house projects or single family residences.
    (D) Federal Veterans Affairs loan guarantees may be used for condominium financing.

79. Discount points are considered
    (A) rate equalization factors.
    (B) police powers.
    (C) origination fees.
    (D) all of the above.

80. Mabel's Savings and Loan is the beneficiary of a trust deed. They sold their interest to an investor for less than the current balance on the note. This is an example of
(A) prepayment.   (C) discounting.
(B) subrogation.   (D) acceleration.

81. Discount points are used to
(A) decrease yields to the primary lender when short term rates are higher than long term rates.
(B) increase yields to the primary lender.
(C) increase the proceeds of the sale to the seller.
(D) do both B and C.

82. One discount point equals
(A) one percent of the sales price.
(B) one percent of the down payment.
(C) one percent of the loan amount.
(D) one percent of the monthly payment.

83. In making a $150,000 loan, what would a lender charge if the loan was being discounted five points?
(A) $3,750   (C) $15,000
(B) $7,500   (D) $37,500

84. The FHA has issued an appraisal for a property in the amount of $150,000 and will insure 97% of the first $50,000 and 95% of the balance. The lender requires a discount of five points. This means that the seller or buyer must pay a discount of
(A) $2,425.   (C) $7,175.
(B) $4,750.   (D) $7,500.

85. Chief Petty Officer Stella Della Bella Vista obtained a federal GI loan for $167,200 to purchase a home. The seller had to pay a discount of $6,688, which was
(A) three points.   (C) five points.
(B) four points.   (D) six points.

86. Lenders sometimes use the term "nominal rate" when talking about interest. This term means
(A) points must be paid because the rate the lender wants would be over the legal rate.
(B) the lender is charging the maximum rate allowed by law.
(C) the rate at closing is higher than the rate originally quoted when the application was made.
(D) the interest rate on the note, which is less than the effective interest rate.

ANSWERS

To practice questions. If you chose the wrong letter, here's the right one! The explanations are designed to clarify your understanding.

1.   **C**   In real estate lending we refer to the "loan to value ratio" as the amount of the loan as a percentage of the sales price or appraised value. For example, a loan of $90,000 on a property acquired for $100,000 is a loan to value ratio of 90%.

2.   **A**   The term "ratio" is just another word for "percentage." Therefore, "loan to value ratio" is the same as saying the percentage of loan in relation to the sales price or appraised value. The secondary market requires that the loan to value ratio be applied to the lower of the sales price or appraised value. A formula to express this would be "mortgage ÷ sales price or appraised value = loan to value ratio." Thus, a mortgage of $90,000 on a property with a value of $100,000 would be a loan to value ratio of 90% ($90,000 ÷ $100,000 = .90).

3.   **C**   The name is "Federal Housing Administration" which is organized under the Department of Housing and Urban Development. It is sometimes confused with the FMHA, which stands for "Farmers Home Administration," the old name of the Rural Economic Community Development Corporation.

4.   **A**   The FHA insures loans made by institutions in the private sector. These institutions, in turn, obtain their funding from investors, mostly by selling the loans to investors in secondary market operations.

5.   **D**   The FHA (Federal Housing Administration, not "Authority") insures loans made by institutional lenders against default. Funds for the loans are provided by the lenders and their investors. Fannie Mae purchases loans originated by other lenders and does not make direct loans.

6.   **B**   Except in rare circumstances, the sole function of the FHA is to insure a loan against default. The loan itself is made by a private institutional lender, and then generally sold in the secondary market. Most are securitized through Ginnie Mae mortgage-backed securities, which are then sold to investors.

7.   **D**   The legislation which created the FHA was the National Housing Act, originally enacted in 1934. Because the country was in the midst of a depression, its function was to stimulate the economy by encouraging home sales. It also provided Title I loans, which were for home improvements. The two main goals of the FHA are to upgrade the nation's housing stock, and to make home ownership affordable for the average American. Over its history, the FHA has been involved in every kind of residential lending, but not commercial real estate lending.

8.   **C**   The two primary goals of the FHA are to make home ownership affordable for the average American, and to upgrade the nation's housing stock. To make home ownership affordable it provides mortgage default insurance, which allows lenders to offer borrowers more liberal terms. To upgrade the nation's housing stock it offers insured home improvement loans. In addition, it has established minimum construction standards for housing.

9.   **D**   The goals of the FHA are to make home ownership affordable for the average American, and to upgrade the nation's housing stock. By creating standardized loans with government insurance the FHA made possible the creation of a secondary mortgage market, which did not exist prior to the FHA. Because it is so large, FHA has been the leader in pioneering new loan programs. Conventional lenders later copy FHA programs.

10.   **A**   The main function of the FHA is to provide mortgage guaranty insurance to borrowers, in effect, lending the government's credit to home buyers. The borrower pays a premium for this insurance. A loan guaranty is not the same as loan insurance, although the result is similar. A loan guaranty is like a co-signature, and is made free of charge (no premium). The FHA does not buy loans as a secondary lender, nor does it make direct loans.

11.   **A**   Loans under Title I of the National Housing Act are for home improvement and upgrading. Title II loans are for home acquisition. Both are insured by the Federal Housing Administration. The National Housing Act does not address loans for veterans or their widows, or loans to farmers and ranchers. Such loans are available under the Department of Veterans Affairs and the Farmers Home Administration, both of which depend on other federal legislation.

12.   **D**   The function of the FHA is to insure home loans made by institutional lenders. The FHA does

not make direct loans, nor is it involved in commercial financing.

13. **C** An FHA insured loan is assumable, provided the buyer qualifies and assumes and agrees to pay the debt. Over the years the FHA has been a principal innovator in providing new home financing alternatives. Although multi-family loan programs are currently not available, in the past the FHA has insured loans for investors in rental housing. Title insurance is provided only by title insurance companies.

14. **B** Because the FHA insures the loan against default lenders are willing to grant the borrower more liberal terms. The FHA has also always had the goal of improving the nation's housing stock. One of the ways it has done this is to establish minimum standards for housing construction.

15. **D** Federal Housing Administration loans are amortized the same as other mortgage loans, that is, the monthly payment for principal and interest is the same, but the amount which is applied to principal is lower at the start of the loan and higher at the end. The FHA insures loans from institutional lenders against default. Loan funds are supplied by the lender, not the FHA.

16. **A** The biggest advantage of FHA financing today is that the FHA insurance entices lenders to make loans with low down payments and with liberal repayment terms. FHA used to set a maximum interest rate which was usually below market, but interest rates today are negotiated without FHA interference. FHA insists that the property meet minimum standards, however, the FHA requires a disclosure that their requirements are not a guarantee to the borrower. Similarly, an FHA appraisal is for loan insurance purposes and is no guarantee that the property is worth what the borrower is paying for it.

17. **D** The function of the FHA is to insure loans made by institutional lenders who participate in the FHA mutual mortgage insurance program.

18. **A** Since the FHA merely insures loans made by institutional lenders, the first step is for the borrower to make application at a lender who participates in the FHA mutual mortgage insurance program.

19. **A** The FHA encourages home lending by insuring home loans made by participating institutional lenders in the private sector. To obtain such a loan the borrower makes application at the lender.

20. **C** The FHA insures loans against default. To cover losses and administrative expenses, it charges borrowers a mortgage insurance premium.

21. **C** The purpose of the FHA is to insure home loans against default. The borrower pays the premium, which is used to cover losses suffered by lenders when borrowers default.

22. **B** The purpose of the FHA mortgage insurance is to pay the lender in the event the borrower defaults and the property does not sell at foreclosure for enough to cover the outstanding loan balance and the lender's expenses of foreclosure.

23. **C** The purpose of the mutual mortgage insurance is to cover losses suffered by lenders when the borrower defaults. The borrower pays the premiums, which cover the losses and administrative expenses of the FHA.

24. **A** The FHA insures loans against default in order to enable the lender to offer the borrower more favorable terms. To make FHA loans acceptable to lenders, the borrower must pay the premiums for the mutual mortgage insurance.

25. **A** The purpose of the FHA mutual mortgage insurance is to cover losses suffered by lenders when borrowers default. Indirectly, this benefits the borrower, because the insurance entices the lender to offer the borrower more liberal terms. However, while the borrower benefits, only the lender is protected.

26. **C** The FHA insures loans made by institutional lenders against default. The borrower pays the premium for the insurance. The lender collects the premium from the borrower and remits it to the FHA. The FHA uses the premiums to cover administrative expenses and losses from defaults.

27. **A** The appraisal fee is normally a borrower expense. No loan program requires it to be paid by the borrower, so if the buyer and seller agree, it can be paid by the seller. In a mortgage loan, the borrower is the mortgagor and the lender is the mortgagee.

28. **B** The maximum amount of the FHA loan origination fee is set by administrative rule of the FHA. Loan origination fees can be paid by anyone, but it is customary to consider it a buyer expense.

29. **A** Most lenders charge a loan fee, which is considered a borrower expense. The FHA sets the maximum loan fee the lender may charge on an FHA insured loan. The official term for the loan fee is "loan origination fee," since its function is to cover the lender's expenses in originating the loan.

30. **C** Federal Housing Administration loans can always be assumed, although if the loan was made after March 1, 1988 the borrower must be qualified and enter into an assumption agreement.

The lender cannot require the new buyer to agree to a different interest rate. There are never prepayment penalties on any government loan.

31.   **D**   No government loan program has ever had a prepayment penalty.

32.   **A**   The FHA has established minimum housing standards. A residence must meet these standards to qualify for an FHA insured loan. In the past, the FHA set the maximum interest rate a lender could charge for an FHA loan, but that has not been true for most loans for many years. In any event, even when there was a maximum interest rate, it was set by administrative rule, not necessarily tied to the going rate in a community. The FHA has always set the maximum loan to value ratio. FHA provides mortgage default insurance for loans made by institutional lenders in the private sector. Loan funds are provided by the lenders, not the government.

33.   **D**   Loans guaranteed by the federal Department of Veterans Affairs are available to qualified veterans to purchase a one- to four-family owner-occupied residence. It can be any kind of residence, including a condominium and a mobile home.

34.   **C**   The federal Department of Veterans Affairs issues loan guaranties for loans to eligible veterans. The purpose is to entice lenders into extending more liberal terms to veteran borrowers. Loans under the program are made by institutional lenders.

35.   **B**   The federal Department of Veterans Affairs issues a loan guaranty. This means that the lender will receive compensation for losses suffered in the event of the veteran's default, up to the maximum amount of the guaranty. The Department does not protect any other parties – only the lender.

36.   **B**   With respect to home loans, the sole function of the federal Department of Veterans Affairs is to issue a loan guaranty to protect lenders from potential losses. The protection is a guaranty, not insurance. "Insurance" would imply that a premium is being paid, which is not the case with loans under the program.

37.   **A**   The purpose of the loan guaranty from the federal Department of Veterans Affairs is to compensate a lender who suffers a loss in foreclosing on a loan. While this is of some benefit to the borrower, in that it entices the lender into offering more liberal terms, it directly protects only the lender.

38.   **D**   There are several ways in which veterans may receive multiple loans. First, if the entire entitlement is not used in the first loan, the veteran may use the rest of the entitlement on a subsequent loan. The veteran may also have his or her loan right completely restored in the event the property is sold and the loan is either assumed by an eligible veteran who uses his or her own entitlement, or the loan is paid off. A veteran may also refinance a home with a new guaranteed loan provided there is already an existing loan guaranteed by the Department.

39.   **A**   The amount of the funding fee is lowered if the veteran makes a down payment. But the federal Department of Veterans Affairs sets no maximum loan amount and requires no down payment. Individual lenders sometimes require a down payment, but this is not a DVA requirement.

40.   **D**   The federal Department of Veterans Affairs issues a loan guaranty, essentially lending the government's credit to the veteran borrower. The loan is normally made by a participating institutional lender. Because of the guaranty, the lender is willing to offer the borrower more liberal terms.

41.   **C**   The federal Department of Veterans Affairs issues loan guaranties to eligible veterans. A guaranty protects a lender from a possible loss in the event of a foreclosure. Loans are almost always made by private, institutional lenders.

42.   **D**   The federal Department of Veterans Affairs normally issues a guaranty for a loan made to a veteran borrower by an institutional lender. If the veteran cannot find a lender willing to make the loan, the Department will make a direct loan. Since there are plenty of lenders, direct loans are practically unheard of. The Department does not regulate participating lenders, except insofar as to ensure their compliance with the rules of the veterans home loan program.

43.   **B**   All properties which secure loans guaranteed by the federal Department of Veterans Affairs must be appraised. The appraisal is called the certificate of reasonable value, usually abbreviated to just "CRV."

44.   **B**   The appraisal of the property for a loan guaranty from the federal Department of Veterans Affairs is called a certificate of reasonable value.

45.   **C**   For all loans guaranteed by the federal Department of Veterans Affairs, the veteran must sign a statement that the property will be occupied by the veteran. There is no penalty for moving out later, however. The property must also be appraised and the appraisal is called a certificate of reasonable value.

46.   **B**   In historical banking practice, the loan origination fee is supposed to cover the cost of making the loan. This includes the compensation paid

to new loan staff and any other expenses directly attributable to making the loan. Interest, on the other hand, is simply paid to the investors who provided the capital to make the loan.

47.   **C**   The official term for the federal GI appraisal is the certificate of reasonable value, produced by appraisers approved by the U.S. DVA. The certificate of reasonable value can be ordered through an approved lender whether a veteran buyer has been found yet or not. Owners of properties around military installations frequently order the certificate of reasonable value when putting the property on the market, so they will be ready if a veteran wishes to buy.

48.   **D**   Since the certificate of reasonable value (appraisal) is the basis for the amount of the loan, there is no way the loan could be transferred to another property without an appraisal of the new property. Although the loan to value ratio for loans guaranteed by the Department of Veterans Affairs can be as high as 100%, some lenders may not be willing to lend the full amount of the certificate of reasonable value. In those cases, secondary financing is permitted, up to the amount of the certificate of reasonable value. The second lien instrument must be approved by the DVA, the interest rate cannot be higher than the rate on the first, it must be amortized over at least five years, and cannot have a balloon payment.

49.   **B**   All properties which secure loans guaranteed by the federal Department of Veterans Affairs must be appraised and a certificate of reasonable value issued. The veteran borrower is free to pay more for the property than the amount on the certificate. Because the loan to value ratio for federal GI loans can be as high as 100%, additional financing is rarely necessary.

50.   **A**   A loan secured by real property is a lien on that property. No lender will ordinarily agree to a substitution of collateral because the paperwork would be prohibitive. For all loans guaranteed by the federal Department of Veterans Affairs the veteran must sign a statement that the property will be occupied by the veteran.

51.   **B**   Loans guaranteed by the federal Department of Veterans Affairs are available to all eligible veterans regardless of need. To obtain the loan guaranty, the veteran must have served the minimum amount of time and under the conditions prescribed by law. When the Department has verified this, it will issue a certificate of eligibility. The property must also be appraised. The appraisal is called a certificate of reasonable value.

52.   **B**   As evidence that a veteran's service qualifies him or her for a loan guaranty, the federal Department of Veterans Affairs will review the veteran's service record and issue a certificate of eligibility.

53.   **B**   Loan guaranties are available to eligible veterans whether or not the veteran has need or is handicapped. The federal Department of Veterans Affairs will review the veterans service record and, if qualified, issue a certificate of eligibility.

54.   **D**   No government loan program has ever had a prepayment penalty.

55.   **D**   No government loan program has ever had a prepayment penalty.

56.   **B**   To obtain a loan guaranteed by the federal Department of Veterans Affairs the veteran borrower must sign a statement agreeing to be personally liable for the full loan balance, even if the property is later sold at foreclosure for less than the remaining balance. Loans under the program can be assumed by anyone, but the veteran is released from the personal obligation only if the loan is assumed by another veteran who uses his or her own entitlement.

57.   **B**   Federal GI loans may be assumed by anyone, whether a veteran or not. However, for loans made after March 1, 1988, the buyer must qualify and must assume the loan. But the lender cannot require an increase in the interest rate.

58.   **D**   When the buyer takes over the old loan the buyer always takes title subject to the loan. When the buyer also assumes the old loan, the buyer agrees to be personally liable for the debt and can be held responsible for any deficiency if the property fails to sell for enough at a foreclosure sale to pay off the debt. If the buyer assumes the existing loan and qualifies for the credit, it is common for the federal Department of Veterans Affairs to obtain a release of liability from the lender for the veteran.

59.   **A**   The maximum loan to value ratio for a federal GI loan is 100% of the certificate of reasonable value. Maximum loan fees and other costs are set by the DVA and if they were not set, lenders would charge more, which would hardly be an advantage. No government loan program has ever had a prepayment penalty.

60.   **D**   Loans through the Rural Economic Community Development Corporation are available for farm purchase and improvement, construction and rehabilitation of farm homes and outbuildings, low-income farmers, housing for the elderly in a rural setting, rehabilitation of rural communities, and

purchase of property by tenant farmers. Loans are generally insured and must meet secondary market requirements. The parent organization is the U.S. Department of Agriculture.

61.   **A**   The purpose of the Rural Economic Community Development Corporation is to provide financing for rural properties of the size of small, family-sized farms.

62.   **C**   The Rural Economic Community Development Corporation provides a multitude of financing programs for rural property. These programs include special financing for low-income borrowers and rural housing for the elderly, among others.

63.   **B**   State GI loans can be used to acquire or construct an owner occupied single-family home, including mobile and floating homes, manufactured housing, and fee title and leasehold condominiums. Loans are also available for home improvement, especially weatherization and alternate energy devices, but the home improvements cannot be luxury items. At one time the program allowed refinancing, but that is no longer possible.

64.   **D**   Acceptable collateral for a loan from the Oregon Department of Veterans Affairs include any single-family residence. It must be owner-occupied and remain owner-occupied until the loan is repaid, or the Department will raise the interest rate to the non-veteran assumption rate. Additional financing may be obtained, within the limits of the veteran's remaining unused eligibility, for home improvements, but no luxury items will be financed. The Department will not make loans to refinance existing loans.

65.   **B**   Loans to eligible veterans from the Oregon Department of Veterans Affairs must be for owner-occupied residences only. The property must remain owner-occupied during the term of the loan, or the Department will raise the interest rate to the non-veteran assumption rate.

66.   **A**   All properties financed with ODVA loans must be owner-occupied. Farm loans are technically available, although not being made at this time; but in any event a farm loan can only be obtained if the property is being worked as a farm. Remodeling cannot be for luxury items.

67.   **C**   All state GI loans must be on owner-occupied property. The property can be any kind of residence, including manufactured dwellings, with or without land, floating homes, and fee or leasehold condominiums.

68.   **C**   Except for mobile and floating homes, loans for personal property are not allowed. As long as the borrower has not used the entire entitlement, junior financing can be obtained for home improvements, especially weatherization and alternate energy devices.

69.   **D**   To protect the Department from claims by borrowers, the Oregon Department of Veterans Affairs specifically disclaims any responsibility for the condition of the property.

70.   **C**   The Oregon Department of Veterans Affairs requires that the discharge be honorable; general discharges or less than honorable discharges are not adequate. In addition, the veteran must demonstrate to the ODVA that he or she is separated from the service. The veteran's discharge papers are normally sufficient. Notice of discharge is waived for surviving spouses, since they may not have ever been in the service.

71.   **A**   All lenders require a mortgagee's title insurance policy insuring that the lender has a good and valid lien. All lenders also require that the improvements be insured with fire and extended coverage. A loss payable clause in the insurance policy is a clause that requires the insurance company to pay any claims directly to the lender, to the extent of the remaining loan balance. Many creditors request credit life and disability insurance, but few require it, including the Oregon Department of Veterans Affairs.

72.   **D**   A loan right can be restored if the veteran loses the property by fire, flood, condemnation, sale due to a job transfer or change of employment, or divorce settlement, among other reasons. To qualify for restoration of loan right the original loan must be paid in full or assumed by another veteran who uses his or her entitlement. In no case can the veteran obtain more than two loans.

73.   **C**   Normally, a veteran is entitled to only one loan from the Oregon Department of Veterans Affairs. Exceptions are made for circumstances beyond the veteran's control.

74.   **D**   Normally, a veteran is entitled to only one loan from the Oregon Department of Veterans Affairs. Exceptions are made for circumstances beyond the veteran's control such as divorce, job change, fire, flood, and so on.

75.   **B**   By having his or her loan right restored, a veteran can obtain a new loan for another home. But the existing loan cannot be transferred to a new property; to obtain a loan on a new property requires

a new loan application. State GI loans are assumable at the discretion of the Oregon Department of Veterans Affairs. Currently, they are assumable even by a non-veteran, although the interest rate will increase.

76. **D** There is no prepayment penalty on any government loan program.

77. **B** No federally insured or guaranteed loan has a prepayment penalty. Federal GI loans require the veteran borrower to agree to be personally liable for the loan until paid in full, even if the loan is later assumed by another. If the loan is assumed by an eligible veteran who uses his or her own entitlement, the Department of Veterans Affairs usually agrees to release the original veteran borrower from liability.

78. **A** There are three main federal agencies which support residential mortgage lending – the Federal Housing Administration, the Department of Veterans Affairs, and the Farmers Home Administration. None of them supply funds to the lenders. Their main function is to insure or guarantee loans made by private financial institutions, in effect, lending the government's credit to the borrower.

79. **A** When a lender makes a loan sometimes the interest rate is below the rate demanded by secondary lenders. If a secondary lender bought the loan at less than the amount due (for a discounted amount), the secondary lender's yield (rate of return) would be higher. The amount of the discount is usually stated in terms of points, where one point is one percent of the loan balance. Therefore, points are used to equalize a below-market rate with market rates demanded by the secondary mortgage market.

80. **C** Selling a loan for its balance due is called selling at face, or par value. Selling for less than the balance due is called selling at a discount.

81. **B** Discount points increase the yield to the lender. When the interest rate is below market, the loan must be sold in the secondary market at a discount, thus the primary lender loses money. The discount is to reimburse the primary lender for this loss.

82. **C** To keep from getting confused, lenders use the term "percent" when referring to the interest rate on the loan, and the term "points" when referring to the discount. For example, a loan at 8% with 2% discount would be stated as "eight percent interest with two points discount." One point is one percent of the loan balance.

83. **B** If one point is one percent of the loan balance, then five points discount on a $150,000 loan would be 5% of $150,000, or $7,500 ($150,000 × .05 = $7,500).

84. **C** First, calculate the loan amount. FHA will insure 97% of the first $50,000 and 95% of the remaining $100,000 ($150,000 conditional commitment – $50,000 = $100,000 balance). This comes to $143,500 ($50,000 × .97 = $48,500; $100,000 × .95 = $95,000; $48,500 + $97,000 = $143,500). If one point is one percent of the loan balance, then five points is five percent of the loan balance (5%). Five percent of $143,500 is $7,175 ($143,500 × .05 = $7,175).

85. **B** The correct way to solve this problem is to divide the discount by the loan balance to find the discount rate (number of points). This comes to four points ($6,688 ÷ $167,200 = .04). An easier way is to try each answer until you find the one that works. For example, three points of $167,200 comes to a discount of $5,016 ($167,200 × .03 = $5,016). Since this is not the discount the seller paid, three points cannot be the correct answer. But when you try the same calculation with four points, you get the correct amount of the discount ($167,200 × .04 = $6,688).

86. **D** "Nominal rate" is a synonym for "note rate." Most of the time the lender's actual yield is slightly higher than the note rate. For example, if the note bears interest at seven percent, but the lender has charged loan origination and other fees, the actual cost to the borrower (and income to the lender) is higher. The "effective rate" is a way to state the lender's actual yield as a percentage, after taking into consideration the additional income. Effective rate is similar to the concept of the annual percentage rate, required by the Truth in Lending Act.

CONVENTIONAL FINANCING PROGRAMS

IN THE EARLY DAYS OF REAL ESTATE FINANCE THE TERM "CONVENTIONAL LOAN" did not exist. All real estate loans were simply called "mortgage loans." But in 1934 the Federal Housing Administration (FHA) was created and a new breed of mortgage loan became available. The FHA was created to insure loans and these loans needed to be distinguished from regular mortgage loans. As a result the term ***conventional loan*** was coined to differentiate ordinary mortgage loans from FHA insured loans. A conventional loan is any loan which is not insured or guaranteed by a government agency, or made directly by a government body.

Later many other government loan programs were created. Loans guaranteed by the Veterans Administration, direct loans from the Oregon Department of Veterans Affairs, farm loans from the Rural Economic Community Development Corporation and the Farm Credit System – all were added to the list of government loan programs. Through it all, the conventional loan retained a solid market share.

Today conventional loans comprise the vast majority of all new loan originations in spite of some of the advantages of government loans. For one thing, not everyone qualifies for government programs. And even those who qualify, may not need the extra assistance that government programs offer and prefer what they perceive as better service in the private sector. Until FHA loans came on the scene, residential mortgage lending was largely a function of the commercial banks, although the thrift industry was making serious inroads into their business. During the depression, however, real estate lending by all lenders dropped to a trickle. Commercial banks took to the new FHA loans because of the liquidity they offered – the fact that FHA loans all met minimum standards and were insured made them salable, so a secondary market could be developed.

The thrifts were less concerned with liquidity and so conventional loans became their standard. Many thrifts did make FHA loans, but the majority of thrift lending was on a conventional loan basis.

When the Federal National Mortgage Association (Fannie Mae) was created in 1938, a dependable secondary market was finally available. At this time mortgage bankers sprang up all over the country. Mortgage bankers do not have customer deposits to lend, so they are completely dependent on the existence of a secondary market. At that time Fannie Mae was a government agency, and did not buy anything but government loans. Therefore, there was no secondary market for conventional loans.

This situation did not change until the early 1970s. The result was that from 1934 until the 1970s, commercial banks hardly ever made conventional loans and mortgage bankers never did. Commercial banks insisted on the liquidity of the secondary market. Mortgage bankers had no choice but to make government loans only, because they were completely dependent on the secondary market as a source of funds. This left the conventional market to the thrift institutions. Most thrifts in Oregon made nothing but conventional loans until very recent years. Even today, the conventional loan still comprises the bulk of the loan activity at thrift institutions.

Starting in the early 1970s, however, Fannie Mae and the (then) newly created Freddie Mac, began buying conventional loans. Suddenly a secondary market for conventional loans opened up. And the result was that commercial banks and mortgage bankers started making conventional loans as well as government insured and guaranteed loans. Nevertheless, there is a strong sense of history in the lending business, and when a thrift institution makes a real estate loan today it is most likely a conventional loan. Still, thrifts have lost a lot of market share in the past several years, and real estate agents place more conventional loans with commercial banks and mortgage bankers today than they do with thrift institutions.

Mortgage insurance

The Federal Deposit Insurance Corporation, the Federal Reserve Board, the Comptroller of the Currency, and the Office of Thrift Supervision have established uniform maximum loan to value ratios for different kinds of property that apply to the various kinds of lenders they regulate.

For land acquisitions, the maximum is 65% and for land development, 75%. For multi-family and commercial properties the maximum is 80%. And for one- to four-family properties the maximum is 85% loan to value ratio. For residential loans the maximum is waived, as long as the amount of the loan over 85% is insured against default.

Government insurance and guaranties have allowed lenders to make loans with little or no down payment for a long time. To allow conventional loans to compete with government loans, *private mortgage insurance* (*PMI*) has been developed by various private insurance companies. Although lenders can make residential loans up to 85%, as a rule, lenders require private mortgage insurance for all loans over 80% loan to value ratio, and some lenders even insure loans over 75% loan to value ratio.

Borrowers pay the premiums for the private mortgage insurance. The premium varies considerably according to the risk. For example, loans with buydowns, adjustable interest rates, and other features which allow the amount of the payment to change will be more likely to go into default than loans with fixed payments. Similarly, the lower the down payment, the greater the risk and the higher the premium.

The premium to insure the loan over its entire life can be paid up front at closing or it can be paid monthly with just the first month's premium at closing. Some lenders also allow the borrower to pay the entire premium at closing by borrowing it and adding it to the principal balance. Many lenders include it in the cost, and then charge a higher interest rate for insured loans as opposed to uninsured loans. For a homebuyer, the latter is desirable, as the interest is tax deductible.

Once the loan balance drops to 80%, the borrower can ask the lender to discontinue the insurance. After all, the private mortgage insurance company no longer has any liability, so paying the premiums is pointless. Secondary market guidelines indicate the private mortgage insurance can be dropped

- On loans at least two years old if the loan to value ratio has been lowered to 80% or less by additions or remodeling,
- On loans from two to five years old if the loan to value ratio has been lowered to 75% due to appreciation, or
- On loans five years old or older, if the loan to value ratio has been lowered to 80% due to appreciation.

Conforming and nonconforming financing

The secondary market establishes the maximum loan amount for the various types of conventional loans. Loan limits are adjusted in January each year according to changes in the national average house price as published by the Federal Housing Finance Board.

Conventional lenders are happy to lend up to the maximum, and such loans are called ***conforming loans***. Loans which exceed the maximum are ***nonconforming loans***, and must be sold to alternative secondary markets or kept in the lender's own portfolio. Nonconforming loans are less desirable for lenders, so the yield they demand tends to be slightly higher. Many lenders call a nonconforming loan a ***jumbo mortgage***.

Exercise a

A conventional loan is any loan that is not government _____ or _____ or made directly by a government body Until the early 1970s there was no _____ _____ for conventional loans. As a result, they were made primarily by _____ institutions only. Today, all types of lenders offer conventional loans.

Conventional loans can be _____ , the same as government loans. This is commonly referred to as _____ _____ _____ , (PMI) to distinguish it from insurance on FHA and RECDC loans. The premium would be the least for (choose one)

- ❑ *A fixed rate 30-year conventional loan.*
- ❑ *A fixed rate 30-year loan with a balloon payment at five years.*
- ❑ *A 30-year adjustable rate loan.*

Most lenders insure only the amount of the loan which exceeds _____ % loan to value ratio.

Loans which are under the maximum loan amount established by the secondary market are called _____ loans. Loans over this amount are called _____ - _____ , or jumbo loans.

Fixed rate loans

The fixed rate conventional mortgage loan (FRM) remains the most popular conventional loan, by far. While the interest rates for a FRM will be higher than for an adjustable rate mortgage loan (ARM), many borrowers are willing to pay the higher rates in exchange for the security of knowing that the principal and interest will not change.

Why are interest rates higher for fixed rate loans? Very simply, lenders are hedging their bets. Being able to change the interest rate in the future helps the lender remain profitable in periods when interest rates increase.

Throughout most of its history, the **amortization** (payoff through periodic payments) of a fixed rate loan has been 30 years. In recent years, however, lenders have offered amortization terms of 20 years, 15 years and 10 years as well. Although 30-year amortization remains the most popular with borrowers, amortization over 15 years is the second most popular. The reason for its popularity is really very simple – enormous interest savings. The following chart shows the interest that would be paid on a loan amortized to the full term over various terms on a $200,000 loan at 7% –

Term	Monthly payment	Total interest over life of loan
30 years	$1,330.61	$279,017.80
25 years	$1,413.56	$224,967.52
20 years	$1,550.60	$172,143.49
15 years	$1,797.66	$123,578.18

Of course, the borrower has to be able to afford the higher payments to take advantage of the interest savings on a 15-year loan. However, there is an additional savings on the 15-year loan. The fact that the term is shorter means that the lender is less concerned with inflation and increasing interest rates in the future. Therefore, it is not uncommon for lenders to offer 15-year loans at about ¼ of 1% below the rate for 30-year loans. If you consider the interest at 6¾% on the 15-year loan in the example on the preceding chart, the monthly principal and interest payment would be slightly less ($1,769.82) and the total interest over the life of the loan would be only $118,567.41.

Of course, if you are clever you have already perhaps thought, "why not just get a 30-year loan, and make extra principal payments when you can?" This would give borrowers the greatest flexibility – in tough times they could make just the minimum payment, and when times are good, they could pay extra on the mortgage. In principle this sounds good. In practice, there are several drawbacks, not the least of which is the loss of the preferential interest rate of the short term loan. Furthermore, the notes required by secondary lenders today provide that if the borrower prepays, the prepayment must be an amount equal to an entire payment. The borrower cannot just add an extra little amount to the payment. In addition, the terms state that, even if the borrower does prepay an amount equal to an entire payment, this does not excuse the borrower from making the next payment. In other words, the extra amount will be subtracted from the principal balance and the borrower will end up paying less interest over the life of the loan, but the borrower is not ahead a payment. And another reason borrowers consider the 15-year amortization is that they know they are less likely to adhere to a plan of making higher payments unless they are forced to do so.

A few lenders offer **bi-weekly loans**. The idea is fairly simple, the repayment is structured with payments every two weeks instead of once a month. Other than the convenience of having a house payment come due exactly on payday, the borrower would ordinarily find no significant advantage to a bi-weekly loan. However, if we look at the way bi-weekly mortgages are structured, the borrower can end up paying the loan off significantly earlier. Calculating the payments on a monthly amortization and dividing it by two would mean 24 payments every year. However, there are 52 weeks in a year, so with a bi-weekly mortgage, 26 payments are made. If we keep the amount of the payment half as much as the monthly payment, an extra payment gets made every year with the bi-weekly mortgage. The extra payment starts a snowballing effect and the result is a significantly faster payoff. A loan of $100,000 at 8% for 30 years would have monthly payments of $733.76 and total interest of $164,155.24 over the life of the loan. Dividing the payment in half means the payments would be $366.88, but making 26 per year means the loan would be paid off in only 23 years, nine months, and the total interest cost would be only $117,926.72.

Payoff of an ordinary 30-year mortgage loan of $100,000 with 360 equal monthly payments of 733.76. The halfway mark is reached at approximately 22½ years.

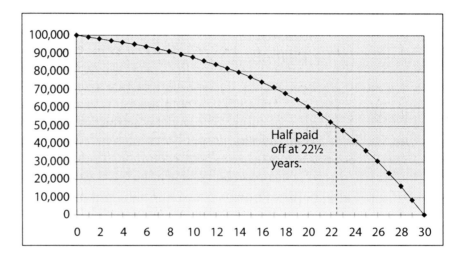

Payoff of a bi-weekly mortgage loan of $100,000 with equal payments of 366.88 every two weeks. By making bi-weekly payments each of which is half of the payment for the 30-year mortgage above, the borrower makes one extra payment each year. The halfway mark is reached at approximately 16 years instead of 22½ years for the 30-year loan.

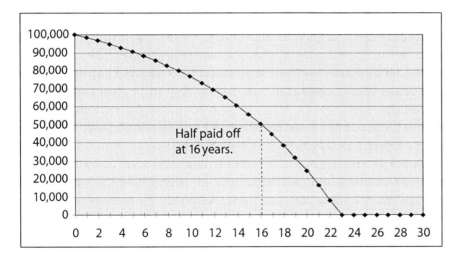

As you can see, bi-weekly loans offer the borrower a payoff better than six years sooner, with a substantial interest savings over the life of the loan. And all of this can be done fairly painlessly, since most borrowers wouldn't notice the slight increase in total principal and interest payment.

Some conventional lenders offer loans with ***balloon payments***, or a ***call feature***. A balloon payment means that the entire remaining principal balance must be paid in full at some point in the future (usually five years or seven years). Some balloon payment mortgages contain a ***rollover clause***, which allows the borrower to continue the loan. A balloon payment loan with a five-year rollover clause would be called a "5/25 convertible mortgage." Similarly, a seven-year rollover clause would make it a "7/23 convertible mortgage."

Balloons and call features are, quite naturally, unpopular with borrowers. What would you do if the due date arrived and you were unable to refinance or sell the property to pay off the loan? The potential for foreclosure is great. Lenders usually lose money on foreclosures, so balloon payment loans are not popular with secondary market investors either. In order to make balloon payment loans more palatable, they are generally made at a slightly lower than market interest rate. They also commonly contain a roll-over clause. Even then, the borrower is required to meet certain tests in order to exercise the rollover privilege, and the rollover is usually at a rate slightly higher than the lender's current rate for new loans. The idea is to give the borrower an escape route, but make it less attractive than refinancing.

Adjustable rate loans

When the interest rate on the loan is tied to an index, we call it an *adjustable rate mortgage* (ARM). Adjustable rate mortgages are more popular with lenders than with borrowers, although many borrowers also find plenty of advantages in ARM loans.

The chief benefit to the lender is a hedge against inflation and interest rate increases in the future. The lender is so thrilled with this benefit that the borrower may find the lender offering very enticing interest rates – two to three percent below the rate for fixed rate mortgages is not uncommon. So enticing, in fact, that ARMs score very high in the area of affordability. When the buyer cannot qualify for a fixed rate loan high enough to buy the property, an ARM frequently saves the sale.

There are also hybrid loans which combine the features of a fixed rate and an adjustable rate loan. Usually these loans start out with a fixed rate for the first seven or ten years, then switch to an adjustable rate. This kind of loan is usually called an *introductory rate ARM*.

Lenders tie their ARM loans to all kinds of different *indexes*. There are many published interest rate indexes and each lender will have a favorite. Some of the more popular are –

- *One-year, three-year and five-year treasury indexes* – Averages of U.S. government bills and bonds adjusted to a constant one-year maturity. Published by the Federal Reserve Bank.
- *Six month treasury bill index* – Based on the results of the weekly auction of 180-day treasury bills, quoted as a bank discount basis.
- *Cost of Funds Index (COFI)* – The average monthly cost of deposits and other funds for thrifts. Some indexes are compiled for individual Federal Home Loan Bank districts. By far the most popular among Oregon lenders is the 11th District Cost of Funds Index, published by the Federal Home Loan Bank of San Francisco. The 11th District is comprised of thrifts in Arizona, California and Nevada.

Regardless of the index, the loan must also stipulate the adjustment period. Most lenders today prefer to adjust the interest rate once every six months, although one-year adjustments are also common. Lenders offer ARMs with a wide range of adjustment period options. At one extreme a few lenders offer adjustments at three years and five years; and at the other end of the spectrum there are lenders who adjust as often as monthly. A *two-step mortgage* is a special kind of ARM that is adjusted just once during its lifetime; usually at the fifth or seventh year.

Although ARMs offer the lowest interest rates of all conventional loans, lenders still charge more than the index rate. For example, suppose the lender wants 7%, but the index is at, say 4½%. In this case the note will call for interest to be charged at the index rate plus the *margin* – in this case 2½%. The margin is a constant and does not vary over the life of the loan. Now, if the margin is 2½% and the index climbs to, say 6%, the borrower's interest rate will be adjusted to 8½% (6% + 2½% = 8½%). The index rate plus the margin is called the ***fully indexed rate***.

Of course, if market interest rates were to skyrocket, borrowers with adjustable rate loans would be in deep trouble, indeed. It is common practice to adjust the payment every time the interest rate changes. A 30-year ARM loan of $200,000 at an initial rate of 6% would have monthly payments of $1,199.10. If the index rate goes up 2% six months later, the new interest rate will be 8%. The monthly payment would then be recalculated to amortize the loan over its remaining term (29½ years), or $1,473.56. This could cause what lenders call ***payment shock***.

To guard against the inevitable defaults this would cause, lenders offer a variety of safeguards in the form of ***caps***. A cap is a ceiling, usually on the interest rate. For example, a ***lifetime cap*** is a maximum amount the interest rate can increase to over the life of the loan. An ARM loan at 5% initially with a 7% lifetime cap can never increase to more than 12%. An ***interim cap***, also called ***adjustment cap*** or sometimes ***annual cap***, is the maximum amount the loan interest can increase in any one period. If the adjustment period is annual, then it is called an annual cap, and so on. There are loans with interim caps as long as three years, and as short as monthly. The longer the period, the less the gamble. Lenders prefer shorter adjustment periods. But if rates are falling, borrowers would benefit from shorter adjustment periods too.

Another kind of cap is a ***payment cap***. Some lenders agree not to raise the payment by more than a certain percentage in any one year (7½% is common). Then, if the interest increases and the increase would cause the payment to exceed this percentage, the lender accepts the lower payment and adds the unpaid interest to the principal balance. This is called ***negative amortization***. Lenders use payment caps in order to calm a borrower's fears about an ARM loan, yet not be constrained to very restrictive interest caps. Needless to say, payment caps are not popular with borrowers.

In fact, this is really a type of ***graduated payment adjustable rate mortgage*** (GPARM) – essentially the same as a GPM (see above), but where the interest rate is tied to an index. In the past many lenders offered formal GPARM loans with payment caps for the first five or ten years. Quite a few were made. But because they can easily create negative amortization, GPARMS are no more popular than GPMS and, hence, rare today. On the other hand, it is still not uncommon for lenders to offer a ***teaser rate***. A teaser rate is a special below-market rate used for the first year – an additional incentive for the borrower to choose an ARM loan.

Some ARM loans have a ***conversion privilege***. A conversion privilege allows the borrower to convert the ARM to a FRM. The exact terms of the conversion privilege vary dramatically from one lender to the next. Most of the time the borrower can only exercise the conversion privilege during the first few years of the loan. In most cases, the interest rate at conversion will be the lender's (then) current rate for new fixed rate loans. In most cases, interest rates would have to decline substantially before exercising the conversion privilege would make sense.

Growing equity mortgages

A ***growing equity mortgage*** (GEM) is a special kind of 15-year fixed rate loan. Unlike regular 15-year FRMs it has graduated payments like a GPM. Most GEMs have payment caps, so there is negative amortization. The major difficulty with GEM loans is that the payments start too low, which means they have to increase to rather high amounts later in order to complete the amortization in 15 years.

Most lenders list GEM loans as available, but there are few actually written today. Some lenders refer to an ordinary 15-year FRM as a GEM, although that is not technically a correct usage, since a GEM is supposed to have graduated payments, at least according to the standard definition.

Buydowns

What do you do when the buyer cannot qualify for the loan? If the buyer fails to qualify because the payments are too high, it may be possible to save the day with a buydown. A *buydown* is a lump sum paid to the lender up front, in exchange for which the lender agrees to lower the interest rate. In effect, it is prepaid interest. In fact, buydowns are the same as discount points (see the previous section, Government Financing Programs), although they don't always work exactly the same way.

The first thing to remember about buydowns on conventional loans is that it generally does not matter who pays the buydown. Typically it is the seller, but it is also common for friends or relatives of the borrowers to pay it. There are qualifying restrictions, however. Lenders want to see the borrower pay some of his or her own funds to buy the property, so if too much of the down payment or amounts to buy the loan down come from the seller or as gifts, this can cause the loan to be denied.

The second thing to bear in mind about buydowns is that they can be used with either fixed rate mortgages or adjustables. Of course, if the interest rate on an adjustable is bought down, it is really the margin that is bought down. For example, with an index that started at 4½% and a margin of 2½%, the initial interest rate is 7%. If the interest rate is bought down 1%, it is the margin that is reduced from 2½% to 1½%.

In conventional financing there are two kinds of buydowns – *permanent buydowns* and *temporary buydowns*. A permanent buydown operates precisely the same as loan points to lower the interest rate over the life of the loan. A temporary buydown, on the other hand, lowers the interest rate only for the first year or first few years of the loan.

In conventional financing permanent buydowns are not nearly as common as temporary buydowns. The main reason for this is the cost. As discussed in the previous section, the rule of thumb for buydowns is eight points for every percent the loan is bought down. So to buy a FRM down permanently from 8% to 7% would require a discount of eight points (8% of the loan balance). On a $200,000 loan, this is going to cost someone – probably the seller – $16,000.

But a temporary buydown may be sufficient. Buydowns are commonly used only when the borrower cannot qualify because the payments are too high. So if the lender will qualify the borrower on the initial, lower payments, then a temporary buydown should be all that is necessary. Lenders will not always agree to qualify the borrower on the initial payment, however. Temporary buydowns commonly run for one, two or three years.

If a temporary buydown is for more than one year, it can be a flat rate or it can be graduated. A *flat rate buydown* is a buydown where the amount of the buydown remains constant. For example, suppose you bought a loan down 2% for each of the first three years of the loan. This would be a flat rate buydown. But suppose instead that you bought the rate down 3% the first year, 2% the second year, and 1% the third year. This would be an example of a *graduated rate buydown*. Some lenders offer a *flex fixed rate* temporary buydown – the same as an ordinary buydown but where the rate increases every six months instead of every year.

Regardless of whether a temporary buydown is flat rate or graduated, it is very easy to get an approximation of what the lender would charge. Just add up the interest that the lender is losing each year because of the buydown. However, this is only an estimate. In reality, the lender is getting the money up front and can reinvest it and earn interest on it, so the actual cost tends to be slightly less than the estimate. For example, a 3–2–1 buydown would cost the lender 3% interest (3% of the loan balance) the first year, 2% the second year, and 1% the third year. Therefore, the total interest the lender would lose is 6%, so someone has to pay 6% of the loan balance (six points). But by getting the money up front, the lender may be willing to discount the six points to, say, 5¾ points. Buydowns are commonly used when the property is being sold by a corporation due to an employee relocation. The corporation will agree to pay the buydown in order to facilitate their employee's transfer.

As an alternative to charging someone points to buy the loan down, lenders today also offer to lower the interest rate for the first few years, in exchange for a higher interest rate over the remaining term of the loan. For example, in a market where FRMs are going for 7½%, a 3–2–1 buydown could be cast at an initial rate of 5¼%, a second year rate of 6¼%, a third year rate of 7¼%, and a rate of 7¾% for the fourth through the 30th year. The extra ¼ of 1% for the last 26 years allows the lender to recover the interest lost the first three years.

Graduated payment mortgages

A *graduated payment mortgage* loan (GPM) is a type of FRM where there is a special reduced payment for the first few years (usually five years). This results in **negative amortization**, that is, the payment is not even high enough to cover the interest, so the unpaid interest is added to the principal balance. In today's market, negative amortization is no more popular with lenders than it is with borrowers.

There is an additional difficulty with GPMs. For a five-year GPM, the payment would be higher for years five through 30 than if it were an ordinary FRM. This is necessary to pay back the negative amortization incurred during the first five years. To lessen the amount of negative amortization, the payment are scheduled to increase every year. Theoretically, there is no limit to how low the first year's payments can be made. But if they are made too low, the annual payment increases can cause payment shock. Secondary market investors do not like loans where the payments can increase more than 7½% a year, so most lenders structure GPMs with 7½% as the maximum annual increase.

Graduated payment mortgages are useful mostly in a market with rapid property appreciation. In such a market the GPM allows the borrower greater purchasing power. However, if future appreciation does not materialize as expected and the borrower needs to move during the adjustment period, the GPM can be a disaster.

Assumability

Where government loans are always assumable (although the buyer is sometimes asked to qualify), conventional loans usually are not. Adjustable loans are the major exception. Since the lender has a means to maintain the interest rate close to market, it becomes less important to enforce the due on sale clause on ARM loans.

Still, there are occasional fixed rate mortgages which do not have a due on sale clause. Real estate agents should always verify from the actual documents whether or not the loan is assumable, and if so, under what terms. Over the last 20 years there have been many different forms used and policies followed. For conventional loans, there are no standards when it comes to due on sale clauses. It is also not uncommon to find lenders' employees giving incorrect information about assumability of a loan. The only way to be sure is to get a copy of the recorded document.

Exercise b

The most popular conventional loan today is the _____ _____ mortgage loan with repayment over a _____ -year term. Shorter term loans can offer enormous savings in _____ paid over the life of the loan. A ____ - _____ loan is a loan where the borrower gains a shorter amortization and less total interest by making an extra payment every year. A _____ _____ requires the borrower to pay the loan off after a certain number of years. If the borrower has the option to renew the loan after this time, we say the loan had a _____ _____ .

When a lender makes an adjustable loan with low interest for the first several years, we call it an _____ _____ ARM. The interest on an ARM loan is tied to an _____ , the most popular of which is the _____ District _____ ____ _____ . An ARM loan which can be adjusted only once during its term is called a _____ - _____ mortgage. Some adjustable loans have a _____ _____ instead of a limit on the interest rate increase, so as not to cause _____ _____ . When the payments are not high enough to cover the interest, this causes _____ _____ . In mortgage lending, the initials "GEM" stand for _____ _____ _____ . Adjustable loans usually have an _____ _____ which sets the maximum the interest rate can be increased in any one period. A _____ _____ establishes the absolute interest limit over the entire term of the loan. When a lender sets a very attractive initial rate, this is called a _____ rate.

Buydowns can be _____ (over the life of the loan) or _____ (just for the first few years of the loan). If the buydown is just for the first few years, it can be a _____ rate buydown, where the amount of the interest reduction remains the same for each year of the buydown, or it can be a _____ rate buydown. When the payments do not cover the interest and the unpaid interest is deferred, this is typical of a _____ _____ mortgage.

Conventional loans almost always have a _____ _____ _____ clause, which means the borrower must pay the loan off if the property is sold. Lenders use this clause to force the buyer to assume the loan and to agree to an _____ in the interest rate to current market.

Construction financing

Of all kinds of mortgage financing, construction lending entails the greatest risk to the lender. In fact, a common rule of thumb is to add an extra 2% to the rate for ordinary real estate loans if the loan is for construction purposes. The reasons for this are many, but one reason is simply because a half-finished structure makes pretty poor collateral.

Although in the past there have been government programs for construction financing, today these programs are virtually nonexistent. Practically all construction financing today is conventional lending.

Construction financing (also called *interim financing*) is short term (not usually more than a couple of years at the most) and designed to be replaced by a new loan to be taken out by the eventual buyers. The new loan is called the *permanent* or *takeout loan*. The term "takeout loan" refers to the fact that the permanent financing "takes out," or pays off the construction financing. A few lenders have made available a one-stage construction loan where the borrower is the eventual buyer, the interest rate is at the higher "construction" rate until the construction is completed, and then the rate is reduced to the mortgage prime rate and the loan is amortized over the usual term. To be sure that permanent financing is available the construction lender sometimes issues a *standby commitment* to the builder, usually at a specific interest rate.

A major problem with construction financing is the possibility of *construction liens*. A construction lien is placed by a worker who claims that a bill for labor or materials was not paid. The problem is that, under Oregon law the priority of the claim predates all other recorded liens. If the contractor does not pay the workers and materials suppliers, the construction lender could easily find itself in second position to all the construction liens.

To guard against this happening construction lenders use a number of safeguards. First, they carefully scrutinize the contractor's financial ability. But most important, they need to be sure that all the workers, subcontractors and materials suppliers are paid. Construction lenders commonly disburse the loan proceeds in stages as the construction progresses. These are called *construction draws*. And the money is usually disbursed directly to the workers, subcontractors and materials suppliers. These people bring their bills to the general contractor who approves them for payment, and then the lender issues checks to pay the bills. The lender uses an endorsement on the checks where the endorser waives the right to a construction lien. Note that this process takes considerably more paperwork than an ordinary mortgage loan. This is probably the greatest reason construction loans are more expensive than permanent financing.

The possibility of construction liens not only makes the construction financing hazardous, it also frequently creates problems for the permanent loan. If the buyers want to close their purchase right after the construction is complete, the lender has to remember that workers, subcontractors and materials suppliers have up to 75 days after substantial completion in which to file their claims. Due to the priority of construction liens, these claims would predate the new permanent mortgage. The usual solution is to pay an extra premium for an *early issue* lender's title insurance policy to cover this possibility.

Another construction problem occurs when a property owner orders improvements built. The owner needs to be sure the builder will finish the project. A common solution is for the owner to insist that the contractor obtain a *completion bond* from an insurance company.

Exercise c

Construction financing is also called _____ financing because it is short term. The construction loan is to be paid off by permanent financing, also called the _____ loan. The priority of a _____ lien is ahead of a construction loan, which creates a problem for construction lenders. To protect themselves, construction lenders disburse the construction loan in _____ .

 KEY TERMS

The key to understanding any new field is the vocabulary used in that field. To maximize your comprehension of the material presented in this chapter, be sure you know the meaning and significance of the following terms. Remember that the majority of test questions primarily test knowledge of vocabulary.

Adjustable rate mortgage (ARM)	Graduated payment mortgage (GPM)
Adjustment cap	Graduated rate buydown
Amortization	Growing equity mortgage (GEM)
Annual cap	Index
Balloon payments	Interim cap
Bi-weekly loans	Interim financing
Buydown	Introductory rate ARM
Call feature	Jumbo mortgage
Cap	Lifetime cap
Completion bond	Margin
Conforming loan	Negative amortization
Construction draws	Nonconforming loan
Construction financing	Payment shock
Construction liens	Payment cap
Conventional loan	Permanent buydowns
Conversion privilege	Permanent financing
Early issue	Private mortgage insurance
Fixed rate mortgage (FRM)	Rollover clause
Flat rate buydown	Standby commitment
Flex fixed rate buydown	Takeout loan
Fully indexed rate	Teaser rate
Graduated payment adjustable rate mortgage (GPARM)	

? ANSWERS

To chapter exercises. If you couldn't figure out what to put in the blanks, find the answer here!

Exercise a

A conventional loan is any loan that is not government ___INSURED___ or ___GUARANTEED___ or made directly by a government body Until the early 1970s there was no ___SECONDARY___ ___MARKET___ for conventional loans. As a result, they were made primarily by ___THRIFT___ institutions only. Today, all types of lenders offer conventional loans.

Conventional loans can be ___INSURED___, the same as government loans. This is commonly referred to as ___PRIVATE___ ___MORTGAGE___ ___INSURANCE___, (PMI) to distinguish it from insurance on FHA and RECDC loans. The premium would be the least for (choose one)

- ■ A fixed rate 30-year conventional loan.
- ❑ A fixed rate 30-year loan with a balloon payment at five years.
- ❑ A 30-year adjustable rate loan.

Most lenders insure only the amount of the loan which exceeds __80__ % loan to value ratio.

Loans which are under the maximum loan amount established by the secondary market are called _____CONFORMING_____ loans. Loans over this amount are called ___NON___ - _____CONFORMING_____, or jumbo loans.

Exercise b

The most popular conventional loan today is the _____FIXED_____ _____RATE_____ mortgage loan with repayment over a __30__ -year term. Shorter term loans can offer enormous savings in _____INTEREST_____ paid over the life of the loan. A __BI__ - _____WEEKLY_____ loan is a loan where the borrower gains a shorter amortization and less total interest by making an extra payment every year. A _____BALLOON_____ _____PAYMENT_____ requires the borrower to pay the loan off after a certain number of years. If the borrower has the option to renew the loan after this time, we say the loan had a _____ROLLOVER_____ _____CLAUSE_____ .

When a lender makes an adjustable loan with low interest for the first several years, we call it an _____INTRODUCTORY_____ _____RATE_____ ARM. The interest on an ARM loan is tied to an _____INDEX_____, the most popular of which is the ___11TH___ District _____COST_____ _____OF_____ _____FUNDS_____ . An ARM loan which can be adjusted only once during its term is called a _____TWO_____ - _____STEP_____ mortgage. Some adjustable loans have a _____PAYMENT_____ _____CAP_____ instead of a limit on the interest rate increase, so as not to cause _____PAYMENT_____ _____SHOCK_____ . When the payments are not high enough to cover the interest, this causes _____NEGATIVE_____ _____AMORTIZATION_____ . In mortgage lending, the initials "GEM" stand for _____GROWING_____ _____EQUITY_____ _____MORTGAGE_____ . Adjustable loans usually have an _____INTERIM_____ _____CAP_____ which sets the maximum the interest rate can be increased in any one period. A _____LIFETIME_____ _____CAP_____ establishes the absolute interest limit over the entire term of the loan. When a lender sets a very attractive initial rate, this is called a _____TEASER_____ rate.

Buydowns can be _____PERMANENT_____ (over the life of the loan) or _____TEMPORARY_____ (just for the first few years of the loan). If the buydown is just for the first few years, it can be a _____FLAT_____ rate buydown, where the amount of the interest reduction remains the same for each year of the buydown, or it can be a _____GRADUATED_____ rate buydown. When the payments do not cover the interest and the unpaid interest is deferred, this is typical of a _____GRADUATED_____ _____PAYMENT_____ mortgage.

Conventional loans almost always have a _____DUE_____ _____ON_____ _____SALE_____ clause, which means the borrower must pay the loan off if the property is sold. Lenders use this clause to force the buyer to assume the loan and to agree to an _____INCREASE_____ in the interest rate to current market.

Exercise c

Construction financing is also called _____INTERIM_____ financing because it is short term. The construction loan is to be paid off by permanent financing, also called the _____TAKEOUT_____ loan. The priority of a _____CONSTRUCTION_____ lien is ahead of a construction loan, which creates a problem for construction lenders. To protect themselves, construction lenders disburse the construction loan in _____DRAWS_____ .

PRACTICE QUESTIONS

The following practice questions are representative of the questions you will find on the final examination and on the licensing examinations given by the Oregon Real Estate Agency.

1. The loan to value ratio on a mortgage is
    (A) the mortgage loan as a percentage of insured value.
    (B) the monthly payments as a percentage of the remaining balance of the loan.
    (C) the loan as a percentage of the sales price or appraised value, whichever is lower.
    (D) none of the above.

2. A borrower obtained a home improvement loan which was neither insured nor guaranteed by a government agency. The security for the loan was the borrower's house which was owned free of any encumbrance. This borrower obtained which type of loan?
    (A) Wraparound
    (B) Package money
    (C) Subordinated
    (D) Conventional

3. Imelda Lopez obtained a mortgage in order to make repairs on her home. The mortgage is not insured or guaranteed by a government agency. The mortgage document secures the amount of the loan, as well as any future funds advanced to Lopez by the lender. Lopez has obtained a
    I. wraparound mortgage.
    II. conventional open end mortgage.
    (A) I only
    (B) II only
    (C) Both I and II
    (D) Neither I nor II

4. August Summers was approved by a bank for a mortgage loan where additional funds could be borrowed in the future. The loan was not warranted by any government agency. August obtained
    (A) a conventional loan.
    (B) an open end loan.
    (C) both A and B.
    (D) neither A nor B.

5. A borrower wishes to get a home improvement loan from Thunderbucks Bank and Trust Co. The security will be the borrower's home which is owned free and clear. The loan would not be insured or guaranteed by any government agency. The borrower is looking for a
    (A) conventional loan.
    (B) package loan.
    (C) wraparound loan.
    (D) securitized loan.

6. A conventional mortgage is
    (A) guaranteed by the FDIC.
    (B) not guaranteed by a government agency.
    (C) made at a rate of interest set by a government agency.
    (D) subject to revocation by the state Department of Commerce.

7. Mortgages which are not insured by a government agency are called
    (A) FMHA mortgages.
    (B) FHA loans.
    (C) VA mortgages.
    (D) Conventional mortgages.

8. A loan made with real estate as security and not involving government participation in the form of insuring, guaranteeing, or direct lending is known as a
    (A) conventional loan.
    (B) standby loan.
    (C) Bancroft bond.
    (D) budget mortgage.

9. Conventional loans are made from
    (A) private sources.
    (B) FHA funds.
    (C) Fannie Mae funds.
    (D) Home Owners' Loan Corporation.

10. Who will insure conventional loans?
    (A) Federal Housing Administration
    (B) Private mortgage insurance companies
    (C) Federal Savings and Loan Insurance Corporation
    (D) Oregon Housing Agency

11. Conventional mortgage loans are
    I.   sometimes partially insured by private mortgage insurance companies.
    II. insured by the FHA or guaranteed by the federal DVA.
    (A) I only   (C) Both I and II
    (B) II only   (D) Neither I nor II

12. Most conventional lenders consider a safe and prudent loan to value ratio to be
    (A) 75%.   (C) 90%.
    (B) 80%   (D) 95%.

13. The direct source for conventional loan funds is
    (A) private sources.
    (B) Fannie Mae.
    (C) the FHA.
    (D) the Home Owners Loan Corporation.

14. Funds for conventional real estate loans are received from
    I.   the Government National Mortgage Association (Ginnie Mae).
    II. private parties and non-government financial institutions.
    III. mortgage brokerage activities.
    (A) I and II only   (C) II only
    (B) I, II and III   (D) II and III only

15. In order to increase their yields on fixed rate conventional loans, lenders have been known to charge
    (A) loan fees.   (C) both A and B.
    (B) prepayment penalties.   (D) neither A nor B.

16. If a conventional lender's loans do not carry government insurance or guaranties, what would the lender do as a result?
    (A) Charge higher interest rates
    (B) Require higher down payments than government sponsored financing
    (C) Both A and B
    (D) Neither A nor B

17. When compared to FHA loans, conventional loans generally offer
    (A) lower interest rates.
    (B) lower loan to value ratios.
    (C) lower down payments.
    (D) longer terms to maturity.

18. Lenders charge higher interest rates on fixed rate conventional loans because they
    I.   fear increasing inflation.
    II. know fixed rate conventional loans are more popular with the public.
    (A) I only   (C) Both I and II
    (B) II only   (D) Neither I nor II

19. In real estate lending, the letters "ARM" stand for
    (A) Annuity Return on Mortgage.
    (B) Ability to Repay Mortgage.
    (C) Adjustable Rate Mortgage.
    (D) Appraised Remodeling Money.

20. An older borrower with substantial income would probably be most interested in
    (A) an ARM loan.   (C) a GPARM loan.
    (B) a GPM loan.   (D) a 15-year FRM loan.

21. A borrower is told that the seller will pay for a "3-2-1" buydown. This means that the
    I.   interest rate will be lowered by 3% the first year, 2% the second year and 1% the third year.
    II. seller will have to pay approximately 6% of the buyer's loan amount.
    (A) I only   (C) Both I and II
    (B) II only   (D) Neither I nor II

22. Negative amortization
    I.   is not permitted on conventional loans.
    II. would result in the principal balance increasing.
    (A) I only   (C) Both I and II
    (B) II only   (D) Neither I nor II

23. A borrower applied for a loan at 6½% interest. The lender told the borrower that the loan will have a lifetime "cap" of 5%. This means that the
    I.   loan is an ARM.
    II. interest charged can never exceed 11½%.
    (A) I only   (C) Both I and II
    (B) II only   (D) Neither I nor II

24. The Glombux Bank holds a conventional fixed rate mortgage at 7% on a property you have listed. The current market rate for new fixed rate loans is 8½%, but Glombux is willing to make a fixed rate conventional loan to your buyer at 8%. This kind of loan is called
    (A) a blended loan.
    (B) a two-step loan.
    (C) an adjustable rate mortgage loan.
    (D) a wraparound loan.

25. A "GPM" mortgage will
    (A) decrease the monthly payments over the life of the mortgage.
    (B) increase the borrower's purchasing power.
    (C) decrease the lender's yield on the loan.
    (D) decrease the term over which the mortgage will be paid off.

26. You are attempting to sell a house to a buyer who cannot afford the payments on the loan needed to buy the house. The buyer wants a fixed rate loan and has good potential for future income increases. Your buyer would be most interested in
    (A) a GPM.
    (B) a GEM.
    (C) a GPARM.
    (D) any of the above.

27. Conventional loans typically
    I. contain a due on sale clause.
    II. are insured if over the 80% loan to value ratio.
    III. do not require the approval of a government agency.
    (A) I only
    (B) I and II only
    (C) II and III only
    (D) I, II and III

28. A prepayment penalty can be charged on a
    I. loan insured by the Federal Housing Administration.
    II. conventional loan.
    (A) I only
    (B) II only
    (C) Both I and II
    (D) Neither I nor II

29. Construction financing is usually designed as
    (A) high interest, long term loans.
    (B) low interest, long term loans.
    (C) high interest, short term loans.
    (D) low interest, short term loans.

30. A construction loan is
    I. a permanent form of financing.
    II. a method of self-financing for the homeowner.
    III. a form of interim financing.
    IV. usually distributed in installments.
    (A) I and II only
    (B) I and IV only
    (C) II and III only
    (D) III and IV only

31. In real estate financing, reference is sometimes made to a "takeout loan." This refers to a
    (A) blanket encumbrance.
    (B) construction loan.
    (C) long term loan taken out after construction.
    (D) net amount after points and prepaid interest are deducted.

32. As used in real estate practice, the phrase "takeout" loan refers to
    (A) net amount after points and prepaid interest are deducted.
    (B) a blanket encumbrance.
    (C) construction loan.
    (D) long term loan taken out after construction.

33. Which of the following pairs of terms are synonymous?
    (A) Takeout loan — Freddie Mac loan
    (B) Interim financing — Construction loan
    (C) Permanent financing — Takeout loan
    (D) Both B and C

34. In large construction projects the developer usually obtains financing from two main sources. The first is the interim lender who specializes in short term loans to cover construction financing. Before lending any money, however, the interim lender normally requires a commitment by a permanent lender to agree to take over the mortgage as a long term investment when the building has been completed. The second phase is called
    (A) takeout financing.
    (B) subjacent support.
    (C) subrogation.
    (D) a junior mortgage.

35. The Landslide Development Company wishes to build a commercial building. The interim lender wants to make sure permanent financing is available. In real estate lending terminology, the permanent financing is called the
    (A) takeout loan.
    (B) junior loan.
    (C) subrogation mortgage.
    (D) secondary loan.

36. A lender on a construction loan for an apartment building expects to be paid off through
    (A) long term amortization.
    (B) permanent takeout loans.
    (C) both A and B.
    (D) neither A nor B.

37. Which of the following statements regarding real estate finance is true?
    I. Residential construction financing entails higher risk for the lender than permanent financing.
    II. In construction financing the builder frequently receives the loan proceeds in stages.
    (A) I only
    (B) II only
    (C) Both I and II
    (D) Neither I nor II

38. When financing new construction, the lender usually releases the final payment to the builder
    (A) when the owner accepts the property.
    (B) after the lien period has expired.
    (C) when the work has been completed.
    (D) after recording the notice of completion.

39. In a construction loan mortgage
    (A) the funds are advanced before construction begins.
    (B) the funds are not normally advanced until construction is completely finished.
    (C) the loan is normally advanced in installments at various stages of construction.
    (D) interest on the total loan begins at the beginning of construction.

40. In a construction mortgage the funds loaned are normally disbursed to the builder in
    (A) a lump sum upon acquisition of title to the land.
    (B) two equal sums, one at the outset of construction and the other at completion of the job.
    (C) a series of installments, after each inspection of progress on the job.
    (D) daily installments that minimize interest payments on the outstanding balance of the loan.

41. A completion bond is for the protection of the
    I. borrower on the permanent loan.
    II. developer.
    III. lender.
    (A) I only
    (B) I and II only
    (C) I and III only
    (D) I, II and III

42. A "standby commitment" means
    (A) that a lender has assured another lender that a construction loan will be paid when it falls due.
    (B) that a lender has extended credit to a builder without actually lending any funds.
    (C) either A or B.
    (D) neither A nor B.

43. Under the terms of an insured mortgage loan, the
    (A) lender is insured against loss should the borrower default.
    (B) borrower is protected against loss of the property if the borrower is unable to make the required mortgage payments.
    (C) lender is protected against loss resulting from fire or other events damaging the property.
    (D) interest rate is always lower than it would be under the terms of a conventional mortgage.

44. A mortgage insurance premium would likely be paid by a borrower who obtained
    (A) a 90% conventional loan from a thrift.
    (B) an FHA loan from a commercial bank.
    (C) a federal DVA loan from a mortgage banker.
    (D) either A or B above.

45. A borrower is allowed to pay in excess of the appraised value of the home on a
    I. Federal Housing Administration (FHA) loan.
    II. U.S. Department of Veterans Affairs (DVA) loan.
    III. conventional loan.
    (A) I only
    (B) I and II only
    (C) III only
    (D) Any of the above

46. A loan where the lender can change the interest rate as market rates change would be available from
    (A) a participating Federal Housing Administration lender.
    (B) an approved federal Department of Veterans Affairs lender.
    (C) a conventional lender.
    (D) any of the above.

47. The down payment would likely be the lowest on
    (A) an uninsured conventional loan.
    (B) a loan insured by the FHA.
    (C) a loan guaranteed by the federal DVA.
    (D) an insured conventional loan for a property that will not be owner-occupied.

ANSWERS

To practice questions. If you chose the wrong letter, here's the right one! The explanations are designed to clarify your understanding.

1. **C** The "loan to value ratio" is the amount of the loan as a percentage of the sales price or appraised value. The secondary market requires that the loan to value ratio be applied to the lower of the sales price or appraised value.

2. **D** Before the existence of government insured and guaranteed loans, the term "conventional loan" did not exist. The term was coined to distinguish loans which were not government insured or guaranteed from those that were. A wraparound loan is a loan which encompasses an underlying loan. A subordinated loan is one where the lender has agreed to be junior in priority to another loan even though the other loan was recorded later.

3. **B** A loan which is not government insured or guaranteed is called a conventional loan. Conventional loans come in all types, including open end loans. An open end loan is like a credit line, where the borrower has a credit limit and can borrow any amount at any time up to the limit.

4. **C** A conventional loan is any loan not made, insured, or guaranteed by a government agency. An open end loan is a loan which operates in much the same way as a credit line. Funds can be borrowed, paid back, reborrowed, repaid again over an indefinite period of time, up to a maximum amount, usually up to a maximum percentage of the appraised value.

5. **A** "Conventional loan" means any loan that is not insured or guaranteed by a government agency, or made directly by the government.

6. **B** The term "conventional loan" was coined to distinguish ordinary bank loans from loans insured or guaranteed by the government.

7. **D** Prior to the creation of the FHA in 1934 the term "conventional loan" did not exist because all loans were conventional loans. The FHA introduced the government insured loan, and the term "conventional loan" was coined to distinguish ordinary real estate loans from the new FHA loans. In time, other federal programs came into existence to insure and guarantee loans, such as programs through the Rural Economic Community Development Corporation and the Department of Veterans Affairs (DVA).

8. **A** The term "conventional loan" was coined in 1934 when FHA came into existence. The FHA insures loans against default, so "conventional" means a regular loan, not insured or guaranteed by a government agency.

9. **A** Institutional lenders provide the funds to originate residential loans. Most are subsequently sold in the secondary market, which replenishes the lender's funds. This is true of conventional loans as well as government insured and guaranteed loans.

10. **B** The first mortgage insurance was through the FHA, created in 1934. Later the Veterans Administration began issuing loan guaranties. It was not until the late 1960's that conventional loan insurance became available. Since conventional loans are not government insured or guaranteed, the insurance is through private mortgage insurance companies.

11. **A** In order to remain competitive with government insured and guaranteed loans, conventional lenders have had to offer lower down payments. Private mortgage insurance has made this possible. Private insurance companies insure all conventional loans today over 80% loan to value ratio, and many loans under 80% loan to value ratio as well.

12. **A** During the 1920's lenders formulated the idea that a 75% loan to value ratio was prudent banking practice. During the post-World War II period banks were highly regulated and were allowed by law to lend up to 80% without insurance. Although bankers would have preferred 75% loan to value ratios, they mostly offered 80% loans in order to meet the competition.

13. **B** Conventional loans are sold or securitized today mainly through Freddie Mac and Fannie Mae, which means that investors in the primary capital markets are the original source of funds, but the direct source is Fannie Mae or Freddie Mac.

14. **C** Ginnie Mae's secondary market activities are limited today to securitizing FHA, VA and FMHA loans originated by primary lenders. Conventional loans are sold or securitized today mainly through Freddie Mac and Fannie Mae, which means that investors in the primary capital markets are the prime source of funds.

15. **C** All fees received are a contribution to profit and overhead. Even though prepayment penalties are seldom charged on conventional loans today, such a charge would still increase the lenders yield.

16. **B** As a rule, lenders charge interest to cover their cost of capital and profit, not according to risk. In order to remain competitive conventional lenders cannot realistically charge more interest than the interest being charged on similar government insured or guaranteed loans. Conventional loans over 80% loan to value ratio are insured against default by private mortgage insurance companies. The only way to avoid loan insurance is to make a down payment of at least 20%.

17. **B** Except for loans guaranteed by the U.S. Department of Veterans Affairs, the lowest down payments available today are on FHA insured loans. Although conventional loans today can rival the loan to value ratio of FHA loans, it is more difficult to qualify when the loan to value ratio is high. Federal GI loans require no down payment and FHA insured loans frequently go as high as 95-100% financing. Because the FHA allows the borrower and the lender to negotiate the interest rate, rates are usually very competitive between FHA insured loans and conventional loans. As for terms to maturity, residential loans over 30 years are rare, regardless of the type of loan. The reason is simply because extending the term longer than 30 years lowers the payment by such a slight amount that borrowers gain little benefit.

18. **C** Since adjustable mortgages are tied to an index, the lender has a much better chance of retaining profitability over the life of the loan. Therefore, the lender can offer a lower rate. There is little doubt that the rates charged on adjustable rate mortgages represent the true rate at which the lender can be profitable. The fact that lenders charge higher rates for fixed rate mortgages is clearly an indication that lenders are hedging their bets. The fact that fixed rate loans are more popular with the public is a fact which is not wasted on conventional lenders. Like all businesses, they charge what the market will bear.

19. **C** "ARM" stands for "Adjustable Rate Mortgage," a mortgage in which the interest rate is tied to an index.

20. **D** An ARM (Adjustable Rate Mortgage) has the chief advantage of a lower interest rate and greater affordability, something which an older borrower with substantial income does not need. A GPM (Graduated Payment Mortgage) is a fixed rate loan with artificially low payments at the beginning, resulting in negative amortization which makes it also not desirable for an older borrower. A GPARM (Graduated Payment Adjustable Rate Mortgage) combines the features of the ARM and GPM, and would also not be suitable for an older borrower with substantial income. The early payoff and security of a 15-year FRM (Fixed Rate Mortgage) would probably best meet the needs of such a borrower.

21. **C** To calculate the approximate cost of a temporary buydown, figure how much interest the lender will lose. In a 3-2-1 buydown the interest is lowered 3% the first year, 2% the second year and 1% the third year. This totals 6% of the loan amount (3% + 2% + 1% = 6%). In reality, the lender will receive the cash up front and can invest it, so the actual discount may be slightly less than 6% of the loan amount. Nevertheless, this is a good approximation of the cost.

22. **B** Negative amortization occurs whenever the borrower's payments are not high enough to cover the interest. The unpaid interest is added to the principal balance. Negative amortization is a feature of graduated payment mortgages.

23. **C** A cap is a ceiling on how high the interest can be increased on an adjustable rate mortgage (ARM). An annual or adjustment cap sets the maximum that it can be increased in any one year or adjustment period. A lifetime cap sets the absolute maximum over the life of the loan. A lifetime cap of 5% over the base of 6½% would mean that the interest on the loan can never exceed 11½%, regardless of what happens to the index.

24. **A** A blended loan is a loan where the lender already holds a loan on the property, but it is at a below-market interest rate. In order to encourage the borrower to refinance, the lender offers a rate that is higher than the rate on the existing loan, but less than the current market rate on new loans. A two-step loan is an adjustable rate mortgage with only one adjustment point. A wraparound loan is a junior lien that encompasses the senior lien.

25. **B** "GPM" stands for "graduated payment mortgage, which is a loan where the initial payments are set lower than the amount needed to pay the interest. The unpaid interest is added to the principal balance. The payments are then increased in stages over the life of the loan so that the loan is eventually amortized.

26. **A** "GPARM" stands for "Graduated Payment Adjustable Rate Mortgage," not a fixed rate loan. "GEM" means "growing equity mortgage" which is a

loan amortized over a short period, so the payments tend to be quite high.

27. **D** Conventional loans almost always contain a due on sale clause today. Lenders use the due on sale clause to force a new buyer to qualify for credit approval, to agree to be personally liable for the debt, and to agree to adjust the interest rate to market. Most lenders insure all loans over 75% loan to value ratio today. By definition, a "conventional loan" is a loan without government insurance, guarantee or other intervention.

28. **B** Loans insured by the FHA cannot have prepayment penalties, by federal regulation. By definition, a "conventional loan" is a loan without government insurance, guarantee or other intervention. Conventional lenders are free, therefore, to impose whatever requirements they wish, consistent with the requirements of the secondary market and negotiation with the borrower.

29. **C** The purpose of construction financing is to provide the funds to pay for the construction of new improvements. It is supposed to be paid off as soon as the builder sells the property, therefore it is almost always short term financing. It is also more risky than regular real estate financing, and involves a lot more paperwork, so the interest rate is usually higher than other real estate loans.

30. **D** The purpose of construction financing is to provide funding for the construction of new improvements. Normally, the construction lender expects the loan to be paid off as soon as the property is sold, therefore construction loans are designed to be short term, interim financing. It is also customary to fund the loan in installments as the construction progresses.

31. **C** A construction loan is normally made on a short term basis, to be paid off when the builder sells the property. The buyers will obtain new, permanent financing. Since the buyers new loan "takes out" the construction loan, it is called the "takeout" loan.

32. **D** A construction loan is normally a short term loan designed to be paid off when the builder sells the property. The buyer usually obtains a regular, permanent loan. The buyer's permanent loan pays off, or "takes out" the construction loan, so "takeout loan" is a slang expression for the permanent financing.

33. **D** The permanent financing is called the "takeout loan" because when it is made it "takes out" (pays off) the construction financing. Construction lending is usually designed to be short term financ-

ing for the construction of the improvements, and repayment is to come through the permanent loan to the eventual buyer. Thus, construction financing is frequently referred to as "interim financing."

34. **A** The final permanent financing is usually obtained by the buyer of the property when construction is completed. The slang expression for the permanent loan is the "takeout" loan, because it "takes out" the construction loan.

35. **A** The term "takeout loan" is used as a synonym for the permanent financing because the permanent loan "takes out," or pays off the construction loan.

36. **B** Most construction loans are short term financing. They are usually amortized, although they are sometimes interest-only loans. Even if amortized, the amortization will usually only be for a short time as the builder will pay off the construction financing as soon as the property is sold to a buyer. The buyer will obtain permanent financing.

37. **C** In order to reduce the risk, a construction lender disburses the funds only as the construction progresses. This way, every time money is advanced, the property value has also increased. Construction loans are considered the riskiest of all real estate financing.

38. **B** One of the risks to the lender in construction financing is that construction liens are prior to the construction mortgage, regardless of when the mortgage is recorded. Anyone who supplies labor or material for the construction can claim a lien against the property, for up to 75 days after substantial completion. Therefore, it is customary to withhold the final loan draw from the builder until after the lien deadline has passed.

39. **C** There are various ways to structure a construction loan. The lender must make sure that the property is worth enough to cover the amount lent, and must also provide protection against construction liens, which are ahead of the lender's lien in priority. One common way to make sure the property is worth at least the amount lent is to disburse the loan funds in stages (draws) as the work progresses. The last draw is usually delayed until after the deadline for filing construction liens is past (75 days after substantial completion).

40. **C** A construction lender must take care that the value of the collateral (the land and partially completed structure) is greater than the amount owing. A common way to ensure this is to disburse the

loan proceeds in stages (draws) as the work progresses. How many draws there will be depends on the nature of the project and is a matter which is negotiated between the lender and the builder.

41.   **C**   A completion bond is like insurance. In fact, it is issued by an insurance company. If the builder (bonded party) does not perform according to the terms of some contract, the other party to the contract can look to the bonding company for redress. Also sometimes called a "performance bond." Consider that the term "borrower on the permanent loan" means the eventual buyer.

42.   **C**   It is typical for a lender to refuse to make a construction loan unless there is a source of new permanent financing to pay off ("take out") the construction loan. Therefore, it is common for a builder to arrange a standby commitment from a permanent financing lender to refinance the property once construction is completed. In this case, the lender of the permanent financing has actually "extended credit" to the builder, even though no funds have changed hands yet and the funds will be lent to the builder's customer, not to the builder directly.

43.   **A**   "Insured loan" means the loan is insured against default. If the lender suffers a loss during a foreclosure, the insuring agency will reimburse the lender. The insurance is called "mortgage guaranty insurance," and has nothing to do with fire or disability insurance.

44.   **D**   Mortgage insurance is required on all Federal Housing Administration (FHA) loans. In fact, practically the sole purpose of the FHA is to insure loans. Conventional loans must also be insured if they exceed 80% loan to value ratio. But the U.S. Department of Veterans Affairs guarantees loans; it does not insure them.

45.   **D**   A borrower may always pay more for a home than the lender appraises it for. With Federal Housing Administration (FHA) and U.S. Department of Veterans Affairs (USDVA) loans the borrower is required to sign a statement acknowledging that the price exceeds the appraised value.

46.   **D**   If the lender can change the interest rate it must be an adjustable rate mortgage (ARM). The most common ARM loans are conventional loans, but ARM loans are available through the Federal Housing Administration (FHA) and the U.S. Department of Veterans Affairs (USDVA).

47.   **C**   The Federal Housing Administration (FHA) requires a down payment of 3% of the first

$50,000 and 5% of the amount that exceeds $50,000 on most programs, although there are special FHA programs where the down payment is even lower and the loan to value ratio frequently approaches 100%. Loans guaranteed by the U.S. Department of Veterans Affairs (USDVA) do not require a down payment at all. Conventional loans up to 100% loan to value ratio are also available, but qualifying is very difficult and the loan would have to be insured and for an owner-occupied property only.

LOAN UNDERWRITING

FOR REAL ESTATE AGENTS, UNDERSTANDING HOW TO QUALIFY THE BORROWER IS just as important as knowing about loan programs and financing arrangements. After all, it makes little sense to sell a house only to have the sale fall through because the buyer cannot get the necessary financing.

In lending circles, the process of credit qualification is called ***underwriting***. Buyers, sellers and real estate agents complain about the convolutions that are required to gain loan approval. Yet, we also have to remember that the average mortgage loan today is a substantial amount of money. Lenders would be foolish to approve such loans without careful scrutiny of the borrower's ability to repay the debt, as well as the borrower's past credit history, and the quality of the collateral.

Lenders have an old saying – "you've got to have the three C's of credit to qualify." The three C's of credit are *collateral*, *character* (or *credit*), and *capacity*. Collateral refers to the value of the property being offered as security for the debt. Character (credit) refers to the borrower's past credit history. And capacity refers to the borrower's income and ability to meet the payments necessary to amortize the debt.

The quality and value of the collateral is demonstrated by an appraisal report. In real estate, if the appraisal is not high enough, the loan will usually be approved for a lesser amount which meets the lender's standards for security. In the final analysis, the collateral is the most important consideration in granting the loan because the lender must be prepared for the worst possible outcome. For the lender, that would be a foreclosure, so the lender must be sure to limit the risk to the amount that could be recovered by taking title to the property at the foreclosure sale and reselling it. Lenders normally apply the loan to value ratio to the lesser of the appraised value or the sales price.

An appraisal will not only tell the lender the market value of the property, but appraisal reports also give the remaining economic life of the improvements. Since it would be imprudent to lend for a term which exceeds the time over which the improvements will have a useful life, lenders must be concerned with their economic life. For most residential properties, this is seldom an issue. Usually it the economic life becomes a matter of concern only of the property is residential, but zoned for commercial use, or there is some other reason to believe the improvements have a limited remaining life. Economic life and other appraisal topics are complex concepts which are discussed in detail in the section on Real Estate Appraisal.

Character refers to the borrower's credit rating. Lenders start with a credit report from standard credit reporting agencies. There are three national agencies –

- Equifax, P.O. Box 740256, Atlanta, Georgia 30374-0256, 800-997-2493, www.consumer.equifax.com.
- Experian (formerly TRW), P.O. Box 9595, Allen, Texas 75013-0036, 888-397-3742, www.experian.com
- Trans-Union, P.O. Box 1200, Chester, Pennsylvania 19022, 800-916-8800

The ***Fair Credit Reporting Act*** requires credit reporting agencies to furnish a borrower with a copy of their credit report at no charge if the borrower was declined for a loan. Borrowers who have not been turned down can also obtain a copy of their credit report for a nominal charge. Credit reporting agencies are required to verify and correct any errors on a borrower's credit report when the borrower advises them of the error. In addition, borrowers have the right to have an a statement included with their credit report to explain derogatory information. Real estate agents should begin their relationship with new buyers by having a frank discussion of these issues and having them make sure their credit report is as clean as it can be.

The borrower's credit rating has to meet secondary market requirements for the loan. It used to be that the secondary market had only one standard – all borrowers had to have impeccable credit or the loan was not salable. Today there are many options, including loans for persons with impaired credit. For less than perfect credit, the interest rate is increased, unless there are offsetting factors such as a very high down payment. Loans rated less than perfect also take much longer to close, as it will take a lot longer to find a lender willing to make the loan. Very highly rated loans can be approved and funded within a few days, since they can be immediately sold to Fannie Mae and Freddie Mac investors.

In gauging a borrower's credit history, there are always exceptions to every rule. Even a past bankruptcy is not necessarily a bar to getting a real estate loan, provided the cause of the bankruptcy is not likely to be repeated. Suppose, for example, that the borrower was found at fault for an accident that resulted in a large personal injury judgment. Or suppose a family member died of cancer after years of medical expenses. Such catastrophes could force a person into bankruptcy, but after re-establishing good credit history, the bankruptcy need not be a bar to obtaining new credit.

Of course, not only do different lenders have different requirements, but the rules change according to the loan type as well. For example, it is common knowledge among real estate professionals that FHA and Federal GI loans offer fairly liberal qualifying standards.

Determining the borrower's capacity is, in the final analysis, an art, not a science. Nevertheless, lenders have rules and guidelines and real estate agents should be aware of them. In times past, real estate agents were taught to find the maximum price home the buyer could afford just by multiplying the buyer's gross annual income by two and a half Such simplistic rules are not adequate in today's lending market.

Lenders today qualify the borrower by placing their major emphasis on two ratios. The first is the ratio of the borrower's monthly housing costs to total gross income (commonly called the **housing cost ratio,** or sometimes the **front-end ratio**. Monthly housing costs include the amounts necessary for principal and interest, one-twelfth the annual property taxes and one-twelfth the annual fire insurance premiums, plus the amount needed each month for association dues (required in condominiums and some subdivisions). Most lenders insist that the ratio not exceed 28%, although FHA will allow up to 29%. The following example of a typical borrower demonstrates the calculation –

Assume buyers with $54,000 annual gross income, buying a new home for $170,000 with a $20,000 down payment. The loan will be a fixed rate conventional, and market interest rates at the time are 7%. Property taxes on the home will be $2,400 per year and the annual premium for the homeowner's insurance policy will be $480. There are no homeowners' association dues.

Monthly principal and interest on $150,000 at 7% for 30 years	$998
One-twelfth annual property taxes ($2,400 ÷ 12)	200
One-twelfth annual insurance premium ($480 ÷ 12)	40
Total monthly housing cost	$1,238

Gross monthly income ($54,000 ÷ 12) = $4,500
Ratio of monthly housing expense to gross income ($1,238 ÷ $4,500) = 27.5%

The second factor is the ratio of the borrower's total debt payments (including the proposed mortgage loan) to the borrower's gross monthly income. This ratio is frequently called the **total debt service ratio**, or sometimes the **back-end ratio** Total debt payments include car payments, credit cards, alimony and child support, student loans – everything that the borrower is obligated to pay each month. The FHA and the federal Department of Veterans Affairs will go as high as 41%, and most conventional lenders will allow the ratio of total debt payments to gross income to go as high as 43%, although some are more strict.

Assume the same buyer as in the previous example, and assume that the buyer has a monthly car payment of $220 and monthly credit card and other installments of $320.

Total monthly housing costs (from above example)	$1,238
Car payment	220
Credit card and other payments	320
Total debt service	$1,778

Gross monthly income ($54,000 ÷ 12) = $4,500
Ratio of total monthly debt service to gross income ($1,778 ÷ $4,500) = 39.51%

In the preceding examples, the borrower qualified comfortably on both ratios. In the real world, it is not uncommon for lenders to encounter a borrower who qualifies comfortably on one ratio, but does not quite qualify on the other. Depending on the circumstances, lenders may bend the rules by a percent or two on one ratio if the borrower qualifies well on the other.

Lenders also take into account the reliability and stability of the borrower's income. Length of time on the job and the type of occupation all have a bearing on underwriting. Overtime pay and bonuses, for example, may be included if they are sufficiently regular that they can be counted on. In some cases, the law requires lenders to include certain income. For example, the Equal Credit Opportunity Act (see the next section on Lending Regulations) requires that both incomes be counted when the borrowers are husband and wife.

Both the debt ratios above are modified somewhat when the initial interest rate is lowered, as in a GPM loan, an ARM loan, or a loan with a buydown. Lenders are aware that the payment may increase, so the qualifying ratios tend to be slightly higher.

Credit scoring

Most lenders today use credit scoring, a system of assigning point values to aspects of the borrower's profile. Credit scoring started in the last half of 1970s when the Equal Credit Opportunity Act went into effect. The Act prohibited discrimination against borrowers, and lenders were initially afraid they would be sued if they turned a loan down. Point scoring was seen as a way to neutralize the loan approval process and safeguard the lender against discrimination claims.

Although lenders are now comfortable with discrimination issues, credit scoring has become the norm because it avoids personal attitudes of the loan officer from coloring the approval process. The majority of residential loans today are brokered, and the mortgage broker receives no compensation unless the loan is made. Therefore, the institution making the loan knows the broker will try to present the loan in the best light possible. Credit scoring helps balance the broker's excess enthusiasm.

The score looks at past delinquencies, derogatory payment behavior, current debt level, length of credit history, types of past credit and the number of inquiries. For example, if the borrower has a past history of a loan from a finance company or other high-risk lender, this has a negative impact on the score. Similarly, if the borrower has a lot of recent credit inquiries from other lenders, it is a caution sign – the borrower may be attempting to solve financial problems by seeking additional loans.

Point scoring today is based on a statistical analysis system developed by Fair, Isaac Company (commonly called the FICO score). All three of the above national credit bureaus do it the same way, although they call it by different names. Equifax calls it the "Beacon," Trans Union calls it "Empirica," and Experian uses the original name "Fair, Isaac." The score is reported in a range from 350 to 900 points. A score of zero means there was insufficient data in the credit file to generate a score. The following chart gives an idea of what most lenders consider in credit scoring. Notice that even an A+ loan can have a couple of revolving past dues and one installment past due –

	Credit Score	Debt Ratio	Max LTV	Mortgage Past Dues			Revolving Past Dues			Installment Past Dues		
				30	60	90	30	60	90	30	60	90
A+	670+	36%-	95%	0	0	0	2	0	0	1	0	0
A	660	45%	95%	1	0	0	3	1	0	2	0	0
B	620	50%	85%	2	1	0	4	2	1	3	1	0
C	580	55%	75%	4	2	1	6	5	2	5	4	1

Borrowers with a score above 670 will qualify for an A+ loan. Credit approval will be completed within minutes, probably through a computerized automated underwriting system. The loan can be closed as soon as the appraisal is complete, usually within a few days. Interest will be at the best rates current in the market. A score of 660 to 670 (an A rating) will probably also gain a good interest rate, but the approval process will take longer, as the lender will have to take a look at supplemental credit information. Inquiries to explain the delinquencies are to be expected. Borrowers with a B rating will not qualify for Fannie Mae and Freddie Mac guidelines, so the loan originator will have to find an alternative secondary market for the loan. It may take some time before a suitable market is found, and investors in such markets demand rates one to two percent higher than prime mortgage rates.

Here are some samples to demonstrate how the statistics work out –
- Scores below 601 yield eight good loans for each bad one
- Scores between 700 and 729 yield 129 good loans for each bad one
- Scores above 800 yield 1,292 good loans for each bad one

Creditors, of course, receive the full statistical breakdown from the credit reporting agency so they can assess the exact odds that a given score will be loan.

Among professional lenders, however, "FICO" has come to be distrusted. Its purpose is just to alert the lender that more investigation is in order. Unfortunately, a lot of lenders just go by the score and little else.

Professional lenders know that the FICO score is just statistics and nothing more. The Fair, Isaac Company created their models based on various criteria, but those issues don't necessarily apply in all cases. For example, although the Fair, Isaac Company maintains their statistical models as proprietary, they have recognized that they use five categories –
- Previous credit history
- Current amount of debt
- Amount of time the borrower has used credit
- How often the borrower has made application for credit
- Types of credit available

Looking at these criteria it's easy to see inconsistencies and faults. For example, look at how often the borrower has made application for credit. This could be an indication that the borrower is desperately trying to borrow money in order to stave off defaults on other obligations. Or it could mean that the borrower is shopping for the best loan terms. Or it might mean absolutely nothing at all. The problem is that the credit agency furnishes the lender with the final FICO score with no explanation of how it was derived. Professionals know that the score is not necessarily a correct indicator.

Fannie Mae and Freddie Mac publish guidelines for loans they will purchase or securitize. In addition to credit qualifications and income to debt ratios above, these guidelines include –
- Loans greater than 80% loan to value ratio must be insured for the amount of the loan exceeding 80% by an insurance company outside of the lender's control.
- Buydowns are permitted for all loans except ARMS.
- The seller cannot contribute toward the borrower's closing costs more than the lesser of 6% of the sales price or appraised value on 90% loans, and 3% on loans over 90% loan to value ratio.
- The borrower may receive gifts for most loan programs, but only from relatives and, if the loan is over 80% loan to value ratio, the borrower must have a personal investment of at least 5%. Gift funds must be documented with a gift letter stating that the funds need not be repaid, and must be verified to be sure the donor did not secretly borrow the money.
- Co-borrowers, co-signers and guarantors do not need to take title to the property. Their income is considered, providing they sign the promissory note. If the loan is over 90% loan to value ratio, the co-borrower must occupy the property to have his or her income considered.

No-doc and low-doc loans

Many borrowers have a difficult time demonstrating their income. Perhaps they are self-employed, receive income irregularly from commissions, or live off investments. Other borrowers insist on maximum privacy. For such borrowers there are options that may be preferable to the standard loan process with its reams of paperwork and intrusive investigations.

There are three kinds of loans borrowers like this might wish to consider –

Stated income loan A **stated-income mortgage** is good for a borrower who works, but doesn't draw regular wages or salary from an employer, such as a self-employed borrower or someone who makes a living off commissions. The borrower on a stated-income mortgage must disclose annual earnings, usually for the past two years, by showing tax returns, bank statements, assets and debts, and possibly other documentation. The borrower must also list debts so the lender can determine the debt to income ratio. A stated-income mortgage would cost anywhere from one-eighth of a percentage point above the conventional rate to more than a whole percentage point higher.

No-ratio loans A **no-ratio** loan is a loan where the usual debt and income ratios are ignored. The borrower is expected to list assets, however. The interest is generally about a half a percent to two percent higher than mortgage prime. For the lender to remain secure, loan to value ratios are 80% or less; for non-owner occupied property 70% loan to value ratios are common. No-ratio loans are favored by real estate investors who would otherwise have very high debt ratios.

No-doc loans **No-doc** or NINA (no income/no asset verification) mortgages are for creditworthy people who want maximum privacy and are willing to pay for it. Interest rates are generally one to three percent higher than mortgage prime. No-income/no-asset verification mortgages require the least documentation. In some cases the borrower provides his or her name, Social Security number, the amount of the down payment and the address of the property. The lender gets a credit report and a property appraisal and that's all. The borrower does need to have an excellent credit report.

Exercise a

Deciding whether or not to make a loan is called loan _____ , which is an _____ , not a science. It includes the lender's evaluation of the three C's of credit, which are _____ , _____ , and _____ . The most important of these is the _____ , which is evidenced by an _____ report. Character is demonstrated by a _____ report.

The _____ _____ ratio is the percentage that the total monthly housing costs will be of the borrower's gross monthly income. The _____ _____ _____ ratio is the percentage that the borrower's total outstanding bills will be of the borrower's total gross monthly income.

Lenders today use _____ _____ to rate loans. Most lenders would give an _____ category to a loan over 670 points. Such a loan can be funded very quickly and at the mortgage interest rate current in the market.

A _____ - _____ loan is a loan at a low loan to value ratio which makes the lender feel sufficiently secure that debt and income ratios are ignored. Such loans are favored by _____ .

🔑 KEY TERMS

The key to understanding any new field is the vocabulary used in that field. To maximize your comprehension of the material presented in this chapter, be sure you know the meaning and significance of the following terms. Remember that the majority of test questions primarily test knowledge of vocabulary.

Back end ratio

Credit scoring

Equal Credit Opportunity Act

Fair Credit Reporting Act

Front end ratio

Housing cost ratio

Low-doc loan

No-doc loan

No income/no asset verification

No-ratio loan

Stated income loan

Total debt service ratio

Underwriting

REFERENCES

The following is required reading to ensure your success on the exams. Many of the practice questions at the end of this chapter, as well as state exam questions, are drawn from the following reading.

Three of the dozens of forms that a residential borrower must complete at time of loan application –

Uniform Residential Loan Application, Form 1003, pages 202–204

Fannie Mae Request for Verification of Employment, Form 1005, page 205

Fannie Mae Request for Verification of Deposit, form 1006, page 206

❓ ANSWERS

To chapter exercises. If you couldn't figure out what to put in the blanks, find the answer here!

Exercise a

Deciding whether or not to make a loan is called loan ____UNDERWRITING____, which is an ___ART___, not a science. It includes the lender's evaluation of the three C's of credit, which are ____CHARACTER____, ____CAPACITY____, and ____COLLATERAL____. The most important of these is the ____COLLATERAL____, which is evidenced by an ____APPRAISAL____ report. Character is demonstrated by a ____CREDIT____ report.

The ____HOUSING____ ____COST____ ratio is the percentage that the total monthly housing costs will be of the borrower's gross monthly income. The ____TOTAL____ ____DEBT____ ____SERVICE____ ratio is the percentage that the borrower's total outstanding bills will be of the borrower's total gross monthly income.

Lenders today use ____CREDIT____ ____SCORING____ to rate loans. Most lenders would give an __A+__ category to a loan over 670 points. Such a loan can be funded very quickly and at the mortgage interest rate current in the market.

A __NO__ - ____RATIO____ loan is a loan at a low loan to value ratio which makes the lender feel sufficiently secure that debt and income ratios are ignored. Such loans are favored by ____INVESTORS____.

Uniform Residential Loan Application

This application is designed to be completed by the applicant(s) with the Lender's assistance. Applicants should complete this form as "Borrower" or "Co-Borrower", as applicable. Co-Borrower information must also be provided (and the appropriate box checked) when ☐ the income or assets of a person other than the "Borrower" (including Borrower's spouse) will be used as a basis for loan qualification or ☐ the income or assets of the Borrower's spouse will not be used as a basis for loan qualification, but his or her liabilities must be considered because the Borrower resides in a community property state, the security property is located in a community property state, or the Borrower is relying on other property located in a community property state as a basis for repayment of the loan.

I. TYPE OF MORTGAGE AND TERMS OF LOAN

Mortgage Applied for:	☐ VA ☐ Conventional ☐ Other: ☐ FHA ☐ FmHA	Agency Case Number	Lender Case Number

Amount $	Interest Rate %	No. of Months	Amortization Type:	☐ Fixed Rate ☐ GPM	☐ Other (explain): ☐ ARM (type):

II. PROPERTY INFORMATION AND PURPOSE OF LOAN

Subject Property Address (street, city, state & zip code)	No. of Units

Legal Description of Subject Property (attach description if necessary)	Year Built

Purpose of Loan	☐ Purchase ☐ Construction ☐ Other (explain): ☐ Refinance ☐ Construction-Permanent	Property will be: ☐ Primary Residence ☐ Secondary Residence ☐ Investment

Complete this line if construction or construction-permanent loan.

Year Lot Acquired	Original Cost $	Amount Existing Liens $	(a) Present Value of lot $	(b) Cost of Improvements $	Total (a + b) $

Complete this line if this is a refinance loan.

Year Acquired	Original Cost $	Amount Existing Liens $	Purpose of Refinance	Describe Improvements ☐ made ☐ to be made Cost: $

Title will be held in what Name(s)	Manner in which Title will be held	Estate will be held in: ☐ Fee Simple

Source of Down Payment, Settlement Charges and/or Subordinate Financing (explain)	☐ Leasehold (show expiration date)

III. BORROWER INFORMATION

Borrower	Co-Borrower
Borrower's Name (include Jr. or Sr. if applicable)	Co-Borrower's Name (include Jr. or Sr. if applicable)

Social Security Number	Home Phone (incl. area code)	Age	Yrs. School	Social Security Number	Home Phone (incl. area code)	Age	Yrs. School

☐ Married ☐ Unmarried (include single, divorced, widowed) ☐ Separated	Dependents (not listed by Co-Borrower) no. ages	☐ Married ☐ Unmarried (include single, divorced, widowed) ☐ Separated	Dependents (not listed by Borrower) no. ages

Present Address (street, city, state, zip code) ☐ Own ☐ Rent No. Yrs:	Present Address (street, city, state, zip code) ☐ Own ☐ Rent No. Yrs:

If residing at present address for less than two years, complete the following:

Former Address (street, city, state, zip code) ☐ Own ☐ Rent No. Yrs:	Former Address (street, city, state, zip code) ☐ Own ☐ Rent No. Yrs:

Former Address (street, city, state, zip code) ☐ Own ☐ Rent No. Yrs:	Former Address (street, city, state, zip code) ☐ Own ☐ Rent No. Yrs:

IV. EMPLOYMENT INFORMATION

Borrower	Co-Borrower
Name & Address of Employer ☐ Self Employed	Years on this job:	Name & Address of Employer ☐ Self Employed	Years on this job:

	Years employed in this line of work/ profession:		Years employed in this line of work/ profession:

Position/Title/Type of Business	Business Phone (incl. area code)	Position/Title/Type of Business	Business Phone (incl. area code)

If employed in current position for less than two years or if currently employed in more than one position, complete the following:

Name & Address of Employer ☐ Self Employed	Dates (from - to):	Name & Address of Employer ☐ Self Employed	Dates (from - to):
	Monthly Income $		Monthly Income $
Position/Title/Type of Business	Business Phone (incl. area code)	Position/Title/Type of Business	Business Phone (incl. area code)

Name & Address of Employer ☐ Self Employed	Dates (from - to):	Name & Address of Employer ☐ Self Employed	Dates (from - to):
	Monthly Income $		Monthly Income $
Position/Title/Type of Business	Business Phone (incl. area code)	Position/Title/Type of Business	Business Phone (incl. area code)

V. MONTHLY INCOME AND COMBINED EXPENSE INFORMATION

Gross Monthly Income	Borrower	Co-Borrower	Total	Combined Monthly Housing Expense	Present	Proposed
Self Empl. Income *	$	$	$	Rent	$	
Overtime				First Mortgage (P & I)		$
Bonuses				Other Financing (P & I)		
Commissions				Hazard Insurance		
Dividends/Interest				Real Estate Taxes		
Net Rental Income				Mortgage Insurance		
Other (before completing, see the notice in "describe other income," below)				Homeowner Assn. Dues		
				Other:		
Total	$	$	$	Total	$	$

* Self Employed Borrower(s) may be required to provide additional documentation such as tax returns and financial statements.

	Describe Other Income	Notice: Alimony, child support, or separate maintenance income need not be revealed if the Borrower (B) or Co-Borrower (C) doesn't choose to have it considered for repaying this loan.	Monthly Amount
B/C			$
			$
			$

VI. ASSETS AND LIABILITIES

This Statement and any applicable supporting schedule may be completed jointly by both married and unmarried Co-Borrowers if their assets and liabilities are sufficiently joined so that the Statement can be meaningfully and fairly presented on a combined basis; otherwise separate Statements and Schedules are required. If the Co-Borrower section was completed about a spouse, this Statement and supporting schedules must be completed about that spouse also.

Completed ☐ Jointly ☐ Not Jointly

ASSETS Description	Cash or Market Value	Liabilities and Pledged Assets. List the creditor's name, address and account number for all outstanding debts, including automobile loans, revolving charge accounts, real estate loans, alimony, child support, stock pledges, etc. Use continuation sheet, if necessary. Indicate by (*) those liabilities which will be satisfied upon sale of real estate owned or upon refinancing of the subject property.		
		LIABILITIES	Monthly Payt. & Mos. Left to Pay	Unpaid Balance
Cash deposit toward purchase held by:	$	Name and address of Company	$ Payt./Mos.	$
List checking and savings accounts below				
Name and address of Bank, S & L, or Credit Union				
		Acct. no.		
		Name and address of Company	$ Payt./Mos.	$
Acct. no.	$			
Name and address of Bank, S & L, or Credit Union				
		Acct. no.		
Acct. no.	$	Name and address of Company	$ Payt./Mos.	$
Name and address of Bank, S & L, or Credit Union				
Acct. no.	$	Acct. no.		
Name and address of Bank, S & L, or Credit Union		Name and address of Company	$ Payt./Mos.	$
Acct. no.	$			
Stock & Bonds (Company name/number & description)	$	Acct. no.		
		Name and address of Company	$ Payt./Mos.	$
Life Insurance net cash value Face amount: $	$			
Subtotal Liquid Assets	$	Acct. no.		
Real estate owned (enter market value from schedule of real estated owned)	$	Name and address of Company	$ Payt./Mos.	$
Vested interest in retirement fund	$			
Net worth of business(es) owned (attach financial statement)	$	Acct. no.		
Automobiles owned (make and year)	$	Name and address of Company	$ Payt./Mos.	$
		Acct. no.		
Other Assets (itemize)	$	Alimony/Child Suppport/Separate Maintenance Payments Owed to	$	
		Job Related Expense (child care, union dues, etc.)	$	
		Total Monthly Payments	$	
Total Assets a.	$	Net Worth (a minus b) $	**Total Liabilities b.**	$

VI. ASSETS AND LIABILITIES (cont.)

Schedule of Real Estate Owned (if additional properties are owned, use continuation sheet.)

Property Address (enter S if sold, PS if pending sale or is it rental being held for income)	Type of Property	Present Market Value	Amount of Mortgage & Liens	Gross Rental Income	Mortgage Payments	Insurance, Maintenance, Taxes & Misc.	Net Rental Income
		$	$	$	$	$	$
	Totals	$	$	$	$	$	$

List any additional names under which credit has previously been received and indicate appropriate creditor name(s) and account number(s):

Alternative Name	Creditor Name	Account Number

VII. DETAILS OF TRANSACTION

a. Purchase price	$
b. Alterations, improvements, repairs	
c. Land (if acquired separately)	
d. Refinance (incl. in debts to be paid off)	
e. Estimated prepaid items	
f. Estimated closing costs	
g. PMI, MIP, Funding Fee paid in cash	
h. Discount (if Borrower will pay)	
i. otal costs (add items a through h)	
j. Subordinate financing	
k. Borrower's closing costs paid by Seller	
l. Other Credits (explain)	
m. Loan amount (exclude PMI, MIP, Funding Fee financed)	
n. PMI, MIP, Funding Fee financed	
o. Loan amount (add m & n)	
p. Cash from/to Borrower (subtract j, k, l & o from i)	

VIII. DECLARATIONS

If you answer "Yes" to any questions a through i, please use continuation sheet for explanation.

a. Are there any outstanding judgements against you?
b. Have you been declared bankrupt within the past 7 years?
c. Have you had property foreclosed upon or given title or deed in lieu thereof in the last 7 years?
d. Are you a party to a lawsuit?
e. Have you directly or indirectly been obligated on any loan which resulted in foreclosure, transfer of title in lieu of foreclosure, or judgement? (This would include such loans as home mortgage loans, SBA loans, home improvement loans, educational loans, manufactured (mobile) home loans, any mortgage, financial obligation, bond, or loan guarantee. If "Yes," provide details, including date, name and address of Lender, FHA or VA case number, if any, and reasons for the action.)
f. Are you presently delinquent or in default on any Federal debt or any other loan, mortgage, financial obligation, bond, or loan guarantee? If "Yes," give details as described in the preceding question.
g. Are you obligated to pay alimony, child support or separate maintenance?
h. Is any part of the down payment borrowed?
i. Are you a co-maker or endorser on a note?
j. Are you a U.S. citizen?
Are you a permanent resident alien?
l. Do you intend to occupy the property as your primary residence? If "Yes," complete question below.
m. Have you had an ownership interest in a property in the last three years?
  (1) What type of property did you own -- principal residence (PR), second home (SH), or Investment Property (IP)?
  (2) How did you hold title to the home -- solely by yourself (S), jointly with your spouse (SP), or jointly with another person (O)?

Borrower Yes No / Co-Borrower Yes No

IX. ACKNOWLEDGEMENT AND AGREEMENT

The undersigned specifically acknowledge(s) and agree(s) that: (1) the loan requested by this application will be secured by a first mortgage or deed of trust on the property described herein: (2) the property will not be used for any illegal or prohibited purpose or use; (3) all statements made in this application are made for the purpose of obtaining the loan identified herein; (4) occupation of the property will be indicated above; (5) verification or reverification of any information contained in the application may be made at any time by the Lender, its agents, successors and assigns, either directly or through a credit reporting agency, from any source named in this application, and the original copy of this application will be retained by the Lender, even if the loan is not approved; (6) the Lender, its agents, successors and assigns will rely on the information in the application and I/we have a continuing obligation to amend and/or supplement the information provided in this application if any of the material facts which I/we have represented herein should change prior to closing; (7) in the event my/our payments on the loan indicated in this application become delinquent, the Lender, its agents successors and assigns, may, in addition to all their other rights and remedies, report my/our name(s) and account information to a credit reporting agency; (8) ownership of the loan may be transferred to successor assign of the Lender without notice to me and/or the administration of the loan account may be transferred to an agent, successor or assign of the Lender with prior notice to me: (9) the Lender, its agents, successors and assigns make no representations or warranties, express or implied, to the Borrower(s) regarding the property, the condition of the property, or the value of the property.

Right to Receive Copy of Appraisal. I/We have the right to a copy of the appraisal report used in connection with this application for credit. To obtain a copy, I/We must send Lender written request at the mailing address Lender has provided. Lender must hear from me/us no later than 90 days after Lender notifies me/us about the action taken on this application, or I/we withdraw this application.

Certification: I/We certify that the information provided in this application is true and correct as of the date set forth opposite my/our signature(s) on this application and acknowledge my/our understanding that any intentional or negligent misrepresentation(s) of the information contained in this application may result in civil liability and/or criminal penalties including, but not limited to, fine or imprisonment or both under the provisions of Title 18, United States Code, Section 1001, et seq. and liability for monetary damages to the Lender, its agents, successors or assigns, insurers and any other person who may suffer any loss due to reliance upon any misrepresentation which I/We have made on this application.

Borrower's Signature	Date	Co-Borrower's Signature	Date
X		X	

X. INFORMATION FOR GOVERNMENT MONITORING PURPOSES

The following information is requested by the Federal government for certain types of loans related to a dwelling, in order to monitor the Lender's compliance with equal credit opportunity, fair housing and home mortgage disclosure laws. You are not required to furnish this information, but are encouraged to do so. The law provides that a Lender may neither discriminate on the basis of this information, not on whether you choose to furnish it. However, if you choose not to furnish it, under Federal regulations this Lender is required to note race and sex on the basis of visual observation or surname. If you do not wish to furnish the above information, please check the box below. (Lender must review the above material to assure that the disclosures satisfy all requirements to which the Lender is subject under applicable state law for the particular type of loan applied for.)

BORROWER

Race/National Origin:
☐ I do not wish to furnish this information
☐ American Indian or Alaskan Native
☐ Asian or Pacific Islander
☐ White, not of Hispanic origin
☐ Black, not of Hispanic origin
☐ Hispanic
☐ Other (specify)

Sex: ☐ Female ☐ Male

CO-BORROWER

Race/National Origin:
☐ I do not wish to furnish this information
☐ American Indian or Alaskan Native
☐ Asian or Pacific Islander
☐ White, not of Hispanic origin
☐ Black, not of Hispanic origin
☐ Hispanic
☐ Other (specify)

Sex: ☐ Female ☐ Male

To be Completed by Interviewer	Interviewer's Name (print or type)	Name and Address of Interviewer's Employer
This application was taken by: ☐ face-to-face interview ☐ by mail ☐ by telephone	Interviewer's Signature Date	
	Interviewer's Phone Number (incl. area code)	

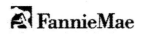 **FannieMae**

Request for Verification of Employment

Privacy Act Notice: This information is to be used by the agency collecting it or its assignees in determining whether you qualify as a prospective mortgagor under its program. It will not be disclosed outside the agency except as required and permitted by law. You do not have to provide this information, but if you do not your application for approval as a prospective mortgagor or borrower may be delayed or rejected. The information requested in this form is authorized by Title 38, USC, Chapter 37 (if VA); by 12 USC, Section 1701 et. seq. (if HUD/FHA); by 42 USC, Section 1452b (if HUD/CPD); and Title 42 USC, 1471 et. seq., or 7 USC, 1921 et. seq. (if USDA/FmHA).

Instructions: Lender — Complete items 1 through 7. Have applicant complete item 8. Forward directly to employer named in item 1.
Employer — Please complete either Part II or Part III as applicable. Complete Part IV and return directly to lender named in item 2.
The form is to be transmitted directly to the lender and is not to be transmitted through the applicant or any other party.

Part I — Request

1. To (Name and address of employer)	2. From (Name and address of lender)

I certify that this verification has been sent directly to the employer and has not passed through the hands of the applicant or any other interested party.

3. Signature of Lender	4. Title	5. Date	6. Lender's Number (Optional)

I have applied for a mortgage loan and stated that I am now or was formerly employed by you. My signature below authorizes verification of this information.

7. Name and Address of Applicant (include employee or badge number)	8. Signature of Applicant

Part II — Verification of Present Employment

9. Applicant's Date of Employment	10. Present Position	11. Probability of Continued Employment

12A. Current **Gross Base Pay** (Enter Amount and Check Period)
☐ Annual　☐ Hourly
☐ Monthly　☐ Other (Specify)
☐ Weekly
$ _____

12B. Gross Earnings

Type	Year To Date	Past Year 19____	Past Year 19____
Base Pay	Thru ____ 19__ $	$	$
Overtime	$	$	$
Commissions	$	$	$
Bonus	$	$	$
Total	$	$	$

13. For Military Personnel Only

Pay Grade	
Type	Monthly Amount
Base Pay	$
Rations	$
Flight or Hazard	$
Clothing	$
Quarters	$
Pro Pay	$
Overseas or Combat	$
Variable Housing Allowance	$

14. If Overtime or Bonus is Applicable, Is Its Continuance Likely?
Overtime ☐ Yes ☐ No
Bonus ☐ Yes ☐ No

15. If paid hourly — average hours per week

16. Date of applicant's next pay increase

17. Projected amount of next pay increase

18. Date of applicant's last pay increase

19. Amount of last pay increase

20. Remarks (If employee was off work for any length of time, please indicate time period and reason)

Part III — Verification of Previous Employment

21. Date Hired	23. Salary/Wage at Termination Per (Year) (Month) (Week)
22. Date Terminated	Base _____ Overtime _____ Commissions _____ Bonus _____
24. Reason for Leaving	25. Position Held

Part IV — Authorized Signature - Federal statutes provide severe penalties for any fraud, intentional misrepresentation, or criminal connivance or conspiracy purposed to influence the issuance of any guaranty or insurance by the VA Secretary, the U.S.D.A., FmHA/FHA Commissioner, or the HUD/CPD Assistant Secretary.

26. Signature of Employer	27. Title (Please print or type)	28. Date
29. Print or type name signed in Item 26	30. Phone No.	

Fannie Mae
Form 1005　　July 96

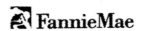 **FannieMae**

Request for Verification of Deposit

Privacy Act Notice: This information is to be used by the agency collecting it or its assignees in determining whether you qualify as a prospective mortgagor under its program. It will not be disclosed outside the agency except as required and permitted by law. You do not have to provide this information, but if you do not your application for approval as a prospective mortgagor or borrower may be delayed or rejected. The information requested in this form is authorized by Title 38, USC, Chapter 37 (If VA); by 12 USC, Section 1701 et.seq. (If HUD/FHA); by 42 USC, Section 1452b (if HUD/CPD); and Title 42 USC, 1471 et.seq. or 7 USC, 1921 et.seq. (If USDA/FmHA).

Instructions: Lender — Complete Items 1 through 8. Have applicant(s) complete Item 9. Forward directly to depository named in Item 1.
   Depository — Please complete Items 10 through 18 and return DIRECTLY to lender named in Item 2.
   The form is to be transmitted directly to the lender and is not to be transmitted through the applicant(s) or any other party.

Part I — Request

1. To (Name and address of depository)	2. From (Name and address of lender)

I certify that this verification has been sent directly to the bank or depository and has not passed through the hands of the applicant or any other party.

3. Signature of lender	4. Title	5. Date	6. Lender's No. (Optional)

7. Information To Be Verified

Type of Account	Account in Name of	Account Number	Balance
			$
			$
			$

To Depository: I/We have applied for a mortgage loan and stated in my financial statement that the balance on deposit with you is as shown above. You are authorized to verify this information and to supply the lender identified above with the information requested in Items 10 through 13. Your response is solely a matter of courtesy for which no responsibility is attached to your institution or any of your officers.

8. Name and Address of Applicant(s)	9. Signature of Applicant(s)

To Be Completed by Depository
Part II — Verification of Depository

10. Deposit Accounts of Applicant(s)

Type of Account	Account Number	Current Balance	Average Balance For Previous Two Months	Date Opened
		$	$	
		$	$	
		$	$	

11. Loans Outstanding To Applicant(s)

Loan Number	Date of Loan	Original Amount	Current Balance	Installments (Monthly/Quarterly)		Secured By	Number of Late Payments
		$	$	$	per		
		$	$	$	per		
		$	$	$	per		

12. Please include any additional information which may be of assistance in determination of credit worthiness. (Please include information on loans paid-in-full in Item 11 above.)

13. If the name(s) on the account(s) differ from those listed in Item 7, please supply the name(s) on the account(s) as reflected by your records.

Part III — Authorized Signature
Federal statutes provide severe penalties for any fraud, intentional misrepresentation, or criminal connivance or conspiracy purposed to influence the issuance of any guaranty or insurance by the VA Secretary, the U.S.D.A., FmHA/FHA Commissioner, or the HUD/CPD Assistant Secretary.

14. Signature of Depository Representative	15. Title (Please print or type)	16. Date
17. Please print or type name signed in item 14	18. Phone No.	

Fannie Mae
Form 1006   July 96

PRACTICE QUESTIONS

The following practice questions are representative of the questions you will find on the final examination and on the licensing examinations given by the Oregon Real Estate Agency.

1. Determining a prospective borrower's abilities with respect to a particular property is part of
   (A) loan underwriting.
   (B) what a secondary maket investor does.
   (C) both A and B.
   (D) neither A nor B.

2. A lender needs an appraisal so as to be sure that the loan
   I. amount does not exceed the market value.
   II. term does not exceed the remaining economic life of the property.
   (A) I only   (C) Both I and II
   (B) II only   (D) Neither I nor II

3. When making mortgage loans a lender should guard against
   I. physical deterioration.
   II. lending for longer than the remaining economic life of the improvements.
   (A) I only   (C) Both I and II
   (B) II only   (D) Neither I nor II

4. In real estate lending, "loan to value ratio" refers to which of the following relationships?
   (A) Loan amount ÷ Insured value
   (B) Loan amount ÷ Appraised value
   (C) Loan amount ÷ Price paid by the borrower
   (D) The lower of B or C

5. In real estate lending, the loan to value ratio is the
   (A) mortgage loan expressed as a percentage of the insured value.
   (B) monthly payment expressed as a percentage of the remaining principal balance.
   (C) loan as a percentage of the sales price or appraised value, whichever is the lower.
   (D) percentage of the loan which is insured against default.

6. The lower the loan to value ratio, the higher will be
   (A) the borrower's equity.
   (B) the lender's risk.
   (C) the appraised value.
   (D) all of the above.

7. The amount of the owner's interest in the property, being the value over and above the mortgage indebtedness, is called
   (A) the principal amount.
   (B) an equity.
   (C) surplus productivity.
   (D) the assessed value.

8. A seller is considering accepting a note and second trust deed from the buyer for part of the sales price. The seller's most important protection would be the
   (A) buyer's equity in the property.
   (B) buyer's credit rating.
   (C) buyer's ability to repay the debt.
   (D) amount still owing on underlying encumbrances.

9. When making a loan to be sold in the secondary market, a savings and loan association would be least concerned with
   (A) the borrower's credit report.
   (B) a bankrupcty eleven years ago.
   (C) the borrower's stable monthly income.
   (D) Fannie Mae and Freddie Mac guidelines.

10. In considering protection of investment in making long term amortized loans having a high loan to value ratio, lenders tend to emphasize both the value of the collateral as a marketable asset and the
    (A) selling price of the property.
    (B) borrower's potential for converting assets to cash.
    (C) credit of the borrower.
    (D) marital status of the borrower.

11. A couple are making an application for a loan to purchase a new home. In evaluating their application, the lender would consider which of the following to be the least important?
(A) The wife's salary
(B) The husband's overtime pay
(C) Their total overall debts
(D) Their past credit history on previous loans

12. When looking at the borrower's ability to repay a loan, the lender should consider
(A) the amount of the borrower's monthly income.
(B) the stability of the borrower's income.
(C) the borrower's current total debt service.
(D) all of the above.

13. A lender will lend only if the borrower's monthly payments will not exceed 28% of the borrower's net monthly income. By "monthly payment" the lender means
(A) interest only.
(B) principal and interest only.
(C) principal, interest and ¹⁄₁₂ the annual taxes.
(D) principal, interest, ¹⁄₁₂ the annual taxes and ¹⁄₁₂ the annual fire insurance premium.

14. Which of the following would be used to calculate the front-end qualifying ratio for a real estate loan?
(A) Total monthly payment including taxes and insurance divided by the gross monthly income
(B) Total monthly payment including taxes and insurance plus payments on other debt, divided by the gross monthly income
(C) Net monthly income after withholding divided by the total monthly payment including taxes and insurance
(D) The gross monthly income minus the monthly payment

15. The "seasoning" of a loan refers to the
(A) type of market in which it would be most advantageous for the lender to sell it.
(B) borrower's payment history on the loan.
(C) final maturity date of the loan.
(D) amortization schedule of the loan.

16. From a lender's standpoint, the most important consideration in granting a loan is the
(A) risk of default by the borrower.
(B) cost and availability of mortgage funds.
(C) borrower's need for the loan.
(D) neighborhood in which the property is located.

17. A lender under a conventional loan may compensate for any additional risk when underwriting a loan by doing which of the following?
 I. Requiring higher down payments than normally would be required
 II. Charging higher interest rates
(A) I only   (C) Both I and II
(B) II only   (D) Neither I nor II

18. A lender gets the best protection against foreclosure
(A) by lending to a stable, high-income borrower.
(B) by lending on a property in a good neighborhood.
(C) if there is an increase in the value of the dollar.
(D) by making a high loan to value ratio loan.

19. For a lender with a low down payment loan on the books, the best protection against foreclosure would be
(A) high monthly payments.
(B) rapid inflation.
(C) a high interest rate.
(D) efficient loan servicing.

20. From a lender's point of view, the most important consideration commonly considered in granting a mortgage loan is the
(A) risk of default.
(B) availability of mortgage money.
(C) condition of the property.
(D) neighborhood where the mortgaged property is located.

21. Loan processing includes, among other things, an analysis of which of the following?
 I. Collateral's value   II. Borrower's credit
(A) I only   (C) Both I and II
(B) II only   (D) Neither I nor II

22. When making the loan the mortgagee's risk of default may be lessened by which of the following?
    (A) Increasing the amortization period
    (B) Reducing the monthly payments
    (C) Reducing the gross debt service ratio
    (D) Reducing the loan to value ratio

23. When a conventional loan exceeds Fannie Mae/Freddie Mac maximum loan amounts, we call it
    (A) an adjustable rate mortgage.
    (B) a nonconforming mortgage.
    (C) a hypothecated mortgage.
    (D) a jumbo loan.

24. The premium for private mortgage insurance on a conventional loan is typically based on the
    (A) original loan balance.
    (B) average balance of the loan for each year.
    (C) amount of the loan which exceeds 80% loan to value ratio.
    (D) bottom 80% of the loan.

25. A commercial bank required a borrower to maintain a minimum balance on deposit. This would be called
    (A) collaterally secured financing.
    (B) a discount loan.
    (C) a compensating balance.
    (D) a violation of the Equal Credit Opportunity Act.

ANSWERS

To practice questions. If you chose the wrong letter, here's the right one! The explanations are designed to clarify your understanding.

1.   **A**   "Loan underwriting" is the term used by professionals to refer to the process of approving a loan. The process involves evaluation of the collateral, the borrower's character (credit) and of the borrower's capacity (income and existing debt service). Secondary market investors purchase securities issued by Fannie Mae and Freddie Mac, who have already approved the loans backing the securities.

2.   **C**   The appraisal is required primarily so the lender can be sure the loan does not exceed the value of the property, after allowing for the costs of recovery. A secondary, but also important, purpose of the appraisal report is to determine the remaining economic (useful) life of the improvements. In appraisal theory, at the end of their economic life, the improvements have no further value. Therefore, a lender would want to be sure that the amortization schedule provided that the loan be paid off before the end of the economic life. To ensure this the lender usually refuses to make a loan where the term is longer than three-fourths of the remaining economic life as stated on the appraisal report.

3.   **C**   In appraisal theory, at the end of their economic life the improvements have no further value. Therefore, a lender would want to be sure that the amortization schedule provided that the loan be paid off before the end of the economic life. The appraisal report will also reveal the condition of the property, which has a bearing on its salability, and therefore the quality of the collateral.

4.   **D**   The loan to value ratio is the percentage that the loan will be of the sales price or the appraised value, whichever is the lesser amount. In other words, if a property was listed for $200,000, sold for $180,000 but was appraised for $160,000, a borrower obtaining an 80% loan to value ratio loan would be able to obtain a loan of 80% of $160,000.

5.   **C**   In real estate lending, "value" means the the sales price or the appraised value, whichever is less. A ratio is a percentage, so "loan to value ratio" means the percentage of the value the lender is willing to lend. Insured value is the value of the improvements only, and usually for the replacement cost, not necessarily the market.

6.   **A**   Since the loan to value ratio expresses the percentage of the value which will be mortgaged, the difference is the owner's equity in the property.

7.   **B**   "Equity" refers to the amount of the borrower's investment in the property. If you put 10% down on a $200,000 property, then your equity is $20,000. As the property increases in value and the loan is paid down, the equity increases.

8.   **A**   The bigger the down payment, the more easily the lender can recover without a loss in the event of a foreclosure. The borrower's credit report only evidences good intentions; it is not a guarantee of future performance. The borrower's income could similarly be interrupted. That the value might go down is the least likely disaster, therefore, for the borrower to have a large equity in the property is the lender's best protection.

9.   **B**   Under the Fair Credit Reporting Act, credit reporting agencies are not allowed to report bankruptcies over ten years old. Furthermore, Fannie Mae and Freddie Mac underwriting guidelines do not consider a bankruptcy that old as a negative credit factor.

10.   **C**   The three C's of credit are capacity (income), character (credit report) and collateral. Lenders generally do not lend unless the borrower and the property qualify for all three.

11.   **B**   Lenders are required by the Equal Credit Opportunity Act to consider all income of a husband and wife when they are co-borrowers. Analysis of the borrower's overall debt and past credit history are essential parts of the loan approval process. Overtime pay, however, will probably not be counted, unless the borrower can demonstrate a history of continuously receiving it for a long period of time.

12.   **D**   The three C's of credit are collateral, character, and capacity. Collateral is evidenced by the appraisal report. Character is proved by the credit report. And the borrower demonstrates capacity to repay the debt by showing employment history and income verification from the employer. Most lenders use two ratios in determining the borrower's capacity to repay the debt. The housing cost ratio is the ratio of the monthly payment including principal, interest, taxes and insurance as a percentage of the

borrower's gross monthly income. The second is the total debt service ratio. This is the total of all the borrower's monthly payments, including the payment on the proposed loan, divided by the borrower's gross monthly income.

13. **D** Lenders use two ratios in determining the borrower's ability to repay the debt. The housing cost ratio is the ratio of the monthly payment including principal, interest, taxes and insurance, as a percentage of the borrower's gross monthly income. The second is the total debt service ratio. This is the total of all the borrower's monthly payments, including the payment on the proposed loan, divided by the borrower's gross monthly income.

14. **A** The front-end ratio is the total monthly payment divided by the monthly gross income. The back-end ratio is the total monthly payment plus all other payments which have ten months or more, divided by the gross monthly income.

15. **B** When lenders say a loan has been seasoned, it means there is a history of regular, timely payments. The opposite of a seasoned loan is a green loan. The fact that a loan is seasoned means that it has a higher market value if the holder should desire to sell it.

16. **A** The cost and availability of funds influences the interest rate, but not the underwriting decision. The neighborhood in which the property is located influences the value of the collateral, and therefore the amount the lender is willing to lend, but does not influence the underwriting decision. The borrower's need for the funds is the least likely to affect the underwriting decision. The major factor influencing the lender's decision to make the loan is the risk of loss.

17. **C** The more collateral, the more secure the lender feels. Requiring a higher down payment increases the value of the collateral in relation to the loan amount. Higher interest rates are used to compensate for higher risk when the amount of risk cannot be reduced.

18. **A** A high loan to value ratio loan is inherently risky because the higher the loan to value ratio, the less the borrower's equity in the property. Lending to a borrower with high, stable income lowers the lender's risk, as does lending on a property in a good neighborhood. Nothing protects the lender as well as a high equity in the property. Increasing inflation, therefore, causes property values to rise, creating less risk. However, increasing the value of the dollar is the opposite of inflation, that is, property values will decline in terms of the dollar.

19. **B** During bad economic conditions property values tend to go down as demand decreases and the volume of real estate sales declines. A low down payment loan is riskier than a high down payment loan because the borrower would have a harder time selling the property for the amount owed in such times. The borrower may have no choice but to walk away from the property, where a borrower with a larger equity may be able to lower the price enough to avoid a foreclosure.

20. **A** The borrower's ability to repay and credit report are the most important considerations in making a loan decision. The condition, location and type of property merely influence whether the loan is salable, and to which secondary market. In today's world, mortgage money is always available.

21. **C** Lenders speak of the "three C's of credit" – capacity, character and collateral. Capacity is demonstrating reasonable income amounts required to make the payments. Character is determined from the credit report. Collateral is the security offered for the loan.

22. **D** There are various ways to make a default less likely. Making it easier for the borrower to comply with the terms of the loan is one way – e.g., making the payments lower or making sure the borrower has more than enough income to service the debt. However, the most effective way is to lower the loan to value ratio. If the borrower has sufficient equity in the property, the borrower can always sell the property, if necessary.

23. **B** Fannie Mae and Freddie Mac publish their joint underwriting standards for conventional loans they will buy. They also publish the maximum loan amounts which are changed each year based on the cost of housing as reported by the Department of Housing and Urban Development. A loan which does not meet underwriting standards is not salable at all. A loan which merely exceeds the maximum amount is called a nonconforming loan and may be salable, although usually at a slightly higher interest rate.

24. **C** The mortgage insurance premium on an FHA loan insures the entire loan balance. Federal GI guaranties are limited to the amount of the guaranty for the loan. Conventional loans are insured by private mortgage insurance companies. Lenders can elect various percentages of coverage, but the norm is to insure everything above 80% loan to value ratio, although many insure everything above 75% loan to value ratio.

25.   **C**   Lenders frequently require commercial borrowers to do the rest of their banking at the same institution, keeping their funds on deposit there. This is called a compensating balance requirement. One benefit to the lender is that the lender effectively lends the borrowers own money back to the borrower, thus increasing the yield on the loan. Another benefit is security, as the lender has the legal right to seize the funds on deposit to offset the loan in the event of default. And the lender usually also earns service fees on funds in a checking account, increasing their return.

LENDING REGULATIONS

L ENDERS IN TODAY'S WORLD MUST DEAL WITH A MULTITUDE OF LAWS AND RULES. While many regulations involve government organizations which insure and guarantee loans, such as FHA and the Department of Veterans Affairs, even lenders who make nothing but conventional loans have to deal with rules. The secondary mortgage market, for example, dictates what kind of loans they will buy. In addition, to these rules, there are a variety of consumer protection laws that lenders must observe. In this section we will explore those consumer laws which affect lending practices.

Of all consumer protection laws, the most significant for lenders is the Consumer Protection Act of 1968. This law is so large it is divided into various separate areas. Title I of the Consumer Protection Act includes the Truth in Lending Act, a thorough knowledge of which is not only essential today for lenders, but for real estate agents as well.

The Truth in Lending Act empowers the Board of Governors of the Federal Reserve Bank to create reasonable regulations as are necessary to implement the purposes of the Act. The resulting rules are called Federal Reserve Regulation Z, and have the force and effect of law. You may hear lenders refer to these laws just as "Truth in Lending" or just as "Regulation Z," but in fact lenders use either term loosely to refer to both the Act and the Regulation together.

The concept of the Truth in Lending Act and Regulation Z is simple – lenders must disclose loan terms to prospective borrowers so the borrowers can shop for credit more easily. There are countless ways to calculate interest, most of which the average consumer does not understand. Furthermore, lenders might make a loan at a low interest rate, but make up for the low rate by requiring loan fees, discount points and other charges. Prior to the Truth in Lending Act and Regulation Z it was virtually impossible for consumers to know which lender offered the best terms. Now, not only must loan terms be disclosed, but all lenders must use the same rules when calculating the actual cost of the financing.

One thing the Truth in Lending Act and Regulation Z do not affect is the interest rate and the fees lenders are allowed to charge. Many states set the maximum interest rates for different types of loans. These are called usury rates. In some states, charging usurious interest can result in forfeiture of the interest or even of the principal balance. However, there are no federal usury laws, and Oregon generally does not regulate the amount of interest a lender is allowed to charge. The point to understand is that the Truth in Lending Act and Regulation Z are strictly disclosure laws. Lenders can charge whatever they want; they just have to disclose it in meaningful ways as required by the law.

Although Regulation Z was created by the Federal Reserve Bank Board of Governors, both it and the Truth in Lending Act are enforced by other federal agencies. For non-institutional lenders and real estate agents, the Federal Trade Commission has the responsibility to ensure compliance. Intentional violations can result in a fine of up to $5,000 and/or imprisonment for up to one year. Unintentional violations are a civil matter between the lender and the borrower. The borrower can sue the lender for actual damages, and in addition, punitive damages equal to twice the amount of the finance charge (minimum $100, maximum $1,000), and the borrower is also entitled to recover reasonable attorney's fees. The $1,000 maximum does not apply to class action suits.

Who must comply   Only persons and entities who regularly extend credit (creditors) or who arrange credit (arrangers of credit) must comply with the Truth in Lending Act and Regulation Z. For residential real estate, Regulation Z defines such a person or entity as one who has made five loans during the current or preceding year. Note that real estate agents regularly arrange credit, so every real estate agent must know how to comply with the Truth in Lending Laws.

However, certain loans are exempted. Business, commercial and agricultural credit is exempt. Loans to corporations and entities other than natural persons are exempt. Loans over $25,000 on personal property are exempt, although this exemption does not apply if the loan is secured by real estate. Loans are also exempt if they are to be repaid in four or fewer installments (in addition to the down payment). A loan where no finance charge is made is exempt; but if a creditor gives discounts for cash to buyers of the same merchandise, the cash discount normally granted to such buyers is considered a finance charge for those who elect to use credit.

How to comply   There are various disclosures required under the Truth in Lending Act. Not all disclosures must be made in all situations. In general, the law distinguishes between disclosures required in the actual extension of credit, and disclosures required when advertising the availability of credit. Real estate agents arrange and advertise credit, but do not usually extend credit, so agents generally need to be concerned only with disclosures required when advertising the availability of credit.

Note, however, that if a real estate licensee takes a loan application for a lender, the licensee is acting as agent of the lender, and will probably be required to make disclosures on behalf of the lender.

Before making disclosures to the borrower, the annual percentage rate, finance charge and total amount financed must be calculated. These are discussed below.

The Annual Percentage Rate (APR)   When interest rates are stated, they must usually be stated as an ***annual percentage rate***, although in advertising, the term may be abbreviated to "APR."

Although there are exceptions, the general rule for stating the annual percentage rate is that it should be stated as an annual rate, not as a periodic rate (for example, "12% APR," not "1% per month APR." The rate must be accurate to within ⅛ of 1%.

The idea of the annual percentage rate is to divide the total finance charge (see below) by the number of years the loan will be in force, and again by the amount financed. However, this does not work for loans with more than one payment. For real estate loans, which typically involve many payments on a declining principal balance, calculating the annual percentage rate involves extremely complex formulas. In some cases it may be possible for a real estate agent to calculate the annual percentage rate with a financial calculator, but in most cases it is best to get the lender to make the calculations.

Disclosing the annual percentage rate is a special problem for adjustable rate loans. In this case, disclosure must be made that the rate can increase, whether or not there are caps, and if there are caps, how high the maximum rates are. Also, if the initial rate is a "teaser rate" not related to the index, then the method by which the increases or decreases are calculated must be disclosed. The usual way to do this is to show a range of payments for the high and low possibilities.

Calculating the total finance charge Lenders and arrangers of credit must disclose the **total finance charge** when offering or extending credit. Obviously, interest usually constitutes the bulk of the total finance charge, however, certain other charges must be included as well –

- Service charges, transaction charges and activity charges
- Points paid by the buyer, including loan fees and assumption fees
- Appraisal and credit report fees in non-residential loans
- Mortgage insurance premiums, including FHA and private mortgage insurance on conventional loans

The following items are *not* included in the total finance charge –

- Application fees, if they are charged to all applicants, whether or not credit is actually extended
- Late payment, return check and similar penalty charges
- Points paid by the seller
- Title insurance premiums
- Document preparation fees, including notarization and recording
- Amounts required to be paid into reserves for taxes and fire insurance
- Appraisal and credit report fees on a residential real estate loan

Certain other items must be included only in special cases. For example, premiums for credit life and/or disability insurance must be included as part of the total finance charge if the lender requires the borrower to carry it. Premiums for fire insurance must be included only if the lender requires the borrower to obtain the fire insurance from an agent of the lender's choosing. And fees for services rendered by third parties need not be included if the lender does not require the service and if the lender does not retain the fees.

Calculating the total amount financed The total amount financed is the original loan balance plus other amounts financed by the lender which are not part of the total finance charge, less any prepaid finance charges.

For example, suppose a lender makes a $200,000 residential home loan. As we have seen above, the appraisal and credit report fees are not part of the total finance charge. So if the borrower pays these items separately at closing, then no disclosure need be made. But if the lender pays for the appraisal and credit report and then increases the loan amount to cover them, they must be included when calculating the total amount financed.

Prepaid finance charges must be subtracted in figuring the total amount financed. A prepaid finance charge is any part of the finance charge which the borrower pays directly to the lender or to a third party. A prepaid finance charge also includes any part of the loan amount which is withheld from the loan proceeds (not disbursed to the borrower).

Prepaid finance charges are common in real estate loans. For example, it is normal practice for lenders to require the payments to be due on the first of the month, with a full month between each payment. If a real estate loan closes on, say, April 16, then the lender will require that the borrower pay 15 days interest on closing (for the 16th through the 30th of the month), so the interest will be paid to May 1. The first monthly payment will be due June 1. The June 1 payment will include the interest which accrues during May.

What must be disclosed (in extending credit) Although the following list is not exhaustive, lenders must usually disclose –

- The interest rate as an annual percentage rate
- The identity of the creditor
- The total finance change
- The loan amount, stated as the total amount financed
- The payment schedule
- The total of all payments

And where applicable, lenders must also disclose –

- If the loan is secured, and a description of the collateral
- The amount of any prepayment privilege charge (prepayment penalty)
- The date the finance charge begins, if different from the note
- The amount of any late charges or other penalties for default
- Whether or not the loan is assumable, and under what conditions
- The amount of any discounts or prepaid interest
- The amount of any tax and insurance reserve requirements
- Any other of the repayment terms

What must be disclosed (in advertising credit) Full disclosure is required in advertising credit terms only if the advertisement contains specific statements about any of the following –

- The amount of the down payment
- The number of payments or the period of repayment
- The amount of any of the periodic installments
- The amount of any of the components of the total finance charge

General statements such as "low down payment" or "no down payment," "budget terms," "monthly payment terms" and the like do not trigger full disclosure. Also, stating the annual percentage rate does not trigger full disclosure, such as "9% APR loan available." Examples of statements which trigger full disclosure are "only 5% down," "pay off in 15 years," "only $825 per month" or "total move-in costs only $1,500."

Full disclosure requires that the advertising include at least the following –

- The annual percentage rate
- The down payment required
- The terms of repayment

The terms of repayment generally include the total finance charge as well as the number of payments, the amount of each payment and the period of payments (e.g., "360 equal monthly payments of $1,300"). However, if there are special terms such as irregular payments, balloon payments, call features, adjustable rates and the like, these terms must also be disclosed.

There is considerable latitude in the exact language used, as long as the disclosure is clear. For example, if the purchase price is $200,000 and the down payment is $40,000, this could be stated as a dollar amount ("$40,000"), as a percentage ("20% down") or even as a loan to value ratio ("80% financing").

Sometimes the annual percentage rate will be different from the actual rate on the note. This happens when there are loan fees and other charges which raise the annual percentage rate above the actual rate. In this case, it is acceptable to state the note rate, as long as the annual percentage rate is also stated, e.g., "Note rate 9% (9.5% APR)".

ADVERTISING REQUIREMENTS SUMMARY

Triggering Items

- Down payment
- Number of payments
- Term of the loan
- Amount of the payment
- Any part of the total finance charge

Items Which Do Not Trigger

- General statements
- The cash price
- That there is no down payment
- The annual percentage rate

Usual Advertising Requirements if Full Disclosure Triggered

- The annual percentage rate
- The down payment required
- The total finance charge
- Number, amount and period of payments
- Any additional special terms

Right of rescission In some credit transactions, borrowers may have a three-day right of rescission. This means the borrower can notify the lender in writing of the borrower's intent not to go through with the transaction. The parties then return to their original position; the lender's security position is void and any loan funds which have already been disbursed must be returned to the lender. If the right of rescission applies, the lender must give the borrower notice of this right.

The right of rescission applies only if the loan will result in a lien on the borrower's principal residence. However, loans for the *acquisition* of a personal residence are exempt from the right of rescission because at the time of obtaining the loan the property was not yet the borrower's residence. Also, even a loan to refinance a principal residence is exempt if the lender is also the existing creditor. Loans for business purposes are also exempt from the right of rescission, even if they result in a lien on the borrower's existing principal residence.

Miscellaneous The Truth in Lending Act and Federal Reserve Regulation Z are very complicated laws. The material presented here should be considered a simplified overview of the subject. We have deliberately concentrated on real estate loans and largely ignored special requirements for unsecured loans and loans secured by personal property. Furthermore, you should always bear in mind that changes are constantly being made to reflect new loan programs. Real estate agents should always be careful to check with appropriate reliable sources before making loan disclosures.

Exercise a

The Truth in Lending Act and Federal Reserve Regulation Z (choose one) ❑ *do* ❑ *do not set the maximum interest rates lenders can charge. The law applies to all lenders who regularly extend or _____ credit in the normal course of their business. Exempted loans include personal property loans over $ _____ ,*

loans of _____ or fewer installments, as well as loans for _____, _____
and _____ purposes. Loans are also exempt if there is no _____
_____. In advertising of credit terms, real estate agents need make no disclosure unless full disclosure
is triggered. Which of the following statements in an ad would trigger full disclosure?

- ❏ Listed at only $195,000"   ❏ "Name Your Terms"
- ❏ "Low, low down payment"   ❏ "Total Payoff in 10 Years!"
- ❏ "Total Finance Charge $232,565"   ❏   "Only $965 per month PITI"

When calculating the total finance charge for a mortgage, which of the following must be included?

- ❏ A two point loan fee   ❏ Late payment fees
- ❏ The down payment   ❏ The appraisal report fee
- ❏ Recording fees   ❏ The mortgage insurance premium

The Real Estate Settlement Procedures Act

During the early 1970s, the Department of Housing and Urban Development (HUD) conducted a study of the costs of closing a residential loan transaction. The study revealed that closing costs varied significantly, not just from one area to another, but even within the same community there were frequently large differences in closing costs required by different lenders.

The Department concluded that some lenders were successful in charging more for their services, largely because of the ignorance of consumers. To remedy this situation, HUD asked Congress to pass the Real Estate Settlement Procedures Act (RESPA). The law was originally passed in 1974 and substantially amended in 1979. Its purpose is to require lenders to disclose closing costs to borrowers, to encourage competition among lenders and to eliminate referral fees and kickbacks.

Real estate agents should take careful note that RESPA is similar to the Truth in Lending laws, but where the Truth in Lending Act and Federal Reserve Regulation Z require lenders to disclose *credit* costs, RESPA requires lenders to disclose *closing* costs associated with the purchase – that is costs such as prorates for taxes, escrow and recording fees, title insurance charges, etc.

The Real Estate Settlement Procedures Act applies only to first mortgage loans incurred to acquire a one- to four-family personal residence made by a ***federally related lender***. A "federally related lender" means any lender which –

- Is federally chartered, or
- Is federally regulated, or
- Has accounts which are federally insured, or
- Makes loans under a federal program such as FHA, RECDC, or DVA, or
- Sells loans to Fannie Mae, Freddie Mac or Ginnie Mae, or
- Makes more than $1 million worth of real estate loans per year.

Notwithstanding the above, the following loans are exempt –

- Loans to acquire land of 25 acres or more
- Junior financing (not a first lien)
- Loans for vacant land unless acquired as a site for a mobile home or for construction of a residence
- Construction loans where the borrower already owns the lot
- Transactions where the buyer takes title subject to an existing loan

What lenders must do to comply Compliance with RESPA does not usually involve real estate agents directly. Lenders, escrow agents and, to a lesser extent, title insurers are more directly concerned with RESPA. However, anything which affects these parties will also indirectly affect real estate agents, so it is good for real estate agents to be aware of the basic provisions of the law. In addition, as real estate agents become more and more involved in computerized loan origination, an understanding of RESPA promises to become more and more important.

When RESPA applies to a loan, the closing statement must be on a form created by HUD called a **Uniform Settlement Statement** (HUD-1). Within three days of obtaining a loan application the lender must give the borrower (at no additional charge) a **good faith estimate** of the closing costs, which must reference the lines on the Uniform Settlement Statement so the borrower can compare to the final settlement statement at closing. (See pages 220 – 222.) If the borrower requests it, the borrower is entitled to review a copy of the final settlement statement not less than one day before the closing, again, on the Uniform Settlement Statement. The idea is that everything must refer to the Uniform Settlement Statement so the borrower can compare the actual costs with the original estimate, line by line. The closing agent is not allowed to charge extra for the preview of the statement, nor may the lender charge for the good faith estimate.

Under RESPA a reserve account is referred to as a **escrow account** (which is also sometimes referred to as an **impound account**). Within 45 days of closing the lender or closing agent (escrow) must also provide the borrower with an **Initial Escrow Statement**. The Initial Escrow Statement itemizes the estimated taxes, insurance premiums and other charges anticipated to be paid from the escrow account during the first twelve months of the loan. It lists the escrow payment amount and any required cushion. Thereafter loan servicers must deliver to borrowers an **Annual Escrow Statement** once a year. The annual escrow account statement summarizes all escrow account deposits and payments during the servicer's twelve month computation year. It also notifies the borrower of any shortages or surpluses in the account and advises the borrower about what the servicer is doing about any shortages or surpluses. Any excess of $50 or more must be returned to the borrower.

During the course of the loan a lender may not charge excessive amounts for the escrow account. Each month the lender may require a borrower to pay into the escrow account no more than $\frac{1}{12}$ of the total of all disbursements payable during the year (usually just taxes and insurance), plus an amount necessary to pay for any shortage in the account. In addition, the lender may require a **cushion**, not to exceed an amount equal to two months worth of the total disbursements for the year.

Within three days of the loan application, the lender must give the borrower a copy of a settlement costs booklet which has been published by HUD. The booklet is designed to explain the Uniform Settlement Statement and to inform the borrower about all the costs which might be involved in purchasing a home. The booklet also encourages the borrower to shop for the services needed.

Also within three days of loan application the lender must give the borrower a **Mortgage Servicing Statement**. This is required only if the provisions of the loan allow the lender to sell the loan servicing. But since practically all loans today give the lender the right to sell the servicing of the loan, the Mortgage Servicing Statement is almost always required.

If the loan servicer sells or assigns the servicing rights to another loan servicer, a **Servicing Transfer Statement** must be given to the borrower. Generally, the loan servicer must notify the borrower 15 days before the effective date of the loan transfer. As long the borrower makes a timely payment to the old servicer within 60 days of the

GOOD FAITH ESTIMATE
(Not a Loan Commitment)

This Good Faith Estimate is being provided by a mortgage broker and no lender has yet been obtained

The information provided below reflects estimates of the charges which you are likely to incur at the settlement of your loan. The fees listed are estimates – actual charges may be more or less. Your transaction may not involve a fee for every item listed.

The numbers listed beside the estimates generally correspond to the numbered lines contained in the HUD-1 or HUD-1A settlement statement which you will be receiving at settlement. The HUD-1 or HUD-1A settlement statement will show you the actual cost for items paid at settlement.

HUD-1	DESCRIPTION OF CHARGES	AMOUNT
801	Loan Origination Fee @ % + $	
802	Loan Discount Fee @ % + $	
803	Appraisal Fee	
804	Credit Report	
805	Inspection Fee	
806	Mortgage Insurance Application Fee	
807	Assumption Fee	
808	Mortgage Broker Fee @ % + $	
809	Tax Related Service Fee	
810	Processing Fee	
811	Underwriting Fee	
812	Wire Transfer Fee	
813	Application Fee	
814	Commitment Fee	
815	Lender's Rate Lock-in Fee	
901	Interest @ /day for days	
902	Mortgage Insurance Premium	
903	Hazard Insurance Premium	
904	County Property Taxes	
906	Flood Insurance	
1001	Hazard Ins. @ /mo. for months	
1002	Mortage Ins. @ /mo. for months	
1004	Tax & Assmt. @ /mo. for months	
1006	Flood Insurance @ /mo. for months	
1008	Aggregate Escrow Adjustment	
1101	Settlement or Closing/Escrow Fee	
1102	Abstract or Title Search	
1103	Title Examination	
1105	Document Preparation Fee	
1106	Notary Fee	
1107	Attorney's Fee	
1108	Title Insurance	
1201	Recording Fee	
1202	City/County Tax/Stamps	
1203	State Tax/Stamps	
1204	Intangible Tax	
1301	Survey	
1302	Pest Inspection	

"S"/"B" designates those costs to be paid by Seller/Broker   "A" designates those costs affecting APR.
"F" designates financed costs.

These estimates are provided pursuant to the Real Estate Settlement Procedures Act of 1974, as amended (RESPA). Additional information can be found in the HUD Special Information Booklet which is to be provided to you by your mortgage broker or lender, if your application is to purchase residential property and the Lender will take a first lien on the property.

Mailing Address | Property Address

Proposed Loan Amount | Loan Type | Estimated Intereset Rate
Preparation Date | ❏ FHA ❏ VA ❏ Conventional | Loan Number

_____ Date   _____ Date

_____ Date   _____ Date

Page 1 of 1   GFE 3/95

Good Faith Estimate as required by RESPA. Note the references to line numbers which match the HUD-1 form to the right.

A. **Settlement Statement**

U.S. Department of Housing and Urban Development

OMB Approval No. 2502-0265

B. Type of Loan

1. ☐ FHA	2. ☐ FmHA	3. ☐ Conv. Unins.	6. File Number:	7. Loan Number:	8. Mortgage Insurance Case Number:
4. ☐ VA	5. ☐ Conv. Ins.				

C. Note: This form is furnished to give you a statement of actual settlement costs. Amounts paid to and by the settlement agent are shown. Items marked "(p.o.c.)" were paid outside the closing; they are shown here for informational purposes and are not included in the totals.

D. Name & Address of Borrower:	E. Name & Address of Seller:	F. Name & Address of Lender:

| G. Property Location: | H. Settlement Agent: | |
| | Place of Settlement: | I. Settlement Date: |

J. Summary of Borrower's Transaction

100. Gross Amount Due From Borrower	
101. Contract sales price	
102. Personal property	
103. Settlement charges to borrower (line 1400)	
104.	
105.	
Adjustments for items paid by seller in advance	
106. City/town taxes to	
107. County taxes to	
108. Assessments to	
109.	
110.	
111.	
112.	
120. Gross Amount Due From Borrower	

200. Amounts Paid By Or In Behalf Of Borrower	
201. Deposit or earnest money	
202. Principal amount of new loan(s)	
203. Existing loan(s) taken subject to	
204.	
205.	
206.	
207.	
208.	
209.	
Adjustments for items unpaid by seller	
210. City/town taxes to	
211. County taxes to	
212. Assessments to	
213.	
214.	
215.	
216.	
217.	
218.	
219.	
220. Total Paid By/For Borrower	

300. Cash At Settlement From/To Borrower	
301. Gross Amount due from borrower (line 120)	
302. Less amounts paid by/for borrower (line 220)	( )
303. Cash ☐ From ☐ To Borrower	

K. Summary of Seller's Transaction

400. Gross Amount Due To Seller	
401. Contract sales price	
402. Personal property	
403.	
404.	
405.	
Adjustments for items paid by seller in advance	
406. City/town taxes to	
407. County taxes to	
408. Assessments to	
409.	
410.	
411.	
412.	
420. Gross Amount Due To Seller	

500. Reductions In Amount Due To Seller	
501. Excess deposit (see instructions)	
502. Settlement charges to seller (line 1400)	
503. Existing loan(s) taken subject to	
504. Payoff of first mortgage loan	
505. Payoff of second mortgage loan	
506.	
507.	
508.	
509.	
Adjustments for items unpaid by seller	
510. City/town taxes to	
511. County taxes to	
512. Assessments to	
513.	
514.	
515.	
516.	
517.	
518.	
519.	
520. Total Reduction Amount Due Seller	

600. Cash At Settlement To/From Seller	
601. Gross amount due to seller (line 420)	
602. Less reductions in amt. due seller (line 520)	( )
603. Cash ☐ To ☐ From Seller	

Section 5 of the Real Estate Settlement Procedures Act (RESPA) requires the following: • HUD must develop a Special Information Booklet to help persons borrowing money to finance the purchase of residential real estate to better understand the nature and costs of real estate settlement services; • Each lender must provide the booklet to all applicants from whom it receives or for whom it prepares a written application to borrow money to finance the purchase of residential real estate; • Lenders must prepare and distribute with the Booklet a Good Faith Estimate of the settlement costs that the borrower is likely to incur in connection with the settlement. These disclosures are manadatory.

Section 4(a) of RESPA mandates that HUD develop and prescribe this standard form to be used at the time of loan settlement to provide full disclosure of all charges imposed upon the borrower and seller. These are third party disclosures that are designed to provide the borrower with pertinent information during the settlement process in order to be a better shopper.

The Public Reporting Burden for this collection of information is estimated to average one hour per response, including the time for reviewing instructions, searching existing data sources, gathering and maintaining the data needed, and completing and reviewing the collection of information.

This agency may not collect this information, and you are not required to complete this form, unless it displays a currently valid OMB control number.

The information requested does not lend itself to confidentiality.

Previous editions are obsolete

Page 1 of 2

form **HUD-1** (3/86)
ref Handbook 4305.2

Uniform Settlement Statement (HUD-1), required by RESPA.

L. Settlement Charges

700. Total Sales/Broker's Commission based on price $ @ % =		Paid From Borrowers Funds at Settlement	Paid From Seller's Funds at Settlement
Division of Commission (line 700) as follows:			
701. $ to			
702. $ to			
703. Commission paid at Settlement			
704.			
800. Items Payable In Connection With Loan			
801. Loan Origination Fee %			
802. Loan Discount %			
803. Appraisal Fee to			
804. Credit Report to			
805. Lender's Inspection Fee			
806. Mortgage Insurance Application Fee to			
807. Assumption Fee			
808.			
809.			
810.			
811.			
900. Items Required By Lender To Be Paid In Advance			
901. Interest from to @$ /day			
902. Mortgage Insurance Premium for months to			
903. Hazard Insurance Premium for years to			
904. years to			
905.			
1000. Reserves Deposited With Lender			
1001. Hazard insurance months@$ per month			
1002. Mortgage insurance months@$ per month			
1003. City property taxes months@$ per month			
1004. County property taxes months@$ per month			
1005. Annual assessments months@$ per month			
1006. months@$ per month			
1007. months@$ per month			
1008. months@$ per month			
1100. Title Charges			
1101. Settlement or closing fee to			
1102. Abstract or title search to			
1103. Title examination to			
1104. Title insurance binder to			
1105. Document preparation to			
1106. Notary fees to			
1107. Attorney's fees to			
(includes above items numbers:)			
1108. Title insurance to			
(includes above items numbers:)			
1109. Lender's coverage $			
1110. Owner's coverage $			
1111.			
1112.			
1113.			
1200. Government Recording and Transfer Charges			
1201. Recording fees: Deed $; Mortgage $; Releases $			
1202. City/county tax/stamps: Deed $; Mortgage $			
1203. State tax/stamps: Deed $; Mortgage $			
1204.			
1205.			
1300. Additional Settlement Charges			
1301. Survey to			
1302. Pest inspection to			
1303.			
1304.			
1305.			
1400. Total Settlement Charges (enter on lines 103, Section J and 502, Section K)			

loan transfer, the borrower cannot be penalized. The notice must include the name and address of the new servicer, toll-free telephone numbers, and the date when the new servicer will begin accepting payments.

A principal feature of RESPA is that kickbacks and referral fees are prohibited. If a fee is charged, a service must have been provided. Moreover, if anyone involved in the transaction (including a real estate agent) refers a buyer to another company, and the referring party has an ownership interest in the entity to which the buyer is referred, the ownership interest must be disclosed to the buyer using an ***Affiliated Business Arrangement Disclosure***. For example, a real estate brokerage company may offer a package of services such as title insurance, escrow, insurance, mortgage lending, home inspections, etc., as long as the package is offered by an independent business organization. Such an arrangement is called a ***Controlled Business Arrangement*** (CBA). When an agent refers a borrower to a CBA the broker must ensure that the borrower understands the relationship between the agent and the CBA and that the borrower may wish to shop for the services elsewhere. The agent cannot receive a referral fee from the CBA, although the agent is entitled to participate in any profits made by the CBA, the same as any owner of a business.

When RESPA applies to a transaction, the buyer cannot be required to obtain financing from any particular lender, nor may the buyer be required to secure title insurance from any particular title insurance company. Note that the seller and the real estate agent cannot require the buyer to secure these services from a particular provider, but there is nothing wrong with the seller or the agent making suggestions or giving the buyer price and quality information relative to providers of financing and title insurance.

Exercise b

The Real Estate Settlement Procedures Act applies to all loans to acquire a _____ - to _____ - family residential property when the loan will be a _____ lien and made by a _____ _____ lender. The Act requires lenders to give borrowers a _____ _____ _____ of closing costs within three days of the loan application. The lender must also give borrowers a booklet which explains the borrowers' rights and encourages borrowers to _____for the services they need. A real estate agent must disclose to the borrower if the agent has an _____ interest in another entity to which the agent refers the borrower. The Act prohibits _____ .

The Equal Credit Opportunity Act

In 1974 Congress passed the ***Equal Credit Opportunity Act*** (ECOA) as Title VII of the Consumer Credit Protection Act. Similar to the Truth in Lending Act, ECOA authorizes the Board of Governors of the Federal Reserve Bank to create such reasonable regulations as are necessary to implement the purposes of the Act. Pursuant to this authority, the Board created Federal Reserve Regulation B. Lenders must comply with both the Equal Credit Opportunity Act and with Federal Reserve Regulation B.

The Equal Credit Opportunity Act requires the extension of credit without regard to race, color, religion, national origin, sex, marital status, age (provided the applicant is of legal age), the fact that all or part of the applicant's income is derived from public assistance, or that the applicant has in good faith exercised any rights under the Consumer Credit Protection Act.

Discrimination under the Equal Credit Opportunity Act includes not only refusal to grant credit, but also discouraging an applicant to apply for credit because the applicant falls into one of the protected categories listed above.

When creditors file reports with a credit reporting agency, if the account is a joint account of a husband and wife, the report must be made in both names and the credit reporting agency must maintain separate files for each spouse. Creditors are not permitted to ask the borrower's marital status and credit applications must be neutral as to sex and marital status. When creditors use loan rating systems, they cannot include sex or marital status as factors.

When an applicant is married, or formerly married, creditors cannot ask for credit information about the applicant's spouse, unless the applicant is relying upon child support or alimony from the spouse. If an applicant who receives child support or alimony does not wish to reveal it to the creditor, the creditor cannot require that it be disclosed, or discriminate if it is not disclosed. However, if it is not revealed, then the creditor need not count it as income in making the credit decision.

Creditors cannot ask an applicant about child-bearing plans or birth control practices. If the applicant, or the spouse of an applicant is of child-bearing age, the creditor violates the law by assuming that the applicant might experience even a temporary interruption in income as a result of child bearing. However, the creditor may ask about the number and ages of the applicant's children and other dependents.

If a credit application is denied, the creditor must give notice to the applicant and the notice must state the specific reason. Statements such as "failed to score high enough on our point-scoring system" or "we have changed our loan policy" are not sufficient.

The Equal Credit Opportunity Act contains specific provisions prohibiting real estate agents from discriminating or discouraging applications because the applicant is a member of a protected category.

Exercise c

The Equal Credit Opportunity Act bars discrimination based on race, color, religion, sex, _____ , marital status, that an applicant's income is from _____ _____ , or that the applicant has exercised any consumer rights under the law. Discrimination includes _____ a potential applicant from applying for credit because the person is a member of a protected category.

Credit reports for joint accounts must be made in both names separately. Creditors are not allowed to ask the applicant's _____ _____ and if an applicant is or was married, the creditor cannot ask for credit information on the applicant's spouse unless the applicant is relying on _____ _____ or _____ . The creditor cannot require an applicant to disclose income from _____ _____ or _____ . Creditors are also prohibited from asking about an applicant's _____-_____ plans and a creditor is not allowed to assume that

an applicant's income will be interrupted because of _____ - _____ .
Real estate agents are also prohibited from _____ or _____ appli-
cants based on the fact that they are members of one of the protected categories.

The Community Reinvestment Act

The Community Reinvestment Act requires regulated lenders to serve the communities in which they operate and prohibits **redlining**. Redlining is the practice of refusing to lend in certain areas based on the fact that people living in the areas belong to a protected category.

Lenders must also prepare a map of the community in which they are located and the map must include all low and moderate income areas. Each lender must then file a statement with the government listing the types of credit they offer and how much they have actually extended in each area in their community.

The Fair Credit Reporting Act

The Fair Credit Reporting Act was enacted in 1970. Its purpose is to ensure fair practices in credit reporting. As a result of its passage, consumers now have the right to know the contents of their credit file. Consumers may also make a statement disputing or explaining derogatory information in their file and the credit bureau must include the statement in any reports it issues.

The Fair Credit Reporting Act differentiates between a **credit report** and an **investigative report**. A credit report is ordinary computerized credit information, where an investigative report includes information gained by specific inquiries made by the reporting agency. A credit report can be ordered on anyone, with or without their permission, provided the person ordering the report has a legitimate business purpose. An investigative report, on the other hand, cannot be ordered without notice to the loan applicant and their permission.

Usury laws

The maximum amount of interest which a lender is allowed to charge is the **usury rate**. Although many states still set usury rates, they have been largely discontinued in Oregon. The rationale for eliminating usury laws is that they discourage venture capital and loans to marginal borrowers. If a lender cannot obtain a yield commensurate with the risk, then the lender will not make the loan. Venture capital is essential for the production of new jobs and industry. Therefore, usury laws hurt working people more than any other group.

Oregon does recognize a **legal rate** of interest. The legal rate (not to be confused with the usury rate) is the rate which applies when interest is called for, yet the amount is not specified. For example, if you sue someone for damages resulting from a car accident and obtain a judgment, you will be entitled to interest on the judgment until paid. Since there is no pre-agreed upon interest rate, the legal rate will apply. The legal rate is set by statute in Oregon and is currently 9%.

Private Mortgage Insurance Act

The **Private Mortgage Insurance Act** was passed on July 29, 1999 and requires that lenders inform borrowers at closing that they have private mortgage insurance (PMI), what the insurance is, and how and when the borrower can cancel it. After that, the borrower must be notified annually by the lender about when the borrower can cancel the PMI.

The law applies only to loans made after July 29, 1999. However, both Fannie Mae and Freddie Mac have adopted the policy that the borrower is entitled to cancellation of the PMI once the midpoint of the loan is reached, even for loans made prior to July 29, 1999.

For loans made after July 29, 1999 the law states that after the borrower has paid off 20 percent of the original value of the house, the borrower can contact the lender and ask to have the PMI canceled. And once there is 22 percent equity in the house the lender must automatically cancel the PMI coverage. Loans insured by the FHA are exempt from the law.

There are two ways to prove that the equity in the property is high enough to cancel the PMI. The simplest is when the loan balance has been paid down to the 78% level. There is no way the lender can argue about this – the loan has been paid down to that level and the borrower is entitled to cancellation of the PMI by law.

As an alternative, the borrower can prove that the equity is high enough by hiring an appraiser to prove that the value has increased. Note that the law allows the lender to choose the appraiser, so the borrower is advised to contact the lender and obtain a list of approved appraisers before incurring the expense of an appraisal.

Nationwide there are only eight insurers who provide PMI insurance. The existence of these insurers has made low down-payment mortgage loans available for millions of buyers who would never have been able to save a large enough down payment to purchase their first home. Private mortgage insurance has been a godsend to the real estate and mortgage lending industries. The purpose of the Private Mortgage Insurance Act is to ensure that lenders use it fairly and wisely.

Exercise d

The Community Reinvestment Act prohibits _____ and also requires lenders to file reports on the number of loans they make in low and moderate income neighborhoods.

The Fair Credit Reporting Act requires credit reporting agencies to allow consumers access to their _____ _____ . Consumers are allowed to make a _____ and have it included when credit information is reported. Creditors must _____ consumers before ordering a credit report.

The maximum rate allowed by law is called the _____ rate. The rate that is applied when interest is called for, but the rate is not specified, is called the _____ rate.

The _____ _____ _____ Act requires lenders to cancel the _____ _____ _____ when the borrower's loan balance is less than _____ of the value, to notify borrowers at closing when the loan is covered by _____ _____ _____ , and to notify borrowers _____ as to how close they are to being able to cancel the insurance.

⚲ KEY TERMS

The key to understanding any new field is the vocabulary used in that field. To maximize your comprehension of the material presented in this chapter, be sure you know the meaning and significance of the following terms. Remember that the majority of test questions primarily test knowledge of vocabulary.

Affiliated Business Arrangement Disclosure | Good faith estimate

Affiliated Business Arrangement Disclosure   Good faith estimate
Annual Escrow Statement   Investigative report
Annual percentage rate   Legal rate
Community Reinvestment Act   Mortgage Servicing Statement
Controlled business arrangement   Private Mortgage Insurance Act
Credit report   Redlining
Cushion   Right of rescission
Equal Credit Opportunity Act   Servicing Transfer Statement
Escrow account   Total amount financed
Fair Credit Reporting Act   Total finance charge
Impound account   Truth in Lending Act
Initial Escrow Statement   Uniform Settlement Statement
Federally related lender   Usury rate

❓ ANSWERS

To chapter exercises. If you couldn't figure out what to put in the blanks, find the answer here!

Exercise a

The Truth in Lending Act and Federal Reserve Regulation Z *(choose one)* ❑ *do* ■ *do not* set the maximum interest rates lenders can charge. The law applies to all lenders who regularly extend or ___ARRANGE___ credit in the normal course of their business. Exempted loans include personal property loans over $ ___25,000___ , loans of ___FOUR___ or fewer installments, as well as loans for ___BUSINESS___ , ___COMMERCIAL___ and ___AGRICULTURAL___ purposes. Loans are also exempt if there is no ___FINANCE___ ___CHARGE___ . In advertising of credit terms, real estate agents need make no disclosure unless full disclosure is triggered. Which of the following statements in an ad would trigger full disclosure?

❑   Listed at only $195,000"   ❑   "Name Your Terms"
❑   "Low, low down payment"   ■   "Total Payoff in 10 Years!"
■   "Total Finance Charge $232,565"   ■   "Only $965 per month PITI"

When calculating the total finance charge for a mortgage, which of the following must be included?

■   A two point loan fee   ❑   Late payment fees
❑   The down payment   ❑   The appraisal report fee
❑   Recording fees   ■   The mortgage insurance premium

Exercise b

The Real Estate Settlement Procedures Act applies to all loans to acquire a ___ONE___ - to ___FOUR___ - family residential property when the loan will be a ___FIRST___ lien and made by a ___FEDERALLY___ ___RELATED___ lender. The Act requires lenders to give borrowers a ___GOOD___ ___FAITH___ ___ESTIMATE___ of closing costs within three days of the loan application. The lender must also give bor-

rowers a booklet which explains the borrowers' rights and encourages borrowers to ____SHOP____ *for the services they need. A real estate agent must disclose to the borrower if the agent has an* _____OWNERSHIP_____ *interest in another entity to which the agent refers the borrower. The Act prohibits* ____KICKBACKS____ *.*

Exercise c

The Equal Credit Opportunity Act bars discrimination based on race, color, religion, sex, __AGE__ *, marital status, that an applicant's income is from* ____PUBLIC____ ____ASSISTANCE____ *, or that the applicant has exercised any consumer rights under the law. Discrimination includes* ____DISCOURAGING____ *a potential applicant from applying for credit because the person is a member of a protected category.*

Credit reports for joint accounts must be made in both names separately. Creditors are not allowed to ask the applicant's ____MARITAL____ ____STATUS____ *and if an applicant is or was married, the creditor cannot ask for credit information on the applicant's spouse unless the applicant is relying on* ____CHILD____ ____SUPPORT____ *or* ____ALIMONY____ *. The creditor cannot require an applicant to disclose income from* ____CHILD____ ____SUPPORT____ *or* ____ALIMONY____ *. Creditors are also prohibited from asking about an applicant's* ____CHILD____ - ____BEARING____ *plans and a creditor is not allowed to assume that an applicant's income will be interrupted because of* ____CHILD____ - ____BEARING____ *.*

Real estate agents are also prohibited from ____DISCRIMINATING____ *or* ____DISCOURAGING____ *applicants based on the fact that they are members of one of the protected categories.*

Exercise d

The Community Reinvestment Act prohibits ____REDLINING____ *and also requires lenders to file reports on the number of loans they make in low and moderate income neighborhoods.*

The Fair Credit Reporting Act requires credit reporting agencies to allow consumers access to their ____CREDIT____ ____REPORT____ *. Consumers are allowed to make a* ____STATEMENT____ *and have it included when credit information is reported. Creditors must* ____NOTIFY____ *consumers before ordering a credit report.*

The maximum rate allowed by law is called the ____USURY____ *rate. The rate that is applied when interest is called for, but the rate is not specified, is called the* ____LEGAL____ *rate.*

The ____PRIVATE____ ____MORTGAGE____ ____INSURANCE____ *Act requires lenders to cancel the* ____PRIVATE____ ____MORTGAGE____ ____INSURANCE____ *when the borrower's loan balance is less than* _78%_ *of the value, to notify borrowers at closing when the loan is covered by* ____PRIVATE____ ____MORTGAGE____ ____INSURANCE____ *, and to notify borrowers* ____ANNUALLY____ *as to how close they are to being able to cancel the insurance.*

PRACTICE QUESTIONS

The following practice questions are representative of the questions you will find on the final examination and on the licensing examinations given by the Oregon Real Estate Agency.

1. Federal Reserve Board's Regulation Z (Truth in Lending)
   I. controls the maximum interest rate that can be charged on a mortgage loan.
   II. requires disclosure to consumers of the effective interest rate charged, expressed as an annual percentage rate.
   (A) I only   (C) Both I and II
   (B) II only   (D) Neither I nor II

2. The purpose of the Truth in Lending Act is to
   (A) protect the lender against credit losses.
   (B) establish uniform interest rates for FHA and federal GI loans.
   (C) establish credit approval standards for federal loans.
   (D) make information available concerning the cost of credit.

3. The primary purpose of the Truth in Lending Act (Regulation Z) is to
   (A) save the general public money in their installment purchases.
   (B) establish a more uniform set of charges.
   (C) disclose to the consumer the cost and conditions of the installment purchase.
   (D) assist the federal government in controlling, "shady" lending practices.

4. Regulation Z of the Federal Reserve Board, the so-called Truth in Lending Law, requires lenders to inform borrowers about
   (A) finance charges.
   (B) usury rates.
   (C) minimum and maximum interest rates.
   (D) mortgage instruments.

5. The Federal Reserve Regulation Z (Truth in Lending) prohibits
   I. the advertising of credit terms.
   II. advertising in general terms such as "reasonable monthly payments."
   (A) I only   (C) Both I and II
   (B) II only   (D) Neither I nor II

6. The purpose of "Truth in Lending" (Regulation Z) is to
   (A) protect the lender against credit losses.
   (B) establish uniform interest rates.
   (C) establish standards for the approval of credit applications.
   (D) make information available concerning the cost of credit.

7. The purpose of Regulation Z, the Truth in Lending Law, is to
   (A) assure a meaningful disclosure of credit costs.
   (B) establish a maximum annual percentage rate.
   (C) regulate usurious charges for credit.
   (D) limit the cost of credit to the consumer.

8. Regulation Z of the Truth in Lending Act
   (A) establishes loan interest rates.
   (B) limits the amounts that may be loaned.
   (C) requires loan cost revelations.
   (D) restricts loan closing costs.

9. Truth in Lending laws apply to
   (A) commercial loan transactions involving real property.
   (B) residential real estate mortgages.
   (C) all personal property transactions.
   (D) real property loans made to corporations.

10. The Truth in Lending law seeks to
    (A) limit the number of discount points to be charged by lenders.
    (B) limit the interest rate charged on mortgages.
    (C) disclose the effective interest charged and express it as an annual percentage rate.
    (D) steer residential mortgage borrowers to savings and loan associations instead of commercial banks.

11. The Truth in Lending Laws do not apply unless the loan in question
    I. contains more than four installments.
    II. is for personal, family or household purposes.
    (A) I only   (C) Both I and II
    (B) II only   (D) Neither I nor II

12. The Truth in Lending laws apply to all loans except
    (A) commercial loans.
    (B) assumptions of existing loans.
    (C) refinance loans.
    (D) A and B above.

13. Truth in Lending laws are applicable to
    (A) commercial transactions involving real property.
    (B) residential real estate mortgages.
    (C) all personal property transactions.
    (D) unconscionable contracts.

14. The Truth in Lending Law (Regulation Z), a portion of the Federal Consumer Protection Act, became effective July 1, 1969. Regulation Z applies to real estate loans for
    (A) personal, family and household purposes.
    (B) agricultural purposes.
    (C) business purposes.
    (D) both A and B.

15. According to the federal Truth in Lending Act, which of the following applicants for a $230,000 first loan must be told the annual percentage rate of the loan by the lending agency?
    I. An applicant for a residential loan
    II. An applicant for a commercial loan
    (A) I only   (C) Both I and II
    (B) II only   (D) Neither I nor II

16. Under the Truth in Lending laws the total amount of the finance charge need not be disclosed
    (A) on first trust deed loans used for the acquisition of the borrower's personal residence.
    (B) in advertising by real estate brokers.
    (C) on commercial loans to corporations.
    (D) on either B or C.

17. Under Truth in Lending laws, all of the following could be credit "arrangers" or "extenders" except
    (A) real estate brokers.
    (B) subdividers carrying purchase money loans on subdivided lots.
    (C) investors purchasing existing trust deed loans.
    (D) mortgage companies.

18. The disclosure requirements of Truth in Lending laws apply to real estate agents if they
    I. assist the buyer in filling out a loan application.
    II. accept a commission from a lender for securing the loan.
    (A) I only   (C) Both I and II
    (B) II only   (D) Neither I nor II

19. In order to comply with federal law,
    I. mortgage bankers need not make full disclosure of loan terms if the loan is to be sold in the secondary market.
    II. real estate brokers must be sure the interest rate is reported correctly if they assist the lender by taking the loan application.
    (A) I only   (C) Both I and II
    (B) II only   (D) Neither I nor II

20. The Truth in Lending Act allows a borrower to rescind a loan agreement if the loan is to
    (A) acquire a personal residence.
    (B) acquire an investment property.
    (C) refinance a personal residence.
    (D) do either A or B.

21. Under the provisions of the Truth in Lending laws, a borrower has the right to rescind a loan agreement within three days from the date the
    (A) earnest money receipt was accepted by the seller.
    (B) loan funds are disbursed by the lender.
    (C) loan documents are recorded.
    (D) borrower received the disclosure statement.

22. When a buyer finances the acquisition of a personal residence through an institutional lender, the buyer will have the right to
    I. disclosure of the annual percentage rate.
    II. rescind the transaction within three business days.
    (A) I only
    (B) II only
    (C) Both I and II
    (D) Neither I nor II

23. The Truth in Lending Laws provide that the cost of credit on certain amounts must be disclosed to the borrower as
    (A) a monthly percentage rate.
    (B) a minimum percentage rate.
    (C) a maximum percentage rate.
    (D) an annual percentage rate.

24. On those loans where the Federal Reserve's Regulation Z (Truth in Lending) applies, the total of the finance charges must be expressed to the nearest ⅛ of 1% as
    (A) an approximate percentage rate.
    (B) an annual percentage rate.
    (C) a minimum percentage rate.
    (D) a maximum percentage rate.

25. When calculating the annual percentage rate for a disclosure statement under the Truth in Lending Act, which of the following items would not be included?
    (A) Discount points
    (B) Tax prorations paid by the buyer
    (C) Loan fees paid by the buyer
    (D) Service charges paid by the buyer

26. The Federal Reserve Board's Regulation Z (Truth in Lending) requires the annual percentage rate of a real estate related loan to reflect
    (A) interest, loan initiation fee, and discount points.
    (B) title fees, loan service costs, and closing costs.
    (C) appraisal fee, prorated property tax, and special assessments.
    (D) all of the above.

27. Which of the following would not be disclosed when calculating an APR?
    (A) A loan broker's fee paid by the buyer
    (B) Buyer's tax prorates
    (C) Buyer's loan fees
    (D) Loan service charges paid by the buyer

28. When computing an annual percentage rate for disclosure purposes under Regulation Z (Truth in Lending), include as finance charges
    I. the service charge for making the loan.
    II. mortgage insurance premiums.
    (A) I only
    (B) II only
    (C) Both I and II
    (D) Neither I nor II

29. When calculating an annual percentage rate, which of the following must be included?
    (A) Recording fees to be paid by the buyer
    (B) Fee for the mortgagee's extended coverage title insurance policy
    (C) Notary fees to be paid by the buyer
    (D) Discount points to be paid by the buyer

30. When the interest rate is disclosed it must be stated to the nearest
    (A) ⅒ of 1%.
    (B) ⅛ of 1%.
    (C) ¼ of 1%.
    (D) ½ of 1%.

31. The most important thing for a real estate agent to know about Truth in Lending laws is
    (A) advertising requirements.
    (B) the amount of the finance charge when advertising loan terms.
    (C) the annual percentage rate.
    (D) the current federal reserve discount rate.

32. A broker wishes to advertise a listing which has attractive terms. Which of the following may not be stated in the ad without full disclosure?
    (A) "Easy financing terms"
    (B) "Monthly payment only $575"
    (C) "Low down payment"
    (D) "7½% APR loan available"

33. If unaccompanied by other facts, an advertisement under Truth in Lending may state
    (A) "low down payment."
    (B) "$200 down."
    (C) "6½% interest."
    (D) "$3,000 down."

34. Under Regulation Z (Truth in Lending) which of the following ads would be legal without full disclosure of all credit terms?
    I. "Low down payment on contract Seller will carry contract with small down payment to qualified buyer."
    II. "Only $2,000 down! will move you into this lovely home. Monthly payments of $350."
    (A) I only
    (B) II only
    (C) Both I and II
    (D) Neither I nor II

35. Which of the following terms may not be used in advertising, according to Regulation Z (Truth in Lending) without full disclosure of all credit terms?
    (A) "Small down payment accepted"
    (B) "Financing available at 11% interest"
    (C) "Liberal terms available"
    (D) "VA or FHA financing available"

36. A real estate office could advertise which of the following without full disclosure of all credit terms and be in compliance with Regulation Z (Truth in Lending)?
    I. "Small down payment OK"
    II. "Only $1,000 down"
    (A) I only
    (B) II only
    (C) Both I and II
    (D) Neither I nor II

37. Under Truth in Lending, it is permissible to advertise which of the following statements without disclosing all the terms of the credit?
    (A) "$2,000 down"
    (B) "10% interest"
    (C) "Reasonable monthly terms"
    (D) "3% interest"

38. When writing an ad, which of the following would be acceptable without any further disclosure?
    (A) "Assume 7½% mortgage"
    (B) "Assume 7½% APR loan"
    (C) "Assume 7½% first trust deed"
    (D) "Assume 7½% APR first mortgage"

39. In advertising, even if the real estate broker is not the source of the loan, the broker must state
    I. all of the items which make up the finance charge.
    II. a description of the security interest the lender will hold.
    (A) I only
    (B) II only
    (C) Both I and II
    (D) Neither I nor II

40. Which of the following must be disclosed according to Truth in Lending statutes?
    (A) The finance charge as an annual percentage rate
    (B) The number, amount and timing of payments
    (C) The amount charged for any late payment
    (D) All of the above

41. The Truth in Lending Act requires disclosure of discount points paid by the
    I. seller.   II. buyer.
    (A) I only
    (B) II only
    (C) Both I and II
    (D) Neither I nor II

42. The disclosure statement given by a lender to a buyer of a personal residence must include all of the following costs of the financing except the
    (A) total of all the payments over the life of the loan.
    (B) fact that there is a prepayment privilege charge.
    (C) attorney's fees for the lender, which the buyer will not pay.
    (D) annual percentage rate.

43. Which of the following must be disclosed according to the Truth in Lending Statutes?
    I. The number, amount and timing of payments
    II. The amount charged for any late payments
    III. The finance charge as an annual percentage rate
    (A) I only
    (B) I and II only
    (C) I and III only
    (D) I, II and III

44. The disclosure statement used under the Truth in Lending Act (Regulation Z) is concerned with the
    I. real estate taxes assessed on the property.
    II. legal fees charged to prepare the deed to the property.
    (A) I only
    (B) II only
    (C) Both I and II
    (D) Neither I nor II

45. Under the Truth in Lending Act, all of the following must be in the disclosure statement except
(A) total finance charges.
(B) payoff penalties.
(C) lawyer's fees.
(D) annual percentage rate.

46. Under the Truth in Lending Law, which of the following need not be disclosed on the purchase of a single family dwelling that the owner will occupy?
(A) The recording fees
(B) The prepayment penalty
(C) The length of the loan
(D) The amount of the monthly payment

47. A first mortgage is used to finance a purchase of a residential dwelling. According to Regulation Z (Truth in Lending) the lender must disclose to the borrower the
I. annual percentage rate of the loan.
II. finance charge payable during the term of the loan.
(A) I only
(B) II only
(C) Both I and II
(D) Neither I nor II

48. Which of the following is not regarded as a "finance charge" under the Truth in Lending provisions?
(A) Loan fee
(B) Loan finder's fee
(C) Borrower's attorney fees
(D) Service charges

49. Which of the following would be considered part of the financing charge when figuring the annual percentage rate under the Truth in Lending Act (Regulation Z)?
(A) Credit report fees
(B) Title insurance
(C) Notary fee
(D) Discount points

50. According to Regulation Z (Truth in Lending),
I. an advertisement offering new homes at "$1,000 down" is in violation if the seller will not usually accept this amount as a down payment.
II. the Federal Trade Commission is responsible for enforcement of the regulation.
(A) I only
(B) II only
(C) Both I and II
(D) Neither I nor II

51. Who enforces the Truth in Lending Law?
(A) Fair Employment Practices Commission
(B) Federal Trade Commission
(C) Real Estate Commissioner
(D) Secretary of State

52. In real estate, the initials "RESPA" stand for
(A) Real Estate Special Protection Account.
(B) Real Estate Settlement Procedures Act.
(C) Real Estate Sales Production Accounting.
(D) Real Estate Services Provisions Act.

53. The Real Estate Settlement Procedures Act (RESPA) is designed to regulate which of the following?
I. Disclosures of closing information
II. Procedures for recording titles to real estate
(A) I only
(B) II only
(C) Both I and II
(D) Neither I nor II

54. The Real Estate Settlement Procedures Act (RESPA) provides
(A) that real estate advertisements must include the annual percentage rate, including all charges.
(B) a secondary market for mortgage loans.
(C) that the mortgagor must be given an estimate of the closing costs before the time of closing.
(D) that real estate syndicates must obey "blue-sky" laws.

55. Which of the following lenders must comply with the provisions of the Real Estate Settlement Procedures Act (RESPA)?
(A) A lender who lends more than $1,000,000 per year
(B) A lender who has deposits which are federally insured
(C) A lender who sells to FNMA, FHLMC or GNMA
(D) Any of the above

56. When the loan is to acquire a residence, the Real Estate Settlement Procedures Act would apply to
(A) a first mortgage loan through the Oregon Department of Veterans Affairs.
(B) a second mortgage loan from a finance company.
(C) a land sales contract carried by the seller of the property.
(D) all of the above.

57. The main burden for implementing the provisions of the Real Estate Settlement Procedures Act (RESPA) falls upon
(A) brokers engaged in commercial transactions.
(B) lending institutions making first mortgage loans for residential purchases.
(C) title insurance companies.
(D) sellers in transactions involving land contracts.

58. The Real Estate Settlement Procedures Act (RESPA) applies to the activities of
I. licensed real estate brokers when selling commercial and office buildings.
II. savings and loan institutions lending money on a first mortgage for the purchase of a home by the borrower.
(A) I only
(B) II only
(C) Both I and II
(D) Neither I nor II

59. The federal Real Estate Settlement Procedures Act
(A) applies to all mortgage loans.
(B) is administered by the Federal National Mortgage Association.
(C) requires the use of a Uniform Settlement Statement.
(D) requires lenders to account for referral fees received by firms issuing mortgage insurance.

60. The Real Estate Settlement Procedures Act (RESPA) applies to
(A) second mortgages.
(B) land sales contracts.
(C) equity mortgages.
(D) first mortgages.

61. Under the provisions of the Real Estate Settlement Procedures Act, upon request of the borrower, an escrow is required to give the borrower a copy of the final settlement statement at least
(A) one day before closing.
(B) three days before closing.
(C) five days before closing.
(D) ten days before closing.

62. Under the provisions of the Real Estate Settlement Procedures Act, the maximum amount that an escrow can charge the borrower for preparation of the Uniform Settlement Statement is
(A) $0.00
(B) $25.00
(C) $50.00
(D) $100.00.

63. Under the provisions of the Real Estate Settlement Procedures Act, the maximum amount that a lender can charge the borrower for preparation of the good faith estimate is
(A) $0.00.
(B) $25.00.
(C) $50.00.
(D) $100.00.

64. A lender agrees to pay a fee to a real estate broker in exchange for which the broker will refer all residential borrowers to the lender exclusively. This would be
(A) a violation of federal Truth in Lending Laws.
(B) a violation of the federal Consumer Protection Act.
(C) a violation of RESPA.
(D) legal, provided the real estate broker is also licensed as a mortgage broker.

65. The federal Real Estate Settlement Procedures Act
I. requires the lending institution to give the borrower a good faith estimate of closing costs.
II. applies to first mortgages.
III. applies to seller-financed transactions.
(A) I only
(B) I and II only
(C) I, II and III
(D) II only

66. Which of the following statements regarding the Real Estate Settlement Procedures Act (RESPA) is false?
(A) A Uniform Settlement Statement must be given to the borrower at or before closing.
(B) An information booklet published by HUD (Housing and Urban Development) must be provided to the purchaser by the lender.
(C) The lender must furnish a good faith estimate of likely settlement charges within three days of the loan application.
(D) Its regulations cover all residential mortgages.

67. Which of the following statements about the Real Estate Settlement Procedures Act (RESPA) is false?
    (A) All persons obtaining a federally regulated new mortgage loan to purchase a single family residence must receive a copy of Housing and Urban Development's brochure."
    (B) It covers all sales of one-to four-family residences when the purchaser is obtaining a federally related mortgage loan to purchase the property.
    (C) Real estate brokers may not split a commission with cooperating members of their multiple listing service.
    (D) A lender may not receive a referral fee for sending a seller to a specific title insurance company.

68. A real estate company offers its buyers a complete package of services including title insurance, closing, and financing. This kind of arrangement is known as
    (A) a limited liability company.
    (B) a multiple agency.
    (C) a controlled business arrangement.
    (D) a consolidated real estate company.

69. Under the Fair Credit Reporting Act, when a property manager obtains a credit report on a prospective tenant from a credit reporting agency, the property manager must
    I. first get the permission of the prospective tenant.
    II. provide a copy of the credit report to the prospective tenant upon request.
    (A) I only   (C) Both I and II
    (B) II only   (D) Neither I nor II

70. With respect to the Equal Credit Opportunity Act, a lender may not discriminate against a borrower on the basis of the borrower's
    I. sex.   II. marital status.
    (A) I only   (C) Both I and II
    (B) II only   (D) Neither I nor II

71. The Equal Credit Opportunity Act would prohibit discrimination based on a borrower's
    I. mental or physical handicap.
    II. age.
    (A) I only   (C) Both I and II
    (B) II only   (D) Neither I nor II

72. A married couple make application for a mortgage loan. Which of the following acts by the lender would be a violation of the Equal Credit Opportunity Act?
    I. Not counting the income of the wife because she is of child-bearing age
    II. Refusing to count regular, stable part-time income because of the sex of the earner
    (A) I only   (C) Both I and II
    (B) II only   (D) Neither I nor II

73. May Williams, a divorced woman who has custody of her two children, receives alimony and child support payments from her ex-husband. When she applies for a loan, the lender may
    I. require that she disclose these sources of income or deny her the credit if she refuses.
    II. check up on the reliability and stability of the alimony and child support payments if she needs to income to qualify for the loan.
    (A) I only   (C) Both I and II
    (B) II only   (D) Neither I nor II

74. It would be a violation of the Equal Credit Opportunity Act for a mortgage lender to
    I. deny credit to a married female applicant because she may become pregnant and therefore her source of income may be interrupted.
    II. refuse a loan to a woman on property she owns alone unless her husband also signs.
    (A) I only   (C) Both I and II
    (B) II only   (D) Neither I nor II

75. The Equal Credit Opportunity Act prohibits lenders from
    I. discriminating on the basis of sex.
    II. refusing to grant credit on the basis of the applicant's marital status.
    III. inquiring into the applicant's child-bearing plans.
    (A) I only   (C) I, II and III
    (B) I and II only   (D) II and III only

76. The term "usury" refers to
    (A) the flow of benefits coming from the ownership of real property.
    (B) the remaining economic life of the property.
    (C) the fact that some properties are more useful.
    (D) charging rates of interest in excess of the maximum allowed by law.

77. If a lender charged an interest rate in excess of the legal ceiling, the lender would be in violation of
    (A) the Truth in Lending Act.
    (B) usury statutes.
    (C) the Statute of Frauds.
    (D) Federal Reserve Regulation Z.

78. The amount of interest that is agreed upon between the borrower and the lender is called the
    (A) legal rate.   (C) usury rate.
    (B) contract rate.   (D) statutory rate.

79. If a lender charges over 50% annual interest in Oregon, the lender may have to forfeit
    (A) all the interest on the loan.
    (B) the principal balance of the loan.
    (C) both A and B.
    (D) neither A nor B.

80. The legal rate of interest in Oregon is
    (A) 9%.   (C) 36%.
    (B) 29%.   (D) 50%.

81. A borrower is entitled to cancellation of private mortgage insurance when the loan balance is at what percentage of the value of the property?
    (A) 20%   (C) 78%
    (B) 75%   (D) 80%

ANSWERS

To practice questions. If you chose the wrong letter, here's the right one! The explanations are designed to clarify your understanding.

1. **B** The Truth in Lending Act does not regulate the amounts that a lender may charge. Its sole purpose is to require the lender to disclose to the borrower the costs of the financing. One of the required disclosures is the annual percentage rate, which must be calculated in a manner to make it comparable to an annual percentage rate as disclosed by other lenders.

2. **D** Loans are frequently insured or guaranteed against loss caused by the borrower's default, but such insurance or guarantee is unrelated to the Truth in Lending Act and Federal Reserve Regulation Z. The Truth in Lending Act and Federal Reserve Regulation Z merely require disclosure of the terms and cost of a loan.

3. **C** The Truth in Lending Act does not regulate how much a lender may charge. Its sole purpose is to require disclosure of the costs of financing on consumer loans.

4. **A** The Truth in Lending Act and Federal Reserve Regulation Z require disclosure of financing costs associated with consumer loans.

5. **D** Advertising of credit terms is completely legal under the Truth in Lending Act, as long as full and accurate disclosure is made when the Act requires it. The only difference between general terms and specific statements is that general terms do not trigger full disclosure. Either is permitted.

6. **D** The Truth in Lending Act is a consumer protection law which requires full disclosure of the costs of financing. It does not limit the amount of any charge – it merely requires disclosure.

7. **A** The purpose of the Truth in Lending Act is to require disclosure of the costs of financing on consumer loans. The Act does not regulate in any way how much a lender may charge. Usury laws are always state laws.

8. **C** The Truth in Lending Act and its administrative regulation, Federal Reserve Regulation Z, are disclosure laws. Neither regulates how much a lender may charge for any service, the interest rate charged, or anything else about lending.

9. **B** The Truth in Lending Act is a consumer protection law, therefore it applies only to consumer loans. However, the purpose of the loan is irrelevant – it applies equally to real estate, personal property, and unsecured loans.

10. **C** The purpose of the Truth in Lending Act is to require disclosure of the costs of credit on consumer loans. It does not regulate how much lenders may charge. One of the disclosures is the annual percentage rate, which is the interest rate on the loan expressed as an effective interest rate.

11. **C** The Truth in Lending Act and Federal Reserve Regulation Z are consumer protection laws, and therefore apply only to loans for personal, family or household purposes. Exemptions include loans for business, commercial or agricultural purposes, loans of four or fewer installments and loans where there is no finance charge.

12. **A** As consumer protection laws, the Truth in Lending Act and Federal Reserve Regulation Z apply only to loans for personal, family or household purposes. Exemptions include loans for business or commercial purposes. A lender must make disclosures to a home buyer assuming an existing loan.

13. **B** As a consumer protection law, the Truth in Lending Act exempts commercial and agricultural loans. The purpose of the loan is irrelevant – a loan for a business to buy a single family house is exempt, but the same loan for an individual is not.

14. **A** The Truth in Lending Act is a consumer protection law, therefore it exempts commercial, business and agricultural loans.

15. **A** The Truth in Lending Act is a consumer protection law. All commercial loans are exempt from its provisions.

16. **C** If discloser is required, the total finance charge must be included. The Truth in Lending Act is a consumer protection law, so commercial loans and loans to corporations are exempt.

17. **C** The Truth in Lending Act and Federal Reserve Regulation Z define a lender as one who regularly extends or arranges credit in the normal course of business. Making five loans or more in a year, or having made at least five loans the previous year, qualifies the person or entity as one who regularly extends or arranges credit. Buying a loan,

however, does not make the purchaser an extender or arranger of credit.

18.   **C**   When real estate agents assist a borrower in filling out a loan application or accept commissions from the lender, they are acting as the agents of the lender, and therefore must make all disclosures that would be required of the lender.

19.   **B**   A person or entity who buys a loan is exempt, but the party who originated the loan (i.e., a mortgage banker) is not exempt. The interest rate must always be specified as an annual percentage rate and must be accurate to at least ⅛ of 1%. When real estate agents assist a borrower in filling out a loan application or accept commissions from the lender, they are acting as the agents of the lender, and therefore must make all disclosures that would be required of the lender.

20.   **C**   The Truth in Lending Act allows the borrower the right to rescind the transaction within three business days if the transaction will result in a lien on the borrower's personal residence. Note that a loan to acquire a personal residence will not result in a right of rescission because at the time the loan is made, the property is not yet the borrower's principal residence. Loans for investment, business or commercial purposes are exempt.

21.   **D**   The right of rescission applies only to loans which will result in lien on the borrower's personal residence. The borrower must exercise the right within three banking days of receiving the disclosure statement. If the lender never gives the borrower the disclosure statement, the borrower can rescind any time, even years later. However, "rescission" means all parties must give everything back as though the transaction never took place, so the borrower would have to return the borrowed money.

22.   **A**   The annual percentage rate must always be disclosed for all loans to which the Truth in Lending Act applies. The right of rescission applies to all loans which will result in a lien on the borrower's personal residence. An acquisition loan does not meet this test, because at the time of signing the loan documents, the borrower does not yet own the property.

23.   **D**   The term prescribed by the Truth in Lending Act is "annual percentage rate." Preference is to disclose it as an annual rate, rather than monthly.

24.   **B**   The legal term for the interest rate which the Truth in Lending Act requires disclosure of is "annual percentage rate."

25.   **B**   The annual percentage rate is based on the total finance charge and the original loan balance. The total finance charge includes (in addition to interest) all charges that the lender requires as a condition of granting the credit. However, expenses the borrower pays to others (such as tax prorations to a seller) are not included.

26.   **A**   The annual percentage rate is based on the loan amount and the total finance charge. The total finance charge must include (in addition to interest), service charges, transaction charges, points (discounts) paid by the borrower, including loan fees and assumption fees, appraisal and credit report fees (for non-residential loans only), and mortgage insurance, including FHA and conventional mortgage guaranty insurance. Closing costs paid to entities other than the lender are generally not included.

27.   **B**   Application fees, late payment and other penalty charges, title insurance premiums, document preparation, notarization and recording expenses, taxes and fire insurance premiums and appraisal and credit report fees for residential loans need not be included when calculating the annual percentage rate (APR).

28.   **C**   The annual percentage rate is based on the loan amount and the total finance charge. The total finance charge must include (in addition to interest), service charges, transaction charges, points (discounts) paid by the borrower, including loan fees and assumption fees, appraisal and credit report fees (for non-residential loans only), and mortgage insurance, including FHA and conventional mortgage guaranty insurance. Closing costs paid to entities other than the lender are generally not included.

29.   **D**   Items which must be included when calculating the annual percentage rate (APR) include service, transaction or activity charges, points paid by the buyer (but not if paid by the seller), appraisal and credit report fees (but not if the loan is residential) and mortgage insurance premiums. Application fees, late payment and other penalty charges, title insurance premiums, document preparation, notarization and recording expenses, taxes and fire insurance premiums and appraisal and credit report fees for residential loans need not be included.

30.   **B**   The interest rate must always be specified as an annual percentage rate (APR) and must be accurate to at least ⅛ of 1%.

31.   **A**   Real estate agents rarely act as agents of the lender, so the portion of the Truth in Lending Act which is of major importance to real estate agents is

that part which deals with advertising the availability of credit. The annual percentage rate (APR) is almost always available from the lender.

32. **B** Advertising need contain no disclosures at all unless a specific fact about the financing is included, other than the sales price or the APR. General statements do not trigger full disclosure. Stating the exact amount of the payment would, therefore, trigger full disclosure.

33. **A** Specific statements about financing (other than the annual percentage rate or the sales price) trigger the requirement for full disclosure. General statements do not trigger full disclosure.

34. **A** Under the Truth in Lending Act, specific statements about financing (other than the annual percentage rate or the sales price) trigger the requirement for full disclosure. General statements do not trigger the requirement for full disclosure. Private party loans are exempt.

35. **B** Under the Truth in Lending Act, stating the annual percentage rate or the sales price does not trigger the requirement for full disclosure. All other specific statements require full disclosure. General statements do not trigger full disclosure. If "11% interest" were stated as an annual percentage rate it would not trigger full disclosure.

36. **A** Full disclosure is required only if a triggering phrase or statement is included in the advertising. General statements do not trigger full disclosure. Also, the annual percentage rate and the sales price may be stated without triggering full disclosure.

37. **C** Full disclosure is triggered if any specific statement is made other than the annual percentage rate or the sales price. General statements do not trigger full disclosure.

38. **B** The terms "mortgage" and "trust deed" refer to specific documents, so they trigger full disclosure. The term "loan" is generic to all financing instruments and does not trigger full disclosure. Furthermore, stating an interest rate which is not calculated as an annual percentage rate (APR) triggers full disclosure.

39. **D** When advertising credit terms, the broker must disclose the APR, the down payment, the number, period for, and amount of the payments, the total finance charge, and any additional special features of the loan such as call features, balloon payments, adjustable interest rates, and the like. When extending credit, lenders must make further disclosure as the lender's identity, all of the items which make up the finance charge and the description of the security for the loan, among other matters. These additional items are not required, however, when advertising credit.

40. **D** The lender must disclose to the borrower the annual percentage rate, the total finance charge, the down payment, the number of payments and the amount and period for the payments, any special charges, plus any special terms such as prepayment penalties, balloon payments, due on sale clauses, and so on.

41. **B** As long as the borrower does not pay an expense, the disclosure need not include the item.

42. **C** In lending, borrowers must be given all the disclosures which must be given in advertising, and in addition the total of the payments, among other matters. Expenses which the borrower will not pay, however, never need be disclosed.

43. **D** When full disclosure is triggered, the lender must disclose to the borrower the annual percentage rate, the total finance charge, the down payment, the number of payments and the amount and period for the payments, any special charges, plus any special terms such as prepayment penalties, balloon payments, due on sale clauses, and so on.

44. **D** The Truth in Lending Act requires lenders to disclose the costs of financing. The lender need not disclose expenses the borrower will incur if they are to be paid to others and not to the lender.

45. **C** When full disclosure is triggered the lender must disclose to the borrower the annual percentage rate, the total finance charge, the down payment, the number of payments and the amount and period for the payments, plus any special terms such as prepayment penalties, balloon payments, due on sale clauses, and so on.

46. **A** The Truth in Lending Act requires disclosure of the cost of credit, not closing expenses that will not be paid to the lender. Closing expenses must be disclosed as well, but the law which requires their disclosure is the Real Estate Settlement Procedures Act.

47. **C** Full disclosure requirements include the interest rate as an annual percentage rate, the total finance charge, the down payment, the number of payments and the amount and period when they are due, and any other special terms, such as prepayment privilege charges, balloon payments, due on sale clauses, and so on.

48. **C** The total finance charge must be calculated by adding certain charges to the interest. These include discount points and loan fees paid by the borrower, service and transaction charges, loan origi-

nation fees, loan finder's fees, mortgage guaranty insurance fees, and the like. If the borrower retains an attorney, it is not included because it was an expense at the discretion of the borrower, not required by the lender.

49. **D** The total finance charge must include (in addition to interest), service charges, transaction charges, points (discounts) paid by the borrower, including loan fees and assumption fees, appraisal and credit report fees (for non-residential loans only), and mortgage insurance, including FHA and conventional mortgage guaranty insurance. Closing costs paid to entities other than the lender are generally not included.

50. **C** As the name would imply, the Truth in Lending Act prohibits false statements in advertising of credit terms. Although many federal agencies have partial jurisdiction over the Truth in Lending Act and Federal Reserve Regulation Z, most of the regulation is performed by the Federal Trade Commission.

51. **B** There are numerous federal agencies which administer the Truth in Lending Act and Federal Reserve Regulation Z, however, the majority of the regulation (especially with respect to real estate agents) is through the Federal Trade Commission.

52. **B** The acronym "RESPA" stands for "Real Estate Settlement Procedures Act." There are no such things as a "Real Estate Special Protection Act," a "Real Estate Services Provisions Act" or "Real Estate Sales Production Accounting."

53. **A** The main thrust of the Real Estate Settlement Procedures Act is to ensure open competition in the lending process and to encourage borrowers to shop for services needed in acquiring a personal residence. Therefore lenders are required to give the borrower a good faith estimate of closing costs at the time of loan application.

54. **C** Disclosure of annual percentage rates is required by the Truth in Lending Act, not the Real Estate Settlement Procedures Act (RESPA). The purpose of RESPA is to encourage buyers of owner-occupied personal residences to shop for services they need in closing the transaction. Therefore, RESPA requires lenders to give the borrower a good faith estimate of closing costs at loan application.

55. **D** All "federally related" lenders must comply with the Real Estate Settlement Procedures Act. A federally related lender is one who is federally chartered, insured by any federal agency, eligible to make FHA, federal GI or Rural Economic Community Development Corporation loans, eligible to sell loans to Fannie Mae, Freddie Mac or Ginnie Mae, or makes over $1 million in residential loans a year.

56. **A** The Real Estate Settlement Procedures Act applies only to loans which are first liens on a property which is to be the borrower's residence, and only if the residence is a one- to four-family structure. All other loans, including second mortgages, are exempt.

57. **B** Anyone involved in a loan transaction to which the Real Estate Settlement Procedures Act (RESPA) applies may be impacted, but the main thrust of RESPA is to ensure open competition in the lending process and to encourage borrowers to shop for services needed in acquiring a personal residence. Private party financing is exempt, as are all commercial loans.

58. **B** The Real Estate Settlement Procedures Act applies strictly to first mortgage loans from institutional lenders for the acquisition of a one- to four-family home which will be owner-occupied.

59. **C** The Real Estate Settlement Procedures Act exempts numerous mortgage loans, including, for example, private party loans. Enforcement is through the Department of Housing and Urban Development. At loan application the lender must provide the borrower with a good faith estimate of closing costs which must refer to the lines on the Uniform Settlement Statement.

60. **D** The Real Estate Settlement Procedures Act applies strictly to first mortgages from institutional lenders to acquire an owner-occupied personal residence.

61. **A** Upon request of the borrower, the closing agent (usually the escrow) must give the buyer a copy of the final closing statement on the Uniform Settlement Statement form not less than one day before closing. The closing agent is prohibited from charging any extra fee for this service.

62. **A** The closing agent is prohibited by the Real Estate Settlement Procedures Act from charging any special fee for preparation of the settlement statement.

63. **A** Lenders are prohibited from charging for the good faith estimate, the same as closing agents are prohibited from charging any special fee for preparing the final settlement statement or for providing a copy to the borrower prior to closing at the borrower's request.

64. **C** Receiving a fee without providing a service is a kickback as defined by the Real Estate Settlement Procedures Act (RESPA), and is illegal. The Act applies only to residential loans.

65. **B** The Real Estate Settlement Procedures Act exempts direct loans from sellers (purchase money financing from private parties) and loans other than first liens. It is a disclosure law. At loan application the lender must provide the borrower with a good faith estimate of closing costs which refers to the lines on the Uniform Settlement Statement.

66. **D** The purpose of the Real Estate Settlement Procedures Act (RESPA) is to encourage the borrower to shop for costs associated with purchasing a personal residence. It requires lenders to give the borrower a good faith estimate of closing costs which refers to the lines on the Uniform Settlement Statement and a booklet written by the Department of Housing and Urban Development explaining the statement. The final closing statement must be on the same form. RESPA applies to all first mortgage loans to acquire a home which will be owner-occupied. Private party loans are exempt.

67. **C** The Real Estate Settlement Procedures Act requires lenders to give the borrower a good faith estimate of closing costs which refer to the lines on the Uniform Settlement Statement and a booklet written by the Department of Housing and Urban Development explaining the statement. It applies to all loans from institutional lenders to acquire an owner-occupied personal residence of one to four units, but exempts all other mortgage loans. Kickbacks (such as a fee from a title insurance company to a lender for a referral) are prohibited, but brokers sharing a commission with cooperating brokers is not considered a kickback, even if the buyer pays it.

68. **C** The Real Estate Settlement Procedures Act requires any provider of a service needed in the closing of a loan to disclose to the borrower an ownership interest in another provider of a service if the first provider refers the borrower to the second provider. It further defines a controlled business arrangement as a provider such as a real estate company which offers a package of services from other providers including title insurance, closing, property insurance, and mortgage origination. Controlled business arrangements are legal as long as the relationship is disclosed to the borrower and no fee is charged for the referrals to the other providers.

69. **D** The Fair Credit Reporting Act makes a distinction between a "credit report" and an "investigative report." A credit report is simply computerized information, whereas an investigative report includes information about the applicant's lifestyle and other matters. A creditor, including a property manager or landlord only needs to have legitimate business reason for ordering a credit report and need give the applicant no advance notice before obtaining one. For an investigative report, however, the creditor must obtain the permission of the applicant. The Fair Credit Reporting Act requires credit reporting agencies to give the consumer a copy of their credit report upon request, but does not require lenders to give a copy to their loan applicants, even if the credit is denied.

70. **C** The Equal Credit Opportunity Act prohibits discrimination on the basis of the borrower's race, color, religion, national origin, sex, marital status, age, source of income or that the borrower has in good faith filed a complaint under consumer protection laws.

71. **B** The protected categories under the Equal Credit Opportunity Act are race, color, religion, national origin, sex, marital status, age, source of income or that the borrower has in good faith filed a complaint under consumer protection laws.

72. **C** The Equal Credit Opportunity Act prohibits a lender from presuming that an applicant's income will be interrupted because of child-bearing and from inquiring as to the applicant's child-bearing plans. One of the protected categories under the Act is the sex of the loan applicant.

73. **B** Lenders are prohibited from requiring a borrower to disclose income from child support or alimony. However, if a borrower does not disclose such income, the lender need not count it. If income from child support or alimony is disclosed and the borrower needs the income to qualify for the credit, then the lender is justified in verifying the reliability of the income, including a credit report on the ex-spouse.

74. **C** Married persons are entitled to have credit in their own name and when a creditor reports information on a joint account it must be reported in both names and the credit bureau must keep separate files. A lender cannot deny credit to a married person borrowing alone unless the person does not have sufficient income to qualify for the credit, or the signature of the spouse is required under state laws in order to perfect the lender's security interest in the property. In Oregon, if a married person owns property alone (the spouse is not in title), the lender would not be justified in demanding the spouse's signature.

75. **C** Under the Equal Credit Opportunity Act the protected categories are race, color, religion, national origin, sex, marital status, age, source of income or that the borrower has in good faith filed a complaint under consumer protection laws.

76.   **D**   "Usury" means charging more than the maximum rate allowed by law. Usury statutes vary from state to state. In Oregon, usury laws have been repealed, so a lender can charge any amount of interest the borrower agrees to.

77.   **B**   There are no federal laws setting the maximum rates a lender may charge. Many states have such laws, which are called usury statutes. Oregon repealed its usury statutes, so lenders are free to charge whatever the borrower agrees to.

78.   **B**   The usury rate is the maximum allowable rate (no ceiling in Oregon), the contract rate is the actual rate agreed upon in the loan contract, and the legal rate is the rate which applies when interest is called for but the rate is not specified by contract.

79.   **D**   In those states where there are usury statutes, the usual penalty is either forfeiture of interest (all interest or at least the usurious portion), or even of the principal balance. Since Oregon no longer has usury laws, charging 50% interest is legal.

80.   **A**   In Oregon, the legal rate is set by the Legislature. The current legal rate is 9%. Do not confuse "legal rate," which is the rate called for when the contract between the parties fails to specify a rate, and "usury rate," which is the maximum rate allowed by law. Oregon has no usury laws.

81.   **C**   The Private Mortgage Insurance Act of 1999 requires lenders to cancel private mortgage insurance on loans when the loan balance is 78% or less of the value of the property. The lender does not have to cancel the private mortgage insurance until the borrower requests it.

REAL ESTATE APPRAISAL

THE STUDY OF APPRAISAL IS ESSENTIAL FOR ANYONE ASSOCIATED WITH REAL estate. Brokers not only need to understand how market forces affect the value of their listings, but they must also be sufficiently conversant with appraisal theory and practice to be able to interpret professional appraisal reports to their clients. This short introduction presents an overview of real estate appraisal sufficient to meet the needs of a beginner, and to point the direction for additional study for those who wish to appraise professionally.

In any introductory work on appraisal, the first need is to define what an appraisal is. A synonym for *appraisal* is *valuation*. That is, the function of a professional appraiser is to estimate the value of the property. Note that appraisers do not "set" value, nor do they determine or create value. Only the activity of buyers and sellers in the open market can create value. Appraisers merely estimate the value of a property from the evidence they find in the marketplace and report their findings to the client.

The public perceives of an appraiser as being hired by buyers or sellers. Although buyers and sellers are certainly common appraisal clients, the vast majority of appraisal assignments today are ordered by financial institutions. Because many appraisals are required by financial institutions and by government agencies, many appraisers work as full-time employees. Yet others, including many of those who appraise for lending institutions, operate independently.

Appraisers who take appraisal assignments independently are sometimes called *fee appraisers* or *independent fee appraisers.*

When an appraiser works independently, the relationship with the client is usually that of *principal* and *agent*. A principal hires an agent because of the agent's special expertise, and frequently grants the agent authority to perform tasks on behalf of the principal. Because of this special relationship, the agent is held to a high standard of loyalty toward the principal – to the exclusion of all others. This is commonly referred to as the agent's ***fiduciary*** duty to the principal. Fiduciary duties include such obligations as full disclosure, confidentiality and due diligence.

While an appraiser usually acts as an agent, there is a special difference between an appraisal agency and a normal agency relationship. For example, a real estate broker is usually the agent of the seller or the buyer, and represents the client's best interests. If the broker represents the seller, then the broker has a duty to obtain the highest price and best terms possible from the buyer. This is called ***advocacy***. An appraiser is also an agent, but does not advocate the position of any of the parties when reporting the opinion of value. The value conclusion must be impartial without regard to the best interests of the client. Note that the appraiser is still obligated to the other aspects of the agency relationship – confidentiality, due diligence and full disclosure.

Exercise a

A synonym for appraisal is _____ . *The majority of appraisals ordered by private parties are required by* _____ *institutions.*

An appraiser normally operates in a relationship of _____ *and* _____ . *This means that the appraiser owes a duty of* _____ *to the principal, as well as full* _____ , _____ *and due* _____ . *These are referred to as the* _____ *duties of the agent. Nevertheless, an appraiser does not act as an* _____ , *that is, the opinion of value is to be rendered impartially without regard to which party is the appraiser's client.*

Value

Since the function of an appraiser is to report value to the client, the first issue is to clarify the definition of value. To say that value is elusive is an understatement, considering the effort appraisers make in its specifying its meaning with precision. There are numerous kinds of value, all of which would result in different dollar amounts.

Appraisers generally recognize two categories of value – ***value in use*** and ***value in exchange***. Value in use is the value a commodity has to the owner. This may be subjective, as the result of emotion or other personal considerations. It may also relate to a property which was custom made for a specific purpose.

Value in exchange, on the other hand, is a value that an ordinary, informed buyer would pay in comparison to other choices available in the marketplace. As such, value in exchange is objective. Although there are numerous definitions of ***market value***, market values are always values in exchange.

Example An owner builds a large and expensive home, but with only one bedroom. The value to the owner may equal what the owner paid for construction of the home (cost), but the average buyer would probably want more than one bedroom in such a home, and would therefore likely be unwilling to pay as much as the owner. The market value (value in exchange) is less than the value in use.

Example You buy some land and have a commercial building constructed at a cost of $500,000, custom built to suit your needs. Later you go to sell the property, but discover that many of the features of the building are useless to a typical buyer. As a result, the price an ordinary buyer would pay for this property is only $250,000. We would say then, that the value in use was $500,000, but the value in exchange was only $250,000.

It is true that either owner in the above examples may be able to sell the property for what it cost if the owner can find the one-in-a-million buyer for whom the special features had value. But appraisers ordinarily define market value as the value to the typical or average buyer who can be found after a reasonable marketing time.

Market values are representative of trends. For example, if a comparable property was recently sold for $200,000, this does not prove that the property being appraised will sell for $200,000. But it does start a *trend*. Suppose now the appraiser locates several other recently sold comparable properties, and their sales prices corroborate the trend. The market value becomes clear when the trend is evident.

Appraisers consider that any commodity has value only when four factors are present –

- Utility
- Scarcity
- Effective purchasing power
- Demand (Desire)

For example, if a commodity has no *utility* (is useless), it will have no value, regardless of the other factors. Similarly, the greater the *scarcity* of a commodity, the greater the value. Buyers must also have the ability to buy, or no sales will occur, so *effective purchasing power* is an essential element of value. (Some texts refer to effective purchasing power as *transferability*.) And finally, there must be *demand* (also sometimes stated as *desire*) for a commodity before it can possess value. If any one of the above elements of value is completely lacking, the commodity has no value at all.

Assuming that the above four elements of value are present, the value of the commodity is also affected by the four great forces which affect the value of all real property. These forces are –

- *Social*
- *Governmental*
- *Economic*
- *Environmental*

Sometimes these forces – social forces, for example – are not rapid. Attitudes towards minorities in this country, for example, have improved steadily, although slowly over recent years. As a result, values of properties in areas where minorities predominate have tended to increase in value faster than properties in other areas. On the other hand, some of these forces have an almost overnight effect. For example, if the local government decides to rezone an area, the governmental influence can change the value of properties in the affected area in the time it takes for the news media to break the story. Economic and environmental forces can also change values relatively quickly. (Some texts refer to environmental forces as *physical* forces.)

Clearly, the appraiser's normal task is to report the market value (value in exchange) of the property, not its value in use. Yet, even the way appraisers define market value varies according to the circumstances and the needs of the client. In other words, there is no such thing as "the" market value. One of the most common is the definition used in the Uniform Residential Appraisal Report (URAR), a form required by secondary lenders today –

"The most probable price which a property should bring in a competitive and open market under all conditions requisite to a fair sale, the buyer and seller, each acting prudently, knowledgeably and assuming the price is not affected by undue stimulus. Implicit in this definition is the consummation of a sale as of a specified date and the passing of title from seller to buyer under conditions whereby: (1) buyer and seller are typically motivated; (2) both parties are well informed or well advised, and each acting in what he considers his own best interest; (3) a reasonable time is allowed for exposure in the open market; (4) payment is made in terms of cash in U.S. dollars or in terms of financial arrangements comparable thereto; and (5) the price represents the normal consideration for the property sold unaffected by special or creative financing or sales concessions granted by anyone associated with the sale."

Note that the basis of this definition is the "willing buyer, willing seller" concept. The essence of this definition is that the value of a property is its ability to command something else (usually money) in exchange.

Another aspect of value is that it is dependent upon the anticipated future benefits which the owner could derive from the property. In other words, the greater the anticipated benefits of ownership, the more a buyer would be willing to pay and the more a seller would demand in exchange for the property. This concept becomes crucial in appraising income properties, where the anticipated benefit of ownership is the income potential of the property.

But not all clients want the appraiser to report the value according to the URAR definition above. In many cases the request is not for the "most probable" price the property would bring, but rather the highest price possible. Yet other clients might want the most probable price, but want to know what they could expect to get for the property within the constraints of a short marketing time. Or a seller might want to know how much could be obtained for their property if special financing concessions were offered to the buyer. All of these are variations on the definition of "market value," yet each would result in a different value to report.

There are also various other types of value which are important in certain contexts. A partial list includes –

Assessed value The **assessed value** is a percentage of the true cash value used for property tax purposes. The tax collector multiplies the tax rate by the assessed value to find the amount of the tax bill. See also "real market value" below.

Book value (also sometimes called *depreciated value*) **Book** or **depreciated value** is the value of a property as carried on the books of a business. Property held for business or income use is subject to cost recovery (depreciation) expense for income tax purposes. Every year the cost recovery claimed must be deducted from the cost on the books of the business. The result at any given time is the remaining book value of the property. Book value is generally a fiction created for accounting purposes and has little relation to market value.

Insurance value The amount the improvements should be insured for is called the **insurance value**. In theory, insurance value is the reproduction cost of the improvements without subtracting an allowance for depreciation. This is because (1) the land cannot be destroyed, so only the value of the improvements need be insured and, (2) the insurance company is generally required to reproduce the structure, not just replace it with another with similar utility located elsewhere. Older properties tend to be insured for amounts far in excess of their market value. At the same time, newer properties can be reproduced for about their market value, but because insurance value does not consider land value, the total market value tends to be higher than the insured value.

Intrinsic value The **intrinsic value** of a commodity is the value of the thing in and of itself, without regard to market forces. Intrinsic value is the utility value alone, even if demand, scarcity and effective purchasing power are not present. Many appraisers consider it to be a misuse of the word "value," since value cannot exist without the presence of the other factors in addition to utility. Certainly, intrinsic value is not market value.

Liquidation (liquidated) value What a property would sell for at auction, under distress conditions or with limited exposure in the marketplace is the **liquidation value**.

Loan value Lenders refer to the **loan value** as the value of a property for mortgage loan purposes. Greater reliance is placed on the earnings potential of the property and its liquidation value in the event of a foreclosure.

Salvage value (also sometimes called *residual value*) When a property has been fully depreciated (see "book value" above), the remaining value is its **salvage** or **residual value**. For example, an owner of an apartment building can claim cost recovery as a deductible expense, but only on the structure, not on the portion of the cost attributable to the land. Thus, when the building has reached the end of its useful life and has been fully depreciated, its book value will be zero. The book value of the property will then be just the land value. In this case the land value is the salvage or residual value.

Real market value **Real market value** is the value for property tax purposes. The Administrative Rules of the Oregon Department of Revenue require each county tax assessor to value all property in the county for its highest price, among other considerations. Therefore, real market value may differ from more common definitions of market value.

In our discussion of value we have occasionally used the term **cost**. Cost, as would seem obvious, is what an owner paid for a property. The cost was paid either as a purchase price or as the sum of the land and construction expenses. What is not so obvious to lay persons is that cost does not equal value. What an owner paid for a property could easily have been a value in use, rather than a value in exchange, and therefore not market value. Market prices change with market conditions too, so even if an owner paid market value for the property, its cost would have little to do with its market value at some point in the future. Furthermore, an owner could pay $200,000 to build certain improvements, but even though brand new, a bad design might cause the market value of the improvements to be substantially less than the cost.

Another term we have already used is **price**. Appraisers use the word "price" to mean the amount an owner is or was asking for a property, or the amount a buyer paid for a property. Naturally, the price an owner is asking for a property does not establish its value. Even the price a buyer paid for a property does not indicate anything more than a value in use for that property. However, the prices paid for various comparable properties do establish a trend, and therefore is indicative of market value for a comparable property.

Principles of value

Various principles of value are fundamental to the appraisal concept of value. Although many of these principles are derived from general theories of economics, here they are applied to a particular economic unit – a parcel of real property. As a result, appraisers sometimes employ these concepts differently than an economist would –

Highest and best use The **highest and best use** of the property is basic to the appraisal process. To determine the highest and best use of the property the appraiser applies four tests; that is, the proposed use must be –

- Physically possible,
- Legal, or can be made legal,
- Financially feasible, and
- That which maximizes benefits to the owner.

For example, soil which will not support a proposed structure makes that use physically impossible, therefore the proposed structure cannot be the highest and best use of the land. Similarly, zoning and availability of financing at reasonable rates to support the project are necessary if the proposed use is to be the highest and best use. Because of the first three of these constraints, the highest and best use of a developed property (land with improvements already in place), is usually the current use. In fact, zoning constraints alone are usually sufficient to dictate the highest and best use.

Of greater difficulty, however, is determining the highest and best use of property where many uses may be legal, physically possible and financially feasible. Such is frequently the case with undeveloped land. Even improved property may require substantial effort to determine the highest and best use, such as where the current use of the structure is coming to an end and the improvements will have to be converted to a new use.

In these cases the appraiser must determine which use will maximize the benefit to the owner. Benefits are not always financial; for example, the benefit of owning a house is use and enjoyment (shelter), not financial reward. Even where the benefits are financial it is not always an easy task to determine the highest and best use. You might think that when the rewards are financial, the highest and best use is simply that use which provides the greatest net return. On the face of it, this would seem to be so, but what if all the proposed uses would bring in the same net revenue, but one shows greater potential for stability or longevity of the income than others? An appraiser must take all these factors into account when analyzing the highest and best use of a property.

A highest and best use analysis is most problematic when the property is vacant land. Economists speak of the ***four agents in production*** – land, labor, capital, and entrepreneurial expertise (management). In classic economic theory, all four are necessary to produce income, but not always in the same proportion, and the amounts of each can be changed according to prevailing economic conditions. If labor becomes more expensive, for example, management will attempt to compensate by utilizing the other factors in different ways. Of the four agents in production, land is the most passive, therefore, the income allowed to it us usually last after the others have been paid. We sometimes speak of the income attributable to the land as residual income.

Substitution Simply stated, the principle of ***substitution*** is that no prudent and knowledgeable buyer would pay more for a commodity than it would cost to acquire an identical substitute, assuming the buyer is acting in his or her own best interests and not under undue pressure. In real life, the available substitutes are never identical, but the principle still holds. For example, if there is a shortage of potatoes and they become very expensive, people will eat bread or rice – equivalent, if not identical substitutes.

Anticipation According to the principle of ***anticipation***, buyers pay and sellers demand more or less for properties in direct proportion to the anticipated future benefits of ownership. While this is true of all properties, it is especially true of income-producing properties. Note that the buyer is motivated by anticipated future benefits, not past performance of the investment. Buyers rely on the past only as a guide to what they can expect in the future.

Example You are listing an apartment building. The owner has not raised the rents for some time, so the rents are half of what they should be. You must value the property using the market rent, not the existing rent. (You should, however, subtract a small allowance from your final estimate to compensate a buyer for vacancies and inconvenience which could occur when the new owner raises the rents.)

What effect does the anticipation of inflation have on property values? In general, it will drive dollar values up because investment in real estate is a classic hedge against inflation. However, inflation will generally drive the values of all properties up more or less equally, since the inflation rate will affect all properties in much the same way.

Externalities The principle of ***externalities*** holds that value is affected by outside forces (extrinsic factors) as well as features of the property itself (intrinsic factors). For example, if the property is in poor condition, this is an intrinsic problem. But if the property is in a poor neighborhood, then the neighborhood is causing the property to lose value, not the property itself; therefore we say the property lost value due to externalities. Because of its inherent immobility, real estate is at the mercy of externalities more than any other commodity.

There are many, many forces which have an effect on property values. In fact, externalities are generally more powerful forces than intrinsic factors. External forces can be international, national, regional or local in scope. Interest rates, for example, are national and international in scope today, and have a profound effect on market values. Or consider that the same house will sell for more in San Francisco than in Portland. The externality in this case is regional supply and demand forces. On the other hand, forces such as zoning decisions would be local externalities. An externality can be as narrow in focus as the fact that the neighbors do not maintain their property well.

Change ***Change*** is constant and unavoidable. Because of this we say that an appraisal report is valid for the date of the report only. In fact, we should be even more precise and say that it is valid for the moment it is delivered to the client. Events occurring after that time may easily change the value. And since future events are unforeseeable, it is impossible to appraise a property for what it will be worth on a future date. It is, however, possible to appraise a property for a past date, simply by using historical data.

When the principle of change is applied to analysis of a neighborhood it becomes evident that neighborhoods go through stages. The first stage is ***growth***, during which improvements are constructed. At some point the neighborhood is fully built and relatively little further change occurs. This is called the period of ***stability*** or ***equilibrium***. There is no set time period over which this period will last, nor is it tied to the age of the improvements. Many older residential neighborhoods, for example, are extremely stable and show no signs of impending change; yet many newly constructed developments may be in imminent danger of being razed to make way for some other use. When a neighborhood reaches the stage where properties are being torn down or converted for other uses, then we say that the period of stability has ended and ***decline*** has begun.

Note that the declining stage really merges with the growth of the next use pattern. Although different neighborhoods change in different ways, a common change is for a residential neighborhood to give way to commercial or industrial use. Thus, when a house is torn down to make way for a shopping center, the decline of the residential use pattern is merging with the growth of the commercial use. Some appraisers refer to this as ***revitalization***.

Revitalization, however, should not be confused with ***gentrification***. Gentrification is the process where older neighborhoods are salvaged and reborn with the same use pattern. Revitalization, in contrast, occurs when the use pattern shifts, as where a residential neighborhood goes commercial.

Conformity The principle of ***conformity*** simply means that property values are maximized when a neighborhood is composed of structures which are generally of the same character. This does not mean that the structures are the same to the point of monotony, but rather that they are generally the same; for example, all single family detached residences.

When a neighborhood has a high degree of conformity, the neighborhood will be able to withstand change better. The better the neighborhood can withstand change, the longer will be the period of stability, so the useful life of the structure will be longer. Logically, the longer the anticipated remaining useful life of the structure, the greater its value, hence, the greater the conformity, the greater the market value.

Progression and *regression* Properties which do not conform because they are underimproved in relation to other properties in the neighborhood frequently benefit in value by **progression**. For example, a small home in a neighborhood of larger homes will command a higher price than if the same home were located in a neighborhood of similar small homes. Conversely, a property which does not conform because the owner has overbuilt suffers from **regression**. In this case, the owner may never be able to recover the costs.

Balance According to the principle of **balance**, a property will bring the highest value when all of its components – land and structure – are in optimum equilibrium with each other. For example, a new five-bedroom house with only one bath is in disequilibrium and its value will suffer, perhaps to the point where its value is less than the cost of construction. The principle of balance also requires that the land and structure be appraised for the same use.

Example Suppose an owner wishes you to take a listing on a home which is located on a 100 × 100 foot commercially zoned lot. The owner feels that the structure (as a house) is worth $200,000, based on the value of similar structures in the area. The owner also feels that the land is worth $200,000, based on the value of nearby similar commercial lots. Therefore, the owner wishes you to take a listing at $400,000.

However, the reality is that the owner has appraised the structure according to its residential value and the land according to its commercial value. Suppose the residential value of the land is only $80,000. Adding this to the residential value of structure gives a market value of $280,000. If we appraise the property according to its commercial value, the land is worth $200,000, but suppose the structure requires $60,000 worth of alterations to bring it up to commercial code. Then the value for commercial purposes is $340,000 ($200,000 land value + $200,000 structure value – $60,000 cost of alterations = $340,000).

Clearly, the highest and best use of this property is for commercial use, but its value as such is only $340,000, not the $400,000 the owner thinks it is worth. The owner's appraisal is incorrect because the owner misapplied the principle of balance in valuing the land for one purpose and the structure for another.

Contribution According to the principle of **contribution** all components of the property – land and structures – contribute to the overall value of the whole, but not necessarily in direct proportion to their cost. For example, a **plottage increment** is an increase in value that can occur when smaller parcels are joined. Sometimes the value of the large parcel is greater than the total of the value of the smaller pieces from which is was made up. Or consider the owner of a house in Oregon who spends $20,000 to install an in-ground swimming pool on an $160,000 house. It is doubtful that buyers will pay a great deal extra for the swimming pool, so the amount the swimming pool contributes to the overall value is far less than its cost. People who rehabilitate properties for resale need to keep the principle of contribution uppermost in mind.

Competition The market value for any commodity is established by **competition**. However, if there is little competition, there is likely to be excessive profit. Excessive profit, on the other hand, attracts competition, which dilutes the profit. In fact, excess profit usually attracts too much competition which ultimately becomes ruinous. In a free market these forces always equalize themselves within a short period of time.

Surplus productivity A measure of the value of any commodity is its productive capacity. In other words, the more productive an item, the greater its desirability, and therefore the greater its value. We can derive a portion of the productivity attributable to one component of an investment and calculate the value of that one component separately from the whole. This is an example of determining the value of one segment of the property by the **surplus productivity** applicable to that segment.

For example, suppose an income property produces an annual net operating income of $50,000 (income after all expenses but before payments on debt). Assume further that there is a $400,000 mortgage with interest payments of $40,000 per year. The net income attributable to the owner's equity is therefore $10,000. We can now ascertain the value of that $10,000 annual projected income, and thereby determine the value of one component of the property – the value of the owner's equity.

Exercise b

A value to the owner of a property is its value _____ _____ , which is _____ and dependent on emotion. A value _____ _____ is the value to an ordinary buyer in a market transaction and is _____ . To establish value, appraisers attempt to find the _____ . The four factors which must be present for a commodity to have value are _____

_____

The forces which influence value are _____

Which of the following would be closest to the market value as defined in the Uniform Residential Appraisal Report? ❑ *Assessed value* ❑ *Book value* ❑ *Insurance value* ❑ *Loan value* ❑ *Real market value* ❑ *Liquidation value* ❑ *Intrinsic value*

What an owner paid for a property is its _____ which is not normally the market value of the property. The _____ of a property is the amount an owner is or was asking for the property, and is also not necessarily market value.

To be the highest and best use of a property, the use must be _____ , physically possible, financially _____ and finally, the use which produces the _____ benefit to the owner. The principle which holds that no one would pay more for a commodity than it would cost to obtain an identical commodity is the principle of _____ . The fact that market value is dependent on the future benefits which can be derived from owning the property is the principle of _____ . When appraisers say that extrinsic forces change the value of a property, this is a reference to the principle of _____ . According to the principle of _____ , an appraiser can make an appraisal report as of the current date or a date in the _____ , but not for a date in the _____ . The three typical stages of a neighborhood are _____ , _____ or equilibrium, and _____ . When upscale buyers move into a neighborhood and restore it, this is called _____ . When properties are of a homogenous character in a neighborhood, the neighborhood will be able to withstand _____ better, thereby increasing the useful _____ of the improvements and increasing the value. This is the appraisal principle of _____ . A small house in a neighborhood of larger houses benefits from the principle of _____ ; the opposite example is a large house in a neighborhood of smaller houses, which suffers from the appraisal principle of _____ . When all components are in optimum _____ the property reaches its highest and best use and therefore its highest potential value. According to the principle of _____ , *all components add to the overall value, but not necessarily in proportion to their _____ . The principle of _____ tells us that excess profits can be ruinous. The principle of _____ _____ allows us to isolate a portion of the income of a property and thereby determine the value of the portion of the asset which created that income.*

Overview of the appraisal process

In conducting an appraisal the first step is to define the task. This usually means creating a clear understanding with the client as to the definition of market value the client desires and the client's reason for ordering the appraisal. On the other hand, it could mean that the appraiser must first complete a highest and best use analysis before the actual valuation can begin, or perhaps extensive discussions with the client will be necessary to determine precisely what the client's needs are.

In an ordinary request for the simple appraisal of a single-family home – such as where the appraisal is ordered by a lender – determining the appraisal task is fairly routine. Lenders are sufficiently sophisticated that they know exactly what to ask for and can communicate their needs easily. And the highest and best use of most improved property is constrained by the zoning, so determining the appraisal task becomes relatively simple.

The second step in the appraisal process is to gather the necessary data. Data required will include information about the region and the neighborhood as well as the property itself. After all available data has been collected, the appraiser is ready to apply the data to the property. In doing this, there are three recognized *approaches to value* – the market approach, the cost approach and the income approach. Each of these approaches will be the subject of extensive discussion later.

Not all of these approaches may be suitable for a given property and, even when appropriate, the appraiser usually finds that the results of one or two of the approaches are more reliable or credible than the results of the other(s). To ensure optimum accuracy, the appraiser uses a process called *reconciliation* or *correlation* to make the final estimate of market value. Reconciliation or correlation means taking a weighted average of the results of the approaches which were used.

For example, in the appraisal of a 20-year old single-family dwelling, the market approach is usually the most accurate, although the cost approach can sometimes be used with fair accuracy. The income approach, however, is less reliable. Therefore, to reconcile the value estimates derived from each of the three approaches, the appraiser might take 75% of the value from the market approach, 25% of the value from the cost approach, and 0% of the value from the income approach. Reconciliation or correlation is a matter of judgment, dependent on the appraiser's skill and experience.

Having made the final value estimate, it is time to complete the appraisal report. Most appraisal reports today are made on the *Uniform Residential Appraisal Report* (URAR), which is the form required by most secondary market lenders. In addition, all appraisers must adhere to the Uniform Standards of Professional Appraisal Practice (USPAP), which dictate the minimum requirements for appraisal reports. The USPAP allows an appraiser to report on a self-contained appraisal report, a summary appraisal report or a restricted use appraisal report. The difference in the three types of reports lies in the amount of detail included in the report. The URAR is considered a summary report.

Regardless of the form in which the report is made, Oregon Revised Statutes provide that appraisals can only be made by persons licensed or certified by the Oregon Appraiser Certification and Licensure Board –

674.100 Persons engaged in real estate appraisal activity required to be certified or licensed; exclusions; violations. (1)(a) No person shall engage in, carry on, advertise or purport to engage in or carry on real estate appraisal activity within this state without first obtaining certification or licensure as provided for in ORS 674.310.

(b) Real estate appraisal activity is the preparation, completion and issuance of an opinion as to the value on a given date or at a given time of real property or any interest in real property, whether such activity is performed in connection with a federally related transaction or is not performed in connection with a federally related transaction. Notwithstanding any other provision of law, a state certified appraiser or a state licensed appraiser:

(A) Is not required to be licensed under ORS 696.025 [the Real Estate License Act, under which real estate agents are licensed] to perform any real estate appraisal activity or any other activity that constitutes the giving of an opinion as to the value of real property or any interest in real property; and

(B) Is not subject to regulation under ORS 696.010 to 696.495 and 696.600 to 696.995 [the Real Estate License Act] in connection with the performance of any real estate appraisal activity or the performance of any activity which constitutes the giving of an opinion as to the value of real estate or any interest in real estate.

(2) Real estate appraisal activity excludes any activity that is not performed in connection with a federally related transaction and that: ...

(g) Constitutes a letter opinion or a competitive market analysis as those terms are defined in ORS 696.010 that, by administrative or judicial order or subpoena, is compelled from a person licensed to engage in real estate activity under the provisions of ORS 696.007 to 696.495, 696.600 to 696.627 and 696.800 to 696.855 ...

Note that the statute specifically exempts real estate brokers from having to be licensed or certified by the Appraiser Certification and Licensure Board, provided the "appraisal" work is performed in the course of taking a listing or making a sale and is in the nature of a competitive market analysis.

Exercise c

The first step in making an appraisal is to _____ the appraisal task. In some cases this may include an analysis of the _____ and _____ _____ of the property.

Making a judgment by taking a weighted average of the results of the different approaches to value is referred to as _____ or _____ .

A common report is the _____ _____ _____ _____ .

The market data approach to value

Appraisers most commonly call this approach the ***market data approach***, although it is also sometimes just called the ***market approach***, and sometimes also called the ***sales comparison approach***. The market data approach is the easiest to explain to lay people because it echoes exactly what buyers and sellers do in the marketplace. Buyers and sellers simply compare one property in the marketplace to others.

Although all principles of value are used in all approaches, the market data approach relies most heavily on the principle of substitution. A buyer will simply not offer to pay more than it would cost to get another property of equal desirability and a seller will not accept less than what other similar properties are selling for.

Needless to say, the market data approach requires the availability of adequate comparable properties. Whenever possible these should be properties which have been sold, and the sales must have been *arms length transactions*. An arms length transaction occurs when the property was exposed in the open market for a reasonable period of time, both parties were knowledgeable and both parties acted prudently in their own self-interest without undue stimulus. Note that the definition of an arms length transaction contains essentially the same elements as the definition of market value.

Example property is very comparable to the subject property in all respects, but sold the day it was listed. The appraiser must conclude that the transaction locates the bottom of the market for the value of the subject property. Clearly it might have sold for much more if it had been exposed to a greater range of potential buyers.

Example You find an excellent comparable for the property you are appraising. When you research the data relating to the sale, you note the seller's name is Georges LeRoux and the buyer's name is Etienne LeRoux. Can you use this sale as a comparable? The parties are obviously related, therefore love and affection may have been part of the consideration, so the price reflected on the deed is not necessarily representative of the market.

Example A sale of a comparable property was recorded 120 days after the property was listed. The grantee on the deed was the Perpetual Savings and Loan Association and the consideration is stated as $72,369.42. If further investigation reveals that this was a deed in lieu of foreclosure, or a sheriff's or trustee's deed, then the transaction was under undue stimulus and is not representative of the market.

The most serious problem with the market data approach occurs when there are few or no comparable properties. Obviously, the better the comparables, the more accurate the results of the market data approach. Appraisers refer to a market with high activity level as an *efficient market*. Real estate markets tend to be inefficient in comparison to markets for other commodities.

When there are no comparable sold properties, can an appraiser use comparable properties currently listed for sale? Properties on the market are generally not used by appraisers because there is no guarantee that the property will ultimately command the price the owner is asking. On the other hand, if the property has been on the market for a time and has not sold at its asking price, one fact becomes clear – the asking price must be higher than market value. Therefore appraisers do occasionally use listed properties as comparables, but use the data only as evidence of the upper limit of value.

Lack of good comparables is also typical of *single-purpose properties*, also called *single-use properties*. A single-purpose property is a property which was specially built for just one use. Examples include properties such as gymnasiums, schools, library buildings, bowling alleys, theaters, churches, among many others.

If you determine that conversion to another use is the highest and best use of a single-use property, then you can use *appraisal by anticipated use* (also sometimes called *appraisal by development cost*) as a technique to appraise the existing structure. To appraise by anticipated use, simply find comparables for the property *as it will be when converted*. This should yield the market value after conversion. Then subtract the anticipated cost of conversion, which will give the present value of the property in its current condition.

The "Sales Comparison Analysis" section of the Uniform Residential Appraisal Report (URAR) has been reproduced on the following page. To illustrate our discussion of

ITEM	SUBJECT	COMPARABLE NO. 1		COMPARABLE NO. 2		COMPARABLE NO. 3	
Address	120 S.W. Lois Lane	123 S.W. Lois Lane		345 S.W. Lois Lane		678 S.W. Lois Lane	
Proximity to Subject		Across street		Two blocks		Four blocks	
Sales Price	$	$ 169,900		$ 171,000		$ 175,950	
Price/Gross Liv. Area	$	$ 112.52		$ 117.93		$ 119.29	
Data and/or Verification Source		MLS		MLS		MLS	
VALUE ADJUSTMENTS	DESCRIPTION	DESCRIPTION	+(-)$ Adjustment	DESCRIPTION	+(-)$ Adjustment	DESCRIPTION	+(-)$ Adjustment
Sales or Financing Concessions		None		Seller buydown	-3,000	None	
Date of Sale/Time		Current		3 months	+2,600	6 months	+5,300
Location	Average	Average		Average		Average	
Leasehold/Fee Simple	Fee	Fee		Fee		Fee	
Site	7,000	7,000		7,000		10,000	-25,000
View	None	None		None		None	
Design and Appeal	Ranch/Avg	Same		Same		Same	
Quality of Construction	Average	Average		Average		Average	
Age	15/15 effective	Same		Same		Same	
Condition	Average	Average		Superior	-5,000	Average	
Above Grade Room Count	Total 7 / Bdrms 3 / Baths 2	Total 7 / Bdrms 3 / Baths 2		Total 7 / Bdrms 3 / Baths 2		Total 7 / Bdrms 3 / Baths 2	
Gross Living Area	1,500 Sq. Ft.	1,510 Sq. Ft.	-1,100	1,450 Sq. Ft.	+5,900	1,475 Sq. Ft.	+3,000
Basement & Finished	None	None		None		None	
Rooms Below Grade	Average	Average		Average		Average	
Functional Utility	Standard	Standard		Standard		Standard	
Heating/Cooling	FAGas	FAGas		FAGas		FAGas	
Energy Efficient Items	Standard	Standard		Standard		Standard	
Garage/Carport	2/None	2/None		2/None		2/None	
Porch, Patio, Deck, Fireplace(s), etc.	One fireplace 10 x 20 deck	Same No deck	+2,000	Same No deck	+2,000	Same No deck	+2,000
Fence, Pool, etc.	None	None		None		None	
Net Adj. (total)		X + ☐ - $ 900		X + ☐ - $ 2,500		☐ + X - $ 14,700	
Adjusted Sales Price of Comparable		$ 170,800		$ 173,500		$ 161,250	

Comments on Sales Comparison (including the subject property's compatibility to the neighborhood, etc.): Due to uncertainty of effect of buydown on Comparable #2, and of effect of oversized lot on Comparable #3, weight was placed 100% on Comparable #1. Value change per Marshall and Swift.

ITEM	SUBJECT	COMPARABLE NO. 1		COMPARABLE NO. 2	COMPARABLE NO. 3
Date, Price and Data Source, for prior sales within year of appraisal	7/9/__ MLS	7/1/__ MLS	4/2/__ MLS	1/10/__ MLS	

Analysis of any current agreement of sale, option, or listing of the subject property and analysis of any prior sales of subject and comparables within one year of the date of appraisal.

INDICATED VALUE BY SALES COMPARISON APPROACH . . . . $ 170,800

the market data approach, it has been completed with appropriate adjustments as an appraiser would have filled it out for a sale as described in the narrative below.

Sales Comparison Narrative

Subject property is a three-bedroom ranch style house of 1,500 ☐ (☐ means "square feet"), built 15 years ago on a 70 × 100 lot (7,000 ☐). It is in average condition and has two full baths, one fireplace and a double garage. The neighborhood is average as is the quality of construction. There is no basement or unusually large front porch, but there is a 10 × 20 foot deck off the back of the house. There are no other special amenities or recent remodeling.

Comparable #1 sold two weeks ago for $169,900. It is in the same block as the subject and was built by the same builder at the same time. Its amenities are the same as the subject and are in the same condition, except that the structure is 1,510 ☐. Its lot is slightly irregular, but totals 7,000 ☐. There are no other special amenities or recent remodeling.

NOTES

Comparable #2 sold three months ago for $171,000. It is located two blocks from the subject property in the same subdivision and was built by the same builder at the same time. Its amenities are the same as the subject, but they are in superior condition, although the structure is only 1,450 ⬜. Investigation of the sale revealed that the seller paid $3,000 to a bank to buy the interest rate down for the buyer.

Comparable #3 sold six months ago for $175,950. It is located four blocks from the subject property in the same subdivision and was built by the same builder at the same time. Its amenities are the same as the subject property and in the same condition, but there is no fireplace and the structure is 1,475 ⬜. A major difference is that the lot is 100 × 100 (10,000 ⬜).

Because the comparable properties above are not identical to the subject property, adjustments must be made. Note that all the adjustments were made *to the comparables*. The adjustments must be made in order to find out how much each comparable would have sold for if it had been identical to the subject. This means that if the comparable is larger or better, the adjustment must be subtracted, and vice-versa.

Note also in this report that the appraiser reconciled the results from the three properties into the final value conclusion by taking a weighted average of the results. In this case the appraiser weighed 100% on Comparable #1 and gave no weight to Comparables #2 and #3. This judgment appears to be justified from the nature and reliability of the data in this report.

In other situations, an appraiser may have comparables where the appraiser feels each should be given at least partial weight. Still, the least reliable comparable should receive the least weight. This is why appraisers try to use at least three, but not usually more than six comparables. Additional comparables would create a substantial amount of extra work, and since they would be given decreasing weight, would not significantly influence the appraiser's final value conclusion.

Exercise d

The market data approach is usually very powerful and accurate when there are a sufficient number of _____ sales, such as would be found in an _____ market. Appraisers compare the subject property to recently sold properties, but only where the sale was an _____ _____ transaction. Appraisers can also use properties which are currently being offered for sale, but these tend to fix the _____ limit of value, since there is no guarantee they will eventually sell for their asking prices.

When the subject property is a _____ _____ property it is unlikely there will be any comparable sales. Still, an appraiser can conduct an appraisal of such a property by making it an appraisal _____ _____ _____ .

Adjustments to value are _____from the sales price of the comparable when the comparable is better than the subject property, and _____ to the sales price of the comparable when the comparable is poorer than the subject.

In the reconciliation (correlation) of the results from the comparable properties, the appraiser uses a _____ average.

The cost approach to value

Like the market data approach, the cost approach to value relies primarily on the principle of substitution. Unlike the market data approach, however, in the cost approach the appraiser uses the cost to reproduce the property as a measure of the upper limit of value. In other words, if a buyer could have the property reproduced for a certain amount, then by the principle of substitution the buyer would not pay any more than that amount.

Example A builder offers you a brand new house on a lot in a new subdivision for $250,000. You contact other builders and determine that you can have the house reproduced (identical in all respects) for $150,000 total construction costs. There are also vacant lots, equivalent to the site on which the builder's house is situated, still available in the subdivision at a price of $60,000. Obviously then, you can get an identical substitute for $210,000, so there would be no point in paying the builder the asking price of $250,000. The reproduction cost of the structure, plus the land value, equals the upper limit of value.

Note that the cost approach can be used only on the improvements. The cost approach assumes either reproduction or replacement, and land cannot be reproduced or replaced. Therefore, to complete the appraisal of a property by the cost approach the appraiser estimates the reproduction or replacement cost of the improvements, and then adds the land value. The land value is ascertained by other approaches, usually simply by comparison with sales of similar vacant parcels (market data approach).

Of course, in the above example we used a brand new structure. It is easiest to explain the cost approach by beginning with a brand new structure. But most improvements are not new. And clearly, the value of a used structure is not as high as a new structure of exactly the same size and style. To account for this most appraisers use **replacement cost** when appraising a used structure rather than **reproduction cost** (**cost to reproduce new**). Replacement cost is the cost of acquiring a structure which offers the same utility and amenities, but with modern materials, construction techniques and floorplans. Reproduction cost, on the other hand, requires calculation of the cost to create an identical reproduction of the structure. For most properties this would be very time-consuming, and usually adds nothing to reliability or accuracy.

But even if an appraiser uses replacement cost, the structure may have suffered from **depreciation**. Depreciation is defined as a loss in value from any cause. There are three types of depreciation –
- Physical deterioration
- Functional obsolescence
- Economic (external) obsolescence

Physical deterioration means just what it sounds like – maintenance has been deferred, so the building is in poor condition. In contrast, **functional obsolescence** refers to those conditions which render the structure outmoded. For example, if the gutters are falling off, this is physical deterioration. But if the property has four bedrooms and only one bath, the property is out of date by today's standards, so this is functional obsolescence. **Economic obsolescence** (sometimes called by its newer name **external obsolescence**) is caused by outside forces (externalities). Poor economic conditions in the region, for example, would cause economic obsolescence.

Regardless of the type of depreciation, it causes the improvements to lose value, and so it must be subtracted from the cost to reproduce or replacement cost. The complete theory of the cost approach is now apparent. The following diagram captures its essence –

$$\frac{\text{Replacement (or Reproduction) Cost}}{\text{Less Accrued Depreciation}}$$

$$\frac{\text{Value of Improvements (Upper Limit)}}{\text{Plus Land Value (by Market Approach)}}$$

$$\text{TOTAL VALUE (Upper Limit)}$$

Calculating cost Determining the replacement or reproduction cost of the improvements is the first step in appraising a property with the cost approach. There are three commonly recognized methods for calculating cost —

- Quantity survey
- Unit in place
- Comparative unit

The ***quantity survey method*** is the most comprehensive and accurate method of estimating cost. It essentially repeats what a contractor would do to make a construction bid. Determining the cost by quantity survey means the appraiser must determine the cost of all materials and labor which would be required to replace or reproduce the structure. Because this is time-consuming, the quantity survey method is used only in unusual circumstances.

Measuring costs by the ***unit in place method*** means that the cost of each whole component of the structure is calculated separately. For example, suppose that an appraiser determines that a typical foundation costs a certain number of dollars per cubic yard of concrete used when it is poured (cost factor per cubic yard). Then the cost to reproduce any typical foundation can be estimated easily just by measuring its volume in cubic yards and multiplying the results times the cost factor per cubic yard. Similar techniques can be developed to determine the cost to reproduce other components such as the roof, flooring, siding, and so on.

While quantity survey and unit in place are used occasionally, the most commonly used method to determine cost is by a ***comparative unit***. For example, suppose you are appraising a warehouse. Warehouses have high ceilings, but the height of the ceiling may vary from one warehouse to the next. Therefore, the reproduction or replacement cost would be more closely related to the volume than to the floor area, so cubic footage would be an appropriate comparative unit. To determine the overall cost, an appraiser needs to determine only the cost per cubic foot, and then multiply this cost by the number of cubic feet in the subject property.

The unit of comparison can be any unit, but cubic foot and square foot are the most commonly used units. In residential and office structures, ceilings tend to be of fairly uniform height, so square footage is the most commonly used comparative unit. If a property has high ceilings (i.e., vaulted ceilings) which would increase the cost, the appraiser can just adjust the cost per square foot. Measurements of square footage for appraisal purposes are generally based on the outside dimensions.

Cost factors per square foot are readily available. Appraisers subscribe to commercial cost service bureaus which provide detailed information with periodic updates. The most popular of these is the *Marshall Valuation Service* published by Marshall and Swift Publication Company. Two sample pages from their *Residential Cost Handbook* are reproduced on the next page. Most appraisers today automate the process by using the on-line or the computerized edition.

Measuring Depreciation Depreciation is said to be ***curable*** or ***incurable***. Curable depreciation is a loss in value which is repairable, from a practical standpoint. Incurable depreciation includes problems which either cannot be remedied at all, or which are impractical to repair or remedy.

ONE STORY
Square Foot Costs — *Average Quality*

RESIDENCE

STUD FRAMED

Total Area	Plywood or Hardboard	Metal or Vinyl Siding	Stucco	Wood Siding	Wood Shingles	Synth. Plaster (EIFS)
600	$58.41	$59.53	$59.49	$59.61	$59.74	$61.26
800	55.35	56.38	56.34	56.45	56.57	57.97
1000	53.08	54.05	54.01	54.12	54.23	55.54
1200	51.30	52.22	52.18	52.29	52.39	53.64
1300	50.54	51.43	51.40	51.50	51.60	52.82
1400	49.84	50.72	50.68	50.78	50.88	52.07
1500	49.20	50.06	50.03	50.13	50.22	51.39
1600	48.61	49.45	49.42	49.52	49.61	50.76
1700	48.06	48.89	48.86	48.95	49.05	50.17
1800	47.55	48.37	48.33	48.43	48.52	49.62
1900	47.07	47.87	47.84	47.93	48.02	49.11
2000	46.62	47.41	47.38	47.47	47.56	48.63
2100	46.20	46.98	46.95	47.03	47.12	48.18
2200	45.80	46.57	46.54	46.62	46.71	47.75
2400	45.06	45.81	45.78	45.86	45.95	46.96
2600	44.39	45.12	45.09	45.17	45.25	46.25
2800	43.78	44.49	44.46	44.54	44.62	45.59
3000	43.22	43.91	43.89	43.97	44.04	44.99
3200	42.70	43.38	43.35	43.43	43.51	44.44

STUD FRAMED — MASONRY

Total Area	Rustic Log	Masonry Veneer	Concrete Block	Stucco on Block	Common Brick	Poured Concrete (SIP) Forming
600	$65.28	$65.62	$61.75	$63.57	$69.02	$65.62
800	61.52	61.84	58.40	59.97	64.88	61.87
1000	58.75	59.06	55.94	57.31	61.85	59.11
1200	56.59	56.88	53.99	55.23	59.48	56.94
1300	55.66	55.95	53.16	54.34	58.46	56.02
1400	54.82	55.10	52.41	53.53	57.54	55.17
1500	54.04	54.32	51.71	52.79	56.70	54.40
1600	53.33	53.60	51.07	52.10	55.92	53.69
1700	52.67	52.94	50.47	51.46	55.19	53.02
1800	52.05	52.32	49.92	50.87	54.52	52.41
1900	51.47	51.74	49.40	50.32	53.89	51.83
2000	50.93	51.19	48.91	49.79	53.30	51.29
2100	50.42	50.68	48.45	49.30	52.75	50.78
2200	49.94	50.19	48.01	48.84	52.22	50.30
2400	49.05	49.30	47.21	47.99	51.26	49.41
2600	48.25	48.50	46.49	47.21	50.38	48.61
2800	47.52	47.76	45.82	46.51	49.59	47.87
3000	46.85	47.09	45.22	45.86	48.86	47.20
3200	46.23	46.46	44.65	45.27	48.19	46.58

SQUARE FOOT ADJUSTMENTS

ROOFING:
Composition shingle or
  Built-up, small rock ...... (base)
Clay tile .... + $4.57
Concrete tile .... + 2.82
Metal, preformed .... + .89
Wood shake .... + 1.38
Wood shingle .... + 1.19
Composition roll .... – .66

ENERGY ADJ: Mod. Climate (base)
Mild climate .... – $ .78
Extreme climate .... + 1.29
Superinsulated .... + 2.77
FOUNDATION ADJ: Mod. Climate (base)
Mild climate .... – $1.66
Extreme climate .... + 3.05
Hillside, moderate slope .. + 1.53
Hillside, steep slope ...... + 4.58

Add for SEISMIC ZONES (Z)/HURRICANE (Wind) ADJ.: See Intro–9; maps. D–12.
Frame (Z2) +$1.04, (Z3–4/wind) +$1.82   Masonry (Z2) +$.73, (Z3–4/wind) +$1.51
See Pages Avg–27 & Avg–28 for other Sq. Ft. Adjustments, Basements, Porches, Garages, etc.

RESIDENTIAL COST HANDBOOK
1998 by MARSHALL & SWIFT. L.P. All rights reserved.   **page Avg–19**

REFINEMENTS
Square Foot Costs — *Average Quality*

SQUARE FOOT ADJUSTMENTS

SUBFLOOR:
Wood subfloor .... (base)
Concrete slab .... – $1.86
Asphalt (for garage or carport) – 1.37

PLASTER INTERIOR: .... + $2.29

FLOOR COVER:
Allowance (if not itemized) + $2.33
Carpet and pad .... + 2.03
Ceramic tile .... + 8.01
Wood flooring .... + 7.29
  Parquet blocks .... + 7.63
Terrazzo .... + 7.79
Vinyl comp. sheet or tile ... + 1.47
Vinyl sheet .... + 2.68

FLOOR INSULATION:
Mild climate .... + $ .62
Moderate climate .... + .78
Extreme climate .... + 1.00

HEATING/COOLING:
Forced air .... (base)
Oil-fired .... + $ .51
Floor or wall furnace ...... – 1.19
Electric, radiant .... – .28
  Baseboard or panel ...... – .19
Hot water, baseboard .... + 1.33
Warm and cooled air .... + 1.37
Heat pump .... + 1.79
Evap. cooling w/ducts .... + 1.68
Air-to-air exchange system + 1.06

LUMP SUM ADJUSTMENTS

PLUMBING: 8 fixtures + rough-in (base)
Per fixture .... + or – $770
Per rough-in .... + or – 285

DORMERS: per linear foot
Hip or gable roof $97.50
Shed roof 82.50

FIREPLACES:
Single one story ...	$1,975 –	$2,425
Single two story ...	2,450 –	3,000
Single three story ..	2,925 –	3,575
Double one story ...	2,625 –	3,550
Double two story ...	3,225 –	3,950
Double three story .	5,100 –	6,250

BUILT-IN APPLIANCES:
Allowance (if not itemized) + $2,100
Dishwasher .... + 525
Exhaust Fan or Bath Heater + 125
Garbage Disposer .... + 190
Hood and Fan .... + 205
Oven .... + 690
Oven, microwave combo .. + 1,350
Range and Oven .... + 1,075
Range top .... + 375
Radio Intercom .... + 730
Refrigerator or Freezer .... + 675
Res. security sys., wireless .. + 1,025
Trash compactor .... + 470
Vacuum cleaner system ... + 1,400

BASEMENTS

Unfin. basements	200	400	800	1200	1600	2000	2400
Concrete walls 6"	$20.50	$15.56	$12.48	$11.04	$10.31	$10.01	$ 9.59
8"	22.00	16.61	13.25	11.66	10.85	10.52	10.03
12"	24.50	18.38	14.53	12.68	11.75	11.38	10.78
Conc. block walls 6"	18.66	14.26	11.54	10.29	9.64	9.38	9.04
8"	19.93	15.15	12.19	10.81	10.10	9.82	9.42
12"	22.26	16.80	13.38	11.76	10.94	10.61	10.11
Add for fin., minimal	4.86	4.35	4.05	3.91	3.84	3.81	3.76
partitioned	20.48	17.92	15.79	15.30	15.05	14.48	14.33

Outside Entrance: $775 – $1,075   For radon removal fan and alarm, add $245.

PORCH/BREEZEWAYS

Square Feet (Each)	FLOOR STRUCTURE: Open Slab	Open W/Steps	Wood Deck	WALL ENCLOSURE: Screen Only	Knee Wall W/Glass	Solid Walls	Add For Roof	Add For Ceiling
25	$4.36	$11.78	$18.82	$11.76	$43.20	$26.38	$9.58	$3.94
50	3.98	9.86	16.88	7.84	28.80	17.59	8.43	3.11
75	3.88	9.06	14.30	6.53	24.00	14.66	8.14	2.83
100	3.78	8.27	11.73	5.88	21.60	13.19	7.85	2.69
150	3.71	7.83	10.53	4.57	16.80	10.26	7.56	2.55
200	3.65	7.38	9.32	3.92	14.40	8.79	7.27	2.48
300	3.53	6.49	8.91	3.27	12.00	7.33	6.69	2.41

RESIDENTIAL COST HANDBOOK
1998 by MARSHALL & SWIFT. L.P. All rights reserved.   **page Avg–27**

For example, an older house with no garage suffers from functional obsolescence today. Normally, the owner can add a garage, in which case we would say that the depreciation is curable. But if there is no place on the site to put a garage, then the problem is incurable. Physical deterioration and functional obsolescence can be curable or incurable. However, economic (external) obsolescence is, by its very nature, outside of the owner's control, and therefore incurable.

The measurement of curable depreciation is most accurate when the appraiser determines the **cost to cure** – that is, how much it will cost to repair the problem. A more difficult problem is measurement of incurable depreciation. Obviously, if the problem is incurable there cannot be a cost to cure. For example, a residence located next to a used car lot suffers from economic obsolescence, but measuring the loss of value in dollars is difficult because the problem cannot be cured. Appraisers have various techniques for estimating the amount of incurable depreciation. These techniques rely on the concepts of **economic life** and **physical life**.

Economic life and *physical life*   The concept of "life" as used in real estate appraisal can only be applied to the improvements. To speak of the life of the land is meaningless, since the land is indestructible, immovable and perpetual. Every improvement has both a physical life and an economic life. The physical life is the length of time it could actually remain in existence, and is normally longer than the economic life. The economic life, on the other hand, is the *useful life* of the improvements. When the improvements no longer produce a benefit beyond the benefit which could be derived if the land were unimproved, then we say the improvements have reached the end of their economic life.

In real life, the only time the physical life turns out to be shorter than the economic life is in the event of a catastrophe which results in the destruction of the improvements (end of the physical life) before the end of their economic life. This principle is exemplified by the saying "more houses are torn down than fall down." That these concepts are true is proved by what happens when there is a catastrophe — if the improvements are destroyed, but still had remaining economic life at the time of their destruction, the owner will use the insurance money to rebuild. If the improvements were at the end of their economic life anyway, the owner will probably just put the insurance money in the bank and sell the vacant lot. When there are vacant lots in a neighborhood where the improvements have been destroyed and not rebuilt, this is a symptom that the structures in the area are reaching the ends of their economic lives.

Example You own a single-family residence in a blighted area. The land has been rezoned for general commercial use. You are able to rent the property as a residence for $1,000 per month ($12,000 per year), which nets you $9,000 per year after expenses. However, due to its zoning, the land value alone is $120,000. If you tore the house down and sold the land, you could place the $120,000 realized from the sale of the land into another investment. If the rate available for an alternative investment is 9%, then you could realize $10,800 per year. This is greater than what you are currently getting from the land and the building together, so keeping the building on the land is a diseconomy and a violation of the appraisal principles of balance and highest and best use. In this case the building has reached the end of its economic life.

Chronological (actual) age and *effective age* The **chronological age** of the improvements is simply the number of years since they were first constructed. A building which was built 70 years ago has a chronological age of 70 years. However, the **effective age** may be more or less than the chronological age, depending on the remaining economic life.

For example, consider a structure which would have a projected economic life of 50 years if new today with today's amenities, style and design. If the structure currently has a remaining economic life of 30 years, then it is 20 years old effectively —

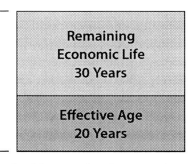

If the chronological age of the building in the drawing above is 70 years, we can conclude that there is some condition which has made the effective age (20 years) dramatically less than the chronological age (70 years). Perhaps the owner has rehabilitated the structure, perhaps it is of a historic style that is in great demand, or perhaps there is a shortage of similar properties in the area.

The effective age is frequently incorrectly thought of as being determined by the manner in which the improvements have been maintained. A longer economic life generally means a shorter effective age (and greater value). But the remaining economic life is determined more by externalities than by factors intrinsic to the property.

For example, it is possible to find properties which have been maintained in excellent condition, even though the owner knew the property would likely be torn down soon to make way for a different land use. If we judge the economic life from the condition, we would erroneously conclude that the improvements have a long remaining economic life. Even more common is the opposite – a property in poor condition located in an excellent neighborhood. When a property in a good neighborhood has been poorly maintained it does not mean that the remaining economic life of the property is shorter than its neighbors. The proof can be seen if the poorly maintained property is offered for sale. The buyer will usually restore the structure, or if it has deteriorated to the point where it cannot be restored, the owner will tear it down and replace it with a new structure of similar utility. This is because the new owner senses that the economic life is sufficiently long to justify the expense of rehabilitation or rebuilding. Notice that it was the externalities – the area surrounding the property, that determined the economic life, not the condition of the property itself.

However, appraisers do tend to equate good maintenance with a shorter (younger) effective age, and poor maintenance with a longer (older) effective age. As a rule, this tends to work, because owners usually maintain their properties in good condition if the remaining economic life is long enough to justify it. But care must be taken to remember that effective age is related to the remaining economic life of the structure, not to its condition. The current condition of the improvements is merely a symptom or indication of the probable remaining economic life.

Using the concepts of life and age, an appraiser can determine the dollar amount of accrued depreciation. Take the property in the graphic on the preceding page, for example. If a new property with today's amenities, style and design would have a projected economic life of 50 years, and the subject property has a remaining economic life of 30 years, then the effective age is 20 years, and we can conclude that 20 years of the economic life is used up. In other words, depreciation on this structure – from all sources – is $^{20}\!/_{50}$, or 40%. Now if the appraiser has determined that the cost to reproduce the structure would be $200,000, then the current depreciated value can be computed by subtracting 40%, that is, $200,000 − $80,000 = $120,000 current value.

The problem with the above method is that it requires accurate judgment as to the remaining economic life and the projected economic life if the property were new. This is not possible. Appraisers, therefore, try to arrive at the amount of accrued depreciation in more scientific ways. One way is by ***observed condition***. This means that the appraiser rates different components of the property to determine their condition and arrives at conclusions as to the remaining economic life and effective age from the results. The problem, however, is that observed condition still assumes that the remaining economic life is tied to the condition of the property, which we know is not always the case.

Another technique used by appraisers is to observe the amount of difference between the market value of different types of properties and their replacement or reproduction cost. If an appraiser can determine from studying market transactions that bungalow style houses in a certain neighborhood tend to depreciate at a rate of, for example, ½ of 1% per year, then this fact can be used the next time the appraiser has an assignment to appraise a similar property. This technique requires experience to use effectively, but in most cases is probably the most accurate.

NOTES

Regardless of the technique used to calculate the amount of accrued depreciation, it is not easy to be accurate. The result is that the more accrued depreciation in the improvements, the less reliable the cost approach. Measuring accrued depreciation is the weak link in the cost approach. Therefore, when correlating the results of the three approaches, the results of the cost approach should be weighted heavily as an indication of the upper limit of value if the property is a newer property with little or no incurable depreciation. The older the property, however, the less the results of the cost approach should be relied upon.

Exercise e

The cost approach relies primarily on the principle of _____ , and the resulting value is generally the _____ _____ of value. Because the cost approach relies on reproduction or replacement cost, it cannot be used on _____ . A loss in value from any source is called _____ . When the property has not been maintained well, this is called _____ _____ . When it is out of date, we call this _____ _____ . When the property has suffered a loss in value as a result of outside forces, we call this _____ _____ . If it is feasible to remedy the problem, we say it is _____ ; if not, it is _____ depreciation.

When an appraiser estimates the cost by computing what a builder would charge to reproduce the structure, this is called _____ _____ . When the cost is calculated in whole components, it is called _____ ____ _____ . The most common method uses a _____ _____ , and the most common of these is _____ _____ .

The number of years since a structure was built is its _____ (actual) age. However, the _____ life of a property is the time over which it is anticipated to remain useful. The projected _____ life of a property if new today, less its remaining life as the structure exists today, is the _____ age of the structure.

The income approach to value

The *income approach to value* (also sometimes called the *income capitalization approach to value* or just the *capitalization approach*) rests squarely on the principle of anticipation. That is, the greater the anticipated future benefits the property will produce, the greater the present value.

The income approach is the most powerful approach for income properties such as office and apartment buildings, warehouses, and even going businesses. Even if a property does not currently produce an income, such as, for example, an owner occupied residence, a potential income can be imputed on which to base the value.

The first step in appraising a property by the income approach is to determine the income the property can produce. To find this, the appraiser must determine the **market** or **economic rent**. Market rent is the income the property could and should be producing, and is determined by comparison with other similar income-producing properties in the area. The process of finding the market rent is called a ***market (economic) rent survey***.

Market rent must be contrasted with ***contract rent***. Contract rent is the rent the owner is currently receiving from the property. If the investment is properly managed, the contract rent should be the same as market rent. But it is certainly possible for the contract rent to be higher or, more likely, lower than the market rent. However, if the property is leased at a fixed rate (flat lease), then the contract rent is the market rent because the owner does not have the option to raise the rents.

If the rent is payable in installments, the appraiser computes what the total annual income would be. This is called the ***potential gross income*** (PGI). Similarly, all expense figures are also computed on an annual basis. Keeping all figures on an annual basis helps avoid computational errors.

The potential gross income is the first figure on the appraisers ***projected operating statement***, also sometimes called a ***pro-forma***. The projected operating statement is the appraiser's estimate of the amount of income the property will produce, net of expenses, in the current economic climate, under optimum management.

It is easier to understand the income approach if we take it from the standpoint of a specific property. Look at the projected operating statement for the *Barkdust Apartments* –

BARKDUST APARTMENTS
Projected Operating Statement

Income
Potential Gross Income (**PGI**)
15 Units × $900 per month = $13,500; × 12 months = ... $162,000
Less Vacancy and Credit Loss $8,100
Effective Gross Income (**EGI**) 153,900

Operating Expenses
Fixed Expenses
    Property taxes 18,500
    Fire and liability insurance 2,500

    Subtotal 21,000
Variable Expenses
    Management (@10% of PGI) 16,200
    Utilities (water/sewer, outside lights, trash) 6,000
    Normal maintenance 5,500
    Reserves for replacements 6,500
    Advertising 500
    Miscellaneous (accounting, landscaping, etc.) 1,000

    Subtotal 35,700
Total Operating Expenses .... (56,700)

Net Operating Income (NOI) $97,200

Notes to Projected Operating Statement Vacancy and credit loss from market at 5% of PGI. Property taxes based on current tax assessed valuation of $1,215,000 at current tax rate of $15.00 per thousand. Normal maintenance includes ongoing expenses for ordinary repairs. Reserves for replacement is allowance for replacement or maintenance of major structural items, such as roof, exterior paint, appliances, carpeting and the like. All income and expense figures obtained from sources deemed to be reliable.

The Barkdust Apartments consist of a 15-unit complex located in an average metropolitan neighborhood. The structure is 12 years old and in generally good condition. All units have two bedrooms, one bath and no other unusual amenities. A market rent survey has disclosed that the units should be rented for $900 per month. The tax assessed value is $1,215,000 and the tax rate is $15 per thousand. All other expenses on the projected operating statement were verified by the appraiser personally from independent sources.

The Projected Operating Statement Referring to the projected operating statement on the preceding page, note that the appraiser has deducted 5% of the potential gross income as an allowance for *vacancy and credit loss*. In order to reflect the real world as accurately as possible the appraiser must adjust for the fact that a certain vacancy factor is inevitable. *The vacancy and credit loss factor is not an arbitrary percentage; it must be derived from the market.* If the appraiser calculates projected rents as derived from the market area surrounding the subject property, then an owner who rents the units at the market rent will experience the same vacancy factor as is being experienced by owners of other properties in the area. The gross income after subtracting vacancy and credit loss is currently called the *effective gross income* (EGI), although some older texts may still refer to it as the *gross operating income*.

Operating expenses are those expenses which are required for the property to produce an income, exclusive of principal and interest on loans or owner's income taxes. (Why these items are excluded is discussed later.) Many appraisers prefer to categorize expenses as those which are *fixed expenses* and those which are *variable expenses*. Fixed expenses are those expenses which the owner would incur whether all units are rented or the building is completely vacant. Variable expenses, on the other hand, are expenses which increase with occupancy. For example, if the management company charges their management fee on the rent *as collected*, then their fees are variable with the rate of occupancy. If their fees are based on the potential gross income, whether collected or not, then their fees are a fixed expense.

After subtracting all expenses, the result is called the *net operating income* (NOI). The net operating income is the amount the owner could expect to realize net of all expenses attributable to the property, exclusive of principal and interest on loans. Note that the net operating income also represents what the property would net if completely managed, assuming the owner's investment is totally passive.

Principal and interest on loans is disregarded at this point because the purpose of the projected operating statement is to determine what income the property would produce if the investment were all cash. At the same time, complete management expense has been duly subtracted. While it is true that in the real world many properties are financed, and it is also true that many owners manage their own properties, at this point in the appraisal we wish to disregard these factors. The reason is that we now wish to use the principle of substitution and compare the income potential of this investment with investments in the marketplace other than real estate. And most other investments – stock, bonds, certificates of deposit – are all-cash, completely passive investments. Structuring the projected operating statement to determine what net income the apartment building could produce if it were an all-cash and completely passive investment allows us to make it as comparable to these other investments as possible.

The capitalization process Now that we understand the purpose of the projected operating statement, we can proceed with the process of finding what an owner would pay for the investment, based on the projected net operating income. This process is called *capitalization*.

The investment marketplace is full of investment opportunities, each with its particular advantages and disadvantages. For our purposes, however, it does not matter which type of investment we choose, because they are all competing with each other continually. Since they all constantly seek their own level with each other, by comparing the apartment building investment to any one type of non-real estate investment, we automatically compare to all. It is common practice, therefore, to compare to the simplest non-real estate investment, usually a deposit at a financial institution.

Before we can begin the comparison, we must learn a few formulas. If you invest $100 in a bank deposit for one year, the amount of interest (income) you will receive is determined by the interest rate. In other words, if the bank will pay, say 9%, then at the end of the year you will have earned $9.00. This is expressed by the formula

$$Income \ = \ Rate \times Investment$$

Of course, we can also calculate the rate an investor is getting on an investment. The formula is

$$Rate \ = \ Income \ \div \ Investment$$

For our purposes, there is another formula that is the most important – the formula to compute the amount of the investment when the rate and income are known. This formula is

$$Investment \ = \ Income \ \div \ Rate$$

Of course, these formulas are used primarily by investors. Appraisers need to change the terminology slightly. An appraiser would recast the investment formula as

$$Value \ = \ Income \ \div \ Rate$$

Now we are ready to think about what a buyer would pay for the Barkdust Apartments. We already know the net operating income is $97,200, so if a buyer were willing to accept rate of, say 8%, our formula above indicates the buyer must be willing to pay $1,215,000 ($97,200 ÷ .08 = $1,215,000).

Of course, depending on the current market interest rates, a given investor may be happy with an 8% rate on a bank deposit, but would the same investor be satisfied with 8% on the apartment investment? If not, then an adjustment must be made. Consider the following chart showing what happens to the value of the apartments as rates demanded by investors change –

$97,200	÷	8.00%	=	$1,215,000
$97,200	÷	8.25%	=	$1,178,182
$97,200	÷	8.50%	=	$1,143,529
$97,200	÷	8.75%	=	$1,110,857
$97,200	÷	9.00%	=	$1,080,000
$97,200	÷	9.25%	=	$1,050,811
$97,200	÷	9.50%	=	$1,023,158
$97,200	÷	9.75%	=	$996,923
$97,200	÷	10.00%	=	$972,000

The above chart shows what happens when the rate demanded by investors changes. As the rate increases, the value decreases, and vice-versa. If you think about the bank account – our point of comparison – this makes sense. The higher the interest rate, the less you have to put on deposit to get the same annual interest income. Therefore, if the bank will pay 10% interest, it would take a deposit of only $972,000 to get an annual interest income of $97,200. Because the income from the apartment building is constant at any point in time, we would expect an investor to be unwilling to pay more for the apartment building than $972,000.

Think of the relationship among the rate, the income and the value like a teeter-totter. At any point in time the net operating income (NOI) is unalterable, so as the rate changes the value changes in the opposite direction –

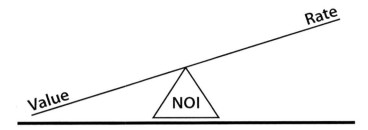

Even having made the net operating income (NOI) appear as similar as possible to the return on other investments – all cash and completely passive – we must still adjust the rate. Appraisers recognize that investors may be willing to accept a certain rate on a bank deposit, but the same investor may demand a different rate for an investment in an apartment building.

There are several reasons the rate must be adjusted. Most obvious is that the investment in the bank account is generally regarded as safer than the investment in the apartment building. Furthermore, real estate investments have a reputation of being less liquid – harder to sell for cash – than other investments; certainly less liquid than the bank deposit. Less obvious, but still important, is the fact that investment in improved real property offers an investor income tax advantages which would not be available if the money were invested in a bank account.

One of the most important differences between an investment in a bank deposit and a real estate investment is the potential for capital gain. In other words, if you put your money in a bank account for a number of years and then withdraw it, the money has lost purchasing power because of inflation. But if you put your money into a real estate investment, when you sell the investment years later, your will get more dollars in return. Even though the dollars you get back when you sell the investment are not worth as much, you get sufficiently more of them to make up for their lost value. This is called a ***hedge against inflation***.

Special note Although unsophisticated investors do not usually understand the difference, professionals know that "hedge against inflation" is not the same as "appreciation." Hedge against inflation occurs when you invest in a hard asset such as real estate, gold, classic cars, art, and the like, and then sell the asset for more, albeit cheaper, dollars later. Inflation raises the number of dollars you can get for the investment, and does so equally for all investments, but does not raise the real value.

Appreciation occurs when some unforeseen event raises the value of an investment more than the value of other similar investments. If you buy an apartment building for $1,000,000 and later sell it for $2,000,000 because the dollar has devalued to half its former value, you have benefited from a hedge against inflation. If you buy an apartment building for $1,000,000 and are later able to sell it for $2,000,000 because a shopping center was built next door making the apartment building more desirable to an investor, you have benefited from appreciation. Some appraisers use the older term ***unearned increment*** to describe both appreciation and hedge against inflation. Sophisticated investors know that true appreciation accounts for little of the increase in market value. Properties almost always increase in market value over time, but mostly from the effects of inflation, not appreciation.

To summarize the adjustments we need to make, let us suppose the banks are currently offering about 7% on deposits. Appraisers call this the ***safe rate***, or sometimes ***bank*** *rate*, **guaranteed rate** or **annuity rate**. Let us further suppose that investigation of market data leads us to the conclusion that we should further adjust the safe rate as follows –

Safe rate	7%
Add for additional risk	+ 1%
Add for lack of liquidity	+ 1%
Subtract for tax shelter benefits	– 1%
Subtract for hedge against inflation	– 4%
Adjusted return on investment required	6% (Yield Rate)

The above adjustments were not meant to be accurate; they were made solely for the purpose of illustration. Therefore, the conclusion that an investor would accept 6% return on the apartment building investment when banks are paying 7% on deposits, is not necessarily correct. Later in our discussion we will discover a technique which allows appraisers to determine an accurate and reliable rate. However, there is another factor which must be considered first.

When an investor will get the entire principal back at the end of the investment period, such as when the money is deposited in a bank account, the proper rate to use is a **yield rate** (as above), also sometimes called a **return on the investment**.

But in some investments, the amount invested is used up over the life of the investment. For example, if you invest in an oil well, the investment becomes worthless as the oil is pumped out and sold. When the well is dry, it is worth only the value of the used pumping equipment and whatever the land will bring – little or nothing in comparison to the original value of the well. At the end of the bank account investment, however, the investor will get back the entire amount of the principal invested. The bank account does not become worthless over its term. (Note that we have already adjusted for loss of market value due to inflation in the adjustments above.) If an investor were comparing the rate of return required for the bank account with the rate of return required for an oil well, it would be necessary to add an additional percentage to account for **recapture** of the oil well investment over its useful life. The rate for recapture is also sometimes called the **return of the investment**.

Assets such as oil wells are referred to as **wasting assets** because they are used up and become worthless over their economic lives. Wasting assets include not only oil wells, but real estate as well. If you recall from the discussion of economic life, we discovered that a structure has an economic life, and the value of the structure at the end of its economic life is zero. So if an additional percentage should be added to the bank rate to adjust it for an oil well, an additional percentage should also be added when comparing the bank deposit to a real estate investment.

The next question to be determined is how much the recapture adjustment should be. Apartment buildings usually have a fairly long useful life, so let us assume the Barkdust Apartments have a remaining economic life of 40 years. If the structure will become worthless over the next 40 years, then we must recapture 2½% each year (100% ÷ 40 years = 2.5% per year).

But there is another important fact to consider. Only the building will become worthless at the end of its useful life; there is no economic life for land, so recapture of the land is not necessary. For the sake of the discussion, let us assume that the structure accounts for 80% of the total investment and the land represents the other 20%. In other words, if an investor paid $1,000,000 for the investment, this was really $800,000 (80%) for the improvements, and $200,000 (20%) for the land.

Therefore, we only need to recapture 80% of the total investment. And if we have a 40-year economic life in which to do this, the recapture rate should be 2% (80% ÷ 40 years = 2% per year). Now our adjustments look like this –

Safe rate	7%	
Add for additional risk	+ 1%	
Add for lack of liquidity	+ 1%	
Subtract for tax shelter benefits	− 1%	
Subtract for hedge against inflation	− 4%	
Adjusted return *on* investment required	6%	(Yield Rate)
Return *of* investment required	+ 2%	(Recapture Rate)
Capitalization rate	*8%*	

Note that the rate above is now called the ***capitalization rate***. To an accountant or an appraiser, a capitalization rate is a rate which includes a yield *on* the investment plus a rate for recapture *of* the investment. Non-wasting assets such as bank accounts, bonds, and the like, must be considered in terms of a yield rate; wasting assets such as buildings, oil wells, mines and the like, must be valued with a capitalization rate.

Now it appears that, if all our assumptions and adjustments are accurate, an investor should demand a return of 8% for the Barkdust Apartments. In fact, however, there is no way to be sure that our figures are accurate. If you recall from our previous discussion, raising or lowering the rate has a dramatic effect on the value. On a net operating income of $97,200, if we change the rate by a mere ¼ of 1%, the difference in value is almost $37,000 −

$97,200	÷	8.00%	=	$1,215,000
$97,200	÷	8.25%	=	$1,178,182

It is apparent that appraisers cannot use the income approach properly without an accurate capitalization rate, and the process we just used is likely to be far from accurate. The theory we used is correct, but it is impossible to be accurate about the assumptions and adjustments we made.

To derive an accurate capitalization rate appraisers usually apply a more direct method called ***market extraction***. If you recall, we can calculate the rate of return an investor is getting on an investment with the formula

Rate = Income ÷ Investment

To recast this for appraisal purposes, just change the names of the terms −

Capitalization Rate = Net Operating Income ÷ Value

In other words, appraisers can find the capitalization rate which an investor is getting just by dividing the net operating income (NOI) by the market value of the property. We know that investors base a great deal of the investment decision on the anticipated rate of return. Therefore, an appraiser uses this formula to extract the capitalization rates from several recently sold comparable properties, and correlates the resulting rates to derive an overall market capitalization rate for similar properties. Using market extraction to find the capitalization rate is highly reliable, since it is based directly on the market.

Of course, if appraisers can simply find an accurate overall capitalization rate by market extraction, it would seem that dissecting the capitalization rate into components such as safe rate, risk factor, recapture, and the like, is a pointless academic exercise. Even though the theory of the capitalization rate is not usually very helpful in real-world appraising, the theory is nevertheless correct. In fact, capitalization theory is useful in another way, because it lets us understand better what happens in the marketplace.

For example, at any given point in time, should we use the same capitalization rate on all properties? If you understand the adjustments we made in discussing the theory of the capitalization rate, you will realize that different properties entail different risk and liquidity considerations, and have different remaining economic lives. A new property in an excellent neighborhood will have comparatively little risk and a long remaining economic life, so its capitalization rate should be low. On the other hand, an older property in a poorer neighborhood may entail substantial risk, lack of liquidity and have a short remaining economic life. For such a property, a much higher capitalization rate is needed.

Investors also benefit from understanding capitalization rates. For example, what would happen to the values of properties if interest rates increase? Increasing interest rates would be translated immediately into higher capitalization rates demanded by investors. And higher rates mean lower values. Or what would happen if there is suddenly an anticipation of increased inflation? Or an increase in tax benefits of owning real estate? Both of these are benefits, so investors would lower the capitalization rates they demand, and there would be a corresponding increase in market values.

Gross rent multipliers Let us consider again the Barkdust Apartments. The potential gross income (PGI) was $162,000 and the net operating income (NOI) was $97,200. If market extraction tells us the proper capitalization rate to use is 8%, then the value is $1,215,000 ($97,200 ÷ .08 = $1,215,000).

If this is an accurate reflection of the market, then we can conclude another fact – that the property ought to sell for about 7.5 times its potential gross income (PGI). The number "7.5" here is called a ***gross rent multiplier*** (GRM), or sometimes ***gross income multiplier*** (GIM). Gross rent multipliers are extracted from the market in much the same way as capitalization rates. To find the gross rent multiplier for a recently sold comparable, just divide the sales price at which the comparable sold by the potential gross income of the property when it sold. The formula is

Gross Rent Multiplier = Sales Price ÷ Potential Gross Income

In other words, $1,215,000 divided by $162,000 is 7.5 – ($1,215,000 ÷ $162,000 = 7.500), so the market value is 7.5 times the potential gross income. If we had several recently sold comparable properties, all of which corroborate the fact that such properties tend to sell for about 7.5 times their potential gross income, the number "7.5" could be considered a market gross rent multiplier for all such similar properties.

Using a gross rent multiplier is an easy way to determine the market value of an income property – just multiply the subject property's potential gross income by a multiplier extracted from the market, and you have the market value. But there are several dangers in using a gross rent multiplier.

Gross rent multipliers are derived from the potential gross income (PGI), not the net operating income (NOI). If you wish to use a gross rent multiplier accurately, then you must derive it from properties that are very similar. Whether a property is older or newer, in a poorer or better neighborhood, among many other factors, has great bearing on the ratio of expenses to income, and this ratio must be identical for the gross rent multiplier to be used accurately.

In the Barkdust Apartments, the total operating expenses were $64,800, which is 40% of the potential gross income ($64,800 ÷ $162,000 = .40). If the Barkdust Apartments had been older, in poorer condition, or suffered from some other detriment, the expenses would likely have been much higher, and therefore the ratio of expenses to potential gross income would have been higher. Since gross rent multipliers are based on the potential *gross* income, not the *net* income, their use presumes that the subject property will have the same ratio of expenses to potential gross income as the properties from which the gross rent multiplier was derived. The danger in using a gross rent multiplier is that many novices take the shortcut too quickly and do not verify that the gross rent multiplier is correct for the property they are appraising.

NOTES

Most appraisers today consider a gross rent multiplier effective as a quick estimating tool, but not a satisfactory method for serious appraisal of an income property. Considering that the income approach is the most powerful approach for an income property, it makes little sense to use a questionable technique. However, gross rent multipliers are commonly used by brokers and their customers and clients in establishing an asking or offering price for a property.

Exercise f

The income approach depends primarily on the appraisal principle of _____ . The first step in appraising by the income approach is to determine the _____ rent, also sometimes called the _____ rent for the property to be appraised. This task is called a _____ _____ . What the property is currently rented for is its _____ rent. On an annual basis, this is called the _____ _____ _____ . Subtracting the vacancy and credit loss from this results in the _____ _____ income. Then the expenses are subtracted, which leaves the _____ _____ income. Expenses include _____ expenses, which are those expenses which would be incurred regardless of the income level, and _____ expenses, where the amount of the expense is based on the occupancy level. Converting the income to value is called _____ . The basic formula to convert income to value is _____ .

The higher the rate demanded by investors, the _____ the market value. In appraising an income property an appraiser would use a _____ rate, which is a composite of a market _____ and a _____ rate to account for the fact that the building is becoming worthless over its _____ _____ . Such rates are usually obtained by _____ _____ . Sometimes appraisers, investors and real estate agents use a _____ _____ _____ as a quick estimating tool.

🔑 KEY TERMS

The key to understanding any new field is the vocabulary used in that field. To maximize your comprehension of the material presented in this chapter, be sure you know the meaning and significance of the following terms. Remember that the majority of test questions primarily test knowledge of vocabulary.

Actual age	Approaches to value
Advocacy	Arms length transactions
Agent	Assessed value
Annuity rate	Balance
Anticipation	Bank rate
Appraisal	Book value
Appraisal by anticipated use	Capitalization approach to value
Appraisal by development cost	Capitalization rate

Change

Chronological age

Comparative unit

Competition

Conformity

Contract rent

Contribution

Correlation

Cost

Cost to cure

Cost to reproduce new

Curable depreciation

Decline

Demand

Depreciated value

Depreciation

Economic forces

Economic life

Economic obsolescence

Economic rent

Effective age

Effective gross income

Effective purchasing power

Efficient market

Environmental forces

Equilibrium

External obsolescence

Externalities

Fee appraiser

Fiduciary

Fixed expenses

Four agents in production

Functional obsolescence

Gentrification

Governmental forces

Gross income multiplier

Gross operating income.

Gross rent multiplier

Growth

Guaranteed rate

Hedge against inflation

Highest and best use

Income approach to value

Income capitalization approach

Incurable depreciation

Independent fee appraiser

Insurance value

Intrinsic value

Liquidation (liquidated) value

Loan value

Market data approach

Market extraction

Market rent survey

Market value

Neighborhood

Net operating income

Observed condition

Physical deterioration

Physical forces

Physical life

Plottage increment

Potential gross income

Price

Pro-forma

Progression

Projected operating statement

Quantity survey method

Real market value

Recapture

Reconciliation

Regression

Replacement cost

Reproduction cost

Residual value

Return of the investment

Return on the investment

Revitalization

Safe rate

Sales comparison approach

Salvage value

Scarcity

Single-use property

Social forces

Stability

Substitution

Surplus productivity

Transferability

Trend

Unearned increment

Uniform Residential Appraisal Report

Unit in place method

Utility

Vacancy and credit loss

Valuation

Value in exchange

Value in use

Variable expenses

Wasting assets

Yield rate

 **ANSWERS**

To chapter exercises. If you couldn't figure out what to put in the blanks, find the answer here!

Exercise a

A synonym for appraisal is ___VALUATION___ . The majority of appraisals ordered by private parties are required by ___FINANCIAL___ institutions.

An appraiser normally operates in a relationship of ___PRINCIPAL___ and ___AGENT___ . This means that the appraiser owes a duty of ___LOYALTY___ to the principal, as well as full ___DISCLOSURE___ , ___CONFIDENTIALITY___ and due ___DILIGENCE___ . These are referred to as the ___FIDUCIARY___ duties of the agent. Nevertheless, an appraiser does not act as an ___ADVOCATE___ , that is, the opinion of value is to be rendered impartially without regard to which party is the appraiser's client.

Exercise b

A value to the owner of a property is its value ___IN___ ___USE___ , which is ___SUBJECTIVE___ and dependent on emotion. A value ___IN___ ___EXCHANGE___ is the value to an ordinary buyer in a market transaction and is ___OBJECTIVE___ . To establish value, appraisers attempt to find the ___TREND___ . The four factors which must be present for a commodity to have value are ___DEMAND (DESIRE), SCARCITY,___ ___EFFECTIVE PURCHASING POWER (TRANSFERABILITY), AND UTILITY___

The forces which influence value are ___SOCIAL, GOVERNMENTAL, PHYSICAL (ENVIRONMENTAL) AND ECONOMIC___ Which of the following would be closest to the market value as defined in the Uniform Residential Appraisal Report? ❑ Assessed value ❑ Book value ❑ Insurance value ❑ Loan value ■ Real market value ❑ Liquidation value ❑ Intrinsic value

What an owner paid for a property is its ___COST___ which is not normally the market value of the property. The ___PRICE___ of a property is the amount an owner is or was asking for the property, and is also not necessarily market value.

To be the highest and best use of a property, the use must be ___LEGAL___ , physically possible, financially ___FEASIBLE___ and finally, the use which produces the ___MAXIMUM___ benefit to the owner. The principle which holds that no one would pay more for a commodity than it would cost to obtain an identical commodity is the principle of ___SUBSTITUTION___ . The fact that market value is dependent on the future benefits which can be derived from owning the property is the principle of ___ANTICIPATION___ . When appraisers say that extrinsic forces change the value of a property, this is a reference to the principle of ___EXTERNALITIES___ . According to the principle of ___CHANGE___ , an appraiser can make an appraisal report as of the current date or a date in the ___PAST___ , but not for a date in the ___FUTURE___ . The three typical stages of a neighborhood are ___GROWTH___ , ___STABILITY___ or equilibrium, and ___DECLINE___ . When upscale buyers move into a neighborhood and restore it, this is called ___GENTRIFICATION___ . When properties are of a homogenous character in a neighborhood, the neighborhood will be able to withstand ___CHANGE___ better, thereby increasing the useful ___LIFE___ of the improvements and increasing the value. This is the appraisal principle of ___CONFORMITY___ . A small house in a neighborhood of larger houses benefits from the principle of ___PROGRESSION___ ; the opposite example is a large house in a neighborhood of smaller houses, which suffers from the appraisal principle of ___REGRESSION___ . When all components are in optimum ___BALANCE___ the property reaches its highest and best use and therefore its highest potential value. According to the principle of ___CONTRIBUTION___ , all components add to the overall value, but not necessarily in proportion to their ___COST___ . The principle of ___COMPETITION___ tells us that excess profits can be ruinous. The principle of ___SURPLUS___ ___PRODUCTIVITY___ allows us to isolate a portion of the income of a property and thereby determine the value of the portion of the asset which created that income.

Exercise c

The first step in making an appraisal is to ___DEFINE___ the appraisal task. In some cases this may include an analysis of the ___HIGHEST___ and ___BEST___ ___USE___ of the property.

Making a judgment by taking a weighted average of the results of the different approaches to value is referred to as ___CORRELATION___ or ___RECONCILIATION___ .

A common report is the ____UNIFORM____ ____RESIDENTIAL____ ____APPRAISAL____ ____REPORT____ .

Exercise d

The market data approach is usually very powerful and accurate when there are a sufficient number of ____COMPARABLE____ sales, such as would be found in an ____EFFICIENT____ market. Appraisers compare the subject property to recently sold properties, but only where the sale was an ____ARMS____ ____LENGTH____ transaction. Appraisers can also use properties which are currently being offered for sale, but these tend to fix the ____UPPER____ limit of value, since there is no guarantee they will eventually sell for their asking prices.

When the subject property is a ____SINGLE____ ____PURPOSE____ property it is unlikely there will be any comparable sales. Still, an appraiser can conduct an appraisal of such a property by making it an appraisal ____BY____ ____ANTICIPATED____ ____USE____ .

Adjustments to value are ____DEDUCTED____ from the sales price of the comparable when the comparable is better than the subject property, and ____ADDED____ to the sales price of the comparable when the comparable is poorer than the subject.

In the reconciliation (correlation) of the results from the comparable properties, the appraiser uses a ____WEIGHTED____ average.

Exercise e

The cost approach relies primarily on the principle of ____SUBSTITUTION____ , and the resulting value is generally the ____UPPER____ ____LIMIT____ of value. Because the cost approach relies on re-production or replacement cost, it cannot be used on ____LAND____ . A loss in value from any source is called ____DEPRECIATION____ . When the property has not been maintained well, this is called ____PHYSICAL____ ____DETERIORATION____ . When it is out of date, we call this ____FUNCTIONAL____ ____OBSOLESCENCE____ . When the property has suffered a loss in value as a result of outside forces, we call this ____ECONOMIC____ ____OBSOLESCENCE____ . If it is feasible to remedy the problem, we say it is ____CURABLE____ ; if not, it is ____INCURABLE____ depreciation.

When an appraiser estimates the cost by computing what a builder would charge to reproduce the structure, this is called ____QUANTITY____ ____SURVEY____ . When the cost is calculated in whole components, it is called ____UNIT____ ____IN____ ____PLACE____ . The most common method uses a ____COMPARATIVE____ ____UNIT____ , and the most common of these is ____SQUARE____ ____FOOT____ .

The number of years since a structure was built is its ____CHRONOLOGICAL____ (actual) age. However, the ____ECONOMIC____ life of a property is the time over which it is anticipated to remain useful. The projected ____ECONOMIC____ life of a property if new today, less its remaining life as the structure exists today, is the ____EFFECTIVE____ age of the structure.

Exercise f

The income approach depends primarily on the appraisal principle of ____ANTICIPATION____ . The first step in appraising by the income approach is to determine the ____MARKET____ rent, also sometimes called the ____ECONOMIC____ rent for the property to be appraised. This task is called a ____MARKET____ ____RENT____ ____SURVEY____ . What the property is currently rented for is its ____CONTRACT____ rent. On an annual basis, this is called the ____POTENTIAL____ ____GROSS____ ____INCOME____ . Subtracting the vacancy and credit loss from this results in the ____EFFECTIVE____ ____GROSS____ income. Then the expenses are subtracted, which leaves the ____NET____ ____OPERATING____ income. Expenses include ____FIXED____ expenses, which are those expenses which would be incurred regardless of the income level, and ____VARIABLE____ expenses, where the amount of the expense is based on the occupancy level. Converting the income to value is called ____CAPITALIZATION____ . The basic formula to convert income to value is ____$V = NOI \div CR$____ .

The higher the rate demanded by investors, the ____LOWER____ the market value. In appraising an income property an appraiser would use a ____CAPITALIZATION____ rate, which is a composite of a market ____YIELD____ and a ____RECAPTURE____ rate to account for the fact that the building is becoming worth-less over its ____ECONOMIC____ ____LIFE____ . Such rates are usually obtained by ____MARKET____ ____EXTRACTION____ . Sometimes appraisers, investors and real estate agents use a ____GROSS____ ____RENT____ ____MULTIPLIER____ as a quick estimating tool.

FNMA 1004

Property Description

UNIFORM RESIDENTIAL APPRAISAL REPORT

File No.

SUBJECT

Property Address	City	State	Zip Code
Legal Description		County
Assessor's Parcel No.	Tax Year	R.E. Taxes $	Special Assessments $
Borrower	Current Owner	Occupant ☐ Owner ☐ Tenant ☐ Vacant
Property rights appraised ☐ Fee Simple ☐ Leasehold	Project Type ☐ PUD ☐ Condominium (HUD/VA only)	HOA$ /Mo.
Neighborhood or Project Name	Map Reference	Census Tract
Sale Price $	Date of Sale	Description and $ amount of loan charges/concessions to be paid by seller
Lender/Client	Address	
Appraiser	Address	

NEIGHBORHOOD

Location	☐ Urban	☐ Suburban	☐ Rural	**Predominant occupancy**	**Single family housing**	**Present land use %**	**Land use change**
Built up	☐ Over 75%	☐ 25-75%	☐ Under 25%		PRICE $(000) / AGE (yrs)	One family ___	☐ Not likely ☐ Likely
Growth rate	☐ Rapid	☐ Stable	☐ Slow	☐ Owner	Low	2-4 family ___	☐ In process
Property values	☐ Increasing	☐ Stable	☐ Declining	☐ Tenant	High	Multi-family ___	To:
Demand/supply	☐ Shortage	☐ In balance	☐ Over supply	☐ Vacant (0-5%)	Predominant	Commercial ___	
Marketing time	☐ Under 3 mos.	☐ 3-6 mos.	☐ over 6 mos.	☐ Vacant (over 5%)			

Note: race and the racial composition of the neighborhood are not appraisal factors.

Neighborhood boundaries and characteristics: _____

Factors that affect the marketability of the properties in the neighborhood (proximity to employment and amenities, employment stability, appeal to market, e

Market conditions in the subject neighborhood (including support for the above conclusions related to the trend of property values, demand/supply, and marketing ti -- such as data on competitive properties for sale in the neighborhood, description of the prevalence of sales and financing concessions, etc.):

PUD

Project Information for PUDs (If applicable) -- Is the developer/builder in control of the Home Owner's Association (HOA)? ☐ Yes ☐ No

Approximate total number of units in the subject project _____ Approximate total number of units for sale in the subject project _____

Describe common elements and recreational facilities:

SITE

Dimensions	Topography
Site area	Size
Specific zoning classification and description	Shape
Zoning compliance ☐ Legal ☐ Legal nonconforming (Grandfathered use) ☐ Illegal ☐ No Zoning	Drainage
Highest & best use as improved: ☐ Present use ☐ Other use (explain)	View

Utilities	Public	Other	Off-site Improvements	Type	Public	Private	
Electricity			Street				Landscaping
Gas			Curb/gutter				Driveway Surface
Water			Sidewalk				Apparent easements
Sanitary sewer			Street lights				FEMA Special Flood Hazard Area ☐ Yes ☐ No
Storm sewer			Alley				FEMA Zone ___ Map Date ___
							FEMA Map No.

Comments (apparent adverse easements, encroachments, special assessments, slide areas, illegal or legal nonconforming zoning use, etc.):

DESCRIPTION OF IMPROVEMENTS

GENERAL DESCRIPTION	EXTERIOR DESCRIPTION	FOUNDATION	BASEMENT	INSULATION
No. of Units	Foundation	Slab	Area Sq. Ft.	Roof ☐
No. of Stories	Exterior Walls	Crawl Space	% Finished	Ceiling ☐
Type (Det./Att.)	Roof Surface	Basement	Ceiling	Walls ☐
Design (Style)	Gutters & Dwnspts.	Sump Pump	Walls	Floor ☐
Existing/Proposed	Window Type	Dampness	Floor	None ☐
Age (Yrs.)	Storm/Screens	Settlement	Outside Entry	Unknown ☐
Effective Age (Yrs.)	Manufactured House	Infestation		

ROOMS	Foyer	Living	Dining	Kitchen	Den	Family Rm.	Rec. Rm.	Bedrooms	# Baths	Laundry	Other	Area Sq. Ft.
Basement												
Level 1												
Level 2												

Finished area **above** grade contains: Rooms;   Bedroom(s);   Bath(s);   Square Feet of Gross Living Area

INTERIOR	Materials/Condition	HEATING	KITCHEN EQUIP.	ATTIC	AMENITIES	CAR STORAGE
Floors		Type	Refrigerator ☐	None ☐	Fireplace(s) # ___	None ☐
Walls		Fuel	Range/Oven ☐	Stairs ☐	Patio ___	Garage # of cars
Trim/Finish		Condition	Disposal ☐	Drop Stair ☐	Deck ___	Attached ___
Bath Floor		COOLING	Dishwasher ☐	Scuttle ☐	Porch ___	Detached ___
Bath Wainscot		Central	Fan/Hood ☐	Floor ☐	Fence ___	Built-In ___
Doors		Other	Microwave ☐	Heated ☐	Pool ___	Carport ___
		Condition	Washer/Dryer ☐	Finished ☐		Driveway

COMMENTS

Additional features (special energy efficient items, etc.):

Condition of the improvements, depreciation (physical, functional, and external), repairs needed, quality of construction, remodeling/additions, etc.:

Adverse environmental conditions (such as, but not limited to, hazardous wastes, toxic substances, etc.) present in the improvements, on the site, or in immediate vicinity of the subject property.:

UNIFORM RESIDENTIAL APPRAISAL REPORT

Valuation Section   File No.

ESTIMATED SITE VALUE . . . . = $ _____	Comments on Cost Approach (such as, source of cost estimate site value, square foot calculation and for HUD, VA and FmHA, the estimated remaining economic life of the property): _____

COST APPROACH

ESTIMATED REPRODUCTION COST-NEW-OF IMPROVEMENTS:

Dwelling _____ Sq. Ft. @ $ _____ = $ _____	
_____ Sq. Ft. @ $ _____ = _____	
= _____	
Garage/Carport _____ Sq. Ft. @ $ _____ = _____	
Total Estimated Cost New . . . . = $ _____	
Less Physical Functional External	
Depreciation _____ = $ _____	
Depreciated Value of Improvements . . . . = $ _____	
"As is" Value of Site Improvements . . . . = $ _____	
INDICATED VALUE BY COST APPROACH . . . . = $ _____	Est Rem Econ Life: _____ yrs

SALES COMPARISON ANALYSIS

ITEM	SUBJECT	COMPARABLE NO. 1	COMPARABLE NO. 2	COMPARABLE NO. 3
Address				
Proximity to Subject				
Sales Price	$	$	$	$
Price/Gross Liv. Area	$	$	$	$
Data and/or Verification Source				

VALUE ADJUSTMENTS	DESCRIPTION	DESCRIPTION	+(-)$ Adjustment	DESCRIPTION	+(-)$ Adjustment	DESCRIPTION	+(-)$ Adjustment
Sales or Financing Concessions							
Date of Sale/Time							
Location							
Leasehold/Fee Simple							
Site							
View							
Design and Appeal							
Quality of Construction							
Age							
Condition							
Above Grade	Total Bdrms Baths	Total Bdrms Baths		Total Bdrms Baths		Total Bdrms Baths	
Room Count							
Gross Living Area	Sq. Ft.	Sq. Ft.		Sq. Ft.		Sq. Ft.	
Basement & Finished Rooms Below Grade							
Functional Utility							
Heating/Cooling							
Energy Efficient Items							
Garage/Carport							
Porch, Patio, Deck, Fireplace(s), etc.							
Fence, Pool, etc.							
Net Adj. (total)		+ - $		+ - $		+ - $	
Adjusted Sales Price of Comparable		$		$		$	

Comments on Sales Comparison (including the subject property's compatibility to the neighborhood, etc.): _____

ITEM	SUBJECT	COMPARABLE NO. 1	COMPARABLE NO. 2	COMPARABLE NO. 3
Date, Price and Data Source, for prior sales within year of appraisal				

Analysis of any current agreement of sale, option, or listing of the subject property and analysis of any prior sales of subject and comparables within one year of the date of appraisal

INDICATED VALUE BY SALES COMPARISON APPROACH . . . . $ _____

INDICATED VALUE BY INCOME APPROACH (If Applicable) Estimated Market Rent $ _____ /Mo.x Gross Rent Multiplier _____ =$ _____

This appraisal is made ☐ "as is" ☐ subject to the repairs, alterations, inspections or conditions listed below ☐ subject to completion per plans and specifications

Conditions of Appraisal: _____

Final Reconciliation: _____

RECONCILIATION

The purpose of this appraisal is to estimate the market value of the real property that is subject to this report, based on the above conditions and the certification, contingent and limiting conditions, and market value definition that are stated in the attached Freddie Mac Form 439/Fannie Mae Form 1004B (Revised _____).

I (WE) ESTIMATE THE MARKET VALUE, AS DEFINED, OF THE REAL PROPERTY THAT IS THE SUBJECT OF THIS REPORT, AS OF _____

(WHICH IS THE DATE OF INSPECTION AND THE EFFECTIVE DATE OF THIS REPORT) TO BE $ _____

APPRAISER:	SUPERVISORY APPRAISER (ONLY IF REQUIRED):	
Signature _____	Signature _____	☐ Did ☐ Did Not
Name _____	Name _____	Inspect Property
Date Report Signed _____	Date Report Signed _____	
State Certification # _____ State	State Certification # _____ State	
Or State License # _____ State	Or State License # _____ State	

DEFINITION OF MARKET VALUE: The most probable price which a property should bring in a competitive and open market under all conditions requisite to a fair sale, the buyer and seller, each acting prudently, knowledgeably and assuming the price is not affected by undue stimulus. Implicit in this definition is the consummation of a sale as of a specified date and the passing of title from seller to buyer under conditions whereby: (1) buyer and seller are typically motivated; (2) both parties are well informed or well advised, and each acting in what he considers his own best interest; (3) a reasonable time is allowed for exposure in the open market; (4) payment is made in terms of cash in U.S. dollars or in terms of financial arrangements comparable thereto; and (5) the price represents the normal consideration for the property sold unaffected by special or creative financing or sales concessions* granted by anyone associated with the sale.

*Adjustments to the comparables must be made for special or creative financing or sales concessions. No adjustments are necessary for those costs which are normally paid by sellers as a result of tradition or law in a market area; these costs are readily identifiable since the seller pays these costs in virtually all sales transactions. Special or creative financing adjustments can be made to the comparable property by comparisons to financing terms offered by a third party institutional lender that is not already involved in the property or transaction. Any adjustment should not be calculated on a mechanical dollar for dollar cost of the financing or concessions but the dollar amount of any adjustment should approximate the market's reaction to the financing or concessions based on the appraiser's judgment.

STATEMENT OF LIMITING CONDITIONS AND APPRAISER'S CERTIFICATION

CONTINGENT AND LIMITING CONDITIONS: The appraiser's certification that appears in the appraisal report s subject to the following conditions:

1. The appraiser will not be responsible for matters of a legal nature that affect either the property being appraised or the title to it. The appraiser assumes that the title is good and marketable and, therefore, will not render any opinions about the title. The property is appraised on the basis of it being under responsible ownership.

2. The appraiser has provided a sketch in the appraisal report to show approximate dimensions of the improvements and the sketch is included only to assist the reader of the report in visualizing the property and understanding the appraiser's determination of its size.

3. The appraiser has examined the available flood maps that are provided by the Federal Emergency Management Agency (or other data sources) and has noted in the appraisal report whether the subject site is located in an identified Special Flood Hazard Area. Because the appraiser is not a surveyor, he or she makes no guarantees, express or implied, regarding this determination.

4. The appraiser will not give testimony or appear in court because he or she made an appraisal of the property in question, unless specific arrangements to do so have been made beforehand.

5. The appraiser has estimated the value of the land in the cost approach at its highest and best use and the improvements at their contributory value. The separate valuations of the land and improvements must not be used in conjunction with any other appraisal and are invalid if they are so used.

6. The appraiser has noted in the appraisal report any adverse conditions (such as, needed repairs, depreciation, the presence of hazardous wastes, toxic substances, etc.) observed during the inspection of the subject property or that he or she became aware of during the normal research involved in performing the appraisal. Unless otherwise stated in the appraisal report, the appraiser has no knowledge of any hidden or unapparent conditions of the property or adverse environmental conditions (including the presence of hazardous wastes, toxic substances, etc.) that would make the property more or less valuable, and has assumed that there are no such conditions and makes no guarantees or warranties, express or implied, regarding the condition of the property. The appraiser will not be responsible for any such conditions that do exist or for any engineering or testing that might be required to discover whether such conditions exist. Because the appraiser is not an expert in the field of environmental hazards, the appraisal report must not be considered as an environmental assessment of the property.

7. The appraiser obtained the information, estimates, and opinions that were expressed in the appraisal report from sources that he or she considers to be reliable and believes them to be true and correct. The appraiser does not assume responsibility for the accuracy of such items that were furnished by other parties.

8. The appraiser will not disclose the contents of the appraisal report except as provided for in the Uniform Standards of Professional Appraisal Practice.

9. The appraiser has based his or her appraisal report and valuation conclusion for an appraisal that is subject to satisfactory completion, repairs, or alterations on the assumption that completion of the improvements will be performed in a workmanlike manner.

10. The appraiser must provide his or her prior written consent before the lender/client specified in the appraisal report can distribute the appraisal report (including conclusions about the property value, the appraiser's identity and professional designations, and references to any professional appraisal organizations or the firm with which the appraiser is associated) to anyone other than the borrower; the mortgagee or its successors and assigns; the mortgage insurer; consultants; professional appraisal organizations; any state or federally approved financial institution; or any department, agency, or instrumentality of the United States or any state or the District of Columbia; except that the lender/client may distribute the property description section of the report only to data collection or reporting service(s) without having to obtain the appraiser's prior written consent. The appraiser's written consent and approval must also be obtained before the appraisal can be conveyed by anyone to the public through advertising, public relations, news, sales, or other media.

APPRAISER'S CERTIFICATION: The Appraiser certifies and agrees that: File No.

1. I have researched the subject market area and have selected a minimum of three recent sales of properties most similar and proximate to the subject property for consideration in the sales comparison analysis and have made a dollar adjustment when appropriate to reflect the market reaction to those items of significant variation. If a significant item in a comparable property is superior to, or more favorable than, the subject property, I have made a negative adjustment to reduce the adjusted sales price of the comparable and, if a significant item in a comparable property is inferior to, or less favorable than the subject property, I have made a positive adjustment to increase the adjusted sales price of the comparable.

2. I have taken into consideration the factors that have an impact on value in my development of the estimate of market value in the appraisal report. I have not knowingly withheld any significant information from the appraisal report and I believe, to the best of my knowledge, that all statements and information in the appraisal report are true and correct.

3. I stated in the appraisal report only my own personal, unbiased, and professional analysis, opinions, and conclusions, which are subject only to the contingent and limiting conditions specified in this form.

4. I have no present or prospective interest in the property that is the subject to this report, and I have no present or prospective personal interest or bias with respect to the participants in the transaction. I did not base, either partially or completely, my analysis and/or the estimate of market value in the appraisal report on the race, color, religion, sex, handicap, familial status, or national origin of either the prospective owners or occupants of the subject property or of the present owners or occupants of the properties in the vicinity of the subject property.

5. I have no present or contemplated future interest in the subject property, and neither my current or future employment nor my compensation for performing this appraisal is contingent on the appraised value of the property.

6. I was not required to report a predetermined value or direction in value that favors the cause of the client or any related party, the amount of the value estimate, the attainment of a specific result, or the occurrence of a subsequent event in order to receive my compensation and/or employment for performing the appraisal. I did not base the appraisal report on a requested minimum valuation, a specific valuation, or the need to approve a specific mortgage loan.

7. I performed this appraisal in conformity with the Uniform Standards of Professional Appraisal Practice that were adopted and promulgated by the Appraisal Standards Board of The Appraisal Foundation and that were in place as of the effective date of this appraisal, with the exception of the departure provision of those Standards, which does not apply. I acknowledge that an estimate of a reasonable time for exposure in the open market is a condition in the definition of market value and the estimate I developed is consistent with the marketing time noted in the neighborhood section of this report, unless I have otherwise stated in the reconciliation section.

8. I have personally inspected the interior and exterior areas of the subject property and the exterior of all properties listed as comparables in the appraisal report. I further certify that I have noted any apparent or known adverse conditions in the subject improvements, on the subject site, or on any site within the immediate vicinity of the subject property of which I am aware and have made adjustments for these adverse conditions in my analysis of the property value to the extent that I had market evidence to support them. I have also commented about the effect of the adverse conditions on the marketability of the subject property.

9. I personally prepared all conclusions and opinions about the real estate that were set forth in the appraisal report. If I relied on significant professional assistance from any individual or individuals in the performance of the appraisal or the preparation of the appraisal report, I have named such individual(s) and disclosed the specific tasks performed by them in the reconciliation section of this appraisal report. I certify that any individual so named is qualified to perform the tasks. I have not authorized anyone to make a change to any item in the report; therefore, if an unauthorized change is made to the appraisal report, I will take no responsibility for it.

SUPERVISORY APPRAISER'S CERTIFICATION: If a supervisory appraiser signed the appraisal report, he or she certifies and agrees that: I directly supervise the appraiser who prepared the appraisal report, have reviewed the appraisal report, agree with the statements and conclusions of the appraiser, agree to be bound by the appraiser's certifications numbered 4 through 7 above, and am taking full responsibility for the appraisal and the appraisal report.

ADDRESS OF PROPERTY APPRAISED: _____

APPRAISER:

Signature: _____

Name: _____

Date Signed: _____

State Certification #: _____

or State License #: _____

State: _____

Expiration Date of Certification or License: _____

SUPERVISORY APPRAISER (only if required):

Signature: _____

Name: _____

Date Signed: _____

State Certification #: _____

or State License #: _____

State: _____

Expiration Date of Certification or License: _____

❏ Did ❏ Did Not Inspect Property

PRACTICE QUESTIONS

The following practice questions are representative of the questions you will find on the final examination and on the licensing examinations given by the Oregon Real Estate Agency.

1. An appraiser's normal goal is to
   (A) set value.
   (B) determine value.
   (C) compute value.
   (D) estimate value.

2. Which of the following best describes the function of a real estate appraiser?
   (A) Estimates the safe loan value
   (B) Determines price
   (C) Estimates value
   (D) Determines value

3. A well done appraisal, including consideration of all available data completed by an appraiser of much experience and good judgment, is best defined as
   (A) a scientifically determined value.
   (B) an opinion.
   (C) legal value.
   (D) the market value.

4. Because of the principles of appraisal, an appraisal report is considered valid for a period of
   (A) three months after the appraisal date.
   (B) six months after the appraisal date.
   (C) one year after the appraisal date.
   (D) It is valid for the date of the appraisal only.

5. An appraiser may advocate the client's position
   (A) at no time.
   (B) only on the witness stand.
   (C) in the finding of value only.
   (D) in the written report only.

6. A qualified appraiser has received an assignment from a lending institution to appraise a property on which the lender intends to make a loan. Which of the following should affect the value estimate?
   (A) The neighborhood in which the property is located
   (B) The current Consumer Price Index (CPI)
   (C) The amount of the intended loan
   (D) Credit rating of the person applying for the loan

7. An appraiser completed an appraisal assignment and reported to the owner a value of $160,000. Subsequently, the owner sold the property for $160,000. Shortly thereafter, the new owner received several offers in excess of $200,000 from other buyers. The appraiser
   (A) may be liable for $40,000 in damages.
   (B) cannot be held liable if the appraisal was for exchange purposes.
   (C) cannot be held liable if the appraisal report was for a lender.
   (D) All of the above are true.

8. In an assignment to appraise a home for the owner, the appraiser's responsibility to the owner
   (A) is as an agent to a principal.
   (B) is a fiduciary responsibility involving the utmost loyalty to the owner.
   (C) requires full disclosure of all facts pertinent to the appraisal assignment.
   (D) includes all of the above elements.

9. A "real estate appraisal" is an estimate of value
   (A) based upon replacement costs.
   (B) based upon analysis of facts as of a specific date.
   (C) derived from income data covering at least the preceding six months.
   (D) derived from average tax assessments covering the past five years.

10. An appraiser gives an appraisal as
    (A) of a given time period.
    (B) of a specific date.
    (C) to the economic conditions surrounding the real property at that time.
    (D) a determination of value.

11. An official valuation of property for ad valorem tax purposes is best described as
    (A) a capitalization.
    (B) an assessment appraisal.
    (C) a recapture rate.
    (D) a building residual.

12. Which of the following pairs mean the same?
    (A) Value in use — current use
    (B) Highest and best use — current use
    (C) Both A and B
    (D) Neither A nor B

13. Identify which of the following is not a widely accepted definition of market value.
    (A) The price at which a willing seller would sell and a willing buyer would buy, neither being under abnormal pressure.
    (B) The value of a property to its owner-user which is based on the productivity of the economic good to a specific individual.
    (C) The highest price which a property will bring if exposed for sale in the open market, allowing a reasonable time to find a purchaser who buys with knowledge of all the uses to which it is adapted and for which it is capable of being used.
    (D) It is the price expected if a reasonable time is allowed to find a purchaser and if both seller and prospective buyer are fully informed.

14. An appraiser could define value as
    (A) the ability of one commodity to command others in exchange.
    (B) the present worth of all future benefits arising from ownership of the property.
    (C) both A and B.
    (D) neither A nor B.

15. Market value is primarily based on
    (A) the "willing buyer, willing seller" concept.
    (B) cost of reproduction.
    (C) tax advantages.
    (D) assessed value.

16. Market value is
    (A) the price a willing seller will accept and a willing purchaser will pay.
    (B) cost of lot plus cost of building.
    (C) cost of lot and the capitalized value of the improvements.
    (D) determined by an appraiser.

17. The market value of a property is the highest price in terms of money which a property will bring in a competitive and open market. Among other conditions, which of the following must exist for a property to be considered sold at market value?
    I.   Buyer and seller were typically motivated.
    II. Payment must have been made in cash only.
    III. Both parties were well informed and acted in their own best interest.
    (A) I and II only   (C) II and III only
    (B) I and III only   (D) I, II and III

18. The amount of money which would be paid by a buyer to a seller for property; both buyer and seller being ready, willing, and able to act and both being fully informed, represents that property's
    (A) exchange value.   (C) market value.
    (B) tax value.   (D) equalized value.

19. Of the following, the dollar valuation which normally is the highest is
    I.   mortgage loan value. III. market value.
    II. residual value.
    (A) I only   (C) III only
    (B) II only   (D) I and III only

20. The value of a piece of land
    I.   is an estimate of the present worth of future benefits.
    II. includes a measure of past expenditures.
    (A) I only   (C) Both I and II
    (B) II only   (D) Neither I nor II

21. An appraiser seeking to find market value would be least concerned with
    (A) original cost of material.
    (B) exchange value.
    (C) reproduction cost.
    (D) market data.

22. Which of the following factors would have no effect in estimating the value of commercial property?
    (A) The accessibility to major roads and railroads
    (B) Income from property
    (C) Original cost of the property
    (D) Zoning

23. An economic good must possess three characteristics:
    (A) scarcity, utility and transferability.
    (B) demand, scarcity and value.
    (C) utility, value and scarcity.
    (D) demand, value and transferability.

24. A measure of a property's value is
    I. the degree of its utility.
    II. the scarcity of comparable utilities.
    (A) I only   (C) Both I and II
    (B) II only   (D) Neither I nor II

25. Demand is one of the elements that help determine value. In order for demand to be effective, it must be implemented by
    (A) highest and best use.
    (B) location.
    (C) purchasing power.
    (D) amenities.

26. Which of the following is not a characteristic of value?
    (A) Utility   (C) Transferability
    (B) Scarcity   (D) Cost

27. Which of the following is not one of the four great forces affecting real property values?
    (A) Governmental   (C) Economic
    (B) Conformity   (D) Social

28. If effective demand for real property in an area remains about the same, over time, the market price will tend to
    (A) rise when supply increases.
    (B) fall when supply decreases.
    (C) rise when supply remains the same.
    (D) rise when supply decreases.

29. If the demand for houses remains constant, whereas the supply of housing
    (A) increases, the value should increase.
    (B) remains the same, the value should increase.
    (C) remains the same, the value should decrease.
    (D) diminishes, the value should increase.

30. If the cost of constructing houses is greater than their market value, what will occur in the short run?
    (A) Costs will decrease.
    (B) Construction will decrease.
    (C) Market value will increase.
    (D) The style of new housing will be changed to reflect the increased costs.

31. The development of a parcel of property to its greatest net income-producing potential reflects the principle of
    (A) substitution.   (C) anticipation.
    (B) highest and best use. (D) market value.

32. Highest and best use is defined as
    (A) property purchased for owner use and occupancy.
    (B) use which will yield the highest present value.
    (C) exclusive residential hill top or view lots.
    (D) property used for churches, schools and hospitals.

33. The concept of the highest and best use is most intimately associated with the appraisal concept of
    (A) substitution.   (C) contribution.
    (B) anticipation.   (D) conformity.

34. Of those listed below, which expression best defines the "highest and best use" of land? That use which
    (A) is in compliance with zoning and deed restrictions.
    (B) produces the highest total gross annual income.
    (C) tends to allow the least degree of physical depreciation.
    (D) is most likely to produce the greatest net return over a given period of time.

35. As a concept of value, the highest and best use is the use that
    (A) contributes to the best interest of the community.
    (B) complies with zoning and deed restrictions.
    (C) produces the highest gross income.
    (D) produces the greatest net return on the investment.

36. Which best describes the highest and best use of property?
    I. The use that will produce the highest net income
    II. The use that will produce the highest gross income
    (A) I only
    (B) II only
    (C) Both I and II
    (D) Neither I nor II

37. A property at its highest and best use will
    (A) conform to all land use regulations.
    (B) produce the greatest net income over a period of time.
    (C) perform a socially valuable service to a community.
    (D) not contain any form of functional obsolescence.

38. Which one of the following best describes the concept of highest and best use?
    (A) Gross return
    (B) Natural and legal use
    (C) Greatest net return over a given period
    (D) Homogeneous use

39. Joseph Smith owned an older home on a corner lot. A professional appraiser advised him that considerably more income could be obtained if the house were torn down and a different improvement placed upon the lot. This illustrates the principle of
    (A) regression.
    (B) supply and demand.
    (C) substitution.
    (D) highest and best use.

40. Certain economic principles are of considerable importance in the valuation of real estate. The principle that "no prudent person would pay more for a product than that for which he or she could buy a reasonable duplicate, allowing for no undue delay" is known as the princple of
    (A) balance.
    (B) competition.
    (C) conformity.
    (D) substitution.

41. "Anticipation" means that value is created according to the
    (A) expected future benefits of ownership.
    (B) benefits which have accrued to the current owner in the most recent past.
    (C) benefits which are derivable as of the appraisal date.
    (D) inevitability of change.

42. The appraisal principle of change means that
    I. an appraisal can only be made as of a specified date.
    II. everything is in constant change.
    (A) I only
    (B) II only
    (C) Both I and II
    (D) Neither I nor II

43. Growth, stability and decline are concepts associated with the appraisal concept of
    (A) contribution.
    (B) conformity.
    (C) change.
    (D) highest and best use.

44. A homogeneous community typically has what effect on real estate values?
    (A) Causes real estate values to be stable
    (B) Causes values to increase
    (C) Causes values to decrease
    (D) Builds an inherent instability into real estate values

45. Which of the following tends to lower values?
    (A) Neighborhood conformity
    (B) Deed restrictions
    (C) Transferability
    (D) Deferred maintenance

46. To realize the maximum value of property, a reasonable degree of sociological and economic homogeneity is necessary, but it should not become monotonously uniform. In real estate, this concept is called the principle of
    (A) progression.
    (B) contribution.
    (C) conformity.
    (D) correlation.

47. The most important factor needed to maintain the value of residential property is
    (A) residents have a substantial income.
    (B) homes in the area conform in size, age, condition, value and style.
    (C) ratio of rentals to owner occupied homes be nearly equal.
    (D) majority of the homes were purchased with low down payments.

48. In a properly developed community, values are upheld by
    (A) conformity to land use objectives.
    (B) minimum use of land.
    (C) blocking freeway access.
    (D) lack of deed restrictions.

49. In which of the following situations is it most likely that a single-family home will hold its value? Where that home is located in a neighborhood where:
    (A) There is a similarity of socio-economic status of the owners.
    (B) There is a mixture of average quality and good quality homes.
    (C) The number of rented homes is approximately equal to the number of owner-occupied homes.
    (D) Financing permitting no down payments is available to home purchasers.

50. Construction of homes costing $290,000 in an area of homes valued at $140,000 would affect the lesser value homes in accordance with the principle of
    (A) regression.   (C) progression.
    (B) substitution.   (D) conformity.

51. If a person constructed a high quality home costing $300,000 in a neighborhood where other homes were valued at $150,000, there would be an immediate loss in value. This type of loss in value is called, in appraisal terminology,
    (A) regression.   (C) progression.
    (B) contribution.   (D) scarcity.

52. Which of the following statements is the best example of the appraisal principle of progression?
    (A) A home of lesser value placed among homes of greater value will increase in value.
    (B) A home of lesser value placed among homes of greater value will decrease in value.
    (C) A home of greater value placed among homes of lesser value will decrease in value.
    (D) Any of the above can be correct, depending on the neighborhood.

53. The value of the best property in the neighborhood will be adversely affected by the presence of comparatively substandard property in the same neighborhood. This is a statement relating to value and is known as the principle of
    (A) balance.   (C) regression.
    (B) contribution.   (D) progression.

54. An appraiser was hired to prepare a feasibility study for adding a swimming pool to a 24-unit apartment building. What basic principle of appraising would be used?
    (A) Regression   (C) Competition
    (B) Contribution   (D) Substitution

55. The addition to total property value produced by an additional property component is considered to have resulted from the
    (A) highest and best use.
    (B) principle of substitution.
    (C) principle of anticipation.
    (D) principle of contribution.

56. According to land economic theory, the last agent of production to be satisfied is
    (A) the improvements.   (C) the land.
    (B) management.   (D) the broker.

57. A property owner has a lot valued at $100,000. The owner purchases the adjacent lot, which is identical, for $100,000. Now the combined property is appraised at $300,000. This is an example of
    (A) depth table.   (C) plottage.
    (B) residual.   (D) capitalization.

58. You had a commercial lot which was too small to build on profitably, but you acquired adjoining properties to create a larger holding and to create an overall greater value. This process is called
    (A) plottage.   (C) unearned increment.
    (B) accession.   (D) none of the above.

59. If the rezoning of a property results in the sudden increase of its value, this increase would be known as
    (A) unearned increment.(C) assemblage value.
    (B) aggregate value.   (D) plottage.

60. Which of the following groups includes the three main approaches to value?
    (A) Land residual method, building residual method, property residual method
    (B) Functional, economic, physical
    (C) Replacement cost, income capitalization, market comparison
    (D) Straight line method, sinking fund method, double declining method

61. The use of comparable property to estimate market value best defines the
    I. market method.   II. cost method.
    (A) I only   (C) Both I and II
    (B) II only   (D) Neither I nor II

62. In the market data approach to value the
    I. price of the land on each comparable sale is calculated separately.
    II. comparable sales are adjusted for differences between themselves and the subject property.
    (A) I only   (C) Both I and II
    (B) II only   (D) Neither I nor II

63. The market data approach
    I. is the simplest to learn and to explain to clients.
    II. depends primarily on the appraisal principle of conformity.
    (A) I only   (C) Both I and II
    (B) II only   (D) Neither I nor II

64. The main valuation principle in the market approach is
    (A) anticipation.   (C) conformity.
    (B) substitution.   (D) marginal productivity.

65. The basis of the market data approach to appraising is found in the principle of
    (A) change.   (C) conformity.
    (B) substitution.   (D) anticipation.

66. The sales comparison method of appraisal would lose reliability when
    (A) there is an inactive market.
    (B) the neighborhood experiences rapidly changing land use patterns.
    (C) there is rapidly fluctuating inflation or deflation.
    (D) any of the above occur.

67. In appraising a property by the sales comparison approach, which of the following would be the least acceptable comparable sale?
    (A) A single-family dwelling sold through a multiple listing service
    (B) A single-family dwelling sold by owner
    (C) A sale from a father to a son
    (D) A private party sale on a land sales contract

68. In reconciling the data in the sales comparison approach the appraiser generally gives the greatest consideration to
    (A) the comparables sales that have occurred most recently and have the greatest degree of comparability.
    (B) the comparable properties with the nearest location.
    (C) the comparable properties closest in age to the subject property.
    (D) none of the above, because all factors are given equal weight.

69. When current sales are unavailable appraisers sometimes use listings to estimate market value. Listing prices tend to represent the
    (A) average of the market.
    (B) value reported by appraisers.
    (C) upper limit of market value.
    (D) lower limit of market value.

70. In using the market data approach to value, the appraiser considers
    I. the sale price of comparable properties.
    II. the acquisition cost to the present owner.
    (A) I only   (C) Both I and II
    (B) II only   (D) Neither I nor II

71. Among the following, which would be the most reliable for information on the sales price of a comparable property?
    (A) The title company
    (B) Neighboring property owners
    (C) The buyer
    (D) The seller

72. An appraiser has located a comparable property which was recently sold. Which of the following would be an acceptable source of information regarding the sale?
    (A) The owner's signed statement
    (B) Public records, such as recorded deeds
    (C) Disinterested third party with knowledge of the facts
    (D) All of the above would be acceptable, when verified independently.

73. For which of the following properties would the sales comparison approach not be suitable?
    (A) A train station
    (B) An apartment building
    (C) A warehouse
    (D) All of the above

74. The market data appraisal approach would be best used for which of the following types of property?
    (A) A new home in a new subdivision
    (B) Vacant land
    (C) A government building
    (D) None of the above

75. In the market data approach to value comparable properties must be adjusted for differences in
    I. physical features.
    II. location.
    III. terms and conditions of sale.
    IV. date of sale.
    (A) IV only
    (B) I and II only
    (C) III and IV only
    (D) I, II, III and IV

76. Richard is using the market approach to appraise a home. The analysis of the comparables should include all of the following data except the
    (A) financing terms.
    (B) location of the property.
    (C) date of the sale.
    (D) original cost.

77. An appraiser who is using the market comparison approach to appraise a single family residence should probably not use the selling price of which of the following?
    (A) A similar home that sold over six months ago
    (B) A similar home that sold recently but is located in another neighborhood
    (C) A similar home that was sold by owners who were forced to sell at any price because of financial difficulties
    (D) A home of similar size but situated on a corner lot

78. Two comparables are identical tract type homes in the same subdivision, built in the same year and both sold on resale within 30 days of one another. Lots are of identical value. Comparable #1 was equipped with standard builder's model range and refrigerator, while Comparable #2 had deluxe appliances which cost $1,000 extra when the homes were new. The home with the deluxe appliances was sold for $500 more than the other. The subject property has the standard builder's model appliances. Which of the following is true?
    (A) No adjustment would be made to Comparable #1
    (B) A $500 adjustment would be made to Comparable #2
    (C) Both A and B
    (D) Neither A nor B

79. In making an appraisal by the market approach, an appraiser would give greater weight to
    (A) a similar home with equal amenities which was listed for sale by a real estate broker, but not yet sold.
    (B) a similar home with equal amenities which was sold under market conditions six months ago.
    (C) a nearly identical home with equal amenities which sold last week at mortgage foreclosure.
    (D) none of the above; all would be weighted equally.

80. In valuing a house by the market comparison approach, adjustments are made to the
    I. comparable property.
    II. subject property.
    (A) I only
    (B) II only
    (C) Both I and II
    (D) Neither I nor II

81. The market data approach to value is best used on
    (A) residential properties only.
    (B) either improved residential or improved income properties.
    (C) vacant land only.
    (D) any property where there are good comparable sales available.

82. Amenities are
    (A) changes or revisions in a contract.
    (B) factors of convenience, location, beauty, or utility.
    (C) properties that have few comparables.
    (D) properties similar to the subject property.

83. Amenities are
    (A) changes or revision in a contract.
    (B) beneficial features of a property.
    (C) payments received in satisfaction of injuries.
    (D) not considered by appraisers.

84. The things which usually increase the value of residential property, such as a nice yard, beautiful trees, and pleasant neighbors, are known as
    (A) tangibles.   (C) emptors.
    (B) amenities.   (D) unilaterals.

85. In the sales comparison approach to value, if a comparable property lacks an amenity that the subject property has, the appraiser should
    (A) add an amount for the value of the amenity to the final estimate of value for the subject.
    (B) deduct an amount for the value of the amenity from the sales price of the comparable.
    (C) add an amount for the value of the amenity to the sales price of the comparable.
    (D) subtract an amount for the value of the amenity from the final estimate of value for the subject.

86. Prices in a neighborhood have been rising at an annual rate of 9%. A comparable in this neighborhood sold four months ago for $226,000. In this case, the appraiser should make a adjustment of
    (A) $6,780.
    (B) $13,560.
    (C) $20,340.
    (D) No adjustment should be made.

87. The cost approach in appraisal is based upon the
    (A) value in exchange.   (C) value in use.
    (B) cost of reproduction. (D) cost of acquisition.

88. The value indicated by the cost approach is said to locate the upper limit of value. This is a concrete example of which appraisal principle?
    (A) Balance   (C) Conformity
    (B) Supply and demand   (D) Substitution

89. When using the cost approach to appraising the appraiser deducts depreciation from the reproduction cost of the building. This depreciation represents
    (A) the remaining economic life of the building.
    (B) remodeling costs to increase rentals.
    (C) loss of value due to any cause.
    (D) costs to modernize the building.

90. An appraiser using the replacement cost approach on an older residential property would use all the following except
    (A) depreciation.
    (B) capitalization.
    (C) land value.
    (D) cost of improvements new.

91. Which of the following is included in the cost approach of appraising?
    I. Depreciation of chattels
    II. Estimate of the value of land
    (A) I only   (C) Both I and II
    (B) II only   (D) Neither I nor II

92. Which of the following appraisal statements is correct?
    I. The reproduction cost approach to valuation of real property seeks to determine the cost of construction at current prices of an exact duplicate using the same materials, construction standards, design, layout and quality of workmanship.
    II. The replacement cost of construction determines the cost of a building having equivalent utility or being almost the same as the one being appraised.
    (A) I only   (C) Both I and II
    (B) II only   (D) Neither I nor II

93. When considering the cost approach to appraising, all of the following statements are true, except
    (A) the cost approach is most effective on new buildings.
    (B) the cost approach is difficult to use because of the great amount of knowledge needed regarding current construction cost factors.
    (C) the cost approach is generally used when appraising public service buildings.
    (D) the cost approach tends to set the lower limits of value.

94. The cost method of appraisal would use all of the following except
    (A) quantity survey.   (C) unit in place.
    (B) plottage reduction.   (D) square footage.

95. The most common unit of measure used in the cost approach to value residential properties is
    (A) cubic foot.
    (B) square feet of living area.
    (C) number of doors.
    (D) number of rooms.

96. Which of the following could be used in the cost approach to appraising?
    I.   Unit in place   III. Square footage
    II. Quantity survey   IV. Accrued depreciation
    (A) I and III only   (C) I, II and IV only
    (B) II, III and IV only   (D) I, II, III and IV

97. A two-story building is to be built on a lot which is 110 feet wide by 200 feet deep. Each floor will be 80 feet by 95 feet and will cost $38 per square foot. Landscaping will cost an additional $5 per square foot, for the area exclusive of the building. If the land costs $430 per front foot, what will be the total cost of the project?
    (A) $617,800   (C) $649,600
    (B) $624,900   (D) $696,900

98. If a house was built at a cost of $160,000 when the Construction Index was 100, what would it cost when the Index is 160?
    (A) $240,000   (C) $272,000
    (B) $256,000   (D) $320,000

99. An appraiser sometimes uses the index method to verify cost figures arrived at by another method. In appraising a residence built at a cost of $24,000 in 1967, the appraiser learned that the cost index at that time was 163.7. The current cost index from the same cost reporting service is 900. Based on this information, what is the approximate reproduction cost of the residence?
    (A) $131,950   (D) $240,000
    (B) $212,000   (C) $216,000

100. Les Izmore wanted to buy a two-story building which measured 80 feet by 120 feet. The first floor had a height of 14 feet and the second floor was 12 feet high. The first floor cost $1.28 per cubic foot to reproduce new and the second floor cost $1.12 per cubic foot to reproduce new. The total reproduction cost new was
    (A) $129,024.   (C) $267,920.
    (B) $172,032.   (D) $301,056.

101. To use the cost approach on a residence built in 1925 would require
    (A) determination of labor costs in 1925.
    (B) labor costs in 1925 to be adjusted by an index.
    (C) average labor costs between 1925 and the present.
    (D) replacement cost determined by today's costs less accrued depreciation.

102. Replacement cost is best described as the
    (A) cost of building a property of equivalent utility with modern materials.
    (B) cost of purchasing an equally desirable property.
    (C) cost of building an exact replica of the subject.
    (D) original cost adjusted for inflation.

103. The cost of constructing a new building having utility equivalent to the property under appraisal but built with modern materials according to current standards, design, and layout, is an appropriate definition of
    I. reproduction cost.   II. replacement cost.
    (A) I only   (C) Both I and II
    (B) II only   (D) Neither I nor II

104. Replacement cost is best described as the
    (A) original cost adjusted for inflation.
    (B) cost of building a property of equivalent utility with the same or similar materials.
    (C) cost of purchasing an equally desirable property, constructed of the same or similar materials.
    (D) cost of building an exact replica of the subject.

105. In estimating value by the cost replacement approach, the depreciation estimate is used primarily to value
  (A) the remaining useful economic life of the building.
  (B) the sales prices of similar buildings.
  (C) the depreciated value used for income tax purposes.
  (D) none of the above.

106. An appraisal involving the cost method would most likely be used in every instance with which of the following?
  (A) Single family residence
  (B) Income property
  (C) Vacant lot
  (D) Public service building

107. An appraiser would depend heavily on the cost approach to value when appraising
  (A) an older home which has been converted to apartments.
  (B) an apartment house.
  (C) a single-family dwelling.
  (D) a special-use structure.

108. Which of the following statements concerning the cost approach to appraisal is true?
  I. The cost approach is generally used when appraising public service buildings.
  II. The cost approach tends to set the lower limits of value.
  (A) I only   (C) Both I and II
  (B) II only   (D) Neither I nor II

109. The term depreciation is best defined as loss in value due to
  (A) physical wear and tear.
  (B) physical deterioration.
  (C) functional obsolescence.
  (D) any cause.

110. The gradual decay or decline in value of property from all causes is called
  (A) depreciation.   (C) alienation.
  (B) accretion.   (D) reliction.

111. The term "depreciation" refers to
  (A) costs incurred to modernize a building.
  (B) the value of real estate after the expiration of its useful life.
  (C) a loss of value in real estate due to any cause.
  (D) the capitalized value of rent losses.

112. Depreciation can be attributed to
  (A) economic obsolescence.
  (B) functional obsolescence.
  (C) physical deterioration.
  (D) all of the above.

113. Two of the three principal causes of depreciation are physical and functional. The third is
  (A) economic life.
  (B) economic.
  (C) accrued age.
  (D) exterior deterioration.

114. Which of the following factors is considered in the estimation of depreciation?
  I. Economic obsolescence
  II. Physical deterioration
  (A) I only   (C) Both I and II
  (B) II only   (D) Neither I nor II

115. The term "depreciation" refers to loss in value due to all of the following except
  (A) physical wear and tear.
  (B) functional obsolescence.
  (C) economic obsolescence.
  (D) effective age.

116. Deferred maintenance is the
  (A) amount of depreciation of all kinds which has accrued to a building.
  (B) maintenance needed to cure functional obsolescence.
  (C) part of physical deterioration which can be restored by repairs and maintenance.
  (D) maintenance, which because of tax reasons, has been postponed until the beginning of the next calendar year.

117. A decrease in value brought about by deterioration through wear and tear, action of the elements, or functional or economic obsolescence is
  (A) defeasance.   (C) loss.
  (B) accretion.   (D) depreciation.

118. Physical deterioration refers to
     (A) eccentric design.   (C) obsolescence.
     (B) changing function.   (D) wear and tear.

119. When a lump sum expenditure is required for
     overdue repairs, it is usually identified as
     (A) physical obsolescence.
     (B) functional obsolescence.
     (C) deferred maintenance.
     (D) building residual.

120. Loss of value due to deferred maintenance is
     called
     (A) physical depreciation.
     (B) inherent obsolescence.
     (C) functional obsolescence.
     (D) economic depreciation.

121. In connection with depreciation, the word "dete-
     rioration" most nearly means
     (A) economic obsolescence.
     (B) functional obsolescence.
     (C) wear and tear.
     (D) loss in value from any cause.

122. When a property has suffered a reduction in val-
     ue due to dry rot and termite damage, appraisers
     will refer to such reduction as
     (A) functional obsolescence.
     (B) economic obsolescence.
     (C) residual loss.
     (D) physical deterioration.

123. Physical deterioration most closely means
     (A) obsolescence.   (C) reversion.
     (B) wear and tear.   (D) recapture.

124. Assume that the trend in architectural design
     is toward more contemporary styled homes.
     Because of this trend, a conservatively designed
     home will tend to
     (A) decrease in value more rapidly than the more
         contemporary styled home.
     (B) decrease in value less rapidly than the more
         contemporary styled home.
     (C) stay about the same in value as the contem-
         porary styled home.
     (D) stay about the same in value as the contem-
         porary styled home; and then start appreciat-
         ing in value.

125. A house which has only one bathroom, located
     next to the kitchen, suffers from
     I. functional obsolescence.
     II. economic obsolescence.
     (A) I only   (C) Both I and II
     (B) II only   (D) Neither I nor II

126. Which of the following might be classified as
     functional obsolescence?
     (A) Exterior needs painting
     (B) Property fronts on a busy expressway
     (C) Property has a single car garage
     (D) Neighborhood is 50 years old

127. A small two-story home with a gable roof was
     built in 1935. It has a tile block foundation which
     is sagging inward. The listing broker claims the
     house has not sold because of functional obso-
     lescence, and therefore the seller should lower
     the price. Which of the following is true?
     I. The improvements have depreciated since 1935.
     II. The foundation problem is representative of
         functional obsolescence.
     III. The foundation problem is representative of
         economic obsolescence.
     IV. The gable roof is an example of economic ob-
         solescence.
     (A) I only   (C) I, II and IV only
     (B) I and II only   (D) II and III only

128. Which of the following conditions in a building
     would be referred to by an appraiser as an ex-
     ample of functional obsolescence?
     (A) Worn carpeting
     (B) Narrow hallways
     (C) Blistered paint on the exterior
     (D) Poor landscaping

129. Charlie bought into a new subdivision located
     near the airport. The airport got federal and
     state approval to redirect the flight path of in-
     coming planes over the new subdivision. The
     effect of the change is known as
     (A) physical obsolescence.
     (B) nominal obsolescence.
     (C) functional obsolescence.
     (D) economic obsolescence.

130. What type of reduction in value is present when a hydrogen gas storage tank is located next to a property?
(A) Physical deterioration
(B) Economic obsolescence
(C) Functional obsolescence
(D) Demolition

131. Depreciation is a loss of value from several possible causes. The cause of depreciation most difficult to eliminate is
(A) physical deterioration.
(B) functional obsolescence.
(C) physical depreciation.
(D) economic obsolescence.

132. Economic obsolescence involves all of the following except
(A) zoning.
(B) street layout and access.
(C) effects of the elements and the weather.
(D) uses on abutting property.

133. Which is (are) true about loss in value due to obsolescence?
  I. Extra-large load-bearing columns in a 30-year old commercial building would represent incurable functional obsolescence.
  II. An unattractive storefront window would represent curable functional obsolescence.
(A) I only   (C) Both I and II
(B) II only   (D) Neither I nor II

134. Which of the following represents obsolescence?
  I. A leaking roof
  II. A rusted boiler
  III. Loss in value due to neighborhood changes
(A) I only   (C) III only
(B) II only   (D) I, II and III

135. Which of the following statements is true?
  I. Functional obsolescence is the result of factors within the property.
  II. Economic obsolescence is caused by factors outside the property.
(A) I only   (C) Both I and II
(B) II only   (D) Neither I nor II

136. There are three main causes of depreciation. Which one of these finds its origin in social sources which is the basis for the old axiom known in social circles, that "more houses are torn down than fall down"?
(A) Economic obsolescence
(B) Functional obsolescence
(C) Straight line depreciation
(D) Physical deterioration

137. Which of the following types of depreciation would be most difficult to eliminate?
(A) Physical deterioration
(B) Functional obsolescence
(C) Physical depreciation
(D) Economic obsolescence

138. Which of the following types of depreciation may be curable?
  I. Economic obsolescence
  II. Physical deterioration
  III. Functional obsolescence
(A) I only   (C) I and II only
(B) III only   (D) II and III only

139. Economic obsolescence should generally be considered to be
(A) curable.
(B) incurable.
(C) an outdated concept.
(D) only applicable in residential housing.

140. The period of time through which a property gives benefits to its owner is best described as
(A) investment duration.   (C) value duration.
(B) physical life.   (D) economic life.

141. Compared to physical life, economic life is usually
(A) longer.
(B) shorter.
(C) the same.
(D) shorter or longer depending on the type of improvements.

142. The useful life of a building, or period of time after which the income provided by it is not sufficient to warrant its maintenance, is called
(A) recapture limits.   (C) investment duration.
(B) reversion limit.   (D) economic life.

143. The period over which a property may be profitably utilized is called its
(A) economic life.   (C) income life.
(B) amortized life.   (D) profit life.

144. Which of the following is correct?
(A) Economic life is normally longer than physical life.
(B) Economic life is normally shorter than physical life.
(C) Physical life is normally shorter than economic life.
(D) Residual life is normally longer than physical life.

145. When the landlord makes improvements to the property, the investment should be recovered over a set period of time. The landlord would use
(A) an amortization rate.
(B) a discount rate.
(C) a recapture rate.
(D) a reformation rate.

146. In a real estate analysis one should be more interested in
(A) future economic life of the improvements.
(B) chronological age of the improvements.
(C) effective age of the improvements.
(D) remaining physical life of the improvements.

147. The time period in which a building produces sufficient income to justify its continued use is customarily called
(A) capital investment period.
(B) earning period.
(C) productive life.
(D) economic life.

148. Assume that the trend in architectural design is toward more contemporary styled homes. Because of this trend, a conservatively designed home will tend to
(A) decrease in value.
(B) increase in value.
(C) stay the same.
(D) stay the same and then appreciate.

149. What is effective age?
(A) The remaining economic life
(B) The actual age
(C) The remaining useful life
(D) None of these

150. A house built in 1970 appraised in 2005 would have
(A) an economic life of 35 years.
(B) an actual age of 35 years.
(C) an effective age of 35 years.
(D) a remaining economic life of 35 years.

151. A building had been built fifteen years ago. However, because the owners had maintained it well, the appraiser felt it should be considered ten years old for depreciation purposes. We could say that its
 I. chronological age was 15 years.
 II. effective age was ten years.
(A) I only   (C) Both I and II
(B) II only   (D) Neither I nor II

152. Using the cost approach, if the site is valued at $100,000 and the improvements have been depreciated 40% and have a remaining value of $600,000, what was the cost of improvements new?
(A) $1,100,000   (C) $1,500,000
(B) $1,000,000   (D) $1,600,000

153. A house and a lot were valued at $200,000. The building was valued at $160,000, and $40,000 for the land. If the economic life of the building was 40 years, what was the value of the property after 14 years?
(A) $40,000   (C) $144,000
(B) $96,000   (D) $160,000

154. An office building has depreciated 35% since it was built 20 years ago. If it would cost $510,000 to build today, and if sites similar to the one on which it is located are now selling for $205,000, what is the market value of the property using the cost approach?
(A) $331,500   (C) $536,500
(B) $464,750   (D) $613,000

155. If a building has an estimated remaining economic life of 50 years, the appropriate recapture rate will most likely be
(A) 2%.   (C) 6%.
(B) 3%.   (D) 18%.

156. A home is eight years old and has been depreciating at the rate of 2.5% per year. If its current value is $190,000, what was the original cost, using straight line depreciation?
(A) $228,000   (C) $232,656
(B) $231,496   (D) $237,500

157. Real property improved with a new apartment building costs $1,600,000. The cost of the land was $300,000. It was estimated that the improvements would have an economic life of 30 years. Using straight line depreciation, the book value of this real property at the end of 11 years would most nearly be
(A) $823,000.   (C) $1,123,333.
(B) $1,013,333.   (D) $1,313,333.

158. Capitalization is a process used to
I. determine the value of most residential property.
II. convert income into value.
(A) I only   (C) Both I and II
(B) II only   (D) Neither I nor II

159. "Capitalization" is a process to
(A) convert income into value.
(B) establish loan value.
(C) determine net income.
(D) find the interest rate.

160. What formula would be used to estimate the value of a property using the capitalization approach to appraising?
(A) Capitalization rate multiplied by gross income
(B) The value of the land and improvements minus the depreciation
(C) Net income divided by the capitalization rate
(D) Net income multiplied by the capitalization rate

161. When an appraiser uses the capitalization method of evaluating property, the appraiser will take into account
I. future income.   II. accrued depreciation.
(A) I only   (C) Both I and II
(B) II only   (D) Neither I nor II

162. In the direct capitalization approach, the appraiser
(A) must determine the income of the property.
(B) must determine the applicable capitalization rate.
(C) would probably be appraising commercial or investment property.
(D) All of the above are generally true.

163. An appraiser using the capitalization approach to value must use the future expected income as the basis for valuation of the property. This is because the capitalization approach depends primarily on the appraisal concept of
(A) substitution.   (C) anticipation.
(B) change.   (D) supply and demand.

164. Which of the following would be most significant to an appraiser in appraising an income property?
(A) Corner influence
(B) Net operating income
(C) Vehicular traffic
(D) Pedestrian traffic

165. By averaging the annual expected cash flows and dividing the resulting cash flow by the cash investment required, one can determine the
(A) total dollar return.
(B) average annual return to equity.
(C) cash payback.
(D) internal or discounted rate of return.

166. Which of the following statements about the income approach is correct?
(A) It is the best method to value real estate bought and sold on the basis of the income.
(B) It is preferred for older properties that show little depreciation.
(C) It is based on the interpretation of cost and depreciation factors.
(D) A study of replacement costs is necessary for the capitalization of net income.

167. In regard to the capitalization rate:
    (A) A changing capitalization rate has no effect on the value of the property.
    (B) As the capitalization rate decreases, value of property decreases.
    (C) As the capitalization rate increases, value of property decreases.
    (D) As the capitalization rate increases, value of property increases.

168. The capitalization rate for improvements is the
    (A) recapture rate only.
    (B) interest rate only.
    (C) overall rate.
    (D) interest rate plus recapture rate.

169. The capitalization rate to be used in the income approach to the appraisal of real property provides for return on and a return of the investment in the improvements. A return of the investment is provided for by means of
    (A) return on the land.
    (B) monthly savings.
    (C) depreciation methods.
    (D) principal payments.

170. A capitalization rate incorporates
    (A) return on land and building and recapture of building.
    (B) return on land and building and recapture of land.
    (C) return on land and recapture of land and building.
    (D) return on building and recapture of land and building.

171. Recapture applies to
    (A) wasting assets, such as buildings.
    (B) non-wasting assets, such as land.
    (C) both A and B.
    (D) neither A nor B.

172. Income properties in older neighborhoods where there is increased likelihood of imminent change must generally be capitalized at higher rates because
    (A) the remaining economic life of the improvements is shorter.
    (B) a higher recapture rate will be required.
    (C) there is usually greater risk in older properties.
    (D) of all of the above.

173. A structure has a remaining economic life of 38 years and is valued at $187,000. In straight line capitalization, what rate should be assigned to recapture?
    (A) 2%
    (B) 2.29%
    (C) 2.63%
    (D) 2.98%

174. Referring to the capitalization rate used in the income method, which is not true?
    (A) The higher the risk, the higher the rate
    (B) The higher the rate, the lower the value
    (C) The lower the rate, the higher the value
    (D) The higher the rate, the higher the value

175. It can be said of income producing investments that a low risk leads to a relatively
    (A) high capitalization rate, and thus to a lower value.
    (B) low capitalization rate, and thus to a higher value.
    (C) high capitalization rate, and thus to a lower value.
    (D) high capitalization rate, and thus to a higher value.

176. Which of the following would be the appropriate method of selecting a capitalization rate for an income-producing property?
    (A) Gross income divided by value
    (B) Net income divided by value
    (C) Gross expenses divided by net income
    (D) Value divided by net income

177. A post office and a video store are both leased on a long term basis. In appraising the properties, the
    (A) post office would demand a higher capitalization rate.
    (B) video store would demand a higher capitalization rate.
    (C) same capitalization rate should be used for both.
    (D) type of property in this case has no effect on the capitalization rate to be used.

178. Which of the following statements is correct?
    (A) Contract rent is the actual rent received.
    (B) Economic rent refers to the income shown on the income statement prepared for net income taxes.
    (C) Economic rent refers only to the market rent for property not used for its highest use.
    (D) Typically, economic rent lags behind contract rent.

179. The income that is ascribable to land under its highest and best use is referred to as
    (A) contract rent.
    (B) excess rent.
    (C) investment rent.
    (D) economic or market rent.

180. An owner of a hardware store leased a building for twenty years at a flat rate of rental. After ten years, the economic rent for the building has increased substantially over the contract rent. Which of the following is true?
    (A) This would be an economic advantage to the lessor.
    (B) This would be an economic advantage to the lessee.
    (C) This would have no effect on either the lessor or the lessee.
    (D) The lessee will most likely attempt to break the lease.

181. Which of the following would not be included by an appraiser when establishing the value of a property by the income approach?
    (A) Real property taxes   (C) Both A and B
    (B) Fire insurance   (D) Neither A nor B

182. In figuring the value of a five-unit building by the income capitalization approach, which of the following is not an acceptable procedure?
    (A) Deducting maintenance costs as an operating expense
    (B) Deducting management fees as an operating expense
    (C) Deducting principal payments on a loan as an operating expense
    (D) Deducting an allowance for vacancy and credit loss from the potential gross income

183. May Flowers is using the income approach on an apartment building. Under which of the following circumstances should she make a deduction from effective gross income for management costs?
    (A) The owner manages the property.
    (B) One of the tenants manages the property in exchange for free rent.
    (C) One of the tenants manages the property at no cost to the owner.
    (D) All of the above

184. Which of the following would not be an allowable expense in determining the net operating income to be used in the capitalization approach?
    (A) Maintenance expenses
    (B) Management fees
    (C) Real property taxes
    (D) Interest payments on underlying mortgages

185. When an appraiser adjusts the income of an office building for vacancies and loss of rent, the resulting figure is called the
    (A) net spendable income.
    (B) gross spendable income.
    (C) effective net income.
    (D) effective gross income.

186. A small apartment building with a gross income of $3,256 per month has an annual expense totaling $15,628. A buyer would pay what price for the apartment to show a net 9% return on the investment?
    (A) $173,644   (C) $390,720
    (B) $260,489   (D) $434,133

187. What rate of return was a small office building bringing to its owner who had paid $335,000 for the property if it was netting the owner 65% of the gross receipts of $58,750?
    (A) 9%   (C) 11.4%
    (B) 10.5%   (D) 12.2%

188. A property capitalized at 6% was worth $100,000. If a capitalization rate of 8% were used, the value would be
    (A) $60,000.   (C) $80,000.
    (B) $75,000.   (D) $100,000.

189. Mr. Brown owns an 18-unit apartment building. After he purchased the property a new freeway was constructed close enough to his property to produce vacancies, as compared with other similar properties, that reduced net income by $180 per month. If the capitalization rate of the area is 11% what would be the loss in value of his property caused by the freeway?
    (A) Answer cannot be determined from the information given.
    (B) $1,920
    (C) $19,636
    (D) $23,275

190. Ms. Best owns a property valued at $247,500 which produces a net income equivalent to an 8.5% rate of capitalization. Economic conditions change to the degree that investors would demand a capitalization rate of 11.3% for this type of property. In this case the value of the property would be
    (A) $186,173.   (C) $247,500.
    (B) $219,533.   (D) $308,827.

191. A property earns $900,000 per year and has expenses of 45% of that amount. If the property is capitalized at 12%, what is its value?
    (A) $3,163,000   (C) $4,125,000
    (B) $3,375,000   (D) $4,387,000

192. Determine the estimated value of an income property using a capitalization rate of 6½%. The gross income is $25,000 per year and expenses average $900 per month.
    (A) $167,588   (C) $252,845
    (B) $218,462   (D) $281,488

193. Logan Berry is contemplating buying a piece of land and custom building a commercial structure to rent to a business. The structure will cost $300,000 to build and the projected income would be $5,000 per month with $12,000 annual expenses. If Berry wants a 12% capitalization rate, what should he offer to pay for the land?
    (A) $12,000   (C) $100,000
    (B) $72,000   (D) $150,000

194. Shirley Wright has $85,000 to invest and wants a 12% return. If she invests in real estate, what net income must the property generate for her to meet her investment objective?
    (A) $7,083   (C) $10,200
    (B) $8,500   (D) $12,000

195. The Empty Arms Apartments produce gross monthly income of $4,750 and annual expenses of $25,650. At a sales price of $261,250, what capitalization rate would the buyer get?
    (A) 9.5%   (C) 10.5%
    (B) 10%   (D) 12%

196. An apartment with a net income of $36,000 was appraised for $600,000. What is the capitalization rate?
    (A) 4%   (C) 8%
    (B) 6%   (D) 10%

197. Wyatt Witherspoon had a 12-unit apartment building. He suffered a $1,800 monthly loss of net income because a freeway built next to the apartments made access difficult. Using a capitalization rate of 10%, how much did the property lose in value?
    (A) $21,600   (C) $240,000
    (B) $216,000   (D) $360,000

198. Dan Johnson wants to earn a minimum return of 20% on an apartment complex he wants to purchase. Operating expenses on the twelve-unit building, which rents for $800 per unit per month, are $22,500 annually. What is the maximum Johnson can pay for the complex if he assumes a 10% vacancy allowance?
    (A) $405,900   (C) $676,500
    (B) $463,500   (D) $811,800

199. A man earned a net income of $109,200 from a duplex over a five-year time period. Using a capitalization rate of 8.4%, what was the value of the property?
    (A) $245,000   (C) $455,000
    (B) $260,000   (D) $1,300,000

200. Two appraisers were asked to appraise an apartment property. Both arrived at the same net income, but the first appraiser used a capitalization rate of 6% while the second appraiser used a capitalization rate of 8%. The reason that one appraiser would choose a higher capitalization rate would be due to the fact that the appraiser estimated
 (A) a higher projected income.
 (B) less depreciation.
 (C) a higher value.
 (D) a higher risk.

201. Two appraisers were asked to estimate the value of an income property. If the first appraiser used a capitalization rate of 10% and the second capitalized at 11%, the value arrived at by the appraiser using the higher capitalization rate would be approximately
 (A) 9% lower.   (C) 1% lower.
 (B) 10% higher.   (D) 1% higher.

202. An appraiser has correctly determined that the net annual income of a feed store is $67,250. The appraiser incorrectly selected a capitalization rate of 11½% instead of the correct figure, 12¼%. Because of the mistake, the appraiser's estimate is
 (A) $7,947 too low.   (C) $7,947 too high.
 (B) $35,803 too low.   (D) $35,803 too high.

203. An apartment building was appraised by two appraisers who both agreed the net income was $132,870. Appraiser Frank used a 10% capitalization rate; appraiser Owens used a 12% rate. Appraiser Frank's estimate of value was
 (A) $221,450 higher than appraiser Owens' estimate.
 (B) $221,450 lower than appraiser Owens' estimate.
 (C) $2,655 higher than appraiser Owens' estimate.
 (D) $2,655 lower than appraiser Owens' estimate.

204. Real property taxes on an income property capitalized at 10% increased $900 last year. If all other expenses and income remained the same, the value of the property would decrease by
 (A) $9.   (C) $900.
 (B) $90.   (D) $9,000.

205. Bill Logan owns a property valued at $500,000 which produces a net income equivalent to a 6% rate of capitalization. Economic conditions change to the degree that investors would demand a capitalization rate of 8% for this type of property. In this case the value of the property would be
 (A) $300,000.   (C) $400,000.
 (B) $375,000.   (D) $450,000.

206. The owner of an apartment building rented 24 units for $750 per month per unit without a vacancy factor. The following year, the owner raised the rents 10%, but had a 10% vacancy factor. The owner's income was
 (A) equal for both years.
 (B) 10% more the first year.
 (C) 10% more the second year.
 (D) 1% less the second year.

207. After careful analysis, Joseph determines that if he builds a new commercial building at a total cost of $450,000, he will be able to lease it to others at gross annual rental income of $90,000. His anticipated annual expenses amount to $18,000. Relying on this information and using a 12% capitalization rate to determine the value of his total investment, Joseph learns that the most he can pay for land on which to locate this building is
 (A) $72,000.   (C) $150,000.
 (B) $600,000.   (D) $450,000.

208. A factor by which the appraiser multiplies the total rental income from a property as an estimate of its value is the
 I. gross income multiplier.
 II. land residual process.
 (A) I only   (C) Both I and II
 (B) II only   (D) Neither I nor II

209. To compute a gross rent multiplier an appraiser must obtain from comparable sold properties the
 (A) current reproduction cost and annual income.
 (B) monthly rent and selling price.
 (C) net income, either annually or monthly, and the selling price.
 (D) net income and the rate of capitalization.

210. A property purchased for $144,000 is renting for $1,000 per month. The monthly gross rent multiplier is
    (A) 1.25.
    (B) 125.
    (C) 1.44.
    (D) 144.

211. A rental property was purchased for $144,000. The property produced a monthly gross income of $900.00. Based on the gross rent multiplier for this property, what would be the value of a comparable property having a gross monthly income of $1,050?
    (A) $133,500
    (B) $168,000
    (C) $189,000
    (D) $210,600

212. An investor is considering offering to buy a 30-unit property at a gross rent multiplier of 6½. Eight units are rented for $600 per month, eight units for $700 per month, and the remainder at $800 per month. The investor should offer
    (A) $360,000.
    (B) $1,360,000.
    (C) $1,632,000.
    (D) $1,684,800.

213. An appraiser has determined that the correct monthly GRM for a property is 105. If the annual income is $60,000 and the monthly expenses are $2,000, what is the indicated market value?
    (A) $52,500
    (B) $73,500
    (C) $525,000
    (D) $630,000

214. Which of the following statements is true with respect to the appraisal of a single-family residence?
    (A) Capitalization of net income is most accurate.
    (B) You should appraise the property by at least three methods, total the results and divide by three.
    (C) The reproduction cost method is a valid method on new properties where the cost of replacement of the building and value of the land can be ascertained.
    (D) Capitalizing the average rent of the neighborhood properties is accurate.

215. The approach to value that is considered the most reliable in appraising a single-family residence is the
    (A) income approach.
    (B) capitalization approach.
    (C) cost approach.
    (D) market data approach.

216. When analyzing the various approaches to estimating value,
    I. the income approach is the most important in site valuation.
    II. the approach that requires the gathering, recording and comparing of sales data for comparable sites is the cost approach.
    (A) I only
    (B) II only
    (C) Both I and II
    (D) Neither I nor II

217. Which is the most appropriate appraisal method to use in evaluating a property for fire insurance purposes?
    (A) Market data
    (B) Capitalization
    (C) Replacement cost
    (D) Comparison

218. An appraisal to place a value on a three year old home for fire insurance purposes would give most emphasis to
    (A) the cost approach.
    (B) the market approach.
    (C) the income approach.
    (D) a weighted average of A, B, and C.

219. An appraisal to place a value on a three year-old home for fire insurance purposes would give most emphasis to the
    (A) cost approach.
    (B) market approach.
    (C) capitalization approach.
    (D) reconciliation of all approaches.

220. Bill O'Goodes wishes to make an offer to buy a lot and hires an appraiser to appraise it first. Which approach would the appraiser most likely rely on?
    (A) Market data
    (B) Land residual
    (C) Construction cost
    (D) Replacement cost

221. The market data appraisal approach would be best used for
    (A) establishing the price for new homes in a new subdivision.
    (B) vacant land valuation.
    (C) both A and B.
    (D) neither A nor B.

222. In the valuation of a large apartment building or office building usually more weight is given to which of the following approaches?
(A) Cost approach
(B) Market data approach
(C) Income approach
(D) All are given equal weight.

223. In which of the following approaches to value is it necessary to determine a dollar value for existing depreciation when figuring building value?
(A) Income approach   (C) Market data approach
(B) Cost approach   (D) All of the above

224. A post office of unique design and construction is best appraised by which of the following approaches?
(A) Cost   (C) Land residual
(B) Income   (D) Market data

225. For which one of the following properties would an appraiser be justified in relying on the cost method to determine market value?
(A) A newly constructed church of contemporary design
(B) A 40-year old bungalow which represents the highest and best use
(C) A vacant lot which possesses latent value
(D) A farm located just outside of town

226. When comparing the income method to the cost method of appraising
(A) the income method provides the upper limits of value.
(B) the cost method provides the lower limits of value.
(C) the income method provides the higher value on income property.
(D) the reproduction cost method provides the upper limits of value.

227. An appraiser is evaluating a parcel in an area of town. The appraiser planned to use some comparable properties known to have been recently sold in that area. Which of the common approaches to appraising would the appraiser be using?
(A) The cost approach to appraising
(B) The market data approach to appraising
(C) The replacement approach to appraising
(D) The reconciliation approach to appraising

228. When using the cost approach in appraising, the upper limit of value is quite well determined by which of the following?
(A) Gather market data for properties of about the same size – land area and cubic feet of improvements – and add 10% to the average value of the comparables.
(B) Assign a reasonable gross income for the property; ascertain the net income; use the process of capitalization to determine value; and add 10% for possible error.
(C) Determine the reproduction cost new, with no deduction for depreciation, plus land value.
(D) Determine the reproduction cost new, minus deductions for accrued depreciation, plus land value.

229. There are three approaches to the valuation of real property and, if possible, all three should be used in arriving at a final estimate of value. Depending on the type of property being appraised, however, one approach will have more weight and should afford greater authority. The comparison approach is given greater weight in the appraisal of
(A) apartment property.
(B) service property.
(C) single-family dwellings.
(D) industrial property.

230. Which is the generally preferred appraisal approach for the valuation of land?
(A) The abstraction procedure
(B) Market data approach
(C) Anticipated use or development procedure
(D) Land residual technique

231. In the approach to value, a real estate appraiser would be most concerned with "the present worth for future potential benefits" in relation to the
(A) cost approach.
(B) summation approach.
(C) market approach.
(D) income approach.

232. Improved commercial real property that is seldom sold is best appraised by the
    I.   cost approach.   III. market data approach.
    II. income approach.
    (A) I only   (C) I and II only
    (B) III only   (D) II and III only

233. The income approach would be most widely used for appraisals of
    (A) newly opened subdivisions.
    (B) commercial and investment properties rented to tenants.
    (C) heavily mortgaged properties.
    (D) heavily insured properties.

234. Estimating the probable sales price of a property by considering sales of similar properties is used primarily in
    (A) the market data approach to value.
    (B) the cost approach to value.
    (C) the income approach to value.
    (D) all of these.

235. The cost approach would be most valid for which of the following?
    (A) Twenty-year old subdivision home
    (B) Railroad depot
    (C) Shopping center with total occupancy
    (D) Ladies clothing store with a 15-year lease

236. In appraising a fifteen-year old, single-family, owner-occupied building in a good neighborhood for the purpose of estimating a basis for sales price, which of the following factors would be given the greatest weight?
    (A) Calculations based on the amount of the most recent property tax assessment
    (B) Current replacement costs of the dwelling house, assuming the value of the land can be closely estimated
    (C) Capitalization of typical rental values in the neighborhood
    (D) Current prices paid for similar homes in the same neighborhood

237. Julie Wilson, a licensed appraiser, has been employed to prepare an insurance appraisal of a property. Of special value is that the property includes an elegant old mansion that is vacant. Which approach to value would Wilson principally rely on in making this appraisal?
    (A) Income approach
    (B) Gross rent multiplier approach
    (C) Market data approach
    (D) Reproduction cost approach

238. Sandy Jones is considering buying a lot to build a single-family residence. She hires an appraiser to appraise the lot. If the appraiser has a choice of the three approaches to appraisal, which of the following would the appraiser probably use?
    (A) Reproduction cost
    (B) Market data approach
    (C) Income approach
    (D) Land residual approach

239. Reconciliation is
    (A) choosing the highest value found by the three approaches to value.
    (B) analyzing the results obtained by using the three approaches to value in order to determine the final estimate of value of a property.
    (C) analyzing comparable properties and listing their amenities.
    (D) the same as averaging.

240. Analyzing the separate value estimates obtained by using the three approaches to value in order to determine the final estimate of value of a property is called
    (A) data reduction.
    (B) correlation or reconciliation.
    (C) averaging.
    (D) simulating.

241. The final step by the appraiser in establishing the final estimate of value is to reconcile the three indications of value obtained through the cost, income and market data approaches. The final estimate of value is obtained by
    I. averaging the three individual indications of value.
    II. selecting the middle value.
    (A) I only   (C) Both I and II
    (B) II only   (D) Neither I nor II

242. The analysis of alternative conclusions to arrive at a final value estimate is referred to as
    (A) an addenda.
    (B) an analysis of data.
    (C) reconciliation.
    (D) the market approach.

243. Reconciliation is an appraisal term used to describe
    (A) the appraiser's determination of a property's highest value.
    (B) an average of real estate values for properties similar to the one being appraised.
    (C) the appraiser's analysis and comparison of the results of each approach.
    (D) the method used to determine a property's most appropriate capitalization rate.

244. To a real estate appraiser, correlation or reconciliation is
    (A) comparing comparable properties and listing their features.
    (B) obtained by using different approaches to value.
    (C) deciding the highest value based on any method.
    (D) estimating value by averaging various income approaches.

245. The correlation process in appraisal
    I. is based on a standard mathematical formula.
    II. consists of averaging the cost, market, and income approaches.
    (A) I only
    (B) II only
    (C) Both I and II
    (D) Neither I nor II

246. Given an appraisal situation in which each of the three approaches to the final estimate of defined value can be used, the final step in the appraisal process should be to
    I. average the three values to arrive at the actual value, using the mean as the definition of average.
    II. accept the midpoint in the range of values as being the defined value.
    (A) I only
    (B) II only
    (C) Both I and II
    (D) Neither I nor II

247. The contractual (lease) rental agreement on a property requires the tenant to pay $1,000 per month with the rent to be adjusted each April 1st according to the cost of living index. The cost of living index when the agreement was made was 122.8. It is time to adjust the rent, and neither the landlord nor tenant agree on what it should be. As you are holding forth as an expert in property value matters the tenant asks you to compute the proper total rent per month for the coming year based upon the present cost of living index of 125.8. You respond that the proper rent should be
    (A) $970.00.
    (B) $976.15.
    (C) $1,024.43.
    (D) $1,030.00.

248. To estimate the value of retail business property where lots vary in size, some appraisers use which of the following to make adjustments?
    (A) Depth and corner influence tables
    (B) The land residual technique
    (C) Plottage increment techniques
    (D) All of the above

249. You are employed to select land to be used for an industrial site. You would be least concerned with
    (A) location.
    (B) subsoil.
    (C) topography.
    (D) fertility.

250. If building costs increase by 20%, the purchasing power of the investment dollar decreases by
    (A) 16⅔%.
    (B) 20%.
    (C) 25%.
    (D) 33⅓%.

ANSWERS

To practice questions. If you chose the wrong letter, here's the right one! The explanations are designed to clarify your understanding.

1. **D** Value is determined and set by the actions of buyers and sellers in the marketplace. The function of an appraiser is merely to estimate the probable market value of the property and report the estimate to the client. Value can be observed, but not computed.

2. **C** Although most appraisals are ordered by financial institutions for loan purposes, the function of the appraiser is still to estimate the market value of the property. Appraisers do not determine value, in the sense of setting or dictating value. Appraisers merely report their estimate of what the property will sell for.

3. **B** The definition of an appraisal is an estimate or opinion of value. The market value is not the only value which appraisers find for the client. There are numerous kinds of value which appraisers are called upon to report, e.g., insurance value, replacement value, etc.

4. **D** According to the principle of change everything is constantly changing; that is, not just the property, but market conditions as well. Therefore, the appraisal is not valid without a date, and is valid only for the specified date. Many lenders are willing to accept an appraisal for three months or six months. They do this only because property values are generally rising, so it doesn't really harm the lender's position. The appraisal is still valid only as of the date of the appraisal.

5. **A** An appraiser is the agent of the client, and therefore owes the client fiduciary obligations of good faith, competence, confidentiality, full disclosure and due diligence. However, when it comes to the value of the property an appraiser is unbiased. If the appraiser were an advocate of the client's position, such as where an appraiser for the seller tries to get the highest price for the seller, this would not be unbiased, and would therefor be a violation of professional standards.

6. **A** Only the property is important. Factors relative to motivations of the owner, the buyer, the lender and even the appraiser are irrelevant. The Consumer Price Index is relevant only if doing a historical appraisal (for the value as of a date in the past).

7. **A** An appraiser is liable to the principal for the appraiser's wrongful actions which result in harm to the principal.

8. **D** As an agent, the appraiser owes the client fiduciary obligations of good faith, competence, confidentiality, full disclosure and due diligence. However, when it comes to the value of the property, an appraiser is not an advocate of the client's position, such as where an appraiser for the seller tries to get the highest price for the seller.

9. **B** An appraisal is always valid for just one specific date. It can be the present, or any date in the past, but not a date in the future.

10. **B** Appraisals are generally done as of the present time. They can also be done for the value of a property as of any date in the past, although never for a future value. The appraisal remains valid only for the moment it is handed to the client.

11. **B** The value for property taxes is called the "assessed value," and the appraisal process is called "assessment." The tax assessor uses the same approaches to value and appraisal principles as an independent appraiser. It is only the purpose of the appraisal that is different.

12. **D** A value in use is the value to the owner, as opposed to a value in exchange, which is a value to a buyer in the marketplace. The current use might not represent either the value in use or the value in exchange. The highest and best use is that use which is legal, physically possible, financially feasible, and produces the maximum benefit to the owner. Because owners tend to act in their own financial best interests, the current use is frequently the highest and best use, but need not be.

13. **B** There are many definitions of market value. Most state that the appraiser is locating the price the property will sell for if exposed in the open market for a reasonable period of time, both parties know of all the uses to which the property could be put, both parties act prudently in their own self-interest, and neither party acts under undue stimulus.

14. **C** Most definitions of market value are a value in exchange, as opposed to a value in use. A value in use

is the value to the owner. What a buyer would be willing to pay and a seller would accept for the future benefits of ownership is a common definition of market value.

15.   **A**   Most definitions of market value state that the appraisal assumes exposure in the open market for a reasonable time, both parties knowledgeable about all the uses to which the property can be put, both parties act prudently in their own self-interest, and neither acts under undue influence.

16.   **A**   There are many elements of value and principles of appraisal which influence market value, but in the final analysis, the value rests at the point where the minds meet. Appraisers report market value, they do not determine or dictate it.

17.   **B**   When a property was sold after a reasonable exposure in the open market and the buyer and seller were both fully knowledgeable, both acted prudently in their own self-interest, and neither acted under undue stimulus, we call this an arms length transaction. Only arms length transactions qualify to be used as comparables for an appraisal.

18.   **C**   The definition of market value used in most appraisals is the price which a willing buyer will pay and a willing seller will accept, both parties knowledgeable about all the uses to which the property can be put, both parties acting prudently in their own self-interest, and neither party acting under undue stimulus. An exchange value is the value for exchange with other property, as opposed to a money value.

19.   **C**   Some lenders are willing to lend up to 100% of the market value of the property, although most will not. Residual value is always a portion of the total market value, as where we speak of the land residual value as the amount of value in the land after subtracting the building value from the total.

20.   **A**   The greater the anticipated future benefits of ownership, the more a buyer will pay for a property. But the amount the owner paid for the property is irrelevant.

21.   **A**   A market value is always a value in exchange. The market data approach is usually the most powerful approach to value. Cost to reproduce new today, or replacement cost today, are also valid approaches to value, but original (historical) cost is always irrelevant.

22.   **C**   There are may factors which influence the value of a property, but what the owner paid for it is always irrelevant.

23.   **A**   A commodity without scarcity has no value. Similarly there must be utility, or no one will be

willing to pay anything for it. Transferability means effective purchasing power, which is also an element that must be present for a commodity to have value. The fact that the element of demand was not listed does not mean that the other three need not be present.

24.   **C**   There are four elements of value – demand, utility, scarcity and transferability (effective purchasing power). If any is completely lacking, the commodity has no value at all. The more of each is present, the higher the value.

25.   **C**   There are four elements of value – demand, utility, scarcity and transferability (effective purchasing power). If any one is completely lacking, the commodity is of no value. For example, if there is no demand for a product, it does not matter how scarce it is, how useful it is, or how easy it is to buy it. It still has no value if no one wants it.

26.   **D**   The four elements of value are demand, utility, scarcity and transferability (effective purchasing power). The greater each of these is present in a commodity, the greater the value. If any is completely lacking, the commodity has no value at all. Cost (what the owner paid for it) is irrelevant.

27.   **B**   The four great forces which affect value are physical (sometimes called environmental, economic, governmental and social. Conformity is one of the principles of value, not a force which affects value.

28.   **D**   Supply and demand are the basis of value. Price goes up if either demand increases or supply shrinks. Price goes down when demand decreases or supply increases.

29.   **D**   When supply increase or demand decreases, price goes down. Price goes up when supply decreases or demand increases. Both supply and demand are relative to each other, i.e., if supply goes up but demand goes up the same amount, there will be no change in price.

30.   **B**   The marketplace is always driven by supply and demand. An increase in demand or a decrease in supply raises prices, and a decrease in demand or increase in supply lowers prices. When builders cannot build for the amount they can get for the property they will not build. This will eventually cause supply to shrink or at least remain constant relative to demand. As demand increases, value will increase, until builders will once again find it profitable to build. There will be both an increase in market value and a decrease in construction, but the first to occur will be the decrease in construction.

31.   **B**   The highest and best use of a parcel of land is that which is maximally productive, assuming

the use is legal, physically possible, and financially feasible. Highest and best use, substitution and anticipation are principles of appraisal which affect market value.

32.   **B**   The highest and best use is that use which produces the maximum benefit, assuming the use is legal, physically possible, and financially feasible. In income properties the benefit is the income, so the highest and best use will be that use which yields the greatest income. Investors buy income properties based on the income, so the greater the income, the greater the present value.

33.   **B**   All principles of appraisal are associated with all other appraisal concepts. However, the principle of anticipation is the most important to consider when conducting a highest and best use analysis. According to the principle of anticipation the greater the anticipated future benefits of ownership, the greater the market value. The highest and best use is that use which produces the maximum future benefit to the owner.

34.   **D**   The highest and best use of a property is that use which is maximally beneficial, assuming that the use is legal (or can be made legal), physically possible, and financially feasible. The most important concept is the benefit to be derived from ownership.

35.   **D**   The highest and best use is defined as that use which is legal, physically possible, and financially feasible. Within those constraints, the use which provides the greatest benefit over the longest time is the highest and best use. Income is not the only benefit one can receive from property ownership.

36.   **A**   In considering return on investment, the expenses incurred to earn the income must be deducted. The remainder is called the net income. We always base return on investment on net income, not gross income.

37.   **B**   The highest and best use of a property is that use which is maximally productive, within the uses that are legal, physically possible, and financially feasible. "Maximally productive" usually means "produces the best income flow," but the time for the income is as much a consideration as the quantity of the income.

38.   **C**   Highest and best use is that use which provides the maximum benefit to the owner. A use cannot be the highest and best use unless it is legal (or can be made legal), physically possible, and financially feasible.

39.   **D**   The highest and best use is that use which is maximally beneficial. It is a concept that is most frequently applied to bare land.

40.   **D**   The principle of substitution is the basis of most appraisal work. Although other principles are important, none are as critical as substitution. Substitution is the principle that, in a free market, people shop for the best price. Therefore, no one will knowingly pay more for a product than what they can get it for elsewhere.

41.   **A**   According to the principle of anticipation the greater the anticipated future benefit, the greater the market value. Note that it is the anticipated future benefit, not necessarily the benefit which actually occurs. Whatever the buyer and the seller believe will happen is what they base their negotiations on. The present benefits are a guide to the future, but many times a property will sell for more than is justified by the present income because the anticipation is that future income will be higher.

42.   **C**   According to the principle of change, everything is constantly changing; that is, not just the property, but market conditions as well. Therefore, the appraisal is not valid without a date, and is valid only for the specified date.

43.   **C**   The beginning phase of a neighborhood is the growth period. The improvements are built up during growth. The second phase is stability or equilibrium. The period of stability is roughly equivalent to the economic life. When structures begin to be torn down, this signals the final phase, which is decline.

44.   **A**   Conformity in an area allows the area to withstand change more easily. The less change, the longer the economic life. The economic life is the period over which the owner will derive benefits from the improvements, so the longer the economic life, the greater the market value.

45.   **D**   To lower the value of a property an influence would have to be negative. Conformity slows down change and increases the remaining economic life of the improvements, a positive force. Deed restrictions do the same. Transferability (effective purchasing power) is the ease with which a property can be sold. The easier it is for a buyer to acquire the property, the more the buyer will pay for it.

46.   **C**   The economic life of a structure is the time period over which the owner can derive benefits of ownership. The longer the economic life, the greater the market value. Change is constant and unavoidable, and is the enemy of economic life. The higher the degree of conformity, the more easily the neighborhood can withstand change, therefore, the longer the economic life, and the greater the market value.

47.   **B**   The greater the remaining economic life of the improvements, the greater the time period over which an owner will receive the benefits of ownership, therefore the greater the value. The more highly conforming the improvements in an area, the more easily the area can withstand change, and therefore the longer the economic life. Therefore, the greater the conformity, the greater the value.

48.   **A**   Conformity makes the area resistant to change, thus lengthening the economic life of the improvements. The longer the economic life, the longer the owner will receive the benefits of ownership, so the greater the market value.

49.   **A**   Conformity increases market value by making the area resistant to change. The less change, the longer the economic life, therefore the longer the period of time over which an owner will receive the benefits of ownership. The longer the period of benefits, the greater the market value.

50.   **C**   Regression occurs when an owner has overbuilt for the area and there is a resulting loss of value compared to similar properties built in an area where they are the norm. Progression is the opposite, that is, a smaller property benefits by being in an area where better properties predominate.

51.   **A**   The appraisal principles of progression and regression are opposites. Progression occurs when a smaller structure gains value because it is placed in an area of larger structures. Regression happens when an owner overbuilds in comparison to other properties in the area.

52.   **A**   According to the principles of progression a smaller or poorer structure will gain value if it is located in an area of larger or better structures. The opposite (an overbuilt property) is regression.

53.   **C**   Progression occurs when a smaller structure gains market value because it is located in an area of larger or better structures. The opposite, as where an owner has overbuilt for an area, is called regression.

54.   **B**   According to the principle of contribution, all components of the land and its improvements contribute something to the overall value of the whole, although not necessarily in proportion to their cost. Sometimes the contribution can even be negative. For example, painting the exterior of a house increases its market value more than other things of equal cost. A swimming pool in Oregon contributes little to the value of an average house, but contributes more to the value of a luxury house.

55.   **D**   All components of the land and its improvements contribute something to the overall value of the whole, although not necessarily in proportion to their cost. In fact, some items may produce a negative value. Nevertheless, this is the principle of contribution.

56.   **C**   In economic theory there are four agents in production – land, labor, capital and management. Land is the most passive. The demands for compensation by labor, capital (investors), and management always take precedence.

57.   **C**   In appraisal, we must take into consideration many factors and principles at the same time. If large parcels of land are scarce in an area, combining two smaller parcels into one can increase the market value beyond the value of either separately. This is an example of an unearned increment, or plottage increase. The depth table is a device used by appraisers to determine the relative value of the frontage of a property in relation to the back part.

58.   **A**   When there is a shortage of large parcels in an area, combining two smaller ones can increase the market value of both. This is an example of an unearned increment. Combining the two parcels (the process) is called plottage.

59.   **A**   Any increase in value without the efforts of the owner is called an unearned increment. Plottage is an unearned increment that sometimes occurs when two smaller properties are combined into one and the resulting larger parcel is worth more than the combined value of the original parcels.

60.   **C**   Land and building residual methods are techniques used in income capitalization to isolate the value of the land or the structure. Functional, economic, and physical are forms of depreciation. Straight line, sinking fund and double declining are methods accountants use to calculate depreciation. The three approaches to value are market data (sales comparison), cost, and income capitalization.

61.   **A**   The market data approach to value depends on finding comparable sold properties and adjusting their sales prices to what they would have sold for if they had been identical to the subject property. The cost approach determines the cost to reproduce or replace the improvements new today, less the accrued depreciation, to determine the value of the improvements only.

62.   **B**   In the market data (sales comparison) approach the land value is included as part of the sales price of each comparable. Sometimes adjustments are made to the land value when the lot of the comparable

is not the same as the subject property, but the land values are not broken out as separate figures. The cost approach, however, can be used on the improvements only, so the land value must be obtained separately. In the market data approach we always adjust the comparables to determine what they would have sold for if they had been identical to the subject property.

63.   **A**   The market data (sales comparison) approach to value involves locating comparable properties and adjusting their sales price for those aspects in which they differ from the subject property. This is exactly how buyers and sellers act in the marketplace, so it is easily understood and normally very accurate. It relies chiefly on the appraisal principle of substitution. According to the appraisal principle of conformity the more highly conforming the improvements in a neighborhood, the better the neighborhood can withstand change. The better the neighborhood can withstand change, the longer the economic life of the improvements, therefore the greater their market value.

64.   **B**   According to the principle of substitution, no one will pay more than it would cost to get an identical substitute. The market (sales comparison) approach is based squarely on this principle.

65.   **B**   According to the principle of substitution, no one will pay more for a commodity than it would cost to get an identical substitute. The market data (sales comparison) approach relies on comparing the subject property to sold comparable properties based on this principle.

66.   **D**   Since the essence of the market data (sales comparison) approach is comparison of the subject property to the sales prices of comparable properties, the reliability of the market data approach will suffer when there are few comparables. Similarly, if property values or other conditions are changing rapidly, the prices at which the comparables sold may no longer be representative of current market conditions, so the market approach loses reliability.

67.   **C**   Appraisers normally use only comparable properties which have been recently sold in the marketplace. Part of the definition of market value is that the parties were knowledgeable, acting prudently in their own self-interest and without undue stimulus. Therefore, to appraise for market value, comparable sales where these elements were present are the only comparables which should be used. Such comparables are called arms length transactions.

68.   **A**   In the market data (sales comparison) approach to value adjustments can and must be made for any differences between the subject property and the comparables. The fewer the differences, the more reliable the results. Reconciliation is a process of taking a weighted average of what the comparables would have sold for if they had been identical (i.e., after the adjustments). Therefore, the greatest weight is given to those comparables that are the closest to the subject property in all aspects.

69.   **C**   In a situation where there are no sold properties appraisers could use properties which are currently being offered for sale, although the results of such a comparison would indicate the upper limit of value. There is no guarantee that the owners of the listed properties will actually be able to sell them for the prices which are being asked.

70.   **A**   Cost, as a historical figure, is always irrelevant in determining the present value of a property.

71.   **A**   The title insurance company will report the value according to what is stated on the deed from the seller to the buyer, which is required by Oregon law for almost all transactions. Other parties may have motivations to be less than truthful.

72.   **D**   All appraisal data must be verified. The appraiser owes a duty of full disclosure to the client, so when the statements of the owner are relied upon without independent verification, that fact should be noted on the appraisal report.

73.   **A**   The sales comparison (market data) approach requires comparable sold properties. Comparables for apartment buildings and warehouses are possible, but it would be unlikely that an appraiser could find good comparables for a train station.

74.   **B**   The market data approach is usually the most powerful approach because it echoes what buyers and sellers do in the marketplace. It fails only when there are inadequate comparable sales. A new subdivision may have few sales to compare the subject property to.

75.   **D**   In using the market data (sales comparison) approach to value it is rare that the comparable properties are the same as the subject property. Therefore, adjustments are necessary for the differences in amenities (physical features). If the comparables are located in a more or less desirable location, an adjustment must be made as well. The more liberal the terms, the more the seller can get for the property. The appraiser is usually asked to appraise the subject property for what it would bring given ordinary and reasonable financing. If one of the comparables was sold with more or less liberal financing

an adjustment must be made. And if the sale date of the comparable was more than a few days earlier an adjustment for increase in property prices from the sale date to the date of the appraisal is also in order.

76.   **D**   Historical cost is always irrelevant to considerations of the present market value. What you paid for a property has nothing to do with what you can get for it.

77.   **C**   In the market data (sales comparison) approach some adjustments are more reliable than others. However, the comparables must all be arms length transactions. A sale under undue stimulus is never an arms length transaction.

78.   **C**   When adjusting for differences between the comparables and the subject property the comparables are always adjusted to the subject. The purpose is to determine what the comparables would have sold for if they had been identical to the subject property. If there are no differences, no adjustment is necessary. If the comparable is better, it should have an adjustment downwards for the value of the difference.

79.   **B**   In the market data (sales comparison) approach, the comparables must be arms length transactions. An arms length transaction is one where the property was exposed in the open market for a reasonable period of time, both parties knew of all the uses to which the property could be put, both parties acted prudently in their own self-interest, and neither party acted under undue stimulus. Properties not yet sold are used as comparables only if there are no sold properties available.

80.   **A**   In making adjustments between the subject property and the comparables, the appraiser always adjusts the comparable properties to determine what they would have sold for if they had been identical to the subject property. This is the only way to get an indication of what the subject property will sell for.

81.   **D**   The market data approach depends on the availability of good data about comparable sales. Therefore, the market data approach should always be used on any property for which there are a sufficient number of comparable sales.

82.   **B**   "Amenities" refer to the beneficial improvements and features of a property. The greater the amenities the more desirable the property. In the market approach to value, appraisers must adjust between the subject property and comparables for differences in the amenities.

83.   **B**   The amenities of a property are the features that owners and buyers find useful, enjoyable or desirable.

84.   **B**   When using the market approach, appraisers must adjust between the subject property and the comparables for differences between them, e.g., one property has a fireplace and the other does not. These differences are called "amenities."

85.   **C**   When making adjustments the appraiser's task is to determine what the comparable would have sold for it had been identical to the subject property. If the comparable lacks an amenity the subject has, then the comparable theoretically would have sold for more if it had had the amenity; therefore, the value for the amenity must be added to the sales price of the comparable.

86.   **A**   In the market data approach the appraiser must determine what the comparable would have sold for if it had been identical to the subject property. The date of the sale must also be the same as the date of the appraisal, so an adjustment for inflation to date is required. An annual rate of 9% is the same as ¾ of 1% per month ($0.09 \div 12 = 0.0075$). For four months, the total percentage of inflation would be 3% ($0.0075 \times 4 = 0.03$). Multiplying the sales price by this percentage gives an adjustment of $6,780 ($226,000 × 0.03 = $6,780).

87.   **B**   The basic idea of the cost approach is to determine the cost to reproduce the structure new, then subtract accrued depreciation to find the present value.

88.   **D**   In the cost approach the cost to reproduce the property is the cost for an identical substitute. The principle of substitution is that no one would pay more than it would cost to get an identical substitute, therefore, the cost to reproduce is the maximum anyone would pay for the improvements.

89.   **C**   The term "depreciation" means a loss in value from any cause. The three kinds of depreciation are physical deterioration, functional obsolescence (out of date) and economic obsolescence (loss in value from forces and influences outside the property).

90.   **B**   The theory of the cost approach is to take the cost to reproduce the improvements new and subtract the accrued depreciation. This gives the present value of the improvements, to which the appraiser adds the land value, located by another method. Capitalization is used in the income approach, not the cost approach.

91.   **B**   In the cost approach the appraiser locates the cost to reproduce the improvements new, then subtracts an allowance for accrued depreciation. This locates the value of the improvements. To com-

plete the appraisal, the appraiser must estimate the land value separately and add it to the value of the improvements. Chattels are personal property and would not be included in the appraisal of real estate.

92. **C** In appraising a newer structure by the cost approach an appraiser would use the cost to reproduce new because the accrued depreciation would be minimal or nonexistent. Determining the accrued depreciation is difficult to do accurately. For an older property, it is more accurate to use replacement cost, which is the cost to replace the improvements with similar, but not necessarily identical improvements. The older the property, the more replacement cost is the only alternative. Some older properties were build with materials and techniques that cannot be obtained today.

93. **D** The weak link in the cost approach is determining the amount to subtract for accrued incurable depreciation. For most properties appraisers have standard cost tables available to locate the cost to reproduce or replacement cost. Nevertheless, it is more time-consuming because the tables are complex. The cost approach tells the appraiser what it would cost to reproduce the property. In theory, no one would pay more for the improvements than this because they could simply hire a builder and have a replacement built.

94. **B** There are three ways to determine the cost to reproduce new. Quantity survey echoes what a builder would do, i.e., determine the cost of materials and labor to build the structure. It is time-consuming and seldom used by an appraiser. Unit in place takes entire components of the structure at a time, such as, for example, the roof system. By looking at the marketplace, the appraiser can determine the cost of a roof, complete with trusses, sheathing, underlayment, and roofing, on a per square foot basis. It then becomes a simple matter to determine the cost to reproduce the roof of any property just by measuring the square footage of the roof and multiplying it by the factor. The most common technique, however, is even simpler. By using building cost estimating guides an appraiser can determine the cost per square foot of the entire structure.

95. **B** The cost approach requires the appraiser to determine the cost to reproduce or replace the improvements. There are various ways to do this, but the simplest is just to calculate the square footage of the different areas of the property, and then multiply each area by a cost per square foot factor derived

from the marketplace that is appropriate. For example, it costs less per square foot to build the garage than the living room, the basement is also less, but the kitchen and bath are more expensive per square foot because of the plumbing. Cubic footage is used on warehouses and other structures where the value is in the volume.

96. **D** In the cost approach the appraiser locates the cost to reproduce the improvements new, then subtracts the accrued depreciation. The cost to reproduce new can be found by quantity survey (cost for the bill of materials plus labor expense), unit in place (taking whole components at a time), or multiplying the overall square footage by a factor from building cost estimating guides.

97. **D** There are three costs to be added to find the total cost of the project – the land, the building and the landscaping. The land is 110 front feet and the cost is $430 per front foot, so the total land cost is $47,300 (110 × $430 = $47,300). The building is 7,600 square feet for each of the two floors, (80 × 95 = 7,600), so the total square footage is 15,200. The cost is $38 per square foot, so the total building cost is $577,600 (15,200 × $38 = $577,600). The landscaped area is the total lot area minus the area occupied by the structure. The total lot area is 22,000 square feet (110 × 200 = 22,000). Subtracting the building area leaves a landscaped area of 14,400 square feet (22,000 − 7,600 = 14,400). Multiplying this by the landscaping cost of $5 per square foot, gives the landscaping cost of $72,000 (14,400 × $5 = $72,000). Adding all three costs gives the total cost of $696,900 ($47,300 + $577,600 + $72,000 = $696,900).

98. **B** If the base index is 100 and increases to 160, this means that costs are now at 160% of what they were at the base. Therefore, if the original cost was $160,000, the current cost to reproduce would be $160,000 times 160%, or $256,000 ($160,000 × 1.60 = $256,000).

99. **A** The easiest way to solve this problem is to find out what the property which cost $24,000 at base 163.7 would have cost at base 100. To find this, divide $24,000 by 163.7%, which comes to $14,661 ($24,000 ÷ 1.637 = $14,660.965). Now multiply this "base 100" figure by the current index of 900, which gives the answer as $131,948.69 ($14,660.965 × 9.00 = $131,948.685).

100. **D** The cost to reproduce the first floor is calculated as 80 feet (wide) times 120 feet (long) times 14 feet (high) times $1.28. This comes to $172,032 (80 ×

120 × 14 × $1.28 = $172,032). The cost to reproduce the second floor is calculated as 80 feet (wide) times 120 feet (long) times 12 feet (high) times $1.12. This comes to $129,024 (80 × 120 × 12 × $1.12 = $129,024). Adding the cost of the two floors together gives the total cost of $301,056 ($172,032 + $129,024 = $301,056).

101.   **D**   Historical (acquisition) cost is irrelevant in appraisal unless appraising the subject property for its historical value (as of a date in the past). Current costs can be found by multiplying historical costs by an appropriate construction index, but it is unnecessary because current costs are always available and never more than a few months out of date. The normal method to find the value of the improvements would be to use replacement cost and then subtract accrued depreciation.

102.   **A**   Reproduction cost is the cost to rebuild the improvements exactly as they are. With older properties this may not be possible, because older materials and techniques may not be available today. Therefore, appraisers use replacement cost, which is the cost to replace the improvements with those of similar utility and size, using modern materials, and not necessarily identical to the original.

103.   **B**   In the cost approach reproduction cost is the cost to reproduce the improvements new today, exactly as they are. With older properties, this may be impossible, since the older materials and techniques may not be available today. As a result appraisers use replacement cost, which is the cost to replace the improvements with new improvements of similar utility, but with modern materials and techniques.

104.   **B**   The theory of the cost approach is to locate the cost to reproduce the structure as though new, then subtract the accrued depreciation. In reality, it is easier and more accurate to use replacement cost rather than reproduction cost. Replacement cost means a structure of the same utility and made with similar or equally desirable materials, but not necessarily identical. The reason is that, especially for older properties, the original materials and methods are no longer available or, if available, can be obtained only at extreme cost.

105.   **D**   The cost approach is a means of appraising the present value of the improvements. In theory, the appraiser calculates the cost to reproduce new, then subtracts the amount of accrued depreciation to determine the present value.

106.   **D**   The cost approach can be used with any improved property, but never with vacant land. Even if a property is improved, the cost approach is not always appropriate. However, for a public service building the appraiser may have little choice. Public service buildings generate no income, so the income capitalization approach is useless. There are also probably no comparables, so the market data approach would also be worthless.

107.   **D**   Normally, the market data approach is the most direct and reliable approach, although for income properties, the income approach is usually the most accurate. But when the market data and income approaches are not reliable or valid, the appraiser is left with the cost approach. Such would be the case where there are no comparables or where the subject property does not produce an income. The cost approach loses reliability on properties where there is substantial incurable depreciation because it is difficult to measure the dollar amount of such depreciation accurately. The older the property, the more likely there is incurable depreciation.

108.   **A**   In theory, the cost approach locates the upper limit of value by finding the amount it would cost to reproduce the structure, then subtracting the accrued depreciation. By the principle of substitution, no one would pay more than this for the improvements because they could simply hire a builder and have them reproduced for that amount. The problem is that the cost approach loses reliability with older properties because it can be difficult to calculate the amount to subtract for accrued depreciation. However, for properties without comparables and no income, the market data and income capitalization approaches fail, leaving the appraiser with no choice but to rely on the cost approach.

109.   **D**   Anything which causes a loss of value is called depreciation. There are three kinds – physical deterioration, functional obsolescence (out of date), and economic or external obsolescence (loss of value from forces outside the property).

110.   **A**   Anything which causes a loss of value is called depreciation.

111.   **C**   Depreciation is a loss in value from any source, categprized as physical deterioration, functional obsolescence and economic (external) obsolescence. Capitalizing rent losses is a way of measuring one source of economic obsolescence. Adding up the total cost to modernize is a method to calculate the amount of functional obsolescence. The value of an improvement at the end of its economic life is always zero, since that is the definition of the end of economic life.

112.   **D**   The three types of depreciation are physical deterioration (lack of maintenance), functional obsolescence (out of date) and economic obsolescence (outside forces and influences).

113.   **B**   The three types of depreciation are physical deterioration (lack of maintenance), functional obsolescence (out of date) and economic obsolescence (outside forces and influences).

114.   **C**   Depreciation is a loss in value from any cause. Economic (external) obsolescence is one kind of depreciation (from forces outside the property), and physical deterioration is another (from lack of maintenance).

115.   **D**   The three kinds of depreciation are physical deterioration, functional obsolescence and economic (external) obsolescence. Effective age is the amount of the original economic life that has been used up, which is not necessarily the same as actual (chronological) age.

116.   **C**   Deferred maintenance is curable physical deterioration. It has nothing to do with functional obsolescence, which occurs when a property gets out of date.

117.   **D**   Any loss in value is a form of depreciation. The three kinds of depreciation are physical deterioration, functional obsolescence and economic (external) obsolescence.

118.   **D**   Physical deterioration is a form of depreciation caused by decay and failure to maintain the improvements. Functional obsolescence occurs when the improvements become out of date. Economic (external) obsolescence is a loss of value due to outside influences surrounding the improvements.

119.   **C**   The three kinds of depreciation are physical deterioration, functional obsolescence, and economic obsolescence. Physical deterioration is caused by decay and lack of maintenance. Functional obsolescence is due to the improvements becoming outdated. Economic obsolescence is from forces and influences outside the property or the control of the owner.

120.   **A**   The three types of depreciation are physical deterioration, functional obsolescence, and economic (external) obsolescence. Physical deterioration is generally caused by lack of maintenance. Functional obsolescence occurs when the improvements become outdated. And economic obsolescence is loss of value from forces and influences outside of the property or control of the owner.

121.   **C**   Depreciation is a loss in value from any cause. Of the three kinds of depreciation, only physical deterioration has to do with maintenance or wear and tear. Functional obsolescence means the property is out of date, and economic obsolescence is from forces and influences outside the property.

122.   **D**   The three kinds of depreciation are physical deterioration, functional obsolescence (out of date) and economic or external obsolescence (loss of value from forces outside the property).

123.   **B**   The three kinds of depreciation are physical deterioration, functional obsolescence and economic (external) obsolescence. Functional obsolescence occurs when the improvements become outdated. Economic obsolescence is when outside forces cause a loss of market value, such as economic conditions in the community, or adverse influence from adjacent properties.

124.   **A**   Depreciation is anything which causes a loss of value. The kind of depreciation due to being out of date is called functional obsolescence, and is just as prevalent as other kinds of depreciation.

125.   **A**   Functional obsolescence means the improvements have lost value due to being out of date. Economic (external) obsolescence is a loss in value due to forces and influences from outside the property over which the owner has no control.

126.   **C**   Lack of maintenance is physical deterioration. Being out of date is functional obsolescence. When there is a loss in value from forces and influences from outside the property, it is economic (external) obsolescence.

127.   **A**   The three kinds of depreciation are physical deterioration (wear and tear, effects of the elements, lack of maintenance), functional obsolescence (out of date), and economic obsolescence (loss of value due to forces and influences external to the property). The sagging foundation is an example of physical deterioration. If a gable roof is a considered depreciation, it would be functional, not economic.

128.   **B**   Physical deterioration is depreciation caused by lack of maintenance. Functional obsolescence is depreciation from the improvements becoming out of date. Economic obsolescence occurs when the forces and influences from outside the property cause a loss of value.

129.   **D**   The three kinds of depreciation are physical deterioration, functional obsolescence and economic (external) obsolescence. Functional obsolescence is when the improvements become outdated. Economic (external) obsolescence is when the property loses value as a result of influences and forces outside the property or the control of the owner.

130.   **B**   Physical deterioration means the property has lost value due to lack of maintenance. Functional obsolescence is a loss of value because the improvements are out of date. Economic (external) obsolescence means there has been a loss in value as a result of forces and influences external to the property and outside the control of the owner. Adverse influence from adjacent property would be an example of economic (external) obsolescence.

131.   **D**   All forms of depreciation are curable or incurable except economic (external) obsolescence. Economic obsolescence is a loss in value from forces and influences from outside the property, therefore there is nothing the owner can do about it.

132.   **C**   Economic (external) obsolescence is a loss of value caused by forces and influences from outside the property. Decay, effects of the elements and the weather. and lack of maintenance are physical deterioration.

133.   **C**   Physical deterioration is a loss in value due to lack of maintenance. Functional obsolescence is a loss in value due to the improvements becoming out of date. Economic (external) obsolescence is a loss in value from forces outside of the property. All may be curable or incurable, except economic obsolescence which, by definition, means the owner can do nothing about it. Curable means that it is feasible to repair or remedy the problem. Incurable does not mean "unrepairable," merely that it is not practical to do anything about it.

134.   **C**   The three kinds of depreciation are physical deterioration (effects of the elements and lack of maintenance), functional obsolescence (improvements have become out of date) and economic obsolescence (loss of value caused by forces and influences from outside the property.

135.   **C**   Physical deterioration is depreciation from decay and lack of maintenance. Functional obsolescence means there is a loss of value because the improvements are out of date. Economic (external) obsolescence is loss of value from forces outside the property, such as bad economic conditions in the area, adverse influence from adjacent properties, etc.

136.   **A**   The three types of depreciation are physical deterioration (lack of maintenance), functional obsolescence (out of date) and economic obsolescence (outside forces). Straight line is a method of calculating the depreciation, not a cause of it. Economic obsolescence is incurable, so its effects are cumulative until the improvements reach the point where the owner no longer gains any benefit from the improvements than that which could be gained from the vacant land. This is the end of the economic life. Since the physical life is dependent on maintenance, it could be indefinitely long. The result is that the economic life is almost always shorter than the physical life, which gives rise to the saying "more house are torn down than fall down."

137.   **D**   All forms of depreciation are curable or incurable, except economic (external) depreciation. Since economic depreciation is caused by forces and influences outside of the control of the owner, by definition it is incurable.

138.   **D**   Curable means that it is feasible to repair or remedy the problem. All forms of depreciation may be curable or incurable except economic obsolescence, which is caused by forces and influences outside the property or the control of the owner. Since the owner can do nothing about it, it is always incurable.

139.   **B**   Of the three kinds of depreciation, economic (external) obsolescence is the only one which is always incurable. It is caused by influences and forces from outside the property, therefore the owner has no means to cure it.

140.   **D**   All improvements have an economic life, which is defined as the period of time over which the owner will receive benefits above the benefits which could be derived from the vacant land without the improvements. The physical life is the time over which the property will last physically. Given proper maintenance; the physical life is indefinitely long.

141.   **B**   The economic life of an improvement is the period over which the owner can expect to receive a benefit greater than the benefit which could be derived from the land alone without the improvement. At the end of the economic life the improvements have no value and the owner generally tears them down or rehabilitates them. The physical life is the period of time over which the improvements can last physically. Given proper maintenance, the physical life is indefinitely long. Therefore, economic life is almost always shorter than physical life, the exception being catastrophe such as fire, flood, etc.

142.   **D**   All improvements have an economic life, which is defined as the period of time over which the improvements provide a benefit higher than the amount which could be realized from the land alone without the improvements. At the end of the economic life the improvements have no value.

143.   **A**   The economic life of the improvements is defined as the period over which the owner will receive a benefit above the benefit which could be realized from the vacant land without the improvements. Economic life is a term that applies only to improvements, not to land.

144.   **B**   The economic life of the improvements is the period over which the owner will receive a benefit greater than the benefit which could be realized from the land without the improvements. Given ordinary maintenance, the physical life of the improvements is indefinitely long, but economic life is not determined by the condition of the property; rather it is determined by the forces surrounding the property. Therefore, economic life is almost always shorter than physical life. The exceptions are catastrophes, e.g., a fire. And if the structure had remaining economic life when it burned, the owner will rebuild.

145.   **C**   If you deposit money in a bank certificate of deposit, at maturity the bank will pay the interest and return the principal to you. If you invest in a property that depreciates, at the end of the economic life the property is worth nothing. In both examples you need a return on the investment, but in the depreciating property you need an additional amount to recapture the invested principal over the economic life of the asset. This additional amount is called a recapture rate.

146.   **A**   Economic life is a concept which can be applied to improvements only. The economic life of a structure is the time period over which it will provide benefits above the benefits which could be derived from the land if it were vacant. For example, a rental house eventually becomes so out of date that the rent is at the lowest end of the market. Simultaneously, changing growth patterns may make the land worth a great deal. The income if the land were ground leased for a long term can be compared to the net income from the rental. When they are equal, the structure is producing no benefit and is at the end of its economic life. The economic life is not related to the condition of the structure or its age or how long it will last physically, rather to the zoning and conditions in the area.

147.   **D**   Economic life is a term applicable to improvements only. It is the period over which the improvements will return a benefit to the owner greater than the benefit the owner could realize from the land without the improvements. At the end of the economic life the owner either rehabilitates the improvements or replaces them with new improvements.

148.   **A**   All structures have an economic life. The economic life is the time over which the improvements contribute more than the bare land. Changing fashions can cause a shortening of the economic life. The shorter the economic life, the shorter the time period over which the owner will derive benefit from the property, therefore the less the property is worth.

149.   **D**   The effective age of a property is the difference between the full economic (useful) life of the property if it were new today, and the remaining economic life, i.e., the amount of the original life that has been used up. The actual (chronological) age is irrelevant.

150.   **B**   The effective age is the projected economic life if the building were new, less the remaining economic life, i.e., the portion of the projected economic life if new today which has been used up. The actual (chronological) age of a structure is the number of years since it was built.

151.   **C**   The actual (chronological) age of a structure is the number of years since it was constructed. The effective age is the projected economic life if the building were new, less the remaining economic life, that is, the portion of the projected economic life if new today which has been used up.

152.   **B**   If we only want the improvement value, the site cost is irrelevant. If the improvements have been depreciated 40%, then the remaining value ($600,000) represents 60% of the original. Therefore, to find the original, divide the present value by 60%. This comes to $1,000,000 ($600,000 ÷ .60 = $1,000,000).

153.   **C**   Assuming straight line depreciation, the amount of annual depreciation can be easily calculated. Only the improvements are depreciable, so to find the annual straight line depreciation, divide the improvement value by the number of years, which comes to $4,000 per year ($160,000 ÷ 40 = $4,000). At the end of 14 years the property still has 26 years of remaining economic life (40 − 14 = 26); so just multiply the annual amount of depreciation by 26 to find the remaining value of the structure. This comes to $104,000 ($4,000 × 26 = $104,000). Adding the land value gives a total value at the end of 14 years of $144,000 ($104,000 + $40,000 = $144,000).

154.   **C**   If it has depreciated 35%, then the remaining value is 65% of what it would cost to build new. If the cost to build new today is $510,000, then the present value is $331,500 ($510,000 × .65 = $331,500). Adding this to the site value gives a total present value of $536,500 ($331,500 + $205,000 = $536,500).

155. **A** A capitalization rate is a composite of a return on the investment and a return of the investment. If you deposit money in a bank certificate of deposit, at maturity the bank will pay the interest and return the principal to you. If you invest in a property that depreciates, at the end of the economic life the property is worth nothing. In both examples you need a return on the investment, but in the depreciating property you need an additional amount to recapture the invested principal over the economic life of the asset. For a structure with an economic life of 50 years, the recapture rate would have to be 2% per year (100% ÷ 50 years = 2% per year).

156. **D** Straight line depreciation means the same amount each year. At eight years of age and an annual depreciation rate of 2.5%, it has depreciated a total of 20% (2.5% × 8 = 20%). Therefore, the remaining value of $190,000 represents 80% of the original value. To find the original value, divide the current value by 80%. This comes to $237,500 ($190,000 ÷ 0.80 = $237,500).

157. **C** Straight line depreciation means the same amount is calculated over each year of the economic life. If the economic life is 30 years, then the annual amount of depreciation is 3⅓% (100% ÷ 30 = 3.33%). The land is not subject to depreciation, only the improvements, so we must subtract the land from the total to get the depreciable amount (value of the improvements). This comes to $1,300,000 ($1,600,000 − $300,000 = $1,300,000). Multiplying this by the annual rate gives a yearly depreciation amount of $43,333.33 ($1,300,000 × 0.033333 = $43,333.3333). To calculate the remaining book value of the improvements at the end of 11 years, multiply the annual amount by the remaining number of years (19 years remaining). This comes to $823,333 ($43,333.33 × 19 = $823,333.33). However, to find the total book value of the property at the end of 11 years we must add back the land value, which gives us $1,123,333 ($823,333 + $300,000 = $1,123.333).

158. **B** The income approach uses a capitalization rate to determine the value of a property based on the income the property is capable of producing. The greater the income, the higher the value, and vice-versa. Although the income capitalization approach can be used on single-family dwellings, it is not very accurate due to the difficulty in determining correct market income and expense figures for a rental house.

159. **A** In the income capitalization approach to value we divide the income by the capitalization rate to find the value, thus the value is derived from the income the property is capable of producing. Determining the net income is part of the process, but not the "capitalization" part.

160. **C** The basic formula for the income capitalization approach is V = NOI ÷ CR, where NOI = Net Operating Income and CR = Capitalization Rate.

161. **A** The income capitalization approach is a method of determining the value of the property from on its income potential. It is based on the principal of anticipation, which holds that the greater the anticipated future benefits of ownership, the greater the market value. The cost approach is concerned with the amount of accrued depreciation.

162. **D** The formula to find the value by the income capitalization approach is V = NOI ÷ CR, where NOI is the Net Operating Income and CR is the Capitalization Rate. Therefore, the appraiser must determine both the income and the capitalization rate to find the value. The income capitalization rate can only be used on properties which do, or could, produce an income.

163. **C** According to the principle of anticipation the greater the anticipated future benefits of ownership, the greater the value, and vice-versa. The benefit of owning an income-producing property is the anticipation of income, so the income approach is based primarily on the principle of anticipation.

164. **B** The income approach is based purely on the net income the property can produce. Any factor is significant if it has a bearing on how much income the property can produce, but the basis is still the net income.

165. **B** An annual cash flow divided by the amount of the investment gives the return on the investment (income ÷ principal = rate).

166. **A** The income approach is based purely on the net income the property can produce. Any factor is significant if it has a bearing on how much income the property can produce, but the basis of the income approach is still the net income.

167. **C** The value of the property is determined by the income it is capable of producing and the capitalization rate the investor requires. The higher rate of return the investor demands, the less the investor can pay for the property, given the same income.

168. **D** All investments require a yield rate, which is a return on the investment. Depreciating assets require an additional recapture rate to recover the amount invested in the asset. A capitalization rate is

a rate that includes both. Land does not depreciate, but improvements do. Therefore, a capitalization rate includes both a return (e.g., an interest rate) plus a recapture rate.

169.   **C**   There are two classes of assets (investments). Wasting assets are assets which become worthless over their economic life (term of the investment). An investor who buys a non-wasting asset receives a return of the investment at the end of the term. A bank certificate of deposit is an example of a non-wasting asset. But if you lend money to a friend who repays part of the principal with each payment, the loan is a wasting asset, because at the end of the loan it will be repaid in full, and the note will be worthless. To value a non-wasting asset, divide the income by a yield rate. To value a wasting asset, a higher rate is needed, a rate which includes an additional amount to recapture the invested principal. The term "capitalization rate" means a rate which includes a recapture rate in addition to the yield rate. To find the amount the recapture should be for a real estate investment we use the amount the structure will depreciate each year.

170.   **A**   All investors require a rate of return on their investments. If the invested capital will be returned at the end of the investment period (e.g., a certificate of deposit at a bank), the rate of return is all the investor requires. If the investment becomes worthless over its life (a depreciating property), then the investor needs an additional amount to recapture the invested principal over the term of the investment. This is called a recapture rate. In real estate, structures depreciate and become worthless over their economic lives, but land does not depreciate. Therefore we need a return on both, and a recapture for the building.

171.   **A**   The rate the appraiser should use when valuing an income property varies according to numerous factors. Of all the elements which make up this rate, the rate available on safe investments such as insured bank accounts, federal obligations, and the like, is considered the starting point. This rate is sometimes called the "annuity rate," "bank rate," or "guaranteed rate." Since most real estate investments involve greater risk and are less liquid than such investments, an additional amount (commensurate with the type of real estate investment) is typically added. However, real estate investments commonly provide investors with a greater hedge against inflation and can also provide tax shelter, so adjustments

are also made downward to compensate for these factors. All of these adjustments are made in order to derive the "yield rate," that is, the rate of return the investor should desire. An important factor which must also be added is the allowance for depreciation. Some assets, such as bank accounts and treasury obligations are called "non-wasting assets" because the investor will get all the money back at the end of the investment term. But other assets, such as mines and natural resources are "wasting assets" because the asset becomes worthless over its life. For such assets, a "recapture rate" must be included as part of the overall rate. The improvements on real estate have an economic life and will become worthless by the time the economic life is over. Therefore, it is customary to add an additional amount to the yield rate for recapture. How much should be added is different for each property, since different properties will have different remaining economic lives.

172.   **D**   The capitalization rate is a composite of a return on the investment (yield rate) and a recapture of the investment over the economic life of the improvements (recapture rate). The shorter the economic life, the higher the recapture rate must be, and therefore the higher the capitalization rate.

173.   **C**   The value is irrelevant in this problem. If 100% of the remaining economic life will be used up in 38 years, then it is being used up at the rate of 2.63% per annum (100% ÷ 38 years = .026315789 per annum).

174.   **D**   Capitalization rates are made up of a rate of return demanded by the investor, and a recapture rate to recover the amount invested over the economic life of the structure. Either a shorter economic life or a higher risk results in a higher capitalization rate. The higher the rate the investor demands the less the investor can pay for the property, so the higher the rate, the lower the value, and vice-versa.

175.   **B**   Investors are willing to accept a lower rate if the risk is less, all other factors being equal. The higher the capitalization rate needed by the investor, the less the investor is willing to pay for the property, and vice-versa.

176.   **B**   Normally, an appraiser determines a capitalization rate by looking at comparable sold properties and determining the capitalization rate the buyer is getting. To determine what capitalization rate (CR) the buyer is getting, divide the net operating income (NOI) by the value (price paid). The formula is CR = NOI ÷ V.

177.   **B**   Risk and longevity of income stream are both important factors in selecting an appropriate capitalization rate. The post office is not likely to default on the lease payments, and will probably occupy the premises for a very long time. Neither can be said with as much certainty for a video store.

178.   **A**   The amount that a property is currently rented for is its contract rent. The rent it could be rented for is called the market, or economic rent. Most properties are rented for the market rent only right at the point when the rents were last raised. Thereafter, until the rents are raised to market again, the contract rent is lower than market rent.

179.   **D**   The contract rent is the amount of rent that a property is currently rented for. Unless the property is leased, the contract rent is irrelevant to an appraiser. The value of the property (by the income approach) is determined by what the property could be rented for in the marketplace. This is called market rent, or by the older term, economic rent.

180.   **B**   Having rent below market is a clear advantage for the tenant (lessee). The lessor should have placed an adjustment clause in the lease allowing the rent to increase to market periodically.

181.   **D**   The income capitalization approach uses the net income and the capitalization rate to find the value. The income must be net of all expenses. Real property taxes and insurance are two of the expenses which the appraiser must deduct from the gross rental income to find the net income.

182.   **C**   An allowance for vacancy and credit loss must also be deducted, unless the property is fully leased. All operating expenses must also be deducted, except principal and interest on a loan (but including taxes and insurance), and the owner's income tax liability. The appraisal is for an all-cash transaction, so loan amounts are disregarded.

183.   **D**   When an owner sells the property the owner does not continue to manage the property for the buyer forever at no cost. Every investor must make an allowance for all expenses of management, maintenance and repair, even if the investor performs the work himself or herself.

184.   **D**   According to the principle of anticipation the greater the anticipated future benefits of ownership, the greater the market value. In an income-producing property the primary benefit of ownership is the income it is capable of producing. Although there are several ways to use capitalization, most capitalization methods compare the income which the subject property is capable of producing to the income which would be generated by other investments in the marketplace. Most other investments (stocks, bonds, and the like) are all-cash investments and completely passive. Therefore, to make the real estate investment as comparable as possible the appraiser must subtract complete management expenses, but nothing for principal and interest payments on a loan. Note that, even if an investor pays all cash, the property must still be insured and property taxes must be paid. Since different investors are in different tax positions the income tax consequences are also ignored, although an adjustment for tax benefits is made when computing the yield the investor would demand.

185.   **D**   In real estate investment, and in real estate appraisal, it is customary to calculate first the maximum income the property could produce if fully rented. This is called the "potential gross income" (PGI). The anticipated market vacancy factor is then subtracted to find the amount which is anticipated would be available to pay operating expenses. This amount is called the "effective gross income" (EGI). Operating expenses (including total management expenses, but not including debt service or investor's income tax consequences) are then deducted to find the "net operating income" (NOI). In direct capitalization, the NOI is then divided by the capitalization rate to find the value.

186.   **B**   First, you must find the annual net operating income. If the monthly gross is $3,256, the annual gross is $39,072 ($3,256 × 12 = $39,072). Subtracting the annual expenses of $15,628 leaves an annual net operating income of $23,444 ($39,072 − $15,628 = $23,444). Dividing this by the capitalization rate yields a value of $260,489 ($23,444 ÷ .09 = $260,488.8889).

187.   **C**   First, find the net operating income, stated as 65% of $58,750. This comes to $38,187.50 ($58,750 × .65 = $38,187.50). To find the value rate the owner is getting, divide this net operating income by the amount of the investment (purchase price). This gives a rate of 11.4% ($38,187.50 ÷ $335,000 = .11399).

188.   **B**   If a property was worth $100,000 when capitalized at 6%, then the net operating income must have been $6,000 ($100,000 × .06 = $6,000. Capitalizing this net operating income at 8% means the new value will be $75,000 ($6,000 ÷ .08 = $75,000).

189.   **C**   You can capitalize a loss or an increase in income directly using the standard formula for value. In this case, the loss of net income was $180

per month, or $2,160 per year ($180 × 12 = $2,160). Dividing this by the capitalization rate of 11% yields a loss in value of $19,636 ($2,160 ÷ .11 = $19,636.3636).

190.   **A**   First, find the net operating income of the property. If it is valued at $247,500 at a capitalization rate of 8.5%, then the income is $21,037.50 ($247,500 × .085 = $21,037.50). Now divide this net operating income by the new capitalization rate to find the new value. The result is $186,173 ($21,037.50 ÷ .113 = $186,172.5664).

191.   **C**   The first thing to do is to find the net income. If the expenses are 45% of the gross, then the net income is the remaining 55%. This comes to $495,000 ($900,000 × .55 = $495,000). To find the value, divide the net operating income by the capitalization rate. The result is $4,125,000 ($495,000 ÷ .12 = $4,125,000).

192.   **B**   The basic formula for determining the value by the income approach is v = NOI ÷ CR, where NOI = Net Operating Income and CR = Capitalization Rate. Therefore, we must first find the NOI. If the expenses are $900 a month, the annual expenses are $10,800 ($900 × 12 = $10,800). Subtracting this from the annual gross of $25,000 gives the NOI as $14,200 ($25,000 − $10,800 = $14,200). Dividing this by the capitalization rate gives a value of $218,462 ($14,200 ÷ .065 = $218,461.5385).

193.   **C**   First, find the net operating income. The potential gross income is $60,000 ($5,000 × 12 = $60,000). Subtracting the expenses of $12,000 leaves a net operating income of $48,000 ($60,000 − $12,000 = $48,000). Dividing the net operating income by the required capitalization rate means the property will be worth a total of $400,000 when completed ($48,000 ÷ .12 = $400,000). Subtracting the cost to construct the building, means the investor can only afford to pay $100,000 for the land ($400,000 − $300,000 = $100,000).

194.   **C**   There are three formulas used with capitalization rates. The basic formula is the formula to determine the dollar amount of return on an investment at a certain rate, that is, I = RV (Income = rate times value). This formula is restructured as v = I ÷ R (Value = Income divided by Rate) in order to find the value (or sales price) of the property when the income and rate are known. And when the formula is rewritten as R = I ÷ v, we have the formula used to extract a capitalization rate when a property was sold and we know the net operating income when it sold and what it sold for. In this problem, just multiply the

investment ($85,000) by the rate (12%) to find the return required ($85,000 × .12 = $10,200).

195.   **D**   First, find the annual gross income and subtract the annual expenses to find the net operating income. This comes to $31,350 ($4,750 × 12 = $57,000; $57,000 − $25,650 = $31,350). Now divide this by the sales price of $261,250 to find the capitalization rate. The result is 12% ($31,350 ÷ $261,250 = 0.12).

196.   **B**   To find the capitalization rate use the formula CR = NOI ÷ v. If the net operating income is $36,000 and the value is $600,000, the capitalization rate is 6% ($36,000 ÷ $600,000 = .0600).

197.   **B**   If the income can be capitalized to find the value (v = NOI ÷ CR), then a gain or loss in income can be capitalized to find the gain or loss in value. In this case the loss of value is $21,600 per annum ($1,800 × 12 = $21,600). Dividing this by the capitalization rate of 10% gives a loss in value of $216,000 ($21,600 ÷ .10 = $216,000).

198.   **A**   The formula for determining value by the income capitalization approach is v = NOI ÷ CR, where NOI = Net Operating Income and CR = Capitalization Rate. First find the gross income, which comes to $115,200 ($800 × 12 months × 12 units = $115,200). Then find the effective gross income by subtracting the vacancy. The vacancy is 10%, or $11,5.200 ($115,200 × .10 = $11,520). The effective gross income comes to $103,680 ($115,200 − $11,520 = $103,680). Next find the NOI by subtracting the annual expenses. This comes to $81,180 ($103,680 − $22,500 = $81,180). Finally, divide the NOI by the capitalization rate to find the value. This comes to $405,900 ($81,180 ÷ .20 = $405,900).

199.   **B**   First, divide the total net income by five to get the income for each year. This comes to $21,840 ($109,200 ÷ 5 = $21,840). Next use the capitalization formula v = NOI ÷ CR to find the value. The value comes to $260,000 ($21,840 ÷ .084 = $260,000).

200.   **D**   The capitalization rate reflects two needs of the investor. The first requirement is a rate of return on the investment. The second is a recapture rate so the investor can recover the amount invested over the useful (economic) life of the property. Risk determines the rate of return needed, and the remaining economic life (amount of depreciation) determines the recapture rate needed. A higher capitalization rate could be caused, therefore, by either a higher risk or more depreciation.

201.   **A**   It is easiest to use a hypothetical property to find the answer. Assume an investment with a net

operating income of $10,000 per year. At a capitalization rate of 10%, the property will have a value of $100,000 ($10,000 ÷ .10 = $100,000). At a capitalization rate of 11% the value drops to $90,909 ($10,000 ÷ .11 = $90,909.0909). The 11% rate resulted in a value which is $9,091 lower, which is about 9% of the first value ($9,091 ÷ $100,000 = .0909).

202.   **D**   You must figure the value with both capitalization rates to determine the difference in value. At a capitalization rate of 11½% the property is worth $584,783 ($67,200 ÷ .115 = $584,782.6087). At a capitalization rate of 12¼% the value is only $548,980 ($67,250 ÷ .1225 = $548,979.5918). The lower capitalization rate made the property worth $35,803 too much ($584,783 − $548,980 = $35,803).

203.   **A**   You must use the formula $V = NOI ÷ CR$ with both capitalization rates to determine the value each appraiser obtained, then calculate the difference. At a capitalization rate of 10% the value is $1,328,700 ($132,870 ÷ .10 = $1,328,700). At a capitalization rate of 12% the value is only $1,107,250 ($132,870 ÷ .12 = $1,107,250). The higher capitalization rate is $221,450 lower than the results at a 10% capitalization rate.

204.   **D**   You can capitalize a loss of income to find out the resulting loss in value. If the expenses increase but the gross income remains the same, then the net operating income will be lower by the amount of the increase in expenses. Therefore, just divide the additional expense by the capitalization rate to find the loss in value. This comes to $9,000 ($900 ÷ .10 = $9,000).

205.   **B**   If the property is worth $500,000 at a 6% capitalization rate, then the net operating income must be 6% of $500,000, or $30,000 ($500,000 × .06 = $30,000). Using this figure, but at a capitalization rate of 8%, the new value would be $375,000 ($30,000 ÷ .08 = $375,000).

206.   **D**   First, calculate the gross income for each year. For the first year the income was $18,000 ($750 × 24 = $18,000). The following year it increased by 10%, or $1,800, so it was $19,800 ($18,000 × .10 = $1,800; $18,000 + $1,800 = $19,800). However, there was a 10% vacancy factor the second year, so the loss was $1,980 ($19,800 × .10 = $1,980). This means the actual gross income for the second year was $17,820, or $180 less than the first year ($19,800 − $1,980 = $17,820; $18,000 − $17,820 = $180). This is 1% less than the first year ($180 ÷ $18,000 = 0.01).

207.   **C**   First, find the value of the total investment, then subtract the cost of constructing the building ($450,000) to determine how much can be paid for the land. To find the value of the total investment, first find the net operating income. The gross is $90,000 and the expenses are $18,000, so the net is $72,000 ($90,000 − $18,000 = $72,000). Divide this by the required capitalization rate to find the value. This comes to $600,000 ($72,000 ÷ .12 = $600,000). Therefore, the amount which can be paid for the land is $150,000 ($600,000 − $450,000 = $150,000).

208.   **A**   A gross rent multiplier is a shortcut to the income capitalization approach. By determining how many times the gross income investors are paying for similar income properties, the appraiser can quickly calculate the value of a building. The land residual process is a method to determine the value of the land under an income property by subtracting the portion of the income attributable to the structure and capitalizing the remainder.

209.   **B**   Only the potential gross incomes and selling prices of comparables are required. The properties must be comparable in style, age, amenities and location.

210.   **D**   The property sold for 144 times its monthly gross income (gross rent multiplier of 144), which is derived by simply dividing the sales price by the monthly potential gross income ($144,000 ÷ $1,000 = 144).

211.   **B**   First, find the gross rent multiplier for the comparable property by dividing the sales price by the income. This comes to a monthly gross rent multiplier of 160 ($144,000 ÷ $900 = 160). Now multiply the monthly gross income of the subject property ($1,050) by the same gross rent multiplier, which gives a value of $168,000 for the subject property ($900 × 160 = $168,000).

212.   **D**   First, find the potential gross income. Eight units at $600 per unit comes to an annual income of $57,600 (8 × $600 × 12 = $57,600). Eight additional units at $700 comes to an annual income of $67,200 (8 × $700 × 12 = $67,200. The remaining units number 14 (30 units − 16 units = 14 units). These 14 units are rented at $800 per month, so their annual total is $134,400 (14 × $800 × 12 = $134,400). Adding all the units makes a total annual gross income of $259,200 ($57,600 + $67,200 + $134,400 = $259,200). Multiplying this by the gross rent multiplier gives the value as $1,684,800 ($259,200 × 6.5 = $1,684,800).

213.   **C**   When using a gross rent multiplier, the expenses are ignored. Since the gross rent multiplier (GRM) given in the problem is a monthly GRM, the annual income ($60,000) must be divided by

12 to find the monthly gross income, which comes to $5,000 ($60,000 ÷ 12 = $5,000). Multiplying the monthly gross income ($5,000) by the gross rent multiplier (105) gives the value as $525,000 ($5,000 × 105 = $525,000).

214. **C** The most powerful and accurate approach for a single-family residence is the market data (sales comparison) approach, since it echoes exactly what buyers and sellers do in the marketplace. The income approach can also be used, but the amount of rental income must be estimated as well as the annual expenses. This is difficult to do accurately for an individual house, so the income approach is not as accurate as the market data approach. The cost approach is also useful in locating the upper limit of value. Its weak link is estimating the amount of accrued depreciation, so it is not of much use on older residences, although it is highly accurate on newer properties. When all three approaches have been used, the appraiser weighs the results of each and takes a weighted average, never a blind, equally weighted average.

215. **D** The income approach and the capitalization approach are synonymous terms. The income approach is hard to use accurately on a single-family house because of the difficulty in obtaining accurate income and cost figures. The cost approach is useful in locating the upper limit of value, but loses reliability on older houses with incurable depreciation. The most powerful approach is the market data (sales comparison) approach, assuming adequate comparables. There are almost always a plentiful supply of comparables for single-family dwellings.

216. **D** Land is best appraised by the market comparison approach to value. The market comparison approach consists of locating suitable sold, comparable properties, adjusting for differences in the amenities, and thereby determining the market value of the subject. The income capitalization approach cannot be used effectively on property which does not produce an income.

217. **C** Insurance policies generally must pay to rebuild the structure. You cannot buy depreciated materials, so the structure will be as new when finished. Therefore, the cost approach, without deducting any allowance for depreciation, is the usual approach to appraise a property for insurance purposes.

218. **A** Insurance appraisals are to determine the cost to replace the improvements, not to sell the property. Therefore, the cost approach, disregarding the accrual for depreciation, is the most appropriate approach.

219. **A** Fire insurance policies usually require the company to rebuild the structure. Therefore, the amount of insurance needed is the amount required to reproduce the property new, disregarding accrued depreciation. The cost approach locates this amount.

220. **A** Vacant land must be appraised by market data (sales comparison) when possible, but if there is a shortage of comparables, land residual is used instead. The cost approach cannot be used on property without improvements.

221. **B** The market data (sales comparison) approach to value depends on an adequate number of good comparable sales. New homes in a subdivision will have a shortage of comparable sales if none have sold yet.

222. **C** Normally the most accurate approach is the market data approach, but the most powerful approach for income producing properties is the income capitalization approach. Investors always ask for the financial information about a listing before they are concerned with its location and other information.

223. **B** The theory of the cost approach is to locate the cost to reproduce the structure new, then subtract an allowance for accrued depreciation. The resulting figure is the value of the improvements today.

224. **A** The market data approach requires adequate comparable sales, which would not be available for a post office building. The income approach is useful on an income-producing property, but a post office is a public service building, not a rental property. The only remaining approach to value is the cost approach, so the appraiser has no choice but to use it.

225. **A** The cost approach can be used on any improved property, but never on vacant land. It locates the upper limit of value, but loses accuracy when used on properties with incurable depreciation because it is difficult to measure incurable depreciation. However, when appraising a single-use property, an appraiser may have no choice because many such properties produce no income, so the income approach is impossible, and there may be no comparables to use with the sales comparison approach.

226. **D** The theory of the cost approach is to subtract accrued depreciation from the cost to reproduce new. This gives the theoretical upper limit of value because a buyer could simply hire a builder and have the structure reproduced for this amount.

227. **B** The market data (sales comparison) approach relies on comparing the subject property to

sold comparable properties based on the principle of substitution.

228.   **D**   The theory of the cost approach is to locate the cost to reproduce the improvements new, then subtract an allowance for accrued depreciation. In theory, a buyer could have the improvements reproduced for this amount, so the buyer would not pay more than this for the improvements. Therefore, we say that the cost approach locates the upper limit of value by the principle of substitution.

229.   **C**   The sales comparison (market data) approach is usually the most powerful when there are good comparables available. Of all real estate markets, the largest and the one with the most comparable sales is the market for single-family homes.

230.   **B**   Sales comparison (market data) is always the preferred method to appraise because it echoes exactly what buyers and sellers do in the marketplace, i.e., they compare a property against others. The land residual technique capitalizes the income attributable to the land in an income property. It is not nearly as direct as market comparison, and used only when the market approach fails due to lack of good comparables. Land for development can be appraised by anticipated use, that is, the appraiser estimates the total value of the lots which can be derived from the parcel, and subtracts the cost of development to determine the present value of the raw land.

231.   **D**   The income capitalization approach is a method of determining the value to an investor of an income property, based on the income the property is capable of producing. The income capitalization approach, therefore, rests mostly on the principal of anticipation. According to the principal of anticipation, the greater the anticipated future benefits of ownership, the greater the market value.

232.   **C**   If comparables are not available the market data (sales comparison) approach to value is worthless. The income approach works best for properties which produce a rental income. If the property does not currently produce a rental income the income approach can still be used by determining what the property could be rented for. The cost approach is used to determine the value of improvements by finding out what it would cost to reproduce them and subtracting the accrued depreciation. It is commonly used on single-purpose structures which have no comparables.

233.   **B**   A newly opened subdivision produces no rental income, so the income capitalization approach would be useless. The amount of the mortgage or insurance on a property are generally irrelevant as to which approach to use. The income approach is designed to locate the value of properties which produce rental income.

234.   **A**   All approaches to value make use of comparable data, but the market data (sales comparison) approach is the only one which does so on whole properties at a time. In the cost approach we might compare the cost per square foot, for example, and in the income approach we might compare rental values, but not the entire property.

235.   **B**   The cost approach determines the value of improvements only. It can be used on any improved property, but the older the improvements the more it loses reliability. Appraisers rely on it mostly when appraising a single-use property for which there are no comparables and income figures are nonexistent or difficult to ascertain.

236.   **D**   Property tax valuations are frequently very out of date and should never be used for listing purposes. The cost approach is relatively accurate for a single-family dwelling as long as it is not too old. The weak link in the cost approach is determining how much to subtract for accrued incurable depreciation. The income capitalization approach is not reliable on a single-family dwelling due to lack of reliable cost and income data. The most powerful approach is usually the sales comparison (market data) approach, given adequate comparables.

237.   **D**   Normally, the cost approach loses reliability when used on older properties because the most difficult part of the cost approach is determining the amount to subtract for accrued depreciation. However, the purpose of an insurance appraisal is to determine the cost to reproduce the structure, disregarding accrued depreciation. Therefore, insurance appraisals are usually based on the cost approach exclusively.

238.   **B**   The cost approach to value can be used only on improved properties, since it is based on the cost to reproduce the improvements. The income approach can be used only on properties which can produce income. A lot for a single-family residence would not produce income. The land residual approach is a method to determine the value of land underlying an income property. The most powerful approach would be the market data (sales comparison) approach.

239.   **B**   The three approaches to value do not enjoy the same validity and reliability for all properties. The appraiser must make a judgment as to how much to weigh the results of each approach in determining

the final value conclusion to be reported to the client. This process is called correlation, or reconciliation.

240. **B**   When the appraiser has finished the three approaches, the value conclusions will each have different validity and reliability. Weighing each value conclusion and using them to determine the appraiser's final value conclusion is called correlation, or reconciliation.

241. **D**   Each of the three approaches is best suited for different types of property, although most properties can be appraised by more than one approach. Even then, due to the reliability and validity of the data, and the relevance of the approach to the subject property, the appraiser cannot take a blind, equally weighted average of the three values. Neither can the appraiser simply take the middle value. The proper procedure is to take a weighted average based on the appraiser's opinion of the results of each approach.

242. **C**   The three approaches to value are market comparison, cost, and income capitalization. Appraisers use these as alternative ways of appraising a property, arriving at different value conclusions for each approach. The final value conclusion is derived by weighing the results of each approach. This step is called correlation or reconciliation.

243. **C**   Reconciliation, or correlation, is the process whereby the appraiser assigns a weighted value to the results of each of the three approaches to value. The weights are based on the reliability and validity of the data and the relevance of the approach to the subject property.

244. **B**   When the appraiser has appraised the property by the three approaches the final value conclusion is never derived by blindly averaging the results of the three approaches. Instead, the appraiser takes a weighted average based on the reliability and validity of the data and the relevance of the approach to the property. This process is called correlation or reconciliation.

245. **D**   The three approaches to value are market comparison, cost, and income capitalization. Each has its strengths and weaknesses. When the appraiser has finished appraising the property by each approach, the final value conclusion is derived by taking a weighted average of each approach based on the reliability and validity of the data and the relevance of the approach to the subject property. This is called correlation. Correlation is never done by blindly averaging the results from the three approaches.

246. **D**   There are three approaches to value – market comparison, cost, and income capitalization.

Each has its strengths and weaknesses. When the appraiser has completed estimating the value by all three approaches the final value conclusion is derived by taking a weighted average of the three approaches, not by taking a blind, equally weighted average. The weight ascribed to each approach is determined by the reliability and validity of the data and the relevance of the approach to the subject property.

247. **C**   This is a ratio problem, where the original rent was $1000/122.8 and the new rent will be X/125.8. To determine the value of X, the equation is $1000/122.8 = X/125.8. To solve the equation, first convert the fraction "$1000/122.8" to a whole number, which comes to $8.143322476 ($1,000 ÷ 122.8 = $8.143322476). Now the equation reads $8.143322476 = X/125.8. To solve for X, multiply both sides of the equation by 125.8. This yields $1,024.43 on the left side ($8.143322476 × 125.8 = $1,024.429967), and X alone on the other side, or $1,204.43 = X.

248. **A**   Depth tables are mathematical devices to determine the relative value of the back portion of a lot in relation to the front area. Similarly, corner influence tables help an appraiser adjust for the benefit of being on a corner. Corner influence and depth make a difference in the market value of all properties, but the amount is slight unless the property is retail, where the amount of space available to show goods is of paramount importance.

249. **D**   The fertility of the land is of importance only for property which will be put to agricultural use. However, even the subsoil is important in all other properties, because the condition of the subsoil affects the buildability of the site.

250. **B**   There is a way to solve this problem with mathematical logic, but it is easier to find the answer by taking a random building cost, increasing it by 20%, and then drawing a conclusion. Assume, therefore, that a building is constructed at a cost of $100,000. If building costs increase by 20%, the same building will cost $120,000 to build. Since $100,000 is 83.33% of $120,000 ($100,000 ÷ $120,000 = .8333), the dollar has lost 16⅔% of its purchasing power (1.00 − .8333 = .1667).

FEDERAL INCOME TAX

F EDERAL INCOME TAXES HAVE A GREAT IMPACT ON REAL ESTATE FINANCING AND on buy-sell decisions. Tax benefits are frequently one of the principal motivations for buying real estate. Even where the tax benefits are not the most important reason for buying, they still influence the amount and nature of the buyer's offer. Sellers also must consider the tax impacts of a sale. When capital gains tax rates are high, sellers may prefer not to sell, or may decide to sell on installment sales or use exchanging instead of selling for cash. The tremendous impact of income taxes on real estate makes it essential for all real estate agents to have a knowledge of income tax basics.

That income taxes are based on income is obvious. What is not so clear is when the income becomes taxable. Wages, interest, dividends and the like generally become taxable when received. Gain on the sale of property is also taxable, but does not ordinarily become taxable until the gain is realized. *Realization* of the gain normally occurs when the property is sold. In other words, if you buy a property and its value increases, no gain is recognized and no tax is due until you sell the property.

The increase in value of an asset is called a *capital gain*. For real estate agents, how taxes are levied on capital gains is the most important part of the Internal Revenue Code. A capital gain should be thought of as profit realized on the sale of the asset. A more complete definition would be "net profit," because taxes are not levied on the costs incurred in making the profit.

The Internal Revenue Code also provides that **capital improvements** are not part of the gain. A capital improvement adds something to the property which was not there when it was purchased. For example, suppose you buy a personal residence, and during your ownership you add a bedroom at a cost of $10,000. The cost of the bedroom will be excluded from the sales price when calculating gain on a sale, because it is actually part of what you paid for the property.

Capital improvements are contrasted with repair or maintenance expenses. If you paint your kitchen, this is maintenance, not a capital improvement. But the distinction between capital improvements and maintenance items is not always clear. For example, painting the kitchen is maintenance, but if it is part of an extensive kitchen remodeling project, it would be considered part of a capital improvement.

The contrast between capital improvements and maintenance items is subjective. In general, if it is a large expense in relation to the total value of the asset, and if it will have a long remaining economic life, it will likely be considered a capital improvement, not maintenance. For example, most tax counsel considers that a new roof is a capital improvement. But re-roofing just part of the structure is generally considered a maintenance item.

To calculate the capital gain, first you must determine your ***adjusted sales price***. The adjusted sales price is the price you sold the asset for, less the costs of the sale. Among other expenses, the costs of the sale include title insurance, escrow and recording fees, as well as the brokerage fee (commission) paid by the seller.

Next, you must calculate your ***cost basis***. The cost basis is the purchase price, plus your costs of acquisition, and any capital improvements. To find the capital gain, subtract the cost basis from the capital gain. The following example shows the calculation of capital gain for the sale of a personal residence for $240,000, which was purchased for $198,000, incurring acquisition costs of $700, a capital improvement of $20,000, and sales expenses of $17,400.

Sales price	$240,000
Less sales expenses	−17,400
Adjusted sales price	222,600
Less purchase price	−198,000
Less cost of acquisition	−700
Less capital improvement	−20,000
CAPITAL GAIN	$ 3,900

Tax is due on the amount of the capital gain. To calculate the amount of the tax, Congress has contemplated various schemes. Central to the debate over capital gains taxes is the fact that a capital gain realized by the taxpayer is not completely profit; in many cases it is just the effect of inflation. In other words, if you bought the house in the above example for $198,000 (plus $20,000 capital improvement) and sold it for $240,000, the "profit" is just caused by the fact that the dollars you sold it for were cheaper dollars than the dollars you used to buy it. The house you sold was the same house you bought (including the capital improvement) so, in reality, there was no "profit" at all.

Of course, sometimes the profit does come from true appreciation. If you buy property and the local jurisdiction changes the zoning in your favor, the resulting increase in value is not due to inflation.

The difficult part is trying to determine how much of the profit is just from inflation and how much is from appreciation. In recognition of this problem, tax rates usually exclude a portion of the gain from taxation. In times past this percentage has been as high as 60%. An alternative philosophy is to index the acquisition cost to the inflation rate, so the taxpayer will pay tax on 100% of the actual profit after inflation. Still another concept is to tax the gain at different arbitrary percentages according to how long the owner held the asset. Since Congress changes the tax laws constantly, you should check with your instructor for the rules currently in effect.

Cost recovery

Under the Internal Revenue Code there are four categories of real property – ***personal use property, trade or business property, investment property*** and ***dealer property***. Personal use property is the taxpayer's personal residence. Trade or business property is property used to produce income in a trade or business. Investment property is property used to produce income by being rented to another or by being held for speculation, such as vacant land. And dealer property is property held as inventory for resale.

These definitions are fairly straightforward, but observe what happens when a taxpayer involved in an incorporated trade or business buys a property. If the taxpayer takes title personally and rents the property to the corporation, it is the taxpayer's investment property. If the corporation buys the property, it is trade or business property of the corporation. Such a taxpayer should always consult with appropriate counsel before acquiring the property to determine the way to take title in order to maximize the tax advantages.

When a taxpayer buys real property, the category in which it falls becomes of great importance. The Internal Revenue Code allows the owner of trade or business property and the owner of investment property to claim an annual expense for loss of market value of the improvements due to depreciation. In real estate appraisal, depreciation is defined as a loss of market value over the economic life of the improvements. (See the preceding section, Real Estate Appraisal.) Note that this deduction applies only to trade or business property or to investment property; but no deduction can be claimed for depreciation of a personal residence. Since land does not have an economic life, vacant land, even the land on which trade or business property and investment property is built, also does not produce a deduction for depreciation. The improvements on trade or business property and investment property are sometimes referred to as ***depreciable*** assets.

When appraising property, appraisers try to calculate the amount of the depreciation as accurately as possible. For income tax purposes, however, an arbitrary amount is typically used. Because of this, depreciation for income tax purposes is now officially called ***cost recovery***, although in the past it was just called "depreciation" and many people still refer to it as depreciation. Note that cost recovery springs from the same concept as depreciation – the improvements are declining in value over their economic life.

Now let us see how the use of cost recovery can benefit an investor. Suppose that you bought an apartment building (investment category) for $500,000, and that $400,000 of the purchase price was the value of the improvements and $100,000 was the value of the land. Let us also assume that the Internal Revenue Code allows a 20-year economic life for this type of asset. (From time to time Congress changes the allowable economic life. Check with your instructor for the current allowable life.)

If you paid $400,000 for the depreciable portion (improvements), and they have a life of 20 years, then the amount of cost recovery allowed would be $20,000 per year ($400,000 ÷ 20 years = $20,000). Let us further suppose that the potential gross income is $96,000, the vacancy and credit loss is 5% ($4,800), and the total expenses before principal and interest are $38,000. This would leave a net operating income of $53,200 –

Potential Gross Income	$96,000
Less vacancy and credit loss	−4,800
Effective Gross Income	91,200
Less operating Expenses	−38,000
Net operating income	$ 53,200

Now let us suppose that you borrow $450,000 at an interest rate of 9% in order to buy the property. This means that your interest expense for the year will be approximately $40,500 ($450,000 × .09 = $40,500). (In reality your interest expense will be slightly less than $40,500 due to amortization, but $40,500 is close enough for purposes of our illustration.) This means that your ***net spendable income*** would be $12,700 –

Potential gross income	$96,000
Less vacancy and credit loss	−4,800
Effective gross income	91,200
Less operating expenses	−38,000
Net operating income	53,200
Less interest expense	−40,500
Net spendable income	$ 12,700

For income tax purposes, the interest is fully deductible, so your taxable income would be $12,700. However, if the Internal Revenue Code allows you to claim an additional $20,000 expense for the loss of market value of the improvements, then you have a tax loss of $7,300 ($12,700 − $20,000 = $-7,300). *This tax loss can be applied on your tax return to offset other taxable income.* Investors can structure investment in depreciable property so the cost recovery will create paper losses. Some investors are able to escape almost all income tax liability. This is commonly called ***tax shelter***.

Of course, the shorter the economic life of the property, the higher the dollar amount of cost recovery. Therefore, investors prefer property with a short economic life. Until 1981, individual taxpayers found themselves constantly battling the Internal Revenue Service over the economic life of the improvements. Today, however, the Internal Revenue Code simply stipulates an arbitrary number of years for the economic life, and both taxpayers and the IRS must use this number of years. The number of years of economic life is the product of politics, and is not intended to reflect reality or even some imaginary average property.

In order to claim cost recovery at a faster pace, investors have developed some creative ways of calculating depreciation. If the law requires the economic life to be 20 years, then you would ordinarily expect to claim 5% of the value of the improvements each year (100% ÷ 20 years = 5% per year). This is another way to perform the calculation we used in the example above –

$$\$400,000 \div 20 \text{ years} \ = \ \$20,000 \text{ per year}$$
$$\$400,000 \times 5 \text{ percent} \ = \ \$20,000 \text{ per year}$$

When the cost recovery is the same amount each year, as in this example, we say the cost recovery is being calculated on a ***straight line*** basis.

Suppose, however, you calculate the depreciation at twice the straight line rate (10% per year instead of 5% per year). And suppose you subtract the amount you claim each year from the basis and recalculate the cost recovery each year on the new basis. This is called ***double declining balance*** (or sometimes ***200% declining balance***) depreciation. Using the same property as above, the following example will illustrate this –

	Straight line	*Double declining*
First year	$20,000	$40,000
Second year	$20,000	$36,000
Third year	$20,000	$32,400
Fourth year	$20,000	$29,160
etc.		

Notice that the amount of cost recovery claimed the first year under double declining balance depreciation is twice the straight line amount, but in the second year the amount is less than twice the straight line amount. This is because "declining balance" depreciation means that the amount claimed each year is deducted from the basis, so the percentage (10%, in our example) is applied to an ever-decreasing basis.

In the preceding chart, the original basis was $400,000, so the first year's depreciation by double declining balance method was $40,000 ($400,000 × .10 = $40,000). Subtracting the $40,000 from the original basis leaves a remaining basis of $360,000 ($400,000 − $40,000 = $360,000). Multiplying the $360,000 by the rate (10%) gives us the second year's cost recovery ($360,000 × .10 = $36,000). To find the third year's cost recovery, subtract the second year's cost recovery from the remaining basis ($360,000 − $36,000 = $324,000) and multiply by the rate. The result is $32,400 ($324,000 × .10 = $32,400). The $32,400 must then be subtracted to find the basis for the fourth year, and so on.

Double declining balance depreciation will never depreciate the property completely to zero because, even after many years, there will always be a small amount left over. Its advantage is that it allows an investor to gain more tax shelter in the early years of the investment. Of course, mathematically speaking, an investor does not have to calculate the depreciation at double the straight line rate — depreciation could be calculated at any percentage of the straight line rate. Commonly used percentages include *125% declining balance* and *150% declining balance* depreciation. In fact, an investor could calculate the depreciation at any multiple of the straight line rate. For example, if the straight line rate is 5% (as in our previous examples), a rate of ten times the straight line rate would result in a first year cost recovery of $200,000!

In addition to the various declining balance depreciation schedules, investors have sometimes used a technique called *sum of the years' digits*. To calculate depreciation by the sum of the years' digits, first add up the numbers for the years in the economic life. For a 20-year economic life, write down the numbers 1 through 20, and add them up, e.g., 1 + 2 + 3 + 4 ... + 20. This comes to a total of 210. Now create fractions working backwards with 20 as the denominator and 210 as the numerator for the first fraction, i.e., $^{20}/_{210}$ and lowering the numerator down to 1; e.g., $^{20}/_{210}$, $^{19}/_{210}$, $^{18}/_{210}$, $^{17}/_{210}$ ... $^{1}/_{210}$. Each fraction represents the portion of the depreciable basis which the investor can claim each year, starting with $^{20}/_{210}$ the first year, and ending with $^{1}/_{210}$ the 20th year. At the end of the 20th year, the investor will have claimed $^{210}/_{210}$, or 100% of the value. Notice that sum of the years' digits depreciation is also much faster than straight line and has not always been allowed.

Because investors could gain immense short term tax shelter by using any multiple of the straight line rate or by using sum of the years' digits depreciation, Congress enacted legislation setting the maximum rate at which investors can claim the cost recovery. In the past the rate has been as high as double the straight line rate, but you should check with your instructor for the current maximum allowable rate. Depreciation schedules which are faster than straight line are called *accelerated depreciation*.

Effect of cost recovery on capital gains

As we have outlined above, investors commonly structure a real estate investment so the cost recovery makes it produce a paper loss. The paper loss can then be used to shelter their other income. But there is a downside to cost recovery. Owners of depreciable real property must claim at least straight line cost recovery, whether they need the tax shelter it creates, or not. And every year the investor claims cost recovery, *the investor's cost basis in the property is reduced by the cost recovery claimed*. This means that when the investor sells the property, the capital gain will be higher.

If you owned the apartment we used in our example above, held it for ten years, and then sold it for $750,000, this is what your capital gain might look like (costs are estimated) –

Sales price	$750,000
Less sales expenses	−60,000
Adjusted sales price	690,000
Less purchase price	−500,000
Less costs of acquisition	−5,000
Less capital improvement	0
Plus cost recovery	+ 200,000
CAPITAL GAIN	$385,000

The $200,000 cost recovery above was calculated at $20,000 per year for ten years. Note that payment of tax on $385,000, all received in one year, would create a tax disaster for most taxpayers. Because of this, many investors use various techniques to avoid payment of capital gains taxes. These techniques will be discussed next.

Exercise a

A capital gain is the _____ profit realized on the sale of an asset. This means that the taxpayer may deduct the _____ incurred in making the gain and also any _____ _____ made to the property. To find the capital gain, the taxpayer must subtract the _____ _____ in the property from the sales price.

"Cost recovery" is the current term used to describe _____ for income tax purposes. Cost recovery can and must be claimed for real property which is held for _____ or _____ and for _____ property, but cannot be claimed for a personal residence or for that portion of any property which represents _____. The most common way to calculate cost recovery is _____ _____, although sometimes the tax law allows the investor to use _____ methods of depreciation such as _____ _____ methods or sum of the years' digits.

Avoiding capital gains

A common technique to avoid capital gains tax is simply not to sell the property. If no sale occurs, no gain is realized, so no tax is due. However, for investment property, this creates a drawback. Investors typically want to sell the property after they have built up a certain amount of equity. For example, recall the apartment building in our previous example –

Potential gross income	$96,000
Less vacancy and credit loss	−4,800
Effective gross income	91,200
Less operating expenses	−38,000
Net operating income	53,200
Less interest	−49,500
Net spendable income	3,700
Less cost recovery	−20,000
Tax loss	$ (16,300)

The potential gross income may be projected at $96,000 when the investor buys the property, but the investor would certainly expect the income to increase with inflation. Although expenses will increase at the same rate of inflation, the dollar amount is less, so the net operating income will increase. As the net operating income increases, the investor's tax shelter (tax loss in the example above) will decrease. Eventually, the property will be producing taxable income. How long this will take depends on a multitude of factors, so an investor's holding period is different for each property.

A common technique to prolong the holding period is simply to borrow additional money against the property. After all, if the net operating income is higher, the value would normally be higher, so the property can support additional financing. The added financing could be in the form of a junior lien or refinance loan. Additional debt will increase the interest expense, thereby reducing the net spendable income, and restoring the tax loss. By judiciously borrowing additional funds against the property, the investor can maintain the tax loss position indefinitely, or at least as long as the economic life under the Internal Revenue Code. What makes this technique especially attractive to investors is that, under normal circumstances, *borrowed money is not taxable.*

Eventually, of course, the owner will die and leave the property to heirs. The owner's estate must pay estate taxes, but capital gains are not recognized in an estate. The estate taxes are levied on the total value of the owner's estate, which includes the net equity in the property at the time of the owner's death. The equity, of course, is the difference between the value of the property (estate value) and the outstanding loan(s) at the time of the owner's death. Real estate agents should be aware that the Internal Revenue Code allows a substantial exemption from estate taxes, so an ordinary investor's estate will owe no estate taxes. An additional benefit is that the heirs will take title to the property at its new estate valuation, and can claim cost recovery all over again from the beginning, as though they had just purchased the property

Another common method to escape payment of capital gains tax is to defer the payment of the tax by an installment sale. In an installment sale the owner sells the property and receives part of the sale price in at least two different tax years. For example, if you sell your property with 20% down, and the buyer pays the balance over a period of years, then you received "part of the sales price in at least two different tax years," so you are eligible for installment sale treatment. Installment sale treatment can be used on any type of property, whether personal residence, trade or business property, or investment property. The Internal Revenue Code does not specify what kind of financing instrument is used – all that is required is that you carried the paper on the property.

If the sale qualifies for installment sale treatment, then you pay tax on the gain only as you receive it. The following example shows a taxpayer who sold a property with $40,000 down on an installment contract for an adjusted sales price of $200,000 in which the taxpayer had a cost basis of $100,000. The taxpayer is in the 28% tax bracket and the interest on the contract is 10% –

Year	Principal Received	Gain Received	Tax on Gain	Interest Received	Tax on Interest	Total Tax Due
1	40,462	23,232	6,504	15,980	4,474	10,978
2	508	254	72	15,930	4.460	4,532
3	564	282	78	15,876	4.446	4,524
4	622	312	88	15,818	4.430	4.518

In the above chart, note that the "Gain Received" is one-half of the "Principal Received." This is because the taxpayer's basis in the example was $100,000, but the adjusted sales price was $200,000. Therefore, for every dollar of the sales price that is received, half is gain and half is simply return of basis. Return of basis is not taxable gain.

The preceding chart also presumes that the gain is 100% taxable at the taxpayer's ordinary rate of 28%. The interest figures are calculated assuming the balance of $160,000 is being amortized at 360 equal monthly payments of $1,370.04 which include principal and interest at 10%.

Selling a property on an installment contract spreads the payment of tax out over the life of the contract, so the taxpayer can avoid being thrown into a high bracket in the year the property is sold. But it does not usually occur to the average seller to think about what would happen if the buyer were to pay the contract off suddenly. In this case, the tax law is clear – the tax on the rest of the gain would be due for the tax year in which the seller received it. To avoid this dilemma, sellers who plan ahead sometimes insist on a clause in the contract providing that only a certain percentage of the principal can be paid in any one year.

For property held for trade or business or for investment property, Section 1031 of the Internal Revenue Code allows an owner to avoid capital gains tax through a ***tax-deferred exchange***, also called a ***like-kind exchange***. Tax-deferred exchanges are also sometimes called ***tax-free exchanges***, although this term is misleading and should not be used. The exchange is not tax-free; payment of the tax on the gain is merely deferred until such time as the substitute property received in exchange is finally sold.

To qualify as a tax-deferred exchange, there are two requirements – the exchange must be of like property for like property, and the exchange must be "simultaneous." Both of these concepts are discussed in detail below.

It is of important to understand that anyone can exchange anything for anything. No tax law can stop you from making any trade you wish. What the tax law means when it says that the properties must be "like for like" is that if one or more of the properties in the exchange do not qualify as "like for like," then the exchange will not be entirely tax deferred. Note also that either party can bring as few as one property to the exchange, or as many as that party owns. The number of properties on each side of the exchange is irrelevant; what is significant is that they must all qualify as like property for the exchange to be completely tax deferred.

Property qualifies as like property if it is of the same nature and character as the property received in exchange. This is interpreted fairly broadly. For example, land can be exchanged for improved property, apartments can be exchanged for commercial space, farm property can be exchanged for urban property, and so forth.

Some types of property are always unlike property. A personal residence, jewelry, cash, property held as inventory (dealer property), and paper (notes, mortgages, trust deeds, land sales contracts) – never qualify as like property. When property which does not qualify as like property is used in an exchange, it is called ***boot***. If a party to an exchange receives boot, that party will have at least some recognizable gain.

Beginners in exchanging frequently become confused by the fact that the properties are usually of dissimilar values. Actually, the values of the properties are irrelevant. In fact, standard exchange contracts do not ordinarily have a place to write in the prices of the properties. The fact is, it is the *equities* which the owners have in their respective properties which must be equal, not the values. For example, if you trade a free and clear $100,000 property for your neighbor's property worth $500,000, the trade is balanced if it turns out that your neighbor's property is encumbered with a $400,000 mortgage.

Originally, the Internal Revenue Code required the exchange to be "simultaneous," which was ordinarily interpreted to mean that the documents had to be recorded at the same time. However, a 1979 decision [Starker v United States, 602 F2d 1341 (CA9, 1979)] resulted in a taxpayer being able to take up to 60 months to find substitute property, under certain circumstances. Subsequently. Congress amended the Internal Revenue Code so that a taxpayer may create a tax deferred exchange provided the substitute property is identified within 45 days and the transaction is closed within 180 days.

Another possible way to avoid tax on a capital gain is to offset the capital gain with a **capital loss**. As the term would imply, a capital loss occurs when the owner sells a property for less than the cost basis. This could easily happen if the property goes down in value. An important fact to remember is that a capital loss can be used only to offset a capital gain – a capital loss cannot be used to offset ordinary taxable income.

Personal residences The foregoing discussion has concentrated mainly on investment properties and the methods investors use to avoid or defer capital gains taxes on them. Although installment sale and other methods described above can be used on a personal residence, tax-deferred exchanging can be used on trade or business property and investment property only. However, owners of personal residences have a huge benefit that is not available for other kinds of property. Owners who wish to sell their personal residence may exclude up to $250,000 of gain ($500,000 for married taxpayers filing jointly). To qualify, the property must be used exclusively as the taxpayer's personal residence for an aggregate of at least two of the five years prior to the sale. The exclusion may be taken as many times as desired, but not more than once every two years. If a personal residence is sold prior to the two year period, the amount of gain is prorated. For example, if you sold a property at a gain of $50,000 nine months after buying it, 9⁄24 of the $50,000 may be excluded from income.

Income taxes and the real estate agent

Most real estate agents act as **independent contractors** under the terms of the Internal Revenue Code. The alternative is to act as an **employee**. If you are an independent contractor your employer need not withhold for taxes or social security. Of course, you must still pay the tax, but you will take the responsibility for paying it yourself. If you are an independent contractor you are required to file an estimated tax return quarterly. Employees, on the other hand, are subject to withholding.

Whether they are independent contractors or employees, real estate agents are entitled to deduct as legitimate business expenses those costs which they incur in producing or attempting to produce an income. These include, travel expenses (including auto expenses), multiple listing service dues, Realtor® dues, license fees, and the like. Education is also deductible, but only if it is required by the employer and where the purpose is to enhance your abilities. Costs of education to enter a field (such as prelicense classes) are not generally deductible.

| A special mention should be made of automobile expenses and expenses of an office in your home. Both of these items are commonly scrutinized by the IRS when they audit your tax return. The IRS may disallow deductions for which you do not have adequate records, so it is imperative that you check with your tax advisor to be sure your auto log and other expense records will withstand an audit.

Exercise b

Capital gains taxes can be avoided altogether if the owner does not _____ the property. Upon the owner's death, the property will become part of the owner's _____ and will be subject to _____ taxes, not capital gains taxes.

The owner of a personal residence can _____ capital gain from the sale of the residence up to _____ , or up to _____ for married taxpayers filing jointly. To qualify, the taxpayer must have lived in the personal residence for an aggregate of _____ years out of the last _____ years. The taxpayer can use the exclusion once every _____ years.

A tax-deferred exchange under Section _____ of the tax code is possible provided the properties are _____ properties. Non- _____ property is called _____ .

A _____ loss occurs when the adjusted sales price is less than the cost basis.

🔑 KEY TERMS

The key to understanding any new field is the vocabulary used in that field. To maximize your comprehension of the material presented in this chapter, be sure you know the meaning and significance of the following terms. Remember that the majority of test questions primarily test knowledge of vocabulary.

Accelerated depreciation	*Double declining balance*
Adjusted sales price	*Employee*
Boot	*Independent contractor*
Capital gain	*Investment property*
Capital improvement	*Like-kind exchange*
Capital loss	*Net spendable income*
Cost basis	*150% declining balance*
Cost recovery	*125% declining balance*
Dealer property	*Personal use property*
Depreciable	*Realization*

ANSWERS

To chapter exercises. If you couldn't figure out what to put in the blanks, find the answer here!

Exercise a

A capital gain is the ___NET___ *profit realized on the sale of an asset. This means that the taxpayer may deduct the* ___COSTS___ *incurred in making the gain and also any* ___CAPITAL___ ___IMPROVEMENTS___ *made to the property. To find the capital gain, the taxpayer must subtract the* ___COST___ ___BASIS___ *in the property from the sales price.*

"Cost recovery" is the current term used to describe ___DEPRECIATION___ *for income tax purposes.*

Cost recovery can and must be claimed for real property which is held for ___TRADE___ *or* ___BUSINESS___ *and for* ___INVESTMENT___ *property, but cannot be claimed for a personal residence or for that portion of any property which represents* ___LAND___ . *The most common way to calculate cost recovery is* ___STRAIGHT___ ___LINE___ , *although sometimes the tax law allows the investor to use* ___ACCELERATED___ *methods of depreciation such as* ___DECLINING___ ___BALANCE___ *methods or sum of the years' digits.*

Exercise b

Capital gains taxes can be avoided altogether if the owner does not ___SELL___ *the property. Upon the owner's death, the property will become part of the owner's* ___ESTATE___ *and will be subject to* ___ESTATE___ *taxes, not capital gains taxes.*

The owner of a personal residence can ___DEFER___ *capital gain from the sale of the residence up to* ___$250,000___ , *or up to* ___$500,000___ *for married taxpayers filing jointly. To qualify, the taxpayer must have lived in the personal residence for an aggregate of* ___TWO___ *years out of the last* ___FIVE___ *years. The taxpayer can use the exclusion once every* ___TWO___ *years.*

A tax-deferred exchange under Section ___1031___ *of the tax code is possible provided the properties are* ___LIKE___ *properties. Non-* ___LIKE___ *property is called* ___BOOT___ .

A ___CAPITAL___ *loss occurs when the adjusted sales price is less than the cost basis.*

PRACTICE QUESTIONS

The following practice questions are representative of the questions you will find on the final examination and on the licensing examinations given by the Oregon Real Estate Agency.

1. An investor sold an office building for $1,000,000. If there is a gain on the sale, the investor will incur
   (A) an income tax liability.
   (B) no income tax liability if the gain is placed in an IRA account.
   (C) no income tax liability if the property was held for at least one year.
   (D) no income tax liability if the property was held for at least two years.

2. Under current federal tax laws, the profit a homeowner receives from the sale of a principal residence is
   I. not subject to federal income tax.
   II. the homeowner's tax basis.
   (A) I only   (C) Both I and II
   (B) II only   (D) Neither I nor II

3. Which of the following improvements would be suitable to increase an owner's cost basis?
   (A) Addition of a patio
   (B) Replacement of an old kitchen sink with a new one
   (C) Both A and B
   (D) Neither A nor B

4. An investor purchased a building to rent for $400,000 and obtained a loan of $380,000. The land was valued at $100,000. What could the investor use as the basis for cost recovery deductions?
   (A) $100,000   (C) $300,000
   (B) $280,000   (D) $400,000

5. Isabel LaBella bought a personal residence for $237,000. She made no improvements and sold it two years later for $287,000. Following the sale she rented an apartment to live in for the next three years. For purposes of her federal income taxes due, she has
   (A) a $50,000 capital gain.
   (B) a $50,000 capital loss.
   (C) $50,000 in earned income to declare.
   (D) no tax to pay.

6. In order to qualify for a cost recovery deduction, real property must be
   (A) improved.
   (B) held for the production of income or used in trade or business.
   (C) both A and B.
   (D) Neither A nor B is required.

7. A real estate broker would be entitled to cost recovery deduction on
   (A) the broker's personal residence, if it is kept for sale.
   (B) the office building from which the broker runs a brokerage business.
   (C) property held for resale as inventory.
   (D) all of the above.

8. Which of the following sales would result in gain being treated as ordinary income?
   (A) The sale of homes in a subdivision by a builder
   (B) The sale of a house owned by a real estate broker for resale
   (C) Both A and B
   (D) Neither A nor B

9. Birdie Gaviota owned an apartment building and deducted $49,000 for cost recovery when filing her income tax return. The $49,000 deduction will
   I. decrease her remaining basis.
   II. lower her taxable income from self-employment.
   (A) I only
   (B) II only
   (C) Both I and II
   (D) Neither I nor II

10. An investor owned a commercial property which was bought for $210,000. The county assessor valued the land at $60,480 and the improvements at $142,120. In determining the basis for depreciation for income tax purposes, if the owner employed the same ratio as that used by the assessor, the value the owner would use would most nearly be
    (A) $123,000.
    (B) $142,120.
    (C) $147,311.
    (D) $202,600.

11. Which of the following would be a type of depreciation schedule?
    (A) Straight-line
    (B) 125% declining balance
    (C) 150% declining balance
    (D) All of the above

12. All of the following are methods sometimes used to calculate depreciation for tax purposes except
    (A) obsolescence.
    (B) 125% declining balance.
    (C) 150% declining balance.
    (D) sum of the years' digits.

13. All of the following would be characterized as accelerated cost recovery methods except
    (A) straight line depreciation.
    (B) 125% declining balance depreciation.
    (C) 150% declining balance depreciation.
    (D) sum of the years' digits depreciation.

14. Which if the following could result in a tax advantage on the sale of investment property?
    (A) An installment sale
    (B) A Section 1031 Exchange
    (C) Either A or B
    (D) Neither A nor B

15. A real estate licensee would most likely encounter the term "boot" when considering a problem involving
    (A) water rights.
    (B) exchanging.
    (C) legal descriptions.
    (D) depreciation.

16. In order for an exchange to qualify as tax deferred, the
    I. properties must be "like for like."
    II. owners' equities in the properties must be equal.
    (A) I only
    (B) II only
    (C) Both I and II
    (D) Neither I nor II

17. In a tax deferred exchange, which of the following would be considered boot?
    (A) Cash
    (B) Note carried back by one of the parties
    (C) Personal property
    (D) All of the above

18. "Boot" is the name used for a factor arising in which of the following cases?
    I. When depreciating property for tax purposes
    II. Where there is a difference between the equity of properties being exchanged
    (A) I only
    (B) II only
    (C) Both I and II
    (D) Neither I nor II

19. A real estate licensee would relate "boot" to
    (A) depreciation.
    (B) amortization.
    (C) capitalization.
    (D) income tax and exchanging.

20. Miss DeMeanour bought a personal residence for $210,000. She lived in the house for two years and then sold it for the same price, paying a real estate broker a commission of $14,070 in the process. On her federal income tax return, she could show
    (A) nothing.
    (B) a $14,070 capital loss.
    (C) a $14,070 capital gain.
    (D) $14,070 in earned income.

21. With certain restrictions, the federal tax laws permit deductions for mortgage interest on
    I. primary residences.   III. rental property.
    II. second homes.
    (A) I only
    (B) I and II only
    (C) I, II and III
    (D) III only

ANSWERS

To practice questions. If you chose the wrong letter, here's the right one! The explanations are designed to clarify your understanding.

1. **A** The only way to avoid tax on a capital gain from investment property is to defer it by tax deferred exchange or installment sale. Placing the profit in a retirement fund has no effect on the taxable nature of the gain. Depending on the tax laws in effect at the time of the sale, the amount of the tax may be different depending on the holding period, but there would always be some tax to pay regardless of the length of the holding period.

2. **D** Profit on the sale of a personal residence is a capital gain and is taxable as such. Most homeowners make use of exemptions and deferrals to avoid having to pay tax on the gain. The owner's basis in a personal residence is the original purchase price, plus costs of acquisition, plus capital improvements made over the years. If the home was sold and the gain deferred by buying a new personal residence, the additional basis from the new residence is also added.

3. **A** Capital improvements increase the owner's cost basis in the property to the extent of the capital improvement. A capital improvement is an improvement which adds something which did not exist at the time the property was purchased. Capital improvements are contrasted with maintenance items. Maintenance items are items which replace or repair that which already existed.

4. **C** The basis in the property is comprised of the purchase price, costs incurred in the acquisition, and capital improvements made since acquisition. The amount of any loans incurred in the acquisition is irrelevant, although loan fees are sometimes considered part of the acquisition cost. The depreciable (recoverable) basis is the total basis less the land value, since you cannot claim cost recovery on land.

5. **A** The gain is classed as capital gain, not earned income. However, the total amount of the gain can be excluded from taxable income since the amount of gain is under $250,000, it was on a personal residence, and the owner lived in the residence for two years out of the five years prior to the sale.

6. **C** Cost recovery is an expense the owner of certain property is allowed to deduct. The theory upon which cost recovery is based is that the improvements are declining in value over their economic life. According to appraisal theory, land does not have an economic life, so cost recovery is possible only for improvements, not for land. Because the owner of a personal residence has other tax advantages, the deduction for cost recovery is only allowed for property held for the production of income (trade or business property) or investment property.

7. **B** When the property is a personal residence, the fact that the owner is a real estate broker is irrelevant. Cost recovery is not allowed on a personal residence. Property owned by a real estate broker and held for resale is inventory (dealer property). Cost recovery is not allowed on inventory property and any profits on resale are considered ordinary income, not capital gain.

8. **C** Whether the owner is a real estate broker or builder, property held for resale is dealer property. Gain from the sale of dealer property is always ordinary income.

9. **C** Cost recovery is allowed as a deduction, even though it is a "non-cash" expense. If the owner of qualifying property has a loan against the property so the interest (also a deductible item) is sufficient that the property produces no taxable income, the further deduction of cost recovery can cause the property to produce a paper loss. The paper loss can be used to offset the owner's income from other sources, thus producing tax shelter. However, every time cost recovery is claimed, the owner's basis in the property is reduced by the amount of the cost recovery.

10. **C** The assessor's total valuation is $202,600 ($142,120 + $60,480 = $202,600). The assessor's ratio is $60,480/$202,600 for the land and 142,120/202,600 for the improvements. Dividing the fractions (converting to decimals) reveals that the land is 29.85% of the total ($60,480 ÷ $202,600 = .29851925), and the improvements are 70.15% of the total ($142,120 ÷ $202,600 = .70148075). Using these percentages on the acquisition cost of $210,000 gives an improvement value of $147,311 ($202,600 × .70148075 = $147,310.9575).

11. **D** Depreciation is another term for cost recovery. In appraisal theory depreciation is a loss of

market value from any source. Appraisers categorize depreciation as physical deterioration, functional obsolescence and external (economic) obsolescence. For income tax purposes, however, the Internal Revenue Code merely prescribes certain amounts. These amounts can be calculated in various ways. Over the years the Code has permitted straight line, 125% declining balance, 150% declining balance, 200% declining balance and sum of the years' digits cost recovery calculations.

12.   **A**   Depreciation is an older term for cost recovery. For income tax purposes, the Internal Revenue Code prescribes certain amounts of cost recovery as allowable. These amounts can be calculated in various ways. In the past the Internal Revenue Code has permitted straight line, 125% declining balance, 150% declining balance, 200% declining balance and sum of the years' digits cost recovery calculations for improvements on real property.

13.   **A**   Straight line depreciation is any method where the dollar amount of cost recovery is the same for each year. Methods where the amount of cost recovery is faster than the straight-line rate are called "accelerated depreciation." These include 125%, 150%, and double declining, as well as sum of the years' digits calculations.

14.   **C**   Neither an installment sale nor a Section 1031 exchange will avoid the tax on the gain, but both techniques can be used to defer the tax.

15.   **B**   The term "boot" refers to property which does not qualify as "like for like" in a tax-deferred exchange. The recipient of boot will not be able to defer tax on the gain from the boot.

16.   **A**   A tax deferred exchange allows the owner(s) to defer the tax on any gain, but only if they exchange for like property. Frequently the equity in one side of an exchange is not equal to the equity in the other side, so one of the parties has to give the other something additional to balance the exchange. If the additional asset is qualifying "like" property, then the exchange is still completely tax deferred. But if the property is non-like kind property, then the receiver of the non-like kind property will receive some of the gain on his or her property, and a taxable event will be created for that party.

17.   **D**   To qualify as a tax-deferred exchange, the properties must be like for like, that is, each property must be investment or trade or business property, and must be real property. Non-qualifying property is called "boot."

18.   **B**   In an exchange the properties are rarely of equal equity value. The parties will not agree to the exchange unless they perceive the values to be the same, therefore the exchange must be balanced. This is accomplished easily just by having one party add something. If the added property does not qualify as "like" property, it is called "boot." The recipient of the boot will have to pay tax on the gain from the boot.

19.   **D**   In a tax-deferred exchange the properties being exchanged must be "like for like," that is, real estate for other real estate, and either held for the production of income or on speculation (investment property). Any property not qualifying as like property can be used, but the recipient will not be able to defer the tax on any gain. Non-like property is called "boot."

20.   **B**   Capital gain or loss is the difference between the adjusted sales price and the cost basis. Since the sales expenses, including a brokerage fee, are deductible from the sales price, the adjusted sales price would be $195,300 ($210,000 − $14,070 = $195,300). When the basis of $210,000 is subtracted from this, the result is a capital loss of $14,070.

21.   **C**   Mortgage interest is deductible as an itemized deduction on a personal income tax return up to statutory maximum amounts for both primary and secondary personal residences. For rental property the mortgage interest is deductible as a business expense.

FINANCIAL ARITHMETIC

B EING A SUCCESSFUL REAL ESTATE AGENT REQUIRES A CERTAIN AMOUNT OF SKILL with financial and other arithmetic subjects. While every real estate transaction involves non-financial mathematical skills, such as estimating buyers' and sellers' costs, square footage of a structure, and many other things, the financial arithmetic is the most critical. If you can't tell a buyer how much the monthly payments will be, it will be hard to get them to sign the earnest money agreement.

Arithmetic is a subject which most people find relatively easy, yet it completely baffles others. Few people are in the middle. This is probably due to early educational experiences, but blaming your parents and elementary school teachers is little consolation now that you want to get into real estate. Luckily the arithmetic questions on the Oregon real estate exams are very easy. And there are only a handful of math questions anyway. There are so few that you could miss every one of them and still pass the exam as long as you did reasonably well on the non-arithmetic topics. Whatever you do, don't let the arithmetic panic you.

One thing that non-mathematically oriented students should keep in mind is that arithmetic is a skill subject and cannot be learned quickly. Facts can be learned quickly, but skills must be practiced. Unless you have many months ahead of you before you plan to take the exams and go into real estate, you probably do not have time to become very proficient in any aspect of real estate mathematics. Nevertheless, even students who are good at mathematics can profit from a review of some simple concepts. And, like learning a foreign language, even if you do not have the time to become fluent, at least you can learn some basics that will become a foundation to build further skills on later.

Basic decimal, percentage and fraction problems

Decimals and percentages are used constantly in real estate arithmetic, so we should start with fundamental decimal and percentage concepts. A ***decimal*** is any number which is less than 1, usually expressed with the ***decimal point*** in front of it – e.g., ".1," ".23," "0.456," and so on. Note that sometimes the "0" is written in front of the decimal point, although it is not necessary. Zeros are also sometimes used at the end, e.g., ".10," ".230," "0.4560," but zeros at the end are also unnecessary and need not be used. The examples used above could be read aloud as "point one," "point two three," and "zero point four five six." They could also be read as "one tenth," "twenty-three hundredths," and "four hundred fifty-six thousandths."

A ***percentage*** is really nothing more than another way of writing a decimal. For example saying "50%" is exactly the same as saying "0.5" (or "0.50," "0.500," and so on). If you note that "50%" is the same as ".50," then you can see that a percentage is just a decimal in which the decimal point has been moved over two spaces to the right, and a percentage sign added. Thus

0.10 = 10%

0.23 = 23%

0.456 = 45.6%

and so forth. *Important note:* On most calculators the "percent key" has the function of automatically moving the decimal point two places to the right for you. Experiment with your calculator to see if this is how it works.

As you can see, percentages and decimals are really just different ways of writing the same thing. Similarly, fractions are another way. For example, "50%" is the same as "0.5," and is also the same as "½." Note the following examples –

.1 = 10% = $\frac{1}{10}$

.23 = 23% = $\frac{23}{100}$

0.456 = 45.6% = $\frac{456}{1000}$

Some people prefer to do their calculations with fractions, and if you are comfortable with fractions, there is nothing wrong with using them. But most people are more familiar with decimals, especially since decimals are easier to use with calculators.

If you wish to convert a fraction to a decimal, just divide the ***denominator*** (bottom number) into the ***numerator*** (top number). For example, to convert $\frac{49}{86}$ into a decimal, just divide 49 by 86, which gives you the decimal equivalent as 0.5697674.

Now, observe that it does not make any difference whether you calculate with a decimal, a percentage or a fraction. Suppose you had a farm which was 1,200 acres and you wanted to know how much $\frac{49}{86}$ of it was. You could calculate it as a –

Decimal: 0.5697674 × 1,200 acres = 683.72088 acres

Percentage: 56.97674% (push % key) × 1,200 acres = 683.72088 acres

Fraction: 49 × 1,200 acres ÷ 86 = 683.72093 acres

Although using the fraction gives a slightly more accurate result, the decimal or percentage is more than close enough, and most people find it easier to deal with tenths, hundredths, thousands, and other decimals.

One of the things real estate agents need to calculate all the time is the dollar amount of a loan discount. Discounts are measured in terms of points. A ***point*** is nothing more than one percent of the loan balance. For example, on a loan of $100,000, a discount of five points would be 5% of the loan amount, or $5,000. The formula is *Discount = Principal × Points ÷ 100*. We have to divide by 100 in order to convert the number of points (expressed as a whole number) to a percentage.

Interest calculations

Calculating interest is basic to understanding other financial arithmetic. The main formula to calculate interest due is $I = PRT$, where I is the interest in dollars and cents, P is the principal balance of the loan, R is the interest rate (percentage rate), and T is the time over which the interest accrues —

$$I = PRT$$

For example, suppose you had to calculate the interest which would be due at the end of a year on a loan of $12,000 at 11%. The calculation would be "I = $12,000 × 11% (or .11) × 1 year" — which comes to $1,320.00 ($12,000 × .11 × 1 = $1,320).

This was a very simple problem. But interest problems are not ordinarily so easy. We usually have to calculate interest over a period of time which is not an even period. In other words, calculating the interest over one year means that the T will be 1. What if the interest were accrued over 188 days instead of one year? Then the T will be $^{188}/_{365}$ (0.5150684 as a decimal). To calculate the interest which will accrue over 188 days, we calculate "I = $12,000 × 11% (or .11) × 0.5150684," or you could substitute "188 ÷ 365" as a fraction for the decimal "0.5150684." The answer will come to $679.89 ($12,000 × .11 × .5150684 = $679.89028).

Note that the T in our calculations above is in terms of "years." For example, if the time is six months, this is one-half of a year, so the T will be 0.5; if the time is nine months, this is three-fourths of a year, so the T will be 0.75, and if the T is 3½ years, the T will be 3.5. The reason the T is in terms of years is because the interest rate (11% in the above examples) is expressed as an annual interest rate.

But what would happen if the interest rate were expressed as a monthly or daily rate instead? The important thing to understand about interest calculations is that the T must be expressed in the same terms as the rate. In other words, if the rate is an annual rate (e.g., 11% per annum), then the T must be the expression of the number of years or fractions of a year. If the interest is expressed as a monthly rate, then the T must be the number of months or fractions of a month. And if the rate is a daily rate, then the T must be the number of days.

This can be very confusing because the rate may be stipulated as an annual rate, but the T is expressed in months. For example, a problem may state "What is the amount of interest that would accrue on a loan of $12,000 at 11% interest over a 9 month period?" — which would lead you to believe that the T must be 9. In fact, since the rate was stipulated as an annual rate, the T must be stated in terms of years, so the proper value for T is 0.75 ($^{9}/_{12}$ of a year). In interest calculations you must always be sure that if the rate is an annual rate, that the T is expressed in years; if the rate is a monthly rate, that the T is stated in months; or if the interest is a daily rate that the T is expressed in the number of days.

So far this discussion has be directed toward calculating interest due. Interest calculations also frequently involve other questions. For example, consider this question —

How big a loan could a borrower afford if the borrower could make annual interest payments of $6,000 and the interest rate will be 9%?

To solve this problem, you need a different formula. You need a formula to calculate the principal balance (P). This formula is actually just a variation of the original interest formula ($I = PRT$) —

$$P = I \div RT$$

Applying this formula to the above problem, we find the answer is $66,666.67 ($6,000 ÷ 0.09 × 1 = $66,666.666). Again, however, this is a simple problem. In the real world the problem is usually much more complex. Suppose the question were —

A couple can afford interest payments of $10,000 per year and the interest on their loan will be ⅞ of 1% per month. What size loan can they afford?

In this case, the solution is simple, once you realize that the dollar amount in interest (I) is based on a year, but the interest rate (R) is expressed in monthly terms. All that is necessary is to convert the interest to an annual rate before solving the problem. A monthly rate of ⅞ of 1% is the same as 10½% per annum (⅞ × 12 = 10½). Using the annual rate of 10½% gives us the answer to the problem, which is $95,238.10 ($10,000 ÷ .105 = $95,238.095).

Another type of problem is the question of what rate is being charged. A problem of this type might be –

Over a year's time, a lender earned $1,350 in interest on a loan of $12,000. What was the rate of return on the loan?

Again, we must recast the original interest formula to solve this type of problem. The formula to find the interest rate is

$$R = I \div PT$$

Using this formula, it is easy to find that the answer to the problem is 11¼% ($1,350 ÷ $12,000 × 1 = .1125). And, as with preceding formulas, the problems are made more complex if the T is more or less than one year. For example, consider the following problem –

A borrower paid $1,100 interest in three months on a loan of $40,000. What was the interest rate?

Since three months is one-fourth of a year, the easiest way to solve this problem is to convert the dollar amount of interest to a full year's worth of interest; that is, multiply it by 4 ($1,100 × 4 = $4,400). Now we can calculate the rate using the formula, which gives us the answer 11% ($4,400 ÷ $40,000 = 0.11).

Sometimes we must find out how long it would take for a certain dollar amount of interest to accrue. For example, consider the following problem –

An investor has lent $190,000 at 11% interest. How long will it take to accrue $2,000 interest?

This means that we must solve for the T, so we must rewrite the formula again –

$$T = I \div PR$$

Using this formula we find that the answer to the above problem is about 35 days. To calculate, first multiply the principal by the rate, which results in $20,900 ($190,000 × 0.11 = $20,900). Now divide the interest ($2,000) by $20,900, which gives the result of 0.0956937. Since the rate (11%) is a yearly rate, this represents the portion of a year that it would take. To convert this to the number of days, just multiply by 365. The final result is 34.9282 days (0.0956937 × 365 = 34.9282).

Compounding

It is a common practice to accrue interest on interest that has already accrued. This is called ***compound interest***. For example, consider the following example of a loan where the interest (at a 10% rate) has been compounded –

	Compounded	Balance	Simple	Balance
Beginning balance		$180,000.00		$180,000.00
Interest for January	$1,500.00	$181,500.00	$1,500	$181,500.00
Interest for February	1,512.50	183,012.50	1,500	183,000.00
Interest for March	1,525.10	184,537.60	1,500	184,500.00
Interest for April	1,537.82	186,075.42	1,500	186,000.00

When interest is compounded the interest that is computed each month it is added to the principal balance, and then the interest for the following month is computed on the new balance – which means that the borrower is paying interest on the interest. If the interest in the above example had not been compounded the monthly charge would have remained $1,500 for each month. When interest is not compounded, it is called *simple interest*. If you look at the chart above, you can see that compounding causes the borrower to pay more interest.

Discount interest

Another way of calculating interest is to discount it from the principal balance. This is called *discount interest*. Interest on certain federal treasury obligations, for example, is calculated this way.

If you buy a ten-year treasury bond for $10,000 at, say, 8% interest compounding annually, the total interest income for the ten years will be $5,368.07. Since the interest will be $5,368.07, you would buy the treasury bond today for $4,631.93. In other words, you lend the government the discounted amount, and the loan matures to the face amount at the end of its term. Calculating discount interest requires a financial calculator or present value table.

Amortizing

Non-amortized loans are sometimes called *straight loans*, or more commonly *interest-only* loans. In an interest-only loan the borrower pays just interest; the principal is all due at the end of the term. Sometimes the interest is paid monthly, or sometimes both the principal and all accrued interest will be due at the end.

However, most real estate loans are made so they are paid off with regular payments and each payment includes a small amount toward the principal. When a debt is retired in regular installments this way, it is called loan *amortization*. The following is a typical loan statement for a bank loan of $180,000 repayable in equal monthly installments of $1,570, including interest at 10% –

Payment	Interest	Principal	Balance
Beginning balance			$180,000.00
1,570.00	1,500.00	70.00	179,930.00
1,570.00	1,499.42	70.58	179,859.42
1,570.00	1,498.82	71.18	179,788.24
1,570.00	1,498.24	71.76	179,716.48
1,570.00	1,497.64	72.36	179,644.12

In the above example the loan was set up with level payments of $1,570 per month. Notice in the chart that the $1,570 payment is applied mostly to interest at the beginning of the loan, but as the loan progresses, the portion of the payment which is applied to interest declines and the portion applied to principal increases. Setting up an amortizing loan requires the lender to determine the monthly payment necessary to amortize the loan over an even period of time, typically 30 years for a real estate loan. The calculation is done today with a financial calculator, although in the past lenders used an *amortization chart*. (For an example of an amortization chart see page 370.)

Some loan amortization schedules take into account that the lender sometimes requires the borrower to include one-twelfth the annual taxes and one-twelfth the annual fire insurance premium with the principal and interest payment. We say such loans are paid "PITI," which stands for "principal, interest, taxes and insurance." If the taxes are included in the payment, but the borrower pays the fire insurance premium, we say it is "PIT." When the taxes and insurance are not included, then we say the loan is just "PI."

When the payments include taxes and insurance the lender normally sets these sums aside in a *reserve account*. In a few cases, Oregon law requires a lender to pay interest on the reserve account, although almost all loans are exempt. If the $180,000 loan in the above example included a reserve account for a $3,000 tax bill and a $350 insurance bill, its amortization schedule might look like this –

Payment	Taxes	Insurance	Interest	Principal	Balance
Beginning balance					$180.000.00
1849.17	$250.00	$29.17	$1,500.00	$70.00	179,930.00
1849.17	250.00	29.17	1,499.42	70.58	179,859.42
1849.17	250.00	29.17	1,498.82	71.18	179,788.24
1849.17	250.00	29.17	1,498.24	71.76	179,716.48
1849.17	250.00	29.17	1,497.64	72.36	179,644.12

The above example shows the first five months payments on the loan. Note that the principal and interest figures are the same as in the previous statement. However, this statement shows that at the end of the five months the bank will be holding $1,250 in the borrower's reserve account for property taxes and $145.85 for the fire insurance policy.

In the preceding two examples of loan amortization, the payments would be calculated so that each month the amounts applied to interest and to principal would change, yet the amount of the payment itself would remain constant.

Although not common today, it is also possible to amortize a loan with equal installments of principal, but variable amounts of interest. In this case, the amount of the payment would change each month. For example, suppose you made a loan of $180,000 to be amortized in 360 principal payments of $500, *plus* interest at 10%. The chart might look something like this –

Payment	Interest	Principal	Balance
Beginning balance			$180,000.00
2,000.00	$1,500.00	$500.00	179,500.00
1,995.84	1,495.84	500.00	179,000.00
1,991.66	1,491.66	500.00	178,500.00
1,985.50	1,485.50	500.00	178,000.00
1,983,34	1,483.34	500.00	177,500.00

... Continuing, until the last few payments look like this –

Balance after payment #355			2,500.00
520.84	20.84	500.00	2,000.00
516.66	16.66	500.00	1,500.00
512.50	12.50	500.00	1,000.00
508.34	8.34	500.00	500.00
504.16	4.16	500.00	0.00

Notice that the total payment starts out high, and declines over the life of the loan. The reason this method of amortizing loans is not popular today is that it is difficult for young people starting out to make high payments at the beginning of the loan. In fact, some modern loan programs actually make the payments artificially smaller at the beginning, perhaps not enough even to cover the interest expense, and compensating with larger payments at the end of the loan. A "plus-interest" amortization schedule is the opposite of what today's typical borrower needs.

Present value and loan discounting

What if you had the legal right to receive $10,000 one year from today. Suppose further that you wished to sell this right in order to derive cash today. Since money has a time value, your buyer would not likely pay $10,000 today for the right to receive $10,000 in one year – this would mean that the buyer's rate of return would be 0%.

The amount a buyer would pay would be less than the face amount of the obligation. In fact, the less your buyer pays for the right to receive $10,000 in one year, the greater your buyer's return on the investment.

For example, if your buyer paid $8,000 for the right to receive $10,000 in one year, your buyer would stand to make a $2,000 profit on an investment of $8,000. This would be a return of 25% ($2,000 ÷ $8,000 = 0.25). But if your buyer paid $9,000 for the right to receive $10,000 in one year, the profit would be only $1,000, so the rate of return would be 11.1% ($1,000 ÷ $9,000 × 1 = 0.1111111).

Figuring the **_present value_** of a potential future income requires that you begin with an assumption as to the rate the investor or lender will require. Since rates of return in the marketplace can be readily ascertained, appraisers sometimes use the present value concept when appraising income properties. By calculating the present values of future anticipated incomes, an appraiser can determine what an informed investor ought to be willing to pay for an income property.

Present value calculations sometimes involve a lump sum future income, as in the above example, but more commonly there is a stream of regular payments to be received. A stream of regular payments to be received in the future is called an **_annuity_**. Calculating the present value of a lump sum payment or of a series of regular payments can be accomplished with a table, but modern investors use a financial calculator.

Now, if you think about it, from a lender's viewpoint, a loan is really an annuity. In fact, "present value" is just a loan calculation in reverse. Instead of starting with a loan amount and calculating the payments needed to amortize it at a certain interest rate, the investor starts with the proposed payments and interest rate, and calculates the principal balance that can be lent.

This concept is constantly used in real estate transactions where the seller will carry a contract or trust deed, but then sell the paper to an investor. The investor determines what he or she will pay for the paper according to the yield (rate of return) the investor demands. This concept will be developed further in the next section, Alternative Financing.

Exercise a

A percentage is the same as a decimal, except that the decimal point has been moved _____ places to the _____ and the percent symbol (%) has been added.

The basic formula to calculate interest accrued on a loan is _____ . To calculate the principal balance, the formula is _____ . The formula _____ is used to calculate the interest rate. And to calculate the time necessary to accrue a certain amount of interest, the formula is _____ . When calculating interest, be sure that the time and the _____ match, that is if the _____ is expressed annually, then the time must be expressed annually also. If the time is monthly, then the _____ must be expressed as a monthly _____ .

When interest is paid on interest already accrued, this is called _____ interest. It is called _____ interest when a loan is made at a net amount, to mature to the principal balance at the end of the term. When a loan is to be paid off in regular installments, we call this _____ . On most real estate loans, the repayment term is many years, which means that the borrower's _____ *will be higher at the beginning of the loan, and the* _____ *will be higher at the end. Most real estate lenders also require the borrower to pay into a account for property taxes and fire insurance. Such loans are said to be paid "* _____ *." The* _____ _____ *is the amount an investor would pay for the right to receive a future income payment.*

🔑 KEY TERMS

The key to understanding any new field is the vocabulary used in that field. To maximize your comprehension of the material presented in this chapter, be sure you know the meaning and significance of the following terms. Remember that the majority of test questions primarily test knowledge of vocabulary.

Amortization	Interest-only loan
Amortization chart	Numerator
Annuity	Percentage
Compound interest	Point
Decimal	Present value
Decimal point	Reserve account
Denominator	Simple interest
Discount interest	Straight loan

❓ ANSWERS

To chapter exercises. If you couldn't figure out what to put in the blanks, find the answer here!

Exercise a

A percentage is the same as a decimal, except that the decimal point has been moved ___TWO___ *places to the* ___RIGHT___ *and the percent symbol (%) has been added.*

The basic formula to calculate interest accrued on a loan is ___$I = PRT$___ *. To calculate the principal balance, the formula is* ___$P = I \div RT$___ *. The formula* ___$R = I \div PT$___ *is used to calculate the interest rate. And to calculate the time necessary to accrue a certain amount of interest, the formula is* ___$T = I \div PR$___ *. When calculating interest, be sure that the time and the* ___RATE___ *match, that is if the* ___RATE___ *is expressed annually, then the time must be expressed annually also. If the time is monthly, then the* ___RATE___ *must be expressed as a monthly* ___RATE___ *.*

When interest is paid on interest already accrued, this is called ___COMPOUND___ *interest. It is called* ___DISCOUNT___ *interest when a loan is made at a net amount, to mature to the principal balance at the end of the term. When a loan is to be paid off in regular installments, we call this* ___AMORTIZATION___ *. On most real estate loans, the repayment term is many years, which means that the borrower's* ___INTEREST___ *will be higher at the beginning of the loan, and the* ___PRINCIPAL___ *will be higher at the end. Most real estate lenders also require the borrower to pay into a account for property taxes and fire insurance. Such loans are said to be paid "* ___PITI___ *." The* ___PRESENT___ ___VALUE___ *is the amount an investor would pay for the right to receive a future income payment.*

PRACTICE QUESTIONS

The following practice questions are representative of the questions you will find on the final examination and on the licensing examinations given by the Oregon Real Estate Agency.

1. The loan to value ratio is the loan amount divided by
   (A) the appraised value.
   (B) the selling price.
   (C) either A or B, whichever is higher.
   (D) either A or B, whichever is lower.

2. If the loan to value ratio is 85%, and the property was appraised for $169,000 and sold for $174,000, how much would the purchaser usually be allowed to borrow?
   (A) $143,650   (C) $152,100
   (B) $147,900   (D) $177,892

3. How much additional cash must a buyer furnish in addition to a $4,500 deposit if the lending institution will lend 85% on a $195,000 home?
   (A) $19,500   (C) $24,750
   (B) $22,500   (D) $29,250

4. A prospective buyer has $34,000 for a down payment on a home and wants to finance the balance of the purchase price on a first mortgage (conventional loan). Lending institutions generally will make an 85% loan up to the purchase price. The most expensive home which the buyer will be able to purchase would have a price of
   (A) $40,000.   (C) $226,667.
   (B) $205,320.   (D) $249,680.

5. A 12% earnest money deposit is required on a $360,000 property. If the bank finances the property with a 70% loan, what is the total amount needed by the buyer to close the transaction, in addition to the earnest money, assuming no other costs?
   (A) $43,200   (C) $108,000
   (B) $64,800   (D) $151,200

6. The selling price of a property is $195,000. The purchaser has applied to a lender for mortgage funds and been told that the maximum loan is $132,600. The lender's appraiser feels that a long term conservative estimate of the property's value is $166,500. Which one of the following statements is true?
   (A) The value of the property for loan purposes is $133,200.
   (B) The loan to value ratio on this loan is 80%.
   (C) The loan to value ratio on this loan is 70%.
   (D) The value of the property for loan purposes is $195,000.

7. The value of property above the total liens or mortgages is the
   (A) assessment.   (C) equity.
   (B) valuation.   (D) surety.

8. Which of the following types of interest is usually charged when financing a house?
   (A) Simple interest   (C) Compound interest
   (B) Straight interest   (D) Add-on interest

9. Interest paid on original principal and also on the accrued and unpaid interest which has accumulated is
   (A) simple interest.   (C) annuity interest.
   (B) compound interest.   (D) interest rate.

10. When using the fully-amortized level payment mortgage,
    (A) the amount of payment on the principal stays the same.
    (B) the interest payment is always greater than the principal payment.
    (C) each payment remains the same.
    (D) a lump sum payment is made at the end of the mortgage term.

11. Discount points are considered
    (A) interest rate equalization factors.
    (B) police powers.
    (C) origination fees.
    (D) all of the above.

12. The monthly payment on a loan remains the same, yet the amount applied to interest decreases and the amount applied to principal increases as the loan gets older. This is an illustration of
    (A) amortization.   (C) acceleration.
    (B) depreciation.   (D) reduction.

13. One discount point is equal to
    (A) one percent of the sales price.
    (B) ten percent of the down payment.
    (C) one percent of the loan amount.
    (D) one percent of the down payment.

14. Discount points would most directly affect
    (A) how much the borrower owes.
    (B) the reserve account required.
    (C) the interest rate on the loan.
    (D) the remaining term of the loan.

15. Loan discounts are normally calculated on the
    (A) sales price of the property.
    (B) buyer's loan amount.
    (C) broker's commission.
    (D) amount of the down payment.

16. Lenders sometimes refer to "nominal rate" when financing real estate. This means
    (A) points will be demanded because the desired rate of interest would exceed the legal rate.
    (B) the maximum rate of interest allowed by law is being obtained by the lender for making the real property loan.
    (C) the interest rate finally agreed to is in excess of the original commitment.
    (D) the rate of interest specified in a note or contract, which may differ from the effective interest rate.

17. A seller was charged an amount equal to 4% of the buyer's loan. This is called
    (A) points.   (C) an origination fee.
    (B) a finder's fee.   (D) a loan fee.

18. In making a $150,000 loan, what would the lender charge if loans were being discounted five points?
    (A) $3,750   (C) $15,000
    (B) $7,500   (D) $75,000

19. A mortgage lender agreed to lend 90% of the value of a property at 7% interest. The lender will only lend at 7% if the borrower pays a discount of eight points. If the appraised value is $180,000, approximately how much would the loan be?
    (A) $149,040   (C) $165,600
    (B) $162,000   (D) $175,000

20. John Johnson borrowed 95% of the appraised value of his house at 8½% interest. In order to get his loan, he had to pay three discount points. If he had additional closing costs of $3,900, what sum did he need for settlement if the house was valued at $180,000?
    (A) $12,900   (C) $18,030
    (B) $18,000   (D) $18,300

21. James Smith bought a home from Peter Thomas for $125,400. Smith got an 80% loan from Commercial Mortgage Company with a mortgage guaranteed by the federal Veterans Affairs. The lender charged Thomas a discount of $5,016, or
    (A) three points.   (C) five points.
    (B) four points.   (D) six points.

22. A borrower went to a lender to obtain a $39,000 second mortgage on the borrower's home. Which of the following is (are) true?
    I. A service charge of three points on this loan would be $390.
    II. A prepayment penalty of three points on this loan would be $390.
    (A) I only   (C) Both I and II
    (B) II only   (D) Neither I nor II

23. A mortgage company agreed to lend a sum of money equal to 90% of the appraised value, at an effective interest rate of 9%. This rate could only be achieved after a discount of 8% was paid on the actual face amount of the note. What sum of money did the borrower actually achieve if the appraisal of the property is $178,500?
    (A) $128,520   (C) $160,650
    (B) $147,798   (D) $164,220

24. A property sold for $240,000. The buyer paid $24,000 earnest money payment. The buyer obtained a loan for the balance. The mortgage lender charged a fee of 1½% of the loan. What was the total cash used by the buyer for this transaction?
    (A) $3,240
    (B) $3,600
    (C) $27,240
    (D) $27,600

25. The beneficiary of a second trust deed sold the interest in the property for a lessor amount than the current unpaid balance of the note. This action is most commonly described as
    (A) subrogating.
    (B) discounting.
    (C) leverage.
    (D) exchanging.

26. Mr. and Mrs. Branbrain sold their home and carried a second trust deed for $50,000. The interest rate on the second is 12%. They wish to sell the loan to an investor, who will only buy it if it produces an 18% yield. In this case, the
    (A) investor will not agree to buy the second trust deed.
    (B) investor cannot legally buy the second trust deed without the borrower's permission.
    (C) investor would probably pay about $33,333 for the second trust deed.
    (D) sellers will have to discount the second trust deed by about 50%.

27. An investor bought a loan for $142,500. The principal due on the loan was $190,000. This means that the discount was approximately
    (A) 25%.
    (B) 33.33%.
    (C) 50%.
    (D) 75%.

28. An investor bought a second trust deed with a principal balance of $54,000 at a discount of 20%. The borrower paid interest payments of $1,500 per month for one year, and then paid the balance in full. The investor's yield was
    (A) 25.00%.
    (B) 33.33%.
    (C) 41.67%.
    (D) 66.67%.

29. Payments periodically made to reduce an outstanding indebtedness on real property are called
    (A) depreciation.
    (B) appreciation.
    (C) quitclaim reduction.
    (D) amortization.

30. The gradual liquidation of a mortgage loan by regular payments to reduce principal and interest over a given period of time is called
    (A) amortization.
    (B) accretion.
    (C) accession.
    (D) prepayment.

31. Amortization is the process of
    (A) paying an acceleration clause in a mortgage.
    (B) converting net income into an indication of value.
    (C) redemption.
    (D) liquidation of a debt.

32. The word "amortization" is best defined as
    (A) a gradual extinction of a monetary obligation by periodic contributions to extinguish the debt together with the payment of interest thereon.
    (B) an annual income.
    (C) gradual redemption.
    (D) the transfer of property and possession of lands, or other things, from one person to another.

33. A buyer obtained an FHA insured loan to finance the purchase of a home. The buyer was offered a choice of a 25-year term or a 30-year term for the loan. What would be the advantage to the buyer of taking the longer term loan?
    I. The amount of total interest paid would be lower.
    II. The monthly payments on the loan would be lower.
    (A) I only
    (B) II only
    (C) Both I and II
    (D) Neither I nor II

34. When interest is calculated on the principal balance, plus interest on the interest which has already accrued, this is called
    (A) discount interest.
    (B) compound interest.
    (C) accumulated interest.
    (D) simple interest.

35. Interest on residential loans is usually calculated as
    (A) compound interest.
    (B) discount interest.
    (C) simple interest.
    (D) daily interest.

36. When a lender collects all the interest at the time the loan is made, this is called
    (A) accelerated interest.   (C) prepaid interest.
    (B) compound interest.   (D) discount interest.

37. An investment of $46,500 bearing interest at 6½% per annum would earn approximately how much per month?
    (A) $248   (C) $265
    (B) $252   (D) $290

38. Bunny LaVoom, a retired performer, has an annuity investment which has a principal balance of $120,000. If the rate of return is 8%, her monthly income from this investment is
    (A) $800.   (C) $9,600.
    (B) $1,000.   (D) $12,000.

39. What will the quarterly interest payments amount to on a straight note of $90,000 at 8% interest?
    (A) $1,800   (C) $7,200
    (B) $5,400   (D) $14,400

40. What is 18 days interest on the unpaid balance of a second trust deed of $20,000 at 11% simple interest?
    (A) $43.71   (C) $102.22
    (B) $96.15   (D) $108.49

41. Interest on a $150,000 straight note at 9% per annum for a seven month period is
    (A) $4,500.   (C) $11,250.
    (B) $7,875.   (D) $13,500.

42. If a mortgagor pays $350 monthly to the holder of a second mortgage, to be applied first on 9% interest and the balance on the principal, how much is applied to principal when the unpaid principal balance is $18,240?
    (A) $136.80   (C) $243.20
    (B) $213.20   (D) $297.50

43. An investor borrowed $30,000 at a rate of 7½% interest. If the principal and interest were repaid in one payment at the end of five months, what was the total amount owed?
    (A) $30,625.00   (C) $31,312.50
    (B) $30,937.50   (D) $32,250.00

44. A note is dated June 6 in the amount of $195,000. The interest rate is 9.07% per annum (simple interest). How much interest will be due on the following May 6, if no interest has been paid until then? (Use the 365-day calendar year)
    (A) $7,035.55   (C) $16,184.35
    (B) $11,841.00   (D) $17,686.50

45. A buyer obtained a loan of $95,000 at 11% interest to buy a home. The transaction closed on March 3, but the first payment was not due until May 1. As a result, the lender charged the buyer interest from March 3 through the end of the March. This amount was
    (A) $801.64.   (C) $1,045.00.
    (B) $870.83.   (D) $2,926.00.

46. A borrower made $985 monthly payments which the lender applied first to interest and then to principal. If the balance was $96,521 and the interest was 11%, how much was applied to principal?
    (A) $100.22   (C) $884.78
    (B) $750.00   (D) $985.00

47. What is the amount applied to the interest for the first month, assuming a $300,000 loan at 8% interest with equal monthly payments to principal and interest amortized over 20 years at a total interest cost of $602,280?
    (A) $509.50   (C) $2,000.00
    (B) $1,800.00   (D) $2,458.00

48. There is a principal balance of $63,000 on a mortgage. The interest rate is 9% per annum. The taxes and insurance total $4,450 per year. The monthly payment is $1,760, including interest, taxes and insurance, with the remainder applied to reduce the principal. What is the principal balance after the next payment?
    (A) $62,083.33   (C) $62,555.80
    (B) $62,454.20   (D) $62,666.10

49. There is a balance of $90,000 due on a real estate contract which requires monthly payments of $800 plus interest at 6% per annum, payable monthly. What would be the total payment for the third month?
    (A) $1,190   (C) $1,242
    (B) $1,238   (D) $1,246

50. A young couple bought a home for $150,000 and obtained a loan of $135,000 to finance it. The payments are $809.40 per month, including principal and interest at 6%, which will pay the loan off in 30 years. After the first payment was made, what was the new principal balance?
(A) $134,325.00
(B) $134,865.60
(C) $135,140.40
(D) $135,675.00

51. A loan had a balance of $120,000 and was written at an interest rate of 12%. It was to be amortized over 30 years with equal monthly payments of principal and interest. The total interest charged over the life of the loan was projected to be $323,330.60. What was the interest charge for the first month?
(A) $898.14
(B) $1,200.00
(C) $1,231.47
(D) $1,440.00

52. There is a balance of $120,000 due on a real estate contract that requires monthly payments of $1,200 plus interest at 9% per annum on the declining balance, payable monthly. The total payment for the third month will be
(A) $1,330.
(B) $2,060.
(C) $2,082.
(D) $2,100.

53. A couple bought a home for $250,000 and financed 80% of the purchase price over 30 years at monthly payments of $2,054.37 which included principal and interest at 12%. As a result of the financing, they paid what percent additional above what it would have cost if they had paid cash?
(A) 196%
(B) 216%
(C) 296%
(D) 316%

54. If the annual 19% interest payment on a loan amounts to $8,800, what is the amount of the principal of the loan?
(A) $46,315.79
(B) $48,190.10
(C) $55,532.20
(D) $88,652.50

55. If the rate of interest is 15% per annum and your monthly interest payment is $1,250, what is the amount of your loan?
(A) $83,333
(B) $100,000
(D) $225,000
(C) $187,500

56. If the current annual 7½% interest payment amounts to $45,000, the amount of the unpaid mortgage will be
(A) $337,500.
(B) $400,000.
(C) $500,000.
(D) $600,000.

57. The interest rate is 10¾% and the monthly interest payment is $252.25. The principal sum is
(A) $28,158.
(B) $29,001.
(C) $29,733.
(D) $32,599.

58. If the annual interest rate on a loan is 8% and the monthly interest payment is $120, the principal sum owed would be
(A) $8,000.
(B) $14,000.
(C) $18,000.
(D) $24,000.

59. An investor purchased a commercial lot and is paying an annual interest rate of 11⅕%. The amount of interest last month was $1,713.00. The principal sum owing is
(A) $15,295.
(B) $138,000.
(C) $183,536.
(D) $209,370.

60. Monthly interest payments on Ms. Bray's second trust deed loan are $459.00. The loan was obtained at 12% interest. What is the original principal amount of this loan?
(A) $36,200
(B) $36,800
(C) $45,900
(D) $61,225

61. Last month Steven's monthly payment for the interest portion of his mortgage amounted to $910.50. Steven pays an interest rate of 9¼%. Based on this information, what was the balance of the loan prior to the last payment?
(A) $102,535.23
(B) $118,118.92
(C) $128,053.50
(D) $129,310.92

62. An investor purchased a straight note which matured in five years, including interest at 14.4%. At maturity the investor collected interest totaling $41,400 from the borrower. The note balance was
(A) $29,500.
(B) $57,500.
(C) $148,500.
(D) $287,500.

63. An investor desires an income of $50,000 per year. The investor is considering two different investments which will meet the investor's goal, one yielding 11% and another which yields 13%. What is the dollar amount of difference between the two investments?
    (A) $69,930 more for the 11% investment
    (B) $69,930 more for the 13% investment
    (C) $69,930 less for the 11% investment
    (D) $45,454 more for the 11% investment

64. A buyer got a 50% loan on a new home at an annual interest rate of 11.3%. The first month's interest was $807.64. What was the purchase price of the home?
    (A) $171,534.16   (C) $237,099.04
    (B) $198,060.84   (D) $250,156.64

65. The loan on a property is 56% of its appraised valuation. If the interest rate is 8.3% and the first semi-annual interest payment is $5,449.10, what is the appraised value of the property?
    (A) $117,235   (C) $515,701
    (B) $234,471   (D) $905,944

66. Mr. Williams secured an 80% mortgage at 9% interest. If the interest for the first month was $1,170, what was the purchase price of the house?
    (A) $156,000   (C) $234,000
    (B) $195,000   (D) $243,000

67. A commercial bank agreed to lend the owner of a piece of property a sum equal in amount to ⅔% of their appraised valuation. The interest rate charged on the amount borrowed is 8¼% per annum. The first year's interest amounted to $16,500. The valuation placed upon the property by the bank was
    (A) $100,000.   (C) $250,000.
    (B) $200,000.   (D) $300,000.

68. A mortgage company agreed to lend the owner of a lot a sum equal to 57% of its appraised value at an interest rate of 10.2% per annum. If the first year's interest is $15,058.30, what is the appraised value of the lot?
    (A) $182,000   (C) $259,000
    (B) $242,000   (D) $280,000

69. An investor bought an apartment building and obtained a loan at a 75% loan to value ratio. If the loan was for 30 years at 10% interest and the annual interest expense was $37,500, the investor must have made a down payment of
    (A) $37,500.   (C) $125,000.
    (B) $100,000.   (D) $375,000.

70. If an investor paid $1,800 interest on a straight note of $80,000 at the end of three months, the interest rate of the note would be
    (A) 6%.   (C) 8%.
    (B) 7%.   (D) 9%.

71. What is the annual interest rate on a $130,000 loan when the interest payments are $8,255.00 semi-annually on the full amount?
    (A) 4.04%   (C) 8.89%
    (B) 6.02%   (D) 12.7%

72. What is the annual interest rate on a $60,000 loan when the interest payments are $921.40 per quarter on the loan?
    (A) 4.49%   (C) 7.09%
    (B) 6.14%   (D) 9.00%

73. Frank Furter took out a home improvement loan in the amount of $6,000. The quarterly interest payments are $180.00. What is his interest rate?
    (A) 3%   (C) 10%
    (B) 6%   (D) 12%

74. What is the annual interest rate on a $200,000 loan when monthly interest payments are $1,416.60 on the full amount?
    (A) 7.0%   (C) 8.5%
    (B) 8.0%   (D) 9.25%

75. A corporation developing a new industrial park borrowed $6 million, repayable in eight years. If they repaid a total amount of $11,942,400, what was the yearly rate of simple interest charged?
    (A) 7.15%   (C) 9.85%
    (B) 8.58%   (D) 12.38%

76. An investor purchased a property for $500,000 which produced an annual return of 12%. The owner's only expense was 10% simple interest on a loan of $400,000. What was the investor's rate of return on the equity?
   (A) 4%   (C) 12%
   (B) 10%   (D) 20%

77. Mr. Homer borrowed $75,000 on a straight loan at an annual interest rate of 7.2%. His total interest payments were $8,100. The term of the note was most nearly
   (A) 12 months.   (C) 20 months.
   (B) 18 months..   (D) 24 months.

78. Smith borrowed $375,000, giving the lender his note secured by a trust deed. His monthly interest payments were based on a 7.2% annual rate for the full term of the note. His total interest payments amounted to $40,500. What was the term of his note?
   (A) 15 months   (C) 21 months
   (B) 18 months   (D) 24 months

79. Michelle Barrett borrowed $62,000 on which she agreed to pay 9.4% interest per annum. If she paid a total of $910.90 interest, how long did she keep the money? (Use a 365-day calendar year.)
   (A) 27 days   (C) 57 days
   (B) 35 days   (D) 94 days

80. A developer borrowed $620,000 at 9.4% interest as short term funds to purchase a property. If the developer paid the lender a total of $9,109 in interest, how long was the loan outstanding?
   (A) 27 days   (C) 57 days
   (B) 35 days   (D) 94 days

81. When the buyer is taking out a new loan, interest begins accruing on that loan
   (A) when the funds are disbursed by the lender.
   (B) when the buyer is entitled to possession of the property.
   (C) when either A or B has occurred, whichever happens first.
   (D) only when A and B have both happened.

82. There is an FHA insurable value appraisal on a home for $104,000. FHA will insure the loan as follows: 97% of the first $25,000 and 95% of the balance of the appraisal. The investor who is going to make the loan as much as FHA will insure also requires a four-point discount. In order for the loan to be closed, the seller or the buyer will have to pay
   (A) $3,600.   (C) $4,160.
   (B) $3,992.   (D) $4,700.

ANSWERS

To practice questions. If you chose the wrong letter, here's the right one! The explanations are designed to clarify your understanding.

1. **D** The secondary market requires that the loan to value ratio be calculated against the lower of the appraised value or the sales price.

2. **A** The maximum loan amount is determined by multiplying the loan to value ratio by the appraised value or the sales price, whichever is lower. In this case, it is the appraised value of $169,000. Therefore, the maximum loan amount would be $143,650 ($169,000 × .85 = $143,650).

3. **C** If the loan to value ratio is 85%, then the down payment is the remaining 15%. This comes to $29,250 ($195,000 × .15 = $29,250). Subtracting the initial deposit of $4,500 leaves $24,750 additional the buyer will have to furnish ($29,250 − $4,500 = $24,740).

4. **C** If the lender will lend at an 85% loan to value ratio, then the buyer's down payment represents 15% of the sales price. To find the sales price, therefore, divide the down payment by 15%. This comes to $226,667 ($34,000 ÷ .15 = $226,666.67).

5. **B** The earnest money is 12% of the sales price, which comes to $43,200 ($360,000 × .12 = $43,200). The loan amount of 70% means that the buyer will have to make a down payment of 30% of the sales price, which comes to $108,000 ($360,000 × .30 = $108,000). Since the buyer has already paid part of this with the earnest money deposit, the difference between the total down payment and the earnest money is how much additional the buyer will have to deposit at closing. This comes to $64,800 ($108,000 − $43,200 = $64,800).

6. **B** Lenders are allowed to lend on the lower of the sales price or the appraised value. Therefore, the answer cannot be either $133,200 or $195,000. This means that we must calculate the percentage that $132,500 is of the appraised value (the loan to value ratio). To find it, divide the loan amount by the appraised value. This comes to 80% ($132,600 ÷ $166,500 = .796396396).

7. **C** Suppose you buy a property worth $200,000 and put $40,000 down, financing the remaining $160,000. Your equity in the property is then $40,000 less the difference between the total of the financing ($160,000) and the market value ($200,000).

8. **A** Simple interest is usually contrasted with compound interest. Compounding means charging interest on the principal, plus the accrued interest. Savings accounts are usually compounded, so the borrower receives interest on the principal amount, plus the interest as it accrues. Compounding results in higher total interest. Loans, however, are usually calculated without compounding, i.e., simple interest. Straight interest would be interest as charged on a straight note (no installments – all due at the end of the term). Add-on interest is where the interest is calculated for the term of the loan in advance, added to the principal balance, and the periodic payments are then calculated by dividing the number of payments into the total.

9. **B** When interest is allowed to accrue (build up) and is added to the principal balance, and then future interest is calculated on the higher balance, this is called compound interest. If interest is calculated only on the original principal amount, it is called simple interest. An annuity is a guaranteed income from a secure investment.

10. **C** Today's mortgages are paid "including interest," which means that the amount of the payment toward principal and interest is constant over the life of the loan. At the beginning, most of the payment is interest, and only a small portion is applied to principal. Toward the end, the amount toward interest is very small, and most of the payment is applied to principal.

11. **A** By selling a loan at a price below the face amount due the lender increases the yield to the investor who buys the loan. This is a common practice when the interest rate on the loan is below market. Because the lender who originates the loan would lose money by selling it at a discount, it is customary to charge a discount fee to cover the loss. The discount fee is typically measured as a percentage of the loan balance. One percent of the loan balance is called a "point."

12. **A** Today's mortgages are paid "including interest" – that is, the monthly payment is constant over the life of the loan and the amount applied to

principal increases as the amount applied to interest declines. Any time a loan is paid in regular installments, it is called an amortized loan.

13.   **C**   Loan discounts are measured as a percentage of the loan balance. To keep from getting confused between "percent of interest" (the interest rate) and "percent of loan" (as a discount), we use the term "point" for discounts. One point is one percent of the loan amount.

14.   **C**   Lenders typically agree to let the borrower or the seller pay discount points in order to "buy down" the interest rate for the borrower. The more points that are paid, the lower the interest rate that the lender will agree to. Buying down the interest rate can help the borrower qualify for the payments.

15.   **B**   When a loan is sold at a discount it is sold for less than the face amount the borrower owes. Therefore, to calculate the dollar amount of the discount, multiply the loan balance by the percentage of discount.

16.   **D**   The nominal rate refers to the amount as stated on the note or contract. This is the rate at which the borrower is charged. However, because of loan discounting, the investor who holds the loan may actually be receiving a higher yield. The yield to the lender is called the effective rate, in contrast to the note rate.

17.   **A**   By selling a loan at a price below the face amount due the lender increases the yield to the investor who buys the loan. This is a common practice when the loan interest rate is below market and secondary lenders demand a market yield. Because the primary lender would lose in such a sale, it is common practice to charge the borrower (or someone else in the transaction) an amount estimated to cover the loss. This amount is typically measured as a percentage of the loan balance. One percent of the loan balance is called a "point."

18.   **B**   One point is one percent of the loan amount, so a discount of five points would be the same as 5% of the loan balance. In this case, that comes to $7,500 ($150,000 × .05 = $7,500).

19.   **A**   To calculate, first find the loan amount, which will be 90% of the appraised value of $180,000. This comes to $162,000 ($180,000 × .90 = $162,000). Next, subtract the discount, which is to be 8%. Eight percent of the loan amount is $12,960 ($162,000 × .08 = $12,960), so the loan amount will be $149,040 ($162,000 − $12,960 = $149,040).

20.   **C**   First find the loan amount. If the value was $180,000 and the loan to value ratio was 95%,

then the loan amount would have been $171,000. One discount point is 1% of the loan balance, so three discount points is $5,130 ($171,000 × .03 = $5,130). Adding the $3,900 in additional closing costs and the down payment of $9,000 comes to a total cash amount of $18,030 ($5,130 + $3,900 + $9,000 = $18,030).

21.   **C**   One point is the same as one percent of the loan balance. In this case the loan was an 80% loan, so the loan balance was $100,320 ($125,400 × .80 = $100,320). To determine the discount percentage, divide the amount of the discount by the loan amount. This comes to 5% ($5,016 ÷ $100,320 = 0.05).

22.   **D**   One point is the same as one percent of the loan balance. Therefore, three points would be 3% of the loan balance, which comes to $1,170 ($39,000 × .03 = $1,170).

23.   **B**   First find the amount of the loan before the 8% discount. This is 90% of $178,500, or $160,650 ($178,500 × .90 = $160,650). Then find the 8% discount, which comes to $12,852. Finally, subtract the discount from the original loan amount, which comes to $147,798 ($160,650 − $12,852 = $147,798).

24.   **C**   First, find the loan amount. The earnest money comprised the entire down payment, so the difference between the sales price and the earnest money is the loan amount. This comes to $216,000 ($240,000 − $24,000 = $216,000). The loan fee is 1½% of the loan amount, which comes to $3,240 ($216,000 × .015 = $3,240). The total cash used by the buyer was, therefore, the earnest money and the loan fee, which totals $27,240 ($24,000 + $3,240 = $27,240).

25.   **B**   Selling a loan for less than the remaining unpaid balance is a way to increase the yield to the investor who buys the loan. The practice is called loan discounting.

26.   **C**   First, use the formula I = PRT to find the interest the borrower will pay in a year. This comes to $6,000 ($50,000 × .12 × 1 = $6,000). Now use the formula P = I ÷ RT to find what the principal balance could be if the rate (yield) were 18%. This comes to $33,333 ($6,000 ÷ .18 × 1 = $33,333.333). In other words, by paying $33,333 for the right to receive $6,000 per year, the investor enjoys an 18% yield.

27.   **A**   Calculate what percentage $142,500 is of $190,000, which is really nothing more than an ordinary fraction. To convert a fraction to a decimal, divide the denominator into the numerator. In this case, the answer is 75% ($142,500 ÷ $190,000 = .75). If the lender received 75%, then the discount must have been 25%.

28.   **D**   If the borrower paid $1,500 interest per month, then the annual interest payment was $18,000 ($1,500 × 12 = $18,000). Since the investor bought the note for a 20% discount, but received a repayment of the full $54,000, the investor reaped additional profit to the extent of the discount. The dollar amount of the discount was $10,800 ($54,000 × .20 = $10,800). Adding this profit to the interest, means the investor received a total return of $28,800 ($18,000 + $10,800 = $28,800). Dividing this return by the amount invested (the discounted purchase price) will give the investor's percentage return. The discounted purchase price was $43,200 ($54,000 − $10,800 = $43,200). Therefore, the investor's yield was 66.67% ($28,800 ÷ $43,200 = .6666666).

29.   **D**   Loans which are paid off in installments which include principal in each payment are said to be amortized loans.

30.   **A**   There are two kinds of loan repayments – straight and amortized. A straight note is one with no payments toward principal at all until the end of the term, at which time the principal is paid in full. An amortized note calls for regular installments toward the principal over the term of the note.

31.   **D**   Amortization means paying off a loan in installments. An acceleration clause allows the lender to demand the entire loan balance in full in the event of a default. Converting net income into value is a description of capitalization, a process used by appraisers of income property.

32.   **A**   Amortization means paying off a loan in installments. The opposite of an amortized loan is a straight loan, where the entire principal balance is paid at the end of the term.

33.   **B**   The longer the term the more total interest the borrower will pay over the life of the loan. However, in spite of the higher total interest cost, by extending the term, the periodic payments will be lower.

34.   **B**   When interest is allowed to accrue (build up) as part of the principal balance, and then future interest charges are calculated on the new (higher) balance, this is called compounding the interest. Compound interest is interest charged on interest already accrued. The opposite of compound interest is simple interest, where the interest is always calculated on the original principal regardless of how much interest has accrued. Discount interest occurs when the interest is deducted from the principal balance at the beginning of the loan, and only the net amount is disbursed to the borrower.

35.   **C**   When a residential loan is amortized the interest charge for each month is calculated on the balance remaining after the previous payment was made. Lenders ordinarily do this as a simple interest calculation. If the lender compounded the interest each day, then it would be called compound interest.

36.   **D**   An acceleration clause allows the lender to call the entire principal balance due at once in the event of the borrower's default. Prepaid interest is the term used by real estate agents to describe interest on a new loan from the closing date of the purchase until the end of the month. Prepaid interest is charged because the lender usually wants the payments to be due on the first, yet wants exactly one month before the first payment is due. Compound interest is charging interest on the interest that has already accrued. Discount interest means calculating the total interest over the life of the loan and subtracting it from the principal, so the borrower receives a lesser amount.

37.   **B**   First, find the annual interest income by multiplying the principal balance by the rate. This comes to $3,022.50 $46,500 × .065 = $3,022.50). Divide this amount by 12 to get the monthly interest income, which comes to $251.88 ($3,022.50 ÷ 12 = $251.875).

38.   **A**   First, calculate the annual interest on an investment of $120,000 at 8%. Using the formula I = PRT, the result is $9,600 ($120,000 × .08 × 1 = $9,600). Since this is one year's interest, divide it by 12 to find one month's interest, which comes to $800 ($9,600 ÷ 12 = $800).

39.   **A**   First, find the annual interest expense. This comes to $7,200 ($90,000 × .08 = $7,200). Then divide the annual charge by 4 to get the quarterly expense. The result is $1,800 ($7,200 ÷ 4 = $1,800).

40.   **D**   First find the interest charge for one year. This comes to $2,200 ($20,000 × .11 = $2,200). Divide this by 365 to get a daily amount, which comes to $6.03 ($2,200 ÷ 365 = $6.027397260). Multiply this by 18 to find the charge for 18 days, which comes to $108.49 ($6.027397260 × 18 = $108.4931507).

41.   **B**   Find the annual interest charge first. This comes to $13,500 ($150,000 × .09 = $13,500). Then divide this amount by 12 and multiply the result by 7 to find the interest expense for a seven months. The result is $7,875 ($13,500 ÷ 12 = $1,125; $1,125 × 7 = $7,875).

42.   **B**   To find the annual interest amount, multiply the balance by the rate, then divide by 12 to get the monthly interest amount. The annual interest comes to $1,641.60 ($18,240 × .09 = $1,641.60).

Dividing this by 12 gives the monthly amount of $136.80 ($1641.60 ÷ 12 = $136.80). Since the total payment is $350, after subtracting the interest charge for the month, the amount left to apply on the principal is $213.20 ($350 − $136.80 = $213.20).

43.   **B**   To find the interest expense for a period of time, find the amount for a year, and then multiply by the number of years (in this case, ⁵⁄₁₂ of a year). If the principal is $30,000 and the rate is 7½%, then one year's interest is $2,250 ($30,000 × .075 = $2,250). Divide this by 12 and multiply the result by 5 to get five months worth of interest. This comes to $937.50 ($2,250 ÷ 12 = $187.50; $187.50 × 5 = $937.50). Finally, add the repayment of the principal to find the total amount that would be repaid at the end of five months, which comes to $30,937.50 ($937.50 + $30,000 = $30,937.50).

44.   **C**   May has 31 days, so there are 31 days between May 6 and June 6. Subtracting this from the number of days in a year, gives us 334 days between June 6 one year and May 6 of the next year. Next, find the daily interest rate by dividing the annual rate by 365. This comes to 0.0248493% (.0907 ÷ 365 = .000248493). Then multiply the principal amount by this rate to get the daily interest charge, which comes to about $48.46 ($195,000 × .000248493 = $48.456135). Multiplying this by the number of days gives us a total interest charge of $16,184.35 ($48.456135 × 334 = $16,184.34909).

45.   **A**   Among lenders it is common practice to make all real estate loan payments due on the first of the month. It is also common to charge the buyer at closing for interest from the closing date (the day the funds are actually disbursed) through the end of the month. This way there will be exactly one month's interest accrued by the time the first payment falls due, which will be on the first of the following month. In this problem, therefore, the borrower must pay the lender for 28 days worth of interest (March 3 through March 31). Since the rate is an annual rate, it is easier to work the formula (I = PRT) if you find out what percentage 28 days is of a year. Dividing 28 by 365 gives the answer .0767123. Therefore, the interest due is calculated as $801.64 ($95,000 × .11 × .0767123, or $801.64).

46.   **A**   First find the interest charge for one month with the formula I = PRT. If the principal balance is $96,521 and the rate is 11%, then one year's interest would be $10,671.31 ($96,521 × .11 × 1 = $10,617.31). Divide this by 12 to find one month's

interest, which comes to $884.78 ($10,671.31 ÷ 12 = $884.77583). If the total payment was $985, the difference is what the lender would apply to reduction of the principal balance. This amounts to $100.22 ($985 − $884.78 = $100.22).

47.   **C**   To find the annual interest charge multiply the principal by the rate. This comes to $24,000 ($300,000 × .08 = $24,000). To get one month's interest, divide this amount by 12, which comes to $2,000 ($24,000 ÷ 12 = $2,000). The amount of interest paid over the life of the loan is irrelevant to the question.

48.   **A**   First, find the interest charge for the month. Calculate it by multiplying the balance due by the interest rate to get an annual interest expense, then divide the annual interest by 12 to get one month's interest. This comes to $5,670 annual interest and $472.50 per month ($63,000 × .09 = $5,670; $5,670 ÷ 12 = $472.50). Next, calculate ¹⁄₁₂ of the annual tax and insurance expense. This comes to $370.83 ($4,450 ÷ 12 = $370.83). When the bank receives the payment of $1,760 they will subtract the monthly tax and insurance reserves, then the interest, and the remainder will be applied to principal. This means the amount to be applied to principal will be $916.67 ($1,760 − $370.83 − $472.50 = $916.67). Subtracting this amount from the principal balance gives the new principal balance for the coming month of $62,083.33.

49.   **C**   We have to calculate the total payment for the third month, by which time two principal payments of $800 will have been paid. Therefore, the principal balance will be $88,400 ($90,000 − $800 − $800 = $88,400). The interest for the third month comes to $442 ($88,400 × .06 = $5,304; $5,304 ÷ 12 = $442). Adding the interest expense to the principal payment gives a total monthly payment of $1,242 ($800 + $442 = $1,242).

50.   **B**   First find the interest charge for one month with the formula I = PRT. If the principal balance is $135,000 and the rate is 6%, then one year's interest would be $8,100 ($135,000 × .06 × 1 = $8,100). Divide this by 12 to find one month's interest, which comes to $675 ($8,100 ÷ 12 = $675). If the total payment was $809.40, the difference is what the lender would apply to reduction of the principal balance. This amounts to $134.40 ($809.40 − $675.00 = $134.40). Subtract this amount from the beginning balance to find the remaining balance after the first payment. This results in the answer, which is $134,865.60 ($135,000 − $134.40 = $134,865.60).

51. **B** The total amount of interest paid over the life of the loan is irrelevant. To solve the problem, just calculate one month's interest on the principal balance of $120,000 at 12%. One month is .0833333 of a year (1 ÷ 12 = .0833333). Using the formula I = PRT, we get $1,200 ($120,000 × .12 × .083333 = $1,199.9995).

52. **C** This loan is being calculated "plus interest" instead of the more normal "including interest." I.e., the $1,200 per month is just principal and includes no interest. To find the monthly interest charge, multiply the principal balance by the rate and divide the result by 12. However, we have to calculate it for the third month, by which time two principal payments of $1,200 will have been paid. Therefore, the principal balance will be $117,600 ($120,000 − $1,200 − $1,200 = $117,600). The interest for the third month comes to $882 ($117,600 × .09 = $10,584; $10,584 ÷ 12 = $882). Adding the interest expense to the principal payment gives a total monthly payment of $2,082 ($1,200 + $882 = $2,082).

53. **B** First, find the total of the payments. Each payment is $2,054.37 and there are 360, so the total to be paid will be $739,573.20 ($2,054.37 × 360 = $739,573.20). Adding the down payment ($50,000) to this will give us the total amount the couple paid for the property. This comes to $789,573.20 ($739,573.20 + $50,000 = $789,573.20). If they have paid cash, they would have paid $250,000, so the extra they paid because of the financing is the difference, or $539,573.20 ($789,573.20 − $250,000 = $539,573.20). Divide this amount by the $250,000 to find the percentage extra that the financing cost. This comes to 216% ($539,573.20 ÷ $250,000 = 2.1582928).

54. **A** Find the principal balance by dividing the annual interest expense by the rate. This comes to $46,315.79 ($8,800 ÷ .19 = $46,315.78947).

55. **B** To find the loan balance, divide the annual interest expense by the interest rate. To get the annual interest expense, multiply the monthly amount by 12, which comes to $15,000 ($1,250 × 12 = $15,000). The loan balance then comes to $100,000 ($15,000 ÷ .15 = $100,000).

56. **D** To find the loan balance, divide the annual interest by the rate. This comes to $600,000 ($45,000 ÷ .075 = $600,000).

57. **A** To find the principal balance, divide the annual interest amount by the interest rate. The annual interest amount is $3,027 ($252.25 × 12 = $3,027). Dividing this by the annual interest rate (10¾%, or .1075) gives the answer of $28,158 ($3,027 ÷ .1075 = $28,158.14).

58. **C** To find the principal amount, divide the annual interest payment by the rate. First, however, we have to find the annual interest payment, which comes to $1,440 ($120 per month × 12 months = $1,440). Dividing this amount by the rate gives us $18,000 ($1,440 ÷ .08 = $18,000).

59. **C** To find the principal balance, divide the annual interest amount by the interest rate. The annual interest is $20,556 ($1,713 × 12 = $20,556). Dividing this by the annual interest rate (11⅕%, or 0.112) gives the answer of $183,536 ($20,556 ÷ .112 = $183,535.71).

60. **C** You can calculate the principal balance by dividing the annual interest charge by the rate. In this case the interest is given as a monthly amount, so it must be multiplied by 12 to get the annual amount. This comes to $5,508 ($459 × 12 = $5,508). Dividing this by the rate gives a principal balance of $45,900 ($5,508 ÷ .12 = $45,900).

61. **B** To find the loan balance divide the annual interest charge by the rate. The monthly interest expense is $910.50, so the annual expense is $10,926 ($910.50 × 12 = $10,926). Dividing this by the rate gives us the balance of $118,118.92 ($10,926 ÷ .0925 = $118,118.9189).

62. **B** Assuming that the interest was not compounded, divide the total interest paid ($41,400) by the number of years (5) to find the annual interest. This comes to $8,280 ($41,400 ÷ 5 = $8,280). Now solve the problem with the formula P = I ÷ RT, which yields the answer $57,500 ($8,280 ÷ .144 × 1 = $57,500).

63. **A** This is really two problems. Find the principal balance of the investment at 11%, and then repeat the process to find what it would be at a 13% rate. The formula to find the principal is P = I ÷ RT, so at 11% it will require a principal balance of $454,545 to produce an annual income of $50,000 ($50,000 ÷ (.11 × 1) = $454,545.45). At 13%, the principal balance would have to be only $384,615 ($50,000 ÷ (.13 × 1) = $384,615.38). The difference between the two is $69,930 ($454,545.45 − $384,615.38 = $69,930.07).

64. **A** First, find the principal balance by dividing the annual interest by the interest rate. The annual interest comes to $9,691.68 ($807.64 × 12 = $9,691.68). Dividing this by the rate gives the principal balance of $85,767.08 ($9,691.68 ÷ .113 = $85,767.07965). Since this represents half of the purchase price (a 50% loan to value ratio), the purchase price was $171,534.16 ($85,767.07965 × 2 = 171,534.1593).

65.   **B**   First, find the loan balance, which is determined by dividing the annual interest expense by the rate. The interest charge given is semi-annual, so the annual charge is $10,898.20 ($5.449.10 × 2 = $10,898.20). The loan balance then comes to $131,303.61 ($10,898.20 ÷ .083 = $131,303.6145). However, this represents only 56% of the value, so to find the value, divide this amount by 0.56. This comes to $234,471 ($131,303.61 ÷ .56 = $234,470.7402).

66.   **B**   First, find the loan amount, which is calculated by dividing the annual interest by the interest rate. The annual interest comes to $14,040 ($1,170 × 12 = $14,040). Dividing this by the rate gives us a loan balance of $156,000 ($14,040 ÷ .09 = $156,000). However, this is 80% of the value, so to find the value, divide it by 80% (.80). This comes to $195,000 ($156,000 ÷ .80 = $195,000).

67.   **D**   Find the loan amount by dividing the annual interest charge by the rate. This comes to $200,000 ($16,500 ÷ .0825 = $200,000). Since this is ⅔ of the value, the value must be $300,000 ($200,000 ÷ 2 × 3 = $300,000).

68.   **C**   First, find the loan amount. The loan amount is calculated by dividing the annual interest charge by the rate. This comes to $147,630.39 ($15,058.30 ÷ .102 = $147,630.3922). This represents 57% of the value of the property so, to find the value, divide the loan amount by 57% (.57). This comes to $259,000 ($147,630.3922 ÷ .57 = $259,000.6881).

69.   **C**   First find the loan amount by the formula P = I ÷ RT. If the annual interest expense is $37,500 and the rate is 10%, then the principal balance must be $375,000 ($37,500 ÷ (.10 × 1) = $375,000). However, this amount was only 75% of the purchase price, so we must find the purchase price by dividing this answer by 75%. This yields the purchase price as $500,000. The down payment, therefore, is the difference between the purchase price of $500,000 and the loan amount of $375,000, or $125,000 ($500,000 − $375,000 = $125,000).

70.   **D**   Three months is one-fourth of a year, so an interest expense of $1,800 over three months is the same as an interest expense of $7,200 over a year ($1,800 × 4 = $7,200). Now, find the rate by dividing the annual interest by the principal. This comes to 9% ($7,200 ÷ $80,000 = .09).

71.   **D**   To find the interest rate, divide the annual interest charge by the principal balance. Since the interest charge given is semi-annual, the annual interest charge is $16,510 ($8,255 × 2 = $16,510). Dividing this by the principal amount ($130,000) gives us the rate of 12.7% ($16,510 ÷ $130,000 = .127).

72.   **B**   To find the interest rate divide the annual interest expense by the principal balance. If the quarterly interest expense is $921.40, then the annual amount is $3,685.60 ($921.40 × 4 = $3,685.60). Dividing this by the loan balance ($60,000) gives us a rate of 6.14% ($3,685.60 ÷ $60,000 = .0614267).

73.   **D**   To find the interest rate as an annual rate, first find the annual interest. If the interest for one quarter is $180, then the interest for one year would be $720 (4 × $180 = $720). To find the interest rate, use the formula R = I ÷ PT. Using this formula gives the result of 12% ($720 ÷ ($6,000 × 1) = .12).

74.   **C**   To find the interest rate, divide the annual interest charge by the principal balance. The interest given is monthly, so multiply by 12 first to get the annual amount. This comes to $16,999.20 ($1416.60 × 12 = $16,999.20). Dividing this by the principal balance gives the rate as 8.5% ($16,999.20 ÷ $200,000 = .084996).

75.   **D**   To find the rate, divide the annual interest charge by the principal balance. The total amount paid includes repayment of the principal, so first subtract the principal to find the amount for the interest alone. This comes to $5,942.400 ($11,942,400 − $6,000,000 = $5,942,400). The interest here is given for eight years, so it must be divided by 8 to get the annual amount. This comes to $742,800 ($5,942,400 ÷ 8 years = $742,800 per year). Dividing this by the principal balance gives a rate of 12.38% ($742,800 ÷ $6,000,000 = 0.1238).

76.   **D**   First, find the net income from the investment, which can be found by subtracting the expenses from the gross income. The sole expense is interest at 10% on the $400,000 loan, so one year's interest is $40,000, found by the formula I = PRT ($400,000 × .10 × 1 = $40,000). The gross income is 12% of the total $500,000 investment, which is $60,000 ($500,000 × .12 = $60,000). Thus, the net return on the equity is $20,000, the difference between the gross income ($60,000) and the expenses ($40,000). To find out what rate of return this is on the equity, use the formula R = I ÷ PT, which gives the answer of 20% ($20,000 ÷ ($100,000 × 1) = 20%).

77.   **B**   To find the term of a loan in months, find the monthly amount of interest and divide this into the total interest paid. The annual interest comes to $5,400 ($75,000 × .072 = $5,400). Divide this by 12 to get the monthly amount, which comes to $450

($5,400 ÷ 12 = $450). Divide this into the total interest paid to find the term in months. This comes to 18 months ($8,100 ÷ $450 = 18).

78. **B** To find the term of a loan in months, find the monthly amount of interest and divide this into the total interest paid. The annual interest comes to $27,000 ($375,000 × .072 = $27,000). Divide this by 12 to get the monthly amount, which comes to $2,250 ($27,000 ÷ 12 = $2,250). Divide this into the total interest paid to find the term in months. This comes to 18 months ($40,500 ÷ $2,250 = 18).

79. **C** To find the period of a loan, divide the interest charge by the product of the principal and the rate. If you want the results in days, first convert the rate to a daily rate. This comes to 0.0257534% (.094 ÷ 365 = .000257534). The product of the principal and the rate comes to $15.97 ($63,000 × .000257534 = $15.96712329). Dividing this into the interest charge gives the answer 57 days ($910.90 ÷ $15.96712329 = 57.04).

80. **C** To find the term (time) of a loan, use the formula T = I ÷ PR. If the principal is $620,000 and the rate is 9.4%, then "PT" is $58,280 ($620,000 × .094 = $58,280). Dividing this into the interest ($9,109) gives us the portion of a year that the loan must have run, that is 15.62971% ($9,109 ÷ $58,280 = .1562971). To find how many days this is, multiply it by 365. This yields the answer as 57 days (365 × .1562971 = 57.048441).

81. **A** Lenders give nothing for free. The minute their check for the loan proceeds is deposited the interest begins to accrue.

82. **D** This is a two-part problem. First find the amount the FHA will insure of the first $25,000. The FHA will insure 97% of this, so the amount comes to $24,250 ($25,000 × .97 = $24,250). Next, find the amount the FHA will insure of the remainder. The remainder is $79,000 ($104,000 − $25,000 = $79,000), and we need to calculate 95% of this, which comes to $75,050 ($79,000 × .95 = $75,050). Adding the two figures together gives us a maximum loan amount of $99,300 ($24,250 + $75,050 = $99,300). If the price is $104, 000, the down payment the borrower will have to pay will be $4,700 ($104,000 − $99,300 = $4,700).

ALTERNATIVE FINANCING

IN MOST REAL ESTATE TRANSACTIONS THE BUYER PAYS CASH FOR THE PROPERTY. Of course, most buyers do not have the cash in the bank, but they can get the cash from an outside lender — so the seller still receives the entire purchase price in cash at closing. There are cases, however, where this is not possible or even desirable. For example, the seller may wish to create an installment sale in order to spread out a large capital gain. In this chapter we will explore several alternatives to traditional all-cash transactions.

The most obvious circumstance in which the seller does not receive cash for the entire purchase price is where the buyer takes over the seller's old loan and just pays cash for the seller's equity. Or the buyer could take over the seller's old loan and the seller could carry paper for part or all of the equity. The latter is commonly referred to as "carrying a second mortgage" (or trust deed). A popular alternative is for the seller to carry the entire unpaid balance on a contract (land sales contract or purchase money trust deed). Of course, even where the seller carries a second or a contract, the seller could still cash out by selling the second or the contract to a third party. Because these techniques are very common in real estate practice, we will discuss them in detail.

We will also look into other alternative financing concepts such as equity sharing (equity participation), sweat equity (work credits), equity kickers (shared appreciation), seller refinances, buying with no money down and use of leverage in real estate investment, ways in which investments can be syndicated, and sale-leaseback arrangements. From time to time all of these can be useful concepts in real estate transactions.

Seller carried financing

When the seller wishes to carry paper, whether it is a mortgage, trust deed or land sales contract, or a junior lien such as a second trust deed, the first and most obvious issue to address is whether or not there is an underlying loan. If there is an underlying loan, you must scrutinize it carefully to see if it has a ***due on sale*** clause (also sometimes called an ***alienation*** clause).

A due on sale clause, as the term would imply, allows the lender to accelerate (call the loan due in full) if the seller (original borrower) should convey title to the property. To keep a seller from getting around a due on sale clause, lenders today phrase the clause to prohibit sales on land sales contracts, options and long term leaseholds as well as transactions where fee title is conveyed.

What kinds of loans have due on sale clauses? Most (but not by any means all) conventional loans have due on sale clauses. For FHA loans, however, the rules vary. If the loan was taken out prior to December 1, 1986, there is no due on sale clause. For loans made after December 1, 1986 there is a due on sale clause, but it can only be used to force the new buyer to meet credit approval and to take personal liability for the debt. Federal Department of Veterans Affairs loans had no due on sale clause until March, 1988. Loans made after March, 1988 have a due on sale clause. But as with FHA loans, the lender cannot use the due on sale clause to force an increase in the interest rate — only to require the buyer to be approved and qualify for the loan, and to take personal liability for it. As for private trust deeds and land sales contracts, you will find that most contain a due on sale clause, but many do not. As you can see, whether or not a loan has a due on sale clause is complicated. In most cases, the best approach is to obtain a copy of the financing documents every time you take a listing, and read them carefully.

Of course, the advantage of a loan which does not have a due on sale clause is that it allows the seller greater flexibility in selling the property. This is particularly true if the interest rate on the seller's old loan is below market, as we shall see later.

Even when the loan does not contain a due on sale clause, the buyer must consider the difference between taking title to the property subject to the encumbrance or taking title subject to the encumbrance and assuming and agreeing to pay it (***assumption***). If the buyer takes title subject to the encumbrance, and also enters into an ***assumption agreement*** with the lender, then the buyer has agreed to be personally obligated for the debt. Whether the buyer assumes or not, the seller is not relieved of the responsibility to pay (unless there is a novation), so the only issue is whether the buyer would also become personally obligated. Becoming "personally obligated" means that the lender can reach all the buyer's assets in the event that a foreclosure sale does not yield enough to satisfy the obligation. If the lender chooses to sue on the note, ignoring the collateral, again only the seller would be obligated unless the buyer has assumed the debt. A novation, of course, extinguishes the seller's liability. These concepts are covered in more detail in the section, Documents of Real Estate Finance.

The following chart will help clarify the issue of which party is normally liable when a buyer takes over a seller's old loan —

Lender remedy	Assumption	No Assumption	Novation
Foreclose on the collateral	Yes	Yes	Yes
Deficiency judgment against buyer	Yes	No	Yes
Deficiency judgment against seller	Yes	Yes	No
Judgment on note against the buyer	Yes	No	Yes
Judgment on note against the seller	Yes	Yes	No

Many real estate agents feel that it is in the seller's best interest for the buyer to take title subject to the seller's old loan and also assume it. Since the seller is not relieved of liability, this is of questionable value to the seller. The only course which would really benefit the seller is a novation, which lenders generally will not agree to. On the contrary, lenders will attempt to insist on an assumption whenever possible, since they gain an additional person obligated to pay the debt.

Now let us look at some actual cases. Assume that you have a seller who has listed a house for $200,000 and there is an assumable loan in the amount of $100,000. The loan is at 6% fixed rate and has 20 years remaining at monthly payments of 716.43. But suppose the market rate for such loans has risen and would be closer to 9% today. Suppose further that you have a buyer for this house and that the buyer has $20,000 cash for a down payment. For various reasons, the buyer wishes to ask the seller to carry the financing for the $80,000 difference between the balance of the underlying loan, and the balance after the down payment (180,000 − $100,000 = $80,000). The seller is to carry the balance as a second trust deed at 10% interest with a 15-year amortization and monthly payments of 859.69, with a balloon payment (payoff) at seven years –

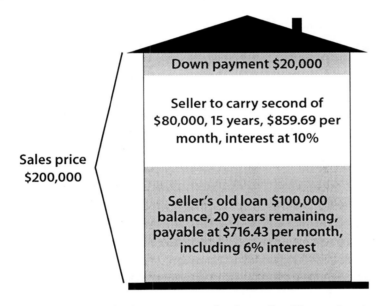

Sales price $200,000

Down payment $20,000

Seller to carry second of $80,000, 15 years, $859.69 per month, interest at 10%

Seller's old loan $100,000 balance, 20 years remaining, payable at $716.43 per month, including 6% interest

There are several ways the buyer can make this offer. The easiest is to have the buyer take title subject to the seller's old loan (assume it or not), and have the seller carry a second trust deed for $80,000, as shown above. The repayment terms on the second trust deed can be as creative as you wish. You can create –
- Adjustable interest rates, tied to an index, with or without caps
- Interest only, for a period of time or for the life of the loan
- Graduated (escalating) payments, with or without negative amortization
- Balloon payments (refinance clause)
- Different interest rates on different portions of the loan
- Additional real or personal property as collateral (blanket or package trust deed)

In short, you can be as creative with the second trust deed as required in order to reach an agreement between the parties.

A popular alternative is for the seller to carry the entire balance ($180,000) on a land sales contract or trust deed. In this case the buyer will write one check to the seller for the principal and interest on the $180,000 contract, and the seller will continue to make the payments on the old loan. In our first example the buyer took over the seller's old loan, so the buyer would be writing two checks every month – one to the seller on the $80,000 second and one to the bank on the $100,000 loan. Suppose the seller carries a contract or trust deed on the balance of $180,000 at 8% for 30 years, with a balloon payment (payoff) at seven years – then the transaction would look like this –

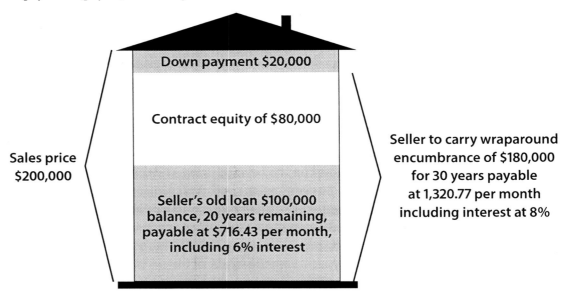

In the above example, notice that the balance of the contract ($180,000) includes the seller's old loan ($100,000). The buyer did not take over the seller's old loan in this case. Since the seller is carrying a contract or trust deed which encompasses the underlying loan, this is called a **wraparound** encumbrance, or just "wrap loan" for short.

Wraparound loans are sometimes better for both the buyer and the seller. The seller can offer a lower interest rate and still receive a good return because the seller is re-lending the underlying loan to the buyer. In the preceding example, the seller borrowed the underlying $100,000 from the bank at 6% interest, and is now re-lending it to the buyer at 8%. The 2% difference in rates is pure profit to the seller, which effectively raises the yield on the wraparound loan. The following chart demonstrates the seller's first year yield on the $80,000 contract equity –

First year interest income on $180,000
(Calculated with a financial calculator) $14,345.66
Less first year interest paid on $100,000
(Calculated with a financial calculator)   5,727.51
Net profit $8,618.15
Profit ÷ Investment = Yield
$8,618.15 ÷ $80,000 = 10.77%

Note that the seller's investment is $80,000 whether the seller carries a second (first example) or a wraparound (second example). But in the first example, the seller's yield is just the rate on the second (10%), where the wraparound increases the seller's yield to 10.77% because the seller gets the 2% override between the first and the contract.

At the same time that the wraparound increases the seller's yield, it is easy to structure it so that the buyer's monthly payment is the same, or even less. If the seller carries a second trust deed (first example), the seller will typically want the repayment to be fairly fast – which tends to make the buyer's monthly payment high. In our example above, the buyer's total payments will be $1,576.12 ($716.43 on the first and 859.69 on the second). But in a wraparound transaction (second example), the seller is usually more amenable to longer repayment terms, so the buyer's total payment can be lower. In our example of the $180,000 wraparound at 8% with 30-year amortization the payment is only $1,320.78 – $255.34 lower.

Both examples require a few extra considerations. If the buyer takes over the seller's old loan and the seller carries a second (first example), then the buyer is in control of the first loan. The seller needs protection to ensure that the buyer will keep the underlying loan current. After all, a foreclosure of the underlying loan will extinguish the seller's second trust deed. Therefore, it is common practice for the seller to record a **request for notice of default**. A request for notice of default requires the underlying lender to notify the seller in the event of a default, so the seller can take steps to bring the first current and avoid a foreclosure. The second trust deed must also have a clause stipulating that a default on the first will also be considered a default on the second.

In the wraparound transaction (second example) there are different considerations. Now the seller retains control of the underlying loan, so the buyer needs protection to ensure that the seller will keep it current. A typical wraparound instrument provides that the seller will keep the first current, and if the seller fails to do so, the buyer can make the payments due on the first and deduct the sums so paid from the amounts due on the wraparound.

The buyer would also want to be sure that the seller did not pay off the underlying loan any faster than required. Since the interest rate on the first is below market, the buyer would like the option of paying the seller the balance of the wraparound down to the balance of the underlying loan, and then taking over the underlying loan. If the seller pays off the underlying loan ahead of schedule, the buyer will be denied this benefit.

Selling paper

Many times a seller will need to carry paper from a buyer, but need to raise more cash in the transaction than the buyer is giving as down payment. For example, in either of the two preceding examples, the seller will receive only $4,000 to $6,000 out of the buyer's $20,000 down payment after deductions for a commission, title insurance, escrow fees and other closing expenses. If the cash normally generated by the transaction is not sufficient for the seller's needs, the seller could generate additional cash by selling the paper to an investor.

Investors might pay face value (par) for the paper, but more commonly it is sold at a discount. To calculate the discount, investors start with the yield they desire. Seasoned paper (paper with a good payment history) is more desirable than green paper (brand new paper). Referring to the first of the preceding examples (seller carries a second trust deed for $80,000), assume that the investor wants a yield of 14%. The $80,000 second trust deed was written at 10% interest with a 15-year amortization and the monthly payments were $859.69.

Now, to calculate what an investor would pay for this second trust deed, just use an amortization chart or financial calculator to find out what could be the principal balance of a loan with 180 payments (15 years) of $859.69 at 14% interest. This is the present value of the second trust deed to an investor who wants a 14% yield. The answer is $64,553.82. In other words, the investor will buy the paper for a discount of $15,446.18 ($80,000.00 − $64,553.82.= $15,446.18).

Of course, the preceding calculation does not take into account the fact that the second trust deed has a balloon payoff at seven years. Using a financial calculator or a loan amortization chart, you can find the payoff at the end of seven years (the 84th payment) to be $45,969.05. In this case an investor would make two calculations in order to decide how much to pay for the paper. The first would be similar to the preceding case, except that the investor would assume a loan of 83 payments of $859.69 at 14% interest (we have to use 83 payments because the 84th payment is the balloon). The principal balance of such a loan would be $45,550.08, so that is what the investor would be willing to pay for the 83 payments.

The investor would make a separate calculation for the value of the balloon payment. To calculate it, the investor must calculate what amount would have to be put on deposit if the interest rate is 14%, compounded monthly, and the deposit is to mature to $45,969.05. Using a financial calculator or present value (present worth) table, you can calculate this to be $17,350.84. Therefore, the investor would pay for this paper –

Present value of 83 payments of $859.69 at 14% yield	$45,550.08
Present value of balloon payment of $45,969.05 at 14% yield	17,350.84
Total value of $80,000 second	$62,900.92

Note that the total value comes to slightly less than the example without the balloon. The interesting point, however, is that the seller could sell to the investor a participation in the paper by selling just the payments (for $45,550.08) or just the balloon (for $17,350.84). Or any other participation could be sold. The seller could also simply borrow money from the investor and pledge the paper as collateral for the loan.

Calculating what an investor would pay for a wraparound loan is more complicated. In a wraparound loan, the benefits are the difference between the payments and the interest rate difference. In the wraparound loan above (second example), the buyer is scheduled to make 360 payments of $1,320.78 to amortize the $180,000 balance at 8% interest. If an investor buys the loan, the investor will receive these payments. But the investor will also have to make the payments on the underlying loan. The underlying loan has a remaining term of 20 years (240 payments) at 6%, and the monthly payments on it are $716.43. Considering that our example has a balloon at seven years (the same as the first example), the balloon will pay off both the wraparound loan and the underlying first. Therefore, the investor will calculate the benefit of receiving the difference between $1,320.78 and $716.43 (which is $604.35) for 83 payments, and then add the present value of the net amount received in the balloon. Using a financial calculator, the calculation would look like this –

Present value of 83 payments of $604.35 at 14% yield		$32,021.07
Payoff amount on wraparound loan at 84th month	$166,458.97	
Less payoff amount on underlying first in 84th month	$77,475.28	
	88,983.69	
Present value of 88,983.69 received in 84th period at 14% yield		33,586.55
Total value of wraparound		$65,607.62

Note that the amount which can be realized from the sale of the wraparound loan is greater than for the second trust deed. This is simply because the wraparound had a higher yield (10.77%) than the second (10.00%), therefore the discount is less.

Exercise a

A buyer cannot take over a seller's old loan if the loan has a _____ _____ _____ clause (also called an _____ clause). If the buyer is to take over the seller's old loan, then the buyer will take the title _____ _____ the encumbrance. The buyer may also _____ the loan, in which case the buyer will become personally obligated to pay it. Only if the lender agrees to a _____ will the seller be relieved of liability.

A seller could carry a portion of the balance either on a contract or trust deed encompassing the underlying loan (called a _____ loan), or the seller could carry a junior lien, such as a _____ trust deed. Typically, the _____ arrangement results in a higher _____ to the seller, especially if the underlying loan is at a rate which is below market. If the seller wishes to sell the paper, the investor will usually offer to buy it at a _____ in order to raise the investor's yield.

Shared appreciation loans

A common technique in commercial lending, the concept of a ***shared appreciation*** loan is also possible in residential financing. (A shared appreciation loan is also sometimes referred to as a loan which has an ***equity kicker.***) In a shared appreciation loan, the lender agrees to an interest rate or other terms which are less than market, in exchange for a share in the future appreciation in market value. For example, if interest rates are about 8%, a lender might agree to lend at only 6%, if the borrower will agree to pay one-half the first five years' appreciation in market value to the lender.

In this example, the amount of the first five years' appreciation could be determined at the end of the five years either by a sale of the property, or by an appraisal. If the borrower wished to keep both the property and the loan at the end of the five years, the amount of appreciation, as determined by the appraisal, could be added to the principal balance. The exact terms of a shared appreciation loan will be different for each transaction.

Shared appreciation loans are common in commercial settings where market interest rates might be too high to make a project financially feasible. A lower interest rate might make it possible for the project to proceed. In residential financing, shared appreciation loans are most common with seller financing. A seller may feel there is great potential for future appreciation, and therefore be reluctant to sell. Having the seller carry a shared appreciation loan can be a useful tool in this situation. Institutional lenders, however, do not make residential shared appreciation loans because there is no secondary market for them.

Equity sharing loans

Because they are similar, many people get the terms "shared appreciation" (discussed above) and "equity sharing" confused. An ***equity sharing*** loan (also sometimes called ***equity participation***) is an arrangement where a buyer teams up with an investor to buy the property together. Using the investor's money, the pair can cash out the seller.

Understanding an equity sharing loan may be easier with an example. Let us suppose you wish to buy a property for $200,000 and you only have $5,000 for a down payment and closing costs. Since this is not enough for most ordinary loan programs, you approach an investor to become your partner in the purchase. The investor will put up $195,000 and you will put up the other $5,000.

At closing you and the investor will become tenants in common. By separate agreement, you will have the right of possession, but also the responsibility to pay for all maintenance. When you go to sell the property, the investor will become entitled to a predetermined percentage share of the appreciation. It is also common for the buyer to make some small monthly payment to the investor, in which case the investor will be entitled to a lesser share of the potential appreciation. The exact terms, of course, are worked out by negotiation between the parties.

In an equity sharing arrangement it is also common for the parties to obtain outside financing. In our preceding example, your $5,000 would be inadequate as down payment for practically any kind of outside loan. But if the investor would add $35,000 (plus some additional amount for closing costs) you would jointly have $40,000 for a down payment. This would allow you to get an 80% conventional loan. You would still become tenants in common, but you would also become co-borrowers on the new loan. Of course, you and the investor would have a separate agreement as to which of you would make the payments (typically, you), perform maintenance (typically, you), and be entitled to possession of the property (typically, you). Again, by negotiation, you and the investor would agree to share the potential appreciation.

Seller refinances

Either as a separate technique, or in conjunction with other financing, the seller could refinance the property prior to the sale. The buyer can then assume the seller's loan. The refinance could be either a new first trust deed or it could be junior financing. Regardless of how the seller refinances, the seller will receive a substantial portion of the equity in cash as loan proceeds. The advantage is that the seller is now in a better position to accept a low down payment from the buyer. The disadvantage of the refinance is that the lender(s) will probably not permit the buyer to take over the seller's loan(s).

However, there are cases where this technique may be useful. Again, an illustration may help to make things understandable. Suppose the seller has a commercial property which is in need of substantial rehabilitation, although it has a current market value of $500,000. There is a buyer who wishes to rehabilitate the property, but does not have any significant amount of cash to put into the transaction, although the buyer would agree to a $100,000 down payment if the cash for it were available.

Here's how the sale could be structured. First, the seller refinances the property for 50% of its market value ($250,000). To do this, go to a commercial lender, not a residential lender. Arrange the loan as a short term loan, which means that the seller should be able to get the lender to agree to waive the typical due on sale clause for at least one subsequent sale. Suppose the proceeds of the refinance (after loan fees and other costs) equals $242,000. The loan proceeds are disbursed to the escrow where the property is being sold to the buyer. Out of the $242,000 loan proceeds, the escrow will disburse $100,000 to the seller as "down payment." The escrow will retain the other $142,000 for the buyer.

The buyer will buy the property for a sales price of $750,000 ($500,000 market value, plus the new encumbrance of $250,000). The buyer will buy on a contract with a balance of $650,000 after the "down payment" of $100,000. The buyer will submit bills for the rehabilitation to the escrow for payment out of the $142,000. When the buyer has finished rehabilitating the property, the buyer can either sell it or refinance it in order to cash out the seller's refinance loan and the contract balance.

Notice how this transaction allowed the seller to gain $100,000 of equity in cash immediately, yet allowed the buyer to obtain the property and rehabilitation expenses with no cash up front. However, there is a grave danger for the seller if the transaction does not leave the $142,000 in the escrow. If the $142,000 is disbursed to the buyer directly, there is the possibility that the buyer could simply leave town with it, never to be seen again. For the seller's protection it is imperative that the funds remain in the escrow to be disbursed only as the rehabilitation proceeds.

Leverage

In real estate investment **leverage** is a tool which can greatly multiply an investor's return. Leverage (also sometimes called **trading on the equity**) is the practice of buying a property with as little cash as possible, then reaping great profit when the property increases in dollar value.

Let us take two examples to illustrate this principle. Assume you have $200,000 cash to invest. In both examples, assume that you invest the $200,000 in real estate and hold the real estate for 10 years. During the ten years, assume a 5% per annum inflation in property value. In the first example, you will use no leverage. In the second example, you will buy with moderately high leverage.

In Example 1, you buy a duplex for $200,000 cash. The monthly rent is $1,000 per unit, but the taxes and insurance are $4,000 per year. Maintenance and other expenses total $5,000 additional per year. Assuming no change in income or expenses, your return on investment would look like this –

Income: $1,000 × 2 units × 12 months × 10 years	$240,000	
Less tax and ins., $4,000 × 10 years	40,000	
Less other expenses, $5,000 × 10 years	50,000	
Income net of expenses		$150,000
Sales price on resale, @ 5% per annum inflation	300,000	
Less original invested amount	200,000	
Profit on resale		100,000
Total net profit		$250,000

$250,000 profit is for ten years; average annual profit is $25,000.
Original investment is $200,000
Profit ÷ Investment = Yield
$25,000 ÷ $200,000 = **12.5%** average annual return on investment

In Example 2, you use the $200,000 to buy ten duplexes identical to the duplex in Example 1, making a down payment of $20,000 on each and financing the balance of $180,000 at a bank at 8% interest. All other considerations remain the same. Your investment would now look like this –

Income: $1,000 × 20 units × 12 months × 10 years	$2,400,000	
Less tax and ins., $4,000 × 10 duplexes × 10 years	400,000	
Less other expenses, $5,000 × 10 duplexes × 10 years	500,000	
Less interest on loans for 10 years	1,363,974	
Income net of expenses		$136,026
Plus sales price on resale, @ 5% per annum inflation	3,000,000	
Less loan balance on payoff	1,579,038	
Less original invested amount	200,000	
Net profit on resale		1,220,962
Total Profit		$1,356,988

$1,356,988 profit is for ten years; average annual profit is $135,699.
Original investment is $200,000
Profit ÷ Investment = Yield
$135,699 ÷ $200,000 = **67.85%** average annual return on investment

Notice that use of leverage can make a vast improvement in the investor's return. The reason for the increase in return is that the interest on the bank loan is 8%, but the net operating income from the investment is an even greater return. In other words, if you have an investment that you are reasonably certain will produce a certain rate of return, then it makes sense to borrow the money to acquire the investment, as long as the cost of the borrowed money is less than the anticipated return on the investment.

Investors who use the leverage principle frequently **pyramid** their investment. Pyramiding simply means cashing out of the investment, and immediately reinvesting the profits in another, larger investment, using leverage again. In Example 2 above, the investor started with $200,000, but when the duplexes were sold, realized an immediate cash flow of $1,207,924 (sales price of $3,000,000 less loan payoff of $1,592,075 = $1,207,924). Using leverage, the investor should be able to use that $1,207,924 to buy 50, 60 or more units.

Of course, there is a downside to leverage. In the preceding examples, a significant portion of the income the properties generated was in the increased market value on re-sale. What would have happened if there had been no inflation? Or worse yet, what if the properties had declined in dollar value over the ten-year holding period? The answer is simple. The investor would make little return, or possibly suffer a serious loss.

In fact, if the dollar value of the properties is not increasing, then it is likely that economic conditions are generally poor and there is a high vacancy factor in the rental market. This means that the leveraged investor will not be able to make the loan payments, and will likely lose the entire investment in a foreclosure. The non-leveraged investor, on the other hand, will be able to weather the storm and hold out for better days. Therefore, while leverage is usually the investor's friend, in a down market, it can be the investors undoing. Each investor should tailor an investment to his or her personal situation and accept only that amount of risk which the investor can comfortably handle.

Buying with nothing down

The less the down payment, the greater the leverage, so buying with nothing down is the ultimate in leverage. Of course, as we noted above, the greater the leverage, the greater the risk, especially for the lender. Still, buying with nothing down may be the right decision in certain cases.

Today we have television real estate gurus who promise to teach us how to get rich in real estate. Their most popular technique is to buy with nothing down and reap the rewards of leverage. But transactions with no down payment are difficult to structure. Nevertheless, since real estate agents encounter such offers, let us look at some practices which can make a "nothing down" transaction more attractive.

Since the party with the greatest risk is the lender, let us look first at ways the lender can be protected. When the buyer puts nothing down, the lender is most likely to be the seller, so we will assume that it is a purchase money financing arrangement. How then, can the seller gain better protection? A lender's position is enhanced by additional sources for repayment. The two traditional sources are the borrower's income, or a sale of the property itself. Therefore, co-signature(s) or additional collateral, or both, would enhance the lender's position. For first-time buyers on a residential sale, co-signatures of relatives is the usual solution. For seasoned investors, additional collateral is more likely.

Looking at a "nothing down" transaction from the borrower's viewpoint, there is also significant risk. The borrower needs protection from the possibility that property values will decrease. A borrower will therefore want to include a **sole collateral** clause in the financing documents. A sole collateral clause states that the property is the sole collateral and the lender cannot obtain a judgment against the borrower, even if the property is sold at a sheriff's or trustee's sale and fails to realize enough to cover the debt.

Negotiating between these opposing interests and desires is what makes it difficult to put together a "nothing down" transaction. In spite of this, most real estate agents can tell you about cases where a "nothing down" sale made sense for the parties involved.

Sweat equity

A time-honored alternative for a down payment is for the buyer to perform work on the property and receive credit for the work. Officially, this is called a **work credit**, but everyone calls it **sweat equity**.

Many lenders recognize a work credit, and FHA even has a formal program. Most lenders, however, prefer not to make such loans because they involve a great deal of extra work. Another problem with a work credit is that the borrower, the seller and the lender have frequent disputes over the quality of the work done and the timeliness with which the buyer completed it. Nevertheless, a property which is run-down is a likely candidate for a work credit financing arrangement, particularly when economic conditions are poor.

Sale-leasebacks

A financing technique which is common in commercial transactions is the **sale-leaseback**. A sale-leaseback is exactly what the term would imply — the seller sells the property (usually to cash out), and then leases the property back from the buyer. The sale-leaseback allows an owner to obtain cash for all the equity in the property, yet retain possession.

In commercial transactions the sale-leaseback is popular, particularly with retailers. A department store wants a building constructed exactly to their specifications, yet wants to use their available capital for merchandise and promotion, not tie it up in the real estate. Therefore, they will build the store, and immediately turn around and sell it to an investor, while leasing it back on a long term lease.

A sale-leaseback transaction is especially valuable in a commercial transaction because the lease payments are a deductible business expense. Ownership of the real estate also produces a tax benefit in the form of cost recovery, but only on the improvements; the Internal Revenue Code does not allow cost recovery on the land. And the investor also gains because there is an assured rate of return from a creditworthy payer.

Syndicates

Many people think that a **syndication** is a type of business organization, the way a corporation is a specific type of legal entity. However, this is not true. The term "syndication" (or "syndicate") merely means any investment in a common enterprise. The vehicle for the syndication is commonly a limited partnership, although when the purpose of the investment is to acquire real estate, a simple tenancy in common is also frequently used. Today, the limited liability company is also popular.

For tax reasons, the corporate form of ownership is not as common for ownership of real estate, although Subchapter S corporations are sometimes encountered. Syndicates are frequently created to provide financing for large commercial projects. Real estate agents should be aware that when the syndicate is a passive investment, it is probably subject to registration and regulation as a security.

The most important consideration in choosing the form of organization is income tax liability. A regular corporation must pay income taxes, and when the after-tax profits are distributed to the investors, they are taxed yet again. To avoid this double taxation, investors could choose to be a Subchapter S corporation. Subchapter S corporations pay no income taxes, so the tax liability (or tax benefit in the case of real property investments) is passed through to the investors. Limited liability companies offer the same pass-through tax benefits, and have some additional flexibility in the number of investors that can be allowed.

Exercise b

In a _____ _____ loan the lender agrees to a below-market interest rate, in exchange for which the borrower agrees to share a portion of the anticipated future _____ in dollar value with the lender. Another term for this arrangement is an _____ _____ . In an equity sharing loan, the borrower and the lender become _____ - _____ in the property and also typically become joint borrowers on the loan. Another technique, commonly used on properties which need rehabilitation is for the seller to _____ the property and then sell it to the buyer, letting the buyer have a portion of the proceeds from the _____ loan in order to make repairs to the property.

In real estate finance, leverage is also called _____ on the _____ . In this situation, the borrower makes a small _____ _____ so as to be able to buy as much property as possible. As the property increases in dollar value, the total investment becomes valuable and the rate of return is enhanced. Leverage is excellent when dollar values of property are _____ , but can be a disaster when dollar values of properties are _____ . The ultimate in leverage is buying with _____ _____ .

A common term for a work credit is _____ _____ .

In commercial transactions, when an owner wishes to obtain all cash for the equity in the property, yet retain possession, the owner should consider a _____ - _____ .

A _____ is a group which is formed for a common business purpose. In real estate transactions, the most common kind is a _____ _____ , although purchases of small investment properties are also made as _____ in _____ . A newer form of organization is the _____ _____ company. The advantage of some types of organizations is that _____ benefits and liabilities are passed directly through to the investors.

🔑 KEY TERMS

The key to understanding any new field is the vocabulary used in that field. To maximize your comprehension of the material presented in this chapter, be sure you know the meaning and significance of the following terms. Remember that the majority of test questions primarily test knowledge of vocabulary.

Alienation clause	Equity sharing
Assumption	Leverage
Assumption agreement	Pyramid
Due on sale clause	Request for notice of default
Equity participation loan	Sale-leaseback
Equity kicker	Shared appreciation loan

Sole collateral clause

Sweat equity

Syndication

Trading on the equity

Work credit

Wraparound loan

ANSWERS

To chapter exercises. If you couldn't figure out what to put in the blanks, find the answer here!

Exercise a

A buyer cannot take over a seller's old loan if the loan has a ___DUE___ ___ON___ ___SALE___ clause (also called an ___ALIENATION___ clause). If the buyer is to take over the seller's old loan, then the buyer will take the title ___SUBJECT___ ___TO___ the encumbrance. The buyer may also ___ASSUME___ the loan, in which case the buyer will become personally obligated to pay it. Only if the lender agrees to a ___NOVATION___ will the seller be relieved of liability.

A seller could carry a portion of the balance either on a contract or trust deed encompassing the underlying loan (called a ___WRAPAROUND___ loan), or the seller could carry a junior lien, such as a ___SECOND___ trust deed. Typically, the ___WRAPAROUND___ arrangement results in a higher ___YIELD___ to the seller, especially if the underlying loan is at a rate which is below market. If the seller wishes to sell the paper, the investor will usually offer to buy it at a ___DISCOUNT___ in order to raise the investor's yield.

Exercise b

In a ___SHARED___ ___APPRECIATION___ loan the lender agrees to a below-market interest rate, in exchange for which the borrower agrees to share a portion of the anticipated future ___APPRECIATION___ in dollar value with the lender. Another term for this arrangement is an ___EQUITY___ ___KICKER___. In an equity sharing loan, the borrower and the lender become ___CO___-___TENANTS___ in the property and also typically become joint borrowers on the loan. Another technique, commonly used on properties which need rehabilitation is for the seller to ___REFINANCE___ the property and then sell it to the buyer, letting the buyer have a portion of the proceeds from the ___REFINANCE___ loan in order to make repairs to the property.

In real estate finance, leverage is also called ___TRADING___ on the ___EQUITY___. In this situation, the borrower makes a small ___DOWN___ ___PAYMENT___ so as to be able to buy as much property as possible. As the property increases in dollar value, the total investment becomes valuable and the rate of return is enhanced. Leverage is excellent when dollar values of property are ___INCREASING___, but can be a disaster when dollar values of properties are ___DECREASING___. The ultimate in leverage is buying with ___NOTHING___ ___DOWN___.

A common term for a work credit is ___SWEAT___ ___EQUITY___.

In commercial transactions, when an owner wishes to obtain all cash for the equity in the property, yet retain possession, the owner should consider a ___SALE___-___LEASEBACK___.

A ___SYNDICATE___ is a group which is formed for a common business purpose. In real estate transactions, the most common kind is a ___LIMITED___ ___PARTNERSHIP___, although purchases of small investment properties are also made as ___TENANTS___ in ___COMMON___. A newer form of organization is the ___LIMITED___ ___LIABILITY___ company. The advantage of some types of organizations is that ___TAX___ benefits and liabilities are passed directly through to the investors.

Amortization Chart

This chart shows the monthly payment for a loan of $1,000 at varying interest rates for one to 30 years. For loans greater than $1,000, multiply the factor below by the number of thousands in the loan. For example, a $258,000 loan at 7% interest for 30 years would use the factor $6.65. This is the amount for a $1,000 loan, so for a $258,000 loan, multiply by 258. The payment is therefore $1,715.70 ($6.65 × 258 = $1,715.70).

Years	6%	7%	8%	9%	10%	11%	12%	13%	14%	15%
1	86.06	86.53	86.99	87.45	87.92	88.38	88.49	89.32	89.79	90.26
2	44.32	44.77	45.23	45.68	46.15	46.61	47.07	47.54	48.01	48.49
3	30.42	30.88	31.34	31.80	32.27	32.74	33.21	33.69	34.18	34.67
4	23.49	23.95	24.41	24.89	25.36	25.85	26.33	26.83	27.33	27.83
5	19.33	19.80	20.28	20.76	21.25	21.74	22.24	22.75	23.27	23.79
6	16.57	17.05	17.53	18.03	18.53	19.03	19.55	20.07	20.61	21.15
7	14.61	15.09	15.59	16.09	16.60	17.12	17.65	18.19	18.74	19.30
8	13.14	13.63	14.14	14.65	15.17	15.71	16.25	16.80	17.37	17.95
9	12.01	12.51	13.01	13.54	14.08	14.63	15.18	15.75	16.33	16.92
10	11.10	11.61	12.13	12.67	13.22	13.78	14.35	14.93	15.53	16.13
11	10.37	10.88	11.42	11.96	12.52	13.09	13.68	14.28	14.87	15.51
12	9.76	10.28	10.82	11.38	11.95	12.54	13.13	13.75	14.37	15.01
13	9.25	9.78	10.33	10.90	11.48	12.08	12.69	13.31	13.95	14.60
14	8.81	9.35	9.91	10.49	11.08	11.69	12.31	12.95	13.60	14.27
15	8.44	8.99	9.55	10.14	10.75	11.37	12.00	12.65	13.32	14.00
16	8.11	8.67	9.25	9.85	10.46	11.09	11.74	12.40	13.08	13.77
17	7.83	8.40	8.98	9.59	10.21	10.85	11.51	12.19	12.87	13.58
18	7.58	8.16	8.75	9.36	10.00	10.65	11.32	12.00	12.70	13.42
19	7.36	7.94	8.55	9.17	9.81	10.47	11.15	11.85	12.56	13.28
20	7.16	7.75	8.36	9.00	9.65	10.32	11.01	11.72	12.44	13.17
21	6.99	7.58	8.20	8.85	9.51	10.19	10.87	11.60	12.33	13.07
22	6.83	7.43	8.06	8.71	9.34	10.07	10.78	11.50	12.24	12.99
23	6.69	7.30	7.93	8.59	9.27	9.97	10.69	11.42	12.17	12.92
24	6.56	7.18	7.82	8.49	9.17	9.88	10.60	11.34	12.10	12.86
25	6.44	7.07	7.72	8.39	9.09	9.80	10.53	11.28	12.04	12.81
26	6.34	6.97	7.63	8.31	9.01	9.73	10.47	11.22	11.99	12.76
27	6.24	6.88	7.54	8.23	8.94	9.67	10.41	11.17	11.95	12.73
28	6.15	6.80	7.47	8.16	8.88	9.61	10.37	11.13	11.91	12.70
29	6.07	6.72	7.40	8.10	8.82	9.57	10.32	11.09	11.88	12.67
30	6.00	6.65	7.34	8.05	8.78	9.52	10.29	11.06	11.85	12.64

In times past real estate agents carried around small booklets of loan amortization tables, similar to the chart above, but broken down by quarters of a percent. Today, agents simply use an inexpensive financial calculator. For beginners, the Texas Instruments BA-35 is one of the most popular. The keystrokes to compute the monthly payment necessary for a $258,000 loan at 7% for 30 years on the BA-35 are –

258,000 **PV** 7 **2nd** **%i** (hit the **%i** key twice) 30 **2nd** **N** (hit the **N** key twice) **CPT** **PMT**

Display – 1,716.48

Note that the answer from the calculator is a few cents off from the results by using the chart. The reason is because the figures in the chart are rounded to the nearest cent, whereas the calculator holds the decimal to many places of accuracy. The factor used above for a 7% loan of 30 years is given as $6.65 in the chart, but the calculator uses the whole decimal – $6.653024953.

The nice thing about the financial calculator is that it allows quick what-if scenarios. If the client asks what the payment would be if the interest rate were 8% instead of 7%, all you have to do is enter the new percentage rate, then hit **CPT** **PMT** and the calculator will recalculate the payment. The calculator remembers what was entered in the **%i** and **N** registers.

PRACTICE QUESTIONS

The following practice questions are representative of the questions you will find on the final examination and on the licensing examinations given by the Oregon Real Estate Agency.

1. Property which is subject to a trust deed in Oregon may not be
   I. sold to another if it contains an alienation clause, without risking foreclosure.
   II. further encumbered with a second mortgage or trust deed carried by the seller.
   (A) I only
   (B) II only
   (C) Both I and II
   (D) Neither I nor II

2. A buyer wishes to take over the seller's old mortgage loan. However, the seller does not wish to remain primarily responsible for making the payments. The seller should insist that the buyer
   (A) take title subject to the mortgage.
   (B) take title subject to the mortgage and assume and agree to pay it.
   (C) purchase the property on a land sales contract.
   (D) agree to a subrogation clause in the contract.

3. A seller sold a property "subject to" the existing mortgage. This means that
   (A) the buyer is now personally obligated to pay the debt.
   (B) the lender's rights to foreclose remain unchanged.
   (C) both A and B above are true.
   (D) neither A nor B above is true.

4. A buyer took title to a property "subject to" the existing trust deed loan. The buyer's greatest risk is
   (A) loss of the buyer's equity in the property.
   (B) the possibility that the lender could sue for specific performance.
   (C) the possibility of a deficiency judgment.
   (D) This creates no risk because the buyer did not assume the loan.

5. Fritz bought a house and obtained a conventional loan in the process. A few years later he sold the house to Fratz "subject to" the existing loan. Fratz subsequently defaulted on the loan. If the lender forecloses and there is a deficit, the lender can collect the deficit from
   (A) Fritz only.
   (B) Fratz only.
   (C) both Fritz and Fratz.
   (D) neither Fritz nor Fratz.

6. A seller sold a property and carried back a trust deed. The trust deed was junior to and included an existing mortgage lien. We would call this trust deed
   (A) a land sales contract.
   (B) a wraparound loan.
   (C) an equity participation loan.
   (D) a collateral trust bond.

7. Theo Thornhump bought a house and obtained a 75% conventional loan. The seller took back a trust deed for an additional 20% of the purchase price. The trust deed the seller carried is called
   (A) a package trust deed.
   (B) a blanket mortgage.
   (C) junior financing.
   (D) a wraparound or all-inclusive trust deed.

8. The main advantage of a wraparound loan is that the
   (A) lender's overall interest rate can be lower than the prevailing market rate for new loans.
   (B) buyer is willing to pay a higher overall rate than the prevailing market rate for new loans.
   (C) originator of a wraparound loan is the holder of the first position encumbrance.
   (D) due on sale clause will not be triggered by a wraparound loan.

9. A "seasoned" loan means that the
   (A) loan has been in default for some time.
   (B) loan was made some time ago and the borrower has paid as agreed.
   (C) loan was made during a time of peak interest rates.
   (D) payments on the loan are current and there is no default.

10. In a shared appreciation loan, the borrower agrees to pay the lender
    (A) the principal balance of the loan.
    (B) the interest on the principal balance per the terms of the note.
    (C) a portion of the equity in the property after some stipulated period of time.
    (D) all of the above.

11. A lender making a large commercial loan agreed to reduce the interest by 1% in return for a 10% interest in the future appreciation in the market value of the property. This would be called
    (A) a participation loan.
    (B) an equity kicker.
    (C) a package loan.
    (D) an open end mortgage.

12. A lender agreed that an investor could be a co-owner and co-borrower with the party who would occupy the property. This is a
    (A) leasehold mortgage. (C) closed end loan.
    (B) shared equity loan.   (D) shut end loan.

13. The Church of the Greater Profit needed a low interest loan to buy a church. They obtained a loan which was 1% under the going rate in exchange for giving the bank a 2% ownership interest in the property. This would be called
    (A) a participation loan. (C) an ownership loan.
    (B) an equity kicker loan. (D) a wraparound loan.

14. Which of the following would be the best example of leverage?
    (A) A borrower who borrowed an amount equal to the down payment
    (B) A buyer who borrowed 100% of the purchase price
    (C) A buyer who paid all cash
    (D) A buyer who traded another property for the seller's equity

15. In a sale-leaseback transaction,
    I. the seller of a property retains a possessory estate.
    II. a leasehold estate and a fee estate exist in the property at the same time.
    (A) I only   (C) Both I and II
    (B) II only   (D) Neither I nor II

16. In a purchase and leaseback transaction, the
    I. seller/lessee retains title to the real estate.
    II. buyer/lessor receives possession of the property.
    (A) I only   (C) Both I and II
    (B) II only   (D) Neither I nor II

17. A property owner sold the property and then leased it back from the buyer. To the lessee, the most important advantage of this arrangement is
    (A) reduced expense for maintenance and fewer management problems.
    (B) release of working capital tied up in the equity in the property.
    (C) increased income tax deductions.
    (D) gaining a leasehold interest in the property.

18. In a sale-leaseback transaction, the buyer would be most concerned with the
    (A) location of the property.
    (B) condition of the property.
    (C) seller's depreciated book value of the property.
    (D) financial condition of the seller.

19. Sale and leaseback transactions are a tool used by firms seeking to
    I. release capital for business expansion.
    II. improve their tax position by increasing deductions.
    (A) I only   (C) Both I and II
    (B) II only   (D) Neither I nor II

20. The term "syndicate" could mean the same as
    (A) joint venture.   (C) group enterprise.
    (B) organization.   (D) any of the above.

21. A real estate syndication can be in the form of
    (A) a real estate investment trust.
    (B) a tenancy in common.
    (C) a limited partnership.
    (D) any of the above.

22. The type of organization used for a real estate syndicate is an important part of the investment decision. Which of the following would not be liable for income taxes?
    (A) Subchapter S corporation
    (B) Real estate investment trust
    (C) Limited partnership
    (D) All of the above

23. The pass-through of profits and tax losses to individual investors in an organization is a feature of
    (A) a general partnership.
    (B) a limited partnership.
    (C) a Subchapter S corporation.
    (D) all of the above.

24. When a wraparound loan is made,
    I. this is an example of leverage.
    II. the borrower borrows funds over and above the balance of the existing mortgage.
    (A) I only   (C) Both I and II
    (B) II only   (D) Neither I nor II

25. Refinancing real estate to obtain funds to buy more property would be an example of
    (A) equity funding.
    (B) wraparound lending.
    (C) pyramiding.
    (D) tax-deferred exchanging.

ANSWERS

To practice questions. If you chose the wrong letter, here's the right one! The explanations are designed to clarify your understanding.

1.   **A**   A typical due on sale (alienation) clause allows the lender to accelerate and foreclose if the property is sold to another without the lender's permission. Although a due on sale clause is not considered an unreasonable restraint on the owner's rights, a prohibition on junior financing probably would be. Furthermore, a foreclosure by a senior lienholder extinguishes junior liens, so it is in the lender's best interests if there is junior financing.

2.   **B**   When a borrower signs a note and mortgage (or trust deed), the borrower agrees to pay the debt, even if the property becomes insufficient collateral. This is why lenders are generally allowed to obtain deficiency judgments. When a property subject to a loan is sold and the buyer takes over the seller's old loan, it does not relieve the seller of the obligation to pay. If the buyer assumes the loan, then the buyer also becomes obligated to pay. Although both buyer and seller are fully liable to pay the entire debt, the lender typically looks first to the buyer, and only to the seller in the event the buyer does not pay. A subrogation clause is used in an insurance policy to allow the insurance company to collect from the party who caused the loss, in the event the loss was caused by someone other than the insured.

3.   **B**   When the property is sold without paying off the loan, the buyer always takes title subject to the encumbrance. The buyer does not become personally obligated, however, unless the buyer also assumes and agrees to pay the encumbrance. Even though the buyer did not assume the loan, the lender can always foreclose.

4.   **A**   Specific performance is a remedy under a land sales contract, not normally done in a trust deed. Since the buyer did not assume the loan, the buyer is not personally liable for a deficiency judgment. There is always the risk of foreclosure, which would mean the buyer would lose all equity in the property.

5.   **A**   When a buyer takes title subject to an existing loan, the buyer has no personal responsibility to pay the debt unless the buyer also enters into an assumption agreement. Whether or not the buyer assumes the loan, the seller is still personally liable.

Therefore, the lender can take deficiency judgment only against the seller, not the buyer.

6.   **B**   When the seller owes money on an existing encumbrance which will not be paid off at closing, and the seller will carry additional financing from the buyer, there are two ways this can be structured. First, the buyer could take title subject to the underlying encumbrance and the seller could carry a second mortgage or trust deed for the difference. Or second, the seller could carry a mortgage, trust deed or land sales contract for the entire purchase price less the down payment. The first example is called "carrying a second mortgage (trust deed)" or just "junior financing." The second example is called a wraparound loan.

7.   **C**   Since the amount of the seller's loan was above the underlying loan and did not include it, the loan was a second trust deed, not a wraparound. Since it is in second position to the first, it is junior financing.

8.   **A**   If the seller carries a second the seller's yield will just be the rate at which the second was written. But if the seller carries a wraparound loan the seller will receive the benefit of relending the underlying loan to the buyer, probably at a higher rate. This override in the rate is additional profit to the seller, which effectively raises the seller's yield above the actual rate being charged the buyer. The purpose of a due on sale clause is to prevent the original borrower (seller) from reaping the benefits of the rate differential; therefore due on sale clauses are normally drafted to prohibit a wraparound loan.

9.   **B**   When real estate paper is being sold to an investor, the amount the investor is willing to pay for the paper is determined by the yield the investor demands. The more attractive the paper (less risk), the lower the yield the investor will demand, and therefore, the more the investor will pay for it. Being "seasoned" means that the buyer has made regular payments for a period of time to establish a pattern of prompt payment. When paper is sold at the moment it is created, we call it "green," or unseasoned paper.

10.   **D**   A shared appreciation loan is a loan where the borrower agrees to give the lender a share of the anticipated appreciation in dollar value of the prop-

erty. In exchange, the lender agrees to some concessions, such as lowered interest rate, lower loan fees, or the like. Shared appreciation loans are sometimes said to have an "equity kicker."

11. **B** A shared appreciation loan is a loan with an equity kicker, which provides that the lender will be entitled to a portion of the increase in value. A participation loan is a loan with a co-borrower (investor) who puts up additional down payment. The investor actually takes title as a co-owner of the property. A package loan is a loan which includes personal property as part of the collateral. An open end loan is a loan where the borrower has the option of borrowing additional funds in the future.

12. **A** There is no such loan as a closed end or shut end loan. A shared appreciation loan is a loan with an equity kicker, which provides that the lender will be entitled to a portion of the increase in value. A participation loan is a loan with a co-borrower (investor) who puts up additional down payment. The investor actually takes title as a co-owner of the property.

13. **A** There is no such thing as an ownership loan. A shared appreciation loan is a loan with an equity kicker, which provides that the lender will be entitled to a portion of the increase in value. A participation loan is a loan with a co-borrower (investor) who puts up additional down payment. The investor actually takes title as a co-owner of the property. A wraparound loan is a loan which encompasses an underlying loan.

14. **B** Leverage in real estate occurs when the buyer borrows money to buy an investment property and the cost (interest) of the borrowed funds is less than the return on the investment. Therefore, the lower the down payment (the higher the loan), the greater the leverage effect. Buying with all cash is using no leverage at all.

15. **C** A sale-leaseback transaction occurs when an owner sells the property to an investor, and then leases the property back from the investor. The advantage to the seller is that all the equity in the property is obtained in cash without having to give up possession. The investor gains an investment property with a built-in lessee and the tax shelter which can accrue from the cost recovery deduction in excess of expense. A leasehold and a fee title occur at the same time in any property which is leased.

16. **D** The term "purchase and leaseback" is a synonym for "sale and leaseback." A sale-leaseback oc-

curs when an owner sells the property to an investor, and then leases the property back from the investor.

17. **B** In a sale-leaseback, the seller becomes the lessee. The advantage to the seller is that all the equity in the property is obtained in cash, without having to give up possession. The investor gains an investment property with a built-in lessee and the tax shelter which can accrue from the cost recovery deduction in excess of expense.

18. **D** In a sale-leaseback transaction the seller will become the lessee, so the buyer/lessor would be most concerned about the seller's ability to make the future lease payments.

19. **C** The advantage to the seller in a sale-leaseback is that all the equity in the property is obtained in cash, without having to give up possession. Businesses do this frequently so they can use the capital for inventory and advertising, instead of having it tied up in the real estate. In addition, the lease payments are a business expense which gives greater tax benefits than cost recovery write-off from ownership.

20. **D** A syndicate is not a type of organization but, rather, means any type of collective enterprise. When only two or three entities are involved, we tend to call it a "joint venture." Corporations, partnerships and business trusts are all examples of syndicates.

21. **D** A syndicate is any group of investors. The form which the syndicate takes is determined by the needs of the parties, especially the tax and liability implications.

22. **D** Partnerships and Subchapter S corporations file only informational tax returns; they are not liable for income taxes. Similarly, business trusts pay no taxes if properly structured. Regular corporations are legal entities which are liable for income taxes.

23. **D** Since partnerships, business trusts and Subchapter S corporations do not pay taxes themselves, all profits and losses are passed directly to the investors.

24. **B** Leverage is using borrowed money to own more real estate than an investor could buy for cash. When the property goes up in value, the investor gains the appreciation on all the value. When the seller owes money on an existing encumbrance which will not be paid off at closing, and the seller will carry additional financing from the buyer, the seller could carry a mortgage, trust deed or land sales contract for the entire purchase price less the down payment. The paper the seller is carrying includes the balance the seller owes underneath. This is called a wraparound loan.

25.   **C**   Pyramiding means investing for increase in dollar value, rather than income, with the idea of reinvesting the increased equity in ever larger investments. Whether the equity which eventually accumulates is taken out by additional borrowing or by selling the investment is irrelevant.

Appendix

On the following pages you will find sections from Oregon Revised Statutes relating to financing –

ORS Chapter 82 – Interest; Repayment Restrictions
Legal rate of interest, notices the lender must give the borrower if the loan contains a due on sale clause or lock-in clause.

ORS Chapter 86 – Mortgages; Trust Deeds
Various provisions relating to mortgages and foreclosure proceedings, late charges, interest on reserve accounts, chattel mortgages (security agreements), and the Oregon Trust Deed Act.

ORS Chapter 93 – Land Sales Contracts and Forfeiture
Chapter 93 contains mostly provisions relating to conveyances (deeds and deed forms), but also contains provisions relating to land sales contracts, specifically the staturoty forfeiture remedy.

Students can obtain the full text of any Oregon statute at most public libraries or on the internet.

Chapter 82 — Interest; Repayment Restrictions
2003 Edition

INTEREST

82.010 Legal rate of interest; effect of violation. (1) The rate of interest for the following transactions, if the parties have not otherwise agreed to a rate of interest, is nine percent per annum and is payable on:

(a) All moneys after they become due; but open accounts bear interest from the date of the last item thereof.

(b) Money received to the use of another and retained beyond a reasonable time without the owner's express or implied consent.

(c) Money due or to become due where there is a contract to pay interest and no rate specified.

(2) Except as provided in this subsection, the rate of interest on judgments for the payment of money is nine percent per annum. The following apply as described:

(a) Interest on a judgment under this subsection accrues from the date of the entry of the judgment unless the judgment specifies another date.

(b) Interest on a judgment under this subsection is simple interest, unless otherwise provided by contract.

(c) Interest accruing from the date of the entry of a judgment shall also accrue on interest that accrued before the date of entry of a judgment.

(d) Interest under this subsection shall also accrue on attorney fees and costs entered as part of the judgment.

(e) A judgment on a contract bearing more than nine percent interest shall bear interest at the same rate provided in the contract as of the date of entry of the judgment.

(f) The rate of interest on a judgment rendered in favor of a plaintiff in a civil action to recover damages for injuries resulting from the professional negligence of a person licensed by the Board of Medical Examiners under ORS chapter 677 or the Oregon State Board of Nursing under ORS 678.010 to 678.410 is the lesser of five percent per annum or three percent in excess of the discount rate in effect at the Federal Reserve Bank in the Federal Reserve district where the injuries occurred.

(3) Except as provided in ORS 82.025, no person shall:

(a) Make a business or agricultural loan of $50,000 or less at an annual rate of interest exceeding the greater of 12 percent, or five percent in excess of the discount rate, including any surcharge on the discount rate, on 90-day commercial paper in effect at the Federal Reserve Bank in the Federal Reserve district where the person making the loan is located, on the date the loan or the initial advance of funds under the loan is made; or

(b) Make a loan of $50,000 or less, except a loan made under paragraph (a) of this subsection, at an annual rate of interest exceeding the greater of 12 percent, or five percent in excess of the discount rate on 90-day commercial paper in effect at the Federal Reserve Bank in the Federal Reserve district where the person making the loan is located, on the date the loan or the initial advance of funds under the loan is made.

(4) Any person who violates subsection (3) of this section shall forfeit the right to collect or receive any interest upon any loan for which a greater rate of interest or consideration than is permitted by subsection (3) of this section has been charged, contracted for or received. The borrower upon such loan shall be required to repay only the principal amount borrowed.

82.020 Computation of interest; charges not included. (1) If, pursuant to any arrangement, understanding or agreement, with the knowledge of the lender, either as a part of the contract of borrowing or collateral thereto, regardless of when made and whether it is made as a special arrangement or in conformity to a regular rule, regulation or practice, there is paid by or at the expense of the borrower to the lender, or the lender's broker, officer, director or agent, with respect to or in connection with any loan to which ORS 82.010 applies, any commission, bonus, fee, premium, penalty or other charge, compensation or gratuity, whether in money, credit or other thing of value, as a consideration, compensation or inducement for obtaining any such loan, or any renewal, extension of forbearance thereof, the same shall be deemed a part of the interest charged on such loan.

(2) In computing interest for the purposes of ORS 82.010, any bona fide commission paid or sustained by the borrower shall be computed for the contract term and not for any accelerated period or prepayment.

(3) Notwithstanding subsection (1) of this section, the following charges shall not be deemed a part of the interest charged on a loan:

(a) Reasonable amounts actually applied in payment of the expense of inspecting any security offered in connection with the loan, investigating the responsibility of the applicant or procuring or extending any abstract of title or certificate of title insurance covering such security;

(b) The amount actually paid for the examination of any such abstract of title or certificate of insurance; or

(c) The cost of the preparation, execution and recording of any papers necessary in consummating such loan.

82.025 Exemptions from application of ORS 82.010 (3) and (4) and 82.020. ORS 82.010 (3) and (4) and 82.020 do not apply to:

(1) Any financial institution or trust company, as those terms are defined in ORS 706.008, any consumer finance licensee under ORS chapter 725, or any pawn-broker licensed under ORS chapter 726.

(2) Any lender approved by the Secretary of Housing and Urban Development of the United States for participation in any mortgage insurance program under the National Housing Act (12 U.S.C. 1701 et seq.).

(3) Any loan secured by a first lien on real property or made to finance the acquisition of real property and secured by any lien on that property.

(4) Any loan which is secured by real property, which is scheduled under the loan agreement to be repaid in substantially equal payments and which is made by a lender described in this subsection. A lender under this subsection is one who makes, invests in or arranges real property loans, including loans secured by first liens on residential manufactured homes, aggregating more than $1 million per year. Under this subsection, payments shall be "substantially equal" if, under the terms of the loan agreement, no single scheduled payment is more than twice the amount of any other scheduled payment.

(5) Any loan wholly or partially secured or covered by guarantees or insurance by the Federal Housing Administration, the United States Department of Veterans Affairs or the Farmers Home Administration of the United States, any department, bureau, board, commission or agency of the United States, or any corporation wholly owned, directly or indirectly by the United States.

(6) Any loan permitted under applicable federal law and regulations from a tax qualified retirement plan to a person then a participant under the plan.

(7) Any bona fide sale or resale of securities or commercial paper.

(8) Any interest charge by broker-dealers registered under the Securities Exchange Act of 1934 for carrying a debit balance in an account for a customer if the debit balance is payable on demand and secured by stocks or bonds.

REPAYMENT RESTRICTIONS

82.150 Definitions for ORS 82.160 and 82.170. As used in ORS 82.160 and 82.170:

(1) "Loan" means a loan of money that is primarily for personal, family or household use made by a person who is regularly engaged in the business of lending money.

(2) "Loan agreement" means the written document issued in connection with a loan that sets forth the terms upon which the loan is made.

82.160 Notice to borrower of penalty for repayment prior to date for repayment in loan agreement. (1) If a loan agreement provides for a penalty to be charged for repaying the loan prior to the date provided for repayment in the loan agreement, the loan agreement shall contain in printing or writing of a size equal to at least 10-point bold or underlined type substantially the following notice:

NOTICE TO THE BORROWER

Do not sign this loan agreement before you read it. This loan agreement provides for the payment of a penalty if you wish to repay the loan prior to the date provided for repayment in the loan agreement.

(2) If a loan agreement does not contain a notice as required by subsection (1) of this section, a lender shall not collect from the borrower a penalty for payment of the loan prior to the date provided for repayment.

82.170 Notice to borrower of lender authority to refuse to accept repayment prior to date for repayment in loan agreement. (1) If a loan agreement authorizes the lender to refuse to accept repayment of the loan prior to the date provided for repayment in the loan agreement, the loan agreement shall contain in printing or writing of a size equal to at least 10-point bold or underlined type substantially the following notice:

NOTICE TO THE BORROWER

Do not sign this loan agreement before you read it. This loan agreement authorizes the lender to refuse to accept repayment of the loan prior to the date provided for repayment in the loan agreement.

(2) If a loan agreement does not contain a notice as required by subsection (1) of this section, a lender shall not refuse to accept repayment of the loan by the borrower prior to the date provided for repayment.

Chapter 86 — Mortgages; Trust Deeds
2003 Edition

REAL PROPERTY MORTGAGES

86.010 Nature of mortgagee's interest. A mortgage of real property is not a conveyance so as to enable the owner of the mortgage to recover possession of the property without a foreclosure and sale. This section is not intended as a limitation upon the right of the owner of real property to mortgage or pledge the rents and profits thereof, nor as prohibiting the mortgagee or pledgee of such rents and profits, or any trustee under a mortgage or trust deed from entering into possession of any real property, other than farmlands or the homestead of the mortgagor or successor in interest, for the purpose of operating the same and collecting the rents and profits thereof for application in accordance with the provisions of the mortgage or trust deed or other instrument creating the lien, nor as any limitation upon the power of a court of equity to appoint a receiver to take charge of the property and collect the rents and profits thereof.

86.020 Covenant to pay money not implied. No mortgage shall be construed as implying a covenant for the payment of the sum thereby secured. When there is no express covenant for such payment contained in the mortgage, and no bond or other separate instrument to secure such payment shall have been given, the remedies of the mortgagee shall be confined to the lands mentioned in the mortgage.

86.030 Absolute deed as a mortgage. When a deed purports to be an absolute conveyance in terms, but is made or intended to be made defeasible by a deed of defeasance or other instrument, the original conveyance shall not be thereby defeated or affected as against any person other than the maker of the defeasance, or the heirs or devisees of the maker, or persons having actual notice thereof, unless the instrument of defeasance is recorded with the recording officer of the county where the lands lie.

86.040 Improvements on mortgaged lands. No person shall sell, dispose of, remove or damage any building or other improvements upon mortgaged lands. All such improvements are deemed a part of the mortgaged property and are subject to the mortgage lien. When any improvements are removed from the mortgaged premises in violation of this section, the mortgagee may follow and regain possession of such improvements wherever found or may recover the reasonable value thereof from the person removing them.

86.050 Payment of taxes and other charges by mortgagee. Whenever a mortgagor fails to pay when due any taxes, assessments, interest on prior mortgages, insurance premiums or other charges necessary to be paid for the protection of the lien of a mortgagee, the mortgagee may pay the same, and such payments shall be added to the mortgage debt and secured by the mortgage held by the mortgagee, and shall bear interest at the same rate as specified in the mortgage. This section applies only to mortgages executed after June 3, 1929, and does not affect the right of parties to specifically contract otherwise than as provided in this section.

86.060 Assignment of mortgage. Mortgages may be assigned by an instrument in writing, executed and acknowledged with the same formality as required in deeds and mortgages of real property, and recorded in the records of mortgages of the county where the land is situated.

86.080 Record of assignment not notice to mortgagor. The recording of the assignment of a mortgage is not of itself notice of such assignment to the mortgagor, or the heirs or personal representatives of the mortgagor, so as to invalidate a payment made by any of them to the mortgagee.

86.095 Acts not affecting priority of lien of credit instrument. (1) Actions that do not affect the priority granted to the lien of a credit instrument at the time it is first received for recordation shall include but shall not be limited to:

(a) Renegotiation or adjustment of the initial interest rate provided in the note or the credit instrument, upward or downward, which may increase or decrease the amount of periodic payments or may extend or shorten the term of the credit instrument, or both;

(b) An increase in the underlying obligation secured by the credit instrument during any part of the term of the credit instrument as a result of deferment of all or a portion of the interest payments and the addition of such payments to the outstanding balance of the obligation;

(c) Execution of new notes at designated intervals during the term of the credit instrument that reflect changes made pursuant to paragraph (a) or (b) of this subsection;

(d) Extension of the term of the credit instrument;

(e) Substitution of a note if there is no increase in the principal amount to be paid under the note;

(f) Modification of periodic payments required under the note if there is no increase in the principal amount due under the note; or

(g) Advances made under ORS 86.155.

(2) As used in this section, the addition of accrued interest to the principal amount of the underlying obligation is not an increase in the principal amount.

(3) As used in this section, "credit instrument" includes a mortgage, a line of credit instrument, a deed of trust and a contract for sale of real property.

86.100 Discharge of mortgage. Any mortgage shall be discharged of record whenever there is presented to the recording officer a certificate executed by the mortgagee, or the personal representatives or assigns of the mortgagee, acknowledged or proved and certified as prescribed by law to entitle conveyances to be recorded, specifying that such mortgage has been paid or otherwise discharged. Every such certificate, and the proof or acknowledgment thereof, shall be recorded at full length..

86.110 Discharge of record by owner and holder of mortgage note who is not the mortgagee of record.
(1) Whenever a promissory note secured by mortgage on real property is transferred by indorsement without a formal assignment of the mortgage, and the mortgage is recorded, the mortgage, upon payment of the promissory note, may be discharged of record by the owner and holder of the promissory note making and filing with the appropriate recording officer a certificate, verified by oath, proving the satisfaction of mortgage and declaring, in substance, that the owner and holder is the owner and holder of the note secured by the mortgage by indorsement of the mortgagee and that the note has been fully paid and proving that fact to the satisfaction of the recording officer.

(2) Upon receiving the certificate, the recording officer shall record the document and index the document as a satisfaction of mortgage. The record shall have the same effect as a deed of release of the mortgagee duly acknowledged and recorded.

86.120 Discharge of mortgage on real property; effect of discharge. No mortgage upon real property shall be discharged except as provided in ORS 86.110 or by the person appearing upon the records of the county where the mortgage is recorded to be the owner thereof. A discharge of the mortgage by such person shall operate to free the land described in the mortgage from the lien of the mortgage as against all subsequent purchasers and incumbrances for value and without notice.

86.130 Discharge by foreign executors, administrators, conservators and guardians. Foreign executors, administrators, conservators and guardians may discharge mortgages upon the records of any county upon recording with the recording officer of the county in which the mortgage is recorded a certified copy of their letters testamentary, or of administration, or of guardianship or of conservatorship. The certificate shall include a statement that the letters are in effect, and the certificate shall be recorded in the mortgage records.

86.140 Liability of mortgagee for failure to discharge mortgage. If any mortgagee or the personal representative or assignee of the mortgagee, after full performance of the condition of the mortgage before or after a breach thereof, shall, within 30 days after being thereto requested, and after tender of reasonable charges, fail to discharge the same, or to execute and acknowledge a certificate of discharge or release thereof, that person shall be liable to the mortgagor, or the heirs or assigns of the mortgagor, in the sum of $500 damages and also for all actual damages occasioned by such failure, to be recovered in an action at law. The owner and holder of the promissory note referred to in ORS 86.110 is deemed the personal representative of the mortgagee for the purposes of this section.

86.150 Loan agreements and promissory notes to state maximum prepayment privilege penalty.
(1) Any person making a loan having a loan period of more than three years secured by a mortgage or by a trust deed on real property located in this state shall, with respect to such loan, expressly and clearly state on the loan agreement and promissory note any maximum prepayment privilege penalty. The statement shall include the maximum prepayment penalty applicable for prepayment during the first year of the loan period and for each year thereafter.

(2) Violation of subsection (1) of this section with respect to a loan agreement or promissory note shall render any prepayment privilege penalty provision in the agreement void.

(3) "Loan agreement" as used in this section means a written document issued in connection with a particular loan which sets forth the terms upon which the loan will be made. "Loan agreement" does not include a mortgage or trust deed which secures a promissory note. Nothing in this section shall be deemed to require a lender to issue a loan agreement.

(4) This section does not apply to any loan agreement executed on or before September 13, 1967, or any loan not primarily for personal, family or household use.

86.155 Priority of line of credit instrument as to certain advances; procedure to limit indebtedness in residential line of credit instrument. (1) As used in this section:

(a) "Credit agreement" means any promissory note, loan agreement or other agreement which provides for advances subsequent to the date of recording of the line of credit instrument which secures such note or agreement.

(b) "Line of credit instrument" means a mortgage or trust deed which secures a consumer or commercial credit agreement and creates a lien on specified real property up to a stated amount, provided that the front page of the mortgage or trust deed, or a memorandum thereof:

(A) Contains the legend "line of credit mortgage," "line of credit trust deed" or "line of credit instrument" either in capital letters or underscored above the body of the mortgage or trust deed;

(B) States the maximum principal amount to be advanced pursuant to the credit agreement; and

(C) States the term or maturity date, if any, of the credit agreement exclusive of any option to renew or extend such term of maturity date.

(c) "Residential line of credit instrument" means any line of credit instrument creating a lien on real property upon which are situated or will be constructed four or fewer residential units, one of which, at the time the credit agreement is entered into, is the borrower's residence or is intended, following construction, to be a residence of the borrower.

(2) A line of credit instrument shall have priority, regardless of the knowledge of the lienholder of any intervening lien, as of its date of recording as to the following advances whether such advances are optional or obligatory advances:

(a) Principal advances made any time pursuant to the credit agreement, to the extent the total outstanding advances do not exceed the maximum principal amount stated in the line of credit instrument under subsection (1)(b)(B) of this section;

(b) Interest, lawful charges and advances made any time pursuant to the credit agreement for the reasonable protection of the real property including, but not limited to, advances to pay real property taxes, hazard insurance premiums, maintenance charges imposed under a declaration or restrictive covenant and reasonable attorney fees, whether or not such interest, lawful charges or advances shall exceed the maximum principal amount stated in the line of credit instru-

ment under subsection (1)(b)(B) of this section; and

(c) Advances made any time after the date of recording and pursuant to a credit agreement that is not secured by a residential line of credit instrument to complete construction of previously agreed-upon improvements on the real property, whether or not such advances exceed the maximum principal amount stated in the line of credit instrument under subsection (1)(b)(B) of this section provided, however, that the front page of the instrument states that the maximum principal amount to be advanced pursuant to the credit agreement may be exceeded by advances to complete construction pursuant to this subsection.

(3) Actions that do not affect the priority granted to the advances set forth in subsection (2) of this section shall include, but not be limited to, those actions set forth in ORS 86.095 (1). If any modification to a credit agreement increases the maximum principal amount to be advanced pursuant to the credit agreement, then principal advances that are made that exceed the original maximum principal amount stated in the line of credit instrument shall have priority as of the date of recording an amendment to the line of credit instrument that states the increased maximum principal amount.

(4) In the case of a residential line of credit instrument, the debtor may limit the indebtedness secured by that line of credit instrument to the amount of the credit outstanding by delivering a notice by personal service upon the lienholder or trust deed beneficiary or by mailing a notice by certified mail, return receipt requested, to the lienholder or trust deed beneficiary at the address given for payment or, if none, to the address of the lienholder or trust deed beneficiary indicated in the line of credit instrument or deed of trust. To be sufficient to limit indebtedness under this subsection, the notice must:

(a) State that it is made under this section;

(b) Contain the legal description in the line of credit instrument or the street address of the real property;

(c) Provide the information necessary to locate the line of credit instrument in the public record;

(d) State the debtor's intention to limit the amount of credit secured by the line of credit instrument to the amount owed at the time the notice is received;

(e) State the date sent; and

(f) Be signed and acknowledged by all debtors obligated under the line of credit instrument.

(5) Not later than the 20th day after receipt of the notice described in subsection (4) of this section, the lienholder or trust deed beneficiary shall:

(a) Indorse on the notice, or on an addendum to the notice, the principal amount of the indebtedness secured by the line of credit instrument on the date the lienholder or trust deed beneficiary received notice;

(b) Sign and acknowledge the notice or the addendum, if applicable; and

(c) Record the notice and addendum in the public record where the line of credit instrument was originally recorded.

(6) If the lienholder or trust deed beneficiary fails to record the notice and addendum, if applicable, within the time period specified in subsection (5) of this section, the debtor may record the notice in the public record where the line of credit instrument was originally recorded, together with proof of receipt by, or personal delivery to, the lienholder or trust deed beneficiary.

(7) Notwithstanding subsection (4) of this section, the line of credit instrument shall continue to have priority as of its date of recording as to:

(a) Principal advances, including any advance the creditor is required to honor, that were made before a notice under subsection (4) of this section is received;

(b) Interest, lawful charges and advances described in subsection (2)(b) and (c) of this section; and

(c) All advances made after a notice under subsection (4) of this section is received which are within the amount owed at the time the notice under subsection (4) of this section is given.

LATE CHARGES

86.160 Definitions for ORS 86.160 to 86.185. As used in ORS 86.160 to 86.185:

(1) "Late charge" means a sum payable by a mortgagor to the holder of a mortgage pursuant to a note or mortgage to compensate the holder for servicing and other costs attributable to the receipt of mortgage payments from the mortgagor after the date upon which payment is due.

(2) "Mortgagor" includes the grantor under a deed of trust.

(3) "Mortgage" includes a deed of trust.

(4) "Residential real property" means a single-family, owner-occupied dwelling and appurtenances.

86.165 Late charge. No lender may impose a late charge:

(1) With respect to any periodic installment payment received by it within 15 days after the due date. However, if the 15-day period ends on a Saturday, Sunday or legal holiday the 15-day period is extended to the next business day.

(2) In a dollar amount which exceeds five percent of the sum of principal and interest of the delinquent periodic installment payment or the amount provided in the note or mortgage held by the lender, whichever is the lesser.

(3) Unless the note or mortgage held by the lender provides for payment of a late charge on delinquent periodic installments and a monthly billing, coupon or notice is provided by the lender disclosing the date on which periodic installments are due and that a late charge may be imposed if payment is not received by lender within 15 days thereafter. However, if the lender and the borrower have provided in the note or other written loan agreement that the payments on the loan shall be made by the means of automatic deductions from a deposit account maintained by the borrower, the lender shall not be required to provide the borrower with a monthly billing, coupon or notice under this subsection with respect to any occasion on which there are insufficient funds in the borrower's account to cover the amount of a loan payment on the date the loan payment becomes due and within the period described in subsection (1) of this section.

(4) More than once on any single installment.

86.170 Prohibited mortgage provisions. Any provision in a mortgage for a late charge except as authorized by ORS 86.160 to 86.185 shall be invalid.

86.175 Scope. ORS 86.160 to 86.185 shall be applicable only to late charges on loans secured by residential real property.

86.180 ORS 86.160 to 86.185 not applicable to certain mortgagees; notice to borrowers. Nothing in ORS 86.160 to 86.185 shall pertain to a mortgage banking company or mortgage servicing company except that if the terms of the mortgage do not conform to the requirements of ORS 86.165, the borrower shall be notified prior to the execution of the mortgage.

86.185 ORS 86.160 to 86.185 not applicable to certain loans. Nothing in ORS 86.160 to 86.185 shall apply to loans insured, guaranteed or purchased by an instrumentality of the federal government, whose regulations establish late charge limitations.

REAL ESTATE LOANS; SECURITY PROTECTION

86.205 Definitions for ORS 86.205 to 86.275. As used in ORS 86.205 to 86.275:

(1) "Borrower" means any person who becomes obligated on a real estate loan agreement, either directly or indirectly, and includes, but is not limited to, mortgagors, grantors under trust deeds, vendees under conditional land sales contracts, and persons who purchase real property securing a real estate loan agreement, whether the persons assume the loan or purchase the property subject to the loan.

(2) "Direct reduction provision" or "capitalization provision" means any provision which is part of a real estate loan agreement, whether incorporated into the agreement or as part of a separately executed document, whereby the borrower makes periodic prepayment of property taxes, insurance premiums and similar charges to the lender or the designee of the lender, who applies such prepayments first to accrued interest and then to the principal amount of the loan, and upon payment of such charges, adds the amount of such payment to the principal amount of the loan.

(3) "Escrow account" means any account which is a part of a real estate loan agreement, whether incorporated into the agreement or as part of a separately executed document, whereby the borrower makes periodic prepayment to the lender or the designee of the lender of taxes, insurance premiums, and similar charges, and the lender or the designee of the lender pays the charges out of the account at the due dates.

(4) "Lender" means any person who makes, extends, or holds a real estate loan agreement and includes, but is not limited to, mortgagees, beneficiaries under trust deeds, and vendors under conditional land sales contracts.

(5) "Lender's security protection provision" means any provision which is a part of a real estate loan agreement, whether incorporated into the agreement or as part of a separately executed document, whereby the borrower prepays, pledges or otherwise commits cash or other assets owned by the borrower in advance of due dates for payments of property taxes, insurance premiums and similar charges relating to the property securing the loan in order to assure timely payment of the charges and protect the lender's security interest in the property, and includes, but is not limited to, escrow accounts, direct reduction provisions, capitalization provisions, and pledges of savings accounts.

(6) "Person" means individuals, corporations, associations, partnerships and trusts, and includes, but is not limited to, financial institutions as defined in ORS 706.008, investment companies, insurance companies, pension funds, and mortgage companies.

(7) "Real estate loan agreement" or "real estate loan" means any agreement providing for a loan on residential property, including multifamily, occupied by the borrower, secured in whole or in part by real property, or any interest therein, located in this state, and includes, but is not limited to, mortgages, trust deeds and conditional land sales contracts.

86.210 Types of lender security protection provisions allowed. A lender may require a lender's security protection provision under ORS 86.205 to 86.275 either as a direct reduction provision, an escrow account, or a pledge of an interest-bearing savings account in an amount not to exceed the maximum amount which a lender may require a borrower to deposit in a lender's security protection provision under ORS 86.240 and bearing interest at a rate not less than the rate required on lender's security protection provisions by ORS 86.245.

86.214 Application of ORS 86.210 and 86.245 to real estate loan agreements. To the extent not inconsistent with provisions of existing real estate loan agreements and provided such agreements are not silent with regard to a lender's security protection provision, the provisions of ORS 86.210, 86.245 and this section shall apply to real estate loan agreements entered into prior to, on and after October 1, 1987. To the extent that the provisions of existing real estate loan agreements are inconsistent with the provisions of ORS 86.210, 86.245 and this section, the existing real estate loan agreements are silent as to a lender's security protection provision, or any part of ORS 86.210, 86.245 and this section is declared unconstitutional as to existing real estate loan agreements, the provisions of ORS 86.205 to 86.275 (1985 Replacement Part) shall govern and be in full force and effect.

86.240 Limit on amount required in security protection escrow account; compliance with federal laws for certain loans as compliance with state laws. (1) No lender, in connection with a real estate loan agreement, shall require a borrower or prospective borrower:

(a) To deposit in any escrow account which may be established in connection with the agreement, prior to or upon the date of settlement, a sum in excess of the estimated total amount of property taxes, insurance premiums, and similar charges which actually will be due and payable on the date of settlement, and the pro rata portion thereof which has accrued, plus one-sixth of the estimated total amount of the charges which will become due and payable during the 12- month period beginning on the date of settlement; or

(b) To deposit in any escrow account, which may be established in connection with the agreement, in any month beginning after the date of settlement a sum in excess of one-sixth of the total amount of estimated property taxes, insurance premiums or similar charges which will become due and payable during the 12-

month period beginning on the first day of the month, except that in the event the lender determines there will be a deficiency on the due date, the lender shall not be prohibited from requiring additional monthly deposits in the escrow account of pro rata portions of the deficiency corresponding to the number of months from the date of the lender's determination of the deficiency to the date upon which the charges become due and payable.

(2) For real estate loan agreements subject to the federal Real Estate Settlement Procedures Act of 1974 (12 U.S.C. 2601 et seq.) and to Regulation X of the federal Department of Housing and Urban Development (24 C.F.R. 3500.1 et seq.), compliance with the Real Estate Settlement Procedures Act and with Regulation X shall be considered to be compliance with this section.

86.245 Interest on security protection deposits; exception. (1) Except as provided in subsections (5) and (7) of this section, any lender who requires a lender's security protection provision in connection with a real estate loan agreement shall pay interest to the borrower on funds deposited in the account at a rate not less than the discount rate.

(2) As used in this section, "discount rate" means the auction average rate on three-month United States Treasury bills, as established by the most recent auction of such Treasury bills, as reported in the Federal Reserve's Statistical Release H.15, less 100 basis points. The discount rate shall be determined with reference to the most recent auction date before May 15 and November 15 each year, beginning November 15, 1995.

(3) The rate of interest payable on the account shall be adjusted semiannually to reflect changes in the discount rate. These adjustments shall be calculated on May 15 and November 15 each year. Adjustments calculated on May 15 shall take effect on the following July 1, and adjustments calculated on November 15 shall take effect on the following January 1.

(4) Interest shall be computed on the average monthly balance in the account and shall be paid not less than quarterly to the borrower by crediting to the escrow account the amount of the interest due.

(5) Except as provided in subsection (6) of this section, this section shall not apply to real estate loan agreements entered into prior to September 1, 1975, or on which the payment of interest on a lender's security protection provision violates any state or federal law or regulation.

(6) If federal law or regulation does not prohibit the payment of interest on a lender's security protection provision by federally chartered or organized lenders, then this section shall apply to the federally chartered or organized lenders and the state chartered or organized lenders that are similar to the federally chartered or organized lenders with respect to a lender's security protection provision executed in connection with real estate loan agreement entered into prior to and in existence on September 1, 1975.

(7) This section shall not apply to real estate loan agreements which are made by the State of Oregon or are made by, or held for sale to, or sold to, the State of Oregon.

86.250 Service charge prohibited where interest required. No lender requiring a lender's security protection provision with respect to which interest is required to be paid by the lender under ORS 86.245 shall impose a service charge in connection with such provision.

86.255 Arrangements where security protection provisions not required; information to borrower. In any real estate loan agreement with respect to which a lender does not require a lender's security protection provision, the parties may mutually agree to any arrangement whereby the borrower prepays, pledges or otherwise commits assets in advance of due dates for payment of property taxes, insurance premiums and similar charges relating to the real property in order to assist the borrower in making timely payments of the charges. Prior to entering any such arrangement, the lender shall furnish the borrower a statement in writing, which may be set forth in the loan application:

(1) That the arrangement is not a condition to the real estate loan agreement;

(2) If it is an escrow account, whether or not the lender will pay interest and if interest is to be paid, the rate of interest; and

(3) Whether or not the borrower must pay the lender a charge for the service. If a charge is agreed to, the charge shall not exceed the amount of interest income earned under subsection (2) of this section.

86.260 Payment of taxes where security protection provision required; credit of discount where taxes not paid; cause of action by borrower. (1) If a lender has a requirement that the borrower pay funds into a lender's security protection provision for the payment of property taxes on property that is the security for the real estate loan agreement, insurance premiums, and similar charges, and there are funds in the account, the lender shall pay the taxes or the amount in the account if less than the taxes due, in time to take advantage of any discount authorized by ORS 311.505, and all other charges on or before the due dates for payments.

(2)(a) If the lender fails to pay the taxes in accordance with subsection (1) of this section resulting in a loss of discount to the borrower, the lender shall credit the lender's security protection provision in an amount equal to the amount of discount denied on account of such failure, together with any interest that has accrued on the unpaid property taxes to the date the property taxes are finally paid.

(b) If the failure of the lender to comply with subsection (1) of this section is willful and results in the loss to the borrower of the discount, or if the failure to comply was not willful but upon discovery of the failure to comply and the loss of discount, the lender fails to credit the lender's security protection provision required by paragraph (a) of this subsection, the borrower shall have a cause of action against the lender to recover an amount equal to 15 times the amount of discount the borrower would have received, together with any interest that accrued on the unpaid property taxes to the date of recovery. The court may award reasonable attorney fees to the prevailing party in an action under this section.

86.265 Effect of lender violation of ORS 86.205 to 86.275. A violation of ORS 86.205 to 86.275 by a lender shall render the lender's security protection provision voidable at the option of the borrower, and the lender shall be liable to the borrower in an amount equal to:

(1) The borrower's actual damages or $100, whichever is greater, and

(2) In the case of any successful action to enforce the foregoing liability, the court costs of the action together with reasonable attorney fees at trial and on appeal as determined by the court if the court finds that written demand for the payment of the borrower's claim was made on the lender not less than 10 days before the commencement of the action. No attorney fees shall be allowed to the borrower if the court finds that the lender tendered to the borrower, prior to the commencement of the action, an amount not less than the damages awarded to the borrower.

86.270 ORS 86.205 to 86.275 inapplicable to certain loan agreements; notice to borrower. ORS 86.205 to 86.275 shall not apply to a real estate loan agreement which is serviced or held for sale within one year by a mortgage servicing company neither affiliated with nor owned in whole or in part by the purchaser and which is made, extended or held by a purchaser whose

principal place of business is outside this state; provided that if the purchaser requires a lender's security protection provision, prior to entering into such agreement, the mortgage servicing company shall furnish the borrower a statement in writing, which may be set forth in the loan application, that the mortgage servicing company is not required by the laws of this state to pay interest on the lender's security protection provision, and specifically informing the borrower why the borrower is not entitled to interest on the account.

86.275 Severability. If any section of ORS 86.205 to 86.275, or the application of any section to any real estate loan agreement shall be held invalid, the remainder of ORS 86.205 to 86.275, and the application of ORS 86.205 to 86.275 to any real estate loan agreement other than the one or those to which it is held invalid, shall not be affected thereby.

CHATTEL MORTGAGES

86.405 Secretary of State to furnish statement of mortgages filed before September 1, 1963; fee. Upon the payment of a fee of 50 cents for each name to be searched for chattel mortgages filed under former ORS 86.370 or 86.390, prior to September 1, 1963, the Secretary of State shall furnish to any person applying therefor a statement of any mortgages noted on the indexes created under former ORS 86.380, or if no mortgages are noted, a statement to that effect. All such fees received by the Secretary of State shall be promptly paid to the State Treasurer and placed in the General Fund.

86.440 Discharge of mortgage recorded with county recording officer. Whenever any mortgage recorded under the provisions of ORS 86.350 (1959 Replacement Part) is paid or otherwise satisfied, it shall be discharged by the recording with the recording officer of a certificate of such owner, executed and acknowledged with the same formalities as are prerequisite to the recording of any such mortgage, showing the date of execution, date of recording, and recording number of the record thereof, and that such mortgage has been fully discharged.

86.460 Discharge of mortgage filed with Secretary of State. In the event of the satisfaction or release of any chattel mortgage, a certified copy of which has been filed with the Secretary of State prior to September 1, 1963; the person so satisfying or releasing the mortgage shall send a duly executed discharge or certified copy thereof, with a fee of 25 cents, to the Secretary of State, who shall note such discharge in an appropriate column of the index kept by the Secretary of State. All such fees received by the Secretary of State shall be promptly paid to the State Treasurer and placed in the General Fund.

86.470 Discharge, assignment and foreclosure of mortgages on chattels registered and licensed by Department of Transportation. The recording officer of counties having less than 50,000 population on the last day of each calendar month, and the recording officer of counties having more than 50,000 population on the last day of each calendar week, shall notify the Department of Transportation, upon forms to be provided by the department, of the partial or full satisfaction, assignment or foreclosure during such period of all mortgages theretofore certified to the department prior to September 1, 1963, as formerly provided in ORS 86.390. The notice shall completely identify the mortgage so satisfied, assigned or foreclosed; and the department thereupon shall note on each index margin such satisfaction, assignment or foreclosure.

INVESTMENTS; FEDERAL HOUSING
ADMINISTRATOR

86.610 Power of financial institutions, fiduciaries and others to make loans secured by property insured by Federal Housing Administrator. Financial institutions as defined in ORS 706.008, trustees, guardians, conservators, executors, administrators, other fiduciaries and all other persons, associations and corporations, subject to the laws of this state, may make such loans, secured by real property or leasehold, as the Federal Housing Administrator insures or makes a commitment to insure, and may obtain such insurance.

86.620 Investment of funds of financial institutions, fiduciaries and others in bonds and mortgages accepted by Federal Housing Administrator, debentures issued thereby, and obligations of national mortgage associations. Financial institutions as defined in ORS 706.008, trustees, guardians, conservators, executors, administrators, other fiduciaries and all other persons, associations and corporations, subject to the laws of this state, may invest their funds, and the money in their custody or possession, eligible for investment, in bonds and mortgages on real property insured by the Federal Housing Administrator, in debentures issued by the Federal Housing Administrator, and in obligations of national mortgage associations.

86.630 Eligibility of securities described in ORS 86.620 as security for deposits, investment or reserve of securities. Whenever, by statute, collateral is required as security for the deposit of public or other

funds, or deposits are required to be made with any public official or department, or an investment of capital or surplus, or a reserve or other fund is required to be maintained consisting of designated securities, the securities described in ORS 86.620 shall be eligible for such purposes.

86.640 Applicability of other laws requiring security or regulating loans and investments. No law of this state requiring security upon which loans or investments may be made, or prescribing the nature, amount or form of such security, or prescribing or limiting the period for which loans or investments may be made, shall apply to loans or investments made pursuant to ORS 86.610 and 86.620.

TRUST DEEDS

86.705 Definitions for ORS 86.705 to 86.795. As used in ORS 86.705 to 86.795, unless the context requires otherwise:

(1) "Beneficiary" means the person named or otherwise designated in a trust deed as the person for whose benefit a trust deed is given, or the person's successor in interest, and who shall not be the trustee unless the beneficiary is qualified to be a trustee under ORS 86.790 (1)(d).

(2) "Grantor" means the person conveying an interest in real property by a trust deed as security for the performance of an obligation.

(3) "Residential trust deed" means a trust deed on property upon which are situated four or fewer residential units and one of the residential units is occupied as the principal residence of the grantor, the grantor's spouse or the grantor's minor or dependent child at the time a trust deed foreclosure is commenced.

(4) "Residential unit" means an improvement designed for residential use.

(5) "Trust deed" means a deed executed in conformity with ORS 86.705 to 86.795, and conveying an interest in real property to a trustee in trust to secure the performance of an obligation owed by the grantor or other person named in the deed to a beneficiary.

(6) "Trustee" means a person, other than the beneficiary, to whom an interest in real property is conveyed by a trust deed, or such person's successor in interest. The term includes a person who is an employee of the beneficiary, if the person is qualified to be a trustee under ORS 86.790.

86.710 Trust deeds authorized to secure performance of an obligation; methods of foreclosure after breach. Transfers in trust of an interest in real property may be made to secure the performance of an obligation of a grantor, or any other person named in the deed, to a beneficiary. Where any transfer in trust of an interest in real property is made pursuant to the provisions of ORS 86.705 to 86.795 to secure the performance of an obligation, a power of sale is conferred upon the trustee. The power of sale may be exercised after a breach of the obligation for which the transfer is security; and a trust deed, executed in conformity with ORS 86.705 to 86.795, may be foreclosed by advertisement and sale in the manner provided in ORS 86.705 to 86.795, or, at the option of the beneficiary, may be foreclosed by the beneficiary as provided by law for the foreclosure of mortgages on real property.

86.715 Trust deed deemed to be mortgage on real property; applicability of mortgage laws. A trust deed is deemed to be a mortgage on real property and is subject to all laws relating to mortgages on real property except to the extent that such laws are inconsistent with the provisions of ORS 86.705 to 86.795, in which event the provisions of ORS 86.705 to 86.795 shall control. For the purpose of applying the mortgage laws, the grantor in a trust deed is deemed the mortgagor and the beneficiary is deemed the mortgagee.

86.720 Reconveyance upon performance; liability for failure to reconvey; release of trust deed. (1) Within 30 days after performance of the obligation secured by the trust deed, the beneficiary shall deliver a written request to the trustee to reconvey the estate of real property described in the trust deed to the grantor. Within 30 days after the beneficiary delivers the written request to reconvey to the trustee, the trustee shall reconvey the estate of real property described in the trust deed to the grantor. In the event the obligation is performed and the beneficiary refuses to request reconveyance or the trustee refuses to reconvey the property, the beneficiary or trustee so refusing shall be liable as provided by ORS 86.140 in the case of refusal to execute a discharge or satisfaction of a mortgage on real property. The trustee may charge a reasonable fee for all services involved in the preparation, execution and recordation of any reconveyance executed pursuant to this section.

(2) If a full reconveyance of a trust deed has not been executed and recorded pursuant to the provisions of subsection (1) of this section within 60 calendar days of the date the obligation secured by the trust deed was fully satisfied, then:

(a) If the obligation was satisfied by a title insurance company or insurance producer or by payment through an escrow transacted by a title insurance company or

insurance producer, upon the written request of the grantor or the grantor's successor in interest, the tender of reasonable charges and the compliance with the notice requirements of subsection (3) of this section, the title insurance company or insurance producer shall prepare, execute and record a release of trust deed.

(b) Upon compliance with the notice requirements of subsection (3) of this section, any title insurance company or insurance producer may prepare, execute and record a release of trust deed.

(3) Prior to the issuance and recording of a release pursuant to this section, the title insurance company or insurance producer shall give notice of the intention to record a release of trust deed to the beneficiary of record and, if different, the party to whom the full satisfaction payment was made. The notice shall:

(a) Provide that the parties to whom the notice is sent shall have a period of 30 days from the date of mailing to send to the title insurance company or insurance producer their written objections to the execution and recording of the release of trust deed;

(b) Be sent by first class mail with postage prepaid, addressed to the named interested parties at their last-known addresses; and

(c) Identify the trust deed by the name of the original grantor and any successor in interest on whose behalf payment was made and by the recording reference.

(4) The release of trust deed shall recite on the first page that it has been executed and recorded pursuant to the provisions of this section. The release shall be properly acknowledged and shall set forth:

(a) The name of the beneficiary to whom the payment was made;

(b) The name of the original grantor of the trust deed and any successor in interest on whose behalf payment was made;

(c) The recording reference to the trust deed that is to be released;

(d) A recital that the obligation secured by the trust deed has been paid in full;

(e) The date and amount of payment;

(f) The date of mailing of notice required by this section; and

(g) A recital that no written objections were received by the title insurance company or insurance producer.

(5) The release of trust deed executed pursuant to this section shall be entitled to recordation and, when recorded, shall be deemed to be the equivalent of a reconveyance of a trust deed.

(6) The title insurance company or insurance producer

shall not record or cause to be recorded a release of trust deed when any of the following circumstances exist:

(a) The 30-day period following notice given under this section has not expired; or

(b) Written objection to such recordation has been received by the title insurance company or insurance producer from any of the parties to whom notice was sent.

(7) The trustee, title insurance company or insurance producer may charge a reasonable fee for all services involved in the preparation, execution, recordation and compliance with this section, to effect the release of trust deed.

(8) Subsection (2) of this section does not excuse the beneficiary or trustee from compliance with subsection (1) of this section.

(9) In addition to any other remedy provided by law, a title insurance company or insurance producer preparing, executing or recording a release of trust deed shall be liable to any party for damages that the party sustains by reason of the negligence or willful misconduct of the title insurance company or insurance producer in connection with the issuance, execution or recording of the release pursuant to this section. Except as provided in subsection (10) of this section, the court may award reasonable attorney fees to the prevailing party in an action under this section.

(10) The court may not award attorney fees to a prevailing defendant under the provisions of subsection (9) of this section if the action under this section is maintained as a class action pursuant to ORCP 32.

(11) As used in this section, "insurance producer" means an authorized issuer of title insurance policies of a title insurance company who is licensed as an insurance producer for that purpose pursuant to ORS chapter 744.

(12) Subsections (2) to (11) of this section shall be applicable only to full reconveyances of the property described in the trust deed and not to reconveyances of parts or portions of the property.

(13) Subsections (1) to (12) of this section are applicable to all trust deeds, whether executed before, on or after November 4, 1993.

(14) A title insurance company or agent is not required to prepare, execute and record a release of trust deed under subsections (2) to (12) of this section if the obligation secured by the trust deed was satisfied prior to November 4, 1993.

86.725 Time within which foreclosure must be commenced. The foreclosure of a trust deed by advertisement and sale or the foreclosure of a trust deed by judicial procedure shall be commenced within the time, including extensions, provided by ORS 88.110 and 88.120 for the foreclosure of a mortgage on real property.

86.735 Foreclosure by advertisement and sale. The trustee may foreclose a trust deed by advertisement and sale in the manner provided in ORS 86.740 to 86.755 if:

(1) The trust deed, any assignments of the trust deed by the trustee or the beneficiary and any appointment of a successor trustee are recorded in the mortgage records in the counties in which the property described in the deed is situated; and

(2) There is a default by the grantor or other person owing an obligation, the performance of which is secured by the trust deed, or by their successors in interest with respect to any provision in the deed which authorizes sale in the event of default of such provision; and

(3) The trustee or beneficiary has filed for record in the county clerk's office in each county where the trust property, or some part of it, is situated, a notice of default containing the information required by ORS 86.745 and containing the trustee's or beneficiary's election to sell the property to satisfy the obligation; and

(4) No action has been instituted to recover the debt or any part of it then remaining secured by the trust deed, or, if such action has been instituted, the action has been dismissed, except that:

(a) Subject to ORS 86.010 and the procedural requirements of ORCP 79 and 80, an action may be instituted to appoint a receiver or to obtain a temporary restraining order during foreclosure of a trust deed by advertisement and sale, except that a receiver shall not be appointed with respect to a single-family residence which is occupied as the principal residence of the grantor, the grantor's spouse or the grantor's minor or dependent child.

(b) An action may be commenced for the judicial or nonjudicial foreclosure of the same trust deed as to any other property covered thereby, or any other trust deeds, mortgages, security agreements or other consensual or nonconsensual security interests or liens securing repayment of the debt.

86.740 Notice of sale to be given to certain persons.
(1) Subsequent to recording notice of default as provided in ORS 86.735 and at least 120 days before the day the trustee conducts the sale, notice of the sale shall be served pursuant to ORCP 7 D(2) and 7 D(3) or mailed by both first class and certified mail with return receipt requested, to the last-known address of the following persons or their legal representatives, if any:

(a) The grantor in the trust deed.

(b) Any successor in interest to the grantor whose interest appears of record, or of whose interest the trustee or the beneficiary has actual notice.

(c) Any person, including the Department of Revenue or any other state agency, having a lien or interest subsequent to the trust deed if the lien or interest appears of record or the beneficiary has actual notice of the lien or interest.

(d) Any person requesting notice as provided in ORS 86.785.

(2)(a) The disability, insanity or death of any person to whom notice of sale must be given under this section shall not delay or impair in any way the trustee's right under a trust deed to foreclose under the deed. If the disability, insanity or death occurs prior to the recording of notice of default, the notice shall be given instead to the guardian, the conservator of the estate of the person or the administrator or personal representative of the person, as the case may be, in the manner and by the time set forth in this section.

(b) If the disability, insanity or death of any person to whom notice of sale must be given under this section occurs on or after the recording of notice of default, the trustee shall, if and when the trustee has knowledge of the disability, insanity or death, promptly give the guardian, conservator of the estate or the administrator or personal representative, as the case may be, the notice provided in ORS 86.745. This notice shall be given by first class and certified mail with return receipt requested, to the last-known address of the guardian, conservator or administrator or personal representative.

(c) In the event there is no administrator or personal representative of the estate of the person to whom notice of sale must be given under this section, the notice may be given instead to the heirs at law or devisees of the deceased person in the manner and by the time set forth in this section.

86.742 Failure to give notice of sale; action by omitted person; defense; pleading and proving knowledge of sale; attorney fees; exclusive remedy. (1) If the trustee fails to give notice of the sale to any person entitled to notice under ORS 86.740 (1)(c), and such person did not have actual notice of the sale at least 25 days prior to the date the trustee conducted the sale, such omitted person shall have the same rights possessed by the holder of a junior lien or interest who was omitted as a party defendant in a judicial foreclosure proceeding, and the purchaser at the trustee's sale or the purchaser's heirs, assigns or transferees, shall have the same rights possessed by a purchaser at

a sheriff's sale following a judicial foreclosure.

(2) The omitted person may also commence an action against the trustee in the circuit court in the county where the real property is located. In an action against the trustee, the omitted person shall be entitled to damages upon proof that:

(a) The trustee did not give notice of the sale to the omitted person in the manner required by ORS 86.740 (1)(c) and 86.750;

(b) A search of the record under the name of the grantor as it appears on the trust deed, or the name of the grantor's successor in interest, would have revealed the omitted person's interest;

(c) The omitted person could and would have cured the default under ORS 86.753; and

(d) The omitted person sustained actual damages as a result of such person's loss of the opportunity to cure the default under ORS 86.753 (1).

(3) In an action against the trustee under subsection (2) of this section, any defendant or third party defendant may move for dismissal on the ground that the omitted person would not or could not have cured the default and reinstated the trust deed if the omitted person had received the notice required by ORS 86.740 (1)(c). The court shall hold a hearing on such motion prior to any hearing on any motion for summary judgment, and prior to trial of the action. The court shall deny the motion only if the omitted person produces affidavits or other evidence sufficient for a reasonable jury to find, applying a standard of clear and convincing evidence, that the omitted person had the financial ability to cure the default under ORS 86.753 prior to the date of the trustee's sale, and that the omitted person would have done so had the omitted person received the notice required by ORS 86.740 (1)(c). If the court grants the motion to dismiss it shall award attorney fees pursuant to subsection (5) of this section.

(4) In any action against the trustee or any other party under this section the omitted person shall plead that the omitted person did not have actual knowledge of the sale at least 25 days prior to the date the trustee conducted the sale, but thereafter the defendant shall have the burden of proving that the omitted person did have such notice.

(5) In all suits brought under this section, the applicable court may, upon entering judgment, allow to the prevailing party as a part of the costs a reasonable amount for attorney fees at trial and on appeal.

(6) The remedies described in subsections (1) to (5) of this section shall be the sole remedies available to a

person entitled to notice of foreclosure by advertisement and sale under ORS 86.740 (1)(c), who failed to receive such notice. Such a person's failure to redeem or to commence an action against the trustee within five years of the date of a trustee's sale under ORS 86.755 shall bar any action under this section or any other applicable law.

86.745 Contents of notice of sale. The notice of sale shall set forth:

(1) The names of the grantor, trustee and beneficiary in the trust deed, and the mailing address of the trustee.

(2) A description of the property covered by the trust deed.

(3) The book and page of the mortgage records where the trust deed is recorded.

(4) The default for which the foreclosure is made.

(5) The sum owing on the obligation secured by the trust deed.

(6) The election to sell the property to satisfy the obligation.

(7) The date, time and place of the sale, which shall be held at a designated time after 9 a.m. and before 4 p.m. based on the standard of time established by ORS 187.110 and at a designated place in the county or one of the counties where the property is situated.

(8) The right under ORS 86.753 to have the proceeding dismissed and the trust deed reinstated by payment of the entire amount then due, together with costs, trustee's and attorney's fees, and by curing any other default complained of in the notice of default, at any time prior to five days before the date last set for the sale.

Note: The 2003 Legislature passed HB 2060 which added three sections to this chapter. The Legislative Council is charged with the obligation to assign statute numbers and a bold face caption to the following sections, but as of this printing they have not done so. We reproduce the sections from HB 2060, as they are now law and part of this chapter.

SECTION 2. (1) Not later than 15 days before the date of a sale of property set forth in the notice of sale under ORS 86.745, the grantor, an occupant, a holder of a junior lien or any other person interested in bidding at the sale may send a written request to the trustee requesting that the trustee provide a written statement of information as described in section 3 of this 2003 Act.

(2) The written request under subsection (1) of this section shall be sent to the trustee at the address given in the notice of sale by:

(a) Certified mail, return receipt requested; or

(b) Personal delivery.

(3) The written request under subsection (1) of this section shall include a mailing address, a facsimile number or an electronic mail address to which the trustee shall send the written statement of information.

(4) The trustee is not required to respond to a written request that does not include an address, facsimile number or electronic mail address described in subsection (3) of this section.

(5) Upon receiving a written request under subsection (1) of this section, the trustee shall send the written statement of information to the address, facsimile number or electronic mail address provided in the written request at least seven days prior to the date of the sale. If the person requesting the written statement of information provided a mailing address, the trustee shall send the written statement of information by certified mail, return receipt requested and by first class mail.

SECTION 3. (1) The written statement of information provided by a trustee under section 2 of this 2003 Act shall include:

(a) A statement of the exact amount required, as of a specified date, to cure the default or satisfy the obligation, including the costs of foreclosure, trustee fees, attorney fees and per diem interest; and

(b) A description of any other performance necessary to cure the default or satisfy the obligation.

(2) If the amount required to cure the default or satisfy the obligation is not calculable to an exact amount, the trustee may estimate the maximum amount required to cure the default or satisfy the obligation.

(3) If the trustee does not provide the written statement of information within the time specified in section 2 of this 2003 Act, the trustee may postpone the sale of the property to provide the person requesting the written statement of information at least seven days between receipt of the statement and the date of the sale.

(4) A person requesting a written statement of information under section 2 of this 2003 Act has the rights of an omitted person under ORS 86.742 if:

(a) The person requesting the statement proves that the person sent a written request under section 2 of this 2003 Act at least 15 days before the date of sale; and

(b) The trustee cannot prove that the trustee sent the written statement of information at least seven days before the date of the sale.

(5) The provisions of this section and section 2 of this 2003 Act do not affect the duty of beneficiaries to provide information to grantors.

86.750 Service and publication of notice; recording proof of compliance. (1) The notice prescribed in ORS 86.745 shall be served upon an occupant of the property described in the trust deed in the manner in which a summons is served pursuant to ORCP 7 D(2) and 7 D(3) at least 120 days before the day the trustee conducts the sale.

(2) A copy of the notice of sale shall be published in a newspaper of general circulation in each of the counties in which the property is situated once a week for four successive weeks. The last publication shall be made more than 20 days prior to the date the trustee conducts the sale.

(3) On or before the date the trustee conducts the sale, an affidavit of mailing notice of sale, proof of service (if any), and an affidavit of publication of notice of sale shall be recorded in the official records in the county or counties in which the property described in the deed is situated.

86.753 Discontinuance of foreclosure proceedings after cure of default. (1) Where a trustee has commenced foreclosure of a trust deed by advertisement and sale, the grantor, the grantor's successor in interest to all or any part of the trust property, any beneficiary under a subordinate trust deed, or any person having a subordinate lien or encumbrance of record on the property, may cure the default or defaults at any time prior to five days before the date last set for the sale. If the default consists of a failure to pay, when due, sums secured by the trust deed, the default may be cured by paying the entire amount due at the time of cure under the terms of the obligation, other than such portion as would not then be due had no default occurred. Any other default of the trust deed obligation that is capable of being cured may be cured by tendering the performance required under the obligation or trust deed. In any case, and in addition to paying the sums or tendering the performance necessary to cure the default, the person effecting the cure shall pay to the beneficiary all costs and expenses actually incurred in enforcing the obligation and trust deed, together with trustee's and attorney fees in the amount of:

(a) A total of $1,000 for both trustee's fees and attorney fees, or the amount actually charged by the trustee and attorney, whichever is less, if the trust deed is a residential trust deed; or

(b) Reasonable attorney fees and trustee's fees actually charged by the trustee and attorney if the trust deed is not a residential trust deed. Any person entitled to cure the default may, either before or after reinstatement, request any court of competent jurisdiction to determine the reasonableness of the fee demanded or paid as a condition of reinstatement. The court may award attorney fees to the prevailing party. An action to determine reasonable attorney fees or trustee's fees under this section shall not forestall any sale or affect its validity.

(2) After cure of the default under subsection (1) of this section, all proceedings under ORS 86.740 to 86.755 shall be dismissed by the trustee, and the obligation and trust deed shall be reinstated and shall remain in force the same as if no acceleration had occurred.

86.755 Sale of property. (1) The sale shall be held on the date and at the time and place designated in the notice of sale. The trustee may sell the property in one parcel or in separate parcels and shall sell the parcel or parcels at auction to the highest bidder for cash. Any person, including the beneficiary under the trust deed, but excluding the trustee, may bid at the trustee's sale. The attorney for the trustee, or any agent designated by the trustee or the attorney, may conduct the sale and act in the sale as the auctioneer of the trustee.

(2) The trustee or the attorney for the trustee, or any agent designated by the trustee or the attorney conducting the sale, may postpone the sale for one or more periods totaling not more than 180 days from the original sale date, giving notice of each adjournment by public proclamation made at the time and place set for sale. The proclamation may be made by the trustee, the attorney, or any agent designated by the trustee or the attorney.

(3) The purchaser shall pay at the time of sale the price bid, and, within 10 days following payment, the trustee shall execute and deliver the trustee's deed to the purchaser.

(4) The trustee's deed shall convey to the purchaser the interest in the property which the grantor had, or had the power to convey, at the time of the execution by the grantor of the trust deed, together with any interest the grantor or the grantor's successors in interest acquire after the execution of the trust deed.

(5) The purchaser at the trustee's sale shall be entitled to possession of the property on the 10th day following the sale, and any persons remaining in possession after that day under any interest, except one prior to the trust deed or created voluntarily by the grantor or a successor of the grantor, shall be deemed to be tenants at sufferance. All persons not holding under an interest prior to the trust deed may be removed from possession by following the procedures set out in ORS 105.105 to 105.168 or other applicable judicial procedure, provided that a

person holding under an interest created voluntarily by the grantor or a successor of the grantor must first receive 30 days' written notice of the intent to remove that person served no earlier than 30 days before the date first set for the sale. Notices under this subsection shall be served by first class mail. "First class mail" for purposes of this section does not include certified or registered mail, or any other form of mail which may delay or hinder actual delivery of mail to the addressee.

(6) Notwithstanding subsection (2) of this section, except when a beneficiary has participated in obtaining a stay, foreclosure proceedings that are stayed by order of the court, by proceedings in bankruptcy or for any other lawful reason shall, after release from the stay, continue as if uninterrupted, if within 30 days after release the trustee gives amended notice of sale by registered or certified mail to the last-known address of those persons listed in ORS 86.740 and 86.750 (1) and to the address provided by each person who was present at the time and place set for the sale which was stayed. The amended notice of sale shall:

(a) Be given at least 20 days prior to the amended date of sale;

(b) Set an amended date of sale which may be the same as the original sale date, or date to which the sale was postponed, provided the requirements of ORS 86.740, 86.750 and this subsection are satisfied;

(c) Specify the time and place for sale;

(d) Conform to the requirements of ORS 86.745; and

(e) State that the original sale proceedings were stayed and the date the stay terminated.

(7) If the publication of the notice of sale was not completed prior to the date the foreclosure proceedings were stayed by order of the court, by proceedings in bankruptcy or for any other lawful reason, after release from the stay, in addition to complying with the provisions of subsection (6) of this section, the trustee shall complete the publication by publishing an amended notice of sale which states that the notice has been amended following release from the stay, and which contains the amended date of sale. The amended notice shall be published in a newspaper of general circulation in each of the counties in which the property is situated once a week for four successive weeks, except that the required number of publications shall be reduced by the number of publications that were completed prior to the effective date of the stay. The last publication shall be made more than 20 days prior to the date the trustee conducts the sale.

86.765 Disposition of proceeds of sale. The trustee shall apply the proceeds of the trustee's sale as follows:

(1) To the expenses of the sale, including the compensation of the trustee, and a reasonable charge by the attorney.

(2) To the obligation secured by the trust deed.

(3) To all persons having recorded liens subsequent to the interest of the trustee in the trust deed as their interests may appear in the order of their priority.

(4) The surplus, if any, to the grantor of the trust deed or to the successor in interest of the grantor entitled to such surplus.

86.770 Effect of sale. (1) A sale made by a trustee under ORS 86.705 to 86.795 shall foreclose and terminate all interest in the property covered by the trust deed of all persons to whom notice is given under ORS 86.740 and 86.750 and of any other person claiming by, through or under such persons, and such persons shall have no right to redeem the property from the purchaser at the trustee's sale. The failure to give notice to any of these persons shall not affect the validity of the sale as to persons so notified.

(2) Except as provided in subsection (4) of this section, no other or further action shall be brought, nor judgment entered for any deficiency, against the grantor, or the grantor's successor in interest, if any, on the note, bond, or other obligation secured by the trust deed or against any other person obligated on such note, bond or other obligation after a sale is made:

(a) By a trustee under ORS 86.705 to 86.795; or

(b) Under a judicial foreclosure of a residential trust deed.

(3) Under a judicial foreclosure of a trust deed that is not a residential trust deed, notwithstanding the purchase money mortgage provisions of ORS 88.070 and 88.075, the judgment shall provide that if the sale proceeds are insufficient to satisfy the judgment, execution may issue, for any amount by which the unpaid balance of the obligation secured by the trust deed exceeds the net sale proceeds payable to the beneficiary.

(4) Nothing in this section shall preclude an action judicially or nonjudicially foreclosing the same trust deed as to any other property covered thereby, or any other trust deeds, mortgages, security agreements, or other consensual or nonconsensual security interest or liens covering any other real or personal property security for the note, bond or other obligation secured by the trust deed under which a sale has been made or an action against a guarantor to the extent of any remaining deficiency following judicial foreclosure. A guarantor of an obligation secured by a residential trust deed shall not have the right to recover any deficiency from the grantor or any successor in interest of the grantor.

86.775 Contents of trustee's deed to purchaser. The trustee's deed to the purchaser at the trustee's sale shall contain, in addition to a description of the property conveyed, a recital of the facts concerning the default, the notice given, the conduct of the sale and the receipt of the purchase money from the purchaser.

86.780 Recitals in trustee's deed and certain affidavits as prima facie or conclusive evidence. When the trustee's deed is recorded in the deed records of the county or counties where the property described in the deed is situated, the recitals contained in the deed and in the affidavits required under ORS 86.750 (3) shall be prima facie evidence in any court of the truth of the matters set forth therein, but the recitals shall be conclusive in favor of a purchaser for value in good faith relying upon them.

86.785 Requests for copies of notice of default or notice of sale. At any time subsequent to the recordation of a trust deed and prior to a recording of notice of default under the deed, any person desiring a copy of any notice of default or any notice of sale under a trust deed as provided in ORS 86.740 (1) may cause to be filed for record in the county clerk's office of the county or counties in which any part or parcel of the real property is situated, a duly acknowledged request for a copy of any notice of sale or default where service is made upon the trustee. The request shall contain the name and address of the person requesting copies of the notice or notices and shall identify the trust deed by stating the names of the parties to the deed, the date of recordation of the deed and the book and page where the deed is recorded. The county clerk shall immediately make a cross-reference of the request to the trust deed, either on the margin of the page where the trust deed is recorded or in some other suitable place. No request, statement or notation placed on the record pursuant to this section shall affect title to the property or be deemed notice to any person that any person so recording the request has any right, title, interest in, lien or charge upon the property referred to in the trust deed.

86.790 Qualifications of trustee; appointment of successor trustee; duty of trustee. (1) The trustee of a trust deed under ORS 86.705 to 86.795 shall not be required to comply with the provisions of ORS chapters 707 and 709 and shall be:

(a) Any attorney who is an active member of the Oregon State Bar;

(b) A financial institution or trust company, as defined in ORS 706.008, that is authorized to do business under the laws of Oregon or the United States;

(c) A title insurance company authorized to insure title to real property in this state, its subsidiaries, affiliates, insurance producers or branches;

(d) The United States or any agency thereof; or

(e) Escrow agents licensed under ORS 696.505 to 696.590.

(2) An attorney who is a trustee under subsection (1)(a) of this section may represent the beneficiary in addition to performing the duties of trustee.

(3) At any time after the trust deed is executed, the beneficiary may appoint in writing another qualified trustee. If the appointment of the successor trustee is recorded in the mortgage records of the county or counties in which the trust deed is recorded, the successor trustee shall be vested with all the powers of the original trustee.

(4) A trustee or successor trustee is a necessary and proper party to any proceeding to determine the validity of or enjoin any private or judicial proceeding to foreclose a trust deed, but a trustee or successor trustee is neither a necessary nor a proper party to any proceeding to determine title to the property subject to the trust deed, or to any proceeding to impose, enforce or foreclose any other lien on the subject property.

(5) Nothing in ORS 86.705 to 86.795 imposes a duty on the trustee or successor trustee to notify any person of any proceeding with respect to such person, except a proceeding initiated by the trustee or successor trustee.

(6) A trustee or the attorney for the trustee or any agent designated by the trustee or the attorney may announce and accept a bid from the beneficiary whether or not the beneficiary is present at the sale.

(7) The trustee or successor trustee shall have no fiduciary duty or fiduciary obligation to the grantor or other persons having an interest in the property subject to the trust deed. The trustee or successor trustee shall not be relieved of the duty to reconvey the property subject to the trust deed to the grantor upon request for reconveyance by the beneficiary.

86.795 Compensation of trustee. The charge of a trustee for the performance of powers and duties of foreclosure by advertisement and sale imposed under ORS 86.705 to 86.795 shall not exceed 50 percent of the compensation allowable to an executor or administrator under ORS 116.173 or a minimum charge of $100. Such compensation shall be based upon the amount due on the obligation, both principal and interest, at the time of the trustee's sale.

PENALTIES

86.990 Penalties. Violation of ORS 86.040 is punishable, upon conviction, by a fine not exceeding $500 or imprisonment in the county jail not exceeding six months, or both.

Chapter 93 — Conveyancing and Recording
2003 Edition

93.290 Risk of loss after contract to sell realty has been executed. Any contract made on or after August 3, 1955, in this state for the purchase and sale of realty shall be interpreted as including an agreement that the parties shall have the following rights and duties, unless the contract expressly provides otherwise:

(1) If, when neither the legal title nor the possession of the subject matter of the contract has been transferred, all or a material part thereof is destroyed without fault of the purchaser or is taken by eminent domain, the vendor cannot enforce the contract, and the purchaser is entitled to recover any portion of the price that the purchaser has paid;

(2) If, when either the legal title or the possession of the subject matter of the contract has been transferred, all or any part thereof is destroyed without fault of the vendor or is taken by eminent domain, the purchaser is not thereby relieved from a duty to pay the price, nor is the purchaser entitled to recover any portion thereof that the purchaser has paid.

93.295 Construction of ORS 93.290 to 93.300. ORS 93.290 to 93.300 shall be so interpreted and construed as to effectuate their general purpose to make uniform the law of those states which enact the Uniform Vendor and Purchaser Risk Act.

93.300 Short title. ORS 93.290 to 93.300 may be cited as the Uniform Vendor and Purchaser Risk Act.

...

FORFEITURE UNDER LAND SALES CONTRACT

93.905 Definitions for ORS 93.905 to 93.940. As used in ORS 93.905 to 93.940, unless the context requires otherwise:

(1) "Contract for transfer or conveyance of an interest in real property" shall not include earnest money or preliminary sales agreements, options or rights of first refusal.

(2) "Forfeiture remedy" means the nonjudicial remedy whereby the seller cancels the contract for default, declares the purchaser's rights under the contract to be forfeited, extinguishes the debt and retains sums previously paid thereunder by the buyer.

(3) "Purchase price" means the total price for the interest in the real property as stated in the contract, including but not limited to down payment, other property or value given or promised for which a dollar value is stated in the contract and the balance of the purchase price payable in installments, not including interest. If the contract provides for the conveyance of an interest in more than one parcel of property, the purchase price shall include only the portion of the price attributable to the remaining, unconveyed interest in real property, if the value thereof is separately stated or can be determined from the terms of the contract.

(4) "Purchaser" means any person who by voluntary transfer acquires a contractual interest in real property, any successor in interest to all or any part of the purchaser's contract rights of whom the seller has actual or constructive notice, and any person having a subordinate lien or encumbrance of record, including, but not limited to, a mortgagee, a beneficiary under a trust deed and a purchaser under a subordinate contract for transfer or conveyance of an interest in real property.

(5) "Seller" means any person who transfers or conveys an interest in real property, or any successor in interest of the seller.

(6) "Unpaid balance" means the sum of the unpaid principal balance, accrued unpaid interest and any sums actually paid by the seller on behalf of the purchaser for items required to be paid by the purchaser, including amounts paid for delinquent taxes, assessments or liens, or to obtain or reinstate required insurance.

93.910 Enforcement of forfeiture remedy after notice of default. Whenever a contract for transfer or conveyance of an interest in real property provides a forfeiture remedy, whether the remedy is self-executing or is optional, forfeiture of the interest of a purchaser in default under the contract may be enforced only after notice of the default has been given to the purchaser as provided in ORS 93.915, notwithstanding any provision in the contract to the contrary.

93.913 Forfeiture allowed for default under certain collateral assignments of interest. In the event of a default under a collateral assignment of the interest of a seller or purchaser in a land sale contract, including a collateral assignment of the proceeds thereof, the assignee may enforce a remedy of forfeiture, as set forth in ORS 93.905 to 93.945, unless the agreement between the parties otherwise prohibits such remedy.

Note: 93.913 and 93.918 were added to and made a part of ORS chapter 93 by legislative action but were not added to any series therein. See Preface to Oregon Revised Statutes for further explanation.

93.915 Notice of default; contents; recordation; time of forfeiture; interim measures. (1) In the event of a default under a contract for conveyance of real property, a seller who wishes to enforce a forfeiture remedy must give written notice of default by service pursuant to ORCP 7 D(2) and 7 D(3), or by both first class and certified mail with return receipt requested, to the last-known address of the following persons or their legal representatives, if any:

(a) The purchaser.

(b) An occupant of the property.

(c) Any person who has caused to be filed for record in the county clerk's office of a county in which any part or parcel of the real property is situated, a duly acknowledged request for a copy of any notice of default served upon or mailed to the purchaser. The request shall contain the name and address of the person requesting copies of the notice and shall identify the contract by stating the names of the parties to the contract, the date of recordation of the contract and the book and page where the contract is recorded. The county clerk shall immediately make a cross-reference of the request to the contract, either on the margin of the page where the contract is recorded or in some other suitable place. No request, statement or notation placed on the record pursuant to this section shall affect title to the property or be deemed notice to any person that any person so recording the request has any right, title, interest in, lien or charge upon the property referred to in the contract.

(2) Notices served by mail are effective when mailed.

(3) The notice shall specify the nature of the default, the amount of the default if the default is in the payment terms, the date after which the contract will be forfeited if the purchaser does not cure the default and the name and address of the seller or the attorney for the seller. The period specified in the notice after which the contract will be forfeited may not be less than:

(a) Sixty days, when the purchaser has reduced the unpaid balance to an amount greater than 75 percent of the purchase price;

(b) Ninety days, when the purchaser has reduced the unpaid balance to an amount which is more than 50 percent but less than 75 percent of the purchase price; or

(c) One hundred twenty days, when the purchaser has reduced the unpaid balance to an amount which is 50 percent or less of the purchase price.

(4) The seller shall cause to be recorded in the real property records of each county in which any part of the property is located a copy of the notice, together with an affidavit of service or mailing of the notice of default, reciting the date the notice was served or mailed and the name and address of each person to whom it was given. From the date of recording, the notice and affidavit shall constitute constructive notice to third persons of the pending forfeiture. If, not later than one year after the time for cure stated in a recorded notice and affidavit or any recorded extension thereof, no declaration of forfeiture based upon the recorded notice and affidavit has been recorded and no extension of time for cure executed by the seller has been recorded, the notice and affidavit shall not be effective for any purpose nor shall it impart any constructive or other notice to third persons acquiring an interest in the purchaser's interest in the contract or the property or any portion of either. Any extension of time for cure executed by the seller shall be recorded in the same manner as the original notice and affidavit.

(5) The statement contained in the notice as to the time after which the contract will be forfeited if the default is not cured shall conclusively be presumed to be correct, and the notice adequate, unless one or more recipients of such notice notifies the seller or the attorney for the seller, by registered or certified mail, that such recipient claims the right to a longer period of time in which to cure the default.

(6) Subject to the procedural requirements of the Oregon Rules of Civil Procedure, an action may be instituted to appoint a receiver or to obtain a temporary restraining order during forfeiture under a land sale contract, except that a receiver shall not be appointed with respect to a single-family residence which is occupied at the time the notice of default is given, as the principal residence of the purchaser, the purchaser's spouse or the purchaser's minor dependent children.

93.918 Continuation of proceedings after certain types of stay ordered by court; procedures. (1) Except when a seller has participated in obtaining a stay, contract forfeiture proceedings that are stayed by order of the court, by proceedings in bankruptcy or for any other lawful reason, shall continue after release from the stay as if uninterrupted, if within 30 days after release the seller gives written amended notice of default by certified mail with return receipt requested, to the last-known address of those persons listed in ORS 93.915 (1). The amended notice of default shall:

(a) Be given at least 20 days prior to the amended date of forfeiture;

(b) Specify an amended date after which the contract will be forfeited, which may be the same as the original forfeiture date;

(c) Conform to the requirements of ORS 93.915 (3), except the time periods set forth therein; and

(d) State that the original forfeiture proceedings were stayed and the date the stay terminated.

(2) The new date of forfeiture shall not be sooner than the date of forfeiture as set forth in the seller's notice of default which was subject to the stay.

(3) Prior to the date of forfeiture, the seller shall cause to be recorded in the real property records of each county in which any part of the property is located, a copy of the amended notice of default, together with an affidavit of service or mailing of the amended notice of default, reciting the date the amended notice of default was served or mailed and the name and address of each person to whom it was given. From the date of its recording, the amended notice of default shall be subject to the provisions of ORS 93.915 (4) and (5).

Note: See note under 93.913.

93.920 Curing default to avoid forfeiture; payment of costs and expenses. A purchaser in default may avoid a forfeiture under the contract by curing the default or defaults before expiration of the notice period provided in ORS 93.915. If the default consists of a failure to pay sums when due under the contract, the default may be cured by paying the entire amount due, other than sums that would not then be due had no default occurred, at the time of cure under the terms of the contract. Any other default under the contract may be cured by tendering the performance required under the contract. In addition to paying the sums or tendering the performance necessary to cure the default, the person effecting the cure of the default shall pay all costs and expenses actually incurred in enforcing the contract, including, but not limited to, late charges, attorney fees not to exceed $350 and costs of title search.

93.925 Failure to cure default; exclusiveness of notice. Notwithstanding a seller's waiver of prior defaults, if notice is given and purchaser does not cure the default within the period specified in ORS 93.915, the contract forfeiture remedy may be exercised and the contract shall not be reinstated by any subsequent offer or tender of performance. The notice required in ORS 93.915 shall be in lieu of any notice that may be required under the terms of the contract itself, except where greater notice or notice to persons other than those described in ORS 93.915 is required by the terms of the contract, in which case notice shall be given for such longer period of time and to such additional persons as required by the contract.

93.930 Recording affidavit after forfeiture; affidavit as evidence. (1) When a contract for conveyance of real property has been forfeited in accordance with its terms after the seller has given notice to the purchaser as provided in ORS 93.915, the seller shall record an affidavit with the property description, a copy of the notice of default and proof of mailing attached, setting forth that the default of the purchaser under the terms of the contract was not cured within the time period provided in ORS 93.915 and that the contract has been forfeited. When the affidavit is recorded in the deed records of the county where the property described therein is located, the recitals contained in the affidavit shall be prima facie evidence in any court of the truth of the matters set forth therein, but the recitals shall be conclusive in favor of a purchaser for value in good faith relying upon them.

(2) Except as otherwise provided in ORS 93.905 to 93.945 and except to the extent otherwise provided in the contract or other agreement with the seller, forfeiture of a contract under ORS 93.905 to 93.930 shall have the following effects:

(a) The purchaser and all persons claiming through the purchaser who were given the required notices pursuant to ORS 93.915, shall have no further rights in the contract or the property and no person shall have any right, by statute or otherwise, to redeem the property. The failure to give notice to any of these persons shall not affect the validity of the forfeiture as to persons so notified;

(b) All sums previously paid under the contract by or on behalf of the purchaser shall belong to and be retained by the seller or other person to whom paid; and

(c) All of the rights of the purchaser to all improvements made to the property at the time the declaration of forfeiture is recorded shall be forfeited to the seller and the seller shall be entitled to possession of the property on the 10th day after the declaration of forfeiture is recorded. Any persons remaining in possession after that day under any interest, except one prior to the contract, shall be deemed to be tenants at sufferance. Such persons may be removed from possession by following the procedures set out in ORS 105.105 to 105.168 or other applicable judicial procedures.

(3) After the declaration of forfeiture is recorded, the seller shall have no claim against the purchaser and the purchaser shall not be liable to the seller for any portion of the purchase price unpaid or for any other breach of the purchaser's obligations under the contract.

93.935 Effect of purchaser's abandonment or reconveyance on interest, lien or claim. (1) In the event of a default under a contract for conveyance of real property, the recorded interest, lien or claim of a person with respect to the real property, by virtue of an assignment, conveyance, contract, mortgage, trust deed or other lien or claim from or through a purchaser, shall not be affected by the purchaser's abandonment or reconveyance to the seller unless the person is given notice in the manner specified in ORS 93.915.

(2) The notice shall specify the nature of the default, the amount of the default if the default is in the payment terms, the date after which the purchaser's interest in the real property will be abandoned or reconveyed to the seller and the name and address of the seller or the attorney for the seller. The period specified in the notice after which the purchaser's interest will be abandoned or reconveyed to the seller may not be less than:

(a) Sixty days, when the purchaser has reduced the unpaid balance to an amount greater than 75 percent of the purchase price;

(b) Ninety days, when the purchaser has reduced the unpaid balance to an amount which is more than 50 percent but less than 75 percent of the purchase price; or

(c) One hundred twenty days, when the purchaser has reduced the unpaid balance to an amount which is 50 percent or less of the purchase price.

(3) If the person having an interest, lien or claim with respect to the real property, by virtue of an assignment, conveyance, contract, mortgage, trust deed or other lien or claim from or through a purchaser whose interest arises under a contract for conveyance of real property, cures the default as provided in ORS 93.920 then such person's interest, lien or claim with respect to the real property shall not be affected by the purchaser's abandonment or reconveyance to the seller.

93.940 Effect of seller's foreclosure or other action on interest, lien or claim. The recorded interest, lien or claim of a person with respect to the real property, by virtue of an assignment, conveyance, contract, mortgage, trust deed or other lien or claim from or through a purchaser whose interest arises under a contract for conveyance of real property, shall be not affected by the seller's foreclosure or other action on the contract unless such person is made a party to the action brought by the seller to enforce or foreclose the contract. In such action, such person shall be entitled to the same rights and opportunities to cure the purchaser's default or satisfy the purchaser's obligations as are granted the purchaser.

93.945 Application of ORS 93.905 to 93.940. (1) The provisions of ORS 93.910 to 93.930 shall apply only to forfeiture remedies enforced after July 13, 1985. The date that the initial written notice of a default is given to the purchaser shall be the date of enforcement of the forfeiture remedy.

(2) The provisions of ORS 93.935 and 93.940 shall apply to all contracts for transfer or conveyance of an interest in real property, whether executed on, before or after July 13, 1985.

Index

*Items in **bold** are main locations where the item is discussed in the text.*